**Cuban
Foreign Policy
and Chilean
Politics**

Studies in the Economic and Social Development
of Latin America
under the general editorship of
Otto Feinstein
Monteith College
Wayne State University
and
Rodolfo Stavenhagen
International Institute for Labour Studies, Geneva

Cuban Foreign Policy and Chilean Politics

Miles D. Wolpin
St. Francis Xavier University

Lexington Books
D.C. Heath and Company
Lexington, Massachusetts
Toronto   London

To Nery B. and his compañeros

Table of Contents

List of Tables

Table

Acknowledgments

A particular debt of gratitude is owed to William Sprague Barns of the Fletcher School of Law and Diplomacy. In the immediate aftermath of Project Camelot, both he and the Ford Foundation risked the Latin American Teaching Fellowship Program by supporting my efforts in an extremely sensitive area. Without their generous aid, the field research would not have been carried out.

At various stages, portions of the manuscript were read and criticized by Ronald Schneider, Douglas Chalmers, William T.R. Fox, and Otto Feinstein. All have contributed to its improvement and none bear any responsibility for the work's shortcomings or conclusions.

For their inspiration along the way, I wish to thank Benedict Alper of Boston College and John Beck of Lexington Books, D.C. Heath and Company. Words cannot, of course, recompense the investment of my wife, Susan Jackson Wolpin, in this undertaking. Her patience, proofreading and encouragement were invaluable.

Special appreciation is due the director of Chile's Institute of Socio-Economic Studies. Not only did Eduardo Hamuy invite me to his home as a total stranger, but he provided unrestricted access to his survey research data.

The librarians at Chile's National and Congressional libraries were always helpful, as was Sister Jean Harris of Saint Francis Xavier University's Library.

Finally, I want to thank Marie Benedict and Mrs. Gladys Blennerhassett for their care and exactitude in typing a rather difficult manuscript.

1 Exporting Revolution

The Substance of the Cuban Allegation

Cuban claims of hemispheric validity and significance for their revolution have been categorical and unqualified. In the course of an address delivered to the members of the United Party of the Socialist Revolution during February 1963, Fidel Castro asserted that mass impoverishment, which he attributed to socio-economic underdevelopment and imperialist exploitation, would inevitably inspire enthusiasm for the Cuban model throughout Latin America:

One frequently hears imperialist contentions alleging that the Cuban Revolution has lost its appeal because of the economic problems confronting it, because of the existing hunger.

I say that this claim is cynical, because it rests upon the following: concentrating all one's power, all his hostility and all his influence in blockading a small underdeveloped country and then saying: "See, they are having difficulties."

The real merit of this Revolution is that the peoples of America are witnessing this, and in spite of it the Revolution is being preserved and moving ahead. . . .

Going further, we could pose a question for the Yankee governors, for the Yankee senators: If Cuba can't be attractive, why are they so pre-occupied with Cuba?

. . . If the Cuban example were not attractive, why that enormous ranting hysteria unleashed in the Yankee senate and press, why the enormous ranting about the danger of subversion that they allege Cuba represents? Why so much fear? Is it not sufficient to view a map of the hemisphere to see the size of Cuba, the geography of Cuba, a tiny island with miniscule territory in the midst of an immense continent in one of whose parts is located the most powerful capitalist country?

Why does Cuba so terrorize them?. . .

The virus of revolution is transported in neither submarines nor ships. It is the ethereal wavelengths of ideas that carry the revolutionary virus, and they prosper wherever there is an abundance of fertile soil. And how much fertile revolutionary soil there is in Latin America!

What is Cuba? Cuba is the example, Cuba is the idea. The force of Cuba is the force of her revolutionary ideas, the force of her example. And since when could ideas be isolated?

It is obvious that the imperialists spend millions on propaganda. But the hunger, the exploitation, the misery are such naked facts that the imperialist lies and all their propaganda will avail them nothing.[1]

In suggesting a relatively simple causal relationship between mass poverty and revolutionary appeal, Fidel Castro enjoyed the company of many other revolutionaries as well as a broad coalition of counterrevolutionaries. Crude economic determinism of this sort was used by United States policymakers to promote support for the Alliance for Progress, and by Chilean anti-Communists to rationalize a new concern for domestic socio-economic reforms.[2]

Although economic stagnation and mass poverty did, in fact, contribute to revolutionary ferment in Chile, Fidel's prediction nevertheless underestimates or ignores crucial system-maintaining relationships which affect the direction of mass political support. The decision to undertake this case study was occasioned by a desire to assess which structural features of Chile's political system effectively limited the transnational appeal of the Cuban Revolution. As will be seen, Allende's unexpected 1970 electoral success was, if anything, correlated with a further decline in mass support for Fidelismo. Among political elites of the center and left, however, there seems to have been a slight rise in sympathy for the Cuban experiment.

Chile's suitability for this investigation is suggested by the widespread socio-economic impoverishment which afflicted between fifty and eighty percent of the citizenry. If one considers that Chilean inflation has been both chronic and severe, the latter figure is probably a good measure of perceived relative deprivation. In any case, economic stagnation, unbalanced development and perhaps "exploitation" can be said to characterize Chilean society. Because of the essentiality of these socio-economic conditions to the *Fidelista* thesis, they are briefly essayed in chapter 2. It also contains comparative Latin American data indicating Chile's similarity to other underdeveloped nations in the region. One cannot appraise the meaning of Chile's most controversial political issues during the past decade without an awareness of and sensitivity to the social plight of her citizenry.

The Significance of Parliamentary Democracy

In prognosticating the transnational appeal of the Cuban Revolution, Fidel drew no distinction between Constitutional and dictatorial regimes in Latin America. Hence, a second objective of this study will be to ascertain the distinctive "strengths" of parliamentary democratic systems when confronted by revolutionary political forces which nevertheless accept the Constitutional "rules of the game."[3]

With this in mind, selected traditional and contemporary aspects of the Chilean political system are described in chapter 3. Their behavioral significance for particular groups was often affected by socio-economic differentials. Thus the property-owning and educated upper classes were more apprehensive of political violence and assigned greater "legitimacy" to the Constitutionalist system. Similarly, blue collar sectors tended to be more radical and sympathetic to the Cuban Revolution.

The classes which appropriate disproportionate material benefits within a stagnant and underdeveloped country represent a small portion of the population.[4] For those experiencing moderate or severe impoverishment, there are few material benefits serving to reinforce the internalization of Constitutionalist norms. This is particularly apparent when we realize that widespread functional illiteracy and apathy, increasing civil violence, periodic suppression of free speech and substantial military autonomy place Chile on a continuum at some remove from a "pure" Anglo-Saxon ideal type of parliamentary democracy.[5] Hence, there is a touch of the ironic in ubiquitous upper class claims that Chileans are "the English of South America." One seldom hears this from their mestizo social inferiors.

United States Intervention

There is no lack of scholarly works emphasizing the "weakness" of civilian institutions in underdeveloped areas.[6] The preservation or attainment of privileged access to raw materials, export markets and investment opportunities (the operative meaning of the "Free World") for the United States may at times require military intervention to ensure the "stability" of the socio-economic system. When in Guatemala (1954), Guyana (1963), Dominican Republic (1963, 1965), and Brazil (1964), the parliamentary system appeared incapable, or unsure, of safeguarding an order in which "free enterprise" could prosper, the essentially instrumental role of parliamentary democracy was manifested by joint United States-local upper class support for violent change in the Constitutional regime. Reflecting a worldwide pattern, analogous interventions which received immediate United States support have occurred in Iran (1954), Congo-Kinhasa (1960), Ghana (1965), Indonesia (1965), and Cambodia (1970).[7]

Because of congressional restrictions, which limit United States economic aid to nationalistic civilian governments, it is undoubtedly simpler for American policy-makers in the executive to rely upon pro-"free enterprise" military "nation-builders." Hence, by 1968 we find Gen. Robert W. Porter, commander-in-chief of the United States Southern Command, candidly recalling for us the continuity in foreign objectives since the pre-Bolshevik "Dollar Diplomacy" era:

Many of you gentlemen are leaders and policy-makers in the businesses and industries that account for the huge American private investment in Latin America. . . . Some misguided personalities and groups in our own country and abroad call you capitalists who seek profit. Of course you do. . . . You can help produce a climate conducive to more investment and more progressive American involvement in the hemisphere . . . the Alliance envisages some $300 million a year in U.S. private investment. . . .

As a final thought, consider the small amount of U.S. public funds that have gone for military assistance and for AID public safety projects as a very modest premium on an insurance policy protecting our vast private investment in an area of tremendous trade and strategic value to our country.[8]

If the Chilean case proves anything, it demonstrates that both an "open door" for North American capital and a parliamentary democracy can be maintained *without the necessity for military intervention;* and despite the legal existence of a Socialist-Communist Popular Action Front (FRAP) with 40,000 dedicated pro-Cuban members and hundreds of thousands of loyal supporters. Furthermore, there was little evidence of any mass commitment to democratic proceduralism. The very marginal political socialization effectuated by the educational system is implied by the fact that less than 40 percent of the economically active population (1960) claimed to be primary school graduates. The maintenance of Chile's system is even more impressive when it is realized that unlike other more pliant Latin American client states, Chile insisted upon the continuation of unrestricted travel and diplomatic relations with Revolutionary Cuba until August 1964 when she was finally forced to sever them. This study centers upon the 1959-1965 period, when the fate of Chile's parliamentary regime was a major political concern in Santiago, Washington and Havana.

How was the system preserved? The attempts by Havana to "export" her revolutionary ideals (described in chapter 4) pale in significance when contrasted to the massive material and ideological assistance which the United States provided sympathetic Chilean political groups and institutions. This extensive intervention (detailed in chapter 5) was possible only because those controlling the Chilean government recognized the international class meaning of "national interdependence."[9]

The relationships examined in chapters 4 and 5 suggest the *differential* "openness" of Chile's political system to revolutionary Cuban and essentially conservative United States infusions. They further indicate—when party, clerical and public reactions to the Cuban Revolution are considered (chapters 6-9)—how closely domestic political institutions are linked to external supporting organizations. The tendency of much contemporary "theoretical" scholarship on political development to *assume* that "less developed" systems are essentially self-equilibrating (autonomous, etc.) functions to obscure these dynamic trans-systemic interactions.[10]

Hence, what we see in this Chilean drama is a pronounced *determination* by Washington to "do everything possible to avoid a second Cuba." The transcending issue in the highly emotional 1964 presidential campaign was the charge that if elected, FRAP nominee Salvador Allende would "transform Chile into another Cuba." By assigning sufficient resources to strengthen sympathetic civilian political actors, the United States enabled them to preserve the socio-economic system without the necessity for military intervention.

Chilean Exceptionalism

The efficacy of external support, however, is affected by the degree of consensual unity, enlightened self-interest and tactical flexibility attained by elites representing upper and upper middle classes. In Chile, a decline in cohesion among these sectors paralleled, and was partially occasioned, by a marked rise in lower class expectations and militance during the 1967-1970 period. These factors along with counterrevolutionary overconfidence and the dysfunctional assassination of the highest ranking officer in Chile's Armed Forces enabled a Popular Unity revolutionary administration to be installed Constitutionally in office on Nov. 4, 1970.

While this Leftist triumph is undoubtedly also due to the consummate political skills and pragmatism of Salvador Allende, it does not thereby invalidate the previously stated hypothesis that parliamentary systems are essentially "closed" to the electoral aspirations of principled socialist parties. To falsify this thesis, not only would the Popular Unity victory and the enlargement of its mass constituency at the next congressional elections have to be honored by the Armed Forces, but there would have to be a pattern of respect for comparable outcomes in other parliamentary systems. Institutional relationships and political socialization variables which are examined in the following chapters suggest why *both* of these possibilities are highly improbable.

Part I:
Background

2 Socio-Economic Environmental Factors

Introduction

Social and economic questions have been prominent among Chilean political issues since the 1940s. Control of inflationary pressures, policies towards wage adjustments, employment and foreign-owned mining firms, expansion of welfare state benefits, public works programs and efforts to raise national production have represented major foci of contention. Yet behind the issues, so to speak, has been a social situation marked by massive and perhaps deepening poverty for a large segment of the nation's citizens. By the early 1960s, proposals for the elimination of this social degradation began to command massive electoral support and emerged as one of the most important political issues—one which effectively contributed to the rise and decline of parties and coalitions. The continuation of mass impoverishment was viewed by *Fidelistas*, those who proposed the Alliance for Progress (AFP) and others as likely to create favorable objective circumstances for—or even "cause"—a social revolution effectively oriented towards the *Fidelista* model. Whether and why such consequences failed to eventuate is a question to be dealt with in succeeding chapters. Before proceeding, however, consideration of what is frequently called "the social problem" is necessary.

The "Marginals"

Frequently viewed as a source of actual or potential resentment in Chile has been not only the pervasive poverty, but the absence of effective social mobility for members of the lower class sectors.[1] Kalman Silvert has suggested the existence of an "effective nation" representing little more than 20 percent of the population. The remaining four-fifths were held to share or participate only marginally—if at all—in the benefits of modern culture.[2] Frederick B. Pike has argued that during the early sixties,

... considerably less than 5,000,000 actually participate or will participate upon reaching maturity in the vital currents of national existence. The other more than 2,000,000 exist in a category that is somewhat similar to serfdom or slavery. Because of their situation they are themselves demoralized, and bereft of hope and vitality. Perhaps worse, the presence of an immobile, inert mass of still docile and fatalistic workers demoralizes, corrupts, and enervates those who take

9

advantage of them and imparts a viciously derogatory connotation to the word labor.[3]

The late Jorge Ahumada, one of the architects of Frei's 1958 and 1964 programs, has focused upon the lack of common values and goals which are necessary for societal cohesion and consensual politics. He has been especially disturbed by the social disintegration evidenced by widespread disrespect for the law.

Chile is not characterized by widespread respect for norms of social behavior which are embodied in laws, regulations and traditions. The obligation to submit to various expressions of majority will is a duty which each individual believes applies only to others. Each Chilean's feeling that he is somehow above the law, the ease with which infractors evade sanctions, the charitable philosophy that conditions legislative attitudes and ethics in the primary schools, the secondary schools and the university adequately explain why infractions occur with the same frequency in matters that are important for collective life as in small things.

In the course of his polemical analysis, Ahumada attributes disrespect for the law by the upper classes to their neo-feudal belief that they are above the law. The masses, he asserts, conceive of the laws as being enacted by and in the interests of the oligarchy.[4]

Chile and Latin America

Patterns of class relations associated with extensive social marginality prevailed in much of Latin America during the late 1950s. From a comparative perspective, however, the material and cultural deprivation experienced by fifty to eighty percent of the Chilean populace was less acute than that which characterized lower class life situations in a number of other Latin American nations. Chile's relatively advantaged position is illustrated by the data on the following page.

Although impoverishment was more widespread in perhaps fifteen Latin American nations, its extensiveness within Chile should not be minimized. More specifically, little if any progress was made in ameliorating social deprivation during the decade preceding the Cuban Revolution. A stagnant economy, inflation and demographic growth contributed to a decline in the living standards of a large sector of the lower classes. The seriousness of the "social question" is evidenced by the following summarization of data in various areas.

Some Dimensions of Mass Impoverishment

Malnutrition. At least since the end of World War II, extensive lower class malnutrition has been known to exist in Chile. A "careful investigation" undertaken

Table 2-1
Selected Cross-National Indicators of Social Deprivation

Nation	Illiterate (% of pop. 15 yrs & over)*		Piped Water (% of dwellings)		Primary Students (per teacher)		Physicians (per 10,000 persons)	
Argentina	8.6	(1960)	53.1	(1960)	19	(1965)	14.9	(1962)
Chile	16.4	(1960)	62.0	(1960)	50	(1964)***	5.8	(1964)
Cuba	23.6	(1953)	55.2	(1953)	34	(1964)	8.9	(1965)
Venezuela	36.7	(1961)	67.1	(1961)	21	(1965)	7.8	(1964)
Mexico	37.8	(1960)	32.3	(1960)	47	(1965)	5.2	(1965)
Peru	38.9	(1961)	42.3	(1961)**	36	(1965)	4.7	(1964)
Brazil	39.4	(1960)	21.0	(1960)	30	(1964)	4.0	(1962)
Guatemala	62.1	(1964)	29.5	(1964)	34	(1964)	2.5	(1964)

*The ages for Mexico and Argentina are six and fourteen respectively.
**Includes only private households.
***Does not include private education.
Source: *Statistical Abstract of Latin America: 1966* (Los Angeles: Latin American Center of the University of California, 1967), pp. 90, 93, 99, 101.

in 1945 indicated that only 14 percent of the primary school pupils "did not show evidence of long term undernourishment."[5] Seven years later a United Nations report concluded that "in Chile there is a clear (caloric) deficit."[6] While there was some improvement in average caloric consumption during the 1950s, by the end of the decade, a decline in protein intake was noted.[7] Several years later, a joint United States-Chilean study in Santiago reported stunted growth among school children as well as an average protein deficiency of 28 percent among the population as a whole.[8] During the same general period, an ILO study concluded that:

Approximately one-half of Chile's population is suffering from malnutrition. Evidence indicates that 37% of the families were getting less than 85% of the standard reference calorie requirement, and 28% were getting less than 85% of the standard protein requirement. This is directly related to economic levels. . . . 11.8% of the population are suffering from mild malnutrition; 26.3% suffer serious malnutrition; and 11% desperate malnutrition.[9]

By the early 1960s the Chilean armed forces were reporting that the average height of conscripts was declining.[10] And in the course of the 1965 congressional campaign, a senatorial aspirant for re-election stated that according to investigations by Chilean health authorities: the growth of 60 percent of the children was stunted; 62 percent were below normal in weight; 42 percent suffered from anemias indicating that they lacked enough red corpuscles; 19 percent had anemias indicating they lacked hemoglobin and 86 percent suffered from bad teeth.[11]

Health. Despite the significant advances which have been made with regard to public health since the 1930s, the lower classes remained particularly vulnerable to infant mortality and tuberculosis.[12] Women from these sectors were the principal victims of complications resulting from induced abortions.[13] Although an estimated 70 percent of the population were able to use the facilities of the National Health Service, the quality of service rendered was clearly inferior to that received by upper middle and upper class persons who could afford private clinics.[14]

Housing. The prevalence of illness among impoverished Chileans during the early sixties was partly conditioned by crowded and unsanitary housing conditions. In 1960, out of 1,325,800 housing units, 573,300 lacked drinkable water and 499,300 did not have toilets. There was an average of 1.7 persons per room.[15]

Due to the decline in the mortality rate, rural migration and limited construction, the estimated number of urgently needed housing units is said to have increased from 400,000 to 500,000 during the 1953-1959 period. By 1967, the housing deficit was estimated at 600,000.[16]

Education. Limited potential earning power, frustration of occupational ambitions and social immobility confronted the lower classes during the late fifties as a consequence of a grave educational deficit. Although primary education has been legally obligatory since 1920, in 1952 only 339,900 of 613,100 children between the ages of six and nine years were attending school. By 1960, the percentage of this age group which was not enrolled had increased to more than 50 percent. In that year, 459,449 were in attendance while 512,902 were not.[17]

While upper middle and upper class children were generally sent to private schools, the quality of instruction and inadequate facilities in most state schools tended to restrict the value of this experience for those who could attend. Similarly, frequent illnesses, primitive and unstable home environments, and an insufficiency of economic resources to finance attendance were probably responsible for many dropouts.[18]

Although the rate of official illiteracy had fallen from about 25 percent in the early 1950s to slightly over 16 percent in 1960, functional illiteracy was substantially higher. Estimates of actual inability to understand the printed word ranged from 25 percent to 40 percent.[19] It is probable that this factor is directly related to mass media usage patterns stressing radio as well as to the simplistic or "demagogic" framework in which some major political issues were framed during the early 1960s.

The lack of educational opportunities for lower class persons was also reflected by university attendance. Frequently cited figures during the early sixties reported that less than 2 percent of University of Chile students came from blue collar backgrounds, and the comparable figure for Santiago's Catholic University was less than 1 percent.[20] This may have limited Marxist appeal among university students. As at other levels, there was a high incidence of dropouts as well as a shortage of facilities and equipment. At both the secondary and university levels, memorization and humanities were stressed.

Public Service and Administrative Outputs. While all social sectors in Chile were encountering some degree of inconvenience as a consequence of the lack of resources and inefficiency of the state and its agencies, those who were unable to afford private substitutes or use personal influence were particularly disadvantaged. Discrimination and arbitrariness in the administration of state services were reflected and facilitated by the ubiquitous use of particularistic and ascriptive criteria for promotions within public agencies. Survey research by the University of Chile's Center of Socio-economic Studies toward the end of 1965 reported that the following percentages "believed that favoritism played a large part in promotions." Administrative elite (52 percent); professionals and técnicos (32 percent); semiprofessionals (43 percent); general office workers (51 percent); technical assistants (52 percent); and service unskilled (55 percent). Between 55 and 70 percent in each category—except the last—attributed this favoritism to personal, family or political "pull" (cuña).[21]

The significance of such a class-biased administrative system is epitomized by the declining efficacy of the state-controlled transportation system. Although increasing imports of unassembled automobiles, converted low duty commercial vehicles and taxis provided effective transport for the upper and upper middle classes, others were forced to rely upon crowded and frequently dilapidated busses. New vehicles, it was alleged, tended to be designated for middle class *barrio* runs, rather than for the slum routes. The discomfort encountered in riding the busses (most being of the type used to transport school children in the United States) may have contributed to the glum expressions of many passengers, and was certainly responsible for advice directed at tourists to avoid them.

In 1965, it was reported that "more than one-half of the rolling stock of Santiago is not in operation, owing to the lack of repair parts. . . . Since the busses are old and worn, the fuel is not burned as it should be, and downtown Santiago has an irritating problem of smog." In addition, because of the piece-work based compensation of most drivers and the absence of any traffic law enforcement with regard to speed, reckless driving was causing many injuries to passengers.[22] While travel on the state railroads was somewhat more safe, most persons were reported to "travel third class in coaches equipped with wooden benches and drawn by coal-burning locomotives. Much of the rolling stock is at least 40 years old."[23]

Since very few, if any, lower class families were able to either obtain or pay for telephones, the high rates and notoriously bad service provided by this United States-owned company did not affect them. Those who benefited from electricity were likewise confronted by high charges. The price of refined gas was so high that most lower class persons probably relied upon kerosene and charcoal for heating and cooking purposes. Both tended to create a smoke problem within crowded living quarters.[24]

Whether it was a question of dealing with social security agencies, the National Health Service, postal authorities or the civil registry, the petitioner who lacked influential friends was confronted by complicated and cumbersome procedures, lengthy delays and at times with patronizing attitudes by the bureaucratic staffs.[25]

Unemployment and Social Insurance. Chilean unemployment increased during the late 1950s, and by the early sixties it was estimated that between 224,000 and 300,000 active job seekers were unable to find work.[26] According to the 1960 census, the economically active population was less than 2,400,000; thus, the real rate may have been as high as 13 percent.[27] More serious, perhaps, was hidden unemployment evidenced by an excessive number of extremely low-paid marginal jobs in the service sector. It has been estimated that this form of underemployment may have accounted for an additional ten percent of the work force.[28] Given these figures, large scale United States budgetary support during the early 1960s may well have averted a serious socio-political crisis which would have further swelled leftist constituencies.

Although Chile was the second nation in Latin America to institute social security "on a wide basis," by the early 1960s its value was marginal for a substantial proportion of the lower or blue collar classes which represented about 75 percent of the population.[29]

According to one report, 50 percent of the worker contributions were used for administrative expenses in managing the "system."[30] There were between thirty and forty-eight different social security funds which were regulated by some 514 different laws.[31] Since the government over-borrowed from many of the funds, United States budgetary support may have been vital here too.

With regard to the lower classes, between 40 percent and 45 percent were without any coverage.[32] It has been alleged that "for every active army officer there are five on pension. But out of every hundred factory workers only one receives a pension."[33] *Empleados* or white collar employees have obtained privileged status under the social security system. And within this very broad classification, special advantages have been secured by particular strata. In general, however, *empleados* or middle class sectors enjoy earlier retirement ages while

the manual workers who represent 74 percent of those covered by social security, receive only 34 percent of the benefits paid by these services. In the case of white collar employees, the majority lack medical attention, illness and maternity benefits. It is estimated that of seven and a half million Chileans, there are at least two million who never receive medical attention, and that more than three million receive neither payments nor other benefits when they suffer illness, become disabled or become old, orphaned or widowed.[34]

Many workers were denied all benefits because they had lost their social security stamp booklets. Others conspired with employers to ignore the "system" altogether.[35] A three-year government study reported in 1962 that pensions lost on the average 85 percent of their purchasing power due to inflation.[36] Hence, payments into the funds were viewed as regressive taxes rather than contributions to future security.

Wage Levels. A fairly accurate indication of the extremely limited purchasing power of the Chilean lower classes may be derived from the average daily earnings in key sections during 1964: copper E4.93; oil E4.81; commerce E3.88; industry E2.47; and agriculture E0.69. At the time, a dollar was worth more than four Escudos on the "parallel" or "black" market which is used widely by the upper middle and upper classes.[37] The wage data cited above and other studies indicate substantial earnings disparities both between and within various sectors. Among blue collar workers, individuals performing similar tasks often receive markedly different wages.

While those in capital intensive and unionized mining or industrial firms have managed to attain a modest degree of security and comfort, a substantial majority of wage earners and a minority of generally better off salary earners brought home earnings of less than $10.00 per week. Hence, during the early 1960s approximately fifty percent of the people "accounted for less than ten percent of the consumption of manufactured goods and nine percent of the services."[38]

Between 1955 and 1965, Chile has been characterized by severe inflation.[39] There is a substantial body of opinion which holds that during this period the real income of the lower classes has in fact declined,[40] with the exception of perhaps half of Chile's 400,000 *empleados* and a much smaller proportion of her blue collar workers—principally those employed in dynamic sectors of industry and mining where unions are most effective, it would seem that the principal consequence of the inflationary process for the lower classes has been a regressive redistribution of personal income.[41]

A number of factors contributed to this situation. Of major importance has been the bargaining weakness of organized labor, which represented about 10 percent of the urban two-thirds of the work force. Since 1956, Chilean governments have generally opposed wage readjustments (election years excepted) that fully compensated for the previous price rises.[42] The Left has vehemently and incessantly attacked the United States for "imposing" this policy upon Chile through its influence in international lending agencies and by means of less formal channels. The tax structure has been heavily regressive, with extensive evasion resulting in very low effective rates for the upper middle and upper classes. Tax payments were withheld from the wage payments to lower middle and lower class employees.[43]

The lack of lower class purchasing power has narrowed the potential internal market and inhibited Chilean industry from operating at full capacity—thus contributing to Chile's economic stagnation in the late 1950s and early 1960s.

Owning groups have consequently invested a small share of their inflation-derived profits in expanding plant and equipment.[44] These funds have either been used for immediate consumption—thus aggravating the chronic balance of payments problems, invested in land as a hedge against inflation, or have been banked or invested in New York or Zurich.[45] Thus, between the mid-fifties and mid-sixties, the growth of Chilean interest and dividend payments was far in excess of the modest expansion of industrial output.[46] The diversion of this inflation-generated surplus from the economy was reflected by a decline of the annual growth in real income from 1.9 percent per capita during 1950-1955 to 1.4 percent per capita from 1955 to 1960. Between 1960-1963, the corresponding percentage had fallen to 0.6 percent.[47]

Rural Differentials. If the life situations of the urban lower classes evidenced a growing distance from those of their social betters during the 1950s, even greater contrasts characterized the rural areas. There were proportionately fewer educational and health facilities. Housing was frequently primitive, and illiteracy more prevalent.[48]

In the mid-1950s, income disparities in rural areas were greater than those in urban sectors.[49] Although the real income of landowners increased by more than 48 percent from 1950 to 1959, per capita agricultural output remained "almost stationary" until the 1958-1962 period when production declined on a per capita basis.[50] Since 1950, it is probable that the real income of the rural peasantry has declined.[51] This has almost certainly been a prime stimulus for the urban migration during the 1950s. In 1952, Chile was 39.8 percent rural, while eight years later the percentage had fallen to 31.8 percent. During this period, the proportion of the national population living in Santiago had risen from about a quarter to a third. Since most of the rural migrants were probably unable to find or hold jobs in commerce or industry, they swelled the ranks of the unemployed and accounted for a major increase of those employed or underemployed in unremunerative "personal services."[52]

While the urban upper class admitted a smaller proportion of individuals from humble origins at midcentury than it had a generation earlier,[53] the class system remained even more closed and hierarchical in the rural areas. The only substantial middle class elements in the countryside were upper middle class purchasers of estates and *chacras* who tended to identify with and assimilate their style of life to that of the older landed families. The latter were, meanwhile, increasing their holdings in urban commerce and industry—or investing funds abroad. Hence, in 1965 approximately one-half of the large businessmen in Chile either owned or were near relatives of those owning large rural estates.[54]

The distribution of farm holdings in 1954 was such that 2.8 percent accounted for 37.3 percent of the arable area, while 54.1 percent held a mere 5.7 percent of tillable land. By 1965, 1.5 percent of the owners owned 70 percent of the tillable land. Fifty percent of the land holders possessed 1 percent of the arable area.[55] The landowning upper classes enjoyed privileged access to government credit facilities, but the loans did not have to be invested in production-increasing improvements.[56] Their tax rates were reported to average 1.9 percent of assessed land values, the assessments being about a third of market value.[57] Similarly, minimum wage and social legislation was often unenforced, while property-owning sectors successfully prevented the organization of peasant co-operatives and unions by landless agricultural laborers, sharecroppers and small plot owners.[58]

Concluding Remarks

Although Chile was on a per capita Gross National Product (GNP) basis among the more "developed" countries of Latin America,[59] the lower classes—with the exception of the *Gran Mineria* copper workers and a few urban sectors of organized labor—had been largely unable to benefit from the amenities of modern civilization. Representing from seventy to eighty percent of the population, they were in society but not really affective participants in what Silvert has termed the "effective nation." In projecting their social revolution as one being made by and for *los humildes* of Cuba and Latin America, the Cuban leadership assumed that the Revolution's programs and reforms would inspire mass support among these sectors in Chile. Even those with little sympathy for the course that Cuba has taken have shared such fears. After concluding his study of the laboring classes in Chile, Argentina, and Brazil, Robert J. Alexander prognosticated that "(t)he widespread feeling of frustration and even desperation among the workers of the three countries might well find expression in one or more of these nations seeking to resolve their dilemma along the lines already made popular in the hemisphere by Fidel Castro."[60]

Argentina and Brazil are today governed by anti-working class military regimes. While Chilean developments seem at first glance to be consistent with the prognosis, it shall be demonstrated that Alexander's prediction is an over-simplified one at best! The succeeding chapters shall explain why mass attention and affective support for the Cuban Revolution was restricted to a small sector of the lower or *"popular"* classes. Although the environmental variables essayed in this chapter were not unimportant, their directional effects upon political behavior were mediated at elite and especially at mass levels by organizational, institutional and tactical variables. And these were differentially and in many cases only marginally affected by Cuba's social revolution.

3

Aspects of Chilean Political Organization and Behavior

Introduction

An understanding of why Cuba's egalitarian social reforms and anti-imperialist mass mobilizations did not evoke widespread sympathy among Chileans requires some consideration of her political heritage and institutions. While the conception of the political system will be broad in nature, only selected aspects will receive attention. These were directly related to differentiated mass and elite identifications with the symbolism of Fidelismo.

Heritage of the Impersonal State and Evolutionary Constitutionalism

The successful struggle by Chileans for national self-determination occurred during the first quarter of the nineteenth century. "On initiating the revolution for independence, the Kingdom of Chile was—of all the Spanish Colonies—the most socially and geographically compact unity. . . . Most of the population was in the Central Valley and it took no more than two or three days to reach anywhere from Santiago."[1]

The setting, then, was not auspicious for the emergence of regionally based caudilloism. Centralized rule was also favored by nearly uninhabitable geographic barriers surrounding the Central Valley. To the north was the desert, while the Pacific Ocean confronted Chileans on the west. Although the largely barren Andes harbored bandit gangs and fugitive slaves during a good part of the nineteenth century, they could not sustain appreciable numbers of permanent settlers.[2] By isolating the country from its northern and eastern neighbors, these natural barriers to external communication prompted the Chileans to construct a respectable fleet of merchant ships and a very large navy during the 1810-1830 period. Given the fact that Chile is more or less shaped like a string bean, naval logistic and blockade support facilitated the maintenance of centralized authority. Southward settlement was limited by inhospitable Mapuche Indians who were not conquered until the 1880s.

Between 1813 and 1830, institutional stability was nonexistent in Chile. The rejection of the traditional authority of the Spanish Crown eliminated the only unifying symbol to which widespread legitimacy was attached. In its absence caudilloist and factional rivalries assumed paramount importance. Heavy taxes,

19

economic difficulties and administrative disorganization and favoritism contributed to a growing consensus among the oligarchy that caudilloism and continued attempts to institute liberal constitutional principles were contrary to their common class interests. With the support of most of the upper classes Diego Portales successfully led a *golpe del estado* (forcible seizure of power) in 1830. This marked the beginning of almost a century of institutionalized authority.

With regard to the regime established by Portales, a noted Chilean historian has remarked that: "The government wasn't Carrera, nor O'Higgins nor this or that general. Government was Authority, the State. The symbolic equivalent of the Crown was established: instead of a King there was now a Constitutional President; it didn't matter who occupied the role; it was Impersonal Authority."[3]

Those who administered the strong presidency established by Portales were said to have viewed it as an agency of government in the common interest and not as an instrument for plunder by a particular clique or faction. Severe, but not barbaric, sanctions were applied to those who organized rebellions. Some purging of corrupt occupants of public office also occurred. Congressional support for the neo-monarchical presidency was assured by presidential intervention in elections for which the franchise was extremely narrow. The president generally nominated similarly ensured the election of his successor.[4]

Evolutionary tendencies and a commitment to constitutionalism marked the period during which political parties began to emerge. Between the 1850s and the 1880s, the scope of the Catholic Church's civil jurisdiction was a political issue of major importance. A lack of upper class consensus on this question catalyzed an acute political conflict, with the Conservative Party identifying itself as the foremost defender of the Church. One wing of the Liberal Party was mildly anti-clerical and inclined to compromise on the issue as were some Conservatives. The more principled anti-clerical wing of the Liberals organized the Radical Party during the 1880s.

From its inception, this group was characterized by a multiclass leadership. In addition to advocating the reformist goals of a small sector of the landed oligarchy, the Radicals assimilated urban-based commercial, industrial and professional elements into the political process. Between the 1860s and 1920s, the Radicals endeavored to widen their electoral base by advocating the extension of suffrage and cultivating the support of white collar employees.[5]

Despite a brief civil war and sporadic military revolts during the 1850s, the traditions of compromise and constitutionalism were strongly reinforced by a presidential precedent in 1858. When congressional hostility to members of the president's cabinet became so intensive that the Congress refused to appropriate funds for the executive budget, instead of declaring a "State of Seige" and assuming dictatorial powers, President Montt acceded to legislative demands that he reorganize his cabinet. The Congress then approved the appropriations.[6] Until

1891, Chilean presidents were willing to respect this constitutional allocation of authority in certain areas to the congressional representatives of the landed oligarchy, the Church and to some degree, business. When a reformist and very nationalistic President Balmaceda was confronted by a similar situation in 1890, he "unconstitutionally" ordered dissolution of the Congress. The British-supported Constitutionalists were victorious in the ensuing civil war.[7] A period of congressional dominance then prevailed until 1925.[8]

Thus, for close to a century, the distribution of legal authority and the procedures governing its exercise by political elites were codified by a single document—the Portales Constitution which had been imposed during the early 1830s. With the exception of a brief interregnum (1924-1933), this tradition also has been associated with succeeding decades. Stability was facilitated not only by the country's geo-physical compactness and isolation, but also by such factors as: 1) the cultural homogeneity and cohesiveness of the landed upper class; 2) its openness during the 18th, 19th and early part of the 20th century to *noveau riche* urban businessmen; 3) the ability to attain and become reconciled with a compromise solution to the anti-clericalism issues of the late 19th century; 4) a consensual willingness to suppress lower class economic and political groups which rejected co-optation during the 20th century; 5) the extension of modest concessions to middle class sectors that accepted co-optation; 6) no mass education; and 7) the exclusion of 90 percent of the adult population from participation in the national political system until the late 1930s.[9]

Hence, although "the traditions of Chilean constitutional and legal practice are those of rigid and inflexible adherence to the forms of constitutionalism rather than to the spirit,"[10] the "forms" have weighed heavily as normative values for political elites associated with Centrist parties and among perhaps 10 percent of the population who have been politically socialized by the nation's educational system.[11] And it shall be seen, this formalistic tradition is also operative in some lesser albeit indeterminate degree upon political elites of the left and right. For many such persons, Cuba's political traditions were "tropical"— hence inferior and inapplicable to the resolution of Chile's developmental problems.

Militarism

A second tradition of particular relevance to Cuba-related group responses during the 1960s concerned the pattern of historic military intervention. In the nineteenth century the Chilean military assumed active political roles during the 1820s, the 1850s, and in the early 1890s. Frequently such armed intervention was solicited by civilian politicians. Liberal and reformist goals were occasionally proclaimed in the 1820s and especially during the 1850s as justification for political involvement. When Balmaceda ordered taxes to be collected without congressional authorization in 1891, the army remained loyal to the president while the naval forces joined the ultimately victorious rebellion. Prior to this Civil War, the armed forces had successfully defeated Peru and Bolivia in the 1830s and again between 1879-1883. Military prestige and satisfaction was also enhanced by army success in decimating the Araucanian natives of southern Chile. These achievements and the pre-1883 restriction of commissioned status to scions of the small and homogeneous upper class contributed to a military tradition of respect for constitutional norms.[12]

During the 1920s and early 1930s, civilian political groups again solicited the intervention of the military. In 1918, the reformist Arturo Alessandri Palma was elected to the presidency. Strengthened by over-representation of rural districts and widespread vote-buying, conservatives in the Congress blocked most of Alessandri's proposed measures. Between 1919 and 1924, the president sought the support of the urban lower and lower middle classes. He actively participated in the 1924 congressional elections which seriously weakened rightist representation in that body.

After its defeat in these elections which brought the first Marxist deputies to Congress, the conservative National Union persuaded the army command to oust Alessandri. In the previous campaign, he had been accused of opening Chile to Communist subversion. The existence of an active reformist faction in the officer corps forced those who deposed Alessandri to pledge that social reforms would be implemented. The National Union-supported military rulers proved to be both inept and disinclined to implement the promised reforms. In January 1925 they were ousted by a pro-Alessandri military faction.[13]

The "Lion of Tarapaca"—as Alessandri was known—returned, and a new constitution establishing a strong presidency was promulgated.[14] A year later, continued Marxist demonstrations and propaganda were used by General Carlos Ibanez del Campo to justify his demand for the resignation of a recently elected "weak" president.[15] Ibanez ran unopposed for the presidency in 1927. In that year he established the Carabineros (a quasi-military national police force), and directed a brutal suppression of the Left.

Ibanez's arbitrariness and heavy-handed methods provoked growing discontent even among the conservative elements which had originally backed his usurpation.[16] In 1932, reformist and socialistic civilian politicians prevailed upon Air Force Gen. Marmaduke Grove and other officers to overthrow Juan Estebo Montero, an inept successor and former minister in the Ibanez regime. A so-called Socialist Republic was proclaimed; it lasted 100 days before conservative officers deposed the cabinet.[17] The military permitted elections in 1932, and Alessandri was again victorious. He had been supported by the Radicals, and various socialistic grouplets, but not by the Communists.

To deter a recurrence of intervention by the military, Alessandri authorized the organization of a Republican Militia in 1933. A total of perhaps 50,000 armed men were assigned to regiments throughout the country. As the Alessandri administration moved increasingly towards the right, these civilian units—many of which were composed of Socialists and workers—began to engender fear among upper class sectors. In 1936, the administration acceded to military wishes that the militia be disbanded.[18]

Three years later, Generals Ibanez and Ariosto Herrera led a military uprising against the Communist-supported Popular Front government of Pedro Aguirre Cerda. Due to poor coordination, vacillations by the plotters and the encirclement of several barracks by the militants of the leftist parties in the course of a general strike, many officers failed to join the conspiracy and the *golpe* proved abortive.[19]

By the late 1950s, the Carabineros and the armed forces represented about 30 percent of all government personnel.[20] In 1959, the military received 22.9 percent of the national budget, and this was apportioned as follows: army 35 percent, navy 47 percent and air force 19 percent.[21] In that year, there were 20,400 men in the army and about 18,000 quasi-military Carabineros.[22] The Carabineros, in addition to suppressing urban demonstrations and peasant land seizures, were assigned the military task of protecting the nation's frontiers.

Although no *golpes* were attempted during the forties or fifties, the Chilean military have been characterized as essentially "autonomous." Their "separation" from politics has been conditioned by a "sort of gentleman's agreement" that "the armed forces' customary 20-25 percent of the national budget must not be revised downward" and that the armed forces must be allowed "to function unmolested and to look after their own affairs."[23]

The Chilean military in recent years haven't drafted *pronunciamientos* about political questions of the day. Nevertheless, their anti-Communist and Constitutionalist sentiments have been publicized occasionally in leading Chilean weeklies. In May 1960, it was reported that a "group of young officers" in the army had drafted an unofficial document urging greater preparations for "subversive war." It warned that "professional agitators" might take advantage of widespread social discontent and stage a series of massive street demonstrations in an effort to take control of the capital. The fate of the military, according to the document, would be the same as that which occurred in Bolivia and Revolutionary Cuba.[24]

About two years later, a retired general who had served as a military attache in Washington and who still retained "solid prestige in the Armed Forces," directed a public call to the Minister of Defense for the outlawing of the Communist Party.[25] And in January 1966, an interview with a general who was about to retire reflected what may be a common army view on the internal security function of the military:

Its duty is to constitute itself as a bulwark of internal security so that the Constitutional government can carry on its work. . . .

Our respect as soldiers of the fatherland, is for the Constitutional government. Its breakdown would bring great harm to the country. Initially, a certain structuring of authority would be maintained, but soon an open struggle would develop for the highest governmental positions. As long as there is a Constitutional government, it will have the unreserved respect of the Armed Forces.[26]

Similar and reinforcing attitudes have been promoted among conscripts and enlistees—virtually all of whom are recruited from the lower classes.[27]

During the 1960s, counterinsurgency training and anti-Communist indoctrination were extended to both the armed forces and the national police. The former established elite "Black Beret" contingents while a special anti-riot "Mobile Group" Carabinero unit was constituted. By the end of the decade the strength of the armed forces had been increased to 60,000 men while the Carabineros had recruited an additional 12,000 officers and men. The combined strength of Chile's national security forces totaled 90,000 in 1969.[28]

That year also witnessed two barracks uprisings due to "professional" grievances concerning pay, retirement, etc.[29] It is worth noting that the interventions of the 1920s were also preceded by a gradual accumulation of professional grievances which were not resolved by politicians. These had involved continued political and social favoritism in the conferral of promotions despite two decades of Prussion supervised professionalization. When civilian political frustrations joined this institutional disquiet, the *golpes* of the twenties occurred.[30]

Unlike the twenties, however, the Frei administration responded by assuaging military economic grievances and also by removing all officers who had collaborated with the *cuartelazo* conspirators. Although Chilean presidents always appoint new chiefs of the various services, this reorganization of commands extended to lower levels by 1970. The armed forces—though not necessarily the quasi-military Carabineros—were finally officered by many Christian Democratic sympathizers. Before the most recent purge, a substantial number were conservative rather than reformist.[31]

Before concluding this discussion, it should be emphasized that the officer corps—as suggested by an earlier quotation—arrogates unto itself the role of preserving "constitutional" government. This implies the authority to decide when a government infringes constitutional norms as was done at the time of the 1891 Civil War. At their mass trial, the officers who had remained loyal to Balmaceda claimed that when he was president of the republic, they had merely obeyed their constitutional commander-in-chief. The victorious foreign-supplied-and-led Chilean rebels were unimpressed by this argument.[32]

In both 1891 and 1924, the interventions by recently enlarged military establishments were catalyzed by congressional recalcitrance to the reform programs of left-leaning presidents. Civilian politicians encouraged intervention in each instance. The second, which was reinforced by professional grievances, did not involve formal violation of the Constitution so much as its perceived abuse by the Congress. A new Constitution substantially enlarging executive authority replaced the Portales instrument. During the late 1960s, the Constitution was amended to vest new authority in the president, to modify constitutional amendments when confronted by a recalcitrant Congress. In such circumstances, Allende could decree a plebiscite which if favorable would enable him to override a hostile two-thirds congressional majority. In any case only simple majorities are required in each chamber for an amendment.[33]

For reasons which will become even more apparent in chapter 5, such conduct could be perceived by civil-military conspirators as an abuse of the president's constitutional authority—particularly if confiscatory socialist economic proposals or a new "peoples" constitution were the source of the congressional-presidential deadlock. Recollection of the fate of the anti-Communist Cuban Armed Forces of 1959 would reinforce such a disposition.

The Party System: An Overview

In addition to being characterized by traditions of military "autonomy," and Constitutionalism, vigorous party competition was integral to Chile's political system during the late 1950s. The absence of dictatorship since the early 1930s and the lengthy nineteenth century period during which political organizations were institutionalized combined to facilitate the emergence of relatively cohesive parties, each manifesting a distinctive tradition. Although some were weakened by internal personalist and ideological factionalism as well as by frequent indiscipline, their basic unity and identity have been preserved and in some cases strengthened.[34]

Between the early 1930s and the late 1950s, all important parties have chosen electoral access as the preferred means for improving or altering the socio-economic and political order. The five major groupings—Conservative (PCU), Liberal (PL), Radical (PR), Christian Democratic (PDC), Communist (PC), and Socialist (PS)—presented the voters with divergent principles and policy prescriptions. In terms of occupational interest groups and social classes, the Centrist Radical and Christian Democratic parties tended to be more broadly aggregative than those to the right and left of them.

During the period in question, all parties evidenced at various times a willingness to compromise their principles in the interests of tactical expediency. *Golpista "partiditos"* on the extreme right and extreme left were unable to emerge as significant political forces, and with the proscription in 1958 of "electoral pacts," the number of parties has declined. Small parties are also discriminated against by the d'Hondt system of proportional representation. Hence, the disastrous decline in support for the right-wing Liberals and Conservatives in the 1965 congressional elections resulted in their merger as the National Party. All parties have at one time or another resorted to informal electoral pacts to enhance congressional representation. This was the major electoral function of the left-wing FRAP between 1957 and 1969.

Party activity is intense during electoral campaigns which tend to be lengthy, especially at the national level. Vote-buying was common until the single ballot was instituted in 1958, but even after that the practice has continued on a lesser scale.[35] Instances of electoral fraud have also occurred, but they seldom have been of determinative significance.[36]

The inability or disinclination of centrist governments to control inflation and significantly raise living standards of the lower middle and lower classes has occasioned a gradual erosion of support from these sectors.[37] The left has been weakened by the outlawry and sporadic suppression of the Communists between 1947 and 1958; similarly, factionalism has plagued the Socialists while traditional animosities and competitiveness have characterized their relations with the Communists even after the two parties created the Popular Action Front (FRAP) in 1956.[38] By 1958, close to a majority of the Chilean electorate—in giving their votes to the Christian Democratic and FRAP presidential candidates—were supporting parties whose announced intention was to effectuate major institutional changes in the socio-economic order.[39] The intense party competition to recruit and register new rural and urban lower class voters ensured that "the social question" would be crucial in electoral campaigns during the sixties.[40]

At the same time, the *opportunity to vote* for parties that alleged they would revolutionize Chile sharply limited any potential popular base for guerrilla warfare—as did the remoteness of suitable terrain from heavily populated areas. The *newness and low educational level of the electorate*—half of those voting in 1964 were doing so for the first time—as well as the large influx of women, placed a premium upon the utility of simplistic anti-Communist (FRAP-Cuban) propaganda. Similarly, the superior financial resources of rightist and centrist parties gave them a distinct advantage in projecting frightening anti-Marxian symbols at the electorate.[41] The dissemination of transistor radios among lower class sectors facilitated such "campaigns of terror" in the bitter 1964 and 1970 presidential campaigns. A legislative proscription (Law No. 16,094) against posters and electronic media political insertions prior to the last fifteen days of the campaign—intended to offset the electoral advantage derived from a disparity in financial resources—was enacted for 1969.

During the congressional elections that year, this "law" was unobserved by "most of the 826 candidates," and unenforced by the government. Nor, for that matter, has there been any attempt to enforce the compulsory voting law for "literates" over 21 years old. In the 1969 congressional elections, for example, only "2,376,084 of the 3,250,436 registered voters exercised their franchise."[42] Even in the bitter 1970 presidential campaign, the abstention rate exceeded 16 percent. Approximately 20 percent of the political electorate remained disfranchised because of age (those between 18 and 21), and an additional 25 percent by reason of illiteracy. Given these considerations and the fact that well under 15 percent of the adult population identify with a particular party,[43] there is some basis for believing that a substantial majority of citizens are psychically marginated from "the party system." This contributes to explaining the ubiquitous fear of leftist mass mobilization and Fidelismo which has been articulated by military and political elites of the center and right.

Attitudes and Involvement

By the early 1960s, it had become fashionable for visiting journalists and scholars to suggest that there was immense socio-economic and political discontent that was about to "explode" Chile's democracy.[44] Although varying degrees of discontent did affect from forty to sixty percent of the adult population, it is unlikely that more than twenty percent were intensely disaffected.[45] Men and blue collar sectors tended to be more dissatisfied than women and the middle and upper classes.[46]

Of equal importance is the fact that at least since the mid-1950s, only a small minority of Chilean adults had internalized Marxist norms. Survey data indicate that between four and ten percent advocated or perceived a class struggle, endorsed expropriation without compensation, etc., as of the early 1960s. Similarly, little more than ten percent held favorable opinions of domestic Communists. Sex and social class were again independent variables functioning as they did with regard to socio-economic discontent and political dissatisfaction.[47]

Within the sector comprised by the roughly half million white collar employees, those in high level managerial positions and professionals tend to exhibit the least of political discontent and the greatest degree of class cohesion. While state regulation and a mixed economy are endorsed, there is minimal support—except among public employees where it is moderate at best—for expropriation or redistributive reforms. Energetic unions are opposed and a substantial proportion favor suppression of the Communist Party. Many at these levels identify with the upper entrepreneurial classes and place the interests of one's business firm before those of their country. The major public policy interest is in ending high rates of inflation—but not via price control. Owners of smaller businesses tend to support more active government control of private monopolies and industry groups which dominate the Chilean economy.[48]

Among the several hundred thousand clerical and semi-skilled white collar employees, there is only moderately greater support for socialism. A surprisingly large proportion of these indebted lower middle class persons identify themselves as "upper class." Their major grievances pertain to low salaries and inflation. In general, there is substantial job satisfaction—especially among public employees! These sectors—except for a minority at the lowest levels—also oppose redistributive reforms. And this attitude is shared by a majority of students preparing for public teaching careers. The lower middle classes do, however, recognize that theirs is a society characterized by gross inequalities of social opportunity. Nevertheless, a majority believe that social mobility should be achieved through little more than an expansion in educational facilities. An appreciable minority does support an expansion of government housing programs.

Among low level public employees in the mid-1960s, approximately 20 percent viewed reforms of agriculture, copper, housing and employment as "high priority" while the remaining 80 percent were divided between inflation and education. Nevertheless, about 40 percent endorsed "collectivism" while only 20 percent supported "free enterprise." Approximately 60 percent favored the prevailing "mixed economy" in Chile. Private white collar employees tend towards greater conservatism.[49]

The existence of perhaps 25 percent of the lower middle class as a potential radical constituency marks a fateful precedent for Chile. Traditionally, the middle classes have identified with and been rewarded modestly by their social betters. Even today middle class identification at both the blue and white collar levels remains as the strongest correlate of anti-radicalism.[50] By establishing the *empleado* employee category and vesting it with greater status, remuneration and security, the upper classes reinforced the socio-political hiatus between the blue collar *obreros* and the moderately better paid clerical employees who rose from less than 10 percent of the work force in the 1930s to more than a third by the 1960s.[51] This ensured socio-political stability by preventing working-class leftist parties from obtaining presidential pluralities or congressional majorities.

As in other nations, a marked lack of political cohesion has characterized the lower classes. Perhaps thirty percent of these strata were legally excluded from political participation due to illiteracy. Between a quarter and a third of the *obreros* and peasants (mis)identified themselves as middle class and hence more often than not opposed Marxist parties.[52] These and others were affected by the middle class ideology transmitted in the school system. Hence, it is not surprising that there is a curvilinear relationship between education and anti-radical predispositions.[53] And women at these levels were markedly more anti-radical than husbands who often backed the working class parties.[54] Many anti-Marxist males were probably: skilled workers employed by high wage capital intensive firms; operatives in commercial or industrial establishments employing fewer than 25 workers—where unions were proscribed and interface contact with middle class personnel was maximal; artisans and tradesmen; and finally, ex-army conscripts.[55]

The foregoing should not obscure the fact that the blue collar classes—especially unskilled, semi-skilled and the lowest income strata—did constitute a stable and slowly expanding constituency for both Marxist parties and Christian Democratic populism. This salient trend and the greater disposition of these classes to evidence generalized discontent than other citizens may be attributed to: 1) greater socio-economic hardship at these levels; 2) the lower class oriented nature of Marxist ideology; and 3) the *relative* freedom of the Marxist parties to organize and defend the economic interests of blue collar workers during much of the previous generation.

The sexual differential may be partly explained by such factors as: 1) less frequent primary experience in hierarchical employer-employee relationships by women; 2) greater female identification with Catholicism; and 3) lower educational levels—hence, abilities to conceptualize about society and the state—among women. Not only are women often not members of the work force, but when employed they tend to be concentrated in tertiary fields where there is high interaction on personal levels with middle class persons. Hence, about two-thirds of those supporting the Marxist parties in 1958 and 1964 were males employed as: 1) industrial *obreros*—particularly in large urbanized areas; 2) miners, and 3) landless agricultural workers. The remainder was comprised of: 1) wives of unionized *obreros* in mining or manufacturing; 2) poor peasants—particularly those residing near unionized mining communities; and 3) a small but increasing number of pauperized white collar (largely government) *empleados.*[56]

Although impressive majorities were willing to express support for social and economic reforms in general terms, attitudinal surveys indicated that very few persons possessed a substantial degree of familiarity with specific issues or problems.[57] Even during the intense 1964 presidential campaign, a larger number of interview respondents indicated that a candidate's personality was of greater importance than did his program.[58]

Similarly, fewer persons—especially among the lower classes—relied upon reading matter for their political information than upon more transitory radio broadcasts.[59] At the same time, during both the 1958 and 1964 presidential contests—when interest was most intense—less than a quarter of the adult population were even marginally involved in the campaigns. The proportion who cast a ballot in the latter and exceptional contest was only moderately higher. Involvement and issue cognizance were lower for women and the blue collar sector.[60]

Among these groups there was probably a widespread failure to comprehend that personal goals could be furthered through the political process. They tended to be susceptible to vote-buying and simplistic anti-Communist (FRAP-Cuba) appeals, both of which were resorted to by those supporting Frei in 1964, and by Christian Democrats and especially nationals in 1970.

Civil Liberties: A Mixed Record

Nearly all commentators on Chilean political history have emphasized the traditional respect for civil liberties which has set this country apart from most other Latin American nations. Associated with Chile's tradition of constitutionalism, they were identified as one of the major values that would be sacrificed if Allende won the presidency in 1964 and 1970. Both the "mixed record" of respect as well as certain legislative provisions to be detailed in the paragraphs which follow may contribute to explaining some of the valid grounds for this very genuine apprehension.

It was not until the last quarter of the nineteenth century that the Chilean Constitution guaranteed the right to exercise a non-Catholic religion or freedom of assembly to discuss political questions.[61] During the parliamentary regime which followed the overthrow of Balmaceda (1894-1924), miners and others who attempted to organize or strike were on quite a number of occasions brutally suppressed by the army.[62] Although there are no longer massacres of scores of laborers, instances of Carabinero or army brutality against demonstrating workers, students and political parties have occurred even during the 1950s and 1960s.[63] There are, however, usually no more than half a dozen deaths caused by the use of firearms or armored vehicles. More or less typical was the El Salvador "massacre." During a sympathy strike at this Anaconda installation in April 1966, army troops surrounded a union meeting hall and ordered occupants outside to place themselves under arrest. When the strikers and some of their wives left the building and began taunting the soldiers with curses and a few stones, they opened fire killing seven and wounding thirty-eight. As one might expect, the left won union positions from Christian Democrats at subsequent elections, and in 1970 Allende received his most solid backing in the four northern mining provinces.[64]

Atypical, but as significant, was the "bloody massacre" at Puerto Montt a few days after the March 1969 congressional elections. Squatters who had "taken" unoccupied land prior to the elections were brutally evicted by Carabineros. The national police wounded eleven and killed fifty-one men, women and children.[65] This historic event contributed to the defection of the populist or Communitarian wing of the PDC before the 1970 election. It also reflected a trend of increased reliance upon the "Grupo Movil" with its tanks, armored cars and gas by the Frei administration between 1966 and late 1969.[66] Although for electoral reasons the "ruano dura" was relaxed thereafter, two students were shot to death by the "Grupo Movil" in the course of a partially effective general strike in 1970.

For more than fifty years, Chilean Marxist parties have been the only consistent defenders of the victims of such brutalities. One of the first campaign pledges carried out by President Allende was the dissolution of the feared "Grupo Movil." Beginning in November 1970, its United States-financed water cannons were used to supply pure water to slum areas.

Communist and infrequently Socialist leaders have suffered from several waves of repression since the early 1920s. Successes at the polls and in leading organized labor—not abortive attempts to initiate a revolutionary insurrection—have been the major catalyzing factors. Eduardo Frei graphically described the violation of civil liberties between 1927-1931 by Ibanez, who "implacably persecuted" the Communist Party which first had been able to elect deputies in 1924.[67] As Frei stresses, all opposition groups were ultimately persecuted.

The Government of Mr. Ibanez, which was born with apparent legitimacy, since elections were called, quickly assumed truly dictatorial characteristics; supported by armed force, it sanctioned neither parliamentary opposition, nor a free press, nor independent labor organizations, nor even the presence in Chile of distinguished personalities who had placed themselves in opposition to it.

The leaderships of the parties were given to those who unconditionally supported his rule, the dailies were intervened and hundreds of persons were imprisoned and exiled; the unions were dissolved, and in their place, as with the parties, were substituted fictitious organizations led by those who were instruments of the Government, while the real leaders of the labor movement were implacably persecuted.

This Government of Mr. Ibanez followed the course of all military dictatorships in South America, characterized by outrages and violence. . . .[68]

By 1932, civil liberties had been restored to all parties, and the leadership of organized labor was no longer subject to persecution. The only serious incident in the late 1930s was the murder by the Carabineros of sixty-one captured Nazis who had previously organized an abortive *golpe*. The Communists and other non-government parties condemned this barbarity.[69] In the aftermath, the Nazis joined the Communists in supporting the presidential candidate of the Popular Front. Without Nazi votes, Aguirre Cerda would not have reached the presidency.[70]

Similarly, Communist votes were crucial to the election of Radical Gabriel Gonzalez Videla to the presidency in 1946.[71] In order to obtain their support, Gonzalez had promised not to obstruct Communist efforts to organize labor unions in rural areas. In addition, the Communists received the Public Works, Communications, and Lands and Colonization ministries. The holding of these three minor ministries between December 1946 and April 1947 enhanced the respectability of the party, and in the April municipal elections the Communists made sweeping gains—receiving over 16 percent of the vote. Because of this and their organizing in rural areas, the Liberals and Radicals who were also in the government, demanded the expulsion of the Communists. Gonzalez first hesitated, but after the ministers from these parties resigned he decided to accept their demands and reconstituted an all Radical cabinet.[72] This kind of resolution of the crisis was probably urged upon the Radical president by United States Embassy personnel, and within months more than forty million dollars in long term credits had been authorized by the Eximbank.[73]

In June 1947, Gonzalez "publicly accused the Communist Party of instigating unrest and subversion through the Chilean Confederation of Labor," and he began to stress the theme that a Third World War was inevitable.[74] After the Soviet rejection of the Marshall Plan, the Communists did in fact launch a wave of strikes.[75] President Gonzalez retaliated, he seized upon a coal strike to justify mass arrests of union leaders, and then successfully proposed legislation that outlawed the party and denied the electoral franchise to all voters who had registered as Communist supporters. Communist publications were suppressed and a concentration camp was established at Pisagua in the northern desert region for arrested Communist union and party leaders.[76]

As early as 1946, the Radical government of Gonzalez had permitted the organization of *Accion Chilena AntiCommunista* (ACHA) by Arturo Olavarria Bravo and other fervent anti-Communists. The organization—financed by Luis Eyzaguirre Infante and Carlos Cruz Eyzaguirre—was permitted to arm itself with machine guns, rifles, hand grenades, etc. ACHA's membership declined to a thousand members after the government outlawed the Communists, and it was then disbanded.[77]

The Socialists had not supported Gonzalez in 1946. The expulsion and subsequent persecution of the Communists was endorsed by a substantial sector of this party which had been struggling with the Communists for leadership of the labor movement. The Socialist Party of Chile then entered the Gonzalez government. A dissident youth faction led by Raul Ampuero withdrew from the party, constituted itself as the Popular Socialist Party, and joined the National Falange (precursor of the PDC) in criticizing Gonzalez's infringement of civil liberties. Although the Ampuero group was not pro-Communist, an agreement was reached with the outlawed party in 1950 to oppose Gonzalez.[78] A year before, there had been a relaxation of governmental suppressive measures. Nevertheless, the "Socialist and Communist parties were badly hit and wholesale desertion of members and supporters was common."[79]

In a bid for Leftist votes during his 1952 campaign, Ibanez promised to legalize the Communist Party. This organization, however, perhaps with remembrance of his conduct during the late 1920s declined to support him.[80] Although the subsequently victorious Ibanez did not advocate the party's legalization, it was allowed to function clandestinely and only persecuted when it actively opposed his measures.

Describing the state of affairs in 1957 after Ibanez had attempted to restrict wage increases in accord with the Klein-Saks recommendations, Kalman Silvert has observed that "the labor unions were without direction, having seen two levels of their leadership peeled off and exiled to towns away from the capital" as a consequence of "the extremely forceful measures President Ibanez had taken in regard to illegal labor demonstrations and strikes."[81] During the same year, the Political Police destroyed the printing press used for Communist and pro-Socialist newspapers after they had supported a student protest over bus fare rises which degenerated into a riot in downtown Santiago.[82]

The Communist and both Socialist parties had organized the FRAP in 1956, and a year later the Popular Socialist Party merged with the Socialist Party. Although FRAP only elected one senator in the congressional elections of 1957, when the Communist Party was finally legalized with Ibanez's support in 1958, six deputies from other parties declared themselves Communists.[83] Ibanez's backing for permanent registration, a single ballot and the legalization of the

Communists was motivated by a desire for revenge against the Conservatives and Liberals who after earlier participation in his government, so bitterly attacked the administration in the course of the 1957 campaign.[84] During that campaign Ibanez had not enforced the Law for the Defense of Democracy against the left. Yet the bill to legalize the PC which Ibanez sent to Congress in 1958, entitled the Law of State Security, contained potentially more repressive provisions "which made the lack of a feeling of patriotism a crime and authorized the president to suspend constitutional guarantees by declaring a state of emergency" even when Congress was in session. "The Chamber of Deputies approved only one of the 49 articles of the Ibanez bill, namely, the article restoring legality to the Communists, and voted to reinstate the pre-1948 Law of Internal Security.[85] Under this earlier legislation, the following commit crimes that can be punished by imprisonment or exile:

Those who aid a foreign power in contravention of the principle of self-determination of the Chilean people or for the purpose of submission to the political domination of said power;

Those who maintain relations with governments, entities or organizations of a foreign origin or receive from them material aid in order to commit acts defined as crimes under provisions cited above; . . .

Those who incite or induce subversion of the public order or revolt, resistance or overthrow of the constitutional government. . . .

Those who gather, arrange or facilitate meetings whose purpose is to advocate or plan the overthrow of the constituted government or to conspire against its stability; . . . .

Those who provoke disorders or any other act of violence intended to disrupt public tranquility.

. . . those who defame, slander or commit calumny upon the President of the Republic, Ministers of State, Senators or Deputies. . . .

. . . (those responsible for public utility strikes or damage). . . .

Those who act as apologists or propagandize in behalf of doctrines, systems or methods sanctioning crime or violence in any form as means for effectuating political, economic or social changes or reforms;

. . . (those who import, sell, ship or manufacture arms or ammunition without authorization). . . .[86]

With their legalization, the Communists increased party membership by 35 percent in 1958, and a 100 percent during the following year.[87] Nevertheless, the party is not unaware of the broad provisions cited above which authorize outlawry at governmental discretion—given Communist doctrine and consistent support for the foreign policies of the Soviet Union. The only provisions of the law that were used to justify the arrest of Communists and Socialists during the early 1960s were those proscribing what were regarded as injurious or slanderous statements concerning the government.[88] Even deputies of the centrist National Democratic Party were prosecuted for "publicly offending and slandering President Jorge Alessandri Rodriguez and his administration outside of Congress through accusations of governmental dishonesty in connection with embezzlement in the Central Bank."[89]

The right's turn came in 1967 when Frei arrogantly ordered the arrest of the entire national leadership of the National Party for publicly charging him with weakness in his handling of Argentine border provocations in the Beagle Canal region of Magallanes Province. An appeal to the Supreme Court resulted in their release and exoneration.[90] Socialist and non-Communist newspaper editors have been jailed for similar published remarks, as was the local *Time* magazine correspondent for a news report which was deemed to injure Chile's foreign prestige.[91] During 1967 Socialist Senator Carlos Altamirano was arrested and tried by a military court for "defaming" President Frei and the armed forces in the course of a speech in Concepción. Upon his release after several months in prison, he vigorously denounced the Frei administration in an interview with the Cuban daily *Granma*.[92]

Early in 1964, Alessandri sent a new "Abuses of Publicity" bill to Congress. It was passed over Christian Democratic and leftist opposition. This law, which was condemned in the official journal of the International Commission of Jurists, proscribed the publication of false news or documents which seriously harm national interests. Criminality even extends to newspaper vendors or advertisers, and its scope includes television, posters, banners and loudspeakers. Socialist and at least one other non-Communist periodical editor was subjected to criminal penalties during 1964 under this legislation.[93] During the late 1960s, similar suppression was periodically inflicted upon the pro-MIR leftwing Socialist bi-weekly *Punto Final*. At the time of the October 1969 *cuartelazo*, several daily newspapers were temporarily intervened.

Although women were given the right to vote in national elections during the late 1940s, illiterates, military and police personnel and those under twenty-one are yet without suffrage rights.[94] Rural districts are over-represented in the Congress which elects the president from the two leading contenders if there is no absolute majority at the polls. While the candidate with a plurality has been traditionally successful in the congressional choice from the two highest vote-getters, unanimity has not generally characterized the final tallies. In 1958, more than a score of leftist congressmen voted for Allende, even though he trailed Jorge Alessandri by almost 30,000 votes. Thus, a precedent was created for Allende's opponents in 1964 and 1970. Following his unexpectedly strong popular showing in 1958, FRAP's opponents also legislated a proscription upon electoral campaign pacts—a measure strongly opposed by the Leftist coalition.[95]

Had the Communists not been outlawed for a decade and had labor leaders not been periodically imprisoned or exiled during the 1950s for violating provisions of the Internal Security Law prohibiting certain strike actions, it is probable that the Left in general and the Communists in particular would have been both stronger and more "adventuristic" during the early years of the Cuban

Revolution. Also, given the provisions of this legislation and the new "Abuses of the Press" law, once in power, the left would have ready means at hand for dealing with some of its long time opponents. Promises to the contrary notwithstanding, Allende's identification with the Cuban Revolution provided further reinforcement for such apprehensions.

Political Violence

Granting that "in the country there is a sense of decency and fair play, respect for freedom of expression and the interchange of ideas,"[96] there is also "within the country" evidence of occasional government prosecution against those it deems responsible for injurious criticism. In addition, periodic violent outbreaks have characterized public life.

The most notorious instance of recent mass violence was sparked by a Chilean Student Federation (FECH) rally in April 1957 against newly authorized increases in bus fares. The Ibanez government—following International Monetary Fund and the Klein-Saks recommendations—was attempting to restrict wage increases to less than preceding price rises. "Two levels" of recalcitrant labor leaders had been arrested and exiled. The rally drew the attention of lower class persons whose real income was suffering, and gradually crowds began to join the protest. Soon a number of people began breaking the windows of commercial establishments. The "downtown area of the city was invaded by great numbers of people from the surrounding 'callampas' to protest runaway prices. But what was supposed to be a simple demonstration turned into a revolutionary movement. . . ."[97] "As the fortissimo was reached, ugliness invaded the crowd, and you have but to recall your favorite story of mob violence to be able to feel what happened. . . . The opposition complained that the government's measures resembled action taken against a foreign invader instead of against the very people of the country. Whether or not this accusation was just, certainly the charge that the forces of law and order did not act in a manner calculated to spare lives seems self-evidently true."[98] The Socialist and Communist newspapers, which had supported the original FECH rally and whose members probably urged workers and other poor persons to attend, were closed down after the Political Police destroyed the equipment on which both were printed.[99]

Violent acts have been regular features of Chilean *election campaigns* since the early 1920s.[100] Until the single ballot was instituted in 1958, gangs of party toughs would assault vote-buyers representing other parties. Although all parties purchased votes, the practice was more frequently resorted to by the right.[101] During the 1957 congressional campaign, several bombs were exploded.[102] On the eve of the 1958 presidential election, there had been at least a month of street fights between FRAPists, Radicals and Alessandristas. Scores were injured and there was some indication of Carabinero brutality.[103] Acid had been thrown at the face of presidential candidate Jorge Alessandri while he was campaigning in Osorno.[104] During the 1961 congressional campaign, at least two parliamentarians were involved in street fighting.[105] Late in the decade, the feeling that Frei's *"officialista"* faction had betrayed the party's 1964 pledge to revolutionize Chile's social order erupted in fisticuffs between supporters of PDC senatorial aspirant Tomas Pablo and backers of PDC *"rebelde"* candidate Alberto Jerez.[106]

Early in 1964, a congressional by-election was held in Curico. In the course of this campaign, a FRAP street agitator was fatally injured by an unknown assailant in an automobile. An attempt by anti-Christian Democratic toughs to break up a parade degenerated into a street battle. The Carabineros were forced to send four armored water-spraying vehicles to the small provincial center. Following the FRAP victory in Curico there was violent street fighting between Duranistas and Allendistas in Santiago, and rightist women began a street battle by attacking the FRAP campaign headquarters with stones. After being dispersed by police, they proceeded to the Communist Party headquarters which they stoned and attempted to set on fire.[107] Several FRAP offices were destroyed by arson during the hate-filled 1964 presidential campaign.[108] FRAPist and Christian Democratic campaign workers were physically assaulted and shot during July and August of that year.[109]

In 1961, Chilean Nazis were probably responsible for bombs which were discovered in the Chilean-Soviet Cultural Institute and at the headquarters of the Communist newspaper *El Siglo*.[110] During the preceding year, Chilean Nazis had attacked Jews and Temples. On another occasion, the police intervened when Leftist youths violently disrupted a Nazi meeting.[111] In August 1963, a gang of toughs shouting, *"Viva Allende"* and *"Viva Frei"* had physically assaulted several women who were attending a social affair in honor of Radical leader Julio Duran's mother.[112] Later that year, the *"Alianza Nacionalista"* which claimed a "membership of 6,000 sworn anti-Semites" nominated ex-General Horacio Gamboa as its presidential candidate.[113] Gamboa had ruthlessly suppressed the April 1957 bus fare riot. During March 1964, a group of FRAP lawyers asked the government to investigate the alleged purchase of 5,000 revolvers and 10,000 rifles by the Nazis who were claimed to have 3,000 members in Valparaiso and 10,000 in Santiago.[114]

In response to increased FRAP support for urban and rural land seizures during the 1967-1969 period, various landowning groups began to stock arms. In late January 1969, a group demanding higher grain prices blocked the main highway south of Santiago. Several months later, a manifesto was promulgated by the "Commandos of Freedom." It called for the outlawry of the left and demanded that the armed forces receive increased appropriations—this shortly after a serious meeting by a regiment stationed in Tacna. The minister of housing was the target of an abortive assassination later in the year and a large cache of arms was discovered by the national police.[115] During 1970, a well-known upper class landowner killed an agrarian reform official who was in the process of expropriating the holding. The presidential campaign of 1970 was marked by the bombing of businesses and public places. After Allende's victory, their tempo increased until a state of seige was declared after the late October assassination of General Schneider. Since then the national security forces have been investigating and suppressing violence-prone anti-Marxist organizations.

The left has also resorted to violence upon occasion. During a June 1961 visit by Adlai Stevenson to Chile, the Communist youth led a demonstration which broke windows at the Chilean-North American Cultural Institute. Several months later, Chilean *Fidelistas* disrupted a meeting of 2,000 anti-Castro protesters, while in late 1964 Maoist students prevented a Venezuelan official from speaking at the University of Chile by throwing eggs, flour, and shouting.[116] During the early 1960s, the Left has supported land seizures by slum dwellers and poorly armed peasants. Bombs were exploded and there was some street rioting during the 1962 missile crisis.[117] A year earlier, the Political Police had arrested forty persons for transporting and storing weapons and explosives. "Many" were Communists. FRAP denounced the mass arrests as a frame-up, while the Communists blamed Trotskyists, Fascists and the CIA. In fact, only a few pistols and a small quantity of dynamite had been discovered and confiscated. The government subsequently admitted that it possessed no evidence of a conspiracy.[118] Given the infiltration of the Socialist and Communist parties at high levels by the Political Police, it is likely that had there been a FRAP plot, some of the leaders of these parties would have been arrested.[119]

The land seizures by peasants and slum dwellers of the early sixties continued into the latter part of the decade. Frei's turn to the right in 1966 was answered by increasing lower class militance which in some cases—particularly during 1969-70—was actively abetted by populist sectors of Christian Democracy. Late in the decade, too, Leftists bombed United States Embassy offices and libraries in Santiago and Concepción, as well as the Right wing pro-Frei daily, *El Mercurio*. Responsibility for these acts probably belonged to the MIR or equally violent Catholic youth organizations which emerged after the death of Camilo Torres—the Fidelista guerrilla priest of Colombia. The rise in militance was also apparent in urban areas where workers began to seize and occupy industrial plants.[120]

Even the halls of the Chilean Congress have not been spared from physical violence which appears to be a recurring adjunct of the legislative process. During 1959 and 1960, at least five deputies and senators from center and rightist parties engaged in altercations within the National Congress building.[121] A year later when President Alessandri was about to address a joint opening session, opposition members were insulted from the public gallery. After calling for the expulsion of the responsible persons, Christian Democratic and FRAP parliamentarians began to advance toward the President. Radical, Conservative and Liberal members defensively encircled Alessandri, and within moments a riot had erupted.

What followed were the most deplorable events of the Plenary Congress. The slaps, taunts and insults were accompanied by vulgarity comparable to that heard during a potato auction at the central market. The ringing of the bell for silence by Herman Videla was wholly ineffective amidst the mixed shouts of parliamentarians, officials, the public and the guards. It was an African "tam tam" in the middle of a Chilean Jungle. . . . The "British of South America" had lost their phlegm and revived the Spanish and Indian heritage that forged this race.[122]

To what extent, then, may it be said that there is a *veneer* of juridicality in Chile? While it is impossible to ascertain precisely the psychological commitment to non-violence, there are grounds for viewing this tradition with caution. The upper and upper middle class persons who, in August 1964, had solidly booked four months of airline departures,[123] may well have feared a potential for mass violence beneath the glum and often sullen expressions on lower class faces. Similar apprehensions were widely shared in September 1970 when hundreds of refugees from Nazi Germany applied at the West German Embassy for restoration of their nationality. Meanwhile, there was a run on banks, thousands fled to Mendoza and Buenos Aires while the dollar soared to over 30 escudos on the black market. Advance airline tickets for foreign destinations were sold en masse as capital was removed from the country by the "patriotic" upper class.[124] As Frederico Gil has noted, this "country seemed, in the last few years, to be on the verge of a social earthquake which the traditional political structures did not appear able to prevent."[125]

Concluding Remarks

The precise importance and direction in which each of the previously discussed factors operated cannot be fully assessed until other matters are examined in the chapters to follow. A tentative synopsis would, however, indicate that the following functioned to limit the appeal of those (FRAP) who were identified with the Cuban Revolution:

1. A Constitutionalist tradition and disdain for Castro's "tropical" style.
2. Intense socio-economic discontent among probably no more than twenty percent of the adult populace.
3. No more than 10-13 percent had internalized Marxist norms; among the lower classes where the level was somewhat higher, there were also lower levels of involvement in the political process and greater ignorance of political issues—thus greater susceptibility to vote-buying and simplistic anti-Communist (FRAP-Cuban) propaganda.
4. Probable fear by many that a FRAP victory would provoke military intervention.

5. Fear that a FRAP victory would result in the use of the Abuses of Publicity Law and the Internal Security Law against pro-United States and anti-Communist leaders.
6. Fear that a FRAP government might encourage or tolerate outbreaks of lower class political violence against propertied sectors or opposition parties.
7. Anti-Communist sentiments among a majority.
8. Mass media usage patterns stressing the radio where financial resources, ownership, and access favored those opposed to the FRAP; this was only slightly less true with regard to the press.
9. Separate voting for women, who tended to identify with Catholicism.
10. Registration of many new voters who might vote for the "Revolution in Liberty" PDC as a protest rather than for the FRAP which was simplistically portrayed as endorsing violence and the destruction of all human dignity.
11. Prohibition of voting by illiterates and those under twenty-one.
12. A weak and fragmented labor movement.

Despite this structural situation, there were several factors which may have increased Marxist appeal:

1. Given the importance of the personalist element in Chilean politics, many of those who were personally registered or cultivated by FRAP militants probably swelled the Leftist constituency.
2. Widespread socio-economic discontent and support for socialistic proposals (probably between 40 percent and 60 percent of the adult population).
3. Superior organization, dedication and discipline of Communist cadres; but this was also true in varying measure for the Christian Democrats—especially the youth.
4. The lower class oriented Marxist ideology during a period of economic stagnation and at best stable living standards for a large blue collar sector.
5. A tradition of fairly consistent and vigorous defense of lower class economic interests within and beyond the Congress.
6. Limited mass commitment to parliamentary democracy.
7. Post-1965 official brutality toward lower class strikes and land seizures.
8. Growing left-wing disaffection within the ruling Christian Democratic party over Frei's unwillingness to communitarianize capitalist institutions.

From a different perspective it should be noted that the possibility of engaging in guerilla warfare was necessarily a remote one for the Chilean left. Only recently the Communist leaders had endured personal hardship and seen their following sharply reduced during the period of outlawry. The leadership of neither Marxist party desired to justify renewed suppression, and in any event their skills were electoral and parliamentary in nature. And so, perhaps, were their ambitions. The leftist parties were both infiltrated by the Political Police up to the central committee level. Furthermore, they would have to confront a national military force which was receiving United States counterinsurgency training. With a wide political spectrum represented at the polls, it would be difficult to develop adequate support for such a struggle. Finally, suitable terrain was far to the south of the Central Valley where most peasants and workers resided. And by sea, Cuban assistance was more than seven thousand miles distant.

**Part II:
External Actors**

4

Revolutionary Cuba Seeks to Inspire Chileans to Defend the Cuban Revolution and to Struggle for National Liberation

Introduction

Without access to the police files, and intelligence reports of the Chilean, Cuban and United States governments, precision is unattainable in endeavoring to assess Cuban proselytization efforts. Hence, only their general character and some of the principal instrumentalities that were utilized will be described.

A Synopsis of the Fidelista Message

It is difficult for one who has not been an *invitado* (officially invited guest) to capture the experience and impressions of others. Those who visited the first "Free Territory of America" were treated as honored guests and shown some of the more striking successes of the Cuban government in such fields as agrarian reform, housing, recreation, education, economic development projects and plans, etc. Many were witnesses to parades or rallies where both mass enthusiasm for the Revolution and Fidel's charisma were demonstrated. The *invitados* were told that by struggle, bravery and determination the Cubans had become masters of their own destiny—albeit with Soviet aid. The opportunity and duty was now theirs to expel imperialism (U.S.) and destroy forever—as the Cubans were doing—exploitation of man by man. Traditional Latin American "fatalism" was the target of Cuban affirmations that here Latin Americans had proven that Washington could be successfully defied provided one was willing to sacrifice and accept temporary economic difficulties. The major enemy was defined as the United States and its allies in the creole military and business establishments. They were jointly indicted for the perpetuation of economic underdevelopment, exploitation and mass misery. These "objective" factors and the Cuban Revolution's very survival and progress in structuring a humanist and later socialist society favored militant revolutionary efforts now in other Latin American nations. Only with such a commitment—to defend Cuban self-determination while simultaneously struggling for internal structural revolution—would the people of each nation ultimately conquer their freedom, equality of social opportunity and national dignity.

Very roughly drawn, this was the message. It varied according to time and the nature of the visitor. But by mid-1960, its basic outlines were quite discernible.[1]

43

The Visitors

It is extremely difficult to estimate the total number of Chileans who traveled to Cuba. In May 1961, the Chilean Ministry of the Interior calculated that during the "first months" of the year, between one hundred and one hundred and fifty persons had traveled to or from Cuba.[2] About two years later, the chairman of the Foreign Relations Committee of the CIA-subsidized Cuban Revolutionary Council informed a United States congressional committee that 173 Chileans had traveled to Cuba during a five-month period in 1962.[3] Thus, from 1959 until 1965, a maximum average of three hundred Chileans may have traveled to or from Cuba each year.[4] Some were making their second or third trip, while others remained in Cuba as students or technicians. In June 1964, Chilean government intelligence agencies estimated that 2,000 nationals were on the Caribbean island for one reason or another.[5]

A majority of those who traveled to Cuba were officially invited guests of the Revolutionary Government. It is difficult to be sure of the criteria which governed the selection of *invitados*. Many were associated with leftist or centrist political parties as legislators or youth leaders. Others were distinguished in some field of professional or artistic endeavor.[6] The following examples are illustrative.

In the summer of 1962, twenty-eight left-wing professionals and a Christian Democratic lawyer went as a group for a two month sojourn as *invitados*. They interviewed Castro, Carlos Rafael Rodríguez, Dórticos and Guevara, and returned to publish a lengthy eulogy of their experiences—with a prologue by Allende.[7] Also in 1962, the Chilean Communist-sponsored "Theatre of the People" organized a competition for playwrights with a trip to Cuba as first prize.[8] During February 1963, several Chilean medical researchers and physicians of repute were invited to Cuba's Tenth National Congress of Medicine. In addressing the delegates, Osvaldo Dórticos described the Revolution's advances in the field of public health and preventive medicine.[9] At the same time, rector of the University of Chile, Juan Gómez Millas, was invited to attend a ceremony at the University of Havana. Its purpose was to award a Doctor Honóris Causa to Chilean scientist and veteran Leftist, Alejandro Lipshutz. During his speech, Gomez promised that he would encourage Chilean technicians to seek employment in Cuba.[10] Later that year, a number of Chilean architects were invited to attend the Seventh International Union of Architects' Congress in Havana. Upon their return, two of them published a well written non-Marxian essay praising social and economic programs of the Revolutionary Government.[11]

Although some Chilean painters, sculptors and singers visited Cuba and responded favorably, it is not clear whether all were *invitados*.[12] In late 1960, the foremost Chilean poet was invited to Havana by the editor of *Revolución*. During the course of his sojourn, Pablo Neruda read a series of "Revolutionary Poems" under the auspices of the *Casa de las Américas*.[13] Both the talent and propaganda value of this eminent Communist were manifested in beautiful poetic tributes which he subsequently rendered to the Cuban Revolution.[14]

The Cubans were less fortunate with another prominent Chilean poet and writer, Matilde Ladrón de Guevara. She visited the Caribbean isle during 1960 and again between April and September, 1961. Her book *Adiós al Cañaveral: Diario de una Mujer en Cuba* was published in 1962.[15] Although marred by the author's egotism and hypersensitivity, the "diary" effectively conveyed the impression that Cuban authorities bestowed preferential treatment upon visiting Communists. The impact of the book upon the Chilean intellectual community was heightened by the fact that Ladrón de Guevara had been president of the Chilean-Cuban Cultural Institute in Santiago during 1960. A non-Marxian anti-Communist, she had joined the Socialist Party in 1960 or 1961. During the 1964 presidential campaign—in which she opposed Allende, her home was the target of gunfire one night.[16]

Potentially more influential than poets were the centrist political leaders who were invited by the Cuban government. In Havana during February 1959, Christian Democratic deputies Alfredo Lorca and Jose Musalem invited Fidel Castro to visit Chile upon behalf of their government.[17] Some months later, Christian Democratic leaders, Jorge Cash, Jaime Castillo, Alejandro Magnet and Radomiro Tomic were invited to the *26 de Julio* celebrations. In addition to being active in the CIA-subsidized Congress for Cultural Freedom, Castillo was director of the PDC organ, *Política y Espíritu*. Both Cash and Magnet were on its editorial board, and Tomic was a frequent speaker and writer. During a rally for a half million persons, Tomic and Salvador Allende were seated as guests of honor next to Fidel's mother. In addition to speaking with Castro, Regino Boti, Raúl Roa and Dórticos, the Christian Democrats conferred with the United States Ambassador, the leaders of the right wing Auténtico party and with members of the fledgling Christian Democratic Movement.[18]

In 1961, it was reported that "more than a few high-ranking Chilean Christian Democratic leaders were invited to visit Fidel Castro's Cuba. . . ."[19] Leaders Patricio Hurtado and Julio Silva were invited during 1962 and 1963.[20] Some of these persons allegedly received funds while in Cuba.[21] A small number of left-wing Christian Democrats and Catholic student leaders continued to visit Havana throughout the decade despite Frei's refusal to restore diplomatic or cultural relations. Cuban trade offers were ignored until the 1970 election year.

The Cuban government also sought to cultivate the sympathy of Radical deputies. Among those invited during 1959 were Ana Eugenia Ugalde and Hernán Brucher. All visited the United States at the same time.[22] Another prominent Radical and forthcoming minister in the Alessandri administration, Luis Escobar Cerda, was apparently also an invitee.[23] An indeterminate number of left-wing Radical leaders visited Cuba during the 1960-1969 period.[24]

Those who visited the "Free Territory of America" most frequently were Socialist and Communist leaders. Their trips often coincided with Cuban political celebrations on January 1st, May 1st or July 26th. Communists Jaime Barros and Orlando Millas were prominent repeaters while party secretary general Luis Corvalán managed at least one trip in 1961.[25] Mathilde Ladrón de Guevara relates an amusing incident which occurred shortly after the defeat of the Bay of Pigs invaders. At the time Corvalán insisted upon wearing his coat and tie while all others including the aristocratic Barros were in shirt sleeves. Ladrón de Guevara then warned the Communist leader that "because of your capitalistic attire they may begin throwing stones at you, Senator." After considering the matter for several moments, his chagrined decision in favor of revolutionary informality was finally made.[26] Socialist leaders such as Aniceto Rodríguez, Salomón Corbalán, Albino Barra, Jaime Ahumada, Raúl Ampuero, Gustavo Horvitz and Oscar Naranjo were also invitees; and Allende probably made the seven thousand-mile journey upon at least six occasions between 1959 and 1963.[27]

The leftist led Chilean labor movement was a major source of invitees. At least fifteen labor leaders were flown to the Caribbean island in 1960 alone. They included Clotario Blest, the aging but dynamic president of the *Central Unica de Trabajadores* (CUT)—the major labor federation in Chile. A year later, four Chilean labor leaders were invited to the Second Conference of Latin American Construction Workers.[28]

Perhaps the largest category of Chilean visitors were youths between seventeen and twenty-nine years of age. In September 1960, a local leader of the Congress for Cultural Freedom claimed that "more than 500" Chilean youths had already visited Havana.[29] Although Christian Democratic student leaders representing five university federations visited Cuba at Dórticos' invitation during the spring of 1960, the Christian Democratic youth declined to participate in the Congress of Latin American Youth which was organized in Havana during July 1960.[30] Of the 600 to 800 delegates and observers, perhaps fifty came from Chile. They included the Socialist labor leader Oscar Núñez, who would soon replace Clotario Blest as the president of the CUT. Many of those attending joined hundreds of Cuban student volunteers who were working on a school city in the Sierra Maestra.[31] Before the Congress closed, delegates from Chile's Radical Youth assumed the responsibility for financing and organizing an open World Federation of Democratic Youth Executive Committee meeting in Santiago during April of 1961.[32] "Labor delegations to the Latin American Youth Congress joined with the *Confederación de Trabajadores de Cuba* in a joint declaration of August 3, 1960, which:

(a) Pledged solidarity by the Cuban and Latin American labor delegates in support for the Cuban Revolution and the signing of a mutual assistance pact between the CTC and the Central Unica de Trabajadores de Chile (CUTCH).
(b) Hailed the Cuban revolution as opening the way to the national liberation of all Latin America, welcomed the support and friendship of the Soviet Union and Communist China, emphasized the threat of aggression by Yankee imperialism and its 'tool,' the Organization of American States, and pledged the

workers of Latin America to give their lives if necessary to repel such aggression.

(c) Endorsed a movement to create a Latin American labor group to support the struggle against internal reactionaries and the forces of imperialist monopolies.

(d) Alerted labor organizations to combat any effort by imperialists to use the OAS at San Jose, Costa Rica, as a means for attacking Cuba.[33]

According to Assistant Secretary of State Edwin Martin, in 1960 the Cubans "very substantially stepped up" their proselytization efforts in the region.[34] This policy priority was partially reflected by the large number of international meetings between January 1961 and January 1963 to which Chileans and other Latin Americans had been invited. They included the following:

Latin American Conference of Plantation Workers, March 1961, Havana.

Celebration of Latin American Solidarity Day, April 1961, in San Antonio de los Banos. Participating were Latin American and European delegates who attended the Latin American Conference on National Sovereignty, Economic Emancipation, and World Peace, held in Mexico City from March 5 to 8, 1961.

Congress of Central American Students, May 1961, Havana.

Seventh Congress of the International Students' Union, May 1961, Havana. Topic: 'Latin America against Yankee imperialism.'

International meeting of voluntary workers, June 1961, Havana; sponsored by the International Students' Union.

International seminar on illiteracy, June 1961, Havana; sponsored by the International Students' Union.

Meeting of Latin American trade union leaders, July 1961, Havana; to exchange ideas regarding the World Trade Union Federation Congress, which was scheduled for December 1961, in Moscow.

Meeting to plan for the Congress of Women of the Americas scheduled for July 1962, July 1961, Havana.

Second meeting of Construction Workers of Latin America, August 1961, Havana.

Congress of Writers and Artists, August 1961, Havana.

Fifth Congress of the World Trade Union Federation, November 1961, Havana.

Fifth Congress of the International Newspapermen's Organization, January 1962, Havana.

Latin American Cultural Congress, January 1962, Havana.

Conference of Peoples (coincident with the conference at Punta del Este), January 1962, Havana.

Congress of Women of America, July 1962, Havana.

Latin American University Games, and Seminar on Sports in Latin America, October 1962, Havana.

First National Congress of the Cuban Federation of Women, October 1962, Havana.

Latin American Music Festival, October 1962, Havana.

Congress of Women of America, January 1963, Havana.[35]

It is worth noting that a majority of these events were scheduled to coincide with May, July and January national celebrations when the Revolution's massive internal backing could be demonstrated.

Some Latin Americans (and presumably Chileans) who visited Havana on their own, as invitees, or to attend some meeting or event, enrolled in a Marxist and/or guerilla training courses.[36] In early 1963, the Central Intelligence Agency (CIA) estimated that between one thousand and fifteen hundred Latin Americans had traveled to Cuba during 1962 for university study, indoctrination, or guerilla training.[37]

Technicians constituted another important category of Chileans who remained in Cuba. They were employed as military and civilian flight instructors, economists, agricultural engineers, radio broadcasting specialists, etc. In September 1963, the current director of the University of Chile's Institute of International Studies reported:

... that at present the Cuban economy is practically being managed by Chilean economists. Of the 700-odd Chilean technical advisers, engineers, medical doctors, and members of other professions who are now in Cuba, more than 100 are economists, and of these, forty-six occupy positions of high responsibility, including vice-ministerial and directorial posts; another sixty-odd work as statisticians, survey managers, agronomists, and managers of State enterprises. ...

The reason for this remarkable influx of Chileans into Cuba is fairly simple. ... Until a generation ago, the Chilean economy was growing at a steady pace and the internal development and growing complexity of urban society easily absorbed every graduate which the University of Chile could produce. But for the last few years—and especially since 1953—the Chilean economy has been practically stagnant and there has been a steady growth of unemployed among the intelligentsia. On the other hand, since 1959 Cuba has lost almost 250,000 people who were allowed to go into exile to the United States. In that group were the immense majority of the professional people who, having attended university under the old regimes, were obviously members of the middle and upper classes and, as such, basically out of sympathy with the communist tendencies of the new regime.[38]

While some of these *técnicos* were certainly Marxists, it is probable that many were no more than mildly leftist. Jacques Lagas returned from a double tour as an air force instructor and wrote an unenthusiastic account of his experiences. Published during the 1964 presidential campaign by the Christian Democrats, it echoed Ladrón de Guevara's work by criticizing alleged favoritism in the Cuban air force for Communists.[39] In 1964, the PDC also published a work by Jacques Chonchol. He had been employed by the FAO to study the Cuban Agrarian Reform during 1960. In *El Desarrollo de América Latina y la Reforma Agraria*,[40] Chonchol viewed the Cuban experiment as "a challenge of extraordinary importance" and argued that unless a structural (i.e. distributive) agrarian reform were implemented, Latin Americans would have to choose between economic stagnation and "establishing dictatorial political regimes" for rapid development. After working as an engineer for the Revolutionary Government during 1963, another *técnico* returned to write a study which manifested sympathy as well as criticism. In *La Nueva Cuba*,[41] Alan Rosman described the lack of rational economic policies and the hostility of Cuban officials to the advice of experts.

This author has been unable to discover one wholly favorable account authored by a technician formerly employed by the Revolutionary Government. John Gerassi quotes one Chilean technician who had been employed for eighteen months during 1961-62: "Castro may have disillusioned us, and I for one left Cuba a very bitter man, but his Revolution also gave us back the right to our dignity. Now we have to earn it. We will."[42]

In their attempts to obtain more favorable coverage than was carried by UPI and other wire services upon which the Chilean mass media rely, the Cubans also extended invitations to Chilean journalists employed by centrist and leftist dailies. Their *reportajes* during 1959 were highly favorable.[43]

It is probable that many of the *invitados* and *técnicos* disseminated oral and written accounts which were favorable to the Revolutionary Government. Several, as noted, reacted quite differently and contributed to negative images of the Cuban experiment among Chilean middle and upper class sectors.

The Cuban investment in *invitados* paid good dividends with the creation of several vigorous organizations by Chilean sympathizers. The National Movement for Solidarity and Defense of the Cuban Revolution (MNSDRC) was launched on the eve of the OAS Foreign Ministers' Conference in San Jose. Led by CUT president Clotario Blest, it sponsored protest rallies, organized at least one assembly of delegates from "Friends of Cuba" clubs which had been established in several cities, published propaganda and released declarations.[44] Persons associated with the FRAP parties were prominent as leaders of this organization.

Initially reflecting a broader spectrum of political opinion was the Chilean-Cuban Institute of Culture (ICCC).[45] Cuban diplomats Roberto Alfon and Julio Cruz were present at its inauguration in December 1959, and the institute subsequently served as a conduit for the dissemination of Revolutionary books and such periodicals as *Bohemia, Verde y Olivo, Vanguardia, Noticiero Sindical de la CTC, Trabajo, Cuba,* and *Cuba Socialista*.[46] It also provided a forum from which Cuban diplomatic representatives could obtain some local publicity.[47] At the time of the Bay of Pigs aggression, an ICCC delegation obtained an audience with the minister of foreign affairs.[48]

The institute appears to have directed special attention to the intellectual community.[49] During 1961 it was reported to be "organizing numerous cultural events, assemblies, conferences, trips, festivals for Cuban films, forums, national tours, etc." In the same year, it joined other cultural institutes representing Communist nations in affiliating with the newly organized pro-FRAP *Instituto Popular*.[50] Two years later, the ICCC sponsored a delegation of two for a three-month tour of Cuba. One was a photographer, and the following account may indicate a typical institute follow-up role:

Upon returning to Chile, Rebecca Yañez selected photographic highlights of the enchanting island. She entitled her presentation 'Greetings to Cuba,' incorporating it into a series of expositions, talks and screenings of Cuban films which were sponsored by the Chilean-Cuban Cultural Institute. The exposition was an immediate success. The constantly filled hall of the Institute in Santiago had to run the exposition for an entire month. Torrents of people jammed the hall. . . .

The workers asked for the exposition, and it .was presented at the Central Unica de Trabajadores (headquarters of the Leftist-led CUT), the students demanded it and it went to the School of Engineering and to other centers of learning. Then the provinces called for it.[51]

While the Instituto Chileno-Cubano continued to function after Chile was pressured into breaking relations with Havana, its activities were considerably reduced and tended to be restricted to Santiago. Similarly, the flow of visitors to Cuba declined to well under a hundred per year. Due to obstacles created by the Mexican Ministerio de Gobernación, many non-official *invitados* were compelled to travel via Spain or Prague.

Fidel Castro's speeches as well as other favorable articles and books about the Cuban Revolution were published in some quantity by the Socialists and Communists.[52] Those items which these parties were unwilling to publish were distributed by Trotskyists and Maoists.[53] The Cubans and Communist nations intensified their propaganda activities during the 1959-61 period. Soviet and Chinese media depicted the Cuban Revolution as a successful anti-imperialist struggle worthy of support and emulation by fellow Latin Americans.[54]

In 1959 *Prensa Latina* was organized to furnish wire service reports of Cuban conditions and viewpoints. Chilean subscribers were the pro-Socialist *Las Noticias de Ultima Hora*, the Communist *El Siglo*, and the Christian Democratic daily *La Libertad* which ceased publication in August 1960. Only *El Siglo* received TASS and ADN, while none of the mass media accepted the free *New China News Agency* wire service. The leftist dailies took UPI. According to one United States Embassy source, this was given without charge to *El Siglo*!

Although both *El Siglo* and *Ultima Hora* sympathetically reported on Cuban developments, the latter was more attentive, less undiscriminating in its support for the Revolution and far more generally disposed to use PL dispatches. Significantly, its director Jose Toha became the highest ranking official in Allende's cabinet, and he personally received a high level Cuban delegation to Allende's inauguration. Another consistently pro-Cuban publication which has been influential among Leftist sectors in Chile was the bi-weekly *Punto Final*. Established in 1965, it has opposed electoralism on the Left and frequently polemicized with the Communist Party daily, *El Siglo*.

Of marginal importance to lower middle and lower class attitudes was the initiation of short wave broadcasting by the Revolutionary Government in May 1961.[55] By the end of 1962, Cuba was directing 109 hours per week of Spanish language broadcasts to Latin America. Her transmissions had increased from about 30 hours per week during 1961.[56] There was a moderate rise in broadcast hours over the 1963-1965 period.[57] No special program was prepared for Chile until April 1966.[58] Soviet and Chinese transmissions—some of which praised the heroic Cubans—also increased during the 1959-1962 period.[59]

In the cultural field, the Cubans managed to send a few performers to Chile. During November 1959, for example, the Cuban Ballet gave recitals in Santiago. And several years later, a Cuban chorus was flown to an Inter-American Choral Group Festival in Antofagasta.[60]

The Cubans discovered that they were able to effectively project their point of view at leftist-organized Latin American congresses and assemblies. The first Latin American Women's Congress was organized by Marxists and their sympathizers in Santiago during November 1959.[61] Although the gathering was denounced by Conservatives, Liberals and Radicals as Communist-inspired, President Alessandri sent the 489 delegates his wishes for a successful meeting.[62] The Cuban delegation was led by Vilma Espin and Alcida Marsh, the wives of Raúl Castro and Ché Guevara. Numbering eighty, it was the largest foreign contingent. Its role at the congress was described by an unsympathetic observer in the following terms:

Evidencing apparent expertise in guerilla techniques, the Cubans displaced their Chilean colleagues who had hoped for a more prominent place in the leadership of the congress. The other delegations . . . acceded to the Cuban drive. . . . There were many delegates of humble origin who remained seated on chairs or the floor for entire hours without knowing what to do or say. From time to time as they sat through lengthy dissertations on the 'Cuban movement,' Fidel Castro and his heroic deeds, a constant theme of the Cuban delegates, they joined some Argentine delegates—especially those who had declared themselves to be anti-Communists—in asking if this were a Cuban congress.[63]

Yet the congress' goal that the legal rights of women should be made effective *was* a dominant theme of the gathering. The Cubans were, however, provided with ample opportunity to emphasize their view that Cuba's problems were those of Latin America and that the United States was largely responsible for obstructing the hemisphere's economic development. In her closing address, Espin maintained that Cuba's only desire was to create a better future for the peoples of Latin America. Her colleagues distributed folders containing pictures of Fidel Castro and one of his speeches.[64]

Delegates of the Radical Party's youth who had participated in the 1960 Latin American Youth Congress at Havana had agreed to assume the responsibility for organizing a meeting of the World Federation of Democratic Youth's Executive Committee in Santiago during April 1961. The Socialist youth had declined to participate because forty of the fifty members of the executive committee were delegates from Communist-led associations. Nevertheless, a substantial number of non-Communist Chilean youth organizations accepted invitations to attend the "open meeting" scheduled for April 16-20.[65]

The executive committee assigned the first three pages of its general resolution to expressing solidarity with the Cuban cause. This declaration blamed the United States for armed attacks upon Cuba and condemned Washington for violating the right of self-determination and for pressuring Latin American nations to break relations with Havana. The statement identified Cuba with the forces struggling against domestic and external economic exploitations and eulogized such measures by the Revolutionary Government as: an agrarian reform that distributed land to 300,000 peasants; an urban reform; the conversion of military barracks into schools and the elimination of illiteracy; the eradication of unemployment; economic planning and a program of industrialization; and the raising of living standards. This section of the general resolution concluded by urging that:

Public demonstrations, the dissemination of the achievements of the Revolution through the press and the radio, forums, broad discussion, the exposure and denunciation of the maneuvers of the enemies of the Cuban people and all other willful manifestations of backing for Cuba by youth are concrete forms of solidarity and collaboration that are fully supported by the WFDY. Today, Solidarity is called Cuba, and the youth of the world have but one desire: to defend the Cuban Revolution. The WFDY regards the first and most fundamental stage in the struggle for liberty, progress and democracy as the consolidation of the conquests of the Cuban people and proclaim the duty and the right of the youth of Latin America to conquer the same destiny for their own peoples.[66]

Similar resolutions were endorsed by the Latin American Conference for National Sovereignty, Economic Emancipation and Peace. It was held in Mexico City six weeks earlier at the behest of Lazaro Cárdenas, the popular former president of that country.[67] A score or more Chileans probably managed the six hundred-mile trip. They included Luis Figueroa, a very high-ranking Communist leader in the CUT, and professor of history at the University of Chile's Institute of Pedagogy and Olga Poblete, who headed the *Movimiento Chileno para la Paz*.[68]

A series of military coups and the rupture of relations by a number of Latin American governments with Havana during the two years which followed the Conference for National Sovereignty, made it more difficult for the Cubans to organize their reply to Kennedy's San José Conference with Central American presidents in early March 1963. The Cuban delegation to the Continental Congress of Solidarity with Cuba was unable to use it as a propaganda forum since the Brazilian government had declined to issue the necessary entry permits. Although more than a thousand delegates and an equal number of guests applauded at the opening session, fully 700 of the delegates and virtually all of the spectators were Brazilians. Of the remaining delegates, 120 were Argentines and 84 represented Leftist groups from Uruguay.[69] At least seven labor leaders were included in the Chilean delegation which was constituted by the National Movement for Solidarity and Defense of the Cuban Revolution.[70] Prominent among the themes of the congress' resolutions were opposition to Yankee imperialism, defense of self-determination, and praise for the Cuban Revolution.

At the 1960 Havana Latin American Youth Congress, a preparatory commission had been appointed to plan a second congress. The Socialist Youth, the CUT Youth Department, and sixteen non-Chilean organizations were represented on this commission.[71] In August 1963, Chilean, Argentine, Venezuelan, Mexican, Panamanian and Colombian members met and agreed upon goals for the Second Latin American Youth Congress which would be held in Chile during 1964.[72] When it opened in March of that year, 419 accredited delegates representing 234 youth organizations participated in the sessions. A sixteen-man Cuban delegation attended, as did a few non-Marxist delegates.[73]

The major questions to which the gathering addressed itself were: 1) Analysis of the Latin American Situation, 2) Youth and the Contemporary World, and 3) Analysis of the Political Situation. The inspiratory significance of the Cuban Revolution was enthusiastically reiterated:

. . . the youth and the working class in general will struggle to achieve, as their Cuban brothers have, an urban reform where each worker can have his own dwelling and truly human living conditions. . . .

Cuba shows the world and all its peoples that it is possible to defeat imperialism, even though it is but a short distance away, and begin the construction of a better life. Geographic fatalism has suffered the great defeat of thoroughgoing structural changes. . . .

These feats move all peoples who desire to implement a program for their liberation and for profound transformations. The attention and thoughts of millions of men are directed at the forementioned achievements (of the Cuban Revolution). The fact is that these measures (nationalization of U.S. firms, economic planning, industrialization, agrarian reform, ending illiteracy, conversion of military barracks into schools, housing, educational opportunities for all youth, an end to racial discrimination, etc.) have been effectively instituted because today we live in a new world.[74]

Although Soviet aid had enabled the Cuban Revolution to remain viable despite economic dislocations, disorganization and the United States trade embargo, there was no certainty in the aftermath of the missile crisis that the Russians would commit their armed forces or retaliate against Berlin in the event of a new military crisis. Thus, the resolutions could threaten only that should there be another invasion, "not one grain of wheat, nor a barrel of oil nor a ton of copper will be delivered to the aggressors." Recognizing the growing isolation of Cuba from the other hemispheric nations, the delegates were urged to pressure their governments for a resumption and expansion of diplomatic, economic and cultural relations with Cuba.

Other resolutions defined the Organization of American States as an agency of United States domination, and characterized the Alliance for Progress as a failure insofar as political liberty and socio-economic structural changes were concerned. The liberation of Puerto Rico was advocated, and students were urged to defend university autonomy and to oppose efforts by United States foundations to modify curricula. Similarly, Peace Corps volunteers were denounced as agents of ideological penetration. The Soviet Union, on the other hand, was praised for its commercial and economic aid which was contributing to Cuban social and economic development. Finally, the 26th of July was declared "the day of the Liberation of Latin America's Youth," and the 13th of March as "the day of the Rebellion of Latin America's Youth."[75]

Between March 1964 and the inauguration of Salvador Allende's "Popular Unity" administration in 1970, international gatherings of a revolutionary nature could not be held in Chile due to hostility manifested by the Frei administration. While a handful of Cubans were allowed to enter the country, subsequent conferences were held in Havana. These included the 1966 Tricontinental Congress and a meeting the following year at which the Latin American Solidarity Organization (OLAS) was constituted. In December 1969, a Latin American Continental Students' Organization was launched. Chilean Communist and Socialist delegates attended the Tricontinental Congress and subsequently representatives of these parties organized a largely symbolic Chilean OLAS committee in August 1967. There was more form than substance to Communist Association with OLAS. Participation in the 1969 student meeting was broadened to include not only the traditional Chilean Left, but also representatives of the Catholic *Movimiento Camilo Torres* as well as the *Movimiento Izquierdista Revolucionario* (MIR).

Economic Aid

More dramatic was Cuba's effort to win friendship by dispatching emergency relief after the disastrous earthquakes which crippled the south of Chile during the latter part of May 1960. Within forty-eight hours of the tragedy, the Cuban Foreign Minister cabled an offer of "any type of assistance which the (Chilean) government needs to aid the victims." Following this, Raúl Roa announced that Castro had decided to give $800,000 worth of sugar and $200,000 in cash to Chile's victims. The Cuban Premier justified these sacrifices as compelled by "American solidarity to help the people of a sister Republic."[76]

About seven weeks later, Cuban Ambassador Juan José Diaz del Real visited the Chilean Foreign Ministry and informed officials that the $800,000 worth of aid had already been shipped. This included 14,000 tons of sugar; about 5,000 were to be distributed in the pro-FRAP southern coal mining region around Lota and Coronel. He also stated that Cuban cultural organizations and labor unions were continuing to solicit donations; that they had already collected $80,000 worth of contributions, and that this too would eventually be shipped. Díaz del Real expressed the government of Cuba's willingness to take care of any future sugar shortages that might develop in Chile as a consequence of the earthquake damage.[77] Cuba, it should be noted, also contributed $13,313 to the OAS special technical assistance fund for the disaster-struck region, and was represented on a special OAS committee which was appointed to plan such assistance.[78]

Within six days of the earthquake, a Cuban transport plane with doctors and medical supplies had arrived in Chile. Similarly, a Cuban helicopter was already engaged in removing the injured from some of the more inaccessible regions. A month later, the Cuban steamer La Habana arrived in Valparaiso with five hundred tons of sugar, clothing and medicines. As the vessel docked, it was met by cheering Chilean students from the school "República de Cuba" who were waving Cuban and Chilean flags. The Chilean government, however, refused to let stevedores unload the 33,000 sacks of sugar; the task was assigned to naval personnel.[79]

The only other assistance reported in the Chilean press was a check given to CUT President Clotário Blest at the closing session of the Havana Latin American Youth Congress. These funds were to be used to aid in the reconstruction of the University of Concepción.[80] Several months after the disaster, students at the Catholic University in Santiago organized a parade of homage to the countries which had aided Chile after the earthquake. Included in the procession were two jeeps with bearded Cuban rebels mounted on them.[81]

In the aftermath of the aid, Chilean rightists charged that Cuban periodicals and other "Communist propaganda" had either been sent with the relief supplies or been disseminated by those who distributed—and in some cases allegedly sold—the Cuban aid in the south.[82] The CUT President replied to these charges by stating that he would cooperate in any investigation of the matter. Allende countered by claiming that only some copies of the Cuban Agrarian Reform periodical INRA had been included.[83]

Cuban Revolutionaries in Chile

Havana's efforts to inspire or assist Chilean sympathizers were not limited to shipments of "economic aid," trips to Cuba, pamphlets, etc. The Cubans also sent a number of their own nationals to Chile. Most arrived during the 1959-1964 period, although a small number continued to be granted entry visas after Chile severed diplomatic relations.

The category of traveling emissaries included delegates to: The National Congress of the Socialist Party (October 1959); The Second National Congress of the Central Unica de Trabajadores (November 1959); The Extraordinary National Labor Union Congress of the Radical Party Youth (April 1960); The First

National Peasants Congress of the FRAP-led National Federation of Peasants and Natives (May 1961); The Third National Congress of the *Central Unica de Trabajadores* (1962); and The Twelfth National Congress of the Chilean Communist Party (December 1962).[84]

Representatives of a different type of delegation was a contingent of nine *barbudos* who were sent on an "Operation Truth" tour of Latin America during February and March 1959. The group included the revolutionary priest Guillermo Sardinas and one woman. During their week in Santiago, they visited leaders of CUT and FRAP as well as some Christian Democrats. In addition to stressing the end of the repressive Batista dictatorship, the *barbudos* stated that the Revolution's goals were "economic independence from the United States" and "social justice." After conferring with Chilean university students, the delegation visited the "José Martí" school in Santiago to which groups of students from other secondary schools had been invited. On the eve of their departure, a reception was offered by them at the Spanish Republic Center for members of the Chilean Congress, representatives of the diplomatic corps and officials in the Alessandri administration. Several days earlier, the *barbudos* had placed a wreath of flowers on the national monument to Chile's nineteenth-century revolutionary hero, Bernado O'Higgins.[85]

Some months later, the Cubans sent Foreign Minister Raúl Roa, Education Minister Armando Hart and Carlos Rafael Rodríguez (director of the Communist daily *Hoy* and a close associate of Castro) to the OAS Foreign Ministers' Conference in Santiago. During the meetings, FRAP and the CUT jointly sponsored a rally to support Cuban demands for sanctions against the Dominican Republic and a hemispheric program for economic and social development.[86] In addressing the rally, Hart proclaimed that only through revolution could the peoples of Latin America win genuine freedom. He also warned the several thousand assembled Chileans that "it would be good for the peoples to know that power cannot be won by elections; only when the people themselves control the armed forces will they have power. It would be good for the people to know that there is where their true destiny resides."[87]

Several days later, Hart, Rodríguez and Gregório Ortega—a journalist from *Revolución*, the organ of the 26th of July Movement—met with more than fifty Chilean and other Latin American politicians. This FRAP-sponsored conference resolved to call a Continental Congress of "democrats and representatives of political parties, social and cultural organizations, in order to analyze the problems of Latin America." The conferees also expressed their repudiation of dictatorships and analyzed the relationship between socio-economic under-development and the creation of tyrannical and totalitarian regimes.[88]

During the OAS conference, Raúl Castro and a party of newsmen and *barbudos* began a flight from Havana to Santiago. When asked the purpose of the trip during a brief stop-over in Caracas, Castro said that in addition to bringing Roa home, we want "to show our sympathies for the Chilean people (who) . . . have shown understanding and solidarity with the Cuban Revolution."[89]

A plane which was carrying twenty-one journalists and thirteen lightly-armed *barbudos* preceded Castro's. When it landed in Santiago, Chilean authorities arrested and expelled the entire group. Chilean Foreign Minister Vergara delivered a note of protest to Cuban Ambassador Carlos Lechuga because the group had failed to obtain entry permits.[90] Although Roa conferred immediately with Vergara, he was apparently unable to do more than obtain permission for Raúl Castro and his five-man party to land without being similarly interned. Upon Castro's arrival in the second plane, he "was greeted by only one leading Chilean, Senator Salvador Allende . . . who became his full-time guide." Allende escorted the Castro party through some of the many slums which surround Santiago, and then took him through the wealthy *barrio alto* to his home where the entire FRAP leadership had been invited to a cocktail party.[91]

When Castro arrived, representatives of Communist youth, Socialist youth, the CUT Youth Department, the 26th of July Movement, *Acción Democrática Juventud*, and the Argentine University Federation were making plans for a Latin American Youth Congress. Raúl Castro reportedly attended one of their meetings and offered to finance the congress if it were held in Havana. Subsequently, a preparatory commission was established which included these organizations, the *COPEI Juventud*, FECH and the *Juventud Radical.*[92] Upon his departure, Castro was accompanied to the airport by Socialists, Communists, other FRAP associates and a few Christian Democrats. His visit had been conspicuously ignored by the Chilean government.[93]

Toward the end of 1959, Cuban Minister of Economy Regino Botí joined three United States professors in attending the University of Chile's International Summer School. Botí spoke on the Cuban agrarian reform.[94] Already registered at the University was Cuba's new cultural attaché in Chile. Upon her arrival as a student of sociology and economics, twenty-five year old Lidia González Huguet announced to the press that "Cuba harbors a great affinity for Chile, and I consider my friends in Chile as brothers."[95]

The Cuban diplomatic representation in Chile was limited to about eight persons. Although they sought to avoid public involvement in Chilean politics,[96] there was considerable covert activity. It has been alleged, for instance, that during 1960 Ambassador Díaz del Real intervened in an attempt to change the leadership of the Chilean-Cuban Cultural Institute. The ousted institute president had opposed Díaz's desire to direct more attention to organized labor and slum dwellers. Ladrón de Guevara claims that Díaz made "a pact" with the Communist Party to support a new president (Baltra) who would accept such a redirection of effort.[97]

In February of the same year, Díaz del Real met with a number of non-Communist politicians including Luis Bossay (the 1958 Radical Party candidate for the presidency, and a senator), Eduardo Frei, Allende and Juan Gómez Millas (the Rector of the University of Chile). Díaz stressed the danger to Cuba from continuing United States-supported attacks by exile groups. He suggested that in view of Chile's "special position," that a letter supporting Cuban self-determination be drafted and signed by leading non-Communist political figures in Latin America. The text of the so-called "Traveling Letter" declared:

The Cuban people are exercising, in these moments, the right to free determination, universally accepted and consecrated in the Charter of the United Nations.

Free determination is the most important guaranty that countries of our America have to enable them to escape poverty and ignorance. The violation of this right would represent a transgression and a danger for all our countries.

Latin American public opinion cannot remain indifferent before any act of economic aggression or any distortion of the truth.

As responsible citizens of free and sovereign countries, we are impelled by our conscience to make a fervorous call to public opinion so that it may be vigilant and alert in defense of the free determination of peoples and, in this case, of the legitimate rights of the Cuban people.

After Frei, Allende and Radical ex-presidential candidate Luis Bossay affixed their signatures, Christian Democratic leader Rafael Augustin Gomucio and writer Manuel Rojas circulated it among non-Communist intellectual and political figures in other countries.[98]

By mid-1961, the Chilean "Foreign Ministry was reportedly beginning to show disapproval of Cuban Ambassador Juan José Díaz del Real for alleged participation in matters of internal politics. He was also criticized for taking part in public acts in company with leaders of the labor confederation Central Unica de Trabajadores Chilenos (CUTCH). The Braden Copper Company refused to allow Díaz del Real, CUTCH general secretary Clotário Blest Riffo, and leaders of the copper unions to enter the Sewell mine to present a program honoring Cuba."[99] Also in July 1961, the rightist *El Mercurio* charged that Cuban and Soviet funds had been used to finance the First National Peasants Congress, referred to earlier in this chapter.[100]

During the first half of 1961, Díaz del Real had been "active in attendance at Communist meetings and toured the country with Socialist and Communist leaders. . . ." By July, the Chilean ambassador in Cuba had asked Havana to withdraw Díaz del Real.[101] A month later he was recalled amidst rightist charges that he had been distributing propaganda and money to pro-FRAP labor unions.[102]

Although the Chileans were unwilling to accept Cuban nominees for the ambassadorial post from then until Santiago severed relations in August 1964, the embassy managed to become involved in at least two "scandals." On October 9, 1962, seven crates weighing a total of 1,700 pounds were unloaded at Valparaiso. Addressed to the Cuban Embassy, they were labeled "samples of Cuban products and cultural and commerical material." Although exempt from customs duty, the shipment was opened and found to contain "Cuban propaganda addressed to various Chileans who a few months before had visited Cuba." In Havana, the Chilean ambassador was instructed to deliver a note of protest which charged that "the quantity of propaganda books and pamphlets was too great for Embassy use and that the material was destined for distribution here." Within a few days, the Cuban Foreign Ministry issued an apology saying that a low ranking official was to blame for erroneously dispatching such a shipment to the embassy in Santiago.[103] A year and a half later, the secretary of the Cuban Embassy was expelled for impersonating a Chilean with forged documents. He had been attempting to enter Peru to recover diplomatic papers carried by embassy couriers who had died in an air crash in that country with which Cuba did not have diplomatic relations.[104]

Less dramatic were the social affairs held by the embassy through which personal contacts were facilitated with important political personalities in Chile. Thus, on July 26, 1964, personal secretaries to the following senators were invited to a reception celebrating the tenth anniversary of the attack upon the Moncada Fortress by Fidel Castro and his followers: Socialist Salomón Corbalán; Christian Democrat Radomiro Tomic; independent leftist Baltazar Castro; Radical González Madariaga; and the Mayor of Renca.[105]

The embassy distributed a certain amount of cinematic and printed propaganda. In 1960, a "brigade" of University of Chile students went south to participate in earthquake reconstruction. The Chilean-North American Cultural Institute supplied them with films and a projector, while the Cuban Embassy gave them a film on the origins of the Revolution.[106] During the same year, the embassy distributed a pamphlet entitled *Cuba Denounces Before the World.*[107] It also disseminated Osvaldo Dórticos' *Letter to the Students of Chile: The Revolution has not Betrayed Cuba; It has Fulfilled its Ideals.*[108] In the course of 1961, the Cuban Embassy contracted with the Socialist Party publishing house to print a fifteen-page report on *Dos Años de Reforma Agraria* by INRA director Antonio Núñez Jiménez.[109]

Concluding Remarks

The extent of the Cuban proselytization effort in Chile was disproportionate to Cuba's limited material resources, yet quite small when compared to that of the United States. It is difficult to assess its over all impact. Apparently, most *invitados* were Marxists, sympathizers or members of centrist parties—either in the left-wing or editors of publications. Upon returning to Chile, a great many expressed sympathy for at least some programs or goals of the Revolution. The Leftists were emotionally inspired and tended to identify in varying degrees with the Revolution. Mixed reactions were common to those on the left-wings of Christian Democracy and the Radical Party, but almost all centrists emphatically affirmed Cuba's right to self-determination. With a few exceptions, little is known about the reactions and subsequent activities of professionals, intellectuals and artistic persons who were either *invitados* or employed by the Revolutionary Government. Within the upper and upper middle class reading sector, the works of Lagas and Ladrón de Guevara appear to have been influential in a negative way.

As for training in "terrorism," the evidence is scanty—an abortive attempt to set off bombs in Santiago during the missile crisis. With regard to economic aid, neither earthquake relief nor the impolitic behavior of Cuban diplomats engendered either friendship or significant diplomatic support from the Chilean government in international organizations.

The printed propaganda probably reached—in large part—radicals already within the FRAP constituency, although some was certainly disseminated among the youth and left-wings of the major center parties. The blue collar sectors are not "readers," and Cuban short wave broadcasts were received almost exclusively by the largely hostile upper and upper middle classes. Thus, the non-participant masses were not directly exposed to the Fidelista "message." Yet, certainly some in this category who were approached by the FRAP activists—especially by those *militantes* who had visited Cuba—did probably read or hear occasional tributes to the goals and programs of the Cuban Revolution.

In summary then, it may be speculated that the most effective Cuban instrumentality was the *invitado* program. It partially circumvented the hostile structure of mass media in Chile, and ensured largely favorable impressions or mesmerization by the opinion or political leaders who were selected. The relatively great expense necessitated for such an undertaking, however, limited the number of invitees to several hundred. Only indirectly and imperfectly could their impressions be conveyed to the Chilean citizenry en masse. Yet, the defection of populistic Christian Democrats and Radicals to the Popular Unity coalition late in the decade may be attributed, in part, to Cuba's revolutionary example. Without these energetic campaign organizers—many of whom had visited Havana earlier in the decade –Allende would never have secured his 40,000 vote plurality in 1970.

5

Aspects of Chilean-U.S. Relations Which May Have Diminished the Potential Appeal of the Cuban Revolution in Chile

Introduction

One of the most important objectives of the Cuban leadership and its FRAP supporters in Chile was the total elimination of United States influence within Chile. This so-called "Strategic Hatred" encompassed nationalization of businesses, severance of military relations, expulsion of the Peace Corps and the USIA, rejection of politically-conditioned economic and technical assistance, etc.

Efforts by Chilean Fidelistas to engender public support for these and related goals were substantially neutralized by certain structural relationships and United States policies.

Legacy of Non-Intervention

Thus, Chilean Fidelistas were unable to reinforce their arguments by recalling a legacy of United States military intervention and occupation. During most of the nineteenth century, relations were fairly cordial. A commercial treaty was signed in 1832, and thirty-nine years later Washington's "good offices" facilitated an armistice with Spain—against which Chile and four neighbors had been unsuccessfully warring for six years.[1]

Although partisanship by the United States Minister at the time of Chile's 1891 Civil War provoked resentment among the victorious rebels—as did United States threats during the "Baltimore Affair" some months afterwards—feelings did not become intense enough to justify a suspension of diplomatic relations. In 1909, Washington did, in fact, serve such an ultimatum upon the Chilean Foreign Ministry. Its purpose was to induce Chile either to pay a million dollars to United States investors or to consent to arbitration where the legality of the claims could not be raised. While mutual concessions and third party intervention resolved the Alsop Company Claims dispute, the prevalent Chilean attitude in the aftermath was again one of resentment.

These experiences may have contributed to frequent Chilean denunciations of United States interventionism in Central America and the Caribbean during the first decade of the twentieth century. Neutralist sentiment was strong during both World Wars, despite the initiation of Eximbank loans in 1937 and technical assistance five years later. Hence, by 1944 Chile's relations had been severed with Berlin.[2]

During the Cold War period, economic and technical assistance were increased and military aid was instituted. In 1947, the Chilean government signed the Rio Treaty. After the outbreak of the Korean War, she acceded to United States pressure in prohibiting the sale of "strategic" commodities to the Sino-Soviet Bloc. With the exception of Yugoslavia, relations with Communist nations were broken after the expulsion of the Communist Party from González Videla's government in 1947. Chile supported the United States at the Caracas OAS Conference which condemned the freely elected Arbenz government of Guatemala. A year later, President Ibáñez introduced legislation reducing the tax rates on copper production—largely controlled by United States firms.

The only minor crisis in relations occurred in 1958 when the State Department supported a bill in the United States Congress which would raise duties on Chilean copper. President Ibáñez reflected Chilean outrage by canceling a planned visit to Washington. Even the prestigious *El Mercurio*, which in recent years has seldom failed to support United States foreign policies, began to advocate expanded trade relations with the Soviet Union.[3] With the support of Ibáñez and businessmen associated with the Liberal and Radical parties, a campaign was begun which resulted in the establishment of several Communist commercial missions during the early 1960s. Thus, not only was there no historic pattern of armed United States intervention, but Chilean governments failed to conform to the "lackey" role portrayed by Fidelistas. Hence, the Frei administration had politely opposed a counterrevolutionary Inter-American standing armed force and has voiced criticism of the 1965 United States invasion of Santo Domingo. Yet, on the maintenance of a favorable investment climate and *major* cold war issues since 1947, Chile's growing economic dependence has been associated with a de facto acceptance of United States policy orientations. Consequently, it was not until late 1970 that relations were established with the Democratic Republic of Vietnam, the People's Republic of China or North Korea. Nor did Santiago seek the reincorporation of Revolutionary Cuba into the Inter-American System prior to Allende's electoral victory. Worth noting, however, is the alignment with the United States on Cold War and "investment climate" issues. As in the case of Guatemala, this superceded Chile's traditional commitment to non-intervention.

Attitudinal Variables

Cuba's growing dependence and association with the Communist nations during the 1959-1962 period was a source of hostility for a major segment of the Chilean public which was sympathetic towards the United States. In 1955, for example, only 14 percent of urban Chileans admitted favorable views of the Soviet Union; comparable figures for People's China and the United States were 5 percent and 62 percent respectively. Similarly, while 12 percent were "anti-

American," the percentages with negative images of the Soviet Union and China were forty and forty-nine. In general, anti-Soviet sentiment was slightly less frequent among the lower classes, and more persons were neutral or opinionless with regard to the Communist powers than the United States. Upper middle class managers appear particularly cohesive in their antipathy towards the Soviet Union and China. Approximately 75 percent of a leftward-biased sample interviewed in 1964-1965 were vigorously opposed to "international communism." Public opinion polls taken in Chile during the late fifties and early 1960s have indicated a slight rise in United States popularity and minor deterioration in the Soviet position.[4]

Other questions put to the Chilean public during the period support the conclusion of fairly widespread United States popularity. Even though Chilean centrists joined leftists in condemning the United States role in overthrowing the elected Guatemalan government in June 1954, when Chileans were asked their opinions of President Eisenhower thirty months later, 63 percent said "good" or "very good," while "bad" or "very bad" views were held by only 2 percent.[5] During 1957 a Greater Santiago sample was asked: "(b)etween Russia and the U.S., which would you have preferred to launch the first satellite?" In the aftermath of Sputnik I, fully 60 percent said the United States while 17 percent opted for the Soviet Union.[6] In 1962, urban Chileans were queried as to whether they thought the United States was "sympathetic" "to the wishes and hopes you have for the future of our country." Fully 65 percent answered in the affirmative, while 10 percent regarded Washington as unsympathetic. The same survey revealed that 54 percent believed the United States supported a redistributive land reform, while 66 percent expressed "considerable" or "very great confidence" in "the ability of the United States to provide wise leadership for other countries in dealing with present world problems."[7]

Despite this strong pro-United States and anti-Communist sentiment, during the 1950s, a majority of Chileans preferred to avoid direct involvement in Cold War conflicts, and only 12 percent supported the "strategic" copper embargo.[8] Similarly, clear majorities supported the initiation of some type of relations with the Communist nations. Trade rather than diplomatic or cultural ties was the form most often favored.[9] While 61 percent wanted foreign aid, only 18 percent thought Chile was receiving enough from the United States "to make a real difference."[10] And a substantial *minority* did not feel that "the United States treats Chile as an equal partner in affairs that concern them both."[11] Yet, when queried in 1962 regarding United States influence in Chile, 59 percent felt that the United States either had "about the right amount" or "should have more."[12]

During the 1950s, very substantial *minorities* of Chileans expressed the view that the United States was not paying enough for the country's copper exports. Smaller yet still significant *minorities* shared the opinion that United States economic policies had harmed the Chilean economy, but very few were able to specify which policies in their replies.[13] Chilean images of the role played by foreign companies in their economy have been on balance positive and fairly stable. In 1955, 54 percent said that "in general . . . foreign companies here in Chile help . . . the progress of the country." Only 20 percent held a contrary view, and union members were more favorably disposed towards the corporations than unskilled labor as a whole.[14]

In 1962, 55 percent felt "that North American business interests in Chile" were "sympathetic to the wishes and hopes" they had "for the future of" their country. Fifteen percent regarded United States firms as unsympathetic. Yet 52 percent favored government expropriation of foreign-owned industries in Chile, and less than half of these endorsed the principle of full compensation. Fewer Chileans preferred state ownership of large locally-owned industries.[15] Despite or perhaps because of the Frei administration's abortive 1965 "Chileanization" of the "Gran Mineria" there seems to have been a substantial rise in popular support for outright nationalization of the three major American copper mining firms—Anaconda, Kennecott and Cerro. Thus, in early 1970, a leading United States financial journal reported: "(t)he prospects for U.S. companies are clouded by rising sentiment for nationalization even among moderates of the younger generation."[16]

The Role of United States Business

Foreign concerns first entered the country with major investments after Chile seized newly discovered nitrate fields from Bolivia in the War of the Pacific (1879-1883). This period also marked the beginning of economic nationalism which has continued to the present day.[17] Until World War I, British investors contributed most foreign capital. "In 1912, United States investment was calculated at 15 million dollars, a sum that rose to 451 million dollars by 1928."[18] Since the great influx of United States capital during the 1920s, North American investments have continued to rise steadily in importance. By the end of the Second World War, they were dominant both in terms of the nation's economy and in proportion to total foreign investment.

Although by 1963 "fears of Fidel Castro and threats of nationalization" had dried up the flow of foreign investments in Chilean extractive industries, Frei's election the following year and his commitment to foreign investor interests— evidenced by the reduction in tax rates on copper production—stimulated approximately $750 million of new foreign investments in copper and dynamic secondary sectors such as steel, petrochemicals, plastics, fertilizers and paper manufacturing. In many cases, shares were purchased in Chilean firms. By the close of the sixties, as much as one-third of all Chilean invested capital was said to be foreign owned. Foreign firms held equity interests in "more than half" of Chile's 160 largest manufacturing corporations.[19] Despite the 1969 purchase by the Chilean government of several North American owned public utilities, United States investment at the end of the decade probably exceeded a billion dollars.[20]

Chile's contemporary similarity to Cuba prior to the overthrow of Batista is not limited to almost identical amounts of American invested capital. Both nations were heavily dependent upon trade with their North American neighbor. In the late 1960s, Chile obtained about 38 percent of her imports from the United States. Much of this was represented by construction equipment, industrial machinery and semi-processed commodities. Between fifteen and twenty percent of her exports—largely copper—were purchased by United States corporations.[21] During the 1960s, the American percentage of Chilean exports declined moderately, while Japan gradually emerged as a major importer of Chilean raw materials.

Although in recent years United States investors have diversified their holdings, the major interests have been in extractive enterprises. The Anaconda and Kennecott-owned copper companies together account for about 60 percent of the nation's foreign exchange earnings.[22] As late as 1969, copper exports accounted for 80 percent of Chilean foreign exchange earnings.[23]

Economic nationalists in Chile have directed unceasing criticism at these firms. The most frequent charge has been that foreign interests have remitted a large multiple of their original investments in the form of dividends, interest and payments for various kinds of services. They have been criticized for urging currency devaluations which have contributed to Chile's inflation. Discontent has also been occasioned by the small percentage of ore which has been refined or fabricated within Chile. Others have complained of their failure to sufficiently expand production. Most of the criticism has focused upon the *Gran Minería* (foreign mining firms).[24]

Despite these problems, the concerns have not found themselves without certain resources. Since the 1920s, most Chilean administrations have endeavored to create a receptive climate for foreign investments.[25] The firms and Chilean governments have argued that such investments increased tax revenues, created new jobs and introduced new technology into the country.

After his election in 1964, Eduardo Frei signed the so-called "Chileanization" agreement with the Kennecott, Anaconda and Cerro corporations. Viewed by Nelson Rockefeller as "a deterrent" to the "growth of Communism," the rapidly negotiated deal was also welcomed by the companies and liberal sectors of the American financial community. Hence, by late 1966 *Business Week* exhorted that "(b)y blunting left-wing demands for nationalization of the copper industry, the new formula has already contributed to political stability in Chile. And by producing new income to finance economic development, the copper program may undercut even further the country's potent Marxist forces."[26]

Despite unprecedented copper prices, neither "economic development" nor "political stability" resulted from this deal which reduced taxes on each ton mined and contributed to unsurpased profits on Chilean operations—funds that were withdrawn from the Chilean economy. Although it did result in an expansion of copper output, increased Chilean control over production and marketing was symbolic rather than real.[27]

Hence, in 1969 both Anaconda and Kennecott were compelled to agree upon a so-called "nationalization" formula with the Frei administration. According to Congressman Thomas M. Rees:

Political pressure to acquire all or a large return of the profits of copper mining have come from Frei's own party as well as parties further to the left. After an attempt to implement a 1967 program giving Chile a larger cut of the copper industry—but which left control of the major mines in the hands of private U.S. companies—the Frei government was finally forced (sic) by continued political pressure to acquire full Chilean control and a much greater share in the profits of the companies. The political pressures to take this step were rendered almost irresistible by the fantastically high copper prices and profits enjoyed by the U.S. companies for the past three years.

In its move to nationalize the companies, the Government of Chile has exercised restraint and shown good faith in its negotiations. It has taken steps to provide prompt compensation to the owners and has scrupulously avoided creating a situation where the Hickenlooper amendment or similar strictures might be applied by the United States. While the economic wisdom of nationalizing the copper companies can be questioned, the domestic political wisdom of nationalizing a key natural resource with foreign ownership is understandable.[28]

The implications of Leftist nationalization proposals were clarified for the Chilean electorate during the 1959-1965 period by the explicit integration of foreign investment goals into the United States foreign aid program. During 1960, Chile signed an agreement with the Inter-American Development Bank which obligated her "to stimulate private investments."[29] In the same year a convertibility guaranty agreement for the expatriation of profits and capital was signed with the United States, as was a second investment guaranty agreement three years later. While both of these agreements ensured North American investors against property losses due to war, revolution, riot, expropriations, etc., the Chilean Congress only ratified provisions pertaining to currency inconvertibility. Despite this limited obligation, the Agency for International Development had insured 125 firms for almost 1.4 billion dollars by April 1969. This insurance coverage included $723,853,865 for inconvertibility, $282,866,600 for expropriation, $11,808,000 for war risk and $376,625,013 for combined coverage.[30]

In addition, the United States Congress had earlier approved the Hickenlooper Amendment to the Foreign Assistance Act of 1963. Section 620(e) directs an automatic suspension of United States economic aid whenever there shall occur: failure to fulfill obligations under investment guaranty agreements; imposition of discriminatory taxes; abrogation of contracts or the repudiation or nonpayment of debts owed to United States firms; or nationalization of United States property without full and speedy compensation. Naturally, no economic assistance funds could be used to compensate United States owners in the event of expropriation.[31] Both the Chile-California Program and the more encompassing Alliance for Progress require that Chile maintain a hospitable climate for foreign investors. Indeed, the promotion of such investment has been viewed as a major goal of the AFP as well as the entire foreign aid program.[32] In 1962, special tax concessions were enacted to encourage United States firms to invest abroad.[33] The promotion of United States investments in Chile has been advocated by President Eisenhower, executive branch officials and congressmen while visiting in Santiago.[34]

North American businessmen have also engaged in what might be called "self-help" programs to further their interests in Chilean politics. With the exception of the Marxist parties, United States firms are said to have regularly contributed to campaign funds of both individual candidates and political parties. Although occasionally done directly, it is more commonly transferred through inflated legal fees. Important political figures are appointed to boards of directors or retained as legal representatives.[35] In 1964, Anaconda and other firms were said to have played a large part in financing the Frei campaign. During the 1970 campaign, Kennecott, Anaconda and Cerro, as well as other major United States investing firms, assumed the rightist Alessandri would win. Investment plans were not curtailed,[36] and funds again were rumored to be subsidizing the major anti-Allende contender. Some firms have ownership shares in the mass media while others engage in institutional advertising.[37]

Because of their superior efficiency and vulnerable position, some United States concerns have been willing to pay relatively high wages to their employees. Technical and managerial personnel in the *Gran Minería* have received remuneration in dollars which could be banked abroad or exchanged at high black market rates. In a number of cases workers have been provided with model living quarters. Anaconda, Braden, Grace and Esso have endeavored to win public favor by widely advertised contests for scholarships or free visits to the United States. The Braden Copper Company has also joined CARE, CARITAS (The Church social welfare agency) and other organizations in subsidizing the anti-Marxist organizing work of the Institute of Rural Education.[38] In the aftermath of the 1960 earthquakes, Braden executives publicly offered to donate medical supplies, clothing, $50,000, and sixty full scholarships for homeless children.

The companies probably receive and disseminate some materials from the United States Information Agency under its "cooperative programs with private organizations." The USIA broadcasts United States opposition to expropriations whenever such views are expressed by officials in the United States.[39]

Foreign Aid

Foreign assistance to Chile began with Eximbank loans in 1937, and was expanded by the addition of a modest technical assistance program during 1943. These forms of aid have been followed by: 1) ICA-AID programs since 1949; 2) military assistance and training since 1953; and 3) the shipment of P.L. 480 surplus agricultural commodities since 1955.

The tables reproduced in appendix III indicate that after fiscal year 1960 there was a 300 percent increase in average annual obligations and loan authorizations.[40] Fiscal 1961 also marked the acceptance by the United States of a commitment to social and economic development in Latin America, provided that certain reforms and other self-help measures were instituted by the recipient nations. Within less than a year, this new approach was incorporated into a program known since as the Alliance for Progress (AFP).

What relationship can be held to exist between this new orientation and the Cuban Revolution? Although Latin Americans had urged such socioeconomic development programs during the 1950s "at Inter-American Conferences, United States delegates merely called for an end to debate, or listened and refused to act."[41] At the Buenos Aires ECLA Conference (April 1959), and at the OAS Foreign Ministers' Conference in Santiago (August 1959), Fidel Castro and Raúl Roa urged such a new program despite previous knowledge of disinclination upon the part of the United States. The deterioration of relations between Cuba and the United States during 1959 culminated in a decision by the Revolutionary Government to accept Soviet assistance in February 1960. Within a month, the United States had begun to train Cuban exiles, and branded the Castro regime as Communist. This was followed by suppression of the island's anti-Communist opposition, physical confiscation of United States—owned sugar plantations and the nationalization of oil refineries.

The suspension of Cuba's sugar quota effectively marked what might be called the point of no return in Cuban-United States relations. Not coincidentally, this intervention was followed within about two weeks by the Eisenhower administration's endorsement of the new socio-economic development program for Latin America. The desire by executive and congressional leaders for diplomatic support in isolating Castro during 1960 was a major factor contributing to the Newport Declaration and the subsequent Act of Bogota.[42] The *emphasis* upon economic and social reforms and development by the United States was "a new departure" as was the multi-lateral approach.

When first proposed the AFP was intended to build upon this reformist approach in an effort to offer an alternative means for socio-economic progress which would avoid the "evils" of Soviet intrusion, and Revolutionary dictatorship in the Western Hemisphere. It might also lessen hostile reactions to the United States in the wake of Castro's anticipated overthrow. After the Bay of Pigs aggression, the AFP was justified before Congress and in Latin America as a "positive" instrumentality for both lessening Fidelista appeal as well as achieving other inherently worthy goals.[43] Integral to a dual policy, it was designed to provide hope for the Latin American masses; at the same time its successes was conditioned upon Latin American support in isolating and crippling the Revolutionary Government of Cuba.[44] United States officialdom, Chilean government leaders and politicians from left to right, and independent observers in both the United States and Chile have stressed the relation of the AFP to the perceived Fidelista challenge.[45]

Although the Alessandri administration publicly eulogized the AFP, its officials and supporters did not "lead the fight for those basic reforms which alone can *preserve* the fabric of their societies." (Emphasis added.) Bills for agrarian reform had been introduced by members of Congress in 1958, 1959, and 1960. None had been enacted.[46] Finally, in August 1962, the government coalition passed an extremely mild bill under which 5,200 peasants were to receive "economic units" during the following year. In fact, only 1,400 were sold such land in 1963, and the figure was even lower in 1964 when the United States Agency for International Development no longer referred to this "reform" to justify appropriation requests.[47] While the agrarian reform bill was being considered by the Chilean Congress, a political analyst reported that:

According to the OAS "wisemen," the Agrarian Reform is not in itself adequate for full-fledged Chilean membership in the Alliance for Progress. The Government must also institute a Tax Reform, balance the budget whose deficit reaches 400 million escudos, and it must comply with the instructions of the Monetary Fund. . . . Chile must devalue her escudo. . . .[48]

Although no tax reform was passed until 1963, the need for foreign funds compelled Alessandri to devalue the escudo at the beginning of October 1962. A week later, the AFP Committee of Nine "Wisemen" approved Chile's Ten Year Development Plan.[49] This "plan" was not a plan for "an action program, as AID has subsequently recognized. Rather, it is largely a series of projections exploring the interrelationships of the major sectors of the economy under certain quantitative assumptions. As such, it provides an analytical framework for Chile's economic development, but *does not set forth clear priorities or definite projects*. In practice, the Chilean government has made vital decisions with little reference to its plan" (Emphasis added.)

The main objective of the plan was to create a favorable climate for private investment—by providing public investment for such necessary infrastructure as electric power and transportation; by stimulating the private sector through public works and direct investments in housing, irrigation, and land settlement; and through the promotion of mining, forestry, and fisheries. It was hoped that the planned level of investment would raise the annual rate of GNP growth to 5.5 percent (3 percent per capita) from the average 3.5 percent per annum during the 1951-60 period.[50]

Although the Chilean economy continued to stagnate during the 1960-70 period, the "plan" did commit Chile to the AFP requirement that foreign investments be encouraged. Fulfillment of this obligation also was reflected by the currency devaluation that contributed to severe inflation during 1963.[51] The tax legislation which became effective in February 1964 hardly deserved to be designated as a "reform." Its most radical provision imposed an added 30 percent income tax rate on income earned in Chile by foreign natural persons. Regular income tax rates were to range from ten to forty-five percent, and the new capital gains tax was set at 20 percent. To reduce evasion, a new inheritance tax restricted gift-giving. Similarly, the legislation simplified administrative procedures and contained provisions to facilitate enforcement. But the principal emphasis of the reform was the reduction of widespread evasion rather than a shift in the burden of taxation.[52]

Inept administration by the Chilean government resulted in the abandonment of the project loans by AID at the end of 1962. More vague criteria were substituted under the heading of "program loans." When the Chilean government failed to meet these requirements during 1963, funds were disbursed anyway for 1964.[53] As a "pilot country," Chile had received through 1965 more AFP aid on a per capita basis than any other Latin American nation.[54]

The continued extension of massive aid despite Chile's failure to implement serious social reforms is probably best explained by the parallel goal of maintaining the type of economic and political system that existed in Chile during the period in question.

In Chile, as we have noted, AID continued budget support and balance-of-payments assistance during the 1964 election year to prevent economic deterioration which would have sparked unemployment and discontent and, presumably, a swing to the far left politically. The assistance was also designed to present the incoming Chilean administration with an economy in reasonably good shape.[55]

There is evidence that as early as March 1962, United States officials were concerned about a possible deterioration of the economic situation because it might contribute to a FRAP victory in 1964.[56] And while it was negatively evaluating the "reform" initiatives of the Alessandri administration, the Goodwin-Moscoso Mission "didn't conceal its opinion. In its judgment, the victory of Marxism-Leninism was inevitable in this country if Christian Democracy failed to win 'regardless of the sacrifice.' "[57] Or in the words of a Christian Democratic leader at the time:

The North American official (Goodwin) knew before his arrival that his mission had no other purpose than to study and estimate the magnitude of the emergency situation confronting the country so that an indispensable minimum of aid could be provided to prevent total bankruptcy of an erroneous policy which would be manifested by paralyzation of the country of galloping inflation.[58]

Although for tactical reasons Christian Democratic leader Eduardo Frei refused to accept an invitation for a meeting with the Goodwin-Moscoso Mission, two weeks afterwards he and Radomiro Tomic were in Washington at the nominal invitation of Georgetown University.[59] And during early 1963 while testifying before a congressional subcommittee, Assistance Secretary of State Edwin Martin was able to boast:

On the positive side, we note the failure of the Communist unions to form a 'neutralist' Latin American Confederation of Workers in Chile in September 1962.

In Chile, all the major student federations are now controlled by the Christian Democrats.[60]

Chilean sensitivities were highlighted during the last months of the 1964 presidential campaign when *El Mercurio* published the following AP report:

Senator Jacob K. Javits, Republican for New York, praised President Johnson last night for having dispelled what he called 'Fears of the anti-Communists in Chile,' that the United States might decide to help a Communist government if it came to power in that South American country.

Javits stated that President Johnson 'completely eliminated that anxiety' during a luncheon speech this week at the Associated Press in New York. . . .

Javits declared that the speech by Johnson should dissipate the anxieties that could 'undermine the forces and fighting spirit of the anti-Communist classes in Chile.'[61]

It will never be known whether fear of the consequences of a termination of United States aid cost Allende enough votes—given the prominence of the anti-Communist issue in the preceding months—to ensure the Christian Democratic victory. In any event, after Frei's triumph, President Johnson happily observed that "the outcome of the Chilean elections remind us of the advances which the Alliance for Progress is making."[62]

Much to his chagrin, President Nixon could not view the outcome of the 1970 Chilean elections with similar enthusiasm. Between 1964 and 1969, Chile's foreign indebtedness had increased from 1.6 to 2.1 billion dollars. Despite fantastic copper prices—ranging up to seventy cents a pound—and an average of 300 million dollars per year in foreign credits, the Frei administration was unable to boast of a higher per capita GNP growth rate than its predecessor Alessandri.[63] Congressman Rees has noted that Chile was "one of the largest recipients of U.S. aid under the Alliance for Progress, receiving some $1.3 billion since 1961. A large part of this assistance has been in the form of program and sector loans (some $534 million) in direct support of the broad program of economic and social reform undertaken by the Christian Democratic government of President Frei."[64] In fact, Chile is second to Vietnam in the world as far as per capita economic aid is concerned.[65]

Although "stability" and its related population control programs of all types have replaced social reforms and rapid economic growth as the contemporary content of the AFP,[66] the former goals remained very central to Chilean politics in the late 1960s. Recognizing this, in mid-1968 Congressman Otto Passman charged that AID funds would be used to reinforce the Christian Democratic position in the 1969 and 1970 elections.[67] It is ironic that Frei's only really successful and completed reform was a high priority AID target—curricula revision and the expansion of educational facilities. Other funds facilitated the organization of peasant laborers by the fiercely anti-Socialist Union of Christian Peasants. This was channeled through the CIA subsidized International Development Foundation which the Frei administration allowed to remain in Chile even after its exposure as a CIA front organization.[68]

North American desperation to prevent the Chilean people from electing a socialist government was reflected by the greatest official equanimity when Frei agreed to barter garlic and beans for Cuban sugar in early 1970. Nor were there complaints when Chile fell two years behind in its dues to the Pan American Union.[69] Election year 1970 also saw the Public Works Ministry exhaust its AID supported budget within ten months. The imperative of utilizing all possible funds to avoid a major depression was again operative as it had been for the 1964 election.[70] This preoccupation was reflected on September 18, 1970, at an "off the record" regional press briefing in Chicago by President Nixon's special advisor on national security affairs. According to one journalist, Henry Kissinger had "warned that Allende's election threatens the neighboring republics—Peru, Bolivia and Argentina—with the spread of Communism." Although former Ambassador Dungan has testified to the geo-physical absurdity of this remark, terming it "ill informed nonsense," it has predictably sparked a widespread anti-Chilean press campaign. By Nov. 27, 1970, Foreign Minister Almeyda had summoned United States Ambassador Edward Korry to lodge an official complaint.[71] Similar press campaigns preceded CIA intervention in Guatemala (1954) and Cuba (1961).

Information Programs

If in its initial years the AFP was urged upon Congress and elsewhere justified as an evocative symbol which might lessen the appeal of the Cuban Revolution and reduce the capital flight from the region,[72] this view was also reflected in USIA programing wherein it was portrayed as a "democratic alternative" to the tyrannical disaster represented by Cuba under Castro. Agency output stressed the Cuban leader's "betrayal" of those who had believed in his public commitments to liberty and anti-Communism, as well as Castro's willing acceptance of the role of a Soviet satellite while enslaving the hungry and suffering Cuban masses. Ignoring the United States-sponsored economic embargo, USIA messages in the mid and late sixties placed great emphasis upon economic shortages and rationing in Havana. The United States was presented as sharing non-conflicting interests with Latin America, and as a model of liberty, democracy and socio-economic progress—goals which Washington promoted in Latin America.[73]

During the 1958-1964 period, USIA utilization of locally held currency in Chile almost doubled. The annual expenditures were $155,007 in 1958 and $294,640 in 1964. There was a smaller yet significant increase in the dollar costs of the program budgeted to Chile: $220,525 (1958); $259,188 (1960); $291,992 (1962); $287,992 (1963 est.); and $294,640 (1964). By 1963-1964, greater amounts were being allocated to only four other and substantially larger Latin American nations: Brazil, Mexico, Argentina and Venezuela.[74] The increase in personnel was also significant during the years in question. In 1961, the agency requested the addition of six locals and three North Americans in Chile. Between 1962 and 1964, six more Chileans and one United States national were added. The total personnel in Chile during 1964 (10 United States and 51 locals) was exceeded only in Mexico and Argentina.[75] USIA officials justified their requests for increased appropriations before congressional committees by emphasizing the need to combat "Castroite" appeal.[76]

In the following paragraphs, the discussion will focus upon specific instrumentalities utilized by the USIA in Chile during the relevant period: shortwave and local radio placement; press and magazine insertions; book, pamphlet and cartoon booklet distribution; the informational media guarantee program; and others.

Before the defeat of Batista, the Voice of America (VOA) was broadcasting less than one hour of short wave programing in Spanish each day.[77] Although no change was made during the following year, in March 1960 a "general intensification of information programs" was begun. At that time, one hour of Spanish "news, features, and commentary" was beamed to the hemisphere for two hours (original and repeat) each evening. "By the end of June, its audience had been increased through a total of 75 local radio stations in 8 Latin American countries, which relayed the programs over their medium wave facilities to their regular listeners."[78] Within a year, the agency reported that "150 local stations in a dozen Latin American countries" were rebroadcasting the programs to an estimated audience "outside of Cuba" of "about 300,000 or 400,000."[79] It is probable that such rebroadcasts occurred within Chile. By June 1963, seven hours per day of Spanish language programs were being directed by short wave to Latin America, excluding Cuba. This level was maintained through 1964, and reduced to 48 hours per week early in 1965.[80]

Because the listening audience possessing short wave receivers was limited to the upper and upper middle classes, the agency has also relied upon "packaged programs" for placement on standard wave bands by local radio stations. Between 1953 and fiscal 1960, the USIA contracted with station WRUL of New York City for the short wave transmission of approved programs. WRUL then paid local Latin American stations for standard wave rebroadcasts. In 1959, local Chilean stations were rebroadcasting sixty quarter hours per week of news, and eight quarter hours per week of features. Twelve broadcasters collaborated in this nation-wide arrangement:

Santiago	*La Serena*
Radio Minería	Radio La Serena
Radio del Pacífico	
	Talca
Antofagasta	Radio Lircay
Radio Libertad	
	Temuco
Concepcion	Radio Cooperativa Vitalicia
Radio Simón Bolivar	Radio La Frontera
Iquique	*Valdivia*
Radio Esmeralda	Radio Baquedano
Punta Arenas	*Vina del Mar*
Radio Austral	Radio Minería

In fiscal 1959, VOA began to "package" programs itself in Washington and Santiago. During that year both WRUL and VOA placed programs on Chilean stations, but no payment was made by VOA to broadcasters who used its materials. The relationship with WRUL was terminated at the end of fiscal 1960. In fiscal 1961, local placement of agency materials in Chile averaged thirty programs per week; 70 percent of them were "substantive" in nature, and 62 percent were broadcast during prime listening time. The thirty programs averaged fifty hours per week, and up to fifty-three broadcasters used a single program. Almost 80 percent of the programs were duplicated by more than one station.[81]

Although no figures have been *published* to document an increase in the use of "packaged programs" by Chilean broadcasters in succeeding years, such inferences may be drawn from regional data.[82] While only 80,000 hours of USIA "packaged program" material were placed on local Latin American standard band broadcasts during fiscal 1959, by March 1961, agency officials were testifying that about 1,350 stations would broadcast 156,000 hours of such USIA insertions during fiscal 1960.[83] In fiscal 1962, this figure had climbed to 468,000 hours—an average of 9,000 hours "every week that passes in the cities, towns, and villages of the continent."

Our general programming includes news summaries and commentaries, dramatizings, and forums, as well as a limited number of musical features.

Examples of typical programs are: 'The Three Villalobos'—an anti-Castro soap opera of 130 half-hour programs done by a Cuban refugee cast, and based on a similar program popular in pre-Castro Cuba; 'The Revolution of Hope,' a weekly 15-minute program on the progress of democratic land reform in Latin America.[84]

Like short wave, television in the early 1960s was primarily heard in Chile by opinion-makers, professionals, businessmen and their families. In 1961, there were 21,000 sets and an estimated audience of 168,000. The estimated figures for 1964 were about 45 percent higher.[85] During the former year, a "one-hour television serial, 'Castro, Communism and Cuba' was sent to 17 posts" in Latin America. By the end of 1962, USIA videotapes for "*Panorama Panamericano*"—a "key American affairs program (that) counters Communist propaganda and stresses the community of interests shared by the United States and its Latin American neighbors"—was being placed on Chilean TV. "The commercial television program, 'Anatomy of Betrayal,' was . . . shown (during the missile crisis) immediately after the telecast of the President's speech to viewers throughout Latin America." During late 1963 or 1964, at least two anti-Castro films were placed on Chilean TV: "Confronting Castro's Subversion" and "Blueprint for Terror." Chilean government officials were given a special private showing of the latter.[86]

In recent years, the agency has also supplied materials to the press and magazines in Chile. During 1961, "USIA posts in Latin America estimated that local press usage ranged from 40 to 70 percent of all Agency materials distributed, and that radio and television usage ran much higher." In the 1963-1964 period, the "press and publications service" was transmitting over short wave nineteen hours of materials per week to agency posts in Latin America.[87] Such materials were being used by the government newspaper *La Nación*, Chile's leading daily *El Mercurio*, a large circulation Santiago tabloid *Las Ultimas Noticias*, and as far south as Punta Arenas in the *Prensa Austral*.[88] In 1966, a USIA employee claimed that as much as ten percent of the reading matter published by the nation's press consisted of agency releases. Only the Socialist *Las Noticias de Ultima Hora* and the Communist *El Siglo* did not receive and use such materials.[89] In general, the press clipping service stressed themes similar to those broadcast by radio and TV.[90]

Agency films are not restricted to television usage. In fiscal 1961, USIA films reached "a Latin American audience of more than 44 million people."[91] During that year, more funds were expended for "the distribution or placement of projectors, screens, and films for the showing of motion pictures to selected audiences" in Chile than in any other Latin American nation. Almost one fourth of the estimated hemispheric budget was allocated to Chile where there was an operating inventory of 83 projection machines on June 30, 1961. The number was to be increased to 92 within three years.[92] During 1961, the "Motion Picture Service . . . produced a one-reel black-and-white film, 'The Unhappy Island,' and another 'The Right to Live,' on the plight of Cuban refugees."[93] And in 1964, a USIA film—"The President"—was shown to 340,000 Chilean theatregoers by a commercial chain.[94]

Although the USIA is not the only agency within the United States government that distributes books in Latin America,[95] it has in recent years financed the translation and publication of a large number of works. "The book translation program in Latin America is designed to stimulate the commercial publication and sale of selected books by American authors in Spanish and Portuguese languages. . . . Emphasis is given to low-priced editions which bring American books within financial reach of the Latin American university student."

Once a book is published, the Agency plays another important role: USIA normally takes from one-fifth to one-third of each edition for its own distribution. Some copies are given to magazine and newspaper editors and radio or television commentators, for review in print or on the air. Many are sent to public, university and school libraries as well as to professors and educators who could be instrumental in having books adopted as texts or supplementary reading material in schools and universities. Copies of appropriate titles are given to government officials, political leaders and others.[96]

This program was initiated several years before the suicide of Getulio Vargas with the publication of four translated works in Portuguese. Between 1956 and 1959, the agency contracted with a Buenos Aires publisher for Spanish translations. During this three year period 440,000 copies were delivered to the agency for distribution and presentations, and three million were distributed through commercial outlets in Latin America.[97] During the first half of 1959, commerical "distribution of 32 low-priced U.S. books, translated and published in Buenos Aires, was expanded to every South American country."[98] By "the end of 1959, the program was producing 9,000 books per day of 35 titles in low-priced Spanish-language editions."[99] Contracted editions and copies in Spanish and Portuguese during the early 1960s increased as shown in Table 5-1.

These books cover a broad range of subjects calculated to further the goals of the Alliance for Progress, to strengthen the sense of identity of interests and values between the United States and Latin America, and to demonstrate that Castro-communism is not the answer to the economic and social problems of the Western Hemisphere.[100]

Table 5-1
USIA Subsidized Book Distribution in Latin America, 1961-1964

Year	Editions	Copies
1961	60	535,000
1962	76	723,000
1963	323	3,550,000
1964 est.	475	4,982,000

Source: U.S. Information Agency, *21st Report to Congress*, July 1 - December 31, 1963. (Washington, D.C.: Government Printing Office, 1964).

In 1948, the Informational Media Guaranty Program (IMG) was instituted by USIA. It "enables certain foreign countries, which have a shortage of U.S. dollar exchange, to import American books, periodicals, films, and other informational materials through normal commercial channels. Foreign importers make payments in their own currency to American exporters, who then exchange the foreign currency for U.S. dollars through USIA. IMG operations in each country are based upon a bilateral agreement between the U.S. government and the government of the participating country. Exports under the program are controlled by the issuance of guaranty contracts made by the USIA and American exporters of informational materials."[101]

Such an agreement for *selected* materials deemed "consistent with the national interests of the United States" was signed with Chile during the Ibáñez administration. The first guaranty contracts were negotiated in May 1955. In fiscal 1958, 53 guarantee contracts totaling $1,093,810 were held by 51 United States publishers or book exporters. During that year $677,202 in dollar payments for Chilean pesos were made under these guarantees. The number of contractors increased to 69 for the 1960-1963 fiscal period. Although 99 contracts totaling $1,476,110 were guaranteed during this period, only $921,915 were paid for Chilean currency.[102]

Another important facet of the information program is the publication by the USIA of its own pamphlets and cartoon booklets. In Chile where in the early 1960s only 40 percent of the economically active population claimed a primary school education,[103] the importance of simplistic illustrated media is fairly obvious. During the first half of 1961, "(m)ore than 800,000 copies of a cartoon booklet on the Alliance were published in Spanish and Portuguese and distributed throughout Latin America."[104] Two years later the agency reported:

The use of booklets has been stressed particularly in Latin America where their purpose has been twofold: to document dramatically Castro's betrayal of the Cuban revolution, and to tell people about the Alliance for Progress and engender support for it.

In the first 6 months of this year, more than 7 million copies of such booklets were distributed in Latin America, thus bringing the total in the 2-year program close to 20 million. Nearly half of the orders were for titles previously published, which indicates a continuing popular demand for the first several editions of these booklets.

Three new titles were published to help meet the great need for direct, graphic, and easily understood appeals to Latin American workers and farmers. 'The Despoilers,' seventh in a series, depicts the way Communism breeds hunger and oppression in every country it blights. Two others deal with the message of self-help under the Alliance for Progress. 'The Turning Point' documents the role Latin American students can play in the program to benefit their respective countries. 'Toward a Better Life' dramatizes successful efforts at community improvement in a hypothetical and typically primitive rural area; orders for more than 1,500,000 of this one broke all records.

USIS posts in Latin America distribute free copies of the cartoon continuities in various ways: through labor unions, through stores where shoppers pick them up, and through instructors who use them as *textbook material for use in reading instruction*. [Emphasis added.][105]

Worth noting is the fact that in 1963, AID established over one thousand literacy centers in Chile, "and more than 10,000 volunteer teachers were recruited to instruct 80,000 adults."[106] Early in the same year, a deputy director of the USIA testified that the agency had "produced six cartoon books on the Castro record in such fields as education, labor, and religion, and these are being distributed in Latin America in some 8 million copies."

After citing three AFP-supporting cartoon booklets of which only 3 million were being distributed, he went on to report that "(o)ur Latin American posts also carry on active field publications programs, tailoring their pamphlets to the local situation, and giving special attention to the Alliance and Communist Cuba."[107] In fiscal 1961, it was estimated that $5,500 was spent in Chile for the local production of pamphlets, leaflets and posters. These materials were "for distribution primarily to student and labor groups."[108]

After Castro's assumption of power, the agency intensified efforts directed at organized labor. It began to publish a new labor periodical in 1959.[109] Within two years, USIA was asking Congress to finance the visit by a United States labor mission to Chile and three other "key" Latin American countries.[110] During 1961, a labor information officer was assigned to Chile.[111] In addition to establishing "rapport with labor unions and workers," his functions included: supplying labor magazines with materials; publishing agency labor newspapers; distributing USIA pamphlets; showing films at labor gatherings; and placing American labor news on local radio and TV stations.[112] The "Washington publications unit provides good backstopping for this program in the form of editorial material, stories and pictures as well as cartoon books particularly aimed at the labor target. An example of the latter is 'Pepe Obrero,' recently published in 585,000 copies and distributed throughout the area."[113]

The Agency also published *Carta Obrera*. This "USIS-Caracas bimonthly magazine for labor, produced by the labor attache and the labor information officer as a joint endeavor has a circulation of nearly 30,000 and is widely circulated throughout trade union circles in Latin America." It "is used in training schools in Latin America set up under the auspices of the American Institute for Free Labor Development. Other USIA posts are reproducing the magazine for their own use in support of their labor programs."[114]

The USIA has carried on a number of other programs in Chile which deserve at least brief mention. "Special presentation items" have been given to students, intellectuals and labor leaders individually and to their organizations. Edited in Santiago, *Estudios sobre el Comunismo* is circulated among intellectuals. By 1963, binational centers were functioning in at least twelve Chilean cities. They sponsored conferences, lectures, courses in English and United States studies,

USIA book distribution, screening, orientation and follow-up of scholarship recipients, exhibits, etc.[115]

It is difficult to measure the effect of all of these activities upon Chilean opinion. At least since 1955, the Agency has been contracting with local market research or public opinion experts for surveys of Chilean views on political questions. The results of such surveys are used in the planning of propaganda activities as well as by other branches of the United States government. They have indicated the existence of anti-Communist attitudes by a large majority of the population at least since 1955. Thus, much of the Agency's work may have constituted little more than reinforcement of such predispositions.

With respect to the Cuban Revolution, negative evaluations increased somewhat during the 1961-1964 period. The opposite was true with regard to the United States. Despite the 1965 invasion of Santo Domingo, this trend probably continued during the latter part of the decade when USIA propaganda zeroed in on the continued refugee exodus and economic deterioration in Cuba. Allende in 1970—again associated with Havana by his opponents—received a lower percentage of the total vote than he had in 1964. Since so much of the mass media use Agency propaganda, it is difficult to clearly distinguish the latter's independent contribution. As early as 1955, "Santiago was found to be on the whole somewhat more pro-United States and anti-Communist than the other Chilean cities surveyed...."[116] There is a concentration of mass media in Santiago, and usage is somewhat higher than in smaller cities and towns.

Cultural Exchange and Related Efforts

State Department educational exchange programs with Latin America were initiated in 1938, on the eve of World War II. They were extended to other areas of the world with the initiation of the Cold War. Although there was a decline in global expenditures after the Korean War, by the end of fiscal 1960 a sharp rise had occurred.[117] During the 1955-1959 period, 77 Chileans received Fulbright Program grants for study, research or teaching in the United States, while 43 North Americans were sent to Chile.[118] In 1959, of 450 Chileans who had received foreign study fellowships during the year, about 300 were going to the United States.[119] State Department grantees under the Mutual Educational and Cultural Exchange Program from fiscal 1959 through fiscal 1965 are shown in Table 5-2.

The exchange of persons program "is not a sentimental gesture. It is not an effort to be generous to foreign students and visitors, nor just a means of providing Americans a personally enriching tour or period of residence abroad. It is a hardheaded investment in our future and the world's future."[120] According to Secretary of State Rusk, "[t]his activity is extremely important for the long-range effect on the lives of nations.... It is through this program as perhaps in

Table 5-2
Chilean and American Grantees under the State Department's Exchange of Persons Program, 1959-1965

Year	Chileans to U.S.	U.S. to Chile	Expenditures incl. P.L. 480
1959	85	25	$371,000
1960	97	28	353,100
1961	69	38	437,561
1962	90	44	475,062
1963	91 est.	47 est.	606,635 est.
1964	130	44	497,869
1965	143	39	521,493

Source: U.S., Congress, House, Committee on Appropriations, *Departments of State and Justice, the Judiciary, and Related Agencies for 1960, Hearings* before a subcommittee of the Committee on Appropriations, House of Representatives, 86th Cong., 1st sess., 1960, pp. 1081-82. U.S., *Departments for 1964*, pp. 1246, 1453. U.S., *Departments for 1966*, p. 882.

no other way that we can take certain leadership in the change that is taking place in the world." Non-educational goals of the program include: 1) the creation of favorable attitudes toward United States society and policies among selected Chileans, and 2) the establishment of relationships of confidence between such Chileans and United States officials or cooperating private organizations.

... the exchange of persons program is designed to provide continuing links of communication, thereby reinforcing democratic orientations and strengthening respect for democratic institutions and processes. Operating as it does among all the levels of the population—the student, the professor, the teacher, the school, and university administrator, the legislator, the artist, the journalist, and the writer—that is, the leaders and potential leaders of the hemisphere—the program provides continuing opportunities for guiding the movement toward mature democratic societies in the area. . . .

It is a program through which ideas are transmitted, contacts and association established, and understanding deepened between the peoples of North and South. These are the bases on which the unity of the Western Hemisphere must be built. . . .

Examples of the contribution the program is making in shaping the leadership in the other American republics necessary to reinforce the goals of the Alliance for Progress, are the many former grantees who now hold high official office in key fields of activity. At a time when the communists are becoming increasingly active in the whole area of exchanges in the other American republics, it becomes all the more imperative that the United States Government continue to strengthen its relationships. . . .[121]

Under the foreign leader program, talented or influential Chilean journalists from centrist or rightist publications have been brought to the United States for from two to eight weeks.[122] Similarly, in early 1962, eight Chilean public relations men were invited for a forty-five day tour.[123] More important have been the many legislators from the centrist and rightist parties who were given such grants.[124] A number publicly extolled aspects of North American culture and viewed their experiences as highly rewarding.[125] Although university students do not generally receive leader grants, an exception was made in 1960 when the presidents of seven university federations toured Puerto Rico and the United States as State Department guests.

The department's cultural exchange program has extended grants to university Rectors, faculty, high level administrators and experts in the Chilean government for participation in conferences or for two to twelve months of study. Labor leaders have also received such grants under the program from AID and its predecessor agencies.[126] Both AID and ICA have financed agreements between United States and Chilean universities for exchanges of faculty and students.

Interchanges of university professors, school teachers, and students with other Latin American countries, either individually or as components of cooperative inter-university projects, are planned to contribute toward strengthening the educational structure of the respective countries. For example, in Chile, under the leadership of the Fulbright program research programs are being developed in Chilean universities in the social sciences which are for the first time preparing Chileans to staff more adequately their university faculty and school teacher needs, thus strengthening the whole base of educational development in the country. . . .

Examples of (broadening the democratic experience of youth) . . . projects carried out in fiscal year 1963 . . . include the interchange of student groups such as the one between the National University of Chile and the University of Texas, which has significantly influenced the student leadership of the National University along democratic lines.[127]

When Chileans who have traveled to the United States on United States government fellowships or leader grants return to their homeland, they may participate in some aspects of the State Department's followup program. In the early 1960s, $200,000 per annum was being expended by the department for such programs in various countries.[128] Those who have studied at North American universities are often invited to join the Women's or the Men's University Club in Santiago. Both cooperate closely with the USIA-directed Chilean-North American Cultural Institute. Some receive North American professional journals for which the Department of State spends about $75,000 annually worldwide.[129] Others may be contacted directly by embassy personnel. In the course of requesting that Congress authorize an increase in the staffs of diplomatic missions in Latin America several years ago, it was emphasized that (t)he Department's staff must be in a position to seek out and meet frequently with persons of influence in many non-official circles, e.g., business, labor, church, student, political and agricultural leaders. United States efforts to influence these groups should be increased and must necessarily be carried on where these people are found rather than in the capital city alone.[130]

The cultural projection efforts of the State Department in Chile have also encompassed the construction and operation of a large binational primary and secondary school near Santiago. In addition, both the USIA and the department have subsidized tours to Chile by selected "patriotic" white and Negro athletes, performing artists and literati. Finally, the embassy has directly sponsored certain cultural activities. During January 1964, for example, the Chilean Supervisory Board of Education and the embassy jointly organized a series of seminars for teachers of history and geography on the evolution of culture in the United States. In the last seminar, no less than 107 teachers participated, as did USIA representatives and the embassy's cultural attaché.[131]

In the early sixties, too, various United States congressmen paid "good will" visits to Chile during which they socialized with their Santiago counterparts.[132]

Peace Corps

Chile and Colombia were the first two Latin American nations to receive contingents of volunteers. The number assigned to Chile increased from 45 in October 1961, to 363 at the end of 1965.[133] A substantial presence was maintained throughout the decade. Hence, by May 1969 there were more than 200 volunteers in Chile, which had the sixth largest contingent in Latin America.[134] Although Peace Corps work is essentially technical, it is not neutral insofar as internal Chilean politics are concerned.

First, in their self-help projects and community development work, the volunteers—who must meet both political and psychological standards to be assigned abroad—tend to establish relations of rapport with the largely unorganized lower class persons with whom they come into contact.[135] Outward-going and willing to live in primitive surroundings, the volunteers are probably the only *Yanquis* that such Chileans have ever seen. This is also largely true for most students in educational institutions where the volunteers are teaching.[136] These Chileans are probably aware that the Peace Corpsmen were sent by the United States government. When a Leftist political organizer approaches such Chileans and charges that the United States is exploiting Chile, taking away all of her riches and the principle obstacle to Latin American development and self-determination, his reception by such *campesinos, pobladores,* or *estudiantes* is unlikely to be ecstatic. Few of these persons comprehend the Leninist theory of imperialism, but most are likely to be impressed by the *simpático Yanqui* who has been sent by Washington to help them help themselves.

Second, the volunteers frequently have worked for or in collaboration with Chilean government agencies.[137] To the extent that they improve social-welfare administrative performance, the volunteers may diminish generalized or agency-directed discontent among the population. Similarly, by *involving* the poor as individuals in *self-help* cooperatives, housing construction, literacy training, etc., the volunteers may neutralize expectations that it is governmental programs that are of primary importance in developing a society.[138] To Peace Corps headquarters in Washington, volunteers' reports detailing their experiences and lower class attitudes are remitted.[139] They are used for the training of future volunteers and are presumably accessible to intelligence agencies and other departments.

Third, since 1961 the volunteers have been assisting one of the most important anti-FRAP organizing efforts in rural Chile. In October of that year, 45 University of Notre Dame trained volunteers arrived in Santiago for a five-week orientation session. They were then assigned to the Institute of Rural Education (IER), which is considered by CARITAS—the major social welfare agency of the Catholic hierarchy in Chile—to be its "Rural Department."[140] The private IER was subsidized in 1962 by the Chilean government, CARE, CARITAS, Braden Copper, Miseror, ILO, UNESCO and "other international organizations." In the same year, AID provided $1,300,000 of which $575,000 was allocated to the construction of five new "schools for the training of peasant leaders."

By early 1962, the IER was operating eleven training schools with 1,650 men and women (fifteen years and older) on full scholarships. The institute's stated goals are: "aiding the peasant by training rural leaders and by promoting the organization of peasants." In the training schools, the peasants were given *moral* education, vocational courses and familiarized with the functioning of cooperatives—fifteen of which had been created by the IER. There were in early 1962, five thousand alumni of these training schools who had joined others in organizing 402 peasant centers. Averaging twenty families in each, the goals of these *centrales* were to promote the social, economic and cultural development of the members.[141] It was in 200 such centers that the Peace Corps volunteers were working by October 1963.[142] These *centrales* were the basis of the *Asociación Nacional de Organizaciones Campesinas* (ANOC), which was organized with IER support in 1962. Other peasant organizations could affiliate with ANOC provided that they also would be "apolitical" and promote a "stable life" among members.[143] ANOC—subsidized also by the CIA-funded International Development Foundation—has been viewed by at least one distinguished Chilean priest and professor of rural sociology at Catholic University as an alternative for peasants who might otherwise have been organized by the pro-FRAP *Federación Nacional Campesina y Indigena.*[144]

The amelioration of lower class discontent and reinforcement of anti-Marxist institutional performance are not the only political ramifications of the Peace Corps presence in Chile. By October 1963, the volunteers were distributing about two million selected books annually on a world-wide basis.[145] Upon occasion they have shown films obtained from USIA or the embassy in Chile, and have participated in forums involving the discussion of political matters.[146] When, however, Peace Corps volunteers publicly criticize United States foreign policy goals, they are withdrawn from the country of assignment. *Within three days* of publishing criticism of the United States occupation of Vietnam during early 1967, volunteer Bruce Murray was shipped out of Chile. Although the alleged reason was his meddling in Chilean politics, the foreign ministry had not suggested Murray's conduct had been improper nor had his removal been requested.

After the FBI investigates the applicant's moral and political background, he undergoes rigid screening and training. The volunteer's instruction includes international affairs, United States government and effective disputation with Marxists.[147] Although they are not propagandists, their selection, training and roles in the field inevitably place them in a value transmitting and image projecting role. Both agency officials and congressmen are cognizant of this function.[148] Unlike foreign aid of an economic nature, both the Peace Corps and the Cultural Exchange Program are exempted from automatic termination when a foreign government nationalizes United States firms without prompt and full compensation, becomes "communist dominated" or commits other acts specified in Sec. 620 of the Amended Foreign Assistance Act of 1961.[149]

Non-Governmental Organizations

The United States foreign aid and cultural exchange programs with Chile have involved significant support for and cooperation with "approved" nongovernmental organizations.[150] Private agencies have received donations of surplus agricultural commodities and shipping reimbursement since 1955 pursuant to Title III of Public Law 480. "Under this program through fiscal year 1965, Chile received over 661 million pounds of food, with an estimated market value of over $47.6 million and freight charges totaling some $11 million." Freight reimbursement for the shipment of other equipment and relief supplies probably amounted to about $12 million.[151]

The largest category of private agencies administering programs in Chile during the early 1960s were associated with United States religious organizations. Many carried on educational and moral instruction in Chilean parochial schools. Other activities often included: distribution of surplus foods labeled "A Gift of the People of the U.S.A.," clothing, medicines or other relief supplies; the operation of social-welfare agencies or hostels; leadership training; and self-help community development projects. By greatly supplementing the material and personnel resources of associated Chilean religious organizations in their work among the urban and rural lower classes, the programs of these agencies almost certainly diminished FRAP's potential for support from these sectors in 1964.[152] It is reasonable to suppose that a desire to counter the threat of Marxist materialism and atheism motivated more than a few of these programs, although purely religious and charitable goals were always intermixed and frequently dominant. Yet, of about forty-seven such programs being implemented in 1964-1965, at least twenty-five were initiated after Castro came to power. And there is some evidence that the new emphasis placed upon aid to Latin America by the United States Catholic hierarchy was at least partly inspired by the perceived "Castro-Communist menace."[153]

One of the largest Chilean programs is supported by the Catholic Welfare Conference of the United States. Between fiscal 1957 and fiscal 1965, the United States government has provided shipping for well over 500,000,000 pounds of supplies.[154] The CWC has supported CARITAS-IER programs in the following areas: community development; construction, housing and planning; cooperatives, credit unions and loans; education; equipment, material aid and relief; food production and agriculture; medicine and public health; and social welfare.[155]

Other Catholic organizations whose programs in Chile have been directly or indirectly subsidized by—or have cooperated with—the United States government are: Association for Cultural Exchange, Inc. (Jesuit Missions); Catholics for Latin America; Daughters of the Holy Ghost; Divine Word Missionaries; Dominican Foreign Missions; Dominican Mission Sisters; Holy Cross Mission; Lorettine Sisters; Maryknoll Fathers; Maryknoll Sisters; National Council of Catholic Women; Papal Volunteers for Latin America; Precious Blood Sisters; and the Sisters, Servants of the Immaculate Heart of Mary.[156]

Similar undertakings have been sponsored by North American Protestant Churches, and two Jewish organizations—all with occasionally direct, but more often indirect United States government material support or cooperation. The largest programs are those of the Church World Service, the Seventh-Day Adventist Welfare Service and Lutheran World Relief.[157] Chilean activities on a less extensive scale were organized by: American Women's Hospitals Service; Board of Missions of the Methodist Church; Christian Children's Fund; Gospel Mission of South America; Interchurch Medical Assistance; Methodist Committee for Overseas Relief; Southern Baptist Convention; United Church Women; United Presbyterian Church in the U.S.A.; World Presbyterian Missions, and World Medical Relief.[158] Government funds have been received by the YMCA, the American Jewish Joint Distribution Committee and the United HIAS Service, Inc.[159]

United States secular organizations have carried on similar programs in Chile with varying degrees of direct or indirect United States governmental support or cooperation. Some have worked with religious groups or the Chilean government. The effect of their efforts almost certainly lessened potential socio-political discontent and in some cases contributed to organizing or promoting Marxist-resistant attitudinal predispositions among the lower classes. The largest program was administered by the Cooperative for American Relief Everywhere (CARE).[160] Efforts were also undertaken by such organizations as the: American Dietetic Association; American Foundation for Overseas Blind; American Fund for Czechoslovak Refugees; American International Association for Economic and Social Development; Association for International Development; Direct Relief Foundation; Foundation for International Child Health; Girl Scouts of the U.S.A.; Institute for Human Progress; Self-Help Inc.; and the Tolstoy Foundation.[161]

Another group of private agencies either assisted the AID program, or provided direct technical assistance. In the first category were the: Council for International Progress in Management; Dairy Society International; International Development Services; National Rural Electric Cooperative Association; and the Public Administration Service.[162] In the second category are the Population Council which has done work in the areas of birth control, and the Meals for Millions Foundation.[163] And in a category alone is the International Schools Services which has probably assisted the *Nido de Aguilas* binational school.[164]

In their programming, several agencies have either cooperated with or provided assistance to the Peace Corps in Chile. They include: CARE; TECHO; Pan American Development Foundation; Experiment in International Living; Volunteers for International Technical Assistance (VITA); and the YMCA of the U.S.A.[165]

Under the "People-to-People" Program, the cities of Minneapolis and Santiago created a "special relationship" in 1962, but it has been only "partly successful."[166] Another "People-to-People" organization, the Engineers and Scientists Committee, was also reported to be operating a program in Chile.[167]

In the related area of cultural and educational exchange, several organizations have carried on active programs—some in very close association with AID or the Bureau of Cultural and Educational Affairs. In the latter category are the: American Institute for Free Labor Development; Cleveland International Program for Youth Leaders and Social Workers; World University Service; Commission for International Development; League of Women Voters; National Council of Catholic Women and the National Farmers Union.[168]

Covert Action

Although it is always difficult to report accurately about "grey" endeavors, their political importance mandates that some attention be devoted to them.

Least dramatic perhaps, has been the role of the International Development Foundation (IDF)—heavily funded by the CIA and AID. Established in 1961, the IDF has concentrated upon "urban and rural leadership training."[169] It, in turn, has subsidized the *Unión de Campesinos Cristianos* (UCC) and ANOC—both vigorous anti-Marxist organizations.[170] Representatives of another CIA "front," the Foundation for Youth and Student Affairs, subsidized such anti-Leftist Chilean organizations as: *Oficina Relacionadora de Movimientos Estudiantiles Universitarios; Pax Romana*; and the International Union of Socialist Youth.[171] In addition, representatives of the National Students Association—a major FYSA grantee—were probably instrumental in affecting the behavior of Chilean student delegates to the Fourth Congress of Latin American Students in Natal, Brazil.[172] On at least one occasion, leaders of Chile's Christian Democratic Youth were brought to the United States by the World Assembly of Youth, also a FYSA beneficiary.[173] The role of the Congress for Cultural Freedom was mentioned earlier. Two other anti-Communist organizations which functionally paralleled the CCF, were the Chilean Committee for the Self-Determination of Peoples and the Chilean Committee for the Juridical Defense of Western Democracy. Their propagandistic activities may well have been underwritten by the CIA, although no reliable disclosure to that effect has yet been published.[174]

During the 1964 presidential election campaign, two acts of intervention appear to have been especially efficacious in reducing Allende's electoral support. The first involved: 1) financial support of major proportions to the Frei campaign, and very probably an advisory role in directing it;[175] and 2) the financing of an extensive anti-FRAP propaganda campaign stressing the "Castroism-Communism" issue.

Frei played his hand with the skill and cunning of a professional Latin gambler. He played his best card—the one that said 'The Only Alternative'—both inside and outside the country. And with equal success.

In Washington he convinced the White House and the State Department that the United States must back him; on Wall Street he convinced the businessmen. No, he kept arguing, we will not nationalize the copper mines (almost all American-owned), but we do want them turned into partnerships. No, we will not expropriate all the land, but we are going to take and redistribute what is being left fallow and we will damned well see to it that what we don't take produces food. Yes, we are going to increase taxes, but you of course realize that taxes are now ridiculously low, so no right-thinking man can mind that.

Backing he finally got. By mysterious ways, not talked about and always officially denied, Frei's campaign was bolstered by Yankee dollars and piles of Chilean pesos. A reasonable estimate is that the Christian Democrats got about $1 million a month, for many months, from American sources, and an estimated $18- to $20-million more from the Christian Democrats in West Germany, Italy and Belgium.[176]

In April 1962, following the departure of the Goodwin-Moscoso Mission, Frei and Tomic received a joint invitation to visit Washington. They arrived in the United States capitol in June, and complaints about a major increase in anti-Communist propaganda date from September 1962.[177] In November of that year, *Chile Libre* was constituted. This anti-Communist propaganda organization was directed by public relations experts.[178] By March 1964, the quantity of propaganda identifying an Allende victory with a tyrannical disaster similar to Cuba increased by "massive proportions."[179] During the months that followed, FRAP access to the mass media was curtailed.[180] Allende was compelled to mortgage his home, and the left continually complained that it was lacking adequate funds.[181] A "letter" from ex-Cuban President Manuel Uruttia to Allende was published in the press, and on the eve of the election a nearly hysterical address by Juanita Castro was broadcast.[182] Impressionistic evidence indicates that her discourse alone probably cost Allende more than a few thousand female votes.[183]

The second intervention involved the activities of Joseph Jova, the counsellor of the United States Embassy. Ambassador Charles Cole, a scholarly and retiring individual, was not particularly adept in manipulating political alignments.[184] Jova appears to have won the confidence of a sector of the Radical Party leadership. After the Curico by-election, he persuaded Julio Durán to solicit the party's renomination by arguing "that unless the PR fielded a candidate, FRAP might obtain a plurality."[185]

Several months later and after the Liberals and Conservatives had thrown their support to Frei, the Radical nominee began to suffer campaign financing problems of a serious nature. A skillful politician, Durán arranged a meeting with Allende—probably as a ploy. At the conference it was allegedly agreed that if the Radicals were given defense, interior and other ministries as well as the leadership of both houses of Congress, Durán would withdraw from the race. Within hours of this meeting, both Frei and Jova held private conferences with Durán. His "agreement" with Allende was disclaimed on the following day.[186] Whether Jova had offered to finance Durán's campaign with PL 480 counterpart or other funds is a question that has not yet and may never be answered.[187] It is quite probable, however, that had Durán withdrawn, many thousands of anti-clerical Radical followers would have refused to vote for the Christian Democratic candidate who was being actively supported by the Catholic hierarchy.[188]

Again in 1970, a very heavily financial "campaign of terror" identified Popular Unity candidate Allende with Communist tyranny and negative aspects of recent Cuban experience. Fidel's July 26, 1970 address on the seriousness of Cuba's economic problems received special emphasis. There were portents of Chile's fate should Allende be elected. So intense was the propaganda against the left that even PDC candidate Tomic supported a leftist proposal for the creation of a congressional committee to investigate the origin of this propaganda. Its effect has been established by the flight of an estimated 14,000 Chileans from their country during the two weeks following the Popular Unity victory in September. At the time, $87,000,000 was withdrawn from banking institutions and the Escudo fell to 55 to the dollar on the Santiago black market.[189]

While there is no reliable evidence of CIA involvement in either the propaganda campaign or the bombings and assassination of General Schneider which followed Allende's triumph, it is quite plausible for several reasons. In the first place, we have the tentative evidence for 1964. During the writer's sojourn in Chile (1966-1967), a PDC Youth leader declared that his party had received funds and would continue to do so from the agency. Furthermore, its operatives seem to have been well entrenched in Chilean institutions. According to Bolivia's former Interior Minister Antonio Arguedas, upon fleeing to Chile "he had been interned, questioned and held incommunicado by the CIA and the Chilean secret police."[190] Even after the exposure of a large number of front organizations in 1967, the International Development Foundation continued to function without official hindrance.

One must also take cognizance of the unrelenting hostility which Washington exhibited towards the 1970 candidacy of Allende. In August of that year, the "National Security Council received a report that if Allende won, a Communist takeover would inevitably (sic) follow."[191] Such certitude is usually reserved for the "dogmatic" followers of Marx. In any case, United States emissaries did what they could to prevent the Popular Unity victory. Ambassador Edward Korry had actually attempted to persuade leading Christian Democrats to moderate their program or withdraw the Tomic candidacy so that a single anti-Marxist nominee could oppose Allende. This act of intervention was, however, unexpectedly "denounced" by one of Tomic's leading campaigners Renan Fuentealba.[192] Even the UP electoral plurality failed to reconcile Washington to the meaning of allowing Latin Americans the right to elect their own leaders. Shortly afterwards, it was reported that "the Nixon Administration is fearful that this could have a contagious effect on other South American countries. The Administration is also sensitive to the fact that the rise of a Chilean Communist regime could become an issue in the 1972 United States Presidential campaign."[193]

Military Relations

Chile signed her first military assistance agreement with the United States in 1952. Total military aid from fiscal 1953 through fiscal 1965 was $111 million. Almost all of this assistance which increased very substantially after June 1960, was in the form of grants.[194] The three branches of the armed services have been largely equipped by the United States. Although joint United States-Chilean anti-submarine maneuvers were begun in 1959, since 1961, United States officers have defined internal security to be the major function of the Chilean military.[195]

Substantial numbers of Chilean officers have been brought to the Canal Zone, Puerto Rico and the United States for training purposes. Between fiscal year 1950 and fiscal year 1965, Chile received more per capita military aid than any other Latin American nation except Brazil. This included $66,100,000 in grant aid and $22,900,000 in generally undervalued equipment.[196] Military aid to Chile during the Frei administration totaled more than thirty million dollars.[197] It has financed the training, organization and equipping of elite Black Beret counterinsurgency army units, as well as the creation of a ruthless Carabinero *"Grupo Movil."* The GM was equipped with laxative, nauseant and laughing gases.

According to the United States Agency for International Development, the following amounts of aid were expended on equipment and training the Chilean national police force during a period when the carabineros expanded from less than 20,000 to a 30,000 man force: $206,000 (FY 1962); $449,000 (FY 1963); $283,000 (FY 1964); $459,000 (FY 1965); $435,000 (FY 1966); $290,000 (FY 1967); $75,000 (FY 1968); $68,000 (FY 1969).

Between FY 1967 and FY 1969, thirty Chilean police officials were flown to the United States for technical training, hospitality and political indoctrination at one or more of the following installations: International Police Academy (Washington); Federal Bureau of Investigation National Academy (Quantico, Virginia); United States Post Office Department Scientific Investigation Laboratory (Washington); International Police Services School (Washington); United States Coast Guard Training Center (Yorktown, Virginia); United States Coast Guard Academy (New London, Connecticut); Criminal Investigation Laboratory (Fort Gordon, Georgia); Southern Illinois University.[198] In 1966, it was reported that at least 2,600 Chilean officers and enlistees had visited or been trained at United States bases.[199] According to the United States Department of Defense, 2,219 Chileans were trained between Fiscal years 1950 and 1963. For the FY 1964-1968 period, the total was 1,448. These figures include external as well as in-country training.[200]

Table 5-3

Chilean Officers Trained in the United States, FY 1964-FY 1969

	FY 1964	FY 1965	FY 1966	FY 1967	FY 1968	FY 1969
Army						
Senior Officers	23	18	19	27	46	1
Junior Officers	13	8	5	7	6	30
Air Force						
Junior Officers	10	19	3	8	8	7
Navy						
Senior Officers	2	2	3	3	3	3
Junior Officers	23	17	17	15	26	33
Total						
Senior Officers	25	20	22	30	49	4
Junior Officers	46	44	25	30	40	70

Source: Data supplied by the Department of Defense.

An additional 412 officers were trained overseas, most probably in the Panama Canal Zone.

That counterinsurgency and other Canal Zone training has included anti-Communist indoctrination is amply illustrated by the following colloquy between Congresswoman Bolton and Gen. O'Meara:

Mrs. Bolton. I think so, too. May I ask you about the training and education of the officers? Do they receive any really thorough grounding in what communism is and how it functions?

General O'Meara. We go into the subject of communism extensively in our schools in the Canal Zone. We have discussion periods. We call in guest lecturers from the services of the countries themselves sometimes through USIS channels—to the armed forces of the countries who request them—literature of it in the form of comic books addressed to the soldiers. (Security deletion.)

Mrs. Bolton. Along the psychological and philosophical lines as well as the more visible things?

General O'Meara. We try to keep it on a pretty practical level.[201]

An examination of anti-Communist and anti-Socialist propaganda used at Fort Gulick in the Canal Zone indicates that its object is to inculcate hatred and fear. The level is that of a ruthless Soviet-run international Communist conspiracy whose primary goal is to enslave mankind.[202] It is reasonable to suppose that anti-Communist sentiments among Chilean officers have been created or more often reinforced by such training.[203]

It is also likely that similar effects were consequential for Chilean officers who trained at Fort Bragg, Fort Knox, Fort Leavenworth or other installations in the continental United States, even though specific anti-Communist indoctrination courses were not given at all of these bases. In early 1963, the United States Advisory Commission on International Educational and Cultural Affairs recommended "(t)he use of these (military) training programs for a broader purpose, concurrent with training in military fields, must be approached with care, but the opportunity is very great and should be seized upon. The recent trend toward giving the military visitors maximum exposure to the United States, to American people, and to the American system in general, is to be commended and encouraged."[204] Between 1963 and 1965, a full-fledged propaganda program was institutionalized at all major training institutions in the United States. Emphasis is upon social hospitality, speaking invitations, meetings with businessmen and politicians, entertainment, recreation, tours, etc. Lectures stress complimentary aspects of United States culture and portray American societal problems as being effectively coped with. Free enterprise is lauded and socialist principles are denigrated. A negative though moderately sophisticated treatment of communism is given secondary attention.[205]

The political aspects of this military training have not been limited to anticommunism and "exposure" to the virtues of North American civilization. A minimal effort also has been made to present the merits of the United States pattern of civil-military relations. Were Chilean officers confronted with a Marxist-led government, however, a conflict would arise between these two values. Not only was the FRAP committed to abrogate the military pacts with the United States, but when he accepted the Popular Action Front's nomination in January 1963, Allende prognosticated changes for "our armed forces who are controlled from abroad."[206] Leftist-oriented officers had been largely purged.[207]

Another important dimension of these military relationships involves the personal friendships established as a direct consequence of the training process.[208] They are maintained through numerous visits to Chile by United States military officers and missions.[209] The cordiality of these relationships has been reflected by the frequent reciprocal bestowal of decorations.[210] In a distinct but analogous context, "(i)t has been said that the most important function of the Caribbean Air Command consists of making friends for the United States with Latin America. The mission responsibilities assigned to the command by Headquarters, USAF are such as to require close personal contact between personnel of the command and representatives of the twenty republics of Latin America. The development of attitudes of mutual trust, respect, and friendship is essential to the successful accomplishment of these missions."[211]

During 1963, while there were 16 military attaches assigned to the United States Embassy in Santiago, an additional 45 officers were attached to United States military missions in Chile.[212] Eight or ten weeks before the 1964 election, "a delegation of 35 officers of various U.S. services arrived in Chile."[213] And at the time of the election, Chilean army units were reported "to be engaging in various parts of the national territory in what they call 'anti-subversive exercises.' "[214] Joint naval and air exercises were scheduled for the period when the Chilean Congress would be choosing the next president if no candidate received an absolute majority at the polls.[215]

North American support for military regimes in Latin America was first declared by Assistant Secretary of State for Inter-American Affairs Thomas Mann on the eve of Brazilian President Goulait's overthrow. It was clearly manifested when the United States Marines invaded Santo Domingo in 1965, in order to save a surrounded and all but vanquished army under General Wessin y Wessin.

Since then this posture has hardened. Testifying before a congressional committee in November 1969, the author of the Nixon Administration's famous "Rockefeller Report" clearly viewed United States ties with the military in Latin America as a means for maintaining a sphere of influence. More equipment and United States training were called for. Although the Marxist threat was most ubiquitously referred to in justification, even Bolivia's nationalistic "revolution" was cited as an unwelcome consequence which could have been avoided.[216]

In Chile, the United States military mission has traditionally maintained its headquarters on the seventh floor of the defense ministry building. The "Rockefeller Report" urged that the size and visibility of these missions be reduced—and that they should not be "called" permanent. It did not recommend their elimination. The apparent reason, according to the Commander-in-Chief of the United States Southern Command General George R. Mather, is that they are useful in communicating with the local military when the United States ambassador wants pressure exerted upon a Latin American government.[217] Testifying in July 1970 that Congress should anticipate *more* military regimes in Latin America and even tolerate some excesses, Gen. Mather went so far as to imply that the United States would *not* accept a freely elected Marxist government dedicated to the socialist transformation of Chilean society:

Mr. Fascell. What is your evaluation on all of your intelligence and other efforts with respect to the trend in Latin America on military governments as against democratic governments.

Gen. Mather. I think we probably will see more, Mr. Chairman, rather than less.

Mr. Gross. How could there be more military dictatorships?

Gen. Mather. [Security deletion.]

Mr. Fascell. What has been your experience with respect to the difference, if any, in dealing with military regimes and nonmilitary regimes, of the U.S. capability in dealing with them in your area?

Gen. Mather. I was happy to see the President's policy as he announced it last October, that we shouldn't isolate ourselves from these authoritarian governments; we should maintain contact with them. I firmly believe—I am firmly convinced in our overall security interests that we have got to keep track of these people, keep in touch with them and have their good offices. The fact that they are authoritarian regimes, not in our image shouldn't poison our official relationship.

Mr. Fascell. You mean we should not automatically disassociate ourselves?

Gen. Mather. That is right. I don't agree with many of the repressive measures that we read of in some of these regimes. On the other hand, I think it can be demonstrated that they do have a basis of support in many of the countries where they are in power; that economically they have brought these countries to a point where the previous regimes had not been able to get to.

I think the main thing is, we must keep contact with them whether they are authoritarian or not.

Mr. Fascell. Whether they are really for us or against us?

Gen. Mather. Well, we want to keep them for us.

Mr. Fascell. . . . [Security deletion.]

Gen. Mather. I think that is very logical to expect, Mr. Chairman, because really, I think the true profile of America in Latin America is the multibillion dollar investment we have here. This is what these economic materialists are after, and causing a lot of our problems. It is $12 billion. About a fifth of our total foreign investment. . . .

Gen. Mather. Exactly. I can't conceive of another Cuba.

Mr. Fascell. The $64 question there is, what happens when a completely new set of circumstances comes into play? For example, in Chile, if an election were held and the Communists actually took over power? Or on a small island in the Caribbean, if through indigenous efforts, agitators, or otherwise, there was a Communist takeover?

I don't see, and I am not asking you to comment on this, how the United States could have a direct (sic) military response to that event.

Gen. Mather. I don't either, Mr. Chairman. I just hope that doesn't happen. As you know, our record of recovery of countries that have gone down the drain is practically nil. We haven't gotten any of them back once they have gone. This is what we have got to stop.

Mr. Fascell. What you are saying here is, that we, as a government, ought to take every action we can which would prevent such an occurrence. Particularly since we are limited in our capability to react?

Gen. Mather. Yes, sir.[218]

The commander-in-chief of the Chilean Army was assassinated during late October 1970. While some of those involved in the conspiracy were reported to have flown to Miami,[219] it is still unclear whether the CIA was implicated. There is no doubt, however, as to why the abortive attempt was made to kidnap army chief Gen. Schneider. According to *Time* magazine, Schneider "was a friend" of Allende. Cuba's *Granma* reported him to be "very unpopular" in pro-United States and rightist circles because of his "firm position" against intervention.[220] Although "Washington intelligence sources believe that (President Allende) can gain effective control of the army within six months through appointment of sympathetic officers and forced retirement of political opponents,"[221] one wonders where officers "sympathetic" to a "Communist" government will be found. As Chilean-American relations deteriorate, military conspiracies will multiply.

Concluding Remarks

The United States "effort" towards Chile may be contrasted with that mounted by Revolutionary Cuba in at least four significant respects:

1) it functioned in such fields as economic aid, military assistance, cultural exchange and propaganda for from six to sixteen years prior to Batista's downfall
2) it operated within an environment of governmental amity and maximum access to the press, radio, television and the universities
3) it effectively prevented a major socio-economic crisis (massive unemployment or inflation)
4) a major undertaking as of 1959, the scale of all programs—economic, military, propaganda—was massively increased after the Cuban Revolution.

In supporting the Catholic Church through PL 480 donations and aid to the Institute for Rural Education, the United States strengthened the influence of one of Frei's major institutional supporters in 1964.[222] More important, the large scale funding of Frei's campaign was crucial to his ability to effectively project himself before the Chilean electorate during the 1962-1964 period. It is also probable that the supporting massive anti-Communist (Cuban-FRAP) "campaign of terror" propaganda was heavily funded and directed by United States government and corporate agencies, as was the repeat performance in 1970.

Therefore propaganda inputs are being dealt with that directly reached a mass audience of hundreds of thousands or more. The "packaged programs" for radio broadcast, films for theatre and mobile screenings, and widespread press and magazine insertions stressed such thematic materials as the AFP as a positive alternative to Castro who had betrayed his countrymen by imposing a blood-thirsty and chaotic Communist tyranny that had led Cuba to economic disaster and mass suffering. And it was this that the "campaign of terror" portrayed Allende and the Marxist led coalitions—largely by virtue of their earlier unreserved defense of Castro's policies—as intent upon effectuating in Chile. The depiction of Cuba as a Soviet satellite—especially during and following the missile crisis—was reinforced by the widely held hostile attitudes towards the Soviet Union and negative dispositions towards Cold War involvement.

The scholarships, leader grants, films, conferences, library facilities, book distribution, informational media guarantee programs and "special" presentation items almost certainly increased pro-United States "understanding" among intellectuals, opinion-makers and university students where the PDC maintained its control of most student federations until late in the decade. Greater anti-Communism among union members than non-union lower class persons may indicate that the AIFLD, labor information officers, and their predecessors have had some effect. And their efforts may also have facilitated some PDC victories in formerly FRAP controlled unions during the early 1960s. Leftist gains in winning leadership of many new unions during the Frei administration almost certainly occasioned the 1968 step-up of AIFLD expenditures. Had Frei not taken a "mano dura" hard line towards urban organized labor, this would not have been necessary.

The Cuban Revolution was largely responsible for the new emphasis upon reforms in United States foreign aid policies towards Chile. While the Chilean "reforms" were minimal, they did contribute to the emergence of such issues as important ones in Chilean politics during the period in question. On the other hand, continuation of massive budgetary and other aid despite the failure of Alessandri's government to undertake major self-help measures reflected the United States desire to maximize Frei's chances in 1964. And fear of its termination may well have lost many middle class protest votes for Allende. Similar tactics were operative in 1970 when the United States was banking on an Alessandri victory. Frei had done little more than his predecessor to reform the basic socio-economic structures of the country.

It is difficult to ascertain the overall "impact" of these programs. Internal opinion and behavior also were conditioned by the schools, tradition, and the conduct of internal political leaderships. Yet these inputs probably ensured Frei's margin over Allende in 1964.[223] They may also have prevented Allende from expanding his constituency between 1964 and 1970.

The urgency attached to preventing a Marxist victory was largely consequential to its identification with the Cuban Revolution and the threat which this signified for United States strategic, economic, and diplomatic interests. Had the FRAP been victorious, the prospective pattern of United States-Chilean relations would have measurably increased the likelihood of an anti-Communist *golpe*. Hence, from a political perspective, United States policies functioned to maintain the parliamentary democratic and capitalist system within Chile. Had they failed or not been maximized during the period in question, a new Communist or more likely militarist system probably would have emerged after some months of instability. This may well be the prospect for the early seventies. In any case, the Popular Unity victory was not a result of any policy "failure" by the United States. As will be seen in subsequent chapters, miscalculations as well as certain internal elite values and decisions that were effectively beyond North American control contributed materially to this unexpected electoral triumph.

Part III:
Internal Actors

Discomfort and Antagonism: The Response of the Chilean Right

Introduction

In this chapter, attention will be focused upon the three most important sectors of the Chilean right: Conservatives; Liberals, and the Alessandri administration.[1] Their role in the Chilean political system and tradition will first be summarized. Then, leadership perceptions and responses to the Cuban Revolution will be delineated. And finally, *these responses* will be related to modifications in party or administration programs, positions and tactics.

United Conservative Party (PCU)

Social Base and Party Principles. The PCU leadership has been recruited in recent decades from landowning, industrial and financial property owning sectors. Until 1958, PCU electoral support was centered in rural areas where the votes of agricultural laborers and sharecroppers were frequently bought. The influence of rural priests and traditional paternalistic attitudes among the peasants were also quite important in assuring a stable constituency. After 1958, the urban middle class and especially female support which the party had also held assumed greater importance. The leadership, however, tended to be upper class in composition. Hence, a recent survey of its parliamentary representatives revealed 78 percent to have university degrees *and* an educational background in private schools. No less than two-thirds listed their vocation as "agriculture," while another 22 percent identified "politics" as their chosen occupation. The remainder reported "other professions." None cited business, law, medicine, education or "worker."[2]

In chapter 3 the confessional origins of the Conservatives were discussed. The party has continued to strongly identify itself as Catholic in recent years.[3] According to its Social Christian philosophy, the following goals inspire the PCU's political action: 1) use of the state to strengthen "natural societies" such as the family, the profession, and local governmental units; 2) promotion of a "corporative" social structure where a person's "value" would be in accord with the "social function" he performed; 3) opposition to "socialism" because of its "materialist character and because of its negation of the true nature of the human being and the ends of society"; 4) furtherance of class collaboration and "spiritual uplifting of the masses" through such devices as profit-sharing, the

99

strengthening of professional organizations and innovations in the field of social policy; and 5) elimination of abuses in the capitalist system which do not serve the common good.[4]

In practice, the PCU has promoted the use of the state as a means for strengthening the Church and its teachings.[5] The party has been fervent in its anti-Communism, and was a driving force in depriving the Communist Party of legal status in 1948. A year later, Eduardo Frei summarized its legislative role:

Studying the voting records in Congress on important bills and examination of its expression in their great organs *El Diario Ilustrado* and *El Mercurio*, enables us to synthesize the attitude of the Right; determined protection for property rights and their exercise; limitation of State intervention to a minimum, reserving a wide sphere to free private initiative; defense of business profits and, contradicting the previous principle, broad protection to the producer by the State; indiscriminate condemnation of all strikes, because they disrupt the social order and interfere with productive activities; opposition to labor organizations and utilization of all opportunities to limit their activities and rights; social benefits for and defense of the patron or employer; attacks upon all tendencies toward socialism, and especially, communism.[6]

Although this description retained its accuracy during the 1950s,[7] objectivity requires that the party's historic support for social legislation also be noted.[8]

1958 Presidential Election

The erosion of the Conservatives' rural following began in 1952 when a sizeable number of peasants defied their patrons' sentiments by casting ballots for the colorful ex-dictator, Gen. Carlos Ibáñez Campos. Nevertheless, the Conservative-Liberal presidential candidate managed to receive 27.8 percent of the vote.

During the mid-1950s, the Conservatives polled about 17 percent of the vote in municipal and congressional elections where local public works and personalities tend to be dominant concerns. While at first opposing the somewhat leftist and nationalistic sounding Ibáñez, they subsequently participated in his government after the withdrawal of the Popular Socialists. By 1957, the image of the Ibáñez administration had been tarnished by scandals and corruption as had the previous Radical government under González Videla.

After declining a bid to support Frei,[9] the reunited Conservatives declared their backing for Jorge Alessandri Rodríguez, a wealthy "independent" industrialist who was president of the Confederation of Production and Commerce.[10] An austere bachelor, Alessandri promised to eliminate waste and dishonesty in government, and reduce welfare spending. He also pledged to: 1) stimulate agricultural production by authorizing higher prices; 2) control inflation; 3) increase social security benefits, especially for blue collar workers who were accorded markedly inferior status under existing legislation; 4) encourage foreign investments and maintain close relations with the United States; 5) attempt to increase the production of both copper and nitrates; and 6) encourage housing construction.[11]

With both the Conservatives and Liberals supporting him, Alessandri managed to secure a narrow plurality of less than 34,000 votes over Allende's 356,493. Supported by FRAP militants who had "invaded" the rural areas to promise the peasants an agrarian reform, Allende had repeated Ibáñez's 1952 success in provoking a major desertion from the rightist constituency.

Perceptions of the Cuban Revolution. Even before Batista's flight from Havana, the leading Conservative-owned daily *El Dairio Ilustrado* declined to express sympathy for the various groups which were struggling to overthrow the dictator. And this during the period when Batista's repression was most sanguinary.[12]

By August 1959, PCU criticism of the new Revolutionary Government first appeared in public. Raúl Roa was condemned for seeking to raise economic development issues at the recent OAS Conference in Santiago. The United States and Chilean governments both had argued that such questions were being properly considered by other bodies. PCU leaders claimed Castro was assisting the Communists in their efforts to disrupt hemispheric unity.[13] Conservative leaders resented Armando Hart's suggestion that "true power is in the people's control over the armed forces rather than in elections" during a FRAP rally protesting the OAS rejection of Cuba's agenda proposals, [14] and they categorically denied Cuban pretensions to speak for the Latin American peoples:

And with this revolution, because nobody now can figure out what it stands for, complexes have made their appearance. Complexes of inferiority and of superiority, racial and social, of class and family name and the most modern of all: the 'Cubanistic complex.' Granting all the respect due Cuba, I consider it an affront to our personality to attempt to make of Chile a second Cuba, as it would be to make Cuba a second Chile. We are different, each people having its own personality, and a personality loved by God.[15]

Well before the end of November 1959, *El Diario Ilustrado* was openly voicing sympathy for the United States in its growing conflict with the Cuban government. Lamenting Major Castro's acceptance of Communist support, the daily condemned his movement in the direction of an overt dictatorship that "openly violated human rights." Particular attention was focused upon the Matos case.[16]

A Cuban exile propagandist with CIA links informed the writer that the Conservatives and Liberals were the only parties that assisted his group in the dissemination of anti-Castro publicity.[17] As early as August 1960, Senator Antonio Coloma, a recent recipient of a State Department leader grant, was unsuccessfully attempting to insert a declaration by the Cuban Revolutionary Democratic

Front (FRD) into the Senate *Diario*. This document stressed the "betrayal" theory.[18] During the same month, PCU Vice-President Luís Valdes Larraín toured the earthquake-struck southern provinces and returned to denounce the dissemination of Cuban and Communist propaganda with Cuban relief supplies.[19] By the end of the year, Valdes was charging in the Chamber of Deputies that Cuban diplomatic officials were in reality political agents sent to intervene in the internal politics of other Latin American countries![20]

The PCU reacted to the Bay of Pigs landing by releasing a declaration supporting the invasion and calling upon Alessandri to immediately sever relations with Havana.[21] In the Senate, PCU President-to-be Francisco Bulnes vehemently argued that Castro's "tyranny" had denied the Cuban people self-determination which was equated with parliamentary democracy.[22] Although they participated in the government after August 1961, PCU leaders continued to criticize Alessandri's Radical foreign minister for his "neutralism" on the Cuban question.[23] The party insistently demanded severance of relations before, during and after the missile crisis.[24]

The 1961 Congressional Election and its Aftermath. During this November 1960-March 1961 electoral campaign, FRAP candidates conspicuously identified the spirit of their newly radicalized program (nationalization of foreign and major domestic firms, withdrawal from the military pacts and other agreements with the United States, severance of ties with the OAS, etc.) with the anti-imperialist and anti-oligarchic orientation of the Cuban Revolution. Socialist and Communist rural gains (and losses by their own party) were a source of great concern to the PCU leadership.[25] About twelve weeks after the March election, Conservative President

Hector Correa told (Alessandri) that the PCU was 'in a state of extreme alarm' following the return of men and women of the Council (of the party) from a trip through all of the national territory. There is a generalized discontent and bitterness. 'We are sitting on a volcano, President,' added the ex-deputy from Chiloe.

The anguish is particularly acute in the countryside among the landowners who witnessed the FRAP electoral advances. They believe that today the agricultural zones are the principal Marxist battlegrounds. . . .[26]

And while addressing the party leadership several days later, Correa warned:

Never has the communist danger been greater. A stepping-stone already exists within the continent (Cuba); social problems have become aggravated due to delays in resolving them; some righteous spirits are disoriented; the democratic parties are deeply divided . . . all of this is promoting the triumph of the enemy. We must prevent this at all costs even though we know that there are some who have a neutralist posture when a ferocious belligerency is called for.[27]

Some weeks after this admonition, the Conservative Youth released a public letter to Alessandri which claimed that the Cuban Embassy was responsible for increasing Marxist penetration in the country. The letter called for a prompt severance of relations with Cuba, and petitioned Alessandri to back a "Democracy in Action" program encompassing: "(t)ax reform, agrarian reform, reform of the laws governing corporations, greater emphasis upon the housing program, a new approach to extractive industries, including the refining of copper within the country, etc."[28]

The party's shift towards mild reformism was also reflected at its 27th General Convention, where "(f)or the first time in its long history, the Conservative Party timidly espoused the division and sale of state lands to individuals in order to create what the party calls 'economic unities' and to promote development of a new rural class of owners of medium-sized farms."[29] By 1964, the PCU was also advocating the promotion of cooperatives, the right of labor unions to bargain and strike for "economic" gains and the obligation of the government to reduce social misery.[30]

Unity of Democratic Forces. A second tactical reaction to the March 1961 congressional election was the PCU decision in August to enter the Alessandri government along with the Liberals and Radicals. Although PCU leaders were sharply critical of the AFP because of their belief that the United States would not supply enough funds to implement the reforms being advocated—hence, more discontent among the masses would result[31]—the party was compelled to formally acquiesce in the new program because of its participation in the government.

Following congressional enactment of a mild AFP agrarian reform bill in July 1962, the three government parties organized a *Frente Democrático* (FD) in an effort to unite anti-FRAP forces around a common candidate for the presidency in 1964.[32] A right-wing Radical, Julio Durán, was the early choice of the coalition, although many younger Conservatives hoped that he would be replaced later by Frei, a fellow Catholic unmarred by the taint of anti-clerical traditions. After further Conservative losses in the April 1963 municipal elections—regarded as indicating a trend for 1964[33]—a factional movement for a new "independent" center-right candidate appeared within the party. At a leadership meeting, PCU President Bulnes defended the existing coalition by warning that unless a PR candidate were supported by the FD parties, many Radical followers would vote for Allende and a Cuban-style tyranny before they would back a non-Radical "independent" (Catholic) candidate. In effect, only a PR leader would hold enough Radical electoral support to prevent Allende from winning a plurality or worse—a majority.[34] The FRAP candidate's impressive showing in 1958 had been wholly unexpected; thus caution was mandatory for 1964.

The Radicals had been the only FD party to maintain their percentage of the vote in the 1963 election. As if to prove Bulnes' point, many Liberals and especially Radicals refused to support an FD candidate *drawn from PCU ranks* in an early 1964 parliamentary by-election at Curico.[35] The unexpected yet narrow FRAP victory, which was obviously due to the personal popularity of its candidate and the ability of FRAP to concentrate resources in the district, was followed by Durán's withdrawal from the FD. With the dissolution of this fragile anti-Marxist coalition, the PCU opted to support Frei as the lesser evil in order to preserve "democracy" in Chile. Although party leaders claimed that this backing and not his reform program was the basis of Frei's margin over Allende, they were unpleasantly surprised in the March 1965 congressional election when their share of the total vote declined to less than six percent. Reform, rather than the Cuban Revolution, had been the major issue of the campaign.

Conclusions. Conservative identification with Chile's tradition of evolutionary constitutionalism as well as the party's Catholicism, commitment to private property and almost fanatical anti-Communism substantially accounted for its early negative evaluations of the Cuban Revolution. Castro's unconservative style and his support for Latin American anti-imperialist and anti-oligarchic revolutionary struggles repelled Conservative leaders as did Cuban support for the FRAP. While Conservatives did not admire equalitarian and materialistic elements in North American culture, they have regarded alliance with the United States as necessary for the preservation of their own institutional order.[36]

By 1961, the Cuban Revolution *clearly symbolized* the destruction of values esteemed by the PCU. The electoral gains of the FRAP which had radicalized its program and openly proclaimed an identity of goals with the Cuban Revolution *increased the sense of urgency* among Conservative leaders that a mildly reformist and anti-Marxist coalitional tactic be adopted. Thus the Cuban Revolution indirectly contributed to the growth in importance of reformism in Chilean politics, as did the AFP.

The Liberals

Social Base and Party Principles. In recent decades, social and especially programmatic distinctions between the two major rightist parties have become minimal. An astute comparison rendered not too long ago by Eduardo Frei was still meaningful during the 1950s:

Both parties have the same social composition: virtually the entire leadership and parliamentary representation belong to the old Chilean aristocracy; they are the owners of the greater part of the agricultural properties where they have a strong electoral base in addition to totally dominating the directing boards of industrial corporations and banks. In a word, they represent in the economy, capital; and in the social system, the old leading class; in politics, necessarily the defense of the liberal-capitalist economic order. While it is true that some sectors of the middle class or artisanry are in their rank and file, and even occasionally become leaders, it is they who are incorporated rather than dominant.

The fact of "incorporation" was evidenced by the educational and occupational diversity that characterized its parliamentary contingent. By the mid-sixties, 58 percent were university graduates while 12½ percent claimed non-university higher education. As for private educational backgrounds, only 25 percent carried this mark of social distinction. Occupationally, 38 percent cited "agriculture," and 46 percent "politics." Four percent referred each to law and business. Limited heterogeneity within the party was also reflected by the establishment of a union department, although its male constituency was essentially white rather than blue collar in nature. There being more cliques and family groupings among the leadership, it was somewhat less cohesive than the PCU.[37]

The origins of the PL were discussed in chapter 3. Although neither a confessional nor self-consciously Catholic, in exchange for an increasing Catholic vote, the party has in recent years supported the clerical positions of the PCU on Church-state questions.[38] While there is no doubt as to the party's anti-communism, there is less traditional Catholic "Holy War" fervor than is the case with the Conservatives. Thus, Liberal leaders have differed from their Conservative colleagues by sanctioning trade relations with the East.[39] El Mercurio, traditionally associated with an influential sector of the party's leadership, constitutes an exception in this regard.[40] Its fierce hostility to Marxism and opposition to all relations with Communist nations have paralleled an almost consistent defense of United States policies, interests and civilization. With minimal irony, then, Salvador Allende defined this "dean" of Chile's press as "a Yankee newspaper written in Spanish" during the 1970 presidential campaign. Owned by financial magnate Agustin Edwards Eastman, this prestigious daily symbolizes the integration of prosperous Anglo-Chileans into the traditional creole upper classes. Nor is it without metaphorical significance that Edwards fled the country after the Popular Unity victory—to become a vice-president of Coca-Cola![41]

As for policies on social and economic questions, it would be fair to say that "differences between them and the Conservatives are so tenuous they can be reduced to matters of degree and sometimes almost of inflection or tone."[42] Although the traditional Liberal commitment to laissez faire principles has been modified somewhat in recent years,

(f)ree enterprise and private initiative are held . . . to be the basis of all human progress and social well-being. Its (1962) program specifically disavows the displacement of private enterprise by the state and, in fact, declares that it is a primary function of government to protect and promote private activities aimed at developing national production. A section of the Liberal program deals particularly with social problems. Though it is worded somewhat vaguely, it seems to center around a fervent mystique of national dedication to service, and it reiterates the conception that the only role of the state is to serve as arbiter between capital and labor. To combat strikes it advocates severe measures, to be taken without any limitation by the laws.[43]

Other policy statements in the early 1960s include: respect for private education; endorsement of parliamentary democracy; the use of the state to inhibit monopolies; and a class system regarded as founded upon differences in natural capacities and the division of labor.[44]

The 1958 Presidential Election. In the 1957 congressional election, the PL had scored substantial gains. The party won about 16 percent of the total vote, and thus ranked third after the Radicals and Conservatives.[45] Declining a written request from Frei for campaign support, the Liberals gave their backing to the "independent" Alessandri who was closely associated with many of the party's leaders.

Despite their candidate's narrow plurality in the September 1958 presidential polling, the Liberals were disconcerted by leftist Allende's rural gains. In November 1959, PL President Gregorio Amunategui began to publicly speak of the need for an agricultural reform or at least a new policy. He noted that a majority of the party's congressmen represented rural constituencies.[46] By January 1960, the three "government parties"—then informally collaborating in Congress—were devoting increasing attention to the problem of raising agricultural productivity. Landowner associations were also expressing support for a new policy, as was *El Mercurio.*[47]

Perceptions and Evaluations of the Cuban Revolution. Although Liberal responses to the Revolutionary Government paralleled those of the PCU, some differences deserve mention. While both parties concerned themselves with Cuba only infrequently, the Liberals devoted even less attention than the Conservatives. Eduardo Moore delivered one of their first public statements in the senate during June 1960. Reflecting his internalization of norms associated with Chile's constitutionalist tradition, Moore contrasted the juridical regularity of Venezuelan democracy with Castro's mass plebiscitary approach:

Venezuelan democracy is not a 'popular democracy.' It is not based upon daily or weekly consultations of the people in mass assemblies before the balconies of the Governmental Palace. . . . It is a democracy that functions within the bounds of legitimacy and the standards of democracy. That is what we Chileans admire and applaud. It differs very little from our own. Despite the differences of climate, race and historical circumstances, it is our impression that a Chilean politician will always feel comfortable in Venezuela. This has been the uniform impression of our friends and Honorable colleagues who have visited that republic and have observed this species of civic miracle that has been produced in America.[48]

By the end of the same year, the PL was sponsoring a speech by Dr. Jesus Valdez Crespo, the permanent delegate in Chile of the CIA-subsidized FRD.[49] And when the exile invasion was launched in April 1961, the PL not only declared its support, but accepted a Conservative invitation to join in requesting that Alessandri sever relations with the Castro government.[50] It was the Conservatives, however, who exercised the initiative in this matter.

During the Senate debate following the abortive episode, Liberal Gustavo Rivera denounced Cuba for attempting to export her revolution and condemned the destruction of civil liberties and legality on the island. After citing many human rights and anti-aggression provisions from the OAS and UN Charters, Rivera called for the imposition of collective non-military sanctions through the inter-American system.[51] This view was reiterated on June 1st at a Congress for Liberty and Democracy (probably United States-subsidized) which was held in Montevideo.[52] El Mercurio had gone further by suggesting that it would support another United States invasion of Cuba.[53] The pattern of the daily's responses accords more with the PCU than with the Liberals: no sympathy for the 26th of July Movement during the insurrectionary period; criticism of Castro's "illegalities" during his first month in power; frequent emphasis upon the Communist and Soviet objectives and support for Castro during 1959-1960; fierceness in tone; and early and unreserved identification with the United States in its conflict with the Havana government.[54]

In August 1961, Hugo Zapeda, President of the Senate and a recent State Department grantee to the U.S., arose before the upper house and delivered a very carefully researched systematic analysis of what he regarded as the negative features of the Cuban Revolution.[55] It is quite probable that this was prepared by some United States government agency, perhaps in collaboration with the FRD; such was the meticulousness of the research. The content of the address focused not only upon the growing role of Communists in Cuba and the regime's dictatorial nature, but stressed declining living standards and Cuba's new satellite role vis-à-vis the USSR. In concluding, Zepeda observed that his speech had been made to counter false Castroite propaganda and because of his love for freedom, since the Chileans were "a people who inherited a 300-year-old struggle for liberty." When asked to inform the Senate of the source for his data, Zepeda declined and replied that they were "responsible persons who merit by faith."[56] Similar views on Cuba were expressed several times during the 1962-1964 period by Senator Pedro Ibáñez.[57]

In the Chamber of Deputies, the Liberals joined the Conservatives and Radicals during the missile crisis in successfully blocking a PDC-supported FRAP resolution which requested an immediate lifting of the United States blockade. Although El Mercurio again called for an invasion, the party leadership only went so far as to accede to PCU proposals that it join in asking Alessandri to sever relations. In March 1963, after the second secretary of the Cuban Embassy was expelled from Chile for impersonating a national, the PL executive board again petitioned Alessandri to end diplomatic relations with the Cuban government.[58]

When Alessandri did sever relations in August 1964, only one Liberal leader was reported to have been opposed to this action. The existence of limited disunity was also indicated by an October 1961 interview of Hernán Videla, then president of the Senate. He declined to adopt the PCU-*El Mercurio*-Rivera position that Castro had waived his right to invoke self-determination against collective sanctions because of his destruction of civil liberties.

Chile must further clarify her international policy. Cuba is a reality in the American continent that can't be brushed aside or ignored. She has the right to give herself the regime that she may want. It is a problem that is related to the internal politics of the island and that involves only the Cubans. But just as we don't seek to export our democracy to Cuba, we demand that she abstain from trying to impose her regime upon our countries. If she did that, we would be compelled to fight her with all of our resources.[59]

Reaction to the 1961 Congressional Election. Despite a small increase in their percentage of the total vote, the Liberals lost a number of seats as the vocally pro-Castro Marxist parties scored new gains in rural zones and elsewhere. By November 1961, the party's national executive committee voted to support a constitutional amendment that would sanction the deferral of cash payment for expropriated lands. The majority had argued:

The land in Chile is held by a few, and here resides the fundamental cause of the enthusiasm for the revolution in Cuba. Was it possible to alter this state of affairs during the last 100 years? Never. But it was necessary to do it today, because tomorrow it would be too late. The State must expropriate the largest holdings and those with idle land; and pay with bonds, not cash, because the State lacks funds.[60]

During Senate debate on the government's agrarian reform bill in July 1962, Julio von Muhlenbrock and Sergio Sepulveda stressed the utility of such a reform in ameliorating peasant discontent and support for Leftist collectivistic "demagogic" proposals. Two other Liberals emphasized that the legislation was directed primarily towards stimulating a rise in productivity.[61]

The party had entered the government with the PR and the PCU in August 1961. Consequently, it was bound by Alessandri's acceptance of the AFP. Unlike the Conservatives, however, PL leaders avoided public criticism of the new Yankee program.[62]

Frente Democratico (FD) and the Defeat of FRAP. The FD was negotiated during the 1961-1962 period when Allende was commonly regarded as the "spokesman of the Cuban Revolution." PL participation in this coalition with the PR and the PCU was motivated by a desire to frustrate a Marxist victory in 1964.[63] Following Durán's withdrawal as the FD candidate after Curico, the PL endorsed Frei as the democratic lesser evil.[64] Although there were a few defections to the

Allende campaign during succeeding months, it is probable that personal animosities were more important than policy differences. After the party declined Frei's letter asking for support in 1958, the PDC candidate requested Jorge Ahumada to edit a program calling for "structural" reforms.[65] From then until 1964, Frei continually attacked the Liberals, Conservatives and Alessandri for being "oligarchic."

By asking their following to support "democracy" (Frei) in 1964, the PL leaders discredited their previous allegations that the PDC was not sufficiently attuned to the danger of communism and that its reform program was demagogic, unnecessary, and in some respects like that of the Marxists. In 1965, Frei argued that if "the only alternative" to communism was to succeed, he now needed a Congress to put through the projected reforms. Apparently many Liberal followers joined a substantial part of the PCU constituency in heeding this appeal.[66] Subsequently, both badly weakened rightist parties merged as the National Party.

Conclusions. The non-confessional nature of the PL accounts for the absence of evangelical anti-Communist compulsiveness. Thus, as Fidel Castro moved toward collaboration and then alliance with Cuban and Soviet Communists, the negative reactions of some Liberal leaders and the party were more restrained than those of their Conservative colleagues. This was also evident in the lack of unity after the Bay of Pigs on the question of whether Castro's alleged violation of human rights or efforts to subvert other governments justified intervention by the OAS.

There was, of course, no equal to *El Mercurio* 's virulent hostility. But on the questions of Chilean-Cuban relations, the Liberals were more reserved than the Conservatives. Although they did join in petitioning for an end of relations on several occasions, it was always at Conservative initiative. This may have been partially due to the sentiment shared by many PL leaders that foreign affairs should be left to the president of the republic—a man who was particularly close to the party leadership.

As with the Conservatives, it is probable that FRAP's gains and identification with an increasingly egalitarian and socialist Cuban Revolution contributed to a sense of urgency that reforms be instituted that would reduce the number of lower class protest votes. The fate of the exiled former anti-Communists and propertied elements in Cuban society as conveyed by the FRD, USIA and North American diplomats, aptly symbolized the probable future of the Liberals under a Socialist-Communist "anti-oligarchic" government.

The Alessandri Administration

The 1958 Campaign. Near the beginning of this chapter, Jorge Alessandri's "program" was summarized. It was characterized by minimal emphasis upon the need for socio-economic reforms. As an "independent," his appeal was to the many voters who had become disillusioned with political demagogy and corruption. He pledged rectitude and an effort to streamline the social security and other over-bureaucratized agencies of public administration.

Despite his personalist and traditional appeal—especially among women—Alessandri would not have secured his narrow plurality over Allende without Liberal and Conservative support. Nevertheless, he appointed a "technical" non-party cabinet. Under the Chilean Constitution, a president is prohibited from holding two consecutive terms of office—and Alessandri was already over sixty at the beginning of his six year term. This reinforced his independence in some measure.

The Shift to Reform. By the end of 1960, a working alliance in support of the government had emerged in the Congress. Of the three constituent parties, only the Radicals managed to hold their own in the March 1961 congressional election. The government's need for foreign funds conditioned its positive response to the shift in United States policies toward socio-economic development as manifested by the Newport Declaration, the Act of Bogota and the subsequent AFP. To ensure adequate legislative backing, Alessandri appointed a political cabinet during August 1961. In chapter 5 reference was made to both the limited scope of the reforms instituted and the government's rationale for endorsing the AFP. To recall the latter, mention may be made of a visit to the White House by the Chilean foreign minister in October 1961. Martínez Sótomayor was reported to have urged that AFP aid be expedited in order to diminish "the danger of installing 'a Cuban style' regime through the democratic process" in 1964. President Kennedy "said 'okey' [sic] and guaranteed that the White House would make a pilot country of Chile in conformity with the program of Punta del Este. The World Bank, the Inter-American Bank and a new organization for public loans will receive orders to support Chile's plans. . . ."[67]

If the reforms proved to be quite mild, the very commitment to them by a rightist government may still be regarded as significant. Furthermore, when he visited Washington in December 1962—after devaluing the Escudo in October, and receiving a United States commitment of $200,000,000 for 1963 budgetary support—Alessandri was disposed to boast that under his administration there had been a 300 percent increase in construction of low cost housing, a 100 percent rise in health spending, and a 55 percent increase in allocations for education.[68] Thus, it is fair to conclude that his government proved less conservative than might reasonably have been expected after the 1958 election. The Cuban Revolution indirectly contributed to this through the AFP and the fear prevalent among the government parties after the 1961 congressional election.

Relations with the Revolutionary Government of Cuba. Evidencing little cordiality, diplomatic relations with Havana were marked by incidents upon more than a few occasions. The Chilean ambassador in 1959, Edwards Bello, was a long time resident of Cuba married to a woman whose family had been closely associated with the Batista regime. Many Batistianos sought refuge in the Chilean Embassy, and problems arose during early 1959 and subsequently in arranging their exit.[69]

Relations became particularly strained in November 1961, when the Cuban Foreign Ministry attempted to compel those who had sought asylum to be lodged in mission offices and ambassodorial residences. It had been announced that when safe conducts were authorized, air fares would have to be paid in dollars.[70] At the same time, the Cuban government manifested its dissatisfaction with Alessandri for refusing to accept Díaz del Real's replacement by creating a difficult personal problem for the Chilean ambassador. He also appears to have been an unwanted emissary!

Emilio Edwards, instead of solving the difficulties between Chile and Cuba, is the greatest problem that Chile has with Cuba. Married to an upper class Cuban woman who was associated with the Batista regime, her house was invaded by Fidelistas who decided that she could occupy only half of it. In the other half were placed three families of the new era. The Chilean Ambassador was unable to protest, because, in truth, he resides in his wife's house and works *ad honores*.[71]

A week later it was announced that Edwards was being withdrawn and would be replaced on an interim basis by a Chargé d'affaires, until Cuba nominated a "professional" ambassador to Chile.[72] Some of Díaz del Real's activities in Chile were related in chapter 4. The Cubans never did appoint a "professional."

As early as August 1959, the Chilean government had indicated its disdain for the style of the Cuban Revolutionary leadership. When a plane filled with *barbudos* arrived near the end of the OAS Foreign Ministers Reunion in Santiago, all of the occupants were interned and then expelled for not having previously obtained visas from Edwards Bello's embassy.[73]

At about the same time, the Chilean government received information of the impending arrival of Raúl Castro. Although not expelled, Castro was completely ignored by foreign ministry officials—Allende being the only important personage to greet him at the airport.[74] Not long after his arrival, the under secretary of the interior ministry was asked at a press conference whether the government had attempted to establish contact with Raúl. Jaime Silva replied: "Look, Comandante Castro did not make his trip official. . . . Our authorities didn't attempt to contact him because it isn't prudent to annoy someone who travels incognito. . . ."[75]

Questions Pertaining to Cuba in the United Nations. If direct Chilean-Cuban relations were less than cordial, their positions in the world organization harmonized upon no more than one occasion. Almost without exception, Chilean delegates to the General Assembly (GA) or the Security Council (SC) voted and argued for the United States position when Cuban complaints were being considered.[76] The consistent Chilean approach was that in order to strengthen the regional organization and system (OAS), the Cuban charges of United States aggression should be considered and resolved by that body. Upon both occasions when Chilean conduct was not identical with that of the United States, the outcomes were not different from what they would have been had there been an identity of position. Whether this fact influenced the Chileans is not known. To illustrate the general Chilean approach and to portray it *when most distinctive* from the United States, the following two events are summarized. (Both were connected with the Bay of Pigs invasion.)

On July 11, 1960, the Cubans requested the SC to consider a complaint that the United States had committed various aggressive acts and was preparing a future invasion of the island. Following debate on the eighteenth and nineteenth of the month, an Argentine-Ecuadorian resolution was adopted. It took note of the complaint, and after observing that Article 33 required the exhaustion of other means for settling disputes, postponed consideration until after the forthcoming OAS Foreign Ministers Conference at San José. Interestingly, the San José Reunión had been called to consider threats to hemispheric peace posed by the Dominican Republic and Cuba, and not to deal with the latter's complaint against the United States. Cuba had claimed that it was useless to appeal to the OAS since it was dominated by her protagonist.[77]

On Nov. 26, 1960, the Cubans directed a letter to the Secretary General of the U.N. charging that the complaint which had been the basis of the July 19th SC resolution had not been considered at San José. A second Cuban letter on Dec. 31st requested an immediate SC meeting to consider United States plans for aggression and cited the existence of CIA training camps in Central America. The charges were considered on the third and fourth of January, with Raúl Roa delivering a lengthy accusation followed by a self-righteous United States denial.

On the second day, Chile and Ecuador introduced a joint resolution urging the United States and Cuba to peacefully resolve their dispute and requesting other states to abstain from acts that might aggravate existing tensions. In defending the joint resolution, Chilean Ambassador Schweitzer argued that Cuban fears had not been substantiated and that the United States had demonstrated that it had no "aggressive intentions." He went on to express faith in the Inter-American System as the proper place to resolve such differences, and referred specifically to the ad hoc mediation committee which had been appointed at San José. Chile and Ecuador decided against moving for a vote on the joint resolution, since France, Britain and China (United States allies) were adamantly opposed to any proposal implying recognition of the charges while the Russians regarded the threat as already clearly demonstrated.[78]

A similar complaint was considered by the GA's First Committee, between

April 15 and April 21, 1961, while the invasion was in process. Draft resolutions were introduced by Rumania, the USSR, Mexico, and seven Latin American nations, including Chile. The seven-power resolution did not even indirectly criticize the United States for organizing the aggression and failed to call upon member states to aid Cuba. It stressed the special regional interest in the dispute, and as amended, requested that the OAS report on its ameliorative endeavors within the current year. The United States had objected to the Mexican draft which: did not specifically refer to the OAS; emphasized non-intervention; and appealed to member states to refrain from permitting their territory to be used in conjunction with the invasion.

Schweitzer considered the omission of any reference to the OAS in the Mexican resolution as a serious defect, but stated that he would vote for it since the resolution complemented the seven-power draft and affirmed principles to which Chile was committed. The Chilean Ambassador did not regard the seven-power draft as prejudicial to Cuba's interests, since in referring to the inter-American machinery, "it had excluded those concepts and actions to which Cuba had taken exception." In the GA, the Mexican resolution failed to obtain a two-thirds majority. Cuba, Chile, Bolivia and Brazil had voted in the affirmative, while the United States and a majority of Latin American states joined in opposition. Except for the provisions referring to the OAS, the seven-power resolution was passed by the GA in plenary session. Chile, the United States and most Latin American nations supported the proposal, while Cuba voted in the negative.[79]

Chile and Cuba in the OAS. The pattern of Chilean conduct in the regional organization is less clear. In general, the Alessandri administration acceded to the United States drive to condemn and expel the Revolutionary Government from the Inter-American System. On the other hand, Chile consistently opposed efforts to force her to sever her own trade and diplomatic relations, as well as the flow of persons to and from Cuba. The latter is largely attributable to Alessandri's concept of national dignity and firm belief that such questions should be self-determined by each sovereign nation. It is also consistent with Chilean resistance to severing relations with the Axis Powers during most of World War II.

When campaigning, Alessandri had committed himself to the maintenance of "close economic ties" and hence, good relations with the United States.[80] During the first half of 1959, a Chilean government mission visited the United States and secured $3,000,000 in credits to finance Alessandri's stabilization program. At a time when Cuba was nationalizing United States agricultural properties, the Vergara mission was inviting United States capital to invest in Chile.[81]

Given this pattern of amicable relations, it is not surprising that Chile wholly supported the United States position in the OAS between May and August 1959, when Cuba was demanding that sanctions be imposed upon the Dominican Republic. Havana was also endeavoring to promote the idea that the United

States should finance a massive economic development program for Latin America by arguing that political democracy and stability were intimately related to high living standards.

In the OAS Council, Cuba had urged that a projected foreign ministers conference consider only her complaints against the Trujillo regime. Chile supported the victorious United States view that all problems associated with existing Caribbean tensions be considered.[82] The Cuban response was to submit a list of twelve items for the agenda then being drafted. Selected for emphasis was the alleged relationship between economic development and the elimination of tyrannical regimes. The Chileans joined the United States in opposing this, arguing that such matters were already being considered elsewhere.[83] And as Alessandri addressed the Foreign Ministers Reunión when it opened in Santiago during August, he argued—with Chile's evolutionary Constitutional tradition in the background—that there was no such simple relation of cause and effect:

Democracy has no exceptions: it is the government of the people, exercised by representatives freely designated in periodic elections that safeguard the popular will and that are founded upon the sacred respect for the human personality and its rights, whose true source is the message of Christian civilization. . . .

We are firmly convinced that a close relationship exists between prosperity and political stability; but even though the former contributes to the maintenance of the latter, it is not sufficient to create it unless there are institutionalized principles which are accepted and determining even during periods of major economic crisis.

Although he stressed the need to develop formulas for the safeguarding of human rights, Alessandri further differed from Cuban Foreign Minister Raúl Roa in warning that such formulas could not contravene "the sacred principle of non-interference."[84] Thus, Chile joined the United States in opposing OAS sanctions for Santo Domingo by invoking the principle of non-intervention.[85]

Although he had signed the Declaration of Santiago upon returning to Havana, Raúl Roa characterized the resolutions as "insignificant verbiage," noting that the declaration had been signed by representatives of the Stroessner, Samoza and Trujillo regimes. Claiming that Cuba had prevented the creation of an inter-American police force that would have been put at the service of various Caribbean dictatorships, the foreign minister continued by stating that he was pleased "by the growing solidarity of Latin American peoples with the Cuban Revolution."[86] Within less than ten days, Revolución was depicting Chile as a prime example of the type of representative democracy advocated by the OAS— one whose economy was "tied to the monopolies." Noting that Alessandri had not been elected by a majority, the writer suggested that FRAP-led miners would soon "be the protagonists of great transformations in their country."[87]

Several months later, Chile's government newspaper La Nación editorialized that Cuba should consider her "permanent interests" in the Inter-American

System and avoid acts that would intensify United States hostility and ultimately prove self-destructive.[88] This followed the Mikoyan visit to Havana, and the signing of a Cuban-Soviet trade agreement. In the first days of February 1960, Wayne Morse, Chairman of the United States Senate Subcommittee on Inter-American Affairs, returned from Santiago declaring that the Chilean "people and their Government are solidly pro-American." He had held several conferences with President Alessandri.[89]

In January, Cuba and the UAR had announced plans to invite all under-developed countries that were members of the U.N. to a special conference in Havana during September. After a February meeting "between Foreign Minister Vergara Donoso and Cuban diplomats Carlos Maria Lechuga and Levi Marrero Artiles, the Chilean Government declined the invitation to attend the Havana conference of underdeveloped countries. In turning down the invitation, Chile explained that it could not commit itself to attend a conference which had not undergone a period of technical preparation."[90] From New York, the U.N. correspondent of the *New York Times* reported that "(m)any countries have declined to attend due to the anti-American policies of Premier Fidel Castro, and also because it might jeopardize the plans of the United States for economic aid to Latin America."[91]

Another source of Chilean-Cuban conflict centered upon a proposal in late 1959 by the Alessandri administration that a conference be organized to consider the reduction of Latin American military expenditures. At the end of November, the State Department expressed its sympathy for the move, and when President Eisenhower visited Chile in late February 1960, both governments agreed that there was a need to control armaments in the hemisphere.[92]

Several days after Eisenhower's departure from Santiago, *Revolución* charged that Alessandri's "Operation Disarmament" proposal had been coordinated with United States plans to convert Cuba into "another Guatemala." The Cuban daily complained that the United States was responsible for the difficulties Cuba was encountering in obtaining European weapons that were necessary to defend the Revolution against growing attacks.[93] The *La Coubre* had just exploded in Havana harbor with a cargo of Belgian arms, and the United States had recently persuaded London to prohibit the sale of seventeen jet fighters to the government of Cuba. The Chilean government, nevertheless, denounced the Cuban allegation that the Alessandri proposal had been coordinated to further United States goals.[94]

Three months before the August 1969 OAS Foreign Ministers Conference opened at San José, Osvaldo Dórticos toured six Latin American capitals in an effort to line up support for Cuba in her growing dispute with the United States. Significantly, he omitted Santiago from his itinerary.[95]

On the eve of the conference, Under Secretary of State C. Douglas Dillon appeared before the Senate Committee on Foreign Relations and requested the authorization of $500,000,000 in Latin American development aid and

$100,000,000 in earthquake reconstruction assistance for Chile. The committee approved the authorization on the second day of the conference, as did the Senate on the fifth day.[96] This was to form the basis of Cuban charges that the conference had been "bought" and represented a "farce."[97]

At the conference, Chile supported the United States position that Cuba be condemned for her relationship with the Soviet Union. In the course of his address, Foreign Minister Ortuzar also denounced the Revolutionary Government for intervening in the affairs of other Latin American nations, and denied that the Cuban Revolution expressed the sentiments or interests of other peoples in the hemisphere. Thanking the United States for its recent offer of developmental assistance, Ortuzar emphasized the urgency of a "solution" for Latin America's "economic and social problems because they are, without a doubt, the factor responsible for continuing discontent among the masses which may take such a hold as to facilitate subversion of the Constitutional order."[98]

The foregoing notwithstanding, the Chilean delegation did attempt to soften the language condemning Cuba that was incorporated into the Declaration of San José. Chile regarded the adoption of an extreme position as likely to increase Cuba's dependence upon the Soviet Union and weaken her already tenuous hemispheric ties. Consequently, Chile joined five other members in forming a special committee that was intended to mediate United States-Cuban differences. Havana declined to cooperate. Attempts to mediate at the conference had failed because the United States insisted that a strongly worded condemnation be adopted.[99]

Within twenty weeks, the United States had severed diplomatic relations with Havana. Upon being apprised of this action in January 1961, the Chilean government indicated that it was not considering such a move. And several days after this announcement, Foreign Minister Vergara attended a reception at the Cuban Embassy to commemorate the second anniversary of the Revolution. This symbolic act was probably designed to undermine FRAP charges during the congressional election campaign then in process, that the government and its supporting parties were "ready to fall into step with Washington in an alleged maneuver to isolate Cuba diplomatically as a prior step for United States intervention in Cuba."[100]

Yet, during the Bay of Pigs, the foreign ministry declined special Cuban appeals that it openly condemn the invasion. The Cubans were told that Chile would cooperate for a peaceful solution within international organizations.[101] And a cable was sent instructing Schweitzer to support the Mexican resolution.[102] This may have been opposed by Alessandri, since his foreign minister resigned shortly afterwards "allegedly for health reasons."[103] On April 20th, the government daily La Nación had editorialized by unequivocally backing the United States and denouncing Cuba's internal regime. This appeared on page four. The first page carried the headline: "100 Million in Aid Approved for Chile," which referred to the approval of this authorization by a subcommittee on foreign aid of the House Committee on Foreign Affairs.

In the aftermath, and following the execution of about twenty counter-revolutionaries for conspiring with the invaders, Alessandri cabled the following plea to President Dórticos:

I am honored to address myself to Your Excellency, certain that I interpret the sentiments of the Chilean people, in requesting that the death penalty no longer be applied to those who oppose your Government. In the hope that this call to your noble humanitarian sentiments will be received favorably, I again convey to you my highest esteem.[104]

Some days later, in the course of a speech to an ECLA conference, Alessandri endorsed the view that Castro's dictatorial methods had violated the right of the Cuban people to self-determination. And solicitous United States diplomats were told that Chile would now support non-military collective action by the OAS against the Havana government.[105]

At the first Punta del Este Conference in September 1961, United States representatives had "quietly" begun "to canvass delegates for support of economic and diplomatic sanctions against Cuba."[106] Chilean Minister of Finance Eduardo Figueroa not only warmly endorsed the AFP goals, but he accepted one of the major United States conditions—that Cuba not be permitted to share the benefits of the AFP until she restored internal democracy and severed her close relationship with the Soviet Union. On the other hand, and pending such developments, Chile opposed proposals by the United States delegation and those of Colombia, Peru, Guatemala and Nicaragua that Havana be expelled from the OAS. Such sanctions would drive Cuba even further into close alignment with the Communist nations.[107]

During November 1961, at "an extraordinary session of the Council of the Organization of American States (OAS), called at the request of Colombian delegate Alberto Zuleta Angel, the latter proposed that an OAS Foreign Ministers' conference be held in January 1962 to discuss the danger to the Hemisphere arising from 'internal subversion and extra-continental threats.' The proposal—reported by the Copley News Service to have been put forward 'after months of collaboration with (U.S.) State Department experts'—did not mention any country by name but was obviously aimed at Cuba. . . . After much deliberation . . . the Chilean Government had decided to reject the proposal. In view of Fidel Castro's December 2 speech asserting allegiance to the Marxist-Leninist doctrine, however, the Foreign Ministry instructed the Chilean Ambassador to the OAS to abstain."[108] Foreign Minister Martínez Sótomayor rationalized Chile's refusal to support the United States-Columbian move on the following grounds: 1) the facts did not justify the invocation of Article 6 of the Rio Treaty; 2) the conference would portray Castro as an embattled nationalist martyr; and 3) any sanctions would drive him into closer alignment with the Soviet Union.[109] But, the Chilean shift from a negative postion to an abstention would also have such an effect, and there is reason to believe that dissatisfaction with the slow release of United States economic aid to Chile was an operative factor here as it may have been at the September Punta del Este conference.

Within several weeks, a high ranking Cuban diplomat visited Alessandri and assured him that Cuba's Marxist-Leninism did not mean that she would depart from the "Belgrade line" of non-alignment in foreign affairs.[110] This, however, did not deter Chile from supporting Cuba's expulsion from the OAS system and the Inter-American Defense Board at the second Punta del Este Conference of Foreign Ministers in January 1962. Chile supported resolutions: denouncing international communism; endorsing the AFP; authorizing the creation of a committee to coordinate anti-subversive measures; and for an embargo on arms sales to Cuba. Foreign Minister Martínez Sótomayor condemned the Cuban government for destroying human rights and representative democracy. But he opposed mandatory trade sanctions, arguing that they would be inefficacious so long as Cuba was free to trade with Europe. Furthermore, socio-economic development would more effectively limit the appeal of the Cuban Revolution.

Although $7.4 million in United States aid was released to Chile on the first day of the conference, it would appear that dissatisfaction with the general slowness in disbursing United States aid commitments played a major role in conditioning firm opposition to mandatory economic and diplomatic sanctions, and especially in Chile's abstention on the expulsion resolution which she actually supported. At the close of the sessions, Goodwin, Woodward and Rostow conferred with Martínez and promised to send a high level mission to expedite AFP funds. This was to be the Goodwin-Moscoso Mission that arrived in Santiago eight weeks later, and whose role was described in chapter 5.[111]

After the Escudo was devalued in early October 1962, and the AFP committee of "Wisemen" approved Chile's Ten Year Plan, Martínez Sótomayor participated in an informal meeting of hemispheric foreign ministers in Washington. It was agreed that "Cuba could not justify taking defensive measures similar to those adopted in other regions of the world." The conferees endorsed the "determination of others" to take action if a situation capable of threatening the peace should develop on this island—after noting the growing Soviet intervention, the arms stockpiling and the necessity of intensifying surveillance and preventing subversion. The assembled representatives further "recognized the Washington position that the Castro regime must eventually be ousted." Although Martínez Sótomayor reportedly opposed a suspension of Chilean trade (about $10 million annually) with Havana, the United States delegate announced an impending blacklist of ships engaging in such commerce.[112]

On Oct. 19th, the foreign ministry delivered an "energetic protest" to the Cuban Chargé d'affaires claiming that the embassy had abused its diplomatic privileges by bringing 1,700 pounds of "communist propaganda" into Chile.[113] Within four days, the Chilean Ambassador to the OAS Council was ordered to vote for its conversion into an Organ of Consultation. Also on Oct. 23, the Chilean representative voted for the United States-backed resolution authorizing individual or collective use of armed force to eliminate the missile "threat" in Cuba. Chile did not join Bolivia, Mexico and Brazil in attaching a reservation stipulating that the resolution should not be interpreted as sanctioning an invasion. Although she failed to offer naval units for the blockade, Chile joined in a unanimous resolution to convoke a second meeting for Oct. 29 in order "to ratify the broad outlines of a plan to send a Continental Liberating Expedition to Cuba."[114]

Subsequently, the Copely News Service reported from Washington that "(t)he United States is particularly gratified at the reversals by Mexico, Brazil, Chile and Ecuador who nine months ago refused to vote for Cuba's dismissal from the OAS."[115] On Oct. 23, the foreign ministry had released a declaration justifying the blockade. It began by observing that "(f)or Chile the situation is clear; it is a simple question of applying the juridical norms to which we have subscribed...." Foreign Minister Martínez explained Chile's endorsement by referring to her commitment to disarmament which Cuba had violated, and subsequently Alessandri claimed that the existence of "offensive" missiles juridically justified the invocation of the Rio Treaty.[116]

The November commitment of $200,000,000 to support Chile's 1963 budget and Alessandri's December visit to Washington have already been commented upon. While Alessandri was at the White House, President Kennedy insisted upon raising the question of Chile's continued relations with Cuba. After repeatedly manifesting his disinclination to discuss this matter, Alessandri began to leave the room. The United States Chief Executive then relented and changed the subject.[117]

At the Punta del Este Conference in January 1962, Chile had opposed the use of the Inter-American Defense Board as a special security committee. When the OAS Council established the Special Consultative Committee (SCCS) on Security in March 1962, Chile had failed to nominate a member. Subsequently, the Chilean ambassador to the OAS urged that the authority of the SCCS be limited to rendering advice or compiling reports *only after a request* by a particular government, but the Chilean position was defeated when the question was voted upon.

On Oct. 24, 1962, the OAS Council had voted to instruct the SCCS to "make an immediate study of the transfer of funds to the American republics for subversive purposes, the spread of subversive propaganda, and the use of Cuba as a training base for subversive techniques." The SCCS report was submitted to the OAS Council on Feb. 8, 1963, and referred to the council's committee on security for review and submission to governments. Chile did not participate in this review which culminated in a report to the council on June 4, 1963, endorsing most of the measures outlined in the SCCS study. When the anti-subversion measures were voted upon by the OAS Council on July 3rd, Chile cast negative votes where recommended action would have clearly violated her constitution—banning travel by Chileans to Cuba, and those requiring virtual outlawry of Marxist political groups.[118]

"In light of the council's far from unanimous vote, U.S. officials quietly pigeon-holed plans to request an OAS embargo against all trade with Cuba. Commerce between Cuba and other Latin American states, never large, had declined to little more than a trickle of Chilean beans and garlic in exchange for Cuban sugar."[119] Within a few months, the United States Congress had enacted the Foreign Assistance Act of 1964, which prohibited the extension of aid to nations that permitted their ships to engage in commerce with Cuba. By early 1964, Chile was no longer trading with Cuba.[120]

With trade relations effectively terminated, there still remained diplomatic ties to be severed. Following the April 1964 overthrow of Brazil's President Goulart, a Foreign Ministers Reunión was called to act upon Venezuelan charges of aggression against Cuba. There was at least one report that its purpose was not only to sanction Cuba but "to serve notice that the rigorous action against Castro would also be taken against 'other areas' if they committed the same sin of violating continental peace and security."[121] The Chilean presidential election was 45 days away, and one of the major charges against FRAP was that it intended to "transform Chile into another Cuba." A severance of diplomatic and trade relations was ordered by the Washington Foreign Ministers Conference in July 1964, and the Cuban people were called upon to overthrow Castro. The Chilean government abstained or voted negatively on most resolutions, ostensibly for juridical reasons. Clearly, it wasn't from sympathy with the Cuban Revolution.[122]

In the weeks preceding the Washington conference, AP and UPI reports of United States-Argentine negotiations in May for a $15,000,000 arms loan were published in Santiago. At the same time, the Argentines began provoking a series of border disturbances in the Palena district by constructing a military post in an area traditionally patrolled by Chilean Carabineros. Viewing these incidents and the projected loan in the context of the intense presidential campaign, *Ercilla* warned "[t]he gravity of these acts is even more serious in view of the persistent rumors circulating in Buenos Aires about the arms that the government had received to be prepared in 'case a government backed by Communists should triumph in Chile.' "[123] The Chilean delegation to Washington had in fact delayed its departure until Buenos Aires ordered a cessation of the "provocations."[124]

During the last days of the Washington conference, there was a renewal of incidents in Palena. Although the Chileans reacted by suspending negotiations with Argentina, on Aug. 3, the foreign ministry dispatched a note to Buenos Aires suggesting that they again be resumed. New incidents were reported on the following day,[125] and no reply was received from Argentina concerning negotiations. At this time, Alessandri was expected to leave the decision on whether to heed the OAS order to sever relations with Cuba to the next president who would be elected shortly.[126] No date had been specified in the mandate, and Mexico had announced that it would not sever relations in the absence of World Court Advisory Opinion on the legality of the OAS resolution. Neither Bolivia nor Uruguay had taken any action.

Unexpectedly on Aug. 11, Alessandri announced that Chile would break relations with Havana. In justifying his decision, the chief executive stated that now the newly elected government would have several months "without pressure" to consider the possibility of a resumption of relations. "On the other hand," said the president, "if relations had not been broken, if an obligatory agreement had been defied, the first months of the future government would be hard for the new chief executive, who would be pressured—and how!—by many governments and some 'militaristically dangerous' ones."[127] "Non-compliance would create a grave precedent which would sooner or later result—in his judgment—in the withdrawal of Chile from the Inter-American juridical system, especially the Treaty of Reciprocal Assistance. The consequences of this, said President Alessandri, could be very grave for Chile, because it is this very treaty that is an especially effective safeguard for the territorial integrity and sovereignty of signatory states."[128] Less than forty-eight hours after announcing his decision, Alessandri was notified that Argentina's foreign minister had delivered a note to the Chilean Ambassador affirmatively replying to the Chilean Aug. 3 request for a resumption of negotiations. "The Argentine Chancellor Miguel Angel Zavala Ortíz, agreed to meet with Chile's Minister of Relations Julio Philippi, to 'arrive at an agreement upon the most efficacious procedures for definitively solving territorial problems and other matters that are a mutual cause for concern.' "[129]

Broadcasting Cuba's response, Radio Havana charged that Alessandri "had capitulated to 'the gross pressures of Yankee imperialism,' and that the rupture would cause more difficulties for Chile than for Cuba. It asserted that the break was intended to influence the outcome of the Sept. 4 Chilean elections."[130] The Chilean government had also regarded one of the goals of the Washington conference as electoral intervention.[131] In addition, direct pressure upon Chile was reported to have been applied by the United States through oral representations.[132] Nevertheless, Alessandri did state that in his opinion compliance with the OAS mandate was legally obligatory for Chile.[133]

The Resurgent Nationals. Following his severance of relations—reportedly after consulting with PDC candidate Eduardo Frei—Alessandri withdrew from Chilean politics for a period of five years. Without his famous name and paternalistic image, the Liberals and Conservatives were deprived of a major source of electoral appeal. As we have seen, these parties were reduced to minor status by the 1965 Frei-PDC onslaught. It is quite probable that the Christian Democratic candidate projected many of the personal qualities—integrity, austerity, and firmness—which had made Alessandri so popular. Furthermore, Frei pledged to effectively cope with inflation and economic stagnation. The Alessandri administration had proved incapable of achieving its goals in these areas.

Hence, much of the traditional constituency opted to give Frei and his party a chance in 1965. In that election, the PL and PCU together won only nine seats in the Chamber of Deputies as compared to 45 in the 1961 election. Whereas the earlier electoral contest had slightly improved the Liberal percentage while the Conservatives suffered a mild decline, the most recent one stunned the leaders of both parties.

Within a year, they had merged to form the *Partido Nacional* (PN). As Frei moved towards the right between November 1965 and May 1966,[134] attacks upon him and the *oficialista* wing of his party, which dominated his cabinet, were moderated. Support was given by both the PN and *El Mercurio* to Frei's crackdown on the Marxist-led labor confederation (CUT) and his wage control policies to reduce inflation. On the other hand, the Nationals bitterly opposed the weak but articulate communitarian or populist wing of the PDC.

Following the militarization and massacre of miners at El Salvador in April 1966, "there were massive firings throughout rural Chile. According to a UCC survey more than 8,000 campesinos were fired, approximately half of whom belonged to unions, many to the UCC." Others, of course, were activists in the FRAP-led *Federacion Nacional Campesina y Indigena.* Through a combination of strikes and government intervention to avoid threatened strikes, all but about 800 peasant unionists were reinstated in their jobs. In some cases, the UCC had actually joined the left in simultaneous work stoppages throughout entire municipalities.[135]

Emboldened by government passivity during this struggle, its *"mano dura"* towards organized labor in urban and mining areas, a general *"oficialista"* lethargy in the social reform area and incipient divisions within the PDC, the Nationals vigorously contested the 1967 municipal elections. They were encouraged by an increase from 12.5 (1965) to 14.2 percent of the total vote. The significance of this lay not only in the PDC's 7 percent decline, but in the latter's association with Frei's emotional declarations that the outcome would constitute a "plebiscite" for the government.

Following Frei's defeat, the Nationals apparently decided that they were in a position to force the administration to crack down on both the FRAP as well as the increasingly restive left-wing of the PDC. The government was vigorously denounced for permitting FRAP leaders to organize a Fidelista OLAS committee on Chilean territory. It was also charged that rural expropriations had exempted *fundos* owned by PDC sympathizers, and demands were made to remove PDC populists from CORA and INDAP—the government agrarian reform agencies. In Congress, Nationals demanded that CORA furnish budgets for each rural settlement project and denounced the use of three year training periods for political indoctrination in communitarianism.[136]

The right was also encouraged by Frei's 1966 curtailment of housing construction, his call for "a truce" that year symbolized also by an absence of references to "Revolution in Liberty" and the expulsion of radical PDC Deputy Patricio Hurtado. And more impressive, perhaps, was the government's disinclination to vigorously enforce existing income tax laws.[137]

In a bold move to garner both military support and an increased mass con-

constituency, the Nationals openly denounced the government for "weakness" in handling a border conflict with Argentina which had erupted in the Beagle Canal during 1967. The PN leaders also accused the government of failing to provide sufficient compensation and equipment to the military. Frei reacted by arresting the PN leadership for violating the Internal Security Law. In this confrontation, both sides had overplayed their hands, for the Supreme Court quickly exonerated Nationals' leaders.[138]

Apprehensive of rising FRAP militance, its continued open identification with the Cuban Revolution and an increasingly active Left Revolutionary Movement (MIR), the Nationals intensified their attacks upon the vacillation of the government. Denouncing Marxists who had allegedly infiltrated the PDC, the Nationals demanded a government capable of restoring respect for authority.

By 1969, the failure of the government's economic and inflation control programs provided additional issues. When the PDC rejected a National offer to back a "moderate" party leader for the presidency in 1970,[139] Alessandri was induced to again run as an independent. Hence the March 1969 congressional election campaign saw the Nationals stressing the following: 1) the Christian Democrats are Chile's Mensheviks and their 1970 candidate Tomic will be our Kerensky; 2) a vote for the PN will ensure Alessandri's candidacy in 1970; and 3) compare Frei's inability to control inflation and the general mismanagement in the PDC administration with the record of his predecessor.[140]

As the Christian Democrats suffered yet another setback many former PDC supporters reverted to the right. This was especially marked in the major urban areas of Santiago, Valparaiso and Concepción where the PN more than doubled its 1965 percentage of 9.7 percent. According to Grayson, "(t)he possibility of an Alessandri candidacy in 1970 proved an enticement to thousands of voters. The absence of a center-of-the-road candidate lured many members of the large urban middle class, who bemoan high taxes, soaring inflation and general unrest, into the National fold." In the rural zones, however, Government losses to the Nationals and other opposition parties were less dramatic. In any case, the PN emerged with 34 deputies and 5 senators based upon a respectable 20 percent of the nationwide vote.[141]

Commenting on the intensity of the 1970 presidential campaign, the United States Embassy in Santiago reported that "polemics associated with it saturate the information media and private conversation at all levels of society."[142] The bitterness recalled 1964. Again the right linked Allende to the Cuban Revolution. Mock photos of Soviet tanks encircling the Chilean presidential palace were distributed as were others of Allende with Fidel. Like Juanita Castro's "Message to the Women of Chile" in 1964, selected exerpts of Fidel's own 26 July 1970 speech were promulgated with the warning that an economic disaster of similar proportions would befall Chile if Allende were elected.[143] Reinforcing this theme was Alessandri's call for a "New Republic a la Portales." This symbolized a commitment to vigorously suppress leftist-led labor class squatters and demonstrators.[144]

After the PDC had declined the offer of a joint candidate, the right persuaded 74 year old Alessandri to campaign energetically throughout the nation. It was charged that Tomic could not win, and in fact most published polls and the United States Embassy reported the PN-supported candidate to be assured of a popular majority.[145] Because of this overconfidence, Alessandri declared that if no candidate obtained a majority, the Plenary Congress should heed tradition and vote for whomever held the plurality.

Alessandri benefited from the backing of fiercely anti-Communist Radicals who left their party to found the *Partido Radical Democratico.* More determinative, perhaps, was the financial backing he received from Anaconda. After a leftist raid on his headquarters, photographs of checks from the giant copper combine were published.[146] This—if true—is quite understandable, since Alessandri was the only candidate not pledged to the nationalization of this highly profitable mining enterprise.

The remainder of Alessandri's program, which was not ready until eight weeks before the election, pertained to the need for "a firm hand on the helm" to control inflation and end Christian Democratic favoritism in selecting *fundos* for expropriation.[147]

On the eve of the election, a mass rally was organized near the Mapocho Railroad Station. For perhaps the first time in Chilean history, thousands upon thousands of upper middle class citizens from the prestigious municipalities of Providencia, Las Condes, Vitacura, and Nuñoa flocked to demonstrate the intensity of their devotion. Unsurprisingly, the election tally on Sept. 4 which brought Alessandri to within 40,000 votes of a plurality demonstrated sizeable middle class and female strength. Although he received 34.9 percent of the total vote, Alessandri was the most popular candidate among women of whom 38.5 percent supported him. In addition to his plurality in Santiago, he was victorious in twelve other provinces of which eleven were predominently rural. Many peasant proprietors and small town petty-bourgeoisie opted for the rightist standard-bearer, as did the descendents of German immigrant farmers who settled in the South during the 19th century.[148]

In an earlier chapter reference was made to the bombings and financial panic which followed the election. United States exporters contributed to the disorderly situation by suspending all lines of routine credit. The executive committee of the National Party called an emergency meeting shortly after Alessandri's defeat. Although Alessandri had urged his supporters in the forthcoming Plenary Congress to act in the traditional manner, he had also announced his prospective resignation if the assembled legislators insisted upon electing him to the presidency. Gripped by their own recent "Campaign of Terror," a majority of the National leaders decided to oppose Allende. Alessandri's resignation would force a new election with a common anti-Marxist candidate. For reasons outlined in subsequent chapters, this tactic was foredoomed to failure. In the Plenary Congress, 35 votes were cast for Alessandri and 7 blank ballots were deposited on

Oct. 24, 1970. It is probable that these ballots represented 90 percent of the Nationals and a handful of right-wing Radicals and Christian Democrats.

Despite Allende's conciliatory style and post-election visit to Alessandri's home, the Nationals have remained unreconciled to the Popular Unity triumph. Beginning in 1969, prominent individuals associated with this sector had "hinted" that perhaps Chile would be better off by following the ever more ubiquitous pattern of military intervention in Latin America. There is also some evidence that neo-fascist mass organizations were constituted to back a future dictatorship, or to carry out a massacre of the left a la Indonesia.[149] Clearly, neither the United States nor the right are prepared to accept the consolidation of a second dedicated socialist regime in Latin America. An international press campaign to discredit the Popular Unity government was initiated in September, 1970.

Conclusions. Like the supporting Liberals and Conservatives, the Alessandri administration reacted negatively within a brief period to Castro's internal measures and his pugnacious anti-United States orientation. Identifying with the Chilean juridical and constitutional tradition as well as with propertied elements in both countries, it was impossible for Alessandri to view the radicalization of the Cuban Revolution with equanimity.

His shift towards a reformist orientation was conditioned not only by the fear of his administration and its supporting coalition of the growth of FRAP-oriented mass discontent, but also by the government's need for foreign funds. Hence, the AFP was welcomed as an aid in preventing the Cubanization of Chile "at the urns." FRAP's 1958 showing, its increased strength in 1961 and the unreserved identification with the Cuban Revolution by Allende and other leaders until well into 1962 clearly demonstrated that not the presidential office, but the system itself was in jeopardy. And a Leftist pro-Cuban victory at the polls would have greatly undermined the counterrevolutionary goals of the AFP.

To some degree, the resistant Chilean attitude towards the SCCS and the Washington Foreign Ministers Conference was conditioned by knowledge that the United States would have to continue providing budgetary support regardless of Chile's position. There was also the traditional nationalistic belief that only Chile should decide certain questions vitally affecting her sovereignty. This was manifested during Alessandri's meeting with Kennedy. Slow disbursement of aid probably influenced the Chilean voting pattern at the Punta del Este Conference as new commitments of aid did during the 1959-1961 period. And a desire to avoid an appearance of *entreguismo* was certainly operative during the 1961 and 1964 electoral campaigns.[150]

The Liberal-Conservative merger did not engender new policy orientations. National Party opposition to social reforms was paralleled by rising fear of left-led mass actions. Invasions of housing sites and privately owned rural estates as well as an increasing number of strikes—supported by both Marxists and populistic Christian Democrats—brought the Nationals to the verge of desperation. The hardening of the right was reflected during 1969-1970 by intimations that military intervention might be necessary to save the social order from anarchy and Castroism. So embittered were the Nationals that they pressured the aging Alessandri, who appeared on television with trembling hands, to campaign. For this election, support of the mildly left-leaning PDC candidate Tomic was out of the question, precisely because he was *much more* committed to egalitarian reforms than Frei's *oficialistas.* While the 1970 "Campaign of Terror" was again effective in frightening potential Allende supporters into backing Tomic or Alessandri, it failed to ensure a plurality. Since Alessandri's 1958-1964 record with regard to inflation control and economic growth was no better than Frei's, most lower class women who backed him in 1970 must have been catalyzed by fear of socialist revolution and radicalism. Some, of course, were attracted by his image of integrity and authority.

Radicalization and Equivocation: FRAP Responses to the Cuban Revolution

Introduction

Rightist responses to the Cuban Revolution were both direct and indirect. The former resulted from the interaction of value structures and the images of the Revolution conveyed by USIA and North American wire services. The latter were consequential to the AFP and the FRAP. Since the relationship of the AFP to the Cuban challenge has already been discussed, we shall now fix our attention upon the responses of Chile's most important Leftist organizations to the Fidelista "message."

Origins of the Popular Action Front (FRAP)

Like the AFL-CIO, a sense of weakness rather than power stimulated the formation of this left-wing electoral coalition. Since 1946, the Chilean Communists and Socialists had been struggling with each other for electoral support and control of important trade unions. Following González Videla's expulsion and outlawry of the PC-related in chapter 3, the PS joined his government. Although the Socialist program at that time called for "progressive" nationalization of the *Gran Mineria* and agrarian reform, it was also stridently anti-Soviet and anti-totalitarian.[1] Within some months, the youth section of the party withdrew under the leadership of Raul Ampuero. Their position was that the integrity and long run viability of the party as a force in Chilean politics mandated that anti-communism be "from the left." That is, be more revolutionary and radical than the Moscow-oriented PC. At the time, the Ampueristas were attracted by the nationalistic and egalitarian policies of the Peron regime in Argentina.[2]

As González Videla moved increasingly towards conservatism in his policies, ever more of the Socialist following defected to Ampuero's new Popular Socialist Party (PSP). The PS withdrew from the Radical government in 1950, and by 1952 it was extremely weak organizationally. In that year the PSP decided to support Ibañez who was running on a Peronist styled program. Carrying a broom, the ex-dictator and *golpista* of 1939 stressed the slogan "out with the Radical thieves." Scandals and corruption in the González Videla administration considerably marred the PR image—its 1952 presidential candidate receiving less than 20 percent of the vote as compared with Ibañez's 48 percent.

Salvador Allende, a prominent PSP member who had served as the minister of public health in Pedro Aguirre Cerda's Popular Front government (1939-1942), had wanted to run as the party's presidential standard-bearer in 1952. Frustrated in this ambition, he negotiated for the support of the rump of the old PS. Although Ibañez had offered to support legalization of the PC in exchange for its support—suppression by González Videla having been relaxed in 1949—the Communists apparently distrusted their ex-persecutor of the late 1920s. At that time, Communists not only had been consigned to concentration camps, but many were tortured and murdered. In addition, the PC was not particularly attracted by the Peronist style, nor, for that matter, by the Argentine leader's anti-Communism. Hence, the party accepted a bid by Allende for its backing. Nevertheless, Allende did poorly—receiving less than 6 percent of the total vote.[3] Miners and peasants provided most of his support. Catholic believers and those with "high" educational status (i.e. white collar sectors) were most solidly opposed to the working class candidate.[4] With the benefit of hindsight, we may say that Allende's role as an architect of Leftist unity was far more significant than the size of his vote. Second, his principled refusal to support Ibañez and concomitant willingness to lead a hopeless campaign help us understand why he subsequently emerged as an unreserved *aficianado* of Cuba's hero of the Sierra Maestra. For Castro too had confronted Batista's United States-equipped and advised army in a seemingly hopeless guerrilla struggle, and he later emerged as an architect of leftist cohesion. Both came from clearly non-Communist radical backgrounds, and neither was disposed to substitute opportunistic anti-communism *a la* Haya de La Torre for principled dedication to the egalitarian transformation of their societies.

Similarly, each of these leaders won constituency recruits because of government repression. In the Chilean case, after the Communists were outlawed, many dismissed union leaders and members returned to the rural village of their birth. They were probably responsible for much of Allende's peasant support. In addition to this latent campaign organization, agrarian areas adjacent to major coal and nitrate mines had been proselytized.[5]

One further Cuban-Chilean parallel worth mentioning pertains to the socio-psychological characteristics of the leftist elites. Just as heterogeniety contributed to sharp cleavages within the 26th of July Movement, so we find evidence of careerism and financial opportunism within Allende's own Socialist Party leadership. Although a large minority were blue collar workers or lower middle class in origin, many apparently used the party as a "stepping-stone" for socio-occupational mobility aspirations.[6] While it is true most anti-Communists had defected during the first decade of Socialist-Communist coalitions, as late as November 1970 the party leadership could be perhaps unfairly depicted as "an unruly mixed bag of Social Democrats, Maoists, Castroites and Trotskyites."[7] Such diversity has been an asset insofar as a non-totalitarian national appeal to Chilean intellectuals is concerned. But with regard to organizing lower class sectors who have always constituted the primary voting and labor constituency of the party, this internal factionalism and indiscipline have placed it in a disadvantageous organizational position vis-à-vis the Communists.

Following their first post-World War II experiment in electoral unity, at a time when many Communist leaders were still in hiding or exile,[8] the Socialists and Communists decided to establish a unified labor confederation for unions under their leadership. The *Central Unica de Trabajadores* (CUT) was largely political in purpose, but never became the powerful organization hoped for by its backers.[9] By the late 1950s its dues-paying membership was less than 25,000 and the CUT's annual budget did not exceed $3,000. About 50,000 workers were said to heed leadership orders.[10] Although controlled by Marxists, some Radical and a few PDC-led unions were affiliated. The CUT nominally represented 4 percent of the economically active population, where a total of little more than 15 percent were organized—the overwhelming number in small and ineffective unions.[11] Thus, in 1959 there were 1,472 unions with average memberships as follows: industrial (243); "professional" (99); agricultural (83). Recorded dues that year for 336,350 members of all legal unions was lower than the period prior to González Videla's repression. This weakness was also a result of class legislation prohibiting industry wide bargaining and unionization—discriminatory laws which remained in effect throughout the nineteen sixties. Hence, as noted in chapter 2, despite numerous strikes under the Ibañez and Alessandri administrations, most workers were unable to keep up with the serious inflation.[12]

During 1954, the PSP had withdrawn from the government after recognizing that it could not induce Ibañez to implement his nationalistic and egalitarian reform commitments.[13] Following losses in the 1956 municipal elections, the PSP responded favorably to a Communist-supported move by Allende to organize an electoral coalition, the FRAP. The Popular Action Front fielded common candidates, sponsored joint rallies and often voted as a congressional bloc. The Communists first had attempted, without success, to attract the PR and the PDC into a broader National Liberation Front (NFL) type coalition.[14] It was their hope that subsequently the centrist parties might be persuaded to join the FRAP, and therefore, socialist goals were excluded from the Communist program for the coalition as late as November 1958.[15] Reacting to their lack of leverage in the Popular Front and Ibañez Governments as well as to relative organizational weakness vis-à-vis the PC, the PSP had adopted the *Frente de Trabajadores* (FT) tactic in 1955. This called for a narrower and especially Marxist-led coalition which would focus upon radical appeals for lower rather than middle class support.

At a socialist "Unity Congress" in 1957, the FT was ratified as the miniscule PS fused with Ampuero's PSP to form the new PS.[16] Ampuero had himself appointed as secretary general and Allende was designated as the FRAP 1958 presidential candidate, since he was one of the few Socialists who could command Communist backing.[17]

The 1958 Campaign

If the coalition rested primarily upon the newly wrought PS-PC alliance, this did not imply total disinterest in securing middle class support. Socialist insistence upon Allende as the presidential nominee had of course ruled out a common effort with the PDC or the PR.[18] Consequently, a number of *partiditos* (small parties) and campaign committees were associated with the FRAP candidacy in an effort to attract white collar support.[19]

More rewarding ultimately was the lesson that FRAP leaders drew from the willingness of a fair number of peasants to reject the 1952 rightist candidate (Matte) in favor of the charismatic father-figure Ibañez.[20] Hence,

during the middle of 1958, a swarm of Communist (sic) agents descended upon the countryside carrying to the peasants the certain hope that they would freely distribute the lands to them as private—not collective—property.

The first stage of the reform was instituted: the free offer of land, tools and seeds.

We possess thorough documentation concerning this campaign which Communism promoted during the months preceding the presidential election. . . . Not a few maps of estates were circulated, some with picturesque drawings, which in red and blue indicated to the delighted peasants what parcels and cattle would be theirs.

It is undeniable that Communism (sic) achieved a major penetration of the rural zones. It is to be expected that not a few peasants were seduced by this bewitching appeal. This cannot be disputed.[21]

And the FRAP did in fact demonstrate "remarkable strength" when the rural ballots were counted.[22] Allende's proposed agrarian reform encompassed:[23]

1) maximum limits upon holdings;
2) payment for expropriated lands with 7 percent negotiable bonds;
3) distribution of expropriated land to individuals or cooperatives in accord with local option;
4) an Institute of Agrarian Reform which would provide credit to those fulfilling state production plans;
5) state farms to be established upon government lands.

Although the FRAP candidate depicted himself as neither pro nor anti-American, his campaign was reportedly marked by "frequent and forceful denunciations of the U.S." Advocating Latin American economic integration and Cold War non-alignment, the FRAP standard-bearer nevertheless "did not propose . . . to annul U.S.-Chilean military pacts." Allende did, however, affirm that Chile would trade freely with the East, and committed his government to the nationalization of the United States-owned Chilean Electric Company. No other United States firms were slated for expropriation. Taxes would be raised to the pre-1955 level on the *Gran Mineria*, and the economy would be subjected to: greater controls; a moderate expansion of the state-owned sector; and an "increase in the working-class share of the national wealth."

In the field of education, the FRAP promised to nationalize all private schools (largely religious) and to institute a massive campaign against illiteracy. Social mobility would be promoted by bringing 600,000 children between six and nineteen into the school system, and through the provision of full primary school-to-university scholarships. Major efforts were also pledged in the fields of public health and the erection of housing for slum dwellers. The purchasing power of the masses was to be increased, and the social security system rationalized and modified to maximize lower class benefits. Income and inheritance tax rates would be raised for the upper classes, and all government officials would be forced to disclose their investments. The armed forces were to be "democratized." Finally, suffrage would be expanded by lowering the voting age to eighteen and giving military conscripts and illiterates that right.[24]

Allende's program did not call for socialism, revolution or even a "democratization" of political institutions. Save for the restoration of the higher pre-1955 tax rates for United States mining firms, it might almost have been acceptable within the 1961-1962 AFP framework. Nor did the right or center base their anti-Allende campaign propaganda upon the premise that a FRAP victory would transform Chile into a Communist tyranny. Years later in 1964, Allende was to attribute this to the fact that nobody expected FRAP to come close to victory as, in fact, it did with about 29 percent of the total vote.[25]

Among other factors, a truly massive PL 480 infusion, Zamorano's candidacy and the unwillingness of most Chilean women to support a Marxist candidate were crucial to the FRAP defeat at the polls.[26] Yet Marxist unity, an energetic rural effort, and a rise in popular discontent and turnout contributed to the impressive showing. Correlations of occupational data and municipal election returns suggest an essentially lower class voting constituency for the left. Allende was strongest among males who were: 1) miners or industrial workers—particularly in the larger urban areas; 2) agricultural laborers, especially those in municipalities near unionized mines. He also received substantial backing from the wives of unionized blue collar workers. Although decidedly weaker in rural areas, the FRAP candidacy was favored by the more fraud resistant single ballot as well as government sanctioned access to formerly isolated rural estates.[27]

Defense of the Cuban Revolution

From early 1959 a pattern of consistent support is evident, although public praise was restricted after 1962 because of the priority assigned to the struggle for governmental power within Chile. During the first two or three years, the Revolution was described as populistic, anti-feudal and anti-imperialist. Its movement towards Marxist-Leninism did not diminish the FRAP commitment to its defense.[28]

How was this defense manifested? Largely through speeches criticizing the Alessandri government for its willingness to cooperate in the United States drive to isolate and ultimately destroy the Havana regime. Other speeches defended the Cuban position toward the OAS and on questions considered by that organization.[29] The United States was incessantly attacked, while programs of the Revolution were detailed and extolled.[30] It is useful to recall that FRAP leaders, members and sympathizers were among the most frequent *invitados* to the "First Free Territory of America." Here they had witnessed many of *their own values* being implemented by Latin Americans in defiance of the Yankee Goliath. Mesmerized by the possibility of what heretofore was believed impossible, their traditional *fatalismo* was consigned to memory during the 1960-1961 period.[31]

Since any victorious electoral coalition must depend upon the support of opportunistically inclined persons and groups, the continued survival and progress of the Cuban Revolution was a psychological asset for a coalition with goals similar to those of the Cuban leadership. This fact was projected to the public not only through articles, Senate speeches and pamphlets, but also by means of mass demonstrations which were intended to condition a less pro-United States position by Alessandri.

Thus, during the Foreign Ministers Reunion in Santiago (August 1959), the FRAP-led CUT organized a rally to protest the OAS and government rejection of the Cuban agenda proposals. Less than 3,000 persons were addressed by Armando Hart and FRAP leaders.[32] FRAP congressmen had already voted to deny use of the National Congress for the conference.[33] And when Raul Castro arrived and was ignored by the foreign ministry, his attention was almost completely monopolized by Allende and other FRAP leaders.[34]

Eisenhower's visit to Santiago in February 1960 was greeted by a FRAP declaration accusing him of touring Latin America to prepare aggression against Cuba. And FRAP congressmen boycotted the joint session which he addressed.[35] Six months later, seven thousand persons attended a mass rally in the Caupolican Theatre to hear FRAP leaders threaten armed revolution if Cuba were the victim of aggression.[36]

Yet, during April 1961, while the FRAP leadership personally requested Alessandri and Vergara to condemn the Bay of Pigs invasion, only "disturbances" were threatened if such action were not forthcoming.[37] CUT then ordered a general strike which caused no more than minor economic dislocations. About 30,000 workers and a similar number of university and secondary students heeded the call. Symbolically, the CUT began to sign up a legion of volunteers to fight in Cuba, but there were no indications of transportation arrangements.[38]

At May Day rallies during the early 1960s, CUT leaders expressed solidarity with the Cuban Revolution. But these assemblies only attracted between 2,500 and 8,000 persons in Santiago.[39] In February 1962, FRAP organized its last rally to praise Cuba. Several thousand persons came to the Caupolican to hear Allende, Communist Secretary General Corvalan and others call upon the Chilean government to withdraw from the OAS now that Cuba had been ousted.[40]

At the time of the missile crisis, a general strike was not even threatened. FRAP leaders urged the government to maintain relations, and a CUT-FRAP rally was organized for perhaps 2,000 persons. But top ranking leaders of the leftist electoral coalition did not address the gathering.[41] Nor did they speak to the three hundred persons who attended a MDSRC-CUT-FECH (PDC-dominated Federation of Chilean Students) rally in a small Santiago theatre to condemn Alessandri for severing relations during August 1964. A delegation of FRAP leaders did obtain an interview with Alessandri and asked him to adopt the Mexican position that a World Court advisory opinion on the juridical validity of the OAS mandate should be a pre-condition for its implementation. Replying that he was "not an Allendista," the Chilean president said the matter was being studied. Following Alessandri's announcement of the rupture, the FRAP leadership bestowed a floral wreath upon the departing Cuban charge d'affaires.[42] And subsequently, Allende challenged the Frei government to implement its campaign pledge to work actively for the reentry of Cuba into the Inter-American System.[43] But except for May Day references to Cuba's "shining example," there were no longer any demonstrations.

By mid-1967, Cuba's support for guerrillas in Venezuela and Bolivia who had broken with the Soviet-oriented Communist parties of those countries occasioned a latent split between the two major FRAP parties. Veiled criticism of Castro by Chile's PC was matched by public emotional expressions of support on the part of Allende and other leading Socialists. Hence, when the Chilean OLAS Committee was constituted after the July 1967 Havana Latin American Solidarity Conference, it was headed by Socialist Senator Aniceto Rodriguez, a close associate of Allende.[44] To ensure nominal Communist association, Nicholas Guillen, an old time Cuban Communist poet, was sent to Chile.

Although they grudgingly consented to attend the Havana OLAS conference and to be formal members of the symbolic Chilean solidarity committee, the leadership—though not necessarily the rank and file—of the PC was secretly relieved by the liquidation of Guevara's last campaign. While the Communist daily *El Siglo* ritualistically deplored his murder after capture and focused upon United States complicity, one can be sure that genuine depression affected many Socialists and MIR members. Until, and after, his accession to the presidency, Allende prominently displayed an autographed copy of Guevara's first edition of *Guerrilla Warfare* in his library.[45]

Hence, when in 1969 three desperate Cuban members of Guevara's band crossed into Chile, Allende "personally conducted the survivors" to Tahiti where they were turned over to French and Cuban officials. The escort by Allende was to prevent them from falling "into the hands of the CIA."[46] With the demise of this adventure and a shift in Castro's attention towards the Revolution's domestic problems, there seems to have been a temporary decline in emphasis upon guerrilla tactics.[47]

During the 1970 presidential campaign in which Allende clearly believed himself to be a sure loser,[48] there seems to have been no conspicuous effort to disassociate Popular Unity from Cuba. Even when Fidel's admission of grave economic errors was disseminated by the anti-UP parties, the typical leftist response was to admire the unusual candor displayed by the Cuban hero. Allende retained a photo of himself and Fidel in his library and sanctioned posters of himself with the Cuban slogan "Venceremos" beneath.[49] The UP campaign song, too, was entitled "Venceremos."

Aftermath of the 1960 Muncipal Elections

Following the 1958 campaign, Allendista Committees which had been organized throughout the country were disbanded.[50] And FRAP, largely Socialist, cadres returned to the urban areas.[51] Thus, for the 1960 municipal campaign, and despite the Cuban Agrarian Reform, the Chilean peasants were temporarily neglected by the left. In addition, for the only time in his administration, Alessandri was presiding over an economic upturn accompanied by only moderate inflation. Other factors which help account for FRAP's inability to poll even 20 percent of the votes include the reduced lower class turnout for such contests, and the greater importance of local personalities and issues.

In the months which followed the April election, the coalition moved in contradictory directions. The newly formed middle class oriented National Democratic Party (PADENA) was induced to enter the FRAP. Controlling about a dozen seats in the Congress, it had emerged from the fusion of two small parties which had formerly supported Ibañez. A non-Marxist entity, PADENA was quite heterogeneous ideologically and committed more to patronage than principles. Insofar as the latter were concerned, the National Democratic Party manifested a vague nationalism and dedication to economic development under middle class tutelage.[52]

Yet, by the close of the year, FRAP was to begin experimenting with new and more militant tactics. In anticipation of the March 1961 congressional elections, FRAP cadres resumed weekend forays into the rural zones.[53] Peasants were entertained by political marionettes, encouraged to register, organized into associations and told about the coming distribution of lands.[54] Some groups *began to seize estates*, and others joined workers in CUT-sponsored hunger marches. Similar FRAP inspired activities were vigorously carried on in rural and urban areas until early 1964.[55] It is quite probable that many of the rural organizers had already visited Cuba and were now beginning *their* struggle for state power in earnest.

Sometime during the latter part of 1960, the FRAP program was radicalized to include: abrogation of military pacts with the United States; nationalization of foreign owned copper, nitrate and iron firms as well as public utilities (all largely U.S. owned); withdrawal of support for Latin American economic integration; "the repudiation of agreements that were harmful to national interests"; nationalization of banking, insurance and foreign trade; and "a constitutional reform which would ensure political and social democracy."[56] The adoption of this set of proposals followed Havana's expropriation of many United States firms and the Soviet commitment to extend large scale economic and military aid to Cuba. Moscow also had offered to purchase those commodities that Cuba was no longer able to market in the United States. Hence, if the Cubans could really—right under Uncle Sam's nose, so to speak—accomplish what all good Latin American Marxists had always dreamed, perhaps the world balance of power had changed sufficiently enough to outdate the 1958 moderate FRAP program. And what better way was there to demonstrate solidarity with the heroic Cuban Revolutionaries than to inflict major economic losses upon *imperialismo*—and from the safer distance of seven thousand miles.[57]

This euphoric militancy was reflected by the Socialist and Communist FRAP candidates for Congress who vigorously identified their campaigns with the anti-imperialist and *anti-oligarchic programs* of the Cuban Revolution. And they denounced Alessandri for complicity in the United States drive and aggressive plans to deny the Cuban people the right of self-determination. The OAS was the "Ministry of Yankee Colonies," which was preparing the setting for an attempt to convert Cuba into "another Guatemala."[58]

At the polls in March 1961, the "FRAP registered a greater increase in voting strength" than any other party. "Disillusioned by the slowness of reforms and impatient with Alessandri's austerity program, the Chilean voter gave solid support to the leftist coalition and to the left-center Christian Democrats. The FRAP obtained more votes than any other party or political bloc." Increasing their share from 9 percent in 1960 to 11.3 percent, the Communists were the biggest gainers in the coalition. The Socialist increase was also more than 20 percent to 11.2 percent. Less remarkable was the fact that "(t)he other two FRAP partners did not fare well this time. The National Democratic Party . . . lost its six senators but was able to elect twelve deputies. Its percentage of the vote was 7.1. The other minor FRAP party, the National Vanguard of the People (Vanguardia Nacional del Pueblo) received about 1 percent of the vote."[59] The VNP was a non-Marxist personalist *partidito* organized by the followers of Baltazar Castro, who was elected to the Senate.

The dismal showing of the middle class parties in FRAP was barely a sign of what was to come. Major gains by the vocally pro-Cuban Marxists on a radicalized program *backed by hunger marches and land seizures* explain the fear that induced the Rightist parties to conceive of a need for a reformist orientation. Similar apprehensions dissuaded middle class sectors from supporting the Popular Action Front. Even more striking was the enlargement of a lower class constituency for Chilean *Fidelistas* despite the relative price stability which had been attained.[60] Inspired campaigning on a radicalized platform reinforced by mass actions best explains the Marxist advance.

Emergence of a Defensive Posture

Allende's impressive 1958 showing and the Marxist 1961 gains ensured that the Socialists would insist that he be the 1964 FRAP candidate. Socialist success in imposing their radical 1957 program upon the FRAP in late 1960 further doomed Communist efforts in 1962 to broaden the coalition to embrace the PR or possibly the PDC.[61] Both of these large parties would have wanted not only programmatic concessions—especially upon those items that were certain to provoke a capital flight and virtual rupture of relations with the United States—but also the presidential candidacy itself. And neither would form an independent coalition with the more moderate, despised and less "Chilean" FRAP party, the Communists. Allende had been the architect of Socialist-Communist unity within a party that was still fundamentally "anti-Communist." Hence, to prevent its own isolation, the PC was compelled to accept the PS *Frente de Trabajadores* tactic in practice while officially yet proclaiming fidelity to the broader NLF approach.[62]

PADENA had apparently entered the FRAP in the hope of securing the presidential nomination for its own candidate, since from a doctrinal perspective the coalition was difficult to rationalize.[63] During the first half of 1962, PADENA President Carlos Montero and a supporting faction unsuccessfully sought to obtain the FRAP candidacy. Adamant Socialist opposition and a probable Communist preference for a centrist party with a more substantial following foredoomed this endeavor. In July, a mildly pro-Allendista faction seized control of the PADENA Central Committee.[64] Following this, the PDC launched a major effort to destroy the party by offering leaders who would defect future administrative appointments or electoral nominations.[65]

Several events created a favorable atmosphere for this strategic objective. As noted in chapters 5 and 6, the *Frente Democratico* and *Chile Libre* were launched in October 1962. Simultaneously, a major anti-Communist propaganda campaign against the FRAP was initiated. Thus, an Allende victory would be transformed into a Communist dictatorship at the service of Moscow. United States military intervention was probable and economic disaster cum violence were certain. Supported by the intensifying USIA propaganda depicting the disastrous Cuban tyranny, anti-Communists in Chile began to republish the glowing praise heaped upon the Castro regime by FRAP leaders—especially Allende—during the 1959-1961 period.

And if Castro's declaration of Marxism-Leninism had greatly reinforced the "betrayal" propaganda and reduced the appeal of the Cuban Revolution to those many Chileans believing Communism was *ipso facto* evil, the outcome of the missile crisis was *portrayed* as proving not only that Havana was a helpless satellite but that in a military confrontation, the Soviets assigned higher priority to peace than the defense of a distant Communist regime; i.e. *fatalismo* was not really outdated. Potential FRAP appeal was also indirectly undermined by a series of military interventions in other Latin American nations during the 1962-1964 period.

Hence, on Nov. 11, 1962, when Allende presented the radicalized FRAP program for 1964, which was essentially that used in the 1961 campaign, he was no longer publicly associating FRAP with the heroism and programs of the Cuban Revolution.[66] According to one of his non-Marxist campaign directors:

Senator Allende, in speaking at the close of the assembly, said among other things, that although the Chilean popular movement had demonstrated its fierce opposition to imperialism this did not mean that Fidel Castro was guilty of trying to export revolution, since here a truly Chilean revolution would be implemented. Following this, Allende clearly distinguished what occurred in Cuba from what would be done in our country. This declaration was opportune, since the enemies of FRAP have been undermining the prestige of the Chilean popular movement by claiming that it was connected and interdependent with that of Fidel Castro.[67]

It was difficult to predict the outcome of the municipal elections scheduled for April 1963. If the anti-Communist campaign caused major losses for the non-Marxist parties in the FRAP, the Allende candidacy or the coalition itself might be jeopardized. Given these uncertainties, the Socialists insisted that Allende be designated as the official FRAP candidate for the 1964 presidential election *before* the April 1963 municipal elections were held. Although the Communist leadership finally agreed to this maneuver, the Socialist move provoked a major crisis within the PADENA leadership. Mildly Allendista Deputy Luis Minchel defended the necessity for joining the PS and the PC in an early endorsement of the Allende candidacy: "(a) clear indication of how reactionaries are taking advantage of FRAP's weakness in not having a candidate is demonstrated by the bastardly anti-Communist propaganda campaign that is inspiring such terror among the middle and lower middle classes."[68] Unimpressed, the Montero faction reacted by boycotting the January 1963 "Presidential Assembly of the People," which designated Allende as the FRAP presidential nominee. As early as September 1962, some members of this faction were publicly denouncing "Soviet intervention" in Cuba.[69]

1963 Municipal Elections

By February 1963 the Christian Democrats had concluded that Cuban prestige was sufficiently tarnished to join the bandwagon. The party's executive council released a manifesto drafted by Jaime Castillo, a prominent Chilean leader of the Congress for Cultural Freedom and a 1960 *invitado*. It proclaimed that the Cuban Revolution was now a revolution of "suppression," and *the* issue in 1964 insofar as FRAP and the PDC were concerned would be the preservation of representative democracy. To this challenge, the Communists rejoined that after FRAP were victorious in 1964, a "similar revolution" would be brought about in Chile *peacefully*, if the reactionary forces abstained from terrorism.[70] Both the PDC and the Marxists were then endeavoring to register as many new voters as possible, the former with Church aid.

The outcome of the April polling, regarded as a precursor for 1964, revealed that the losses suffered by the *non-Marxist* FRAP parties

accounted for the overall loss suffered by the Left. The National Democratic Party (PADENA) fell from 7.1 percent in 1961 to 5.2, and the National Vanguard of the People Party dropped from 1 to 0.1 percent of the total vote. (On the otherhand,) if there was one winner in particular it was clear that it was the Christian Democratic Party. . . . Obviously their triumph had been at the expense of both the government Right-Center coalition and the FRAP. . . . The Communists reached 12.7 percent (11.7 in 1961) and the Socialists 11.5 percent (11.2 in 1961).[71]

Within twelve weeks Montero and several other prominent followers had deserted the PADENA. By September 1964, eight of its twelve deputies were to leave, many entering PDC ranks. Some organized pro-Frei *partiditos* such as the New Democratic Left and the Agrarian Labor Party.[72]

Shortly before this defection of middle class non-Marxists began, the FRAP leadership organized a strategy-planning conference at Las Vertientes. The feeling of those meeting was that the major enemy in 1964 would be Frei, not Duran. Of the FD parties, the PR had managed to hold its own in the 1963 municipal elections, while the rightist Liberals and Conservatives had both suffered defections to Frei. Church support for Frei through the Bishops' Pastoral Letter was probably of major importance in catalyzing this shift. The FRAP leadership expressed concern over the electoral support given to the PDC by the recent Church declaration, and resolved to center its attacks upon Frei's cooperative attitude toward United States interests and the "vagueness" of the PDC program.[73]

Insofar as potential non-Marxist voters were concerned, the FRAP decided to create a number of "movements" directed at different groups (Catholics, women, retired army personnel, etc.). But no modification of the FRAP program or position on a possible Radical presidential candidate was considered. It was also probably decided to stress Allende's commitment to civil liberties, and to *avoid self-identification* with the Cuban Revolution. Virtually all of the twenty-eight pieces of 1964 FRAP propaganda which are held by the National Library reveal a *complete absence* of references to the Cuban Revolution either in defense of it against attacks or stressing its social measures.

The "Campaign of Terror"

Following the municipal elections, the 1964 presidential campaign began in earnest. One anti-Communist observer reports that "the country was deluged with posters, pamphlets, newspaper articles, and radio programs warning the Chilean people that an Allende victory would mean the end of democracy, the installation of a dictatorship on the Cuban model, and the reduction of Chile to the status of a Soviet satellite."[74] And in a more immediate sense, it was charged that "urban and rural properties 'would be robbed' in order to give them to peasants and urban slum dwellers, private automobiles would be confiscated in order to make gifts of them to workers and political opponents would be shot."

The lower classes were warned that as in Cuba their children would now owe first loyalty to the Communist State and even be sent to Russia, people would no longer be able to worship freely, unions would be deprived of their right to strike, better paid workers such as those in the *Gran Mineria* mines slated for expropriation would lose their higher standard of living, rationing would be introduced, etc.[75] As to its effectiveness, Gil and Parrish suggest that "anti-Communism in the campaign . . . was probably the most important factor in the Frei victory."[76] It is obvious that several hundred thousand Liberal, Conservative and Radical supporters—and perhaps a greater number of "independents"— voted for Frei because of their fear of his adversary. Even Socialists deserted the Allende candidacy.[77]

The FRAPists were handicapped by a shortage of funds and an inefficient campaign organization.[78] Some leftist leaders later complained that the FRAP parties hadn't devoted sufficient energy to organizing in urban slums and rural areas.[79] In addition, probably all but three newspapers were opposed to Allende, and access to radio time on eight networks was wholly denied or severely curtailed.[80] There is some evidence of direct involvement in the campaign by the USIA.[81]

The financial backing for the Frei campaign and the "deluge" of anti-Communist propaganda made it impossible for the FRAP leaders to disassociate themselves from the chaos and Communist tyranny that was prognosticated as certain to follow their victory. This propaganda disparity, set in a context of majoritarian anti-Communist attitudinal structures, also precluded an effective defense of the Cuban Revolution by the Allendistas. While a vigorous and straightforward defense of Cuba might have regained a few thousand lower class voters—and this is not certain—it would have detracted from the FRAP emphasis upon domestic issues and have: 1) sacrificed any possibility of obtaining middle class support; 2) indirectly reinforced the portrayal of Allende as "the Communist candidate"; 3) aided in converting this into the central issue of the campaign; and 4) increased the probability of a congressional vote for Frei and/or a military *golpe*. The impact of the United States-backed military intervention in

Brazil during April was not modest upon the FRAP following, nor, for that matter, upon many other politically attentive Chileans. The FRAP was not prepared to effectively confront such an eventuality, and lived in constant if muted fear of the military.[82]

Notwithstanding the Frei landslide victory, the FRAP increased its percentage over 1958 by about a third, no mean achievement considering the forces and resources opposing it in the campaign. In rural areas, less subject to higher propaganda and mass media concentration or "vote-buying" than the *callampas* (urban slums), the increase over 1958 was 58 percent. Similarly, the percentage rise was greater in small urban centers than in large cities.[83] Yet, the basic sexual and occupational variables associated with FRAP voting in 1958 remained operative in 1964: industrial workers in larger urban centers; rural full and part-time laborers; miners and nearby peasant communities; and, of course, males. Only 32 percent of the women voted for Allende while 63 percent backed Eduardo Frei, the Christian Democratic nominee. The percentages of men were 45 percent and 50 percent. Close to a million Chileans voted for the FRAP compared to slightly over 350,000 in 1958.[84] It is probable that a substantial number of Alendista militants who registered new voters and solicited votes were both conscious of and inspired by Cuba. This was their opportunity, even though they had been ordered to omit all mention of either the word "revolution" or "Cuba." This was the great "deception."[85]

Electing a New Congress

In the aftermath, the FRAP leadership declined to adopt a policy of total opposition to the barrage of reform proposals with which Frei innundated the Congress. Similarly, Socialist Senator Ampuero rejected a PDC offer of a Ministry of State. The FRAP and especially the Communists offered selective support for what were regarded as anti-oligarchic legislative proposals. In general, however, leftist leaders rightly regarded this public relations oriented flood of bills as "half-measures which would only delay the day of true reform." With regard to the *Gran Mineria*, FRAP leaders displayed great foresight in charging "that the 'Chileanization' program was going to cost the government much more than the benefits that would accrue to it through higher tax revenues." Yet, "A Congress for Frei" was the major issue in the 1965 election, after the new president had dramatically withdrawn his reform bills when they were confronted by the usual procedural delays as well as rightist, Radical and some Socialist opposition. Cuba and communism had faded from electoral politics.[86] Although the PDC chief executive had rejected a Cuban offer to barter sugar for Chilean products, the FRAP was disinclined to press the issue.

As a result of the polling, the PC added two deputies and two senators to their parliamentary contingent, while the PS only managed to gain three seats in the Chamber of Deputies. The Radicals and especially the two rightist parties suffered devastating losses which, except for the FRAP gains were recouped by the Christian Democrats who won an absolute majority in the lower house and added twelve senators. In percentage terms, the Socialists declined slightly from their 1963 level to their 1961 position, while the Communists gained slightly over 1961.[87] Both parties were handicapped by the prohibition upon electoral pacts, and the advantage which usually accrues to the party of a recently victorious president. Furthermore, Frei made maximum use of captive radio audiences through "obligatory (radio) chains," and his supporters were again charged with vote-buying in the form of 5,000 sewing machines, TV sets and public telephones.[88] The VNP had deserted the FRAP in September 1964, while PADENA severed its ties after suffering crippling losses in the March 1965 election.

The Challenge of Christian Democracy

The fact that these two small middle class parties ended up in the Christian Democratic camp as well as the PS stagnation in the recent congressional contest provoked internal dissention within the faction-ridden Socialist Party. Those who opposed the Communist commitment to a coalition with middle class sectors as futile charged that the tactical moderation required for such an approach had lost to the left many lower class votes and won few from the white collar strata.

Allende intervened personally to maintain a semblance of unity with the Communists by ensuring that his friend Aniceto Rodriguez was selected as secretary general of the party.[89] Nevertheless, those who defined the somewhat ambiguous Workers Front tactic as *excluding* the middle class would ultimately dominate the Socialist Central Committee. Not only this, but a de facto radicalization of tactics was to be forced upon the generally circumspect Communists.

While the PC leadership reacted to the events of 1965 by seeking to support egalitarian PDC measures and simultaneously launching a major drive to organize peasants, it became increasingly difficult to avoid a frontal assault upon the Frei administration. As the latter endeavored to persuade and bargain with oligarchic elements, the "*oficialistas*" not only moderated the pace of their reforms but were also compelled to put organized labor in its place through symbolic suppression (the "El Salvador Massacre" of March 1966) and by creating government supported dual unions.[90]

While the Communists continued to offer selective support for "progressive measures"—and there were some notable ones—Frei's general moderation and his arrogant refusal to similarly bargain with the left, forced the PC to join the Socialists in vigorously denouncing the "betrayal" of the PDC pledge to transform socio-economic structures.

Intense leftist antipathy was evidenced in early 1967 when PS, PC and PR senators united to deny the president of the republic permission to visit Washington. While this is understandable when one considers Leftist indignation concerning United States armed interventions in Santo Domingo and Vietnam, it was an unprecedented exercise of constitutional authority. During the same period, these three parties had elected Allende as president of the Senate. Hence, there had been a symbolic confrontation between the two foremost Chilean leaders.[91]

The April 4, 1967, municipal electoral gains by both the PS and PC were as dramatic as were the PDC losses. In fact, the two Marxist parties increased their 1965 percentage of 22.7 to 28.7. Since Frei had proclaimed this contest to be a plebiscite—and had with his ministers campaigned throughout the country—the opposition parties had been vindicated in their claim that "Frei is not Chile." Within a short time, the Radical Party was taken over by a pro-FRAP faction led by Alberto Baltra. This undoubtedly heartened the Communists who renewed their drive for a broad NLF coalition in 1970.

While the PC ultimately attained this goal in late 1969, it was in form rather than fact. First, many of those who won control of the PR in 1967 were ex-*invitados* and Communist sympathizers. Second, this move was the pretext for a struggle within the Socialist Party between Raul Ampuero, a long time anti-Communist, and the Rodriguez-Allende faction. The former was defeated and defected with a half dozen Socialist congressmen as well as about 15 percent of the PS membership.[92] They organized a Popular Socialist Union which lost all but one parliamentarian in the 1969 congressional election!

Although the PS was weakened by this schism as it was by the desertion of youth to the Leftist Revolutionary Movement (MIR) which advocated armed struggle, the leadership reacted with vigor by adopting the leftist tactics that had been so useful during 1960-1961. After playing an ostentatious role at the Latin American Solidarity Conference where they learned of Guevara's heroism, Socialist delegates returned to again announce their unreserved solidarity with Cuba.[93] Rather than draft new programs, however, the PS began to lead militant strikes, seizures of housing sites, takeovers of *fundos* and university confrontations. Since 1966 the PS had been intently organizing industrial workers.[94] Now, with the "*oficialista*" freeze on urban wages and its lethargy in expropriating *fundos*,[95] a unique opportunity appeared.

Ironically, the Communists were compelled to join these militant mass actions. Between 1967 and 1970, an unprecedented number of strikes were called. Landlords were taken hostage, universities were closed, slum dwellers marched.[96]

While the PDC suffered another and even more serious setback in the March 1969 congressional election, no more than half of the defectors moved over to support the Marxist parties. Most of these were probably slum dwellers, miners, industrial workers and peasants. Many Christian Democratic sympathizers among the lower strata were not brought to the polls and therefore abstained. But it is extremely unlikely that PDC middle class losses defected in appreciable numbers to the left.[97]

Following the election and the "Puerto Montt Massacre" of squatters, the Marxists reacted by increasing mass militance. Because of its obvious appeal to the unintegrated *marginals*, even the PDC was compelled to authorize its militants to lead such actions.

By the end of the year a formal Popular Unity coalition was established to contest the 1970 election. In by-elections during 1967 and 1968, the PR and FRAP had supported common candidates. With difficulty, a common program was adopted by the PS, PC, PR and the United Popular Action Movement (MAPU) as well as the miniscule Social Democratic Party and Accion Popular. The Social Democrats were led by ex-Christian Democratic Senator Tomas Pablo, who became president of the Senate following Allende's inauguration. Accion Popular was intended to appeal to a motley assortment of middle class independents. And MAPU represented about 15 percent of the PDC (*"rebeldes"* who defected after the Puerto Montt mass slaying by the *Grupo Movil*). Their view was similar to that of Fidel Castro after the El Salvador "Massacre" three years earlier: Frei has promised a revolution with liberty, but instead had provided bloodshed with liberty.[98] Interestingly, many MAPU leaders—Chonchol, Gomucio, Silva, Jerez—had been Cuban *invitados*.

The Socialists entered the Popular Unity (UP) coalition only after the Communists pressured them into accepting Radical participation. Until PS assent was forthcoming, the PC declined to withdraw Pablo Neruda as its presidential candidate. Agreement was ultimately ensured by the PDC's refusal to sanction "an opening" via coalition "to the left," and by Communist support for a Socialist rather than Baltra as a UP candidate. In view of the PR's stagnation in the 1969 congressional election, it was also obvious that Baltra could never win.

After first offering the nomination to Senator Carlos Altamirano and Aniceto Rodriguez, the Socialist Central Committee finally gave it to Allende—a three time loser! Both Rodriguez and Altamirano were prominent Chilean *Fidelistas*, as was Allende. As friends of the latter, they declined the proffered opportunity to become the nominee. More significant was their recognition that only Allende held sufficient popularity among the party's cadres who would have to mobilize potential voters.

In contrast to 1964, this time there was no deliberate suspension of mass seizures and demonstrations. Tactical radicalism reinforced a very radical program which committed the new UP government to a working class government. In many respects it was similar to the 1961 and 1964 FRAP platforms. The Popular Unity Program was more revolutionary, however, in that a sweeping constitutional reform was pledged, one that specifically mandated the end of a strong presidency and Chile bicameral legislature. Authority was to be vested in a party dominated People's Assembly. Elections were no longer to be staggered and illiterates would be registered.

While the tone was moderate as were provisos for the military and even limited foreign investment, the sweeping nationalizations and egalitarian social commitments implied an investment strike by capitalists and an eventual confrontation with the United States and its domestic supporters.[99] And if this were insufficient, the organization of 4,000 Popular Unity committees in work places and neighborhoods, initially as campaign organizations and ultimately as the basis for "Popular Power," signaled the end of an era.

The UP campaign focused upon the "failures" of Christian Democracy in such areas as agrarian reform, housing, eliminating illiteracy, inflation and the loss of an extraordinary amount of development capital due to the "Chileanization" giveaway of ore resources.[100] While 80 percent of the Popular Unity Committees were led by Communists, it is probable that Allende's humane and witty demeanor on television brought him some unexpected white collar support as well as urban slum backing.

What is striking, however, is that his percentage of the total vote declined from almost 39 percent in 1964 to less than 37 percent in 1970. As for his total vote, it was 1,075,616—barely 100,000 higher than in 1964. Had it not been for the failure of the Christian Democrats to nominate a candidate considered reliable by the right, Allende would have lost. Most radical PDC followers who might have defected from a moderate Christian Democrat like Leighton had already deserted to the MAPU in 1969 when Tomic received the nomination.

If Tomic was unable to threaten Allende's core blue collar constituency, the question remains as to why the UP lost ground. While Communist cadres again avoided identification with Cuba, this was not so with regard to many Socialists and some MAPU campaigners. The militant mass actions including a violent general strike called by students reinforced the anti-UP "Campaign of Terror." A substantial sector of the left seemed resigned to electoral defeat by Alessandri and eventual repression which would catalyze armed struggle as advocated by MIR and the late Che Guevara. While the Radicals may have brought Allende the support of a few thousand public employees and several thousand nitrate miners—Allende won an overwhelming majority only in the four northern mining provinces—they could not deliver most of their white collar constituency. These sectors voted for Alessandri and in some cases for Tomic.[101] It should be recalled that middle class identification was found to be the strongest correlate with anti-radicalism.

Hence, the Cuban issue at the cognitive level interacted with mass demonstrations and a socialist UP program to deprive the NLF coalition of virtually all middle class appeal. As the egalitarian course of the new UP government becomes manifest, the middle class will—with some exceptions—become increasingly embittered.

Hence, equal participation at the cabinet level by the Radicals will seem as a facade and the party as a "Communist front." Its main function will be to control and reassure the Armed Forces until anti-Communist officers can be removed or the Carabineros can be restructured as a counterbalance. Alejandro Rios, a non-Marxist Radical, is minister of defense while Jose Toha, a *Fidelista* Socialist, controls the Carabineros as interior minister.

MAPU, however, promises to emerge as a Catholic worker-peasant party. Large sectors of the PDC union, youth and peasant departments created it. As socialists and populists, they have no interest in maintaining middle class privileges. It is significant that the Marxist-Leninist Allende attended a Te Deum at Santiago's Cathedral after his inauguration. Also worth mentioning is the qualified support for the new government by Chilean Jesuits and Raul Cardenal Silva, Archbishop of Santiago. As the Church in Cuba has reoriented itself to the Revolution, so has much of the Chilean clergy.[102]

Chile's Revolutionary Government

Within moments of Allende's inauguration, Chile's territory was thrown open to Cubans. A *large* delegation headed by Fidel's confidant Carlos Rafael Rodriguez spent a week in Santiago at the time of Allende's inauguration. Upon departure from and return to Cuba, Premier Castro personally accompanied this delegation. Eight days after being invested with presidential authority, Allende broadcast to the nation that Chile and Cuba were establishing the broadest possible diplomatic, economic and cultural relations. Fidel, who telephoned Allende on the night of his victory to convey congratulations, has offered to visit Chile at the president's convenience.[103]

In his first presidential address, Allende paid tribute to Guevara's heroism and called for a new moral code by public officials—specifying Cuba as an example.[104] Also following Fidel's example, the UP government has frozen rents and imposed severe restrictions upon landlords. Land will be rapidly expropriated and distributed to "indivisible" cooperatives and state farms, although a small number of individual holdings may be sanctioned. As wages are equalized for similar tasks and the privileges of *empleados* are eliminated, class struggle will become the order of the day.

Within months the Popular Unity committees have more than tripled, illiterates were being enrolled in the electoral registry and profits were forced to absorb the burden of inflation control for the first time in Chilean history.[105]

Although both Fidel and Chilean Communists have advised Allende to move slowly in expanding the state sector and in achieving economic independence from the United States—and despite Allende's evidence of heeding this counsel—pressure from the "left" and growing Yankee antagonism have catalyzed accelerating radicalization.[106] The government has established relations with North Korea, China, North Vietnam, East Germany and Nigeria. It is endeavoring to develop military relations with Bolivia and Peru, while raising military salaries, family allowances and pensions. The question, then, is how long 90,000 armed men—officered by United States-indoctrinated anti-Communists—can be deterred from provoking a Civil War or effectuating a *golpe* a la Brazil. Although the odds are against it,[107] if the UP government could survive to the 1973 congressional election, a rapidly expanded lower class constituency would ensure a working majority in both chambers and this would clear the way for a new constitution. Profiting by Cuban errors and Chile's greater resources, there might then be a Chilean as well as a Cuban model to inspire those who aspire for national liberation. Already it is clear that Chile is not endeavoring to "export" her revolution and is doing everything possible to avoid a mass exodus of refugees. Yet in the OAS she will certainly denounce the continued exclusion of Cuba.

Socialists, Communists and the Cuban Revolution

Although united in the FRAP electoral coalition, both parties retained their distinctiveness and autonomy. Thus, beneath the surface electoral struggle against common enemies, reaction to the Cuban Revolution was not necessarily identical.

Castro's Style. Unlike the youth sections of their parties, the Marxist leaders were primarily middle-aged politicians who may have been affected by Chile's evolutionary constitutionalist tradition. Even during 1960 when Allende's praise for the Revolution was most intense, he seldom neglected to observe that the violence and passion in Cuba reflected that country's distinctive history—moral corruption and prior dictatorship. The Chilean revolution would be peaceful and gradual.[108] And after his 1970 victory, it was reported that "Allende insists that he will work within the democratic system, as he has done all his life."[109] Attuned to Chile's legislative system, the Marxist leaders were incapable of adopting the roles appropriate to insurrectionary leaders or charismatic orators. Chileans tend to be formal, restrained and somewhat dour.

While they clearly admired the Cuban leader's heroism during the Sierra Maestra period and subsequently in openly defying the United States, the primary attraction of the Revolution lay in its programs and progress.[110] Yet, between the two parties there was some difference. Still reacting to their hardships endured during outlawry and reflecting the bureaucratic traits of organization-men, at least some Communist leaders disdained the impetuous and "tropical" temperament of Castro and other *barbudos*.[111] A less disciplined, more "open" and romantic political grouping, the Socialists naturally felt greater vicarious identification with Fidelista militancy and "adventurism." Even *before* the downfall of Batista, the Socialists had published a book praising Fidel's heroism.[112] Yet, when a decision on mass struggle confronted them in late 1960, both party elites reacted similarly. On Nov. 3, 1960, the CUT organized a mass rally to denounce the government's wage readjustment bill which was not fully compensatory for the prior inflation. In the course of his address, CUT President Clotario Blest, an ex-Social Christian who had been truly mesmerized by his visit to Cuba, bellowed that "(t)he heroic Cuban people have been capable of standing up to North American imperialism. . . . We Chileans must respond to this call and demonstrate a capability for creating our own Sierra Maestra. From this moment we must struggle with our arms, with our fists, with our strength and courage so that when the people take to the streets, nothing can stop them." As Blest concluded to workers' chants of "Revolution," "Revolution," he called out:

> Fidel, Fidel
> We will do as he did;
> Our next march
> Will be with rifles;
> In the street battles
> The working class will triumph!

The inspired workers then began an unauthorized march towards the central area of Santiago. When the Carabineros attempted to obstruct their way, the workers charged at the police lines. Then the Carabineros opened fire, killing 2 and wounding 35. Eleven members of the national police were injured. Blest was arrested for uttering seditious remarks, and the CUT called a 24-hour general strike to protest the government use of firearms. During the stoppage only 64,000 workers left their jobs.[113] Within a year, the Socialist and Communist leadership had forced Blest's resignation when he attempted to call another general strike, this time to protest a similar government wage bill.[114]

Tactical Questions. Castro never suggested during the period under study that guerrilla warfare or violent revolution was necessary or even desirable for a country with Chile's traditions and political system. Although he informed a Communist delegation in 1962 that the bourgeoisie had never surrendered power peacefully, Castro's attitude towards the "peaceful road" for Chile was skeptical rather than categorically negative.[115] And an electoral orientation was impliedly sanctioned by Che Guevara's admonition in his *Guerrilla Warfare:*

Whenever a government has come to power through some form of popular consultation, fraudulent or not, and the appearance of Constitutional legality is maintained, guerrilla insurrection is impossible since the possibilities of civic struggle have not been exhausted.

Even after Frei's victory in 1964, Fidel's reaction was not to imply that "the possibilities of civic struggle" had been exhausted.[116] And upon Allende's 1970 electoral triumph, Havana explicitly acknowledged the "revolutionary" character of the government-elect. Beatriz Allende Gozzeus was sent flying to meet with Fidel. Upon her return to Chile, she told her father that the Cuban leader knew him to be "a revolutionary"—it was unnecessary to prove it by impetuous measures against the bourgeoisie.[117]

Yet within both parties there emerged factions which advocated the preparation of armed units for an eventual insurrection. In the PC this element tended to draw primary inspiration from China, while the "Cuban example" was more influential within the Socialist Party. Although the dominant Socialist leadership occasionally spoke of the possibility that violent struggle might be necessary, they reacted with the Communist leadership by totally rejecting such proposals. Only when the "reactionaries" first resorted to armed force or trained such units would the Socialists endorse activities of this nature.

Communist Secretary General Corvalan went further and required not only that the "peaceful road" be blocked, but enough mass discontent to provide popular backing for such preparations would also have to exist. In the absence of these conditions, armed training was viewed as likely to provoke military interventions, sectarianism and "adventurism." Advocates of armed training were purged from the PC, while the PS permitted some to remain within its ranks.[118] The leaders of both parties probably feared prosecution under the Internal Security Law or outlawry which the right was insistently demanding. The impact of the 1948-1958 period upon the less respectable Communists conditioned a more unyielding leadership line against advocates of "*la via armada*."

FD vs NLF. Within the framework of electoralism, it seems clear that the course of the Cuban Revolution reinforced the Socialist commitment to the *Frente de Trabajadores* narrow radical coalitional approach. The early expulsion and withdrawal of bourgeois elements from the Revolutionary Government was seconded by Castro's view that the inevitable logic of a truly revolutionary struggle leads one to socialism and ultimately, Marxism-Leninism. This development culminated in his denigration of the "progressive" role of the national bourgeoisie in the Second Declaration of Havana. And if Socialist arguments along these lines were not enough, the desertion of a large PADENA faction and the unattractiveness of the FRAP coalition with its radicalized program to the major center parties clearly demonstrated to the Communists that their National Liberation Front tactic was inapplicable. As perhaps the best disciplined and organized party in Chile, they had the least to fear from a broad coalition,[119] which was not only the best means for dividing the bourgeois opposition but would provide valuable time for the neutralization of the armed forces.

This reasoning probably conditioned Communist efforts to establish a working coalition with the Christian Democrats in 1965 and again with Tomic during 1969. The negative PDC reaction in the first instance was countered by a Communist drive to undermine the rightist leadership of the Radical Party. Successful in this effort, they compelled the Socialists to accept the Radicals and MAPU as equal partners in the 1970 campaign. Hence, the second PDC declination of an "opening to the left"—albeit following an intense intra-party struggle—was accepted without undue disappointment. What was crucial, however, to both Socialists and Havana, was that a dedicated working-class oriented Marxist would wield the substantial powers of the presidency. Hence, the middle class elements were de facto junior partners.

In addition, for reasons already discussed, the left demonstrated great flexibility and courage by leading direct action mass struggles in the 1967-1970 period. In substance, then, the Communists were compelled to adopt quasi-*Fidelista* tactics similar to those sanctioned at the beginning of the decade. This undoubtedly pleased many rank and file PC militants and effectively deprived the NLF coalitional approach of any meaningful content. Hence, in the 1970 election the middle classes—with few exceptions—opted for the rightist candidate, as did many anti-Marxist lower class women.

Nationalism and Internationalism. If the Communists held tenaciously to their NLF principle and refused to heed Castro's developing thesis that only revolutionaries belong in revolutionary coalitions, it was not merely because Castro's own road to power belied this claim. To the Communists, Castro was a newcomer to Marxism and the world movement of which the Chileans had long been a part. Traditionally, they had idealized the Soviet Union and viewed its defense as the *sine qua non* for the ultimate expansion of socialism.[120] That the Russians repaid them by accepting a Frei bid for an invited visit during October 1963, precisely when FRAP was charging that he was so *entreguista* that his claim to be committed to a foreign policy "independent" of "both imperialisms" was sheer demagogery, did not shake the faith of the PC hierarchy.[121] Nor did a subsequent offer of $57 million in low interest credits to the Frei administration. They were fully aware that had it not been for Soviet aid, the Cuban Revolution might have dissolved in a sea of chaos or compromise with *imperialismo*. Hence, Cuban pretensions to tactical wisdom for the revolutionary struggle in other lands were a source of irritation rather than attraction. And the purges of old line Communists in Cuba—friends of the Chilean comrades—failed too as a basis of appeal.

Some of these Cuban phenomena had a different effect upon the Socialists. As an autonomous party which identified more with the revolutionary movements in underdeveloped and colonial regions than with the "Socialist Camp," the last thing the Socialists wanted was to become subject to Soviet discipline.[122] During the late 1950s, they were still articulating the APRISTA ideology of the thirties and early forties.[123] Hence, they reacted with much greater enthusiasm to the 26th of July Movement victory of January 1959 than did the PC.[124]

As Castro demonstrated that coalition with the Moscow-oriented Communists need not always result in domination by the latter, the Socialist commitment to a FRAP based upon a PS-PC alliance was almost certainly strengthened. Similarly, Fidel's continued assertions of relative independence from Moscow (UN inspection in 1962; refusal to sign the Treaty of Moscow; his tactical projections for revolutionaries in "a majority" of Latin American countries; the internal purge of "old" Communists) increased the attractiveness of the Cuban model for the Socialists. A "fashion oriented" party which adopted Titoism after disillusionment with Peronism, had finally discovered a truly worthy Latin American model.[125] Cuba's polemical attack upon the unwillingness of Communist parties in Guatemala, Brazil, Venezuela and Bolivia to support armed struggle during 1967 and 1968 also reinforced the Socialist commitment to OLAS as an evocative symbol.

Thus, the Marxist coalition was strengthened by the latitude for independent conduct which was evident in Soviet-Cuban relations. A FRAP or Popular Unity government would clearly need extensive Soviet aid. If this were extended bountifully to a "Marxist-Leninist" revolutionary government where the traditional Communists were controlled and the foreign policy was in some measure self-determined, then perhaps nationalism and internationalism were compatible.[126]

The Ultraleft

Hostility to FRAP. Beyond the mainstream of the Chilean left were a number of small parties with membership ranging from less than a score to several hundred. Ernest Halperin has described this as "a fringe territory populated by egregarious individuals and tiny splinter groups that incessantly combine and repel each other in the most varied combinations."[127] Mutual repulsion was, however, far more intense between all of these sects and the two major Marxist parties which were accused of bureaucratism and institutionalized reformism.

By virtue of its social nature, reformism is anti-revolutionary. It isn't mistaken nor does it follow an erroneous line: it is inherently and consciously anti-revolutionary. It reflects the retardation of the revolution, the accommodation of its leadership to the existing society. Its union bureaucrats, its political apparatus, its brutal and anti-democratic internal methods, its electoral social-democratic habits all manifest the existence of a basically conservative bureaucracy, whose destiny is intimately tied to the existing order, a bureaucracy, incapable of surviving a revolution.[128]

This statement by the Popular Socialist Party (PSP) youth, a conglomeration of former and neo-Trotskyists led by Clotario Blest and Oscar Waiss, fairly reflects an attitude shared by most of the ultraleftist sector.

The nexus of the conflict with the FRAP leadership centers upon the most appropriate tactics for gaining control of the state. According to Waiss, "(t)he argument that the world balance of power has changed is inapplicable in any real sense to Chile since the geographical proximity of our neighboring imperialist colossus neutralizes all other factors. Only Cuba destroyed that historical and geographical fatalism, but not with an electoral campaign. The Cuban experience continues to be ignored or to mystify those who have gone to the extreme of considering it a 'deviation' when in fact it is an example that should be imitated."[129]

With particular reference to the 1964 presidential campaign, Waiss contended that the FRAP attempt to attract middle class votes by advocating "moderate" reforms was foredoomed because it was quite obvious that once in power, the FRAP would begin a process resulting in the destruction of the existing socio-economic and political order. Hence, the truly damaging consequence of using a deceptively moderate propaganda line was that it prevented the left from demonstrating to the working class that the PDC was itself closely related to property-owning exploiting sectors. This could be made clear only if the FRAP resolved to lead the working class in mass strike actions, the occupation of factories and landed estates, and through the organization of armed self-defense squads during the electoral campaign. Such a militant tactic would force the PDC to adòpt a position which would clarify the demagogic nature of its anti-oligarchic pronouncements, i.e., it would side with the upper classes for "order," rather than "revolution." At the same time, the way would be cleared for the eventual confrontation with the Carabineros and the armed forces. Both would have to be restructured if a revolution were to be made.[130]

This argument was also propounded by the *Vanguardea Revolunionaria Marxista*, another neo-Trotskyist group. After a sector joined Waiss in organizing the PSP, the remaining members reorganized and held their First Congress during the early months of 1964. The resolutions stressed Waiss' points, and espoused the view that in fact the Chilean masses were not deeply committed to the parliamentary system. In addition, the Cuban Revolution was regarded as having proved that with the support of peasants, both the regular army and the police could be defeated—and so might *imperialismo*, provided the revolutionaries were "uncompromising."[131] Both the PSP and the VRM received an infusion of new members from PS resignees and expelees who had attempted to obtain control of that party at its February 1964 Congress.[132]

The assumptions and tactical views of the two previously mentioned groups were shared equally by the Trotskyist *Partido Obrero Revolucionario* (POR). As early as 1961, its leader Luis Vitale was proclaiming that "the Cuban Revolution has clarified the character of the Latin American Revolution and the Chilean one." To support his thesis that the masses had not internalized the values associated with juridical democracy, Vitale cited the fact that only 22 percent of Chilean workers were registered to vote, and but 20 percent actually voted.[133]

A year later, in his prologue to Fidel Castro's *La Revolucion Cubana contra el Sectarismo y el Burocratismo (The Cuban Revolution Against Sectarianism and Bureaucracy)*, which only the POR published, Vitale was to attribute defections from the Radical, Socialist and Communist parties to the impact of the Cuban Revolution.

The Cuban Revolution has clearly highlighted the problem of power, national and social liberation in a short time span for each one of the Latin American countries. It has sharpened the contradiction between the rank and file who want to proceed with haste to the revolutionary road and those leaders who are blocking them.[134]

It seems, however, that Cuba was less important than China to the PC defections. In March 1963, a Chinese Commercial Mission was established in Santiago, and within a short time *Pekin Informa* was being read by an estimated 6,000 subscribers. *Espartaco Editores* was organized by a group of sympathizers in the PC to disseminate Chinese propaganda. Following both a public letter from the Chinese PC to the Chilean one accusing the latter of not accepting the validity of the Cuban experience which proved that armed struggle was necessary to conquer power, as well as a homage to China by Chilean PC members, a quiet purge was instituted. Many of the "Maoists" who resigned or were expelled subsequently entered the *Movimiento Revolucionario Comunista* (MRC) which in turn joined the VRM in organizing the *Movimiento de Apoyo a la Revolucion Antiimperialista*. In 1964, however, the MRC expelled the *Espartaco* group because it was allegedly more interested in distributing propaganda than in organizing a revolutionary party. The MRC then fused with the POR, dissident neo-Trotskyist Socialists, Waiss and Blest in constituting the PSP.[135]

In 1965, less than a hundred university students organized the Leftist Revolutionary Movement (MIR). This and the concurrently launched journal *Punto Final* were explicitly *Fidelista* in nature. Their emphasis was upon the ultimate necessity *to be prepared* for armed struggle.[136] In addition, the struggle for state power required that the left sharpen the awareness of the lower classes concerning the bourgeois and exploitative nature of the state. Hence, it was necessary to foment militant mass attacks upon private property while simultaneously arming workers, peasants and students. Despite surveillance and occasional suppression by the Frei administration, the MIR more than tripled its membership during the 1966-1970 period. It also recruited a small number of slum dwellers and by 1970 had organized several militia units which possessed pistols and a few rifles. The MIR's principal effort, however, has been to polarize socio-political conflicts at universities and among *caliampa* dwellers.[137]

Campaigning for Allende. Despite their criticism and hostility toward the PS and the PC, most of these militant revolutionaries campaigned for Allende in 1964. Admitting that the FRAP program was not fully socialist in nature, Vitale nevertheless concluded that "voting for Allende means voting against the imperialists and the national bourgeoisie; it means voting for socialism, for Cuba, for a new social system." Acting under this assumption, "(t)he revolutionary Marxist groups, (POR, VRM) . . . the pro-Peking groups and the groups that left the SP, have fused with the rank-and-file of the mass Allende Committees . . . they bolster and encourage the radicalization now taking place among the Allendist

workers and help prepare them for the necessary transition of the electoral process into a direct revolutionary mass struggle." The Allendist committees were
regarded not simply as campaign committees, but as organizations which would
demand that the FRAP fulfill its electoral pledges and exert pressure for "direct
revolutionary action." Vitale reported that "some peasant committees also have
plans to immediately invade estates without waiting for 'bureaucratic procedures'." They would demand arms in the event of an attempted military
golpe.[138]

In the aftermath of Allende's defeat, the ultraleft concluded that the outcome had vindicated their view that FRAP tactical moderation had been as
important as the "Campaign of Terror" in contributing to the Frei victory—ideas
similar to those expressed by Waiss and Vitale in 1961 and 1962.[139] The VRM
reiterated its position that "(t)he revolutions of China, Cuba, Algeria, North
Korea, of Africa and Asia show us which is the true road to power."[140] Despite
this endorsement of violent insurrection, the ultraleft adopted the position that
in 1965 followers should cast blank ballots.[141] Nor did any of these groups send
contingents into the barren Andes or the forested south of Chile to establish
guerrilla focos.[142] Interestingly, they were not invited to the 1967 OLAS conference in Havana where the Chilean delegation consisted exclusively of PS and
PC leaders.

Undaunted, the ultraleft continued to reject what it regarded as futile FRAP
electoralism. Encouraged by United States-supported military interventions elsewhere in Latin America, the MIR and other entities began to covertly store arms
and to train followers. In 1969 these sectors encouraged the casting of blank
ballots or abstention from the congressional election. There were almost 39,000
blank ballots cast as well as 61,000 null votes. In addition, abstentions were un-
usually high—26 percent (868,808).[143]

If the electoral tactics of the Socialists and Communists had become radicalized for the 1970 campaign in accord with the earlier ultraleftist critique, so had
those of the latter. The MIR and other groups focused upon mass actions to the
exclusion of vote solicitation.

Following Allende's unexpected plurality, MIR flexibility was demonstrated
by a decision to support Popular Unity and to pressure the government for the
rapid implementation of its program. Days after the September election, a mass
rally was organized at which Allende was symbolically proclaimed president-
elect. General strikes and virtual civil war were threatened if the Plenary Congress declined to heed tradition.[144] The MIRists sparked the rapid growth of UP
committees and continued their mass invasions of private property. This is based
upon their assessment of the Brazilian and Indonesian coups. Only mass mobilization and revolutionary consciousness will, in their opinion, deter the military
from deposing the Popular Unity government and massacring leftists. Allende
has withdrawn all criminal charges against MIRists and may have permitted them
to organize a special Presidential guard under Cuban supervision. In any case,

before the end of 1970, Castro had officially recognized the MIR as part of Chile's revolutionary left.[145] And at their University of Concepcion stronghold, the MIR established a formal coalition with the Socialist youth, MAPU and even the Communist youth, their arch-protagonists.[146]

Los Fidelistas Violentes. Within Chile, the only groups that actually resorted to violence were to be found on the ultraleft. Most of these elements however, limited their activities to vigorous participation in mass demonstrations which were organized by the CUT and/or FRAP.

There is some evidence that in 1961 a group of ultraleftists was stockpiling dynamite and small arms. Although about forty persons were arrested, the police were unable to "prove the existence of an actual conspiracy."[147] In the Senate, Solomon Corbalan charged that mass arrests of PS and PC members represented a "frame-up" against the Left and were intended to justify repression of the Popular Movement and a break in relations with Cuba. The Socialist secretary general claimed that more than half of those arrested were rightist or CIA "provocateurs," and that the remainder were neo-Trotskyists.[148] Subsequently, Oscar Waiss was expelled from the PS when he publicly alleged that the party had received funds from Cuba for arms but had used them for electoral campaigning in 1961.[149]

Actual violence did occur in Santiago during the Missile Crisis. Both the *Vanguardia Nacional Marxista* and the *Movimiento Social Progresista* (ex-Radical youth) were implicated, although the latter group denied involvement.[150] Following an accidental explosion in the apartment of Gasper Gomez Ortin, the Political Police informed the press that:

Found in the flat were 30 sticks of dynamite, 38 detonators, other explosive elements and metal receptacles 11 inches long and having a diameter of two inches. Seventeen cases of Cuban revolutionary propaganda were also discovered in Apt. 51. Preliminary investigations linked the injured bomb-maker with Julio Stuardo Gonzalez, former candidate for deputy of the Radical Youth (Juventud Radical) Party. When police went to Stuardo's home on Monday morning to place him under arrest they also uncovered Fidelista leaflets. Some of the pro-Castro literature was signed by ex-CUT president Clotario Blest, leading to his subsequent arrest. Even though it has not been announced officially as yet, it is assumed that the organization to which Gomez belongs was responsible for some or all of the acts of terrorism which occurred in Santiago last week: one bomb (out of two) exploded near the Teatro Nilo; a similar bomb was set off at San Antonio 318; two 'Molotov Cocktails' and other inflammable material were placed at the entrance to the national headquarters of the Radical Party, Calle Augustinas 620, and a bomb was exploded at the Ford Motor Company's San Borja office. According to documents discovered by the police at the homes of those arrested, a large-scale terrorism campaign was planned. The plot included sabotaging the Cerro San Cristobal electricity center, the Santiago water supply system and other utilities. The bombs being prepared in the Calle Tenderini apartment, it is averred, were destined to be exploded at the offices of the United States Embassy . . . and the U.S. Ambassador's residence on President Riesco. The authorities are attempting to track down the source of the dynamite (the sale of which is restricted) as well as to ascertain whether or not the terrorist movement is being financed by foreign elements.[151]

One of the bombs had been detonated near the residence of President Alessandri. After the explosion in the Gomez apartment, "dozens of people were re-arrested, accused of terrorism and charged with being in the pay of the Cuban Embassy. The homes of several Trotskyists were searched and the POR leaders—among them its secretary, Humberto Valenzuela—had to go into hiding. Clotario Blest was arrested for the third time in a week—he had been arrested 23 times for having defended the Cuban Revolution—and charged while in jail." And a deportation order was issued against Luis Vitale, an Argentine by birth.[152]

Effective police suppression in 1962 probably deterred sectors of the ultraleft from resorting to violence in August 1964 when Alessandri terminated relations with the Cuban Government. During the campaign, however, Jacques Lagas was assaulted by FRAPists and unknown persons fired shots into the home of Matilde Ladron de Guevara. Both of these were ex-*invitados* who had written fiercely anti-Cuban books upon their return to Chile.

The leftist supported general strikes, *fundo* seizures and invasions of housing sites between 1967-1970 were accompanied by rising interpersonal violence. While official repression was often indiscriminate as in the army and Carabinero massacres at El Salvador (1966) and Puerto Montt (1969), the leftists were responsible for only a few kidnapped landlords and virtually no deaths.

In general, MIRists and other militant leftists physically seized university buildings or land. They would then defend their occupied holdings with whatever means were available—most often stones and clubs. While arms were used to deter official assaults against some "liberated" *fundos* and residential communities, this was exceptional in nature. During 1969, the MIR may have been responsible for bombing United States Embassy offices in Santiago and the nearby USIA Library. In Concepcion, a MIR stronghold, the USIA Library was burned down by arsonists. Although there were several spectacular bank robberies during early 1970, the MIR agreed to end violent provocations following Allende's inauguration.

Concluding Remarks

Since the Cuban Revolution symbolized the first hemispheric success in totally destroying capitalism and eliminating United States influence, there is nothing remarkable in the vicarious inspiration felt by Chilean Marxists and anti-imperialists.[153] Given the mass poverty and rigid social structure described in chapter 2, the leftists assumed that their identification with Cuban redistributive social restructuring would, when conveyed to the Chilean masses, aid their effort to obtain control of the Chilean state.[154] Their proselytization efforts were undoubtedly invigorated by visual or other exposure to the Cuban scene. And there is no doubt that the number of persons voting for Allende almost tripled between 1958 and 1964. It is less clear, however, how much of this increase can be *directly* attributed to FRAP identification with the Cuban Revolution. Cuban and FRAP access to the mass media was quite limited, and the overwhelming majority of leftist speeches and propaganda focused upon domestic issues divorced from any relation with Cuba.

The FRAP leadership was adapted to electoral and legislative roles. Hence, those who wished to follow Castro's armed road to power were forced out of the two major Marxist parties, each dominated by a well entrenched leadership. And even these ultra-*Fidelistas* failed to attempt an armed insurrection; nor were they recognized by the Havana government until after Allende's 1970 victory. Within the limits of the constitutional system—safeguarded by the armed forces—the FRAP leadership could only radicalize its program, praise the Cuban Revolution and organize demonstrations which did not draw a large attendance.

They were forced to fight for the presidency within a milieu characterized by majoritarian anti-Communist attitudes and "openness" to United States inputs which provided major aid to an already unfavorable structure of mass media. These reinforced an effective negative portrayal of the economic hardships actually suffered in Cuba after 1961, as well as its transformation into a Marxist-Leninist state. The virtually unreserved defense of every Cuban act by the FRAP leadership—and especially by Allende—during the 1959-1962 period also provided unexcelled source materials for the "Campaign of Terror" which probably accounted for a considerable part of Frei's 7 percent margin over Allende in 1964. The Liberals and Conservatives had jointly received more than 24 percent of the vote in the 1963 municipal elections. There is no doubt that their support for Frei was exclusively motivated by fear of the FRAP coalition; and this was contributed to by its association in an unreserved way with the Cuban Revolution.

The 1970 "Campaign of Terror" was equally, if not more, effective. It prevented perhaps two hundred thousand lower middle class persons who had been hard pressed by government tax increases, salary freezes, inflation and favoritism in promotions from following the newly "revolutionary" Radicals into the UP coalition. And then there were millions of lower class Catholic women as well as many impoverished small peasant owners. Hence, the UP candidates' percentage of the total vote declined by 2 percent (7 percent if we include Duran's 1964 vote).

It should be recalled that in 1969 the Radicals received 13 percent of the vote while the FRAP won about 30 percent if the PSU is included. Since Allende's 36 percent includes a large number of lower class occasional "independents" who don't vote in congressional contests as well as new participants to electoral politics, it is unlikely that the Radicals or MAPU brought more than 100,000 voters. Hence the psychological terror was almost certainly effective—more so because of outspoken Socialist identification with OLAS-Cuba in the 1967-1970 period. It was similarly reinforced by left-led mass militance, mass media disparities, Fidel's 26th of July candor and by the variables and relationships examined in chapters 3 and 5.

Self-Determination and Rejection: Chile's Center Groups

Introduction

The indirect effects of the Cuban Revolution were most portentous for Chile's two major center parties, the Radicals and the Christian Democrats. Between the 1930s and the late 1960s, these multiclass or "aggregative" parties effectively defined the limits of government policy. Symptomatically, they not only failed "to deliver" on their reform commitments, but also suffered progressively from internal ideological schisms. And this lack of factional or middle class cohesion was determinative in facilitating the installation of a Popular Unity government in 1970.

The Radical Party (PR)

Social Base and Programmatic Orientation. In recent years, the social background of the PR leadership has been more diverse than that of the rightist parties. While dominated by wealthy businessmen, landowners and professionals, these have often been the "new rich." The leadership has also included a number of Masons, Lebanese, Jews and Protestants, as well as civil servants and a few trade unionists. Pre-eminently a "middle class" party, its membership incorporated large numbers of government white collar employees, small businessmen, school teachers and better paid unionized blue collar workers.[1]

Traditionally, the PR has been Chile's anti-clerical party. Although many followers continued to share this sentiment, by the late 1950s the leadership was no longer opposing growing State subsidies to clerically operated schools. Similarly, despite some socialistic traditions and programmatic commitments, since the early 1940s the party has functioned more as a brokerage organization than as a force for social reform. Although it had expanded educational opportunities for the lower middle class and some blue collar sectors, much of the party's energy had been expended upon securing state subsidies and risk assumption for import substitution industries. When they became profitable, such protected enterprises were sold by the government to businessmen. By the early 1950s the possibilities of import substitution had been largely exhausted as had those of playing the Socialists off against the Communists. Tarnished by a series of scandals and corruption, the Radicals placed third in the 1952 presidential election with less than 20 percent of the vote, thus ending fourteen years of government rule.[2]

Although the leadership of the party was dominated by conservative, proconservative enterprise and pro-United States elements until 1967, there was a minority left-wing—dominant in the youth section of the party—which drew inspiration from the Socialist and anti-clerical tendencies in the party's heritage. While most public employees, particularly at higher levels, who constituted a major PR constituency tended to oppose structural reforms, a significant minority were sympathetic to state collectivism.[3] There were other factions which were primarily opportunistic or patronage-oriented. Hence, indiscipline and frequent disunity have been consequential to the party's heterogeneous ideological and social composition. This diversity was not apparent from the occupational or educational characteristics of the PR's congressional contingent, probably due to domination of the party by upper strata elements. Hence a survey in the mid-sixties revealed a higher proportion (77 percent) of university graduates than among Liberal parliamentarians (58 percent). At the time, less than one percent of the population held university degrees! Occupationally, 68 percent listed "politics" while 13 percent identified "education." "Agriculture" was indicated by 6.5 percent while "business" was referred to by a bare 3 percent![4]

1958 Presidential Campaign. As a consistent opponent of the directionless and scandal-ridden Ibanez administration during the 1950s the PR had improved its position measurably in the 1957 congressional election. At the party's 20th national convention during June of that year, a program was adopted which failed to stress any need for socio-economic reform. The most radical planks pledged "a more just distribution of wealth" and "defense of the economic interests of the salaried classes."[5] In his campaign for the presidency the following year, PR nominee Luis Bossay, a member of the left-wing of the party, "did not seriously challenge the position of the landed elite," and urged government aided and supervised industrialization. His leftism was manifested by charging that the *Nuevo Trato* copper laws which had substantially lowered taxes in 1955 were "too favorable to American owners."[6]

The left-wing of the PR had urged Bossay to withdraw in order to maximize Allende's chances. Members of the party's right-wing had disregarded his candidacy and worked for Alessandri. And Bossay was subsequently to accuse other "Radical leaders of having sold out his candidacy to Frei." As for Bossay himself, it was charged that "(h)e knew full well that his failure to withdraw his seemingly doomed candidacy might mean an Alessandri victory, yet he chose to remain in the race." In the aftermath, the Radical "candidate" asked those who had actually supported him to abstain in the Congress when the two presidential candidates having the greatest popular support (Alessandri and Allende) were voted upon. But Bossay was overruled by the party's *Comite Ejecutivo Nacional* (CEN).[7] Receiving less than 16 percent of the total vote, he had done worse than the PR candidate in 1952.

Radicals and the Cuban Revolution. Official Radical statements on Cuba during the first seven months of the Castro government were virtually nonexistent. The dominant pattern of response was indicated in August 1959 when the CEN indirectly criticized the Cuban government for not holding elections.[8] At about the same time, however, a prominent Radical professor and Dean of the Economics Faculty at the University of Chile was visiting Cuba as were editorial staff of a pro-Radical daily, *La Tercera de la Hora.* Luis Escobar Cerda, who would subsequently be appointed as Minister of the Economy by Alessandri, had some qualified praise for the Cuban Agrarian Reform.[9] *La Tercera* temporarily adopted a more favorable view of the Cuban position in the OAS.[10] And Luis Bossay observed in the Senate that despite his lack of faith in the OAS, he still hoped that it would intervene in the Dominican Republic which was attempting to subvert "strong democracies" such as those in Cuba and Venezuela.[11] Although the party leadership mildly criticized the Chilean Ambassador to the OAS for voting with three dictatorships—the United States having abstained—against Cuban agenda proposals for the Santiago Foreign Ministers Reunion, the CEN subsequently expressed its approval of both the outcome of the conference and the role of Foreign Minister Vergara.[12] The party ignored the CUT protest rally.

Between April and July 1960, a position of clear hostility to the Castro regime emerged. Although he agreed to sign the "Traveling Letter" defending Cuban self-determination during April, Bossay was reported to be critical of the Revolutionary Government's policies.[13] At about the same time, the Santiago Provincial Council of the PR released a declaration warmly welcoming Eisenhower.[14] And not long before the anti-Castro OAS Foreign Ministers Conference opened at San Jose in August 1960, the CEN resolved to call upon the foreign ministry to sever relations with the Trujillo regime because of its alleged complicity in an attempt to assassinate Romulo Betancourt. This policy-making group also resolved

(t)o deplore that the regime ruling in Cuba, although conceived with the high purposes of overthrowing the dictatorship and instituting social justice, is not on the road towards the creation of an effective democracy despite the fact that eighteen months have elapsed since its inception.

The declaration went on to urge that the OAS assume a major role in "resolving the difficulties which have developed" in United States-Cuban relations.[15]

During August 1960, PR leaders Julio Duran and Ulises Correa denounced the Castro regime for betraying its "fundamental promise" to "constitute a broad and true democracy." Cuba was also charged with "being administered by international Communism"[16] At the time of the Bay of Pigs, the CEN failed to adopt a position due to internal conflict, although a majority were reported to be particularly concerned over Castro's "violation of human rights" and the "menace" which the Cuban regime signified for hemispheric peace and security.

After the United States admitted complicity, the CEN adopted a resolution condemning Castro for destroying representative democracy, recorded itself as being opposed to unilateral intervention that contravened international law and urged that collective action be taken through the OAS. A majority was opposed to joint military intervention.[17] Endorsing the AFP some weeks later, PR Vice President Carlos Martinez Sotomayor—soon to be Alessandri's new foreign minister—urged that efforts be made to bring Cuba back into the Inter-American System through negotiations.[18] This attitude by Martinez and a center-left faction was partially responsible for Chilean opposition to the imposition of mandatory diplomatic and economic sanctions upon Cuba at the Punta del Este Conference in January 1962.[19]

Characteristically, as at the time of the Bay of Pigs, the CEN did not adopt a declaration until the most acute stage of the missile crisis had passed. On Oct. 29, and after "heated debate," a CEN majority forced through a resolution calling upon Alessandri to break relations. The president of the republic had opposed a similar rightist petition with the argument that such a rupture would disrupt important trade! After the CEN vote, Martinez Sotomayor informed the majority of his impending resignation as foreign minister. The CEN majority reacted by amending the resolution to omit the objectionable demand. As amended, the declaration nevertheless "resolved to condemn the Castro regime for violating the Declaration of Human Rights, for its totalitarianism and because it is an ideological and military base of the Soviet Union." In the Chamber of Deputies, Radicals joined the rightists in defeating a PDC-supported FRAP resolution calling upon Kennedy to end the blockade.[20]

Although a CEN majority supported Alessandri's opposition in 1963 to OAS mandatory sanctions upon Cuba, they readily accepted his direction to heed the OAS directive.[21] Campaigning for the presidency—or better said, against Allende—Julio Duran had openly advocated the imposition of such sanctions.[22]

The party's youth and a small CEN minority led by Professor Alberto Baltra had expressed open sympathy for the socio-economic revolution within Cuba during 1960 and 1961.[23] They never denounced Havana either for the adoption of Marxism-Leninism or for that government's close ties with the Soviet Union. During the missile crisis, the youth did criticize the Soviet Union for using Cuba as a "pawn" in the Cold War, but an even more vigorous denunciation was reserved for the United States blockade.[24] This neo-Marxist sector of the PR did not question the Cuban Premier's refusal to schedule elections, and consistently defended Cuban self-determination.

Reaction to the 1961 Congressional Election. Within months of Alessandri's narrow victory, the PR had joined the Rightist parties in collaborating with his administration.[25] By August 1960, following a slight setback in the April municipal elections, the PR had joined the PL and PCU in organizing the Congress. During the same month, Julio Duran denied that the Cuban model was suitable for a Chile characterized by greater "civic maturity." He then suggested the timeliness for agrarian and other reforms in Chile, which might lessen support for extreme revolutionary measures.[26]

After the Radicals failed to do more than hold their own in the March 1961 congressional election, Duran attached a new urgency to his warning that unless the 40 percent of the population residing in rural areas were incorporated into modern society, existing conditions would "invite the adoption of solutions which are offensive to our consciences as free men." The Radical leader supported his argument by referring to President Kennedy's AFP.[27]

The party reacted quickly to the AFP and the Marxist gains in the recent election. At their 21st National Convention in June, a new reformist program was ratified. The assembly also authorized entry into the Alessandri administration provided that it accepted reforms as a means of saving Chile from Marxism.[28] The PR's newly assimilated reformism encompassed an agrarian reform involving a "broad program of expropriation" of non-productive lands as well as "transformations in the social, economic and cultural structures of the country" which would provide "broad access" for the "working classes." It advocated democratization of the educational and cultural system, improvement in the social security system and a tax reform to redistribute existing national wealth.[29]

When the PR joined the rightist parties by accepting posts in Alessandri's Cabinet during August, a large sector of the party's youth resigned.[30] Some of them organized the Progressive Social Movement, which was allegedly implicated in the violence that occurred during the missile crisis. The leaders' sense of urgency was heightened in April 1962 when a CEN member, after touring the party's local *asambleas* in various parts of the country, reported that because of the slowness of the government in proposing reforms, "ninety percent of the members want our party to withdraw from the Government."[31]

The party leadership reacted by both arguing for more emphasis upon land distribution and taking the lead in driving Alessandri's AFP agrarian reform bill through the legislative process.[32] Shortly after the bill was sent to Congress, PR President Jaime Torme declared:

We are going, then, to make this reform with full faith in our democratic capacity to bring about deep social and economic transformations without renouncing our liberty; in a similar way we are going to implement in the near future other equally important reforms in the fields of taxation, customs and education.[33]

The theme of liberty was reiterated during Senate consideration of the proposed agrarian reform legislation. On July 26, 1962, former PR President Aguirre Doolan admitted that the popularity and urgency of the AFP-backed bill was "obviously" due to the "Communization" of Cuba and the related fear that if no action were taken, the peasants would support violent solutions in Chile. Similar motivation was reflected by Julio Duran.[34] A week earlier, *Ercilla* news analyst Hernandez Parker had reported:

Obeying the dictates of Kennedy and of his Alliance for Progress, the majority of the CEN wanted to present before the Conference of Punta del Este, an urgent Agrarian Reform bill to be implemented with the velocity of a satellite by means of decree laws.[35]

Although they also had adopted a fear-inspired reformist orientation, the rightist parties were less closely attuned to the new goals of United States foreign policy. In any event, the Radicals were compelled to restrain their apparent impatience until a carefully considered bill was formulated.

Rise and Decline of the Frente Democratico. Despite strong internal opposition to Alessandri's currency devaluation, the party resolved at an October 1962 National Assembly to remain in the government. During the same month the FD pact was signed with the PL and the PCU. As mentioned previously, its objectives were to save Chile from Marxism by: supporting the government's reform program; running joint candidates in 1963; attracting the PDC, if possible; and supporting a common presidential aspirant in 1964.[36] Duran, already the unofficial nominee for 1964, quickly foreclosed a coalition with FRAP by charging: "(t)oday, Cuba is there; they (Cuba and its Chilean supporters) only want to enslave these lands."[37] Within eight weeks, the PR's National Executive Committee had designated an Anti-Communist National Committee of the Radical Party with the objective of purging any members "who spoke in favor of Cuba."[38] From December 1962 until Frei's victory, Duran was to stress the Cuban-Communist issue in his campaign against Allende.[39]

The Radicals suffered mild losses in the 1963 municipal elections while their rightist allies experienced a major defeat. In the weeks and months that followed, the PR began to be afflicted by desertions, and the view soon prevailed that little was to be gained by remaining in the government.[40] Not only was inflation becoming very severe, but the still popular Alessandri had declined to endorse Duran. A pretext for withdrawal from the government was seized upon in September. This was an issue which hopefully might win the Radical candidate lower middle class support in 1964.

The continuation of the 'illegal' strike of national health (service employees) . . . including close to 20,000 . . . affiliated with the Radical Party, exacerbated longstanding divisions within the governing coalition and plunged the country into political crisis. When Congress, with the support of the Radical Party, passed a Socialist-sponsored bill obliging the Central Bank to provide funds for the striking workers and President Jorge Alessandri Rodriguez vetoed it, four members of the Cabinet, all Radicals, resigned. They were Carlos Martinez Sotomayor (Foreign Affairs), Benjamin Cid (Health), Luis Escobar Cerda (Economy), and Pedro Enrique Alfonso (Agriculture).[41]

Actually, the Radicals had already forfeited the support of many public employees due to their backing for government real salary reductions since 1959.[42]

Hence, within a month, FD President Gonzalez Videla was predicting that only Frei could defeat the Allende coalition.[4 3] This became seemingly obvious when the PCU *Frente Democratico* candidate was sabotaged by Radicals and defeated by Socialist Oscar Naranjo during March 1964 at a by-election in Curico. It is worth noting that little anti-Communist propaganda was distributed in the Curico district despite a vigorous FRAP campaign.[4 4] This is surprising since the area "had always been considered a conservative stronghold";[4 5] hence, at this time and in such a locale a continuation of the "campaign of terror" identifying a Naranjo triumph with an increased chance of victory for the "Communist candidate" Allende should have been particularly effective. When considered in light of Conservative claims that some Liberal and many Radicals sat on their hands, it becomes suggestive of a manipulative effort by Jova and his associates in the Radical and Liberal parties.[4 6] For although the FD candidate still polled almost 33 percent of the votes (to Naranjo's 39 percent), Duran seized the defeat as a pretext for resigning as the FD candidate.

Role of the Duran Candidacy. The left-wing minority faction in the Party CEN countered by demanding a national convention where they believed a majority of local delegates would accept Allende's post-Curico invitation to join a broadened FRAP.[4 7] Following their defeat in the CEN, some remained in the party, others resigned and a number were expelled for publicly endorsing Allende. A majority of the national leadership meanwhile renominated Duran as the party's candidate, even though it was obvious that he had not the slightest chance of securing a plurality.[4 8]

The decision to maintain the Duran candidacy was motivated by a number of factors. Foremost was a desire to prevent those Radical followers and members who would never vote for a Church-backed Catholic candidate from supporting Allende.[4 9] In this way, it reduced the chance that Allende might obtain an absolute majority. Given the unexpected support that he had received in 1958, one could not be certain what might happen even though public opinion survey data indicated Allende would not receive a plurality.[5 0] If Allende received a plurality, the ultimate choice would rest with Congress where in exchange for patronage and a role in the Frei government, the Radicals could have constitutionally elected a second-ranked Frei as president.[5 1] In fact, many Radical activists may have campaigned for Frei.[5 2]

Since Allende offered key ministries and other major concessions to the PR in May if Duran would withdraw, there was nothing to be gained by maintaining the candidacy as a bargaining weapon for a role in a future FRAP government.[5 3] Nor would PR association with the FRAP have reduced its viability as a party. Jova had persuaded Duran that his candidacy was necessary to ensure that Allende would not receive even a plurality. Had Allende secured a plurality, there is some evidence of a pre-electoral intra-party "pact" to vote for Frei in the Congress, where he needed only six PR votes while Allende would require at least 46 non-FRAP votes. And at a press conference on April 7, 1964, Duran had opined that it should not be assumed that a popular plurality for Allende would necessarily be heeded by a congressional majority. Allendista congressmen had refused to vote for Alessandri in 1958, and this time the system was at stake.[54]

In the aftermath of the Frei landslide victory, the Radicals adopted a policy of partial obstructionism in the Congress. Receiving but 5 percent of the presidential vote, Duran charged that Frei's victory reflected mass commitment to representative democracy rather than support for the PDC program.[55] To the dismay of the PR leadership, Duran's token support in 1964 was followed by major losses for the party in the 1965 congressional election, when the Radicals lost nineteen deputies and three senators while obtaining but 13 percent of the vote.

Radicalizing the Radicals. While maintaining their major party status between 1965 and 1969, the Radicals were unable to fully recover the white collar constituency initially lost to Frei, and subsequently to the Nationals. In terms of Chilean social structure, these businessmen, professionals and privileged *empleados* were directly threatened by Marxist egalitarian policies. And ironically, under the Frei government large capital intensive enterprises and limited lower sectors were the recipients of major government subsidies and income transfers.

During the initial two and a half years of Christian Democratic administration, the PR leadership was clearly on the defensive and lacked an effective strategy for challenging the dominant PDC. Hence while there was no difficulty in supporting a lethargic and moderate government agrarian reform,[56] they only offered partial support for Frei's "Chileanization" agreement and a Constitutional Amendment that enhanced potential government control over private property.[57] While the opportunistic Radicals undoubtedly would have liked to follow party tradition by joining the government of the moment, the self-righteous and prepossessive Christian Democratic leadership was disinclined to consider such an option. In part, United States confidence and backing nurtured PDC ambitions to pre-empt Chile's political spectrum from extreme left to extreme right.

All neo-Marxist elements had by no means deserted the PR. And others returned. Meanwhile, in addition to launching an intensive rural organizing effort after 1965, it is here conjectured that the PC encouraged its sympathizers to become active members in many Radical local organizations.

Following a minor improvement (16.1 percent) in the April 1967 plebiscitory municipal elections over their dismal 1965 tally, a national party convention was scheduled for July 1967. When the locally elected delegates assembled at the 23rd National Convention, it became immediately apparent that neo-Marxists—largely from professional and blue-collar occupational constituencies—were in a majority. A ringing declaration denouncing the Frei government for its unwillingness to implement structural reforms was adopted. Similarly, United States imperialism in the Caribbean and Vietnam was sharply impugned. Despite a paucity of references to Cuba, "pro-Marxist" Alberto Baltra Cortez was elected president of the party. Not only had Baltra been president of the Chilean-Soviet Friendship Society, but he had also visited Cuba as an *invitado*. Of equal significance, with the active backing of Cuban Ambassador Juan Jose del Real he had replaced the anti-Communist Mathilde Ladron de Guevara as president of the Chilean-Cuban Cultural Institute in 1960.[58]

Symbolizing a Radical movement toward a coalition with the left, the PR had supported a successful Socialist senatorial candidate in a by-election shortly before the 23rd National Convention. Although the Socialists and Communists reciprocated—once the Ampuero faction was forced out of the PS—by backing unsuccessful Radical candidates in by-elections during December 1967 and May 1968, neither could attain a plurality. Nevertheless, they did very well in light of constituency characteristics.[59]

For perhaps the first time in their history, Radical leaders called themselves "revolutionary" as well as "democratic" as they attacked the Christian Democrats from the left in the 1969 congressional campaign.[60] While their ability to adopt such an electoral approach is suggestive of Frei's failure "to deliver," it also reinforced the Communist strategy of inducing Socialist leaders to accept a traditional middle class party as a coalitional equal. The failure in 1969 of the PR to improve upon its 1965 congressional constituency (about 13 percent both times) and the ominous decline from the 1967 municipal elections when the party had attained 16 percent should be viewed from the perspective of Socialist and Communist gains which amounted to an additional 5 percent of the total vote in 1969. Hence, the Radicals and Communists could not seriously champion Baltra Cortez as a presidential nominee of a unified left-center coalition. This in turn made it possible for the PS to accept the Radicals within the somewhat ambiguous *Frente de Trabajadores* tactic.

But the attainment of Popular Unity also occasioned the defection of Julio Duran and other anti-Socialist Radical leaders. They organized the Democratic Radical Party with the explicit implication that the left-led Radical Party was "undemocratic." The PRD joined the Nationals in campaigning for Alessandri in 1970. Communism and *Fidelismo* were the major themes in the heavily funded anti-UP propaganda campaign. Given white collar attitudinal parameters, it is probable that much of the Radical constituency heeded the PRD's call to support Alessandri.

The Christian Democratic Party (PDC)

Origins. In 1957 the Social Christian Party and the National Falange (FN) merged to form the non-confessional Catholic Christian Democratic Party

(PDC). The former represented a civil libertarian sector that had withdrawn from the Conservative Party over the issue of outlawing Communism in 1948. Conservative Party origins also characterized the FN, which had advocated a movement for "national regeneration" in the late 1930s. Following their forced withdrawal from the party, the Falangists supported the Popular Front government and participated in the Radical administration of President Rios (1942-1945). After opposing Gonzalez Videla's persecution of the Communists, the small FN remained in opposition during the 1950s.[61]

Social Composition and Principles. Professional and managerial offspring of the upper upper classes (i.e. the 'old' families) were more prominent in the PDC leadership than in the PR. At the same time, lower middle class semi-professionals also appear to have played a prominent leadership role. During the early 1960s, a number of peasant and urban labor leaders were incorporated into the directive stratum of the party.[62] Worth some emphasis, however, is the fact that propertied elements played a major role in leading the PDC.[63] In 1965, for example, fifty of eighty-two deputies were owners of rural estates (*fundos*).[64] And during the 1964 presidential campaign, "the financial resources of the PDC were said to have been nearly fifteen times those of the Left."[65]

Inspired by Catholic social doctrine, the new PDC was *formally* committed to Communitarian principles. Although vague in some respects, they implied worker participation in management and profits of large industries as well as a substantial role for the state in introducing new industries and regulating the economy. Ownership, however, was to be vested ultimately in local communities or employees. While major social reforms to raise the cultural and social level of the lower classes were envisaged, the necessity of promoting "class-struggle" was categorically rejected. Persuasion via appeal to Christian conscience and cooperativism were more in harmony with the party's neo-Thomistic philosophy.[66] The PDC was open to non-Catholics and did not propose a merger of Church and state. There were also some corporativist tendencies within the party. Their origin was in the Falange of the 1930s which drew limited and qualified inspiration from then current Italian and Spanish movements. As the FN's association with the Popular Front government suggests, these sympathies were not dominant.

The 1958 Presidential Campaign. Following Frei's refusal *to write a letter* requesting PCU support, both rightist parties rejected his bid for their backing.[67] Jorge Ahumada was *then* assigned the task of drafting a vigorously reformist program advocating "institutional change," "industrialization," and an "immediate rise in lower class living standards." It differed from the FRAP platform by: 1) not calling for an immediate distribution of land to the peasants; 2) not increasing taxes upon United States mining firms; 3) promising to provide incentives to foreign investors; 4) not advocating a "democratization" of the army; 5) not pledging nationalization of the United States owned Chilean Electric Company; 6) advocating an improved security effectiveness for the OAS; and 6) promising to introduce "just prices."

The mild agrarian reform was designed to stimulate an immediate increase in productivity and to provide social benefits for the peasants who would receive land at some future date. Monopolies were to be eliminated and tax rates to become more progressive. Major commitments of expenditure were destined for housing, education and public works. Unemployment and very low wages would be ended while *nonforeign owned* businesses were communitarianized through direct employee participation in management and profits. There would be government economic development planning with both incentives and sanctions for private enterprise in its assured sector. Finally, the social security system and the public administration were to be reorganized. Like the FRAP, the Christian Democrats advocated trade ties with the Soviet Bloc.[68]

Although two factions of the Ibanista *Partido Agrario Laborista* and the *Partido Nacional* supported the PDC candidate, Frei received only 20.7 percent of the total vote. Allende had exceeded this by 8.1 percent, while Bossay polled 5.1 percent fewer votes than Frei. Nevertheless, Eduardo Frei's support was more than double the percentage received by Falangist candidates in the 1957 congressional election, and highlighted the emergence of the PDC as a major political force. While Frei had engendered strongest backing in middle class districts, his appeal was manifest in rural as well as urban areas.[69]

Pattern of Responses to the Cuban Revolution. Although PDC leaders were somewhat more interested in Cuba than those of the Radical Party, their evaluations were remarkably similar. The director of the official party journal was Jaime Castillo, a prominent Chilean member of the Congress for Cultural Freedom who enjoyed the unofficial reputation as party "ideologist."[70] In editorials, articles under his byline and other insertions, *Politica y Espiritu* emerged as an ardent critic of the Cuban regime. As early as his first months in power, Castro was being denounced for the "circus trials" of Batistianos.[71] By July 1959, the journal was reproaching the dictatorial and "anti-anti-Communist" tendencies of the Cuban leadership.[72]

The tempo of these attacks increased during 1960 when they incessantly denounced Cuba's relationship with the Soviet Union. Although the party organ generally justified United States diplomatic moves in the intensifying conflict with Havana, reservations were expressed concerning the wisdom of unilateral or collective military intervention.[73] With very few exceptions, the *small number* of articles reporting Cuban social or economic developments emphasized their "irrationality" and "collectivistic" orientation.[74] Unabridged versions of all major Church documents attacking the Cuban government were printed.[75]

The Party consistently refused to participate in FRAP protest demonstrations against the policies of the Alessandri administration in the OAS, or in opposition to United States policies towards Cuba. In July 1959, a declaration was adopted expressing general sympathy for the Cuban Revolution and its right to self-determination, but no support was voiced for Havana's view that sanctions should be imposed upon the Dominican Republic, nor was Cuba's OAS economic development agenda proposal endorsed.[76]

During the 1960 San Jose OAS Foreign Ministers Conference, *La Libertad*—a PDC daily that ceased publication that same August—enthusiastically endorsed the outcome of the meeting which was considered to be "directed exclusively against Cuba."[77] Officially, the party did not assume a position on the conference.

The first official condemnation of the Cuban regime by the party leadership appeared in the April 1961 Declaration of Millahue. It was reportedly premised upon

Frei's concept of 'anti-Fidelism,' which holds: 1) The Cuban Revolution is legitimate and 'its original program with which it was made and presented to the world abroad was and still is fully valid for Latin America,' 2) Condemns the refusal of Fidel's Government to hold elections and denounces 'the distortions, exaggerations and manifest abuses which notoriously have characterized the revolutionary government's domestic and foreign policies,' and 3) Proclaims its categorical opposition 'to all forms of aggression against the sovereignty of the Cuban people by any other nation, whether American or non-hemispheric.'[78]

Hence, *during* the Bay of Pigs invasion the National Council *politely* petitioned Kennedy *not to intervene* and asked him to support efforts at the U.N. and in the OAS to peacefully resolve the crisis.[79] Yet, the PDC and its entire leadership studiously avoided direct criticism of the United States subsequently for its admitted responsibility for the aggression. Similarly, the Party *boycotted* the CUT general strike and the protest rally.[80]

No declaration was adopted by the party when Cuba was expelled from the OAS. At the time of the missile crisis, PDC deputies supported an abortive FRAP resolution urging Washington to lift the blockade—*but only after provisions criticizing the United States were deleted.*[81] On Oct. 30, the party released a declaration *totally endorsing the United States view* that the "installation of offensive military bases by the USSR on Cuban territory clearly threatened continental security as safeguarded by the Rio Treaty, and that any freely and collectively determined action to verify their presence and eliminate them as a danger which was taken by the hemispheric community was legitimate." It also observed that the expulsion of Cuba from the OAS system due to Cold War bloc rivalry had driven her into closer dependence upon the Soviet Union, and *mildly* admonished the United States for acting unilaterally on the first day. Finally, the resolution urged that a peaceful solution be sought at the OAS, and especially in the United Nations.[82]

In 1962 and 1963 the PDC published a number of books or pamphlets which fiercely condemned the Castro government upon one or more of the following grounds: the growing role of the Cuban Communists; authoritarianism and repression of oppositionists; and efforts to subvert other Latin American nations.[83] During the 1964 presidential campaign, the PDC supported Alessandri's opposition to mandatory diplomatic and economic sanctions.[84] But following the July 1964 Washington accord, Frei and Party leaders refused to become involved in suggesting what course Alessandri should adopt.[85] After relations with Havana were suspended Frei expressed approval and implied that in view of Argentine pressures, the issue should remain non-political.[86] Although he had assailed the economic blockade of Cuba during the campaign, after his victory both Frei and his foreign minister declined to assume any initiative in bringing Cuba back into the Inter-American System. The new government *rejected a trade offer* through Spain, and adopted the position that it would cooperate in a collective effort to reintegrate Cuba *only after* that nation ended its close association with the Russians.[87]

Within the party, there was some variation of opinion regarding the Cuban Revolution. At one extreme were Castillo and those who in early 1959 adopted a hostile view. Others, such as Radomiro Tomic, Julio Silva, Patricio Hurtado and Alberto Jerez were impressed by the "moral purity" of the Castro group and the revolution's mass backing. As individuals they devoted some attention to the social reforms, and strongly criticized the United States. Because of its support for vested Cuban and United States interests in the old Cuba, Washington had literally created a self-fulfilling prophecy by driving Fidel into the arms of his only source of major material support.[88] The party's youth section went so far as to demand the exclusion of the United States from the OAS.[89] Party policy evidently represented a compromise weighted in favor of those sharing the Frei-Castillo pro-United States perspective. This was evidenced in 1965 when the government perfunctorily and with restraint voiced its disapproval of the United States invasion of Santo Domingo.

At the Vina del Mar and Punta del Este Latin American economic conferences later in the decade, the Frei administration joined a majority of nations in complaining that United States trade-aid policies were dysfunctional for economic development.[90] It was not until 1970 that Chile consented to trade garlic and beans for a small quantity of Cuban sugar.[91] And this was clearly an electoral maneuver influenced by Tomic's populistic campaign tactics.

Challenge of the First National Convention. Following Frei's impressive showing in the 1958 presidential balloting, the PDC scheduled its First National Convention for May 1959. This assembly reiterated the goal of a Communitarian and Christian society. Social reforms and a mildly nationalistic foreign policy were set forth as the party program. They included:

1. modification of the OAS so that members might reduce arms spending without jeopardizing security;
2. priority for Latin American economic integration;
3. intensification of all types of relations with West European investors and nations—and "eventually with the Soviet area"—"as an equilibrating factor and counterweight for our present relations with the United States";
4. opposition to Chilean participation in Cold War conflicts;
5. greater attention by the Inter-American System to: the stabilization of export prices; economic and social development and reform; and '(t)he promotion of democracy through agreement upon effective methods of demonstrating solidarity with legitimate governments; and for ensuring that governments respect the liberties and rights of citizens.'

The assembly of PDC leaders expressed its firm commitment to political decentralization, pluralism and civil liberties. Reacting to Allende's near victory in the recent election, the convention emphasized its conviction that Christian Democracy was the "only dynamic" alternative able to save Chile from dictatorship and communism. In so doing, it endorsed the widely shared belief that social injustice and mass poverty within the context of economic underdevelopment would cause such undesired results.[92]

Because the PDC leadership righteously *defined* itself as "the only dynamic alternative" to Marxism, it followed that no coalition was possible with the FRAP so long as the Socialists refused to end their alliance with the Communists.[93] The latter were defined as the principal danger for Chile. As if to prove their dynamism, PDC legislators rivaled FRAPists in presenting bills in the Congress for agrarian reform and rural unionization during 1959.[94]

First Declaration of Millahue. The Christian Democrats had rejected a FRAP invitation to join in condemning Eisenhower's early 1960 visit to Santiago as integral to anti-Cuban diplomatic efforts.[95] When Adlai Stevenson arrived shortly after the chief executive's departure, Frei impressed upon him the PDC view that it was *the only effective alternative* to Communism. And he warned the United States emissary that unless Washington resolved to finance public sector enterprises and increase economic development assistance so as to reduce social inequality there would be a grave danger of Communist success in the country.[96]

Following substantial gains in the 1960 municipal and the 1961 congressional elections, a plenary meeting of the PDC National Council was held at Millahue. A proposal for a coalition with the FRAP that had been drafted by a leftist faction led by *invitados* Rafael Augustin Gomucio, Alfredo Lorca and Alberto Jerez was rejected, as was another for an "opening to the Right" by Juan de Dios Carmona and Tomas Pablo. Radomiro Tomic, also a former *invitado* closely associated with Frei, successfully argued that the party should emphasize its reformist image by assigning higher priority to such goals as agrarian reform, a new labor code and a new corporation law that would aid small business and inhibit monopoly. Insofar as reactions to the AFP, Cuba and the recent PS-PC gains were concerned, it was subsequently reported that

... Christian Democracy maintained its support for the Kennedy Plan 'which in substance acknowledges the viewpoints that have been expressed upon many occasions by our party.' . . .

Agrarian Reform is the most urgent issue for Chilean parties these days. Nobody rejects it outright since President Kennedy transformed it into the pivot of his 'Alliance for Progress.'. . .

It is the simple and unquestionable demonstration of a reality. The Chilean parties, from left to right, know that the existing order is at the edge of a revolutionary abyss. If democratic methods are not used to institute the reforms, the danger persists that they will be effectuated in the Fidelista way, with its consequential blood, pain and suffering.

This explains the attitude of the insurgent and renovating groups in the Conservative and Liberal Parties. It also serves to explain the Radical haste for an Agrarian Reform, the ever more aggressive Christian Democratic hostility to the 'capitalist system' and the semi-revolutionary animus of the FRAP leaders and activists.[97]

Communism, Cuba and the PDC-FRAP Polemic. In the weeks following the Millahue meeting, a public exchange of letters occurred between PC Secretary General Luis Corvalan and Frei, already the unofficial PDC nominee for 1964. Corvalan advocated a united front to enact tax, agrarian and judical reforms, while Frei reiterated the basic incompatibility of the Communist creed (athiest, materialist, class struggle) with that of the PDC (Christian, spiritual, libertarian, opposition to class struggle).[98]

During July 1961, Radomiro Tomic urged that Chile require the mining companies to refine more copper in the country, and introduced the concept of "Chileanization" for the *Gran Mineria*.[99] While addressing the Third World Conference of Christian Democracy two weeks later, Tomic again stressed the need for socio-economic development reforms, and endorsed the AFP.[100] Continued PDC support for the AFP—albeit within a framework of criticism that reforms were being implemented too slowly or that the terms of trade issue was being ignored[101]—prompted Corvalan to charge at the beginning of 1963 that FRAP's principal difference with the PDC centered upon divergent attitudes toward *imperialismo*.[102]

In March 1962, the Christian Democrats had rejected overtures from the rightist and Radical parties for a broad anti-Marxist coalition, claiming again that the PDC was "the only organized force capable of defeating Communism."[103] Although a half-hearted attempt was made some months later to attract PS support for a PDC candidate in 1964, it was rebuffed by the Socialists.[104] In December 1962, PDC President Renan Fuentealba categorically rejected the possibility of coalition with the Socialists since in his view that party was intent upon installing a Castroite dictatorship in Chile.[105] And when the FRAP proclaimed Allende as its candidate in January 1963, the National Council of the PDC released a declaration which warned that a FRAP victory in 1964 would transform Chile into a Soviet satellite and result in a Castroite type of dictatorship with a similarity of both goals *and methods* to those employed by the Cuban leadership.

The joint thinking of the Socialist and Communist Parties can be characterized as an attempt to follow the model set by Fidel Castro's revolutionary Government in Cuba.

In effect, as we all know, not the Cuban revolution itself, but the subsequent course followed by Castro is unconditionally accepted by both parties. We may add that the Communist and Socialist leaders, in unison, have done all in their power to involve the Chilean people in the most fervid types of support for the Cuban Government, its leaders and its acts. On this point there are no grounds for controversy, reservation or reflection. Certainly, nobody can ignore that such sentiments of admiration, carried at times to proxysm, have a very real political significance: It's a question of whether the people will adopt the goals and methods of the Cuban revolution.

And we should all know that among those methods are the elimination of elections, the prohibition of parties, the installation of an official philosophy imposed by the State, the physical persecution of the adversary, etc.[106]

The Communists countered by denying that civil liberties would be violated by a FRAP government in the absence of rightist terrorism, and by charging that the PDC, in turn, was subservient to *imperialismo*. This allegation was vehemently denied by PDC President Renan Fuentealba, who retorted that his party would judge the AFP strictly by its results. Fuentealba again identified his adversaries with *el paredon*, a defamatory symbol of the *Cuban execution wall with which the FRAP would be incessantly associated* in the course of the succeeding twenty months. The PL youth charged that as in 1961 the PDC was only using the "Christian Democracy or Communism" alternative for electoral purposes, while the Conservatives praised the Christian Democrats for their virile anti-communism.[107]

The Second Millahue Conference. Both the PDC and FRAP considered the April 1963 municipal elections as indicating a trend for 1964. During the campaign, PDC propaganda continued to stress the theme first introduced in late 1962—that the FRAP goal was a "revolution without liberty but with *paredon.*" Despite their protestations that distinctive methods would be used, the electoral returns and PADENA disunity indicated that the Marxist coalition was losing middle class appeal. Similarly, FRAP candidates had received only 15 percent of the female votes as compared to 40 percent from males. While the FRAP share of the total vote fell from 31 percent in 1961 to 29.5 percent, that of the PDC increased from 15 percent to 22.7 percent.[108]

Following the April balloting, a second PDC Plenary National Council was held at Millahue. The leadership consensus was that the *Frente Democratico* coalition continued to represent the major threat to their aspirations for a 1964 victory. Radomiro Tomic suggested that an attempt be made to forge a working agreement with the FRAP. Otherwise, he argued, a very large margin over the FD would be needed since "(i)f we defeat the Democratic Front by very few votes, they might elect the second in the Plenary Congress." The National Council rejected this reasoning. In the Chilean Plenary Congress, the PDC had distinguished itself from the FRAP by voting for Alessandri in 1958, after he had won a narrow plurality. The Millahue gathering ratified Jaime Castillo's proposal that the party go it alone with its own candidate in 1964.[109]

The Drive for the Presidency. During August 1963, 6,288 Freista women from all parts of Chile were brought to Vina del Mar for a "Congress of Chilean Women." The reformist program was disseminated and the women returned to their communities to intensively propagandize for "the only alternative."[110] Within eight weeks Frei was visiting Moscow and the Vatican—the former to undermine FRAP charges of *entreguismo* (being a supine retainer of Washington), and the latter to strengthen his identification with Catholicism.[111] The image of "assertive nationalism" was reinforced in May 1964 when Jacob Javits publicly intimated that if Allende were victorious, United States aid might be terminated. The PDC National Council retorted by declaring that "(w)e repudiate the warning of Senator Javits that if the Chilean people should elect our adversary, that such a decision would provoke North American reprisals."[112]

Following the FRAP victory in the Curico by-election, it was reported that "(t)he leaders of Christian Democracy are convinced in the aftermath of the 'breakdown' at Curico that Frei and no other candidate will capitalize upon the fear of Allende. And that his second presidential candidacy will be strengthened by this fear."[113] During April, the PDC intensified its propaganda drive identifying Allende as "the Communist candidate" and a FRAP victory with tyrannical images of the Cuban Revolution.[114] About fifty full time staff personnel had been employed by Frei's campaign organization, as had the services of such public opinion research firms as Salas Reyes and International Research (Associates).[115] Both had previously done contract work for United States government agencies.[116]

April 1964 also was marked by the release of a "Third Declaration of Millahue." Emphasizing Frei's commitment to rapidly introduce major reforms (i.e., the "Revolution in Liberty"), the document pledged:

1. land to 100,000 peasant families within six years;
2. 360,000 housing units during the same period;
3. classrooms for several hundred thousand not in school;
4. 3,000 university loans to needy students;

5. wage readjustments equal to prior inflation;
6. suffrage for illiterates;
7. other goals as outlined in the 1958 and 1961 programs.

Denying that anyone would be deceived, the "Third Declaration of Millahue" announced *the* major issue in the presidential campaign was the choice of

either the revolution in liberty of Frei, or the communist revolution of Allende. No other alternative exists. . . .

And that, in view of recent world events (Cuba, Brazil), it was evident that the immense majority of the nation would swing behind Frei, who would institute revolutionary changes but without violating either the democratic system or the conscience of Chilean women and men.

Insofar as the right was concerned, support would be welcomed "no matter from where it came."[117]

Shortly after the PL and PCU endorsed Frei, the PDC candidate sought to enhance his appeal to Radical supporters by arranging a well publicized meeting with the Grand Mastery of Masonry. Aristoteles Berlendis was assured that the separation of Church and state would be maintained. Frei requested that the Masons not support any candidate. The Grand Master replied that the Masons never supported presidential candidates, but since Allende was a member it was natural that a majority viewed his candidacy with sympathy.[118]

During the last weeks of the campaign, the Freistas sponsored mass demonstrations and carried the "campaign of terror" to unprecedented intensity. Neighborhood committees organized "teas" for maids, and workers were informed that operations would cease if Allende won.[119] In the final hours of the campaign, a frenzied plea to "the women of Chile" was illegally broadcasted. Juanita Castro's script had been prepared and taped under CIA supervision in Brazil and was placed on a nationwide network with the assistance of Christian Democrats and locally-based Cuban exiles.[120] It may have accounted for a fair proportion of the 63 percent of the female votes which were cast for Frei. Although the PDC nominee received 56 percent of the total vote, women accounted for 85 percent of his margin. The relationship of Church influence to their support will be assessed in the following section of this chapter.

Equally striking was the broadly aggregative nature of Frei's constituency. He was particularly strong with urban white collar voters in Santiago and Valparaiso where more than 40 percent of the electorate backed him. Another important supporting group was made up of poorly paid blue collar workers in the tertiary sector—many of which interacted frequently (and identified) with the middle classes. Even among industrial workers—particularly those residing in mixed middle-lower class residential districts—he made major inroads. While a majority in most districts containing more than 40 percent industrial workers opted for Allende, the latter's share was substantially less than it had been in 1958. Similar gains for Christian Democracy were in evidence among better paid miners and in rural areas. Here, medium sized farmers joined small town clerks and tradesmen in flocking to Frei's banners as did numerous isolated tenants yet under landlord influence. While many semi-illiterate PDC supporters were probably attracted by Frei's pledge to institute a "Revolution in Liberty," it is likely that somewhere between 40-60 percent were catalyzed by the rightist-PDC "Campaign of Terror."[121] Some, of course, were simply heeding the advice of local priests, landlords or other employers. During 1969-1970, many of the non-programmatic Frei backers had shifted their support to the Nationals and Alessandri. Of the reformist constituency, the majority remained with Tomic, while perhaps fifty-thousand defected with MAPU to Popular Unity.

Electing "A Congress for Frei." In the aftermath of his "smashing victory," Frei sent missions to the United States and Europe to secure additional external financing for his administration. They reiterated *la unica alternativa* (the only alternative) theme.[122] After resuming relations with the USSR, an attempt was made to divide the demoralized PS by offering a Ministry of State of Raul Ampuero. CLASC, an anti-CUT rival labor confederation, was given additional financial resources.[123]

More effective than these moves was the deluge of "urgent" legislation which Frei sent to a specially convoked congressional session. Reflecting Frei's decision that he "would not try to work with the existing Congress,"[124] Chile's leading newsweekly Ercilla reported:

(t)he Government bills ignited the political atmosphere. They indicated that in La Moneda (the Chilean presidential palace) there was 'a planning machine' that was functioning 24 hours a day. The impact upon public opinion was also significantly reinforced by the coordination of official propaganda, obligatory daily radio chain broadcasts (by all stations), and the trips by Frei and his ministers to various parts of the country.[125]

The requested congressional action embraced the following area: a constitutional amendment permitting the president to dissolve Congress once during his term if an irreconcilable deadlock existed; authorization for him to reorganize the public administration; "Chileanization" of the *Gran Mineria*; a new property tax and an increase in inheritance taxes; a 100 percent wage readjustment to compensate for the severe inflation in 1964; and legalization of *Promocion Popular*, a PDC program to organize and train local leadership within a hoped for stable constituency among slum dwellers. This paternalistic proposal involved the provision of subsidies, equipment and technical advice to Neighbors' Committees, Mothers' Centers, social clubs, etc.

Only the wage readjustment bill was enacted. Congressional delays or opposition to other bills were used by Frei to justify their dramatic withdrawal after only eight weeks of consideration. Charging that the Democratic Front parties had opposed his bills with the rationale that he and not the PDC program had been voted upon in September, Frei declared that this issue would be resolved by the electorate in March.[126] And when the new Congress was elected, the Christian Democrats scored major gains at the expense of all parties save the Communists and Socialists. Securing an absolute majority in the Chamber of Deputies, the PDC also won a plurality in the Senate. "Many Christian Democrats were almost as stunned as were the opposition parties at the extent of their victory." And due to the d'Hondt system of proportional representation, the victors were "heavily overrepresented" in the new national legislature. In the Chamber of Deputies, the PDC held 82 of 147 seats, while 13 Christian Democrats sat in a 45 member Senate.[127] For "revolutionary" anti-oligarchic measures, there were 14 FRAP senators and conceivably two or three left-wing Radicals. In neither house of Congress did the right (Nationals and 75 percent of the Radicals) hold even a third. Frei's party was thus given a mandate and an opportunity to implement its program for a "Revolution in Liberty."

The Frei Administration: Oligarchic Representation and Blue-Collar Incorporation. If "the congressional election gave Frei a 'blank check' in terms of political opportunities,"[128] it is equally true that the government failed to use this mandate. Despite the "anti-capitalist" campaign rhetoric, after five years of PDC rule, a careful student of the Chilean political process concluded:

the basic situation of the lowest income groups had not been altered by the Frei policies, taken as a whole. In fact, those policies have responded much less to the needs of the disadvantaged than to the interests of the privileged entrepreneurial or industrial bourgeoisie.[129]

Before examining how this posture indirectly contributed to the rise of a Popular Unity government, some effort should be devoted to explaining the phenomenon.

Rhetoric notwithstanding, Frei and the dominant faction of the party had always been members of and identified with entrepreneurial strata. Had this not been so, the Liberals would not have been disposed to support his 1958 presidential candidacy. Nor, for that matter, would the Kennedy and Johnson administrations have provided such generous assistance.[130] In fact American Ambassador Ralph Dungan (1964-1967) was compelled to leave Chile because of his open *oficialista* sympathies and intervention. Given these antecedents, the corporate role in financing the 1964-1965 campaigns and Frei's cooperative attitude toward the *Gran Mineria*,[131] it is unremarkable that:

(a)lmost without exception, Frei's cabinet ministers and close advisers have come from the right wing of the PDC and from conservative groups outside the PDC. The tendency to surround himself with men whose orthodox economic and social views inspire confidence was accentuated by Frei's February, 1968 cabinet reshuffle, which made his, as one publication called it, 'a government fit for business.' Even in the one area originally thought to be the preserve of more leftist PDC technocrats, agrarian reform, pressure from the 'officialista' branch of the party and big landowners forced the resignation of Jacques Chonchol, the radical vice-president of INDAP.[132]

This *oficialista* anti-radicalism was even apparent as early as 1965, when the PDC "tacitly" joined the Right in backing a Radical congressional aspirant in Magallanes Province against a FRAP candidate.[133]

Hence, after demonstrating an inclination to bargain with Liberal and Conservative landowners over the pace, extent and nature of agrarian reform,[134] the Chilean President arranged a conference with the Chairman of the SFP (Manufacturing Development Association). At this meeting, Frei asked for employer representation in "planning the national economy," and stated "that co-ordination between the Government and private interests would shortly be considered."[135]

Many businessmen had given early backing to Frei's *oficialistas*. While a substantial number even joined the PDC, they did not thereby consent to "anti-oligarchic" reforms of the socio-economic structures.[136] They were reassured by the appointment of William Thayer as labor minister. He was on the board of directors of the CIA-associated ALFLD. Thayer remained as minister of labor until February 1968. This despite the fact that the August 1966 PDC National Convention had directed party leaders to resign if they also insisted upon holding responsible positions in ORIT or the AIFLD.[137] This followed the public disclosure of CIA links to these organizations.

Thayer, as previously noted, had presided over an effort to undermine the CUT by establishing a dual union movement. In the urban areas, MUTCH was subsidized while in rural areas, the CIA-funded International Development Foundation was permitted to aid the Christian Peasants Union (UCC) in its competition with FRAP to organize agricultural laborers—Allende's major rural constituency![138]

INDAP (Institute for Agrarian Development) officials complained that this was in competition with their own efforts to organize peasants. United States AID subsidized the IDF-UCC campaign while simultaneously denying funds to CORA for the expropriation of large estates.[139] What is particularly important here is that while the government provided limited aid for unionization, it resolutely opposed the creation not only of a united labor movement, but even of strong Christian trade union federations. Thus, the government refused to amend labor code provisions which proscribe industry-wide bargaining and it declined to legalize public sector unions. Similarly, it was unwilling to renounce official authority over determining which unions are "legal." In rural areas, the same pattern of weakness and fragmentation prevailed.

This recalcitrance pleased employers and the United States, as did Frei's *mano dura*[140] crackdown on independent left and Radical led unions. But the same policy also antagonized Christian union leaders who complained of various manifestations of pro-employer bias as early as November 1966.[141] Christian trade unionists also were denied representation in high level party councils and government planning agencies.[142] The neo-corporativistic *oficialista* strategy was to incorporate the masses via weak organizations which were dependent upon official sponsorship. In the process, energetic lower class potential leaders were to be coopted and trained in the official communitarian ideology. At the same time these "leaders" were expected to persuade lower class followers to forsake social reforms which were incompatible with maximizing production, i.e. anything that contravenes investor incentives. The ultimate goal was a "Mexican" type political regime.[143]

The Failure to Reform. Frei's commitment to maintaining a healthy investment climate based upon *oficialista* identification with the entrepreneurial stratum explains the non-fulfillment of the "Revolution in Liberty" program. We do not draw any sharp distinction between the Chilean upper classes and external businessmen. Hence, by the end of the Frei administration, an estimated 50 percent of national industry was directly or indirectly owned by foreign—principally United States—investors. And this denationalized sector was the most modern and dynamic one. While Frei's government sought higher prices for Chilean exports and encouraged foreign mining firms to do more processing in Chile, it also sanctioned major tax concessions as did his predecessor Jorge Alessandri.[144]

Ironically, towards populistic and Marxist representatives of the lower classes Frei adopted a "no-bargaining" attitude. Those who demanded social concessions were denounced with "anti-patriotic" and "counterrevolutionary" invectives.[145] His style towards rural landowners was erratic though generally conciliatory since many PDC leaders owned *fundos* or were closely related to such persons. Hence, while the green light was given to organize rural laborers in 1964 in competition with the FRAP's FNI, bargaining with the right delayed the enactment of a new Agrarian Reform law until after the PDC setback in the 1967 municipal elections. During this period, most expropriations resulted from labor conflicts. There was little in the way of credit or technical aid extended to small farmers. Meanwhile the Frei Government had excluded "productive" estates from expropriation. A few thousand small farms were distributed, and much of the land being prepared for such purposes was of low fertility (if formerly private) or had been transferred from State institutions. Even CIA-funded UCC leaders criticized the government for lack of consultation and a failure to indicate what would and what would not be expropriated.

In many areas new rural minimum wages—decreed in 1965—were unenforced by the government. We have already referred to the May 1966 mass dismissals of peasant union sympathizers. Symbolic of the administration's lethargy was its failure to enact legislation recognizing the right of peasants to organize until

February 1967.[146] Some peasants, had apparently returned to the rightist constituency in the March elections. These 1967 agrarian laws finally provoked a clash with the Nationals who charged that the president was depriving starving Armed Forces of necessary equipment and had acted weakly in the recent Beagle land crisis. Frei reacted violently by unlawfully imprisoning PN leaders.[147]

Although Chonchol's forced resignation in 1968 served to allay the right—so that it was willing to back Leighton in 1970—many prominent notables continued to harbor deep resentment toward Frei's arrogance and haughty style. Their animosity was increased by the government's failure to expropriate a significant number of estates owned by PDC leaders. Heightened mass militance in rural areas compelled the government to increase the tempo of expropriations in 1969-1970.[148] Tomic's campaign was another important consideration as was the ominous defection of PDC populists. Tomic's leftist program did not, however, inhibit the interior minister from ordering the arrest and prosecution of "the Revolutionary Left and Fidelista sectors of the Socialists" who were leading mass assaults against private property.[149]

Notwithstanding this intense mass struggle only 30,000 families had received land mortgaged land titles by September 1970.[150] This was less than a third of what had been pledged in 1963-1965. Actually, more than 50 percent of these plots were not distributed until the 1969-1970 election years when Tomic's campaign and fear of electoral defeat were dominant factors as was PDC disintegration. Hence, as of December 1968, "(o)nly 404 asentamientos . . . had been established, settling 14,594 families; and land had been directly distributed to another 994 families."[151] What truly enraged the landlords was the use of agrarian reform appropriations to indoctrinate peasants in PDC communitarian ideology during the three year asentamiento training period.[152] This is why Chonchol was forced out of INDAP in 1968. In addition to unionizing more than 75,000 peasants—double the percentage recruited by the UCC—INDAP and CORA had organized 123,000 small landowners.

By 1969-1970, more than 500 peasant unions and five times that number of "fundo committees" had been constituted in the PDC and UCC drive to preempt the political system from extreme left to extreme right.[153] By January 1970, all types of unions of rural laborers accounted for but 104,000 out of 230,000 agricultural laborers. There were, however, 394 separate unions.[154] Although they occasionally coordinated their efforts at the communal or even regional level, the government was in general little more than neutral towards landlord dismissals or refusals to obey the minimum wage law of about United States $0.80 per day. Similar indifference was manifested with regard to establishing cooperatives among small farmers.[155] Despite this the UCC had managed to organize about 30,000 laborers by late 1967 and this figure was probably doubled toward the close of the Frei administration.[156]

Although the government only expropriated land of "marginal quality" during its first four years,[157] its credit and price incentives to large farm owners were inefficacious in stimulating a major rise in productivity. Hence, while agricultural output increased by 6.2 percent (4 percent per capita) in 1967, the rate of increase in 1968 was a mere 1.8 percent (−.4 percent per capita).[158] A United States AID-funded study by the Economic Research Center of Santiago's Catholic University which was prepared in 1968 concluded that government policies would engender "at best" a 1.1 percent increase in per capita agricultural output between 1965 and 1980. According to the investigators, this was due to: 1) low prices; 2) inadequate highway construction and maintenance projections; 3) inadequate allocations of public capital for investments; and 4) uncertainty as to tenure rights.[159] A drought in the northern sector of the Central Valley during 1968 reduced 1969 output to 5.2 percent (7.4 percent per capita) less than 1968.[160]

Frei's record in promoting national economic growth has been a total failure. Despite two billion dollars in foreign exchange due to record copper prices, and notwithstanding major foreign investments in mining and secondary sectors, Chile's per capita growth rate was almost identical to the stagnation during the Alessandri period.

Nor has the government eliminated unemployment. Despite, for example, a new inflow of foreign capital of $347 million in 1968, the grossly underestimated rate of unemployed in Santiago during June of that year was about 6 percent. A year later it had risen to 7.1 percent.[161] By 1970, it had reached 11 percent in the industrial center of Concepcion, which gave Allende a plurality.[162] In Santiago, the rate fluctuated around 7 percent in March 1970. In this city Tomic came in third. According to a World Bank study, the real rate of unemployment was about 20 percent.[163]

Even copper output expansion was unimpressive. In 1968 it actually declined by .4 percent. The 1969 increase over 1967 was but 3.8 percent. Copper prices—normally about $.40 per pound—were: $.54 (1966); $.49 (1967); $.53 (1968); $.67 (1969).[164]

Table 8-1
Chilean Gross National Product: Rate of Increase

Year	Total	Per Capita
1961	6.2	3.6
1962	5.0	2.4
1963	5.7	2.1
1964	4.2	1.6
1965	5.0	2.4
1966	7.0	4.6
1967	2.3	0.0
1968	2.9	0.6
1969	3.1	0.7

Source: Economic Report of the Minister of Finance, November 27, 1970. Reprinted in *El Siglo*, 28 de noviembre 1970, p. 16.

In general, as mass militance increased and modest social reforms were promulgated after 1966, capitalists—especially domestic ones—declared an investment strike. Rather than increase productive capacity, they imposed higher prices. Hence, while the rate of inflation had declined from 38 percent in 1964 to 17 percent in 1966, by 1968 it was close to 27 percent. In 1969, the figure exceeded 30 percent as it did in 1970.[165] Frei's failure to control inflation occasioned a defection of many middle class salary earners to the Nationals.

The *oficialista* pro-capitalist bias weakened their price control restraints and debarred a *mano dura* policy towards recalcitrant investors. This bias also prevented the government from inducing expansion by widening the market through rapid Latin American economic integration, another PDC pledge. It was not until May 1969 that an Andean Common Market Treaty was even signed, and as of July 1970 the Chilean government had not even decided upon particular tariff reduction proposals.[166]

Copper prices notwithstanding, economic disaster—as opposed to mere stagnation—was only avoided by large scale foreign credits. In 1968, external debt increased by 2.4 percent while it rose by 14.7 percent during 1969 when major refinancing was arranged. Foreign debt obligations increased from 1.6 billion dollars in 1964 to more than 2 billion in 1969. And the rate of expansion for non-copper exports was lower than it had been under the Alessandri administration.[167]

The failure to stimulate investment cannot be attributed to government support for urban labor. Trade union representatives were not represented in national planning agencies such as ODEPLAN (an office directly associated with the presidency), and as we have noted there was a two year drive to weaken the CUT. According to a scholarly sympathizer with the PDC, by 1969 organized labor was "poor financially, divided politically and hamstrung legally." No more than 25 percent-30 percent of the organizable work force were in unions.[168]

A leftist expert uses the figure of 27.4 percent for December 1969. This includes: 200,404 blue collar members of 1,361 *sindicatos* (unions); 235,000 members of illegal public sector unions—mostly white collar; and 503,261 white collar employees in the private sector.[169] But according to official data, 25 percent of the wage and salary workers were already organized in December 1965 when the average industrial union had 225 members![170] While there was a substantial growth in rural labor unions so that almost 50 percent of the laborers were organized by 1970, government indifference contributed to only marginal urban growth. Hence, between 1963 and November 1966, the Chilean affiliate of CLASC increased from 18,359 to 68,520 members. These, however, were enrolled in 140 industrial and 209 rural unions.[171]

This official apathy strikingly contrasted with the government's zealous efforts to organize slum dwellers in mothers' centers, neighbors' committees, socio-cultural clubs, etc. By the end of 1967, more than 500,000 persons were associated with the 15,000-20,000 *Promocion Popular* entities, while about

70,000 had attended government subsidized courses in PDC communitarian ideology. Although 70 percent of the membership were in Santiago, the PP campaign extended to all urban areas. Child care, cottage industry and various self-help activities were the official goal of these mass incorporating organizations.[172] Unfortunately for the government, quite a few of them elected leftists to leadership positions! Nevertheless, they formed the basis of Tomic's urban constituency and therefore may be viewed as moderately successful. Neeedless to say, they brought some very limited material improvement to the lives of hundreds of thousands of *callampa* residents. This was also consequential to the government's tacit support for the dissemination of artificial contraceptives and the use of experimental injections by North American non-governmental agencies.

Although the government's housing program began with an impressive 50,000 housing starts in 1965, it had fallen to less than 20,000 the following year. For low income persons, the Housing Corporation (CORVI) provided foundations, utilities, some technical advice and loans to purchase construction materials.[173] Gripped by inflation and government opposition to compensatory wage adjustments between 1966 and 1969, many recipients spent their funds for other necessities. By 1970, 200,000 "concrete floors" had been poured. These, however, are undoubtedly encompassed within the government claim that a total of 260,000 units had been constructed.[174] Hence, nothing was erected on many of these foundations. The total of 260,000 falls far short of what had been pledged, and it includes much middle class housing which was also subsidized by the state.

The only "reform" which Frei fully attained was one that was heavily funded and directed by the United States AID. Moreover, as we saw in chapter 3, it was a typically middle class response to social immobility. Education rather than income distribution was the preferred means for attaining "social justice." Hence, whether or not they could afford books or obtain subsequent jobs, schools were provided for all primary age students. By 1966, 1,500 new buildings had been erected, and the total number of schools had tripled by 1970.[175] Primary enrollments increased by 46 percent, secondary by 117 percent and university matriculation rose by 124 percent. Professors were retrained and new curricula were devised with North American assistance. Education, of course, is a primary means of political socialization. In the long run the new texts and teacher training would strengthen the inculcation of anti-Marxian middle class attitudinal orientations.

The "Chileanization" of the *Gran Mineria* was revealed to be "little short of a disaster" according to one Christian Democratic sympathizer.[176] Reduced tax rates and high prices contributed to "fantastically high . . . profits enjoyed by the United States companies."[177] In addition, Kennecott had originally agreed to invest only $12 million of its own funds to expand facilities. For its 51 percent interest in one of the least profitable large mines in Chile, Kennecott not only retained control of management, but was paid $160 million for assets with a book value of $65 million.[178] This was regarded as scandalous! Frei was finally pressured into forcing Anaconda to sell its assets. Because of the generous terms, this too was criticized by the left and even by Tomic—himself "more of a demagogue and an authoritarian than Frei." Ironically, in order to outmaneuver proponents of nationalization, Tomic had coined the "Chileanization" slogan in 1961. By 1970 he was demanding—as a PDC presidential nominee—that Anaconda and all other foreign mine operations be nationalized.[179] After his inauguration, Allende waited but a few weeks before a suitably drafted Constitutional Amendment was sent to the Congress for majority approval.

At the close of the Frei administration there remained: 350,000 landless rural families; 50 percent of the children undernourished; over half of the population surviving on less than $30 a month; an illiteracy rate of 11 percent (down from 16 percent); and many government employed white collar workers were still earning between $30 and $40 per month.[180] The government had failed to reform the social security system.[181] Naturally, the communitarian principle of worker participation in industrial profits and management had been discarded after the 1965 election.

Through 1968 at least, capital gains on the sale of stocks were untaxed. While an 8 percent property tax was imposed, up to 50 percent of one's income tax could be credited against it. With regard to 1965 tax obligations, "(i)neffective enforcement reduced yields to slightly more than one-third of their potential." "More income is concealed from tax authorities than is reported to them." Combined tax yields for 1965 were 3.1 percent of personal income as compared to 10.5 percent in the United States. Most evasion, which persisted at least through 1968, was centered in the 90,000 or so upper class tax payers.[182]

Considering the foregoing, one must be cautious in accepting official claims that the highest fifth of wealth holders possessed 25 percent in 1965 but only 20 percent of the national wealth in 1970. It is similarly alleged that the lowest fifth increased its net holdings from 2.5 percent to 5 percent during the same period. Frei has also stated that official data show a real increase in wages and salaries of 62 percent between 1964 and 1969.[183] Viewed differently, "(i)t is estimated that real wages for urban workers have risen by about 40 percent during 1964-1969."[184]

Ironically, the last mentioned source attributes Frei's failure to control inflation to his "inability to control wages." Considering this and the rise in regressive taxation under his administration, it becomes apparent that Christian Democratic government in Chile cannot claim credit for any redistribution in wealth or income.[185]

Social amelioration through wage increases was generated by mass struggles led by the left. In 1967 strikes resulted in the loss of 1,990,000 man days. This increased to 3,652,000 in 1968 and fell to 972,000 in the 1969 election year. Because "their advice (was) ignored," even PDC union leaders deserted the gov-

ernment to seek unity with the FRAP-led CUT.[186] While it would be unfair to
say that the government did nothing significant for lower class Chileans, it would
be more injudicious to ignore Frei's obvious failure to "transform (Chile's) institutions, accelerate its development, and permit it to end inflation, to create jobs
for its youth and its workers, and to incorporate them into new standards of
living."[187] Both communitarian principles and social restructuring were consigned to memory after the 1965 election. Hence there was some truth in
Castro's view that while he promised a "Revolution in Liberty," Frei delivered
"Liberty with Blood." The massacres at El Salvador in 1966 and Puerto Montt
in March 1969 justified the Cuban denunciation as did frequent brutality by the
Grupo Movil in suppressing demonstrations. Symbolically, one of President Allende's first measures was to order the Carabineros to avoid all confrontations
with workers and peasants. He has also prohibited rent increases and submitted a
law raising wages in excess of prices. Vigorous enforcement of *existing* tax legislation will, according to the UP Finance Minister, yield a 50 percent increase in
tax revenues.[188] Frei's failure attests to the necessity of confronting rather than
cooperating with the oligarchy if one is indeed committed to egalitarian social
reform.

Electoral Decline and Party Disunity. If communitarianism and egalitarian reform commitments were not taken too seriously by Frei and his dominant *oficialista* faction, they were regarded as being of utmost importance by the populist
elements in this aggregative entity. While a distinct minority numerically, the
rebeldes were scattered through various government departments and they were
prominent as party organizers in the PDC peasant, student and trade union departments. A substantial number had visited Cuba where their egalitarian and
anti-imperialist predispositions had been reinforced. Similarly, daily contact with
the underprivileged masses served to heighten their impatience with Frei's commitment to maintaining incentives for foreign and domestic investors.

As early as October 1965, twenty-five PDC congressmen and youth leaders
drafted an internal party statement which concluded with the ringing declaration: "(w)e do not believe that the revolution has begun."[189] During 1966, discontent spread to second rank professionals in the government. One congressman was expelled (the *invitado* Patricio Hurtado) for statements of a critical
nature made during a trip to Cuba, and a second (Lorenzini) resigned.[190]

The June 1966 Second Trade Union Congress of the PDC "strongly attacked
the trade unions' lack of representation both in the government and in the
party." Prior to the August 1966 National Party Congress, *rebelde* leaders (Senator Rafael Agustin Gomucio and Deputies Alberto Jerez and Julio Silva—all
Cuban *invitados*) circulated a document "defining their group's point of view" in
which

they call for a return to the earlier spirit of sacrifice and an orientation more in
tune with the popular classes. Their criticism is aimed at the alleged take-over of

the party by professionals, technicians, and businessmen. They attack these late-comers ("parachutists") for not really being in agreement with the communitarian-socialist program of the party.[191]

There is a strong probability that the populist cadres were *dispirited* campaigners for the 1967 municipal elections. Hence they may be partially responsible for the failure of this presidentially determined "plebiscite" when the party's support declined from 42.3 percent (in 1965) to 36.5 percent. This "ominous decline" may have been consequential to a *rebelde* self-fulfilling prophesy! In any case, the populists redoubled their intra-party proselytization and won a majority on the PDC's National Council in July 1967.

Gomucio was elected PDC president and the National Council released a document edited by Jacques Chonchol (INDAP vice-president and a former FAO adviser to Cuba's Agrarian Reform Institute) calling for a "non-capitalist" developmental program for 1967-1970. It warned the Frei administration that unless it began moving on social reforms that the party would lose mass support in 1969-1970.[192] This admonition was underlined by the recent loss of a senatorial by-election in rural Colchaga Province during June. The widow of Socialist Senator Solomon Corbalan had been backed by both the Communists and Radicals.

Until their takeover of the party's National Council, "(t)he populists' 'greatest problem (had) been their ambivalence toward a government with which, despite short term working relations they share(d) few essential ideals.' " Now the Christian Democracy was "split at the very heart of its organization," it was incumbent upon Frei to adopt a definite position.[193]

In November 1965, President Frei had responded to the October intraparty memo by joining Minister of Lands Jaime Castillo in stating it might take "a generation" to implement the communitarian goals.[194] At this critical juncture and notwithstanding obvious disaffection among PDC trade union leaders, Frei adopted a *mano dura* non-negotiating posture—previously reserved for the FRAP—toward the populist faction within his own party. Although laws for agrarian reform, peasant unionization and property control were *finally* enacted, the *oficialistas* also moved rapidly to regain control of the PDC National Council. By February 1968, Chonchol had been forced out of the government and the party was again safely in *oficialista* hands. This was the *coup d'grace*. Emboldened, a national leader publicly

referred to dangerous 'collectivist, authoritarian' (Marxist) tendencies among the rebels. In the summer of 1968, for example, the newly elected president of the PDC youth was disciplined and nearly expelled from the party for his 'extremist' views and criticisms of the government; earlier . . . the president of the party accused the youth of teaching guerrilla tactics at their summer camp.[195]

The government's arrogant refusal to bargain with those who rejected cooptation delegitimized its non-corporativist participatory and pluralistic pretensions.

Hence, when Frei and his ministers traversed the country in the 1969 congressional campaign, the *rebelde* faction declined to vigorously support most candidates. While they were given their due share of the candidacies, many were in FRAP strongholds rather than in safe constituencies. Hence, only three *rebeldes* were elected. A centrist or *tercera* faction received .14 percent of the candidacies and elected 16 percent of the victorious candidates. Among the *oficialistas* the respective proportions were 64 percent and 73 percent, while for the *rebeldes* they were 17 percent and 5 percent.[196]

If this were intended to reassure the potential Alessandri constituency that the party was not controlled by "Mensheviks," it failed admirably as did the massacre of 51 squatters in Puerto Montt, a conservative area, several days after the election. For Christian Democracy lost a full 25 percent of its constituency—a majority opting for the Nationals.[197] In addition, almost 30 percent of the electorate—mostly lower strata who should have been mobilized by the *rebeldes*—cast blank ballots or abstained. According to one PDC aficionado:

A number of Christian Democrats were apparently puzzled as to the PDC's position because of factional disputes and denunciations of Frei by 'rebel' and Youth leaders. Others were disillusioned over the regime's failure to transcend political bickering and project an image (sic) of revolutionary commitment and disciplined austerity. Some opted for another party; some stayed home. Urban workers have decried Frei's wage policy which they feel places the burden of the administration's anti-inflation campaign on their backs.[198]

In the aftermath the embittered populists suffered two more major defeats. Although the party had declined from 42 percent in 1965 to 30 percent in the 1969 congressional election, the National Council categorically rejected an "opening to the left" for 1970. There would be no coalition with either the *Fidelista* Socialists or the always importuning Communists. Finally, a number of idealistic PDC Youth leaders were suspended from the Party for publicly criticizing the government.[199]

While Frei's "refusal to conciliate foes" was still in the air, he sought to "brighten the image of the PDC regime" by proposing a banking reform, quickening the pace of agrarian reform and forcing Anaconda into an "agreed nationalization"—this time at book value. But it was too late and too little, and too symbolic in an evocative rather than a referential sense. Approximately 15 percent of the PDC—among them the most youthful and energetic campaigners—resigned en masse. They included Senators Gomucio and Alberto Jerez, Deputy Julio Silva, Jacques Chonchol, five mayors and 28 municipal councilmen.[200] This group, led by former Cuban *invitados* and one aged PDC founder (Gomucio, also an *invitado*), organized the United Movement for Popular Action (MAPU) which affiliated with Popular Unity. Symbolically, Chonchol became Allende's minister of agriculture and was dispatched in December 1970 to Cautin Province. There, in the citadel of the Nationals and *oficialista* Christian

Democracy, he was to direct the expropriation of 200 large rural estates. And significantly, the PDC has joined the right in opposing the Popular Unity government's egalitarian reforms.[201]

This would not have been apparent from Tomic's presidential oratory. Recognizing that while 1969 PDC losses had been spread evenly throughout the country they had been heaviest in urban areas, Tomic himself attacked Frei's failure to implement the 1964 PDC program. He called for outright nationalization of the *Gran Mineria*—including Anaconda—and declared that all political tendencies within the PDC would be represented within his government. Tomic unsuccessfully endeavored to win Communist support by declaring that he would accept leftist backing to attain the presidency in Congress—if he "came in a strong second" at the polls. Agrarian reform would become a reality and better relations with Cuba were suggested by the re-establishment of trade in March 1970.[202]

During the early part of his campaign when it appeared that Allende would be a certain loser, Tomic sought to capture the largest possible lower class vote. Towards the end, a reliable yet secret opinion survey revealed that it would be a toss up between Alessandri and Allende who had maintained—if not increased—his hold on the lower class constituency. At this point Tomic shifted his tactics to emphasize middle class appeals, particularly anti-(Castro) communism. This probably cost Allende many votes among white collar strata and Catholic lower class women. For Tomic, despite coming in a poor third with 28 percent of the vote, "obtained percentages much above his national average from women in the working class barrios of Santiago, Valparaiso, and Concepcion, and especially from women in the peasant provinces where in almost every instance he defeated the Popular Unity candidate.[203]

In those areas where land had been distributed or expropriated, Tomic won easily. He secured pluralities in Cautin, Aysen and Valparaiso provinces and did better than average in peasant and mining areas.[204] With regard to the latter, it should be pointed out that in April 1970 Frei had announced large subsidies and technical aid for medium and small copper producers.[205]

Because of Frei's inability to outlaw Marxism, the defection of MAPU and the PDC's failure to fulfill egalitarian aspects of the program, Tomic was unable to make a major dent in the UP constituency. Christian Democracy's limited reforms and UCC efforts did, however, conserve much of the PDC lower class constituency for Tomic. His anti-Marxism notwithstanding, it was impossible for him to engender substantial white collar support. This was due to the party's: failure to control inflation; feeble attempts to increase taxes upon the middle and upper classes; inability to outlaw the left; and above all its choice of a candidate who insisted upon a populist style.

United States Ambassador Edward Korry had sought to unify the Alessandri and Tomic candidacies by advising the latter to moderate his style and proposals. PDC Senator Renan Fuentealba replied to this by denouncing it as open intervention in Chilean internal affairs.[206]

The militant spirit of some of Tomic's campaigners was reflected by their dancing in the streets with Allendistas after the Popular Unity candidates' electoral triumph. Even within the congressional delegation of Christian Democracy, there remained *terceristas* who had been radicalized by Tomic's populistic campaign. They had assured Popular Unity leaders that: 1) there would be no military intervention; and 2) their votes would ensure Allende's election by the Plenary Congress. Therefore, according to these Tomic followers, there was no need to mobilize the masses via general strikes.[207]

But the UP leaders were as frightened as they were surprised by Allende's victory at the polls. He had not even bothered to designate a Cabinet-elect. And several days after the election PDC President Benjamin Prado ominously announced that Chilean Christian Democracy was "the only force capable of saving Chilean liberties." Then on Sept. 24, the PDC demanded that UP accept a "Statute of Guarantees" as Constitutional Amendements exchange for "unanimous" PDC backing.

This decision followed a tumultous meeting at which "the largest party in Congress nearly split over whether or not to support Allende." Tomic had already recognized Allende's right to the presidency and the Left threatened an armed revolution if Chile's "powerful tradition" went unheeded. In fact, Prado had argued within the party that a denial of his popular mandate, similar to Alessandri's in 1958, would vindicate those Fidelistas who disparaged the efficacy of "free" elections.

The central problem was that "there were reports that President Frei's forces were trying to gain support for an alliance with Alessandri's Party." Alessandri would be elected and then resign. Following this, Frei could run again as a joint PDC-PN candidate. Since Allende only needed thirteen votes and considering *tercerista* sympathies as well as the refusal of 32 PDC Deputies to support certain provisions of an *oficialista* Constitutional Amendment vesting increased powers in the presidency during the past year, a deal of this kind was likely to backfire and further divide an already weakened party. In fact, Tomic had previously agreed to support Allende if he received up to 100,000 votes less than Alessandri as a front-runner. Hence, the *oficialistas* opted for a second strategy. The "Statute of Guarantees" contained demands some of which would make it almost impossible for UP to implement its revolutionary program, and might well prove unacceptable for that very reason. They included the following: 1) no government role for "Popular Power" councils; 2) the maintenance of the private—largely Catholic—schools; 3) no press nationalization or withdrawal of advertising; 4) no substantial changes in textbooks or other aspects of the educational system; 5) equal time for the opposition over the state television network; 6) no use of the armed forces for national development programs; 7) military "autonomy," i.e., maintenance of the existing command structure in the armed forces. The first four implied major compromises in the UP program. Numbers three and five denied the Popular Unity government authority previously exercised by the Frei administration. Six had been implicit in the UP program.

A dexterous politician, Allende induced the coalition to accept all except the seventh. This was sufficient to outmaneuver the *oficialistas*, as the *terceristas* demanded PDC acceptance of the compromise. It was clear they would vote for Allende anyway.[208] He needed no more than 13 of the 75 PDC votes.

Following Allende's accession to the presidency, the PDC has been forced into a de facto coalition with the Nationals. This has been occasioned by the class content of many UP measures—Allende's conciliatory demeanor notwithstanding. It is only a matter of time before *oficialistas* join the Nationals in secret conferences with military officers.

The Catholic Church

Dimensions of the Catholic Constituency. Although clerical issues are no longer dominant in Chilean politics, the Church has maintained a keen interest in the governmental process. Despite the "separation" of Church and state, politicians have not been wholly unresponsive to the institutional and proselytizing goals of the clergy. There has been film censorship against sexual ideas not in conformity with Church doctrine at least since 1949. The influence of the Church is so feared that until 1970 no party dared advocate liberty of marital divorce.[209] This, despite a rate of about 2,000 annulments annually, based upon fraudulent allegations.[210]

The proportion of the total student population educated by public schools in 1928 was 88 percent. By 1957 this figure had fallen to 64 percent. In 1962 private instruction was being given to 30 percent of the primary school pupils and 47 percent of those in secondary schools. Two years later, it was reported that more than one-third of all Chilean youths were being educated in Catholic institutions. They included: 1,200 primary schools; 138 technical and professional schools; 149 secondary schools; 12 colleges for the training of teachers; and 3 universities. The government was subsidizing these and other private educational institutions.[211]

Like many other peoples, the Chileans are not particularly religious in terms of living according to Catholic ethical principles or of mastering Church doctrine. Nevertheless, and despite Protestant gains during the 1950s, at least 87 percent of a Greater Santiago public opinion sample identified themselves as Catholics in late 1958. In fact, the national percentage was higher since this survey did not include rural interviews. At the time 3 percent said they were Protestant and 8 percent atheist or without religious preferences. Comparable figures for early 1965 were: 85.3 percent; 3.9 percent; and 8.3 percent. Recognizing that both samples were taken in Santiago, we may conclude that during the intervening period about 90 percent of Chileans throughout the nation identified with Catholicism. And in 1965, at least 7 percent from the Santiago survey stated they participated (5.8 percent "often") in lay organizations of the Church.[212]

An October 1963 survey of four hundred Santiago women revealed that they were less inclined to be irreligious than men, something that has always been known to impressionistic observers. Ninety-two percent said they "belonged to some religion." Eighty-three percent of these stated they went to Church, almost half of them on a weekly basis. *Only 26 percent of the entire sample either did not belong to a religion or went to Church less than once a month.* The 92 percent who "belonged to some religion" were then asked: "Is religion important to you in the choice of a candidate?" Of these, 47 percent replied in the affirmative, 8 percent did not respond to the question and 45 percent said "no." Forty-six percent of the entire sample said their choice of a presidential candidate would be influenced by whether he was a member of their faith. Of the 92 percent who belonged to a religion, greatest and least sympathy for political parties were as shown in Table 8-2.

In November 1964, a large sample of men and women in Santiago were asked if they would support a divorce law. While 53 percent opposed such legislation, 45 percent answered in the affirmative. Of the total sample, 35 percent were opposed because it would increase family instability—the principle argument of the Church. Another 12 percent rationalized their opposition by simply saying that the Church was against divorce, and 4 percent said such a law would be abused.[213]

Although no more than ten to twenty percent of the Chilean population may be classified as "devout,"[214] it would seem that between 35 percent and 45 percent may be responsive to clerical positions on *certain* issues. The latter figure is probably applicable to women and issues at a high level of generality—"favoring Communism," for example.[215] On the other hand, because of low levels of cognition, most of the clerical constituency would not respond where: 1) issues

Table 8-2
Party Sympathies of Female Church Members in Santiago, October 1963

Party	Greatest	Least
Christian Democratic	45%	2%
Conservative	9	4
Liberal	6	4
Radical	10	14
Socialist	10	3
Communist	5	59
PADENA	2	1
Democratic	2	0
None	10	14

Source: Frida Kaplan B., Yolanda Navarrete R., Daniela Rubens, F., "Algunos Factores que Determinan la Conducta Electoral de la Mujer" (Memoria para Optar al Título de Psicológico, Universidad de Chile, Facultad de Filosofía y Educación, Escuela de Psicología, Santiago, 1964).

were obscure or complex, and 2) when significant cleavage existed within the hierarchy. This may be inferred not only from the semiliterate status of most Chileans, but also from a survey of three million practicing Santiago Catholics during the late 1960s. Approximately 31 percent had never heard of the incarnation, 21 percent did not know who Jesus Christ was, 78 percent were ignorant of what the "mystical body of Christ" signified, and 65 percent were unable to identify the Bible.[216]

Instrumentalities of Church Influence. The predispositions of the faithful are structured by clerical utilization of the pulpit, the confessional and Church-operated educational and social institutions.[217] Following World War II, several quasi-political organizations were constituted. Among businessmen, the *Union Social de Empresarios Cristianos* (USEC) has been promoting an interest in Church Social Doctrine since 1947. By 1960, its conferences were analyzing the desirability of an agrarian reform. This paralleled the PDC program.[218]

In the late 1940s, a Catholic labor confederation was organized. *Accion Sindical Chilena* (ASICH) was both confessional and compulsively anti-Communist. Led by William Thayer, destined to be Frei's minister of labor, ASICH was instrumental in establishing the Latin American Confederation of Christian Unionists (CLASC) in 1954. During the late 1950s, ASICH had no more than several thousand members and organized few strikes in urban or rural zones. This Chilean affiliate of the CLASC began serious rural organizational work only *after Allende's 1958 rural inroads.* The *Union de Campesinos Cristianos* (Christian Peasants' Union or UCC) was organized by ASICH during 1960 in cooperation with the Institute of Rural Education—the rural department of CARITAS.[219] As noted in chapter 5, the UCC was supported by the International Development Foundation, the National Farmers Union and AID. In April 1961, the ASICH published a pamphlet for the UCC which advocated an agrarian reform in order to avoid a "Marxist dictatorship," to increase production, and to expand social welfare in rural areas.[220] During the 1964 presidential election campaign, CLASC disseminated propaganda identifying Allende with the "Castro tyranny."[221]

Among Catholic university students, professionals, businessmen and priests, the most influential Church journal is *Mensaje.* Published since the 1940s, this Jesuit monthly was articulating the PDC reformist-communitarian political approach as *la unica alternativa* during the early 1960s. Hector Valenzuela, Hernan Poblete, Radomiro Tomic, and Alejandro Magnet were prominent Christian Democratic contributors during the period in question. In 1958, Magnet, Valenzuela and Poblete were members of the *Politica y Espiritu* editorial board. Clerical declarations and views were disseminated by both *Politica y Espiritu* and *La Libertad.*

The Archbishopric of Santiago published its own weekly newspaper. *La Voz* was distributed on Sundays and increased its circulation from 11,000 as a bi-weekly in 1961 to 15,000 two years later. Both Magnet and Poblete were on its staff. In January 1959, Hernan Poblete was appointed director of the *Radio Escuela del Instituto de Educacion Rural*. The Peace Corps provided volunteers and AID distributed radio receiving equipment for its programming to more than 1,000 rural schools and *centrales* during the early 1960s. At the same time, the Archbishopric of Santiago operated its own major broadcasting station, *Radio Chilena*; and Catholic University owned one of the two television stations in Santiago.[222]

The most prominent Jesuit in Chile was Roger Veckemans. An advisor to Pope John XXIII in the preparation of *Mater et Magistra*, Father Veckemans was in the early 1960s the director of the School of Sociology at Catholic University as well as the director of DESAL (Center for Latin American Economic and Social Development). During the 1964 Frei campaign, DESAL—ostensibly financed by European Catholic institutions and identified as a cooperating agency by the International Development Foundation—employed many of the professionals and technicians who drafted PDC strategy and programs. DESAL was also reported to have paid the salaries of some Frei campaign organizers.[223]

Images of the Cuban Revolution. Early in 1959, *Mensaje* published an article by Jaime Fonseca, Editor of *Noticias Catolicas* in Washington. It defended the necessity—from a Christian standpoint—for agrarian reform measures in Cuba.[224] Subsequent to this, editorials and articles began to appear in *Mensaje* which without exception criticized the course followed by the Cuban leadership. Hostility first centered upon the lack of legal due process. Then during late 1959 and early 1960, it denounced: 1) Castro's acceptance of Communist support and collaboration; 2) collectivistic and statist tendencies in the agrarian reform and other economic programs and measures; 3) political dictatorship; and 4) close relations with the Soviet Union.[225]

By December 1960, CLASC had released a declaration condemning Castro for "betrayal" to both the 26th of July Movement and the Cuban nation.[226] *La Voz* and *Mensaje* joined the Archbishop in sympathizing with the Bay of Pigs invaders.[227] In the aftermath, *Mensaje* endorsed the need for collective sanctions against Cuba and the AFP to diminish Communist potential in the hemisphere.[228] The Alliance was viewed as a direct response to the Cuban challenge.[229]

A large number of the *Mensaje* articles incorporated statements by Cuban Church authorities or members of lay organizations. They stressed the growing role of communism and the post-Bay of Pigs "persecution" of the Church by the Castro regime.[230] During 1962, the Archbishopric of Santiago published a seventy-six page tract entitled *Pasion de Cristo en Cuba: Testimonio de un Sacerdote*. This anonymous polemic recounted the conflict between the Church and the Revolutionary Government, which was held to have begun in June 1959. The principal subjects treated were the growth of Marxist influence, opposition by the Church, its "persecution" and a description of anti-Church propaganda disseminated by the Cuban government.[231]

Affected by the development of social revolutionary tendencies within the Church in several Latin American countries as well as by a new pattern of co-existence between the Fidelista regime, and the Catholic hierarchy in Cuba, the orientation of *Mensaje* was modified during the late sixties.[232] Although we have not done a content analysis for the 1966-1970 period, it is probable that Chilean Jesuits adopted a more moderate and discriminating perspective towards Cuba's social progress and economic difficulties. Even Raul Cardinal Silva Henriquez, Archbishop of Santiago, was willing to offer praise for Fidelista Cuba and the Revolutionary Government's social achievements. This, in the course of a November 1970 interview with a reporter from *Juventud Rebelde.*[233]

Anti-Communism During the Late 1950s. The Christian desirability of social and economic reform was not emphasized by the Catholic hierarchy in Chile prior to Castro's assumption of power. It is true that Bishop Larrain of Talca and a small following within the clergy were quite concerned about the plight of the lower classes. Although stressing the "danger" of communism, Larrain also argued the intrinsic Christian value of eliminating mass social deprivation.[234] Cardinal Maria Caro who presided over the Santiago archdiocese in 1958 was, however, preoccupied with other matters.[235] Simple anticommunist declarations without reference to social reform were considered adequate insofar as this "danger" was concerned. Hence, early in 1958 *La Revista Catolica,* the Archbishop of Santiago's official organ, warned anyone supporting the relegalization of the Communist Party that they were in fact "favoring communism," therefor guilty of sin, and could not receive the Holy Sacraments. The PDC was then backing the repeal of the Law for the Defense of Democracy, as were the Radicals and the FRAP. Cardinal Maria Caro had also warned that Catholics could not licitly register or vote for "the Communist parties," nor could they licitly read, spread or write in books, newspapers or pamphlets "that favor Communist doctrine or activities." This effort at Conservative behest to influence the PDC vote was criticized by Frei as illicit political intervention.[236]

In the presidential election campaign, it was reported to be "evident that Ibanez looked with disfavor upon Allesandri and that the Church opposed Allende, but beyond that the President and the Catholic hierarchy maintained official neutrality." After his victory, and "(u)nlike many predecessors who in avoidance of the suggestion of clericalism had 'promised,' Alessandri 'swore' faithfully to discharge his presidential duties. Then he walked to the cathedral and became the first president since 1931 to attend a Te Deum upon his inauguration."[237] After the December death of Jose Cardinal Maria Caro, Monsenor Emilio Tagle, a man noted for reformist sympathies, was designated as Apostolic Administrator of Santiago. This appointment was enthusiastically received by the PDC journal *Politica y Espiritu.*[238]

During April 1959 the same periodical reported a new Holy Office pronouncement that it was "illicit . . . to give electoral support to candidates who in practice (sic) favor the Communist Party." The editorial noted that the pronouncement had been prompted by the withdrawal of some Christian Democrats from the Sicilian PDC. They had then organized a Social Christian Party which formed a coalition with the Communists. The editorial writer observed that this Vatican ruling would be used against the PDC in Chile.[239]

In May, the text of the Holy Office statement appeared in *La Revista Catolica*. It specifically warned (the Christian Democratic faction, led by Radomiro Tomic, favoring a coalition with FRAP during the First National Convention of the PDC that same month) that Catholics could not licitly "in an election of representatives of the people . . . give their votes to parties or candidates who, although they don't profess principles opposed to Catholic doctrine, and even use the name of Christians, nevertheless are in fact working with Communists and whose efforts help them."[240]

Support for the PDC Reformist Approach. If the undesirability of a PDC working relationship with FRAP was a major concern of the new Apostolic Administrator, Rev. Tagle soon began to please Christian Democrats by evidencing a genuine interest in socio-economic reforms. During the FRAP pro-Cuban congressional election campaign in early 1961, *La Voz* reprinted an interview with Bishop Larrain that had first appeared in *The Sign*, a United States Catholic periodical. In April, the interview was again reprinted, this time in *Politica y Espiritu*. Its theme was the urgency of an agrarian reform because of the Communist threat. But Monsenor Larrain also supported such measures because they would implement the evangelical message. If this were done, there would be no problem of Communism. Larrain praised the new United States foreign aid program and the United States non-governmental organizations then operating in Chile.[241]

In June 1961, newly appointed Archbishop of Santiago Raul Silva Henriquez made a strong plea for Conservative-Christian Democratic unity. Describing the Chilean people as for the most part "miserable," Silva stressed the critical importance of "peaceful and gradual" social and economic reforms.

Either we are going to evolve rapidly or we are going to confront a social catastrophe. . . . Attempting to institute changes through violence is to nullify them, they will be equally unattainable if individuals or special groups seek to take advantage of this (crisis). . . .[242]

And within five weeks, the fears of Larrain and Silva were being echoed by thirteen priests from Los Andes, a district where *Fidelistas* Allende and Jaime Barros had been victorious in the recent congressional election. Of the two rightists who had formerly represented the area with Allende, only Liberal Pedro Ibanez, a model landlord, had survived the FRAP gains. With the apparent approval of their bishop, the priests addressed a public letter to Alessandri warning of "the delicate situation and the necessity to do something in the way of agrarian reform to detain the advance of Communism in the countryside."[243]

In July 1961, Bishop Larrain and Archbishop Silva announced that a model agrarian reform would be instituted on a number of estates within their dioceses. By February 1962, the Pope had elevated Archbishop Silva to the College of Cardinals. And within several weeks, *Ercilla* news analyst Hernandez Parker was reporting that

(e)ven in the upper levels of the hierarchy of the Catholic Church the winds are blowing. There are the gifts of the bishops while other influential ecclesiastics are becoming Christian Democrats. The Rev. Raul Silva Henriquez—an independent priest, but one much closer to the PDC than the PCU—was designated to be Chile's second Cardinal.[244]

With the technical advice of PDC economists, Bishop Larrain was able to inaugurate his first cooperative in June 1962. While Congress was simultaneously considering the AFP agrarian reform bill, the Cardinal publicly warned that it was too moderate. And Larrain declared that several more estates within his diocese were being added to the Church program—an "example" for the rest of the nation.[245] In its May issue, *Mensaje* carried a laudatory analysis of the AFP by Raul Saez, who was destined for a vice-presidency of the Chilean Development Corporation (CORFO) in the Frei administration. Saez conceived the new program as a means for safeguarding liberty and democracy from the threat of dictatorship and totalitarianism.[246]

Church support for reforms was also manifested by two pastoral letters during 1962. Released in May, the first was entitled "The Church and the Problem of the Chilean Peasantry." Endorsing agrarian reform, it proposed that state lands be the first ones distributed. Then unproductive private holdings should be expropriated while ultimately any tracts suitable for parcelization might properly be made subject to the program.[247] Before the Second Pastoral Letter was read, Cardinal Silva personally spoke with President Alessandri "about the desirability of including in agrarian reform legislation some provisions that would encourage the distribution of land to individual peasants, as the archbishopric is now doing."[248]

In September 1962, *Politica y Espiritu* devoted twenty-one pages to the following: "The Bishops of Chile Speak: The Social and Political Duty of the Present Hour"; "Declaration of the Cardinal Archbishop Rev. Raul Silva Henriquez"; and "Agrarian Reform: The Church's Example." The second Pastoral Letter had been signed by three archbishops, seventeen bishops and two apostolic administrators. It asserted the right of the clergy to openly intervene in the political arena: "(w)e have the right and the duty to intervene by indicating the moral, natural and religious fundamentals that must guide us in these difficult circumstances." The document stressed the urgency of structural reforms in order to reduce mass misery which was regarded as the basis of the growing Communist (FRAP) threat. Although no parties were specified, the message clearly implied that given what was known of their past performance, the Liberals, Conservatives and Radicals were not likely to effectuate the desired changes.

It is necessary to promote, through the use of one's vote, a true reform of the structures of the country, so that to the greatest extent possible, its features may conform to Christian principles.
   The voter must take into account the true intentions and the actual possibilities of the political parties. . . .

While collaboration with the FRAP was impliedly sanctioned only for immediate and particular objectives that were intrinsically valued, the pastoral warned in the clearest terms against any coalition or voting support for the FRAP as long as the Communists were within it:

. . . the Church considers communism to be a noxious doctrine for human society. . . .
   Collaboration is not possible with communism. What collaboration, what possibilities can there be with a system or party that has as a basic postulate the destruction of all ideas and institutions to which it is opposed? . . .
   . . . those who collaborate with the communists are sons who have separated themselves from the paternal house. . . .
   The desire to aid communism in achieving power even with the intention of not following its dictates or opposing it once the latter is secured, constitutes an immoral act which cannot be justified and that assumes a lack of tactical adroitness upon the part of the communists, something that is very alien to reality. . . .[249]

   Our inescapable conclusion is that the Church was throwing its moral support behind the PDC. The call for structural reforms paralleled and reinforced the program of the Christian Democrats. And as one observer noted, "(t)he orientation of the Christian Democrats and the Santiago Curia in political, economic and social affairs is too identical for it to be considered purely casual."[250] Silvert has attested to the fact that "many of the most influential Church leaders have been supporting" the PDC, and he views Church advocacy of "social change" to have "been influential in assisting the growth of the Christian Democratic Party."[251]
   One of those who participated in drafting the pastoral was the Jesuit Roger Veckemans, whose role in the Frei effort has already been discussed. In the course of being interviewed during December 1962, Cardinal Silva announced that the Church's political role would be limited to the declaration of general principles. It was for laymen to detail the particular measures needed for their implementation.[252] This was, of course, one of the principal tasks undertaken by DESAL during the Frei campaign.

The principles contained in the pastoral were reiterated within three months by the Jesuits in a special issue of *Mensaje* entitled "*Vision Cristiana de la Revolucion en America Latina*" ("The Christian View of the Latin American Revolution"). The editorial assumed the inevitability of a revolution and admonished that unless Christians assumed leadership, the Fidelistas and Communists (FRAP) would.

And when we talk of revolution we are not now contemplating the barracks revolts and mob attacks of days gone by, but rather something new and different. Almost without wanting to do so, we think of what happened in Russia, China and Cuba.

Revolutionary winds, in effect, are blowing. An immense and each time larger majority is becoming conscious of its strength, its misery and the injustice of that political, juridical, social and economic 'order' which it has been obliged to accept; and that majority is not willing to wait any longer. It demands a change: a rapid, profound and total structural change. If violence is necessary, it is willing to use violence. The masses themselves aspire for power in order to effectuate an authentic 'common good.' Logically, this mass which desires revolution is inspired by the only ideology that is readily available to them: the Marxist ideology.

To deny this fact is to close one's eyes to an obvious reality. . . .

In the face of this 'revolution on the march,' what attitude should the Christian take? Should he without hesitation promote it? Should he cross his arms and await what may come? Should he struggle against it? If revolution involved no more than struggling against injustice, there would be no problem. But revolution can now also be and in fact it has been until now—violence, vengeance, reprisal, persecution, destruction of liberties and rights, the execution wall and exile. Hence, it is not strange that attitudes towards it are varied, even among Christians. The atmosphere is tense and filled with hopes, rancors and fears; ideas are confused and are accommodated to desires and fears; facts are simplified or distorted.

In such circumstances, *Mensaje* is dutybound to lead its readers and through them the Christians of Chile. . . .

It is impossible for one to remain neutral before this 'revolution on the march.' Either one decides he is against it and will openly or secretly combat it, or he decides he is for it; there are simply no other alternatives.[253]

Within fifteen months Communist leader Orlando Millas was to attribute the adoption of a vigorous structurally reformist orientation by the bishops and *Mensaje* to "pressure from the Catholic masses who have joined the popular movement (FRAP), and . . . the many rank and file priests who are more closely acquainted with the lives of the peasants and workers in their parishes or in industrial and mining areas."[254] And indeed the *Mensaje* editorial, if not the pastoral as well, tend to substantiate such claims. Some Chilean priests have publicly "attribute(d) the Church's new attitude to the social effects of the Cuban revolution,"[255] and Martin Needler has suggested that it was catalyzed by the communization of Cuba and the growing appeal of political groups which identified with the policies of the Cuban Revolution.[256]

During January 1963, Cardinal Silva announced that the Church was undertaking a massive campaign to end illiteracy among 800,000 persons. Financed by sympathetic businessmen and possibly AID, 350 volunteers immediately set to work.[257] It would not be unreasonable to surmise that those who mastered the rudimentary skills under clerical auspices would swell the ranks of Frei's supporters once they were registered. And in the same weeks, Father Veckemans publicly called upon the AFP to provide direct aid to unions, cooperatives and student federations without channeling it through governments, since little impact upon mass living standards had been brought about in that manner.[258] The Church continued to distribute large amounts of CARITAS foods during the early months of 1963.[259] Subsequently, Frei was to suggest that the shift in the Church's orientation (1961-1962) and its work among the poor had created a "favorable climate" for the PDC "to work in."[260]

Beginning in 1962, PDC-oriented rural unions such as the UCC and ANOC launched a major drive to organize the peasantry. This campaign was reportedly supported by many rural priests who—both from and beyond the pulpit—implored the peasants to oppose communism.[261] At the time of the municipal elections in early 1963, the Church failed to disassociate itself from thousands of Holy Cards warning female voters of "the Communist plague."[262]

A second special issue of *Mensaje* entitled "*Reformas Revolucionarias en America Latina*" was published in October 1963. The editorial defined it as a continuation of the special issue published ten months earlier which had emphasized the need for a "revolutionary" structurally reformist approach by Catholics due to the Marxist threat. This issue contained a series of well written essays endorsing the AFP and analyzing the assumptions, methods to be used and objectives of reforms in such areas as agriculture, education, the economy, social security, etc.

During December, an interview with Cardinal Silva was published in the Vatican weekly *L'Osservatore della Domenica*. As reported in *El Mercurio*, the Chilean prelate had warned that:

In the year 2,000 Latin America will have 600 million inhabitants. The problem of what the continent's ideology will be is a serious one. I believe that if the political and social situation remains the same as it is at present, there is no doubt that Latin America will become communist.[263]

Within two months INPROA (the Church agrarian reform agency) had received a $40,000 loan from the World Bank to accelerate its formation of co-operatives.[264] In early 1964, INPROA published a simply worded pamphlet characterizing its program as motivated by love, faith and the desire to end class hatred. The fact that the peasants would own their own land—after paying for it over a twenty-four year period—was also stressed.[265]

El Marxismo: Teoria y Accion was released during May 1964. Jointly edited by Father Veckemans and several leading Christian Democrats, it highlighted the negative and despotic aspects of the Soviet and satellite regimes. Another 1964 PDC release was a sixteen page pamphlet entitled *Revolucion en Libertad*. After delineating specific reforms pledged by the party, it defined the "Revolution in Liberty" as "(a) rapid change of the juridical, social and economic structures, economic development planning, and all of this implemented with the support of a majority of the nation." The tract referred approvingly to the Bishops' 1962 Pastoral on page four. And it defined "liberty" as "the power and the right that man has to choose his destiny, to express his thoughts and his faith in God, and to propagate them." Associational freedom, pluralism and civil liberties were also embraced by this term. The Christian Democratic commitment to reform was held to be motivated "not by a desire to attack communism, which we believe is not the solution, but rather because the dispossessed classes demand it with urgency. That is why Christian Democracy calls for a Revolution."[266]

Several months before the September 1964 election, Catholic University published an astutely written 133 page booklet entitled *Gano Allende!* (Allende Won!) It imaginatively portrayed Chile's fate if Allende were victorious. In essence, the argument was that the Communists would inevitably dominate the FRAP government, and Chile would be transformed into a Soviet satellite. First, Allende's claim that his government would be similar to Aguirre Cerda's 1938 Popular Front government was rejected, since the Radicals would no longer constitute a balancing factor. In addition, readers were admonished not "to forget that then the influence of 'Castroism'—a Latin American version of Marxism—did not exist. . . . . the love of the prestige that is consequential to the holding of power will be a determining factor in Allende's desire to be a Castro rather than a Urrutia. . . ." To strengthen his point, the anonymous author then argued that Allende's claim that constitutional legality would be maintained was dishonest by virtue of the FRAP candidate's previous unreserved identification with the Cuban Revolution:

How useful it is now—in order to eliminate any possible doubt—to recall Allende's admiration for Castroite legality in Cuba . . . ! For the ultra-rapid laws that created Peoples' Courts and their rules of procedure, which were more than adequately dealt with by the International Commission of Jurists' investigation. Laws that were preliminaries to the execution wall and arbitrary imprisonment. . . .

One may remember now his admiration for the Cuban legality that abolished union liberty, transforming the island's labor unions into mere instruments of exploitation by the militia . . . !

Then the writer contended that Allende's nationalizations and other economic measures would provoke a disastrous decline in productivity, bankruptcy and a consequential need for Soviet aid: "Fidel Castro has done all this and much more in three years. . . . these days, Cuba lives on Soviet charity with a system of permanent rationing." It also warned that a FRAP government would organize Red Battalions of Communist unionists, assign leftist reserve officers to existing commands in the armed forces and introduce Communist military instructors and equipment into the country. Chile would sign bilateral commercial agreements with the Russians, and the Church would be prohibited, *as in Cuba*, from teaching its social doctrine. The pamphlet claimed that under a FRAP government, children would owe their primary loyalty to the state as in Cuba: "it is not out of cruelty that Fidel Castro has dictated a new law transferring essential jurisdiction over children from the parents to the State. It is purely and simply the application of Marxist-Leninist doctrine."[267]

By June, the presidential campaign was entering its final and most hate-filled phase. On the third of the month *Ercilla* published a statement by the Cardinal which had been made on April 28th in Rio de Janeiro, while the prelate was en route from the Vatican to Chile. It came close to directly condemning the FRAP: "The Chilean communists are employing the same method that was being used in Brazil: to infiltrate themselves ideologically among the masses and trying to obtain key positions in the government."

Two weeks later *Ercilla* published a London *Sunday Times* report of April 19th that "Frei has the backing of the progressive Catholic Church; a true enlightenment is winning for him the devout of Chile."[268] Several weeks earlier, *La Voz* had obtained a six hour interview with Allende. It subsequently appeared under the headline "Allende: Prisoner of the Communist Party."[269] On June 21, *La Voz* published an openly anti-FRAP article entitled "In the FRAP: Maneuvers and Propaganda." And the *Mensaje* issue for June editorialized with a warning that it was sinful to vote for or otherwise support FRAP: "From no possible perspective does it appear to us to be licit for a Catholic to contribute to the installation of Marxism in our fatherland."

On the 23rd of June, Communist Senator Jaime Barros delivered a vitriolic denunciation of clerical intervention in the campaign. Addressing his colleagues, Barros noted that Cardinal Silva had "openly declared himself for the . . . Christian Democratic candidacy, in a class at the Catholic University of Valparaiso." Barros also charged that Bishop Vicuna of Chillan "made the peasant swear while on their knees, that they would not vote for Salvador Allende," and he denounced the publication of *Gano Allende!* by the Church.[270] FRAPists complained that from pulpits and confessionals, as well as outside the Churches, priests were warning that to vote for Allende would be an act of "mortal sin."[271] A PDC youth leader informed the writer that although rural priests had been involved in campaign activities for Frei, such direct support had been avoided in urban areas where anti-clerical sentiment is pervasive.[272]

During 1964, an estimated 13 percent of the population were receiving PL 480 CARITAS foodstuffs from the Church.[273] Socialist Senator Solomon Corbalan charged in mid-June that in many slum districts such commodities were distributed preferentially to those displaying Frei stickers or signs in their windows.[274] Two months later, he informed the Senate that the Carmelite Sisters had permitted anti-Cuban and anti-Hungarian (Soviet) films from the USIA to be shown in their school.[275] It is of course impossible to verify these claims; nor can one ascertain how prevalent such conduct may have been. However, given the orientation of the Church and the transcending issue in the campaign—maintenance of the system—they deserve to be taken seriously.

The Church also assisted in organizing the Institute for Union and Social Leadership Training (INCASIS). During 1964, leadership courses were provided for about 20,000 persons from slums and rural areas. Conducted in Santiago, Valparaiso and Concepcion, the courses included the following subjects: history; politics; *communitarian* theory; comparative social doctrines; social history; economic development; cooperatives; etc.[276]

In July, *Mensaje* carried an article by the Director of *La Voz* defending the PDC against FRAP charges that it was the "other face of the Right." An editorial in the same issue indirectly supported the PDC by: 1) endorsing socio-economic "structural" reforms (this was Frei's, not Duran's approach); 2) opposing a revolution from above imposed by violence; 3) opposing the substitution of "State Paternalism" for "Oligarchic Paternalism"; 4) stressing the importance of mass participation in bringing about changes; and 5) advocating that the present defamatory campaign be replaced by one focusing upon the issues.[277]

On Aug. 23, *La Voz* editorialized directly in support of Frei. An article by *Politica y Espiritu* Editor Alejandro Magnet in the same issue also backed Frei, and observed in part:

When Frei was saying 'Chileans,' this should be understood as meaning 'Liberals' and 'Conservatives'. . . .

And for the first time in the history of Chile and Latin America, an election has focused upon two ways of making a revolution: the Marxist way or the Democratic way.

And again on Sept. 2, *La Voz* reminded its readers that they should heed the Cardinal's message that to vote was "a duty" and an "enormous privilege."

In other words, the vote implies the right of men to govern through persons of their choice. . . . When the fate of the country is at stake, there can be neither vacillations nor indifference because that would be a crime against the community.

Following Frei's victory, *Mensaje* editorialized that "(h)appily, the fourth of September passed, and the triumph of Frei put an end to this long suspense. . . . Frei's victory signifies above all the triumph of Democracy." After summarizing his programmatic commitments and relating them to the 1962 Pastoral Letter, the writer concluded by warning that "(w)e must prove that it is possible to achieve a revolution, without execution walls, without violence, without rancors, without revanchism; a human, and hence, Christian revolution."[278]

Survey data indicated that religion was a major factor influencing Frei's massive support.[279] The more Catholic-oriented women voted separately from their husbands who gave greater, albeit minority support to the FRAP candidate.[280] And according to Donald W. Beatty, "(t)here is no question but that he (Frei) had the support of the Catholic Church."[281] Following Frei's victory, Cardinal Silva was quick to visit Frei's home to congratulate the new president-elect.[282]

In January 1965, a *Mensaje* editorial urged support for Frei's proposed reforms of the educational system. In the same issue, the director of *La Voz* authored an article endorsing Frei's proposed constitutional amendment which would sanction a plebiscite when Congress blocked presidential initiatives for reforms or constitutional amendments. Norman Gall subsequently reported in the *New Leader* that the clergy was urging Catholic voters to support Frei in the 1965 congressional election.[283]

Communitarianism vs. Freism. The gradual realization that Frei's *oficialistas* were ill-disposed towards a rapid transformation of socio-economic structures in a communitarian direction prompted an intense disillusionment by a small but highly active sector of Chilean Catholicism. The lethargic severely circumscribed implementation of egalitarian measures and the emergence of revolutionary Catholic movements elsewhere in Latin America catalyzed the emergence of an active Catholic lower class oriented movement in Chile.

Early in his term, Frei had broken with Father Veckemans' DESAL.[284] Elsewhere in this chapter we have referred to the complaints that were voiced by ASICH, the Chilean affiliate of CLASC during November 1966. But more was involved than lack of access to government and PDC decision making bodies. These Catholic trade unionists also protested Frei's failure to amend the Labour Code so that strong and self-reliant trade unions could be constituted. They also criticized the unhurried tempo of rural expropriation, called for communitarian reforms of economic firms, access by unions to corporation financial records and for profit sharing.[285]

Oficialista indifference to these petitions and others relevant to its lower class constituencies catalyzed the emergence of the *Iglesia Joven* movement of students, workers and priests. During mid-1967, student members of this group had seized control of Catholic University in Santiago.

The rebels sought renewal of the institution to bring it nearer to the Chilean masses, and they made peremptory demands for student participation in the administration, for the right to vote in elections of rector and deans, and for a voice in selection of faculty.[286]

The rector was forced to resign, and within a year the allied *Movimiento Camilio Torres* was also rapidly expanding its mass base at this traditional upper class bastion. By 1970, an invitation in conjunction with other Chilean universities had brought Cuban scholars to Catholic University.[287]

Several months after Chonchol had been forced to resign from INDAP, a group of "seven priests (three of them Spaniards), two nuns, a pro-Marxist Catholic political leader, students from both the Catholic University and the University of Chile, and about 150 men and women (most of them members of the working class) "forcibly locked themselves in Santiago's Cathedral. This seizure coincided with the nationwide emergence of mass protest against Frei's *indifference* to the "revolution" he had so incessantly pledged. With national attention upon them, the Cathedral insurgents released a manifesto proclaiming their egalitarian commitments:

. . . Moved by our love for the church which is our home, we have shut ourselves in the Cathedral. We came here to meditate. We are moved by the truth of the gospel, not by any private interest.

We want to be the church of the people. We want the church to live among the poor. Thus we say No to a church which is enslaved by social concessions. We say Yes to a servant church. Yes to a church which, by its faith in Jesus Christ and in man, dares to side with the poor, to eradicate illiteracy, penury and infant mortality. We say No to a hierarchial scheme which burdens the souls of men instead of redeeming them; Yes to priests who are born out of the masses and fight with them for a richer life; No to a church which is afraid to face history; Yes to a valiant church in battle for genuine emancipation of human beings.

We condemn the violence exercised by the rich; their usurpation of rights is violence. We condemn the exploitation of man by the iniquitous profit system; international imperialism; the subjection of human consciences by the monopolies that own the means of information; racial, cultural and economic segregation; the operation of education in favor of the ruling classes; the division among the masses which only fortifies the power of the dominent classes. We favor a new society that will dignify human beings, where love can actually be practiced.

Thus it is inconceivable that the Holy Father can travel to a land where the oligarchies drown the people in an ocean of pauperism and illiteracy. We believe that the ostentatious display of the Colombian society will but hamper the gospel. Christ came to the world to redeem the poor. The pope will see slavery, not liberation. It is high time that we recapture genuine Christianity.[288]

Although reprimanded by Cardinal Silva, following apologies the Chilean prelate invited the offending priests "to partake with him of holy communion." More than 300 priests from Santiago Province partook of this mass. Manifesting a conciliatory disposition, Cardinal Silva admitted:

Perhaps we have not given ourselves to our priests and to our members in the measure needed today. We must not forget that among our people there are hunger, penury, indigence. The masses want justice. . . .[289]

While it must be acknowledged that a substantial majority within the Church opposed these militant tactics, there was a sizeable and growing minority of revolutionary supporters.

Conservative Catholics had organized the National Council of Chilean Society for the Defense of Tradition, Family and Property.

Members of this group accuse the hierarchy of being harder on them than on those who 'labor night and day to use the church as a channel for the diffusion of communistic ideas among the faithful.' In a message signed by 80,000 persons and forwarded to Paul VI at Bogota it denounced the 'infiltration of communism' into the ranks of Chilean lay people and clergy, particularly the Jesuits.[290]

The hatred which infused this rightist sector of Chilean Catholicism was reflected during *and after* the 1970 presidential campaign through the dissemination of mountainous propaganda associating a Popular Unity victory with Castro-Communism.[291] Significantly, almost 39 percent of voting women opted for Alessandri. Tomic received but 30 percent. Only a small proportion of Allende's 31 percent identified as practicing Catholics.

Yet, as compared to 1964, Allende lost precious little support from women as opposed to a larger percentage decline among generally less Church-oriented males!

Since he attained a plurality of but 40,000 votes, it is likely that vigorous campaign assistance by the explicitly Catholic MAPU ensured his margin. This would be true even if much of their organizing were among the non-Catholic *marginales*. The 15 percent who defected from the PDC included several hundred priests and perhaps ten times that number of lay activists inspired by the social gospel and communitarian ideals. Similarly their failure to work for Tomic almost certainly contributed to his unimpressive showing.

By 1970, this revolutionary Catholic sector was receiving open support from *Mensaje*. In July the Jesuit monthly denounced torture in Brazil and Cardinal Rossi's defense of that government.[292] Two years earlier, the same journal complained that an official assembly which had been called to consider Church "renewal" had failed to discuss social action programs.[293] While *Mensaje* did not support Allende, neither did it oppose the UP candidate. In fact, his answers to reporters were published together with those of Tomic and Alessandri.[294]

Unlike Catholics of the right who responded to the September UP victory by negotiating with *oficialistas* for concerted action in the forthcoming Plenary Congress, *Mensaje* immediately recognized Allende's legitimate claim to be chief of state. Noting that despite "simplistic" Castro-Communist propaganda, the "vast majority of our youth were overjoyed to learn of UP's victory at the polls," the Jesuit monthly called upon its constituency to actively support the government's efforts to implement a revolutionary program similar to that previously outlined in the 1962-1963 special issues of *Mensaje*:

The unimpeachable triumph of Dr. Allende at the ballots has triggered a dangerous panic in the country. Stock quotations are plummeting, bank deposits are being withdrawn, savings and loan banks are shutting their doors, employees are being let go, small industries are folding, many are selling and few are buying, hundreds of Chileans are fleeing abroad.

We have been hoping that Chileans would show more maturity and serenity. But apparently the simplistic and systematic campaign of rumors—as if the triumph of Allende meant firing squads, Cuban-style law, Soviet imperialism, an end to all freedoms, and economic ruin—has had upsetting effects far and wide. The false image that many have of socialism and communism has likewise built up fears.

Some, of course, are deliberately increasing the panic, irresponsibly and unpatriotically, to feather their own little nests. We are not writing for them, obviously, since their attitude merits only scorn. Rather we are writing for those who are fearful but who at heart are patriots and desire Chile's good. For these, we say that their panic is quite groundless, that they should calm down and help restore tranquility to the country.

Liberty does not mean I may do whatever I please, have as many automobiles or houses as I wish, go on pleasure jaunts abroad whenever my heart so desires. To respect freedom means to keep intact a man's right to be fully a man (under our present system, alas, there are many who don't enjoy that right at all); to participate practically, not just in theory, in the national society; to express one's opinions freely and responsibly; to join in associations in order to be heard and to protect one's legitimate rights; and to profess publicly one'e religious beliefs.

Guaranteeing the basic freedom of all Chileans to co-operate actively and conscientiously in the country's historic destiny is what UP (Popular Unity) has proposed. And is that not a perfectly acceptable program?

The neo-capitalistic system has assured the welfare of a few at the cost of making the great bulk of our people "marginal" socially, politically and culturally. Some of our present structures, devised by capitalism, are still at its service. We must, therefore, change them. Capitalism has its eye on profits before all else; it creates artificial needs, yet leaves the basic ones unsatisfied; it connives with the great foreign consortiums that by their subtle and systematic advertising are shaping our modes of thinking, our tastes, our customs—in a word, the most precious thing people has: its own way of life, its authentic culture.

Back in 1962, this Review, in a special issue, denounced the injustice that blankets Chile and all Latin America; another special issue, in 1963 pointed out certain reforms that were urgently required. We are talking about revolution—a necessary revolution, but one to be carried out as much as possible without physical violence, without blood, and of course without injustices, respecting all the basic rights of man. That has been and will continue to be the policy of this Review, and what motivates us are not only social but also Christian imperatives.

Christ came to liberate the poor and give them His good news. The kingdom

He founded will have its culmination in another world, but here on earth He means it to be a just society, one whose social structures help all men, not just certain lucky ones, to fulfill themselves. In that sense we may say that the lack of human corporateness toward which capitalism is leading us is radically anti-Christian.

As human beings, as citizens and as Christians, then, we must struggle to get thousands and thousands of our fellow citizens, our brothers, out from under the asphyxiating, subhuman misery in which they live without hope. We must struggle so that there won't be so many of them undernourished; so that they will have steady, well-paid work; so their children can get an education that will equip them to serve their country well; so that all will have a genuine voice in the major decisions that their country makes, in order that all can thus defend their personal selves and our positive traditions.

These are the goals that UP is proposing. Let us reflect on the enormous gain for many Chileans if these reforms are applied effectively, seriously, without partisan selfishness, without ambitions, without falling into mountains of bureaucratic red tape, keeping in view always the peoples' advantage.

A sober reflection here can help us. The vast majority of our youth are over-joyed to learn of UP's victory at the ballots. They are ready now to leap in, heedless of costs or sacrifices, to realize that party's program. By their idealism, their generosity and dedication, these young people are the country's most sensi-tive antennae to grasp the pulse of the historic future that opens before Chile. Shouldn't all of us Chileans go along with them?

It seems reasonable to expect that this collaboration will be expressed in a variety of ways. Some agree with the UP's entire program; others differ with it, one point or another. But those differences of agreement should always be mani-fested with responsibility and out of a constructive purpose, aiming only at the common good and the furtherance of basic human values.

In any event, we should be ready—all of us, from the President down to the least citizen—to show our seriousness, to work hard and produce more, not seek-ing first and foremost what profits us as individuals, or our particular party, but keeping in view the common good.

Finally, as Christians, we believe that the risen Savior is the supreme force in history. Any progress in freedoms, any profundization of dialogue, any fulfill-ment of man will be growth in the total Christ. His kingdom may reach us in ways that will upset us, but we look for its unerring advance. May this faith and hope of ours be evidenced by our ardent and generous work.[295]

Given this challenge, it is obvious that Christian Democracy had failed to revolu-tionize Chile's socio-economic structures.

Manifesting his respect for Catholic support, Allende was escorted from his inauguration by a "special guard from the military school" to the Cathedral of Santiago. There, this "Marxist-Leninist" Mason attended a Te Deum Mass.[296] Within days, Cardinal Silva officially recognized the participation of Catholics in the UP government (MAPU held three ministerial portfolios). Acknowledging the inequities associated with capitalism, the Chilean prelate admitted that socialist measures might constitute legitimate remedies in unspecified issue-areas! Significantly, this interview with *Juventud Rebelde* was featured in Havana's Granma![297]

Concluding Remarks

The centrist parties did not react identically to the Cuban Revolution. Within the governing coalition, the Radicals were transformed into vigorous advocates of moderate reforms. This was—like a lesser shift by the rightist parties—almost wholly conditioned by the successive electoral gains of a FRAP whose leaders had associated themselves with the policies of the Castro government. The PDC had already adopted a reformist posture by 1958. The decision to accord *much greater stress* to this orientation while emphasizing its role as *la unica alternativa* was attributable to both the party's competition with the Marxists for lower class support as well as a need to accommodate its own left wing, a minority among the national leadership and an overwhelming majority among the party's youth. This new emphasis was reinforced by the AFP and the emergence of the Church as a vigorous advocate of social and economic reform. The clergy's shift appears to have been partially conditioned by fear of growing leftist popular appeal. The fate of the Church in Cuba almost certainly heightened its sense of urgency. For both the Chilean Church and the PDC, material aid from United States corporations, non-governmental organizations, and especially the United States government appears to have played a vital role in their ability to effectively project *la unica alternativa* to the electorate.

The incompatibility of centrist reliance upon entrepreneurial backing while proclaiming dedication to social reforms was first manifested under Popular Front governments between 1938 and 1947. At that time, popular support for the Marxist parties increased due to the respectability accorded them by inclusion in the government. If Christian Democracy wisely abstained from repeating this Radical error, it nevertheless committed even more serious tactical blunders. In some cases, however, decisions were literally compelled by circumstances.

Hence, given the catalyzation of leftist political struggle in the early 1960s which had been inspired in part by the Cuban example, the Christian Democrats—pressured also by their communitarian wing and the United States—had to move to the "left." This demagogic posture raised expectations and heightened commitments of a growing Catholic minority. Reinforced by visits to Cuba and emerging revolutionary tendencies elsewhere in Latin American Catholicism, the PDC communitarians finally realized that only through class struggle could their egalitarian goals be attained. This brought them closer to Chilean Marxists. Simultaneously, a more militant sector of Catholic youth, inspired by Camilio Torres, moved towards tactical unity with the MIR. As the Social Democratic character of the *oficialistas* became increasingly evident these energetic mass organizers joined the radicalized Radicals in affiliating with the Marxist-led Popular Unity coalition.

At the same time, *oficialista* arrogance and Tomic's prior claim on the 1970 nomination fatally undermined PDC tactical flexibility. Hence, a candidate acceptable to the Nationals could not be presented. Middle class disunity, then, provided a weakened but unified left an unexpected electoral plurality. To some extent this was also consequential to counterrevolutionary miscalculations—overconfidence that Alessandri would triumph. Even if he had been victorious, middle class disunity might have contributed to a Popular Unity government. For although many supporters of Tomic had remained in the PDC, they were nevertheless genuinely committed to his populist campaign which had attacked Frei's failure to deliver a "Revolution in Liberty." Thus, "(a) few days after the elections it was revealed that there had been a secret pact of mutual support between Tomic and Allende in the event that one of them should win first or second place; and they agreed to recognize a victory by Alessandri only if he won a substantial plurality of more than 100,000 votes."[298] Since, the UP nominee, considered at the time to be a "right-wing Socialist," needed but 13 of 75 PDC votes in the Plenary Congress, there is good reason to believe that Allende would have been elected anyway. *Neither* Tomic nor Allende had pledged their supporters to back the candidate receiving a mere plurality—although the overconfident Alessandri had!

9 Public Opinion and Activism

Introduction

It may be assumed that the decision by anti-FRAP forces in late 1962 to assign major priority to a *paredon* issue was based in some degree upon knowledge of the general unpopularity of Castro and the Cuban Revolution. Public opinion was, of course, conditioned by the structure of mass media ownership which implied that most information about Cuban events was defined, interpreted and conveyed to United States wire services and the USIA. This was especially true with regard to day-to-day events. Evaluations were also influenced by the educational system, clerical institutions and to a lesser degree by political parties and unions. In many instances Cuba-related opinion was a partial function of pre-existing dispositions towards the Church, constitutionalism and the United States.

Survey Data. During the second half of 1959, a former USIA officer then on an OAS fellowship surveyed several hundred students at the University of Chile and Catholic University in Santiago. Although the results are unrepresentative, they may cast some light upon early student reaction to the Cuban Revolution. Asked to identify their "most favored leader," the students revealed the following order of preference: Castro (10); Mao (17); Nixon (79); Khrushchev (93); Dulles (100); Nehru (158); and Adenauer (178). "Marcus explained Fidel Castro's low popularity by referring to his 'tropical' methods; but, on the other hand, there was a great sympathy for the 26th of July Movement because it overthrew Batista." Fully 71 percent believed the United States was intervening in Cuba, while a mere 13 percent denied the existence of such acts.[1]

By September 1961, large scale nationalizations of domestic and especially United States firms had been carried out in Cuba. In addition, a relationship of dependency upon the Soviet Union and close collaboration with Cuban Communists characterized the Castro leadership. A large majority of the non-Cuban Catholic clergy had left or been forced out of the country. And although Fidel's dictatorship was officially "socialist," United States and rightist propaganda had defined it as Communist since March 1960.

No reliable survey data are available for the period from January 1959 until September 1961. During September, the University of Chile's Center for Socio-Economic Studies (CESO) conducted a survey of heads of households (83 percent male) in Greater Santiago. The following evaluations of Fidel Castro were expressed:

211

Very Good	7.2%
Good	17.8
Undecided	12.2
Bad	37.0
Very Bad	8.9
Don't Know or No Reply	17.0

Forty-four percent agreed that Fidel Castro was a Communist and that the Cuban Revolution was controlled by Communists, while 22.4 percent held a contrary view. These two figures correlate fairly well with the "good-bad" evaluations, although some sympathizers may have held a "good" opinion of Castro while accepting the view that the Revolution was led by Communists. About 20 percent of the respondents declined to agree with either of these alternative characterizations of Fidel and the Revolution, while 13 percent failed to reply or "didn't know."

Open-ended evaluations of Castro as a leader indicated a slightly less favorable distribution:

14.7%	a great leader; a modern Bolivar;
7.5	a hero who defended the people's rights;
10.3	he is responsible for both good and bad deeds;
2.7	is too personalistic and has committed too many errors;
14.1	he is crazy, ambitious, a demagogue, etc.;
11.9	deceives the people; executed and murdered them;
6.9	persecutes Cubans; does not respect liberty of thought, especially religion;
6.0	is a Communist; ruined the country;
9.6	other opinions;
16.8	can't give an opinion; don't know; no reply.

A greater frequency of favorable responses was apparent when the interviewees were asked to assess the "Cuban Revolution," rather than Castro. The percentages were as follows: very good (4.5); good (25.1); undecided (14.4); bad (31.6); very bad (5.5); don't know or no response (18.4).

The fact that there was a smaller proportion of extreme views indicates that Castro—the man—inspired greater emotionality of response than did the Revolution itself. On the other hand, there is little real indication as to the intensity with which the views were held. And there was an element of ambiguity in the term Cuban Revolution. Thus, when the respondents were asked to characterize *the nature* of the Cuban Revolution, their replies to this open-ended question were stratified as follows:

11.1% it liberated Cuba from Yankee imperialism; an example for America; now the Cubans are free;

7.9 they nationalized industry; change and reform was fostered; Cuba was liberated from the economic tutelage of the United States; the country was liberated from a dictator;

0.9 there is an economic crisis, low production and famine, etc.; they damaged the country;

2.6 there is political, ideological or religious persecution; the people are persecuted;

5.7 there is no democracy or liberty; one dictatorship has been substituted for another; no elections were called;

14.7 at the beginning the revolution was good, now it is bad; it shifted its principles and goals; it is good insofar as Cuba was liberated from a dictatorship and a beginning was made for economic development, and bad because of the relationship with the Russians, the religious persecution, the executions and murders;

16.1 now Cuba is Communist; there are executions and murder; it is a failure; there is disorganization; ambition is rampant;

13.0 other opinions;

4.4 cannot give an opinion; doesn't know what is happening; the news agencies distort events there;

15.9 don't know or no reply.

As in the case of Fidel as a person, the ratio here is a 3-2 negative one. As a vague symbol, however, the Cuban Revolution evoked fewer negative responses. Or it may be that more functionally illiterate persons responded favorably to the mention of the Cuban Revolution, but were unable to specify the grounds for such beliefs. Others may have thought of the Cuban Revolution exclusively in terms of its (Castro's) original programmatic commitments, which included civil liberties.

Despite the clear predominance of negative attitudes towards Fidel and to a lesser degree with regard to the Revolution in overall terms, Chilean sentiment opposed overt United States intervention to undermine or destroy the Cuban Government. United States "support" for the Bay of Pigs invasion was evaluated as follows: good (15.6 percent); bad (61.8 percent); the United States did not support the invasion (3.2 percent); don't know or no reply (19.5 percent). The sample was then asked what United States policy should be towards Cuba in the future:

3.0% invade and install a pro-United States government;

20.8 don't invade, but impose economic and political sanctions likely to provoke a change of orientation by the Cuban government;

54.4 respect Cuba's right to have the kind of government she wants, like any other Latin American nation;

12.5 assist and support the Castro government;

9.3 don't know or no reply.

It is impossible to ascertain how important such views were to those who held them. An indication that Cuba was not in the minds of many persons—especially those in the sympathetic category—is manifested by Cuba's position among Latin American countries for which the interviewees had "most" and "least" sympathy (see Table 9-1). Considering the rest of the world, 43.6 percent selected the United States as the nation for which they harbored most sympathy, as opposed to 10.8 percent offering contrary views. We may conclude that far more Chileans were conscious of Cuba as a negative symbol than as an attractive one; and taking both groups together, less than a third of the respondents were willing to single out Cuba at all among the Latin American group. And the fact that six times as many persons viewed the United States with "greater sympathy" indicates that even before Castro adopted Marxism-Leninism, Cuba was not a source of revolutionary inspiration for many Chileans.

In the weeks following the missile crisis, a Chilean public opinion survey in all cities with an excess of 10,000 persons as well as in some rural areas indicated a major decline in Fidel Castro's popularity. When asked "(w)hat opinion do you have of Fidel Castro?," the following replies were given: very good (6 percent); good (11 percent); neither good nor bad (19 percent); bad (24 percent); very bad (27 percent); no opinion (7 percent); hadn't heard of Castro (6 percent).[2] In

Table 9-1

Foreign Sympathies by Heads of Household, Santiago, September 1961

Nation	Most	Least
Cuba	7.7%	23.5%
Argentina	25.8	24.2
Brazil	27.5	0.0
Bolivia	0.0	9.6
Mexico	15.5	0.0
Peru	0.0	7.1
Uruguay	5.7	0.0
Others	4.0	2.0
No Reply	10.5	31.3

Source: "Stratification Survey" by the Centro de Estudios Socio-economicos, Instituto de Economía, Universidad de Chile, September 1961. Unpublished data furnished by Eduardo Hamuy, Director of CESO.

general, rural opinion paralleled that in urban areas, except for a higher proportion of "no opinion." The lower classes are less cohesive and evidenced more leftism.[3]

In the October 1963 survey of 400 Santiago women, the following question was posed: "In Cuba there has been a revolution which has changed the way people live. What is your opinion of it (see Table 9-2)?" Whereas 92 percent of the sample identified themselves as belonging to a religion, this figure was as high as 97 percent for the traditionalists. In general, those identifying with a religion were slightly more hostile to the Cuban Revolution than the average for the total sample. Unmarried girls, and women under forty years of age were slightly less hostile, and more likely to be politically leftist.[4] The lower classes and those without secondary education were most supportive; and this is consistent with the class content of the Cuban Revolution. But even at these levels, a majority of those offering opinions were perjorative. Especially significant was the strong correlation between self-designation as a revolutionary and defense of Cuba. At the time of this survey, both the FRAP as well as Christian Democracy were explicitly committed to "revolutionizing" Chilean socio-economic structures.

Table 9-2
Evaluations of the Cuban Revolution by Santiago Women, October 1963

| Evaluation | Socio-economic Level | | | |
	Upper	Middle	Lower	Average
Good	15.8%	11.6%	25.5%	17.5%
Bad	68.4	65.7	30.9	51.5
Don't know	5.3	8.3	31.5	17.5
No response	10.5	14.4	12.1	13.5

| Evaluation | Years of Schooling | | | |
	0-5	6-8	9-11	12+
Good	24.0%	24.2%	13.7%	13.0%
Bad	32.7	42.1	60.3	70.0
Don't know	32.7	23.2	10.9	1.0
No response	10.6	10.5	15.0	16.0

| Evaluation | Conservatism-Radicalism | | |
	Traditionalists	Reformists	Revolutionaries
Good	1.5%	11.0%	65.2%
Bad	77.0	67.7	8.7
Don't know	16.9	7.9	17.4
No response	4.6	13.4	8.7

Source: Frida Kaplan B., Yolanda Navarrete R., Daniela Rubens F., "Algunos Factores que Determinan la Conducta Electoral de la Mujer" (Memoria para Optar al Título de Psicológico, Universidad de Chile, Facultad de Filosofía y Educación, Escuela de Psicología, Santiago, 1964).

A survey of Catholic clergy and lay activists in Church related organizations during the very early 1960s revealed a greater polarization of opinion towards Havana. The interviewees were asked for their evaluation of the long range effect of the Cuban Revolution upon the people of Cuba (see Table 9-3).

During the second week of May 1964, a Cuba-oriented survey was conducted in Santiago by a local public opinion research firm. The sample was rather small, containing only 200 persons.[5] Opinions of Fidel Castro had improved somewhat over the last USIA-commissioned survey in the weeks following the missile crisis. This time the responses were as follows: very good (5 percent); good (17 percent); neither good nor bad (27 percent); bad (27 percent); very bad (20 percent); don't know (4 percent). The other relevant questions posed were:

Since the Cuban Revolution, the life of the average person has

become better	20%
become worse	58
remained about the same	13
don't know	9

If Castro remains as the head of the Cuban Government, conditions there will

improve	27%
worsen	42
remain the same	25
don't know	6

Should Chile maintain her diplomatic relations with Cuba?

yes	58%
no	39
don't know	3

Venezuela has charged Cuba with engaging in subversive activity against her, and has proposed that the Latin American countries jointly warn Cuba that they will retaliate through the OAS if Cuba "engages in subversive activity against any Latin American country." Should Chile sign this joint warning?

Table 9-3
Views of the Cuban Revolution by Active Catholics in 1959-1961

Perception	Clergy	Lay
Very Good	2.4%	2.2%
More Good than Bad	20.4	30.5
More Bad than Good	46.7	43.5
Very Bad	25.9	23.4
No Reply	4.6	0.4

Source: Joseph Fichter, *Cambio Social en Chile* (Santiago: Editorial Universidad Católica, 1962), p. 47. No date is provided for this survey. It is likely that the sample was from Santiago and largely middle and upper class in composition.

yes	35%
no	58
don't know	7

Widespread opposition to sanctions against Cuba was again revealed in a CESO Greater Santiago survey during the first days of August 1964. To the question of what Chile's attitude should be towards Cuba, the following replies were given: expand relations (8.2 percent); maintain them as they are now (45.1 percent); suspend relations (20.4 percent); break relations and participate in a policy of sanctions (10.1 percent); no answer (15.7 percent). If there was an expected decline in the percentage of those wanting to maintain relations now that the OAS had ordered a severance, more remarkable was the fact that a smaller percentage now endorsed a suspension or break in relations than did so in early May. On the other hand, when one compares the results of this survey to that carried out in September 1961, it is clear that a larger proportion of Chileans now supported coercive measures by the United States towards Cuba. When asked what United States policy should be towards Cuba, they said:

4.1% invade and install a pro-United States government;
42.0 don't invade, but impose economic and political sanctions likely to provoke a change of orientation by the Cuban government;
39.5 respect Cuba's right to have the kind of government she wants, like any other Latin American nation;
6.8 give Fidel all forms of aid to fulfill the revolution;
12.2 don't know;
5.9 no reply.

Interestingly, the percentage who were now confused or otherwise unwilling to reply had doubled over that of 1961.

The importance of the Cuban-Communist issue in the hate-filled electoral campaign then at its climax, may well have been reflected by the refusal of an overwhelming majority of interviewees to offer *any opinion* of either Fidel Castro or the Cuban Revolution. Significantly, those harboring negative views were more outspoken and predominant (see Table 9-4).

When asked to indicate the Latin American nations for which they held the greatest and least sympathy, Cuba was substantially less popular than in 1961, but mentioned somewhat more frequently. This, in turn, may have been a consequence of its importance as a campaign issue at the time (see Table 9-5).

After Chile had severed all relations with Cuba, CESO conducted another survey in Greater Santiago shortly before Frei's inauguration. There had been a marked decline in the number of persons who advocated a resumption in diplomatic relations. On the other hand, a larger majority expressed support for *some type of relations*, and fewer favored total rupture than had during early August.

Table 9-4

Opinions of Castro and the Cuban Revolution, Greater Santiago, August 1964

Opinion	Fidel Castro	Cuban Revolution
Very Good	0.4%	0.4%
Good	3.6	5.8
Neither Good nor Bad	0.1	0.4
Bad	19.1	23.5
Very Bad	6.2	5.0
No Response	70.2	64.9

Source: "Pre-Electoral Survey" of Greater Santiago by the Centro de Estudios Socio-economicos, Instituto de Economía, Universidad de Chile, August 1964. Unpublished data furnished by Eduardo Hamuy, Director of CESO.

What should Frei's policy be towards Cuba?	
Renew relations	29.6%
Establish purely commercial relations	43.2
Maintain broken relations	23.2
Don't know	3.4

They were then asked why Chile failed to have relations with Cuba, while at the same time she maintained them with other dictatorial regimes. The interviewees proffered the following answers: the situation was arbitrary or contradictory (24.6 percent); Cuba was Communist or the Soviet Union had intervened there (33.2 percent); Cuba had intervened in the internal affairs of other nations (7.4 percent); United States pressure (4.2 percent); because of the nature of the present Government of Cuba (0.9 percent); the OAS mandate (1.8 percent); there is no contradiction (2 percent); no opinion or no reply (19.9 percent).[6]

Public Responses to Demonstrations. The very limited and diminishing positive appeal of the Cuban Revolution among the public was also manifested by at-

Table 9-5

Sympathies for Other Nations, Greater Santiago, August 1964

Nation	Greatest	Least
Cuba	5.9%	30.4%
Argentina	19.5	22.3
Brazil	27.1	1.2
Bolivia	0.6	20.7

Source: "Pre-Electoral Survey" of Greater Santiago by the Centro de Estudios Socio-economicos, Instituto de Economía, Universidad de Chile, August 1964. Unpublished data furnished by Eduardo Hamuy, Director of CESO.

tendance figures for rallies and other demonstrations of support. Although participation data may be discounted somewhat by the fact that Chileans in general are not involved in political activities, they nevertheless reflect the unwillingness of even those with sympathetic views to commit themselves to physical expressions of support—a test of their intensity and priority relative to other personal interests.

The homage to Cuba and Venezuela which the CUT-FECH-FRAP organized on Aug. 11, 1959, was expected to attract "hundreds of thousands." Despite the presence of Armando Hart, Allende, etc., the Carabineros estimated that only about 2,500 persons attended. And this was a rally unofficially supported by the PDC through the presence of such prominent party leaders as Musalem, Gomucio and Juan de Dios Carmona.[7] During the same year, more than 500,000 persons were reported to have participated in one Santiago religious procession.[8] Even if these figures are not accurate, the disparity remains significant.

On Feb. 28, 1960, an estimated 400,000 Chileans crowded President Eisenhower's parade route in downtown Santiago.[9] This may be compared with the FRAP 26th of July commemoration which was subsequently organized at the Caupolican to laud the Cuban Revolution and condemn the United States for suspending Havana's sugar quota. It was estimated that 7,000 persons attended this event.[10] Several weeks later, between 2,500 and 5,000 persons participated in an outdoor CUT-FRAP demonstration to protest the OAS Conference of Foreign Ministers at San Jose.[11] El Mercurio reported in its usual "unbiased" fashion:

When the conference was opened in Costa Rica, these elements attempted to organize a movement throughout Latin America, that would provoke street disturbances as a protest against that meeting. But the public did not respond to the call, and the protest only amounted to a few feeble and boresome processions in which communists and their fellow-travelers put on Cuban peasant hats and listened to the same orators who have been addressing them for so many years.[12]

During the Bay of Pigs aggression, 150 Chilean writers, artists and intellectuals signed a declaration condemning United States support of the "mercenary army" as an "attack upon the free determination of peoples, upon the right that our countries have to choose their own forms of government and way of life."[13] The CUT 24-hour general strike resulted in between 29,802 and 88,650 workers leaving their jobs. Another 30,946 students boycotted their classrooms.[14] Ercilla reported that "there was mass agitation and even a third grade general strike which failed to have the consequences hoped for by the leftists and feared by the Government."[15] A protest rally at the Plaza Brazil attracted between 2,000 and 10,000 while the Carabineros estimated that only 102 persons participated in a Valparaiso demonstration. Between several hundred and a thousand students joined a number of workers in parading and chanting in the business center of Santiago, and there were some violent incidents both in the capital city and especially in Concepcion. Molotov Cocktails were thrown at the Grace building, the Chilean-North American Institute of Culture, and an abortive bombing attempt was directed at the United States Embassy.[16] It is probable that most of those who participated in the general strike and the demonstrations were affiliated with leftist or centrist political parties either as members or active supporters.

On May Day, the FRAP and the CUT sponsored a rally dedicated to the "Defense of the Cuban Revolution." Suitable banners were prepared and an announcement was released that 20,000 were expected to attend this event, in the aftermath of the Castro victory at Playa Giron. Nevertheless, a reported 5,000 appeared on May 1 at the Plaza de Artesanos.[17] When Adlai Stevenson arrived for an official visit six weeks later, he "was greeted by anti-U.S. demonstrators who smashed the windows of the U.S. Information Service Office in Santiago. *El Mercurio* reported that the group, "some 50 in number, consisted of youths and also older men and women attempting to pass themselves off as students. The demonstrators . . . carried signs stating 'Stevenson, Go Home' and shouted *Cuba Si, Yanqui, No*.' There were no injuries, and the damage amounted to some 300 Escudos (1.05 Escudos = $1)."[18]

During the first half of 1962, there were two events that deserve brief mention. In February, the FRAP called a rally in the Caupolican to protest the expulsion of Cuba from the OAS.[19] Since the Caupolican Theatre seats seven thousand persons, it is probable that several thousand attended. An estimated 8,000 attended the CUT May Day rally, where the Cuban Revolution was a major theme.[20]

If there was some quite limited *mass* support from the students community and the working classes during the Bay of Pigs events, there was none at the time of the missile crisis. "Some disturbances were reported Tuesday night, but police quickly brought the few roving gangs of students under control. The cries of 'Cuba Si, Yankees, No' evoked little response and no audible support."[21] *El Siglo* reported that 200 FRAP students had filed through the main streets of Santiago, chanting anti-United States slogans. They provoked virtually no violence, and only 25 were arrested, 12 of whom were charged only with parading without a permit. *El Siglo* claimed that "thousands of students and workers" had demonstrated in Valparaiso, and that there were "thousands and thousands" of banners and placards at a "gigantic" and "vigorous" protest rally in Santiago.[22] In both cases, the figures may be prudently reduced to between two and three thousand FRAP militants.

Radio Havana had called upon Latin Americans to defend Cuba by violently attacking United States businesses and government offices.[23] The small group of persons responding to this call and their largely abortive efforts were described in chapter 7. They were highly politicized revolutionaries, and the public was not involved.

During July 1963, the CUT sponsored an assembly at the Caupolican to commemorate the 26th of July anniversary.[24] It is probable that no more than three or four thousand attended. Most were active sympathizers with or members of the FRAP parties. At about the same time, the Chilean-Cuban Cultural Institute organized a program in the Salon de Honor of the University of Chile.[25] This theatre seats no more than several hundred persons, and virtually all of those who attended were probably active or sympathetic leftists.

Finally, when the CUT and the FECH organized a meeting at the Teatro Esmeralda on Aug. 14, 1964 to protest Chile's rupture of relations with Cuba, the event began one-and-a-half hours late with "less than a third of the thousand seats in the theatre occupied."[26] A week later, about eighty persons traveled to the airport to wish the Cuban Charge d'Affaires a farewell as he boarded his flight for Havana.[27]

Concluding Remarks

It is noteworthy that by September 1961, predominantly negative opinions were already held toward Castro (5-3) and the Cuban Revolution (3-2). Of course, *for almost eighteen months* the USIA, *El Mercurio* and other mass media had been charging that Cuba was Communist. The fact that no more than 5 percent spontaneously identified sympathetically with Cuba was also reflected in the low turnout figures for pro-Cuban demonstrations.

During the succeeding three years, these ratios altered very moderately. The only exception occurred in the weeks following the missile crisis when Cuban prestige declined markedly. Its subsequent recovery almost to 1961 levels was not, however, paralleled by the maintenance of the initially overwhelming Chilean opposition to a United States drive to impose economic and diplomatic sanctions upon the Havana government. By May 1964, a bare majority opposed such measures. This may have been conditioned by widely publicized Cuban efforts to subvert pro-United States governments, the "Campaign of Terror," and the improved image of the United States as noted in chapter 5.

There is nothing remarkable in the fact that self-conscious Catholics, women, conservatives and the middle classes tended to be more hostile to the Castro leadership than those associated with opposite variables. It is interesting that the "Cuban Revolution" suffered a greater decline in prestige than its charismatic leader who was initially not as popular as the Revolution. The effect of the "Campaign of Terror" was clearly manifested by August 1964 spontaneous (open-ended) negative views of Cuba by 30.4 percent, while in September 1961 only 23.5 percent had expressed themselves similarly. Well over 60 percent declined to give any opinion of Castro or the Cuban Revolution in August 1964.

Since the economic situation of Cuba continued to deteriorate as the decade progressed, there is no basis for assuming that popular sentiment changed. In fact, Cuba's enforced isolation substantially curtailed the flow of persons between Chile and Havana. While the author is not in the possession of survey data for the late sixties, the enthusiasm with which anti-UP forces used Fidel's 26th of July confessions suggests a similar array of negative attitudes. The only probable development at the mass level was greater ignorance and indifference to the Cuban experiment in creating a new type of man. Unless the Allende government is deposed by the military, there will be a *gradual* rise in mass consciousness of and support for the Cuban Revolution. A modified mass media structure and expanded cultural relations will be reinforced by the UP government's egalitarian and nationalistic program. Eventually, Fidel Castro will receive his first invitation since 1959 to visit a Latin American country. Then hundreds of thousands of lower class Chileans will enthusiastically applaud an honored hero on Chilean soil. For as social scientists are well aware, even in "developed" countries the masses are not strongly committed to the libertarian procedures of "parliamentary democracy."[28] The less politically socialized Chilean masses— consigned under all previous regimes to debt and proverty—have even lower levels of commitment to such norms.[29]

10 Conclusions

In the following pages, differential responses to the Cuban Revolution will be summarized and related where possible to such modifications as occurred in the Chilean political system during the 1959-1970 period. Consideration will then be given to some implications for the study of comparative politics and United States foreign policy.

Three Political Systems and a Symbol

The foregoing inquiry has focused upon the interactive relationships of three political systems. In effect, a small power with a revolutionary and increasingly Communist leadership sought to engender the sympathy of internal actors within another small power which was not only 7,000 miles distant, but also characterized at the elite level by an evolutionary constitutionalist tradition and parliamentary democratic institutions. Chile was, however, beset by mass poverty, economic stagnation, class barriers that inhibited mobility, chronic inflation of a severe nature, slowly escalating mass discontent—and in 1957 there had been large-scale violence and looting during rioting that followed a mass protest against inflation. A third political system—the world's greatest power—countered the Cuban inputs with a variety of its own. They were directed at sympathetic internal elites as well as the mass of citizens.

In the most summary form, this was "the Chilean drama" during the 1960s. Would one of the few parliamentary democracies in Latin America be transformed into "another Cuba" without foreign aggression or even violent revolution? Given both the North American self-fulfilling prophesy that "the Communists have never won a free election" plus the overt threat posed by FRAP to the profits of United States corporate investors, it was necessary to intervene in a variety of ways to ensure that electoral outcomes were compatible with the maintenance of international capitalism. As the pattern of United States "aid and comfort" to Latin American dictatorships suggests, an Open Door for investors is the only operational meaning of the "Free World" slogan.

To politically conscious Chileans, the words "Cuba" or "Castro" were transformed by the end of 1959 from mere standards of reference to highly charged evocative symbols. In essence, "Cuba" exemplified not merely independence from the United States, but an effective assertion of economic sovereignty. To the extent that Cubans succeeded in their economic nationalizations, the ubiquitous *fatalismo* that paralyzes more timid "latino" nationalists would be under-mined. As the following exchange between Congressman Fascell and the Com-mander-in-Chief of the United States Southern Command (Latin America) sug-gests, there is acute recognition by politico-military elites of the threat which nationalism poses for North American investing corporations:

Mr. Fascell. In understanding that factor and in understanding also the political necessity to stay in power, do you agree that each one of these nationalistic regimes, with a change in its political base, will be forced to take a stronger anti-American stand in order to justify their position?

General Mather. I think that is very logical to expect, Mr. Chairman, because really, I think the true profile of America in Latin America is the multibillion dollar investment we have here. This is what these economic materialists are after, and causing a lot of our problems. It is $12 billion. About a fifth of our total foreign investment.[1]

Hence, the necessity—perceived by some and sanctioned by all decision-makers—to isolate and cripple the Cuban economy. By structuring such a self-fulfilling prophesy—that Latin Americans who refuse to cooperate will fail—the United States endeavored to convince Chileans that support for local *Fidelistas* would bring upon them a national disaster. In some measure, too, the early appeal of the Alliance for Progress was reinforced by a series of Cuban administrative er-rors.[2] Despite generous Soviet assistance and marked improvements in social welfare, the Cuban economy has failed to "takeoff," to use Rostow's phrase. Symptomatically, 1971 is the "Year for Productivity."

The Pattern of Internal Responses

The Right. Apparently, the very word "revolution" was a source of discomfort for Liberals and especially Conservatives. At the end of 1958, there is no evi-dence of sympathy for even the *libertarian political goals* of the 26th of July Movement. When the Cuban leadership became preoccupied with egalitarian socio-economic reforms and national self-determination during 1959, the right dwelled almost exclusively upon Castro's failure to "restore" parliamentary democracy in Cuba. In March 1960, they closely paralleled the United States government approach by denouncing Cuba's friendly relationship with the USSR and Fidel's open collaboration with domestic Communists. Hence, by August 1960 the two rightist parties were praising the Alessandri government for signing the anti-Cuban Declaration of San Jose.

Hatred for the Cuban example became so intense by 1961 that sympathy was vehemently articulated for the Bay of Pigs invaders. We find an almost consistent record of support for the United States position in the United Nations on Cuban questions by the Alessandri administration. Its recalcitrance at the January 1962 Punta del Este Conference was not attributable to sympathy for Cuban self-determination or genuine commitment to the view that expulsion would drive Cuba into closer association with the Communist nations. Only to the extent that an influential leftist faction of the PR forced such an approach was it relevant to Chilean conduct at the Foreign Ministers Conference. More determinative was governmental displeasure with the lethargic disbursement of United States aid commitments.

OAS sanctions in the areas of communications, trade relations and diplomatic ties involved elements of what many Chileans regard as "sovereign" rights—matters that ought to be decided upon in Santiago rather than by the vote of other nations. This nationalistic commitment was also manifested by Chilean reluctance to sever ties with the Axis during World War II, and by the "neutralist" sentiment of public opinion during the 1950s. In addition, the maintenance of relations during 1963-1964 excluded the issue from the presidential campaign. Thus, the goal of exclusively identifying the FRAP with the defense of Cuba was not obscured by forcing the PDC to take a stand on the issue. By August 1964 when Alessandri finally opted for a rupture of relations, the momentum of the "Campaign of Terror" had fatally undermined the ability of the left-wing in the PDC to raise the issue.

Given the "traditional" orientation of the rightist parties and their commitment to constitutionalism and order, negative leadership responses to the "tropical" regime in Havana are quite understandable. Furthermore, the widespread Cuban expropriations threatened the sense of identity and security of the propertied elements which dominated the leadership of these parties. Castro's relations with the USSR and the unreserved identification with Havana by their internal enemies (FRAP) reinforced the rightist view that only the United States could help them preserve "Western Civilization" in Chile.

The Church. Clerical reactions to the Cuban Revolution were nearly identical to those of the rightist parties. The hatred for communism which was particularly apparent in *El Mercurio* and PCU responses was also manifested by *Mensaje* and *La Voz.* As with the Conservatives, this antipathy was partly induced by Cuban proscription of Catholic Social Doctrine and expropriation of Church schools and other properties. Naturally the expulsion of foreign priests and holy orders would have rendered the Chilean Church virtually impotent, as would the forced suspension of CARITAS importations from the United States. Although Fichter's survey of clerical and lay activist attitudes indicated some divergence towards the Revolutionary Government, the sympathetic minority was never permitted to present its views in *Mensaje* or *La Voz* after the Church in Cuba resolved in June 1959 to oppose Castro.

Frei's subsequent indifference to communitarian social principles and the new pattern of coexistence between the reorganized Church and the Revolutionary Government of Cuba operated to increase sympathy for the Revolution. Hence, Chilean Jesuits and a minority of Catholics moved to the left, as did similar groups in other Latin American nations after 1964. In some measure, this was reflected by Cardinal Silva's conciliatory attitude toward militant Catholics between 1968 and 1970, as it was by his willingness to say kind words about Cuba after the UP triumph. Quite a change from his role in 1964!

The Center. The responses of the Radicals and Christian Democrats were more restrained. There was some Radical interest in Cuban reforms and OAS proposals during 1959. But the intensifying conflict with the United States they so admired, as well as the internal radicalization of the Revolution's programs and its dictatorship, clearly repelled the dominant right-center faction of the party by early 1960. Although internal divisions were intense, a center-leftist majority maintained that: 1) unilateral armed intervention by the United States was not acceptable, except at the time of the missile crisis; 2) collective nonmilitary sanctions by the OAS were appropriate; and 3) Chile should decide herself when and if diplomatic or trade relations with Havana should be terminated. The neo-Marxist orientation of the Radical youth and a small minority at the national leadership level resulted in praise for the radical reforms and the anti-United States posture of the Cuban leadership.

Christian Democratic reactions to the Revolution were fairly similar to those of the PR. As a more reformist party, somewhat greater attention was focused upon the early social policies and goals of the Revolutionary Government. But the trend toward dictatorship, collaboration with Communists, and with the East resulted in forthright condemnation by April 1961. Nevertheless, until September 1964 the Party "officially" opposed the OAS expulsion and sanctioning of the Cuban government as likely to drive it into closer association with the East. Because of its acceptance of communitarian philosophy and identification with "the West," the left-wing of the PDC never went so far as to ignore Castro's political dictatorship and Soviet dependency, as did the corresponding leftist faction in the PR. The communitarians or populists were, however, dedicated anti-imperialists who derived great inspiration from Fidel's egalitarian social measures and his eradication of much governmental corruption. As the decade progressed and the *oficialistas* continued to deny them access, this sector became less enamored with the forms of parliamentary democracy and somewhat more sympathetic towards the Cuban experiment. The United States invasion of Santo Domingo and Washington's open support for anti-populist militarism elsewhere in the hemisphere disposed them increasingly towards sympathy for *Fidelista* revolutionaries in other Latin American countries. This was not the case for the dominant procapitalist *oficialista* wing of the party which focused almost exclusively upon the Revolution's economic disorganization, dictatorship and its continued dependence upon Soviet aid.

Table 10-1
Party Responses to the Cuban Revolution, 1959-1970

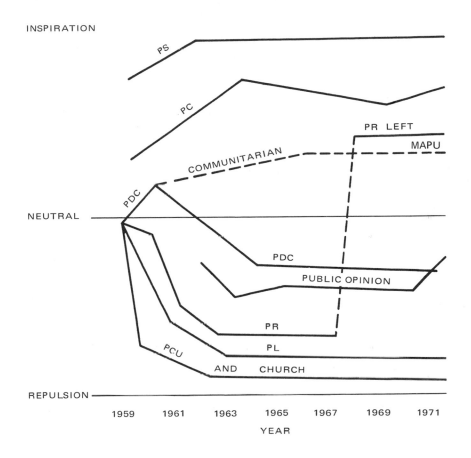

Source: Chapters 6-8.

The Left. What deeply disturbed the center and right, and thus made the Cuban Revolution particularly relevant to the Chilean political system, was the enthusiastic FRAP identification with the programs and policies of the Revolutionary Government. Although both Socialists and Communists always pledged that the methods would be distinctive for the Chilean revolution—in view of the nation's constitutionalist and parliamentary non-"tropical" heritage—they unreservedly defended Castro's authoritarian methods as appropriate to a land with traditions of militarism, violence and corruption.

Castro's willingness to defy Washington and his refusal to purge Communists from his government in 1959 brought belated Communist support which intensified after friendly relations were established with the Soviet Union. As Cuba was socialized, became officially Marxist-Leninist and increased her dependence upon the Soviet Bloc, the PC began to publish Fidel's speeches and defend the Revolution without hesitation. Although little was said about the matter, we may surmise that Castro's purge of some "old" Communists and his active support for guerrilla warfare were responsible for the chauvinistic views of many Communist leaders. They held that Castro was a "tropical" latecomer whose success was wholly due to Soviet aid. Although *El Siglo* dutifully mourned the CIA supervised murder of Che Guevara in Bolivia, there can be no doubt that most of the party's leadership breathed a sigh of relief. This was not necessarily true at the rank and file level where increasing numbers of lower class militants developed an aversion to the Secretary General Corvalan's tactical restraint. By 1970, a militant minority at the central committee level was prepared to challenge the conservative leadership of the Corvalan faction. This was postponed only by Allende's victory.

Unlike the Moscow-oriented Communist elite who continued to prefer Soviet policies and leaders to the "petit-bourgeois" Cuban leadership, the Socialists were the products of a tradition which was both nationalistic and "fashion-oriented." From Peron to Ibanez and then on to Titoism, the party had been a heterogeneous Marxist cum Social Democratic conglomeration in search of a charismatic leader independent of both Cold War blocs. Its and especially Allende's early enthusiasm was certainly reinforced by Castro's demonstration that local Communists could be controlled even with almost total dependence upon the Soviet Union for economic and military aid. If the Soviet concessions during the missile crisis caused some reservations, they were never expressed publicly. The mere survival of the Cuban Revolution as well as its experiment with moral incentives continued to inspire admiration. This was reflected by the party's enthusiasm at the July 1967 OLAS Conference in Havana as it was by Socialist initiative in establishing Chile's own symbolic OLAS Committee afterwards. For the Socialists, Guevara's death was a genuine tragedy. As John Martz has noted, "there can be no denial that the pragmatic example of Fidel Castro in Cuba and the writings of Guevara have touched the imagination of countless Latin Americans searching for a means to rectify historical ills."[3] Following the UP electoral plurality, a large bronze statue of Che was unveiled by the Socialist mayor of the "red barrio" of San Miguel. And when confronted by dozens of youths carrying posters during his first political address at the National Stadium on Nov. 5, 1970, the president of Chile announced: "I'm deeply moved by the sight of portraits of the immortal Che Guevara." But he then asked the revolutionary youth "to think calmly."[4]

The Ultraleft. These perpetually agitated groups traditionally recruited disaffected "left" militants from the two Marxist parties. During the sixties—due to the Cuban example—they received a fair quota of new associates from former Radical and PDC youth sections. Holding a neo-Trotskyist line, the "lesson" of Cuba for them was that only through mass struggle *and preparation for armed insurrection* could control of the state be ultimately wrested from the dominant classes. The rejection of such an approach by the PC and the PS strengthened ultraleftist convictions that these parties were "bureaucratic" and dominated at the leadership levels by a reformist mentality. Their conviction that an ultimate confrontation with the armed forces would necessarily occur before socio-economic structures could be transformed engendered alternating attitudes of indifference and hostility towards electoral participation.

During 1970, the MIR boycotted the election and organized "black beret" militias in a few slums around Santiago. Civil war was expected to follow Alessandri's predicted victory. The unexpected triumph of Allende brought a large Cuban delegation to the inauguration. Members of this group and left-wing socialists—always close to the MIR—induced these *via armada* enthusiasts to support the government by agreeing to a coalition with other UP youth organizations. After several months of bickering and violent confrontations, some degree of operational cooperation had been attained.[5] Upon Allende's inauguration, Cuba had for the first time officially recognized the MIR as "revolutionary."

Public Opinion. As early as October 1959, many middle class university students were definitely unattracted by Castro's "tropical" style, although they sympathized with the libertarian goals of the 26th of July Movement. Unfortunately, no national survey data is available for the 1959-1960 period. But even in September 1961—before Cuba became officially Marxist-Leninist—well over 40 percent of those interviewed held negative views toward the Cuban Revolution and especially Fidel Castro. While approximately 25 percent expressed contrary sentiments, only about 6 percent were intensely sympathetic and relatively few of these participated in demonstrations while only a score engaged in political violence. In general, hostility was more pronounced among women, the middle and upper classes, Catholics and persons of a conservative inclination. Although Castro's standing declined substantially in the immediate aftermath of the missile crisis, there was some apparent recovery by early 1964. Yet, even then his self-identified supporters were reduced to little more than 22 percent while those holding hostile views reached almost 50 percent. Interestingly, the economically disorganized and Marxist-Leninist Cuban Revolution was now even more unpopular than Fidel.

During the entire period, a substantial majority of those with views were opposed to unilateral United States armed intervention or sanctions by the OAS. By 1964, however, there was increased support for sanctions and even a suspension of relations by Chile. This was mirrored by a rise in United States prestige during the period and decline in "neutralist" sentiment. It is likely that the AFP, propaganda intensification by the USIA and the forceful handling of the missile crisis contributed to this modification, as did the Chilean "Campaign of Terror." As we have previously noted, a massive "Campaign of Terror" was financed again during 1969-1970. Allende was directly linked to what was portrayed as a Cuban tyranny.[6] This reflected cognizance of the fact that because of the Revolution's economic problems, "the attractions of the Cuban model have somewhat diminished."[7] A similar decline in United States prestige after Kennedy's assassination and the Dominican invasion probably failed to offset Cuba's loss of appeal at the mass level.

The Operative Variables: An Overview

A brief summary of the numerous factors which affected the Cuban Revolution's impact upon Chile is presented below:

A. Relational Patterns Most Affected
by the Symbolic Role of the Cuban
Revolution

Greater Influence

1. The increased probability that the left would not be permitted to occupy the executive branch of the national government—assuming an electoral plurality.
2. The increased likelihood that the right and the (Catholic) Church would actively support a centrist presidential candidate from the PDC.
3. The increased likelihood that the PDC and especially the Radicals would decline to enter a coalition with the left, particularly one with Allende as its presidential nominee.
4. The intensification of United States inputs (informational, cultural, economic, military and covert).
5. The growing conviction by both the center and the right that cooperation with the United States was vital to the preservation of the Chilean political system.
6. Defection of the PDC left wing.

Lesser Influence

7. Likelihood of a "Campaign of Terror."
8. PS insistence that Allende be the FRAP nominee in 1964.
9. Strengthening of PS and PC commitment to the FRAP coalition.
10. Emergence of moderate and "revolutionary" reform issues as dominant in Chilean politics.
11. Intensification of the competition for registration, organization and political recruitment of lower class persons.

B. The Catalytic Factors: Direct
Affective Responses

1. Early, vociferous and unreserved FRAP, especially Socialist (Allende) support for Cuban goals, policies and programs.
2. Successful Socialist effort to secure anti-American and socialistic radicalization of the FRAP program by early 1961.
3. More inspired proselytizing militancy with some Cuban aid during the 1960-1962 period by FRAP.
4. Willingness of left-wing Radicals and Christian Democrats to join the Marxist coalition.
5. MIR and left-wing Socialist initiatives in leading mass seizures between 1967-1970.

C. Important Intra-Systemic
Structural Factors

1. Mass media
2. Church
3. Disparity of propaganda resources
4. "Openness" to United States inputs
5. Armed Forces, including the Carabineros

} significance of anti-Marxist (Communist) attitudes

D. Secondary Intra-Systemic Factors

1. FRAP-CUT organizational inefficacy.
2. PS-PC rivalry and sectarianism.
3. Experience of the PS in the Ibañez government.
4. Former outlawry of the PC.
5. Adaptation of both PS and PC leaderships to electoralism.
6. Historic political violence and civil liberties violations.
7. Evolutionary constitutionalist tradition and disdain for the "tropical" style.
8. A PDC untainted by a prior governmental responsibility.
9. Separate voting for women and men.
10. Widespread socio-economic discontent; but intense feelings among only about 20 percent.
11. Internalization of parliamentary democratic norms by a relatively small minority of the electorate.
12. Inability of the Frei administration to transform Chilean socio-economic structures due to the *oficialista* commitment to domestic/foreign investor interests; failure to control inflation due to resistance within PDC to more than token suppression of the left.

E. Tactical Variables

1. Flexibility by the right and the Church in adopting a reformist orientation and supporting Frei's candidacy.
2. Greater stress upon reform commitments by the PDC.
3. Vigorous and effective lower class organizing efforts by the PDC and Church-supported organizations.
4. Maintenance of Duran's "anti-Communist" candidacy.
5. The "Campaign of Terror."
6. Restrictions and denial of Radio Access to FRAP.
7. "Vote-buying" and misappropriation of CARITAS foodstuffs.
8. United States determination to do everything possible to avoid the establishment of a second Castro-type regime: intensification of propaganda; budgetary and balance of payments emergency loans; military assistance and training in anti-communism and counterinsurgency; rise in P.L. 480 shipments; AFP; covert activities; Peace Corps; etc.
9. Deceptive FRAP campaign commitment to moderation and democratic norms.
10. Common exclusion of the issue in 1965.
11. Arrogance and unwillingness of Frei to conciliate leftists within and beyond the PDC.
12. Seizure of the PR by a leftist majority.
13. Rigidity of the Tomic candidacy.
14. Pragmatic flexibility of Allende.
15. Rightist overconfidence in Alessandri's image (1970).
16. Rightist miscalculation in assassinating General Schneider.

F. Indirect but Relevant External Events

1. Fate of the Cuban Revolution: personal dictatorship; communism; relationship to East; economic hardship.
2. Bay of Pigs outcome: diminishment of fatalism.
3. Missile Crisis and 1962-1964 *golpes*: restoration of fatalism.
4. Argentine provocations.
5. Mann Doctrine and the invasion of Santo Domingo.
6. Spread of United States supported militarism during the late sixties.
7. Rise of several revolutionary Catholic movements in Latin America; new disposition of Cuban clergy to cooperate with the Revolutionary Government.

The large number of factors and variables itemized above suggest the complexity of interactions which affected the transnational appeal or "impact" of the Cuban Revolution. Some of the more important relationships will be commented upon in the sections which follow.

Dominance of a Reformist Orientation

The perceived threat of "Castroism" in Latin America was probably the most important factor in stimulating a shift in the United States aid program for the region. The new priority upon social and economic development through internal self-help measures and reforms was first announced in the July 1960 Newport Declaration of President Eisenhower, and then formalized in the Act of Bogota. The AFP was justified before Congress as a "positive alternative" to the Cuban challenge. Among other things, it would engender affective support from the impoverished Latin American masses.

When the Alessandri administration and the three government parties accepted this approach, they joined many other observers and officials in viewing the Alianza as a means of preserving the Chilean political order as well as the existing capitalist system. In adopting a reformist posture, they were also reacting to recent congressional gains by Marxist parties which were then publicly extolling the programs of the Cuban Revolution. Thus, these sectors were *catalyzed by fear* of a rise in popular discontent which through support for a radicalized FRAP might well consign them to a fate similar to that experienced by the middle and upper classes who once enjoyed life and politics in pre-Revolutionary Cuba.

The new *sense of urgency* conditioned the April 1961 PDC decision to assign greater stress to its reformist and "anti-oligarchic" image. This was reflected in an emphasis upon *immediate distribution* of land in the party's agrarian reform program, in the pledge to "Chileanize" the *Gran Mineria*, and in specific welfare pledges for 1964. Endorsing the AFP, the Christian Democrats also regarded it as primarily a response to the danger of "Castroite subversion." Similarly, there can be little doubt that fear of increased "Communist" (FRAP) electoral support and strike actions during the early period heightened the sense of urgency within the Catholic clergy. By late 1962, its open advocacy of a reformist approach fully consonant with that of the PDC—and often openly articulated by Christian Democrats in clerical communications media—reflected a decision to support *la unica alternativa* with the moral authority and institutional resources at the clergy's disposal.

Thus, by 1964 all forces seeking the presidency were supporting reform commitments. Since Duran's post-Curico role was to minimize Allende's chances, his candidacy was in fact aiding the Frei drive for power. This contrasted markedly with the 1958 campaign when two of the major candidates were not proclaiming that Chile's "social question" was the major issue. By March 1965, it was evident that the right and the Radicals had temporarily lost many followers to Christian

Democratic reformism. Their defeat, the Marxist ability to hold its own proportion of the vote and the overwhelming PDC triumph confirmed that decisions of how best to reform the system would be central to Chilean politics for the remainder of the decade.

If Christian Democrats were unable to use their popular mandate to fully implement the repeatedly promised "Revolution in Liberty," they performed no less effectively than earlier middle class administrations. In fact, their social measures compared favorably with the innovative Popular Front government of Pedro Aguirre Cerda.

But a generation later, the "delivery" of even a portion of what had been pledged could only be defined as a "failure!" And it was by the Marxists in early 1967. During the succeeding three years, socialistic Radicals and communitarian Christian Democrats also insisted upon "the impossible." As the Alliance for Progress was quietly buried, so were the communitarian commitments. Even Tomic was to turn upon his nation's president. Nor could the *oficialistas* stimulate investment without systematic suppression of the left. And this in turn would have provoked a massive resignation of PDC reformists. And ironically, without such virtual outlawry of the Marxists, control of inflation was rendered impossible. In fact, the government actually lost control of its own Christian-Democrat led trade unions.

Aside from the administration's tangible but limited reforms, Frei's earlier rhetoric interacted with FRAP demands to consolidate a broad and expanding reformist movement dedicated to the elimination of monopolistic capitalism in Chile. This explains the categorical refusal of the Nationals to support Tomic, well known for his dynamic personality and populist tendencies. Hence, "(b)y arousing expectations which could not be fulfilled by its own policies, the Frei government has helped create at least the subjective conditions for a more thoroughgoing change."[8] The intensity of this commitment was reflected by the Tomic-Allende deal for the Plenary Congress as it was by the role of MAPU, *Mensaje* and the radicalized Radicals in 1969-1970. In varying degrees, this leftward movement was inspired by Cuban nationalism and socialism. It is hardly coincidental that the UP elites from all constituent parties—like Tomic—are former Cuban *invitados.* In addition to this direct stimulation, there was the reactive effect upon "moderate" and rightist sectors described at the beginning of this section.

Revolution in Chile: A Less
Probable Outcome

If the existence of the Cuban Revolution and FRAP's association with it contributed to the emergence of issues of social and economic reform as the dominant ones in Chilean politics, FRAP's identification with the Castro leadership also diminished the leftist coalition's chances of effectuating a socialist restructuring of Chilean society.

In late 1960, the Communists and especially the Socialists were enthralled by Fidel's daring and successful defiance of Washington. At the same time, it is likely that United States efforts to isolate and economically cripple Havana had provoked intense FRAP hostility. The consequential inspired proselytizing and radicalization of the FRAP program to include nationalization of the *Gran Mineria* and other large firms, abrogation of the military pacts and other international agreements "not in the national interest" was followed in 1962 with a pledge to withdraw from the OAS.

This programmatic modification made it more difficult for the Marxists to hold the non-Marxist PADENA within the FRAP. Similarly, it further complicated efforts to obtain Radical support for Allende in 1964. Thus, unlike Castro who had broadened his coalition in 1958, the FRAP's response to Cuban "successes" served to further isolate it from the support of non-Marxist and middle class sectors which were vital for an electoral contest.

By provoking a new reformism among the government parties and greater emphasis upon reform by the PDC, the inspired campaigning and radicalization of the FRAP program may have indirectly served to enhance or maintain the lower class appeal of these parties. On the other hand, this radicalization and identification with the Cuban Revolution increased the probability that in 1964 these parties would refuse to vote Allende in as president during a plenary session of Congress, assuming that the FRAP candidate won a plurality. Allende's congressional supporters in 1958 had declined to follow the tradition requiring they cast ballots for Alessandri, and other minorities had done the same in 1946 and 1952. Now, however, not the presidency but the system itself was believed to be in question. A capital flight inspiring counter measures such as strict controls, economic crimes, nationalizations, an end of United States budgetary support and the expulsion of the Peace Corps and the USIA would mark the beginning of a process which might well end in a revolutionary transformation of the Chilean socio-political order.

And even if the FRAP had won *majority* popular support at the polls, the fate of Cuba's armed forces and her social system certainly increased the probability of intervention "to preserve the Constitution" by Chile's armed forces. The purge of Socialist-oriented officers in the 1960-1961 period and the intensification of anti-Communist training at Chilean and United States-operated bases served to reinforce the likelihood of this outcome, as did the *immediate* United States endorsement of the Brazilian "revolution" in April, 1964.

One of the integral aspects of Cuban appeal to the Chilean Left was that this socialist revolution had been made and defended by Spanish-speaking Latin Americans. No longer was it a question of applied Marxism in some remote European or Asian nation where language and cultural heritage were totally foreign to the Chileans. The greater symbolic vividness and meaningfulness which socialism in Cuba represented was also an element which maximized the effectiveness of the "Campaign of Terror." Juanita Castro's quasi-hysterical CIA-taped "Message to the Women of Chile," widely disseminated *paredon* photographs, pamphlets by Cuban students and exiled labor leaders as well as summaries of other types of persecution by Latin Americans speaking the same tongue certainly were more terrifying than reports of Soviet or Chinese outrages against their own peoples, European Slavs, or Magyars. And if this were not enough, Allende's early and glowing praise for the Cuban Revolution and the concomitant radicalization of the FRAP program also provided excellent source material for a propaganda campaign that probably accounted for a substantial part of Frei's margin over Allende. The remainder of his margin was ensured by PCU-PL support and the maintenance of Duran's candidacy. Their apprehension of a FRAP victory was also *heightened* by similar Cuba-related factors. It was, perhaps, as such a catalyzing symbol that the Cuban Revolution most directly influenced the course of Chilean political conflict.

Under the Christian Democratic administration, the Marxists were unable to rapidly expand their lower class constituency. Their demoralization by Guevara's death and the rampant United States backed militarism in Latin America was reinforced by Fidel's own administrative errors. Hence, whereas Allende was unsurprised by the decline in his 1970 percentage, partially attributable to the foregoing events and another "Campaign of Terror," he was stunned by his 40,000 vote plurality.

While one can argue that without MAPU and the Radicals, well over 40,000 votes would have been lost, even with this Cuba inspired support the UP would have lost had the upper and middle classes remained unified behind a common candidate. Their failure to make the necessary compromises reflected overconfidence and miscalculation as well as personal antipathies.

The Communist success in broadening the Marxist coalition to include the MAPU and Radicals reassured the Tomic-oriented members of the PDC parliamentary delegation. Their faith in Allende's integrity as well as the momentum of Tomic's populist and anti-Frei campaign overwhelmed fears of a "Fidelista dictatorship" in Chile. In fact, Allende needed but 13 of 75 PDC congressional votes.

Although the Popular government of Chile will adhere to the forms and procedures of the Constitution, within a few years their formal nature will become increasingly apparent to the rigorously indoctrinated and pro-American officer corps of the Armed Forces. As upper class disinvestment is reciprocated by intensifying leftist pressure from the Marxist cadres, the government will be compelled to accelerate its interventions and expropriations.[9] Gradually, the social and financial constituencies of the Christian Democrats and Nationals will be weakened. As plebiscites and the new Constitution are introduced with the backing of a rapidly expanding UP lower class constituency, sectors of the military will revolt.[10] The fate of the Revolutionary Government of Chile will then be in the hands of a new elite of mass mobilizers. Unless arms are in their possession, Chile may well become the Indonesia of Latin America.

One Factor Among Many

In the preceding paragraphs, such terms as "contributed to" or "increased the likelihood" were commonly used. The fact is that Cuban symbolism did not function independently but was affected by other factors. One may well ask: What if there had been no Cuban Revolution? It is probable—though somewhat less so—that a similar pattern of events would have occurred within Chile.

Allende's agrarian reform commitments and his surprisingly strong peasant backing in 1958 would probably have been followed by a vigorous 1961 rural campaign. Whether the FRAP program would then have been so radicalized is quite problematic. Similarly, it is unclear whether the rightist parties would have adopted even a mildly reformist posture in absence of the AFP and FRAP identification with the Cuban regime in 1961 when the Marxists scored major gains. Even so, the opportunistic and heterogeneous Radicals would have embraced a reformist orientation and the PDC probably would have placed more stress upon its own reform pledges. To minimize the chances of a FRAP victory in 1964, budgetary support and massive P.L. 480 surplus foods would probably have been injected by the United States.

Similarly, a "Campaign of Terror" would have utilized Soviet oppression in Hungary, Chinese despotism, etc. Then there was Allende's 1953 eulogy of Stalin that would certainly have been republished by the CIA-subsidized Congress for Cultural Freedom. Given Allende's 1958 popular support and the death of Cardinal Maria Caro, it is likely that the Church would have moved towards both reformism and more vigorous opposition to the candidate who "favored Communism." The large 1958 vote would have reinforced the FRAP PS-PC based coalition. Socialist insistence that Allende again be the candidate would limit the possibility of attracting a major center party into the FRAP. The probability of a congressional vote against Allende and military intervention against a "Communist Government" would also exist, if in lesser degree. In this case, the issue would be whether Chile was to become "another Guatemala."

The definite, though *limited*, catalytic influence of the Cuban Revolution was also apparent in the *selectivity* with which it was used symbolically by all political sectors. Prior to the missile crisis, which seems to have resurrected widespread *fatalismo* as did the "anti-Communist" *golpes* in other Latin American nations during the 1962-1964 period—and especially before Cuba became officially Marxist-Leninist, the left was quite willing to publicly endorse the Cuban example of *anti-imperialismo*. In this period, Havana was generally ignored by the center and right. During 1962, and especially in the succeeding two years, this situation was dramatically reversed. And at the time of the 1965 congressional elections, all parties tended to omit reference to Cuba. Thus, the Cuban Revolution as a propagandistic symbol was subordinated to the tactical requirements of the struggle for governmental control within Chile.

Related to this was the fact that an examination of speeches, articles, convention proceedings, public rallies, meetings and demonstrations between 1959 and 1965 reveals that *relatively little* day-to-day attention was focused upon Cuba. As a remote and largely non-interdependent political system, Chilean political attention was concentrated upon domestic issues and conduct. Foreign affairs issues were of secondary importance. Within this framework, it is true that somewhat more attention to Cuban policies and self-determination was exhibited by the Marxists and especially by the Socialist Party.

Yet it would be imprudent to confuse Cuba's quantitative importance with her motivational significance at the elite level. There are good grounds for believing that the *insistence* upon PDC egalitarian reforms by populists within the party was catalyzed by earlier visits to Cuba. Socialist Secretary General Aniceto Rodriguez who rejected the exclusionary *Frente de Trabajadores* tactic in 1967-1970 also was the organizer of Chile's OLAS committee in 1967 after his return from Havana. The pragmatic tactical flexibility of both Aniceto Rodriguez and Allende mirror Fidel's in the 1957-1959 period. There can be no doubt that these men were inspired as were the leftist Radicals who captured control of their party in 1967. Baltra, it should be recalled, replaced Ladron de Guevara as President of the Chilean-Cuban Cultural Institute. Similarly, the UP undersecretary of foreign affairs, Aleides Leal, is a Radical former *invitado*.

In a *qualified* sense, then, we may say that without a Cuban Revolution led by Fidel Castro, the profile of Chilean history might well have differed. Had the United States been successful in restoring *fatalismo* by subverting the Cuban Revolution, neither the Radicals nor the MAPU would have been as likely to have joined the UP, and the reformist impetus would also have been much more moderate. The militant mass seizures, strikes and demonstrations which polarized Chile between 1967-1970 probably would not have occurred. And from an antithetical perspective, had Cuba's economic difficulties not engendered rightist overconfidence, Allende would have been denied his plurality. Now, capitalism in Chile can be preserved only through military intervention. As the Rockefeller Report warned: "a Castro on the mainland, supported militarily and economically by the Communist world, would . . . pose an extremely difficult problem for the United States." "Castro" here symbolizes "Marxist solutions to their socio-economic problems."[11] A year earlier, the commander-in-chief of the United States Southern Command reassured an audience of United States investors concerning a major function of military training for Latin American officers. Gen. Porter's formulation was as follows:

Many of you gentlemen are leaders and policy-makers in the businesses and industries that account for the huge American private investment in Latin America. . . . Some misguided personalities and groups in our own country and abroad call you capitalists who seek profit. Of course you do. . . . You can help produce a climate conducive to more progressive American involvement in the hemisphere. . . . the Alliance envisages some $300 million a year in U.S. private investment. . . .

As a final thought, consider the small amount of U.S. public funds that have gone for military assistance and for AID public safety projects as a very modest premium on an insurance policy protecting our vast private investment in an area of tremendous trade and strategic value to our country.[12]

If *fatalismo* was weakened by Cuba's continued assertion of economic sovereignty, it would be doomed by a successful Chilean "road to socialism."[13] Thus, Gen. Mather's prediction—quoted in chapter 5—of more coups in the hemisphere. As Lyndon Johnson's invasion of the Dominican Republic implied, "no more Cuba's" has become an imperative for North American capitalist expansion. And in contradistinction to the Dominican rebels, Chile's leaders *are* enthusiastic admirers of the Cuban example. Thus even in Washington, the Cuban Revolution has increased the urgency assigned to subverting the Popular Unity government. Without Cuba, however, Chile would have received more leisurely CIA-military treatment similar to that which overthrew the freely elected government of Guatemala (1954).

Some Feasible Implications

Two Theses. In chapter 1 Castro's belief that the Cuban Revolution represented the true interests of the peoples of Latin America and could not be isolated from them was quoted. Reference was also made to the related assumption that the objective conditions of mass poverty and socio-economic exploitation were sufficient to create a revolutionary atmosphere in other Latin American political systems. Survey data presented in this study indicate that about 6 percent and certainly no more than 25 percent of the Chilean citizenry sympathized with the Cuban Revolution. While this tends to indicate that Fidel's projection of appeal was a grossly exaggerated one, we should also be aware of the questionable reliability of public opinion polls when an affirmative answer in September 1961 implied support for a regime which had been labeled Communist by much of the mass media since March 1960. Having been legalized only in 1958, the stigma of outlawry was still associated with Chilean communism. Many sympathizers, then, might not have desired to make such identification a matter of public (and perhaps police) record. Furthermore, FRAP leaders had urged their supporters not to cooperate with such polls, and some leftist pollsters at the University of Chile have been known to deliberately falsify results. Hence, although a useful general index of opinion, these polls probably understated radicalism on sensitive questions.

It is difficult to ascertain whether Chilean socio-economic conditions created "objectively favorable" circumstances for revolution particularly if one defines an armed struggle for power as integral to revolution. The emergence and growth of MIR and the *Movimiento Camilio Torres* testify to the belief by growing sectors of Chilean youth that the *via armada* was both practical and necessary. This orientation was shared by a majority of the Socialist youth. And it elicited increasing mass support as the tempo of property seizures accelerated after 1966. Alessandri's election following a popular plurality would probably have sparked the beginning of urban and possibly rural guerrilla warfare by these partisans of "the Cuban road."[14] On the other hand, if one restricts the definition to mass support for rapid and sweeping modifications of existing social and economic institutions in Chile, there was *some* basis for the claim. In 1964, the PDC *alleged* that its reforms would be "structural" in nature and create the foundations of a new and more socially just communitarian social order. Their slogan was "Revolution in Liberty." And it must be assumed that perhaps half of Frei's supporters were principally motivated by this commitment—even though grasped at a high level of generality. Similarly, it cannot be doubted that most of the 980,000 voters backing Allende—if only because of the "Campaign of Terror"—were cognizant of the revolutionary implications of the FRAP program and the coalition's basis as a Socialist-Communist alliance.

We have then, close to two-thirds of the voters supporting some type of revolutionization of Chilean society. For some, sympathetic association with the Cuban experiment was undoubtedly operative, and for most the relationship was both indirect and mediated by the intervening structural relationships and party responses essayed in this study. While it remains unclear what proportion of FRAP's 39 percent of the electorate offered their support because Allende (FRAP) was publicly identified with the Cuban Revolution, this probability cannot be wholly dismissed for three reasons: 1) Allende's backing increased from 350,000 votes in 1958 to nearly a million in 1964; 2) survey data indicate that *at least* a fifth of those interviewed openly sympathized with the Cuban Revolution; and 3) Allende's following was not personalist, as he failed to project a charismatic image. Thus, much of his support was probably related to the radical and lower class oriented programs and economic struggles led by the Communist and Socialist parties.[15] Aside from *directly inspiring a substantial number of organizers and campaigners*, the Cuban Revolution was symbolically associated with and hence reinforced the image of a FRAP committed to a fundamental socialist transformation of the Chilean socio-economic system.

It is also conceivable that had the Popular Action Front leadership adopted the "ultraleftist" tactical proposal of encouraging mass struggles (wage strikes and sit-ins, land seizures by peasants and slum dwellers, etc.) during the last months of the 1964 campaign, that more lower class voters would have perceived the PDC to be substantially less "revolutionary" and "anti-oligarchic" than it claimed to be. But the FRAP leadership regarded such militant tactics—as the old Cuban Communist Party once did Fidel—as "adventuristic."

Even if we admit that Fidel's allegation of *direct* appeal was both overstated and oversimplified, a common characteristic of political rhetoric, on another and related point he appears to have been more accurate. In chapter 7 we quoted Castro's view that the Revolution had exerted a rather substantial impact upon the nature of political conflict within Chile and other Latin American polities: now it was between revolutionaries and reformers whereas formerly reactionaries and reformers had constituted the major contending forces. If we substitute conservative for reactionary, the statement aptly describes the leftward shift in Chilean politics—a transformation catalyzed in part by Cuba's revolutionary challenge to the hemisphere. Thus by the end of the sixties, even vehemently anti-Communist governments in Chile, Peru and Bolivia were desperately seeking domestic support by nationalizing particularly exploitative United States extractive enterprises. Whether this reflects a hemispheric pattern is doubtful as there are conservative military regimes in Argentina, Brazil and a number of other countries. Hence, except for Chile and several other nations, the leftward movement of the early 1960s has been arrested during the Johnson and Nixon administrations.

It would be incorrect to view Alessandri's 36 percent of the vote in Chile's 1970 election as evidence of a return to earlier patterns of political cleavage. Much of his appeal was either personalist in nature or a result of the more gross aspects of the second "Campaign of Terror." More significant was the support by two-thirds of the Chilean electorate for candidates who attacked the moderateness of *oficialista* reform measures. The results of the April 1971 municipal elections attest to the permanent decline of the Nationals. They also reflect the incorporation of illiterate *marginales* into the revolutionary electoral constituency.

Mobilization of Bias. FRAP's decision to avoid self-identification with the Cuban symbol during 1963-1964 was almost certainly conditioned by pre-existing anti-Communist mass attitudes and the unfavorable structure of communication. The Church, the schools, the bulk of the press and almost all of the radio broadcasters projected values and interpretations of reality which did not favor— and often made more difficult—the recruitment of a following by the Marxist-led FRAP. The major restrictions upon leftist access to radio broadcasting as a result of possibly concerted denials of any or prime time were aggravated by the limited financial resources of the leftist parties. Although personal solicitation by perhaps twenty thousand FRAP activists—a minority probably inspired by visits to or accounts of the Cuban Revolution—was partially offsetting, this in turn was more than balanced by massive personal campaigning by the anti-FRAP parties and supporting groups. Given the disparity of total propaganda resources, it was not possible to effectively defend the Cuban Revolution or even to distinguish contemplated FRAP methods from those used by Fidel Castro. An abortive attempt to defend Cuba would have reinforced anti-FRAP efforts to convert this into the central issue of the campaign, and increased the likelihood of a congressional veto and/or military intervention. But even though FRAP leaders sought to concentrate upon domestic issues, they were unable to escape the effects of a propaganda "deluge" that identified them with both the goals and the methods of the Havana government.

A similar pattern of social-psychological "bias" was maintained and intensified during the latter part of the decade. State subsidies were utilized to finance the organization and anti-Marxist indoctrination of *Promocion Popular* slum dwellers and CORA *asentamiento* peasants. Several hundred thousand persons were affected by this effort to incorporate them in a stable PDC constituency. For the more literate, higher education was rapidly expanded, despite a paucity of jobs, and state subsidies were granted to pro-PDC publishing firms through advertising, printing contracts and mailing privileges. These and similar policies as well as the inputs discussed in the following section adversely affected the Marxist efforts to expand their constituencies. Despite the desertion of one major daily, *El Clarin*, to the UP candidacy, it is unsurprising that Allende received a measurably smaller percentage of the popular vote in 1970 than he had in 1964.

Differential Receptivity to "Competing" External Inputs. Radio and press placement as well as other covert and propaganda activities indicate how much more "open" the system was to United States efforts than to the Cubans. Most of the press and radio ignored Prensa Latina and relied upon AP, UPI and USIA for their accounts of Cuban reality and United States intentions. While the Chilean government vehemently protested the importation of propaganda by the Cuban Embassy, it sanctioned not only USIA inserts, cartoon booklets, film showings, book distributions, "special presentation items," publications and attitudinal surveys, but also cooperated with the intensified exchange of persons program for union leaders, military officers, professors, journalists, students, etc.

Although the Cuban government did bring perhaps a score of centrist politicians to Cuba, only Hurtado was wholly and instantly "transformed." The others and *invitado* youth activists probably did become more insistent defenders of Cuban self-determination and advocates of reform within their parties. Of greater importance, after 1959 the Cubans were unable to project their message through neutral mass media to the citizenry at large. This openness to United States inputs facilitated the provision of large scale material and some personnel aid to the PDC and Church-related mass organizing efforts which greatly strengthened the Frei campaign. The activities of the Peace Corps and the many subsidized non-governmental organizations contributed in a more moderate way to creating an unfavorable climate for Marxist recruitment in urban slums and some rural zones.

More determinative significance should probably be attributed to the extensive United States economic aid to Chile after the 1960 earthquakes and during the 1963-1964 period. One has only to imagine the mass unemployment or wholly uncontrolled inflation and food shortages that would have resulted from a decision to deny such budgetary and exchange of payments support. It seems clear that this assistance was intended to maximize the probability of a "democratic" outcome in 1964, as detailed in chapter 5.

Finally, the major increase in military assistance during the period in question—with its concomitant personal relationships, anti-Communist and counterinsurgency training—reinforced the likelihood that the military would not have assumed a neutral role had Allende secured a popular majority in 1964. Of greater importance from the perspective of maintaining the Chilean parliamentary democratic system were the previously mentioned infusions of propaganda and especially financial supports. They diminished the probability and necessity for direct military intervention.[16]

Under the Frei administration, this differential openness was, if anything, more pronounced than it had been under Alessandri. While the government refused to renew cultural or diplomatic relations with the Republic of Cuba, it simultaneously permitted intensified socio-psychological inputs by the United States. These included an AID directed restructuring of public school curricula, de-emphasis of the humanities, and continued CIA assistance to lower class unionization campaigns. Nor were USIA propaganda insertions or public opinion surveys curtailed. Among the lower classes, United States subsidized non-governmental organizations continued to expand their constituencies. Some progress was made in the area of limiting blue collar births by inducing women to accept contraceptive loops and through an experimental injection program in Santiago.[17]

The government's willingness to tolerate massive and systematic inputs extended to blatant acts of diplomatic intervention. While earlier in the decade it had ritualistically deplored "Project Camelot" after this counterrevolutionary survey research was exposed by the Communist daily *El Siglo*, the Frei government was indifferent to less conspicuous research of a similar guise. Nor did the *oficialista* regime demand the expulsion of United States Ambassador Edward Korry when he openly intervened in the 1970 presidential campaign.

On the other hand, following Allende's victory the Cuban delegation was not permitted to even land in Chile until the Socialist interior minister was vested with authority *after* the new Chief Executive was inaugurated. Under the Popular Unity government, these patterns of differential receptivity are being altered rapidly. But it will be several years before North American inputs are eliminated; that is if a military coup does not foreclose this possibility. In fact, the prudent revisions in the UP program—as compared to FRAP's in 1964—for terminating military dependence upon the United States reflect a sensitive fear of the intimate relations between the 32-man United States Military Mission and Chilean officers.[18] As we noted in chapter 5, several hundred were indoctrinated in the United States and Panama between 1965 and 1970.

Impact of Tradition and Legality upon the Left. It is interesting to speculate whether the Socialists and Communists would have categorically rejected preparation for armed struggle had Chile's internal security forces been scaled to those of Costa Rica. Regardless of the way this question is answered, the leaders of the Marxist parties had internalized parliamentary and electoral roles. Their freedom to organize and campaign legally would seem to have reinforced leadership rejection of the Cuban "road to power." When neo-Trotskyist elements sought to win control of the PS in February 1964, the Ampuerist leadership was so desperate that it even violated the party's rules in order to perpetuate its dominance of the party apparatus.

And as for the more "bureaucratic" and entrenched Communist leaders, their recollection of the discomforts and loss of party influence during the period of outlawry and persecution obviously disinclined them towards "adventurism." Thus, an effective military establishment and legal sanction for "revolutionary" parties to function within the Constitution may dispose Marxist leaderships to accept "rules of the game" which prejudice their chances of ever securing control of the state. Various attitudinal, communicational, constitutional, financial and external input factors tending in this direction have been discussed in the preceding paragraphs.

While Allende's election to the presidency was occasioned by counterrevolutionary tactical miscalculations and consequential disunity—and hence may be regarded as fortuitous—a more basic fact was that the left could not appeal to a substantially expanded constituency. Despite favorable "objective conditions," only small gains were achieved. In addition to the system-related social-psychological variables essayed in preceding paragraphs, transcendant importance must be assigned to the effectiveness with which dominant classes diffused middle-class identification to a large sector of the lower classes. This and Catholicism best explain blue-collar recalcitrance when confronted by political programs defined in terms of class struggle. As capitalist elites succeed in subjecting the lower classes to high levels of political socialization, the permanent minority status of class-based appeals becomes an omnipresent reality. This suggests the need for a drastic revision in Marxian theory—as does the obvious inefficacy of the NLF coalitional approach.[19]

Only by recasting socialist egalitarian goals in *populist* terminology and reorganizing Marxist parties as populist movements can the fact of middle-class consciousness be transcended in nations characterized by moderately developed bourgeois political cultures. Whether within such an ideological framework mass property seizures and demonstrations should be promoted is a question best left to pragmatic experimentation. In 1970, *both* the Tomic and Allende forces believed such tactics to be expedient for electoral purposes.

Latin America: One Entity or Distinctive Political Systems?

Abstractions such as "Latin America" are meaningful only within well defined contexts. It is a useful term when understood to refer to a geographical region sharing a common linguistic and colonial background. Hence, a "Cuban example" inspired more identification and intensity of response than would a Soviet or Chinese reference. Yet, it seems clear that even some Leftist leaders recognized the distinction between Chilean traditions of orderly evolution and the "tropical" exhuberance and violence that characterized the mulatto population of Cuba. The view that "the English of South America" were not simply *latinos* but superior in their abilities to others was more pronounced in centrist sectors and especially upon the right. This upper class chauvinism and sense of distinctiveness from Caribbean Americans was also conditioned by the absence of historic humiliation caused by overt United States intervention and occupation. Leftists argued that it was Cuban programs, reforms and self-determination that inspired them, not Fidel's style or treatment of the opposition. And for right-wing Radicals, Liberals and some Christian Democrats, it would seem that there was greater basis for cultural identification with the United States—the bastion of capitalist progress and "Western Civilization"—than with either Cuba or many of the products of their own country.

Whether the masses of Chilean voters distinguished themselves in such a manner from Cuba's civic culture is doubtful. Similarly, one cannot be certain that those who voted anti-Communist (Cuban) were at the same time voting for the parliamentary democratic tradition. They may in large part have been voting against apprehended atheism, religious persecution, loss of patrimony and authority over one's children, military intervention, war with Argentina, violence, economic chaos, etc. There was a countervailing tradition of political and anomic violence, infringement of civil liberties as well as some survey data to indicate widespread distrust of "the people" and faith in "strong" leaders as opposed to laws and speeches. Furthermore, three quarters of the population were uninvolved even in presidential campaigns and more than half of those voting in 1964 had no prior electoral experience. Thus, while appeal to democratic traditions may have reinforced anti-Communist (FRAP-Cuban) propaganda among the citizenry, its importance for voting behavior is not a subject for even safe speculation.

Dictatorship and Revolution. The flexibility of Chile's internal political elites in adopting reformist and coalitional tactics and the crucial supporting infusions by the United States suggests that in general it may be possible to maintain a parliamentary system—given sufficient determination and commitment of resources—despite the existence of a strong and aggressive internal Marxist opposition. But these same attributes of such an "open" system may contribute to explaining why the Fidelista leadership believed it necessary to "close" the Cuban system in order to limit the external resources and maneuverability of those in Cuba who were opposed to radical social and economic restructuring.

In a more measured fashion, the Popular government will be compelled to do the same. Aware however of the military presence, it will necessarily constrict de facto rather than formal liberties of the upper classes and their dependent elites. Because these sectors have been so closely linked with the United States, the gradual deterioration of relations with Washington will fatally weaken their internal position. Alessandri's 1970 campaign was the last to be financed by Anaconda. After an additional sector of Christian Democracy is won over to UP, the rump of the PDC may be allowed to remain as a vestige of opposition. As the left would have been were they defeated in 1970, the Christian Democrats and allied Nationals will be consigned to permanent minority status. This will be ensured through the extirpation of middle-class identification from lower class consciousness. The neutrality of the Church will reinforce such a process. Thus, a distinctive and unique "Chilean road to socialism" will appear. Even if—as seems unlikely—the military do not depose the UP government, the Chilean model will not have widespread appeal. The element of fortune was too paramount in importance and stabilized parliamentary conditions are exceptional in Latin America.

A Tentative Hypothesis. As suggested in the introduction, the findings of this study indicate that investigators or analysts of political systems in underdeveloped regions should not assume that they are essentially autonomous or self-equilibrating. Where groups committed to revolutionizing the system are significant, and perhaps at other times as well, it may often be the case that great power infusions are of major importance to internal political conflicts and outcomes. If such intervention is excluded a priori from examination, the political system will be portrayed lacking one of its essential structural features.

More generally, it may be hypothesized that four factors are of especial importance in maintaining a parliamentary democratic system where the following exist: 1) mass social deprivation; 2) a marginal rate of economic growth and social mobility; and 3) a relatively strong and growing Marxist opposition. First, parties and institutions committed to the preservation of the existing system must be willing in some cases to sacrifice lesser interests to this commitment. Flexibility would be required insofar as the acceptance of socio-economic reforms and the creation of de facto coalitions were concerned. Second, the presence of a strong and reasonably effective internal security force is of vital importance. A third factor relates to the existence of a widespread middle-class identification, anti-Communist attitudes and a favorable structure of mass media. Finally, large scale propagandistic and especially economic inputs by one or more sympathetic external factors would be mandatory, both to prevent a social crisis and to enhance the resources and appeal of internal groups committed to the objective of system maintenance.

Since many political regimes in underdeveloped areas are not characterized by functioning parliamentary democratic institutions, the applicability of this hypothesis might be regarded as quite limited. Yet rather, it may still be useful for orienting research when viewed as a model focusing attention upon several important system-maintaining variables that in varying degree may be relevant to the preservation of many other "imperfect" parliamentary regimes which do exist in Latin America and elsewhere in the "Third World." Nevertheless, from the standpoint of mass welfare and social opportunity, such system-maintenance may function as an obstacle to development and human liberation. The classes which dominate these formal democracies have been unwilling to invest their surplus capital in productive enterprises. Hence the "stability" of mass impoverishment and inequality of opportunity under "democratic" and demagogic Chilean governments since the 1947 Cold War purge. The accession to constitutional office by the Popular government does not vitiate these observations. It merely highlights the determinative significance of counterrevolutionary disunity when confronted by an inspired and principled revolutionary coalition. As both Marx and behavioral scientists have recognized, social-psychological and organizational variables transcend environmental determinism in conditioning political change.[20]

Appendix I:
Attitudinal and Behavioral
Data

Appendix I

Attitudinal and Behavorial Data

A. Some Indicators of Socio-Economic and Political Discontent (Radicalism). A USIA survey taken in all urban centers with 10,000 or more persons late in 1962, posed the following question: "All things considered, how do you feel about your present standard of living?" Only 18 percent said that it was "much less that it should be." Rural responses generally paralleled urban ones, except that there are more "don't knows." United States Information Agency, Research and Reference Service, *The Economic and Political Climate Of Opinion in Latin America and Attitudes Toward the Alliance for Progress* (Washington, D.C.: USIA, R-110-63(R), June 1963), p. 1.

A Greater Santiago "Pre-Electoral Survey" by the University of Chile's Center of Socio-Economic Studies (CESO) during August 1964 revealed that 62 percent of the interviewees "believed that the majority of men don't do better because they lack initiative." A year later the same organization, directed by Eduardo Hamuy, surveyed housewives in the same area. In terms of financial ability to procure what the women regarded as household necessities, only 11 percent reported that they suffered "great penury." Some degree of hardship was claimed by 43 percent. CESO, Centro de Estudios Socioeconomicos, "Patrones Socio-Culturales del Comportamiento Economico," *Informe Preliminar No. 1-* (julio 1966), pp. 1-4.

B. Sex and Class: Relationship to Socio-Economic and Political Discontent (Radicalism). A moderate relationship for both of these variables is indicated by survey findings reported in: CESO, "Patrones Socio-Culturales," pp. 1-4. USIA, *Economic and Political Climate*, p. 1. United States Information Agency, Research and Reference Service, *The Economic and Political Climate of Opinion in Latin America and Attitudes Towards the Alliance for Progress: Appendix I, Breakdowns by Economic Sub-Groups within the Urban Sample* (Washington, D.C.: USIA, R-50-64, April 30, 1964), p. 5. See also the two sections which follow (C and D).

C. Views of Communism and Related Subjects. During 1955, a USIA poll asked urban Chileans: "If the Communists came to power in Chile, how would this affect: (see Table A-1 on p. 252)

Seven years later, urban residents were asked how much influence Communism should have in Chile. Only 10 percent said "more." Lower income sectors were more pro-Communist. USIA, *Economic and Political Climate, Appendix*, p. 5.

Even fewer Chileans appeared to endorse Marxist issue orientations. A repre-

Table A-1

Effect of a Prospective Communist Government on Urban Chileans' Values, 1955

Goal—Value	Favorably	Unfavorably	No Opinion
Your work, your income	11%	56%	33%
Your personal security	10	60	30
Your freedom of ex- pression	9	66	25
Chile's independence	8	67	25

Source: U.S., Information Agency, Research and Reference Service, *Chilean Attitudes Toward Communism and the East-West Conflict* (Washington, D.C.: USIA, Report No. 4, December 16, 1955), p. 8.

sentative sample of Chileans residing in thirty-three cities were asked during June and July 1955: "In your opinion, what is the most important problem facing Chile today?" Although 96 percent listed economic problems (62 percent housing; 5 percent transport; etc.), virtually none cited "foreign exploitation" or U.S. exploitation." This was an open-ended query. On another question, 27 percent said that they thought United States economic policies—on balance—had injured the Chilean economy. When asked to specify how, only 3 percent offered neo-Marxian replies such as "looking for quick profits, exploiting for own profits, being opportunists." Four percent said that the United States was "underpaying for Chilean products, and another 3 percent cited "manipulating the rate of exchange, causing devaluation of currency." No other reply to this open-ended question was given by more than 2 percent. United States Information Agency, Research and Reference Service, *Chilean Attitudes Toward the United States and U.S. Economic Policies* (Washington, D.C.: USIA, Report No. 3, Oct. 31, 1955), pp. 3, 6.

Similarly, during the November-December 1962 survey, 12 percent of the interviewees expressed the view that significant advances would not be made with regard to agrarian reform during the next five years. No more than one quarter of these cited neo-Marxian explanations such as "opposition of vested interests" or that the government is dominated by such interests. Fourteen percent didn't expect significant tax reforms to be instituted during the ensuing five year period. In this case, slightly over half, or eight percent of the entire sample, provided similar rationales. Perhaps equally revealing was another open-ended question which was set in these terms: "There is considerable talk these days about the urgent social changes and economic changes that may be needed in Chile. What specific changes, if any, do you think need to be made in our country to allow the average person here to live a better life?" No more than 2 percent responded with such characteristically Marxist solutions as "radical changes in the system of government, change to a socialist system, eliminate capitalism, nationalize the extractive industries." When asked about expropriating landlords and nationalizing foreign firms, only 4 percent in each case opposed any compensation. While 52 percent supported nationalization of foreign-owned firms, 30 percent said either partial or no compensation should be paid. When asked to explain this, only 5 percent offered neo-Marxian rationales as: "they have exploited or cheated the people or the country, they have operated without conscience, have kept the people in misery, have exploited the workers." USIA, *Economic and Political Climate*, pp. 8, 13, 17, 23, 29, 30, 31. Cf., Sol Arguedas, "El Saldo de las elecciones chilenas," *Cuadernos Americanos*, CXXXVIII (enero-febrero 1965), 36-37.

A 1966 survey by the Center for the Study of Public Opinion (CEDOP), reported that less than 10 percent of the interviewees viewed class struggle as the appropriate means for overcoming social inequalities. "Encuestas: Las Clases Sociales," *El Mercurio: Revista del Domingo*, 8 enero 1967, p. 6.

This result was consistent with an October 1963 survey of a representative sample of 400 Greater Santiago women who were asked: "There are people who think that social classes help each other. What do you think?" The results of this poll are shown in Table A-2. Slightly more than 35 percent expressed dissatisfaction with the existing political situation in Chile. When asked for remedies, less than 7 percent gave the most radical reply: that the system should be changed. Anti-communist attitudinal structures were particularly striking when the women were asked: "With which of the following political parties do you sympathize most, and with which least?" The response is shown in Table A-3.

D. Support for Socialistic and Other Reforms. The 1966 CEDOP survey which asked how social inequalities should be resolved, reported that 25 percent endorsed some redistribution from the upper classes. While 15 percent asserted

Table A-2
Female Perceptions of Class Struggle, Greater Santiago, October 1963

	(White Collar)		(Blue Collar)	
	Upper (19)	Middle (215) (Socio-Economic Sectors)	Lower (166)	Total
Yes, they do	47.4%	39.8%	37.6%	39.3%
No, they don't	36.8%	41.2%	36.4%	39.0%
No, there is a struggle	5.3%	5.6%	6.6%	6.0%
At times, they help each other	10.5%	6.5%	7.3%	7.0%
No Reply	—	6.9%	12.1%	8.8%

Source: Frida Kaplan B., Yolanda Navarrete R., Daniela Rubens F., "Algunos Factores que Determinan la Conducta Electoral de la Mujer" (Memoria para Optor al Título de Psicológico, Universidad de Chile, Facultad de Filosofía y Educación, Escuela de Psicología, Santiago, 1964).

Table A-3
Female Preference for Political Parties—by Social Class, Greater Santiago, October 1963

	Upper		Middle		Lower		Total	
	Most	Least						
Communist	–	73.7%	6.6%	58.7%	8.5%	49.4%	7%	56%
Conservative	10.5%	–	10.6	5.3	6.1	6.0	9	5
Christian Democratic	47.5	–	43.4	3.1	40.0	1.8	42	2
Radical	10.5	15.8	11.5	12.7	6.7	15.1	6	14
Socialist	–	–	7.5	4.4	16.4	1.2	11	3
Liberal	10.5	–	5.8	5.3	4.2	5.4	5	5
PADENA	–	–	1.8	0.4	3.0	0.6	2	1
Democratic	–	–	2.2	–	1.2	–	2	–
No Reply	21.0	10.5	10.6	10.1	13.9	20.5	12	14

Source: Same as in Table No. A-2.

that social differences were natural and couldn't be changed, 50 percent supported the raising of lower class living standards, but not at the expense of wealthier sectors. A parallel finding on support for altering the distribution of income was reported in the November-December 1962 USIA poll, where the figure was 30 percent. When asked to specify particular socio-economic reforms, the following responses were forthcoming: end illiteracy and improve education (18 percent); improve housing (13 percent); industrialization (12 percent); agrarian reform and improvements (7 percent); monetary and tax reforms (5 percent); improvements in public health facilities (3 percent); better working conditions and reforms in the labor laws (1 percent); etc. On a more general level, 24 percent wanted more jobs and 27 percent a halt to the inflationary process. These were open-ended multiple answer questions. When asked specifically whether they supported agrarian and progressive tax reforms, the interviewees replied affirmatively in majorities of eighty-one and seventy-eight percent. "Encuestas: Las Clases Sociales," *El Mercurio: Revista del Domingo*, 8 enero 1967, p. 6. USIA, *Economic and Political Climate*, pp. 6, 7, 11, 20.

A similar lack of consensus on open-ended questions was revealed by the October 1963 survey of Santiago women. They were asked: "Are you satisfied with the present economic situation of the country?" Table A-4 displays their response. The 66.3 percent who replied negatively were then asked what measures they thought would improve the situation. On this multiple answer, open-minded follow-up, the percentages are of the 66.3 percent, as shown in Table A-5.

Table A-4

Female Satisfaction with the National Economic Situation—by Social Class, Santiago, October 1963

	Upper	Middle	Lower	Total
Yes	21.1%	31.0%	26.0%	28.5%
No	78.9	65.8	65.5	66.3
No Reply	–	3.2	8.5	5.3

Source: Same as in Table No. A-2.

Table A-5

Female Proposals to Ameliorate Economic Problems—by Social Class, Santiago, October 1963

	Upper	Middle	Lower	Total
More employment, reduce hardship, common effort	21.1%	14.5%	16.6%	15.8%
Regulation of present economic system, price control, maintenance of standard of living	5.3	11.5	17.4	13.5
Greater governmental efficiency	–	4.9	15.7	8.8
Change the system	–	7.9	7.4	7.2
More equitable distribution of income and wealth	15.7	9.1	0.8	6.2
Increase honesty in government and business	5.3	6.1	2.5	4.6
Expand production and use of natural resources	5.3	4.9	1.6	3.6
Nationalize the riches of the country	–	2.4	0.8	1.6
Can't be improved	5.3	1.2	–	1.0
Others	15.7	17.6	19.9	18.4
No Reply or Don't Know	21.0	18.7	15.7	17.8

Source: Same as in Table No. A-2.

Once again, when asked about a specific reform, the measure received greater support. "Do you think that the state or private firms should control (plan) national production?" Table A-6 shows the response to this question. Two years earlier, a survey by CESO of heads of households revealed greater male radicalism, thus indicating the significance of the sexual factor. The respondents were asked what policy the government ought to implement with regard to the large mining, industrial and public utility firms. While 36.3 percent

Table A-6

Female Support for State Control of the Economy—by Social Class, Santiago, October 1963

	Upper	Middle	Lower	Total
State	21.1%	45.9%	51.1%	47.0%
Private	21.1	17.1	10.9	14.75
Both (Mixed)	52.6	28.7	10.5	22.25
No Reply	5.2	8.3	27.5	16.00

Source: Same as in Table No. A-2.

urged nationalization, 47.9 percent advocated greater control but not ownership by the government. Almost 7 percent said the government had enough control, and 3.4 percent asserted less government control was desirable. Don't Knows and No Responses accounted for 5.48 percent of the respondents. CESO, "Stratification Survey" (September 1961). Later in 1962, the USIA commissioned survey asked: "In general, which do you prefer—government ownership of major industries, or private ownership?" Forty-four percent said "government," 42 percent "private," other answers were offered by 4 percent and 10 percent lacked an opinion. USIA, *Economic and Political Climate*, p. 28.

The results of an October 1966 Greater Santiago survey by Eduardo Hamuy's Centro de Estudios de Opinion Publica appear in *El Siglo*, 27 diciembre 1966, p. 7. The interviewees were asked whether certain types of property were or were not beneficial for the nation. The replies were: la casa propia, 99.2 percent beneficial and 1.1 percent not beneficial; el latifundio, 17.7 and 61.6; la pequena propiedad agricola, 70.6 and 9.1; la gran industria privado nacional, 64.4 and 13.4; la industria artesanal, 68.4 and 7.0; la mediana propiedad agricola, 69.7 and 7.0; la gran casa comercial, 68.4 and 13.4; la mediana industria privada, 66.4 and 11.0; el monopolio privado, 15.4 and 57.0; el pequeno comercio, 67.3 and 16.1; la gran industria del Estado, 67.7 and 11.7; los Bancos privados, 43.1 and 32.0; la propiedad colectiva, 43.9 and 34.4; la propiedad privado sobre la locomocion colectiva, 45.9 and 34.4; la propriedad estatal sobre la locomocion colectiva, 64.9 and 22.3; la gran industria extranjera, 42.2 and 40.4; la pequena industria, 71.5 and 9.3; las cooperativas, 78.6 and 6.6; la gran propiedad agricola del Estado, 59.8 and 18.1; la propiedad communitaria, 48.8 and 24.0. The remainders represent "don't knows." Except with regard to large foreign firms, no more than 13.4 percent could be held to accept Marxist value-orientations in general. The lower classes were slightly more inclined to support State or collective ownership. Thus, the sample was divided into four socio-economic levels, and asked: "Which of the following three sentences is most congruent with your way of thinking: "Private property is a sacred right and no one should inhibit its free exercise," 39.0 percent from the upper group, 37.6 percent from the upper middle, 33.7 percent from the lower middle, 32.7 percent from the lower, and

35.5 percent of the total sample; "Under certain circumstances, the state should limit and control the right of property in the interest of the common good," 39.0, 38.6, 38.2, 30.9 and 37.7; "The State or the collectivity should possess all property that affects the people's welfare or the economic progress of the country," 14.6, 14.9, 16.5, 21.8, and 16.3; Don't Know or No Response, 7.4, 8.9, 11.6, 14.6, 10.5. Other polls have indicated that Santiago is somewhat more anti-Marxist than the country as a whole.

E. Personalism. In a survey which accurately predicted the September 1964 presidential returns, Eduardo Hamuy included the following: "In supporting your candidate, do you consider: his program (49.58 percent Yes, 33.05 percent No), his personality (51.59 Yes, 31.05 No), his religion (32.23 Yes, 50.41 No), the parties that support him (19.45 Yes, 62.19 No), his social class origins (less than 17 percent Yes), his opposition to reactionaries (10.13 Yes, 72.51 No). Less than 10 percent were not asked, since they had not yet selected a candidate; and the remainder failed to reply. Personalism was also manifested by the fact that over three-fifths did not consider the political parties supporting the candidate. The fact that less than 20 percent considered such organizations while close to 50 percent claimed they were attentive to his program indicates—within a context of executive-legislative sharing of powers and an institutionalized and fairly strong party system—the lack of sophistication and rationality which characterize the electorate. CESO, "Pre-Electoral Survey" (August 1964).

The same survey reported that 70 percent expressed the belief that "you can't trust the people." Similarly, the following question was put to them: "A few strong and energetic leaders can make the country progress more than all the laws and speeches: 19.72 percent were "very in accord"; 49.40 were "in accord"; 9.94 were "partly in accord"; 14.15 were "in disaccord"; and 3.92 were "very in disaccord" with the statement." There is also some evidence of peasant (small farmer) distrust of landlords. See Marshall Wolfe, "Rural Settlement Patterns and Social Change in Latin America," Latin American Research Review, Vol. I, No. 2 (1966), p. 27.

During September 1963, four hundred Santiago women were asked: "When you choose a candidate, do you give more importance to: the candidate himself (32.8 percent), the program of his party (20.8), both (29.8), don't vote (13.8), no reply (3.0)." Then, the following open-ended question was set: "What is your ideal type of candidate?" Good moral qualities were cited by 22 percent, that he will help the people's situation improve by 15 percent, that he will do what he promises by 12 percent, that his ideas are similar or not opposed to the interviewee's by 10 percent, that he is able and popular by 7 percent, that he is religious or won't impede the free exercise of religion by 6 percent, reference to the candidate's physical characteristics, age or civil state by 3 percent, that he will change the system by 1 percent, that he is concerned with welfare and education of children by 1 percent, others by 8 percent, and no response from 15 percent. No more than 17 percent of these women referred even in the most general terms to programmatic matters or issues pertinent to reform. Kaplan, et al.

F. Mass Media Usage Patterns and Issue Cognizance. The results of a Greater Santiago mass media usage study by Roy Carter and Orlando Sepulveda during January 1963 are summarized in Table A-7. Average radio listening time was three hours daily. About 75 percent of the self-designated "opinion leaders" (1/3 of the men and 1/7 of the women who claimed that someone had recently asked them for advice concerning a current issue in the news) said that they relied on the radio as their principal source of news, while one quarter cited the newspapers. Similar news source ratios were cited by non-leaders. *El Mercurio, Clarin* and *La Tercera* were the most frequently read, and in that order. Forty-three percent of the radio listeners said they also read newspapers. "Opinion leaders of both sexes were less likely than non-leaders to credit radio news with greater truthfulness and impartiality than was attributed to the daily press." About 92 percent of the opinion leaders and 66 percent of the non-leaders believed that the press should be more objective and truthful. Except for magazine reading, there was no significant difference in mass media usage for the different sexes. Carter and Sepulveda, "Some Patterns of Mass Media Use," 219-24. During 1965, Sepulveda conducted a similar study on a small town in the south. Although there was somewhat less exposure to the

Table A-7

Social Class Differentials in Mass Media Exposure, Greater Santiago, January 1963

Individual says He:	Median Socio-Economic Status	
	Below	Above
Reads newspapers	77%	94%
Read one yesterday	41	61
Reads magazines	55	70
Read one yesterday	19	29
Reads books occasionally	42	68
Read one yesterday	8	20
Listens to radio customarily	84	95
Listened yesterday	63	77
Listened to news yesterday	44	62
Has seen a television program	40	71
Attends the movies	45	79
Saw one yesterday	5	9

Source: Roy E. Carter and Orlando Sepulveda, "Some Patterns of Mass Media Use in Santiago de Chile," *Journalism Quarterly*, XLI (Spring 1964), p. 216.

media, the same reliance upon the radio, especially among the lower classes was discovered. Similarly, the upper classes were better informed, and tended to read more. Orlando Sepulveda, "Medios de Comunicacion de Mases y Cambio Social" (Universidad de Chile, Instituto de Sociologia, Santiago, 1966, mimeo).

Analogous findings were reported in the September 1963 study of Greater Santiago women. While 88.50 percent said they listened to radio news programs, only 54.25 percent stated they also listened to political speeches. Of the former, 27.5 percent tuned in political and other news, 16.6 percent listened to political commentaries, 24.7 percent to general commentaries, 6.5 percent to crime reports, and 24.7 percent didn't answer or said they didn't know. When asked to indicate their favorite station, the results were 22.3 percent Mineria, 10.6 percent Portales, 9.9 percent Magallanes, 8.9 percent Pacifico, 8.2 percent Nuevo Mundo, 8 percent Cooperativa, 6.6 Agricultura, 5 percent Corporacion, 3 percent Balmaceda, etc. Slightly less than 80 percent claimed to read newspapers regularly, and of these, about 83 percent said they never failed to read domestic and foreign news while only 16 percent gave a similar reply with regard to editorials. When 80 percent were asked which paper they read regularly, their answers—stated here in terms of percentages of the 79.5 percent who claimed to read newspapers regularly—were as follows: 39 percent *El Mercurio*, 12.4 percent *La Tercera*, 11 percent *El Clarin*, 9.6 percent *La Nacion*, 9.6 percent *La Ultimas Noticias*, 3.3 percent *La Segunda*, 3 percent *Las Noticias de Ultima Hora*, 2 percent *Diario Illustrado*, 1.7 percent *El Siglo*, 8 percent magazines, 0.4 percent No Reply. Kaplan, et al.

The August 1964 "Pre-Electoral" CESO survey reported that 38 percent of the interviewees stated they didn't read magazines. Thirty percent said they did so occasionally, while 32 percent claimed they read them once a week at least. Almost 14 percent read the centrist *Ercilla*, while less than 2 percent said they bought the Communist weekly *Vistazo*. The same study reported that while 22 percent reported that they listened to the radio once a day on an average, 52 percent claimed they did so more often, and 17 percent said "occasionally." Only 8 percent said they never listened.

Studies by public relations firms in Santiago during 1963 indicated that women listened to the radio an average of three and three quarters hours per day, while the male rate was an hour less. Erica Vexler, "Quien es y como es el chileno," *Ercilla*, XXIX (10 julio 1963), 5. Heavy reliance upon radio is unsurprising, given the fact that only 40 percent of the labor force had a primary education while 6 percent had completed secondary school. United States, *Foreign Aid in Action*, p. 6.

A useful commentary on the findings of these studies is provided by the November-December 1962 USIA thirty-three city urban survey. More than a year and a half after the Alliance for Progress program had been formally initiated, interviewees were asked if they had "heard of a program called the Alliance for Progress." Negative replies were tendered by a third of the respondents, and more than a quarter said they "don't know." Only 14 percent knew when the Alianza was formed (1-1½ years earlier), 21 percent were aware that the United States had suggested this program, and none knew of any specific projects being carried out. USIA, *Economic and Political Climate*, pp. 54, 59, 61-62. Similarly, in the September 1963 study of Santiago women, less than 24 percent could identify either the NAZI or Communist Party symbols. Comparable figures for the Christian Democrats and the Radicals were 16.7 percent and 21.9 percent respectively. Yet 40.25 percent claimed to have an interest in the political programs of parties (58.5 percent said they lacked such an interest), and 42.5 percent reported reading party propaganda (against 57.25 percent who didn't). But of those who exposed themselves to such political materials, almost 80 percent indicated that they were only glanced over. Kaplan, et al. A few months earlier, the Salas Reyes Organization had interviewed a representative sample of 1000 persons in Santiago. Over a third never had heard either of Allende or Frei, and 42 percent could not identify Duran. While 54 percent associated Frei with the PDC, 9 percent had only heard of his name. Thirteen percent said Allende was a Communist, 13 percent that he was a Socialist, 28 percent that he was associated with FRAP or the left, and 12 percent had only heard of his name. With regard to Duran, 28 percent associated him with the Radical Party, 18 percent with the Frente Democratico, 4 percent with the right, the Liberal or the Conservative Parties, and 8 percent had only heard of his name. Fifty percent of those interviewed had never voted in a presidential election. Erica Vexler, "Lenguaje Politico Gastado," *Ercilla*, XXIX (17 julio 1963), 11. A public opinion poll carried out by a leading Santiago weekly during 1966, revealed that "a substantial majority" were ignorant of national events, and even more so with regard to international affairs. Many claimed that they lacked the time to follow the news and sought to present vague answers in order not to appear ignorant. Their main issue concerns were the failure of the Government to control inflation and provide proportionate wage readjustments, and the inadequacies of the mass transit "system." Mary Zajer, "Encuesta a Santiaguinos Chilenos 1966: indiferencia frente al mundo," *Ercilla*, 28 diciembre 1966, pp. 4-7.

G. Participation and Affective Orientation. A September 1958 Greater Santiago study reported that registration and electoral campaign involvement were positively correlated with such variables as higher socio-economic position (occupational and educational status were highly correlated), male sex, and middle age. Table A-8 reflects this, and Table A-9 indicates the very limited electoral campaign participation by the vast majority. It should be noted, too, that only 21 percent of the citizenry were registered. Although big businessmen represented 2.1 percent of the sample population, they constituted 2.6 percent of those registered. Corresponding figures for the remaining categories are: 9 percent and 13 percent, 36 percent and 40 percent (includes small businessmen, clericals and non-university professionals), 22 percent and 18 percent, 31 percent and 26 percent. Since 48 percent of this sample were registered, whereas only 21 percent of the general population of the country was, it is probable that the actual level of non-participation was close to 80 percent for the citizenry as a whole. Santiago, too, is one of the most politicized demographic zones in the country. In the 1958 presidential election, less than 18 percent of the population voted.

Interestingly, in 1964 when 36 percent of the population was registered and 32 percent voted in a campaign without precedent for intensity, a Greater Santiago study indicated that more than 76 percent of the sample had failed to

Table A-8

Degrees of Active Campaign Participation According to Sex, Age and Socio-economic Category, Santiago, 1958

Characteristics	Participation	Socio-Econ. Categories	Participation
Sex			
Men	42% (306)	Big Businessmen	35% (17)
Women	20% (501)	Managers and University trained Professionals	46% (73)
Age			
21-34	25% (230)	Small Businessmen	31% (61)
35-44	32% (223)	Clerical employees and non-Univ. professionals	27% (230)
45-54	32% (133)	Artisans and self-employed	23% (177)
		Wage earning workers	26% (246)

Source: Guillermo Briones, "La Estructura Social y La Participacion Politica," *Revista Interamericana de Ciencias Sociales*, vol. II, no. 3 (1963), pp. 380-81, 385-86, 398, 400. The foregoing pages are also the source of the other data referred to in my text.

Table A-9

Forms of Campaign Participation, Santiago, 1958

	Registered	Non-Registered	Total
Contributed Money	8%	2%	5%
Membership on an Election Committee	11	1	6
Attended Marches	21	6	13
Attended Meetings	15	4	9
Distributed Propaganda	11	2	7
Worked in a Campaign Office	6	1	3
Attempted to Persuade other Persons	25	10	17
Other Forms	2	–	1
No Participation	57	83	71
No Reply	–	1	1
	(385)	(422)	(807)

participate in any campaign activity. With regard to the 24 percent who did become involved: 6 percent contributed money; 4 percent were members of electoral committees; 13 percent attended marches; 13 percent attended meetings; 7 percent distributed propaganda and 3 percent worked in political offices. About 11 percent were involved in only one form of participation, 5 percent in two forms, 3 percent in three, 2 percent in four, 1 percent in five, 1 percent in six, and .36 percent in seven. The percentages are of the total sample. Reports by individuals that they had argued with others in an attempt to persuade them to vote were not regarded as campaign participation. Briones reported ("La Estructura Social," p. 399) that "(t)hese efforts occur most frequently during informal conversations in primary groups such as in the family, among friends or work-mates." Unless the "attempt to persuade" were part of an organized activity, any disagreement with one's tavern mate or wife might be included in this extremely loose definition of "campaign participation." Perhaps the mere act of witnessing a parade or march should also have been excluded as marginal to genuine involvement. The source for the 1964 data is: CESO, "Pre-Electoral Survey" (August 1964).

Electoral and campaign non-participation—most marked among the lower classes—are but manifestations of an internalized non-participant orientation. During 1965, for example, ECLA sociologist Adolfo Gurrieri studied 366 lower class youths from *poblacion* Jose Maria Caro, a Santiago slum where the Carabineros had killed a half dozen persons during a riot several years earlier. The interviewees stated that they and their parents didn't participate in unions, neighborhood centers or political parties. These organizations were viewed as belonging to the middle class. When the males were asked about their major goal in life, 20 percent advocated "struggle for social change." Fifteen percent cited work-oriented goals, while 50 percent wanted to obtain more education. Only 1½ percent indicated an interest in politics. According to Guerrieri: Se ha considerado que el concepto que interpreta mejor la situacion de los jovenes de la poblacion es el de 'desorientacion,' o 'perplejidid'; pretenden un mundo mejor y saben que esa pretension es legitima socialmente, pero el medio social en que se encuentran no les presenta con claridad, y tampoco con facil acceso, los instrumentos eficaces para superar su situacion." Augusto Olivares, "La Juventud en una poblacion callampa," *Desfile* (9 diciembre 1965), 18-19. The rarity of participant roles was also reflected in the study by Kaplan, et al. The 400 women were asked: "Do you attend political meetings or rallies and/or those of occupational interest groups." The responses were: Yes 7 percent, No 92.75 percent, and No Reply 0.25 percent. Less than 2 percent had attended more than two meetings of any kind during the previous year. *Of the 7 percent*, 36 percent were Frei supporters, 32 percent endorsed Allende, 14 percent Duran and 11 percent Prat. It is unsurprising, then, that women play a very limited role in the political parties with few holding posts in them. Julieta Campusano, "The Role of Women in Modern Society (Chile)." *World Marxist Review*, V (August 1962), 79.

A 1963 study of a thousand Santiago residents by the Salas Reyes Organization—which has done a number of the USIA surveys—reported that the lower classes attach less importance to elections. When asked whether they believed that the 1964 presidential election was important, 80 percent of the upper socio-economic group replied in the affirmative, 70 percent of the middle grouping replied similarly, while 60 percent of the lower one did. Only 15 percent of the entire sample were affiliated with any political party. Vexler, "Lenguaje Politico Gastado." During January 1963, a Gallup Poll (Instituto Chileno de Opinion Publica) indicated greater lower class pessimism. Those surveyed were asked whether they thought the economic situation would improve in 1963. Twenty-six percent replied in the affirmative, while 34 percent said it would remain the same. Thirty-eight percent expressed the belief that it would deteriorate, while 2 percent failed to respond. Of the 38 percent, contributions ranged from 10 percent in the upper class to 50 percent among unskilled workers and maids. "Encuesta Gallup en Chile," *Ercilla* XXIX, (20 febrero 1963), 15.

**Appendix II:
U.S. Non-Governmental
Organizations in Chile**

Appendix II

U.S. Non-Governmental Organizations in Chile

A. Catholic Relief Services: U.S. Subsidies. "Catholic Relief Services ships to Chile various supplies that are directly connected with its aid and assistance programs, including United States government-donated foods, used clothing donated by Americans to the annual Catholic Bishops' Thanksgiving Clothing Campaign, medicines, and various other relief supplies. In addition, CRS strives to cooperate with many other organizations that have goals similar to CRS in their programs and we assist these organizations with their shipping needs, if at all possible. Over the years, there have been innumerable organizations, Catholic, Protestant, Jewish as well as non-sectarian, that we have assisted with shipments, but to list them would be a virtual impossibility because of the various and sundry agencies involved."

By years, from 1957 through 1965, the value in tonnage of supplies shipped by CRS to Chile is as shown in Table A-10.

The income of CRS for fiscal 1963 (ending 9/30/63) was $176,525,972.91. This financed activities in 73 countries. Insofar as its Chilean program is concerned, CRS has stated that "(o)cean freight for food and basic relief supplies provided by the United States government; interior freight provided by the government of Chile and local Caritas groups; warehousing provided by government of Chile at central distribution points." Personnel in Chile during fiscal 1963 were three North Americans and four Chileans. American Council of Voluntary Agencies for Foreign Service, Inc., Technical Assistance Information Clearing House, *U.S. Non-Profit Organizations (Voluntary Agencies, Missions*

Table A-10
U.S. Government Subsidized Shipments to Caritas–Chile, 1957–1965

Year	Value in Dollars	Gross Weight in Lbs.
1957	1,561,178.73	10,177,450
1958	11,014,430.53	84,604,472
1959	8,704,010.22	104,360,677
1960	8,661,585.01	81,904,111
1961	7,151,661.43	65,564,014
1962	6,679,259.25	70,953,585
1963	3,592,039.98	36,375,944
1964	4,850,398.71	49,620,277
1965	7,821,674.21	98,350,536

Source: Letter dated June 19, 1967, from Rocco A. Sacci, Public Relations, Catholic Relief Services, New York.

267

and Foundations Participating in Technical Assistance Abroad): A Directory for 1964 (New York: Technical Assistance Information Clearing House of the American Council of Voluntary Agencies for Foreign Service, Inc., 1964), pp. 67, 501. Hereafter cited as American, *USNPO: 1964.*

B. Catholic Relief Services: Activities. "Relief supplies made available by Catholic Relief Services are distributed (in Chile) by the social welfare agencies of the Church, by non-sectarian organizations (again, only those serving the poor) and by governmental welfare agencies. Much of the Catholic Relief Services program in Chile is conducted in cooperation with the local counterpart agency, Caritas/Chile, which helps distribute CRS supplies throughout the country to the impoverished. Many of these programs will also include cooperation between CRS and all the local-level welfare agencies, Church, and government." Letter dated June 19, 1967, from Rocco A. Sacci, Public Relations, CRS.

During fiscal 1963, CRS was responsible for the following activities:

Relief: It distributed 1,800,000 lbs. of clothing to the needy throughout Chile.

Medicine and Public Health: It provided and shipped medicines, medical equipment, books, and supplies to hospitals and clinics affiliated with the nation-wide health program of Caritas; the medicines were provided by the CRS-NCWC and the Catholic Medical Misson Board. Equipment was donated for a rehabilitation hospital in Valparaiso. And CRS was responsible for the distribution of United States-donated foodstuffs to 1,127,499 needy throughout Chile including 173,527 children served through a school lunch project, 38,818 in orphanages, homes for the aged, and other institutions, 838,910 members of families, and 76,244 at summer camps.

Food Production: It provided both equipment as well as funds for seeds and fertilizers to the Institute of Rural Education.

Social Welfare: Caritas was assisted "in its further development as a social welfare and socio-economic development organization." Funds were provided to assist "in the rehabilitation of 3 special health cases."

Community Development: Funds and equipment were given to the Instituto de Viviendas Caritas (INVICA) to facilitate its housing construction program. CRS also supplied: "funds for development and administration of credit and producers' cooperative in Osorno, Valdivia, and Puerto Montt; funds and material to TECHO community development and producers' cooperative movement in Santiago and Antofagasta; funds for community development project in Chol Chol; and equipment to Instituto Indigeno in Temuco."

Education: CRS cooperated with the Institute of Rural Education in its rural training program, "including proposed P.L. 480 Title II feed-grain project." It also provided books and equipment "for technical training schools, equipment to Foundation for Popular Education and funds to 2 training schools." American, *USNPO: 1964*, p. 501.

C. Other Catholic Organizations and Holy Orders. The Association for Cultural Exchange (Jesuit Missions) was created in 1962. During fiscal 1963, it was operating a colegio (private primary and secondary school) in Osorno enrolling 322 students. There were 6 United States Jesuits and 13 local teachers employed. In February 1965, Jesuit Missions registered with AID as an approved agency and changed its name to International Educational Development, Inc. No "excess property was procured and shipped to Chile until January 1966." American, *USNPO: 1964*, pp. 47,500. Letter dated April 11, 1967, from Evelyn I. O'Brien, secretary to Rev. C.J. Ryan, S.J., President.

Catholics for Latin America (TECHO Foundation, Inc.) was also established in 1962. The "organization is guided by three goals: 1. To serve the poor directly, making friends with them and getting to know their immediate important needs; 2. To involve Latin Americans in the needs of the poor, especially the upper and middle classes; 3. To help the poor to help themselves, helping them to stand on their own two feet." Early in 1964, it had 3 United States volunteers and one local working in Chile where they cooperated with the Peace Corps, Chilean civil and local authorities, CRS, religious orders and local clergy. In Concepcion, TECHO was operating a dispensary and clinic and encouraging the development of home industries. A social center and a "mother's center" were also being operated in that city. In Santiago, the agency operated a fundamental education center, recreation and social welfare programs were promoted, and a professional advisory office was maintained where local lawyers, teachers, and medical personnel were assisting the poor. American Council of Voluntary Agencies for Foreign Service, Inc., Technical Assistance Information Clearing House, *U.S. Non-Profit Organizations (Voluntary Agencies, Missions and Foundations in Technical Assistance Abroad): Supplement for 1965* (New York: Technical Assistance Information Clearing House of the American Council of Voluntary Agencies for Foreign Service, Inc., 1965), pp. 20, 270. Hereafter cited as American, *USNPO: 1965*. Letter dated April 22, 1967, from Joan Kinch, TECHO Foundation, Inc.

The Daughters of the Holy Ghost expended $76,100 for foreign assistance "including surplus commodities and gifts in kind" during 1962. Fifteen of the sixteen Sisters who were abroad had been assigned to Chile. They included one dietician, four professors, one registered nurse, and nine full time teachers. The registered nurse and medicines were assigned to a dispensary in Chanaral. Their principal activities were, however, in the field of education. Thus—also in 1962 or 1963—the Sisters: operated two primary schools in Antofagasta and Tocopilla for approximately 400 students; conducted English language courses at the Normal Teacher Training School (Branch of Universidad del Norte), and at the Technical School, both in Antofagasta, and taught English and French courses in the public secondary schools in Chanaral. There is no indication as to when their program was initiated in Chile. American, *USNPO: 1964*, pp. 139, 503.

The Society of the Divine Word was "founded to promote the spiritual, moral and material welfare of underprivileged peoples." The program of the Divine Word Missionaries in Chile began in 1910 and has been educational. In 1964, they were conducting and administering "42 primary schools for 6,137 students; 6 elementary schools for 3,050 students; 1 professional school for 75 students; and 5 high schools and colleges for 4,442 students." The colegios were "located in Santiago (opened 1910), Puerto Varas (1930), Los Angeles (1937) and El Golf, Santiago (1950)." The Missionary Sisters Servants of the Holy Spirit (Techny, Ill.) were also cooperating. Nationalities of the schools' staffs: 2 United States, 24 South American, 64 European and 250 Chileans. Although the Divine Word Missionaries received "surplus foods" and were thus an "approved" agency, it is not clear whether they were distributed in Chile. There is, however, a strong probability that such foods were used for school lunch programs. American, *USNPO: 1965*, pp. 33-34, 270-71.

The objectives of the Dominican Fathers (Sacred Order of Friars Preachers, Province of St. Joseph) are defined as: "(t)o extend the Kingdom of Christ on earth. To provide educational, medical and social welfare assistance." Their program—initiated in 1957—was centered "in an outlying district of Concepcion" where the Fathers: administered a school "giving rudimentary instruction to approximately 200 children"; operated a social center for the poor; and a clinic. As of 1964, the program involved two United States teachers and seven Chileans (two teachers, two doctors, two nurses and one medical technician). The Fathers cooperated with CRS which shipped used clothing for them "under United States government subsidy for transportation." American, *USNPO: 1965*, pp. 35, 271. Letter dated April 18, 1967, from the Very Rev. Richard E. Vahey, O.P., P.G., director of mission.

Established in 1955, the goals of the Dominican Mission Sisters are: "(t)o raise the standards of education and health in various countries by sending missionary Sisters to foreign lands for educational, social and catechetical work among needy persons in. . . ." During 1963, the Sisters were teaching "in a primary school in Las Rocas de Santo Domingo for 173 children; in the primary department of the St. George School—with approximately 1,000 boys—conducted by the Holy Cross Fathers in Santiago; in the primary school of the Colegio San Mateo with 280 students in Osorno conducted by the Jesuit Fathers." Other activities included operation of the Government Health Department Clinic in Las Rocas de Santo Domingo, where "one Sister nurse and one registered nurse paid by the Health Department" were treating an average of 400 to 500 patients a day. Caritas was providing "some material and financial aid," while medicines were supplied by the Chilean government. DMS personnel in Chile included: "11 U.S. Sister teachers, 1 U.S. Sister nurse, 1 Papal Volunteer, 1 local nurse, and 38 local teachers." American, *USNPO: 1964*, pp. 102, 502.

The stated objectives of the Holy Cross Missions (Fathers and Brothers) are: "(t)o educate youth from primary to college level. To raise the economic and social status of the underprivileged by vocational and trade schools; by credit unions and cooperatives; by medical dispensaries, orphanages, leprosaria, etc. To conduct relief programs for the needy." In 1964, the Fathers of the Indiana Province were administering and staffing St. George's Colegio in Santiago with an enrollment of 1,900. They had established this institution in 1943. The Fathers assigned to the colegio totaled thirteen; seventy-five local lay teachers were also employed. One Father staffed "a home to care for and educate poor boys and orphans in Talagante." The 1963 budget was $170,000 for programs in seven countries, including Chile. "Grants" accounted for $30,000, and "surplus commodities" were valued at $5,000. American, *USNPO: 1965*, pp. 59-60, 271.

The goals of the Lorettine Sisters (Sisters of Loretto at the Foot of the Cross) are "(t)o impart the principles of Christian faith and morals and to raise the standards of living of the less developed nations." They report that "(t)wo Sisters are engaged in the training of women in domestic arts in the rural areas surrounding Santiago. The program began in January 1963 and is conducted in cooperation with the Rural Catholic Action Institute." Expenditures "for fiscal year ending 6/30/64 in foreign technical assistance, including gifts in kind and surplus commodities" were $25,466.11. In addition to Chile, programs were being conducted in Bolivia and Peru during fiscal 1964. American, *USNPO: 1965*, pp. 75, 272.

The Maryknoll Fathers listed their objectives as: "(t)o recruit and train American youth for lifetime service overseas; to send its members overseas and to support them in their spiritual programs and technical assistance activities for the benefit of people regardless of race, color or creed; to help develop nationals capable of taking over the operation and administration of all its overseas spiritual and technical assistant programs." Their Chilean program during 1963 may be summarized as follows:

Medicine and Public Health: School-lunch projects were being carried out in Temuco, Santiago, Portezuelo, Ercilla, Curepto, Talca, and Galvarino. The following classes were sponsored: child care in Pemuco and Temuco; first aid in Santiago; Red Cross in Ercilla; and nursing aide instruction in Pemuco and Santiago. Six clinics were being administered in Santiago, Talca and Chol Chol, and dispensaries were being operated in Chillan, Pemuco, Ercilla, and Temuco.

Food Production: The Fathers sponsored an agricultural school in Molina and a soil conservation project in Ercilla. They also organized "Young Christian Farmers in San Gregorio and Galvarino."

Social Welfare: Athletic teams were organized and recreation centers operated in Santiago, Curepto, Talcahuano, Licanten and Galvarino. Social services were provided in Pemuco, Santiago, Curepto, Licanten, Temuco, Galvarino and Chillan. Night-lodging for men was provided in Chillan, and a home for the aged was operated in Curepto. Boy Scout and Girl Scout groups were organized in Talcahuano, Chillan, Portezuelo, and Curepto.

Community Development: The Fathers conducted "leadership training projects for civic and social responsibility in 16 centers in the provinces of Nuble, Concepcion, Bio-Bio, Santiago, Talca, and Cautin." Consumers' and farmers' cooperatives were organized in Pemuco, and credit unions were established in Chillan, Santiago, Curepto, Talca, Galvarino and Temuco.

Education: Literacy classes were conducted in Pemuco, Santiago, and Renaico, while sewing classes were given in Santiago and Temuco. Thirty primary schools were administered in the provinces of Nuble, Concepcion, Bio-Bio, Santiago, Talca, and Cautin for 6,874 students with a staff of 172 teachers. Seven secondary schools were administered in the provinces of Nuble, Concepcion, Santiago, and Cautin for 456 students with a staff of 17 teachers. Vocational schools were operated in Santiago (one) and Talcahuano (one for girls) as was a commercial school in the latter city. A night school for adults offering courses in typing, shorthand, electricity, music and drama was also operated in Talcahuano.

Maryknoll Fathers Mission personnel in 1963 included: "102 U.S. missionaries including 47 Maryknoll Fathers and 6 Maryknoll Brothers, 10 other missionaries, 219 local employees and 340 part time volunteers (5 doctors and 425 volunteer Catechist Leaders). And "Cooperating Agencies" were listed as: "Catholic Relief Services-Caritas/Chile cooperates in distributing U.S. food resources; Chilean government in relief work, education and agriculture; Franciscan Sisters (6) in educational work; Maryknoll Sisters (46) in educational, medical, health and social work; and Papal Volunteers (3) in medical and social work." American, *USNPO: 1964*, pp. 174, 504.

The Technical Assistance Program of the Maryknoll Sisters of St. Dominic, Inc. "aims 1) to promote better social living by providing services geared to helping the people attain a fuller recognition of their personal dignity and by developing professionally trained local personnel and local civic leaders; 2) in general, to promote better socio-economic conditions through educational, medical and social welfare programs with special emphasis on local self-help." Their Chilean program in 1963 may be summarized as follows:

Medicine: A school clinic in Santiago was "serving 400 students and 160 others in surrounding impoverished areas."

Social Welfare: Services were provided "to 2,404 individuals and 652 families through case work, counseling and planned relief." Unwed mothers, the aged and the chronically ill were also assisted.

Community Development: "Leadership training for women and for teenage boys and girls (was) provided in all centers through 35 groups with 3,102 members."

Education: They staffed six elementary and four secondary schools with a total enrollment of 3,793. In addition, 1,300 "children in a grade and high school in Huachipato" were instructed.

This work was being carried on by 44 United States Sisters, "including 41 teachers, 1 nurse and 2 social workers; 81 local employees and 285 local volunteers." Listed as "Cooperating Agencies" were: "Maryknoll Fathers conduct the projects; U.S. Embassy provides educational literature, films, first grade readers for 6 schools; CARE, sewing machines, sports equipment, and children's school kits; Catholic Relief Services, food and clothing; Catholic Medical Mission Board, medical supplies." American, *USNPO: 1964*, pp. 176, 504-505.

Papal Volunteers for Latin America (PAVLA) was established in 1960, "as a department of the Latin American Bureau of the National Catholic Welfare Conference." PAVLA's objectives are "(t)o provide qualified personnel on a long-term volunteer basis to help the Church and the people in Latin America in their efforts to meet pressing social, economic and religious needs." PAVLA believes that the expectations of the Latin American multitudes are rising too fast, and that consequently the Church needs outside aid to "usher in a new social order." Major aspects of its program include: use of mass media; strengthening Catholic schools; a religious education program; and recruitment of clergy. In Chile during 1963, nine volunteers were engaged in community development projects in Temuco and Talca. In addition: two volunteers were teaching at a secondary school in Antofagasta; one was instructing at a similar institution in Santiago; one was teaching at Catholic University in Santiago and four were assigned to the Catholic University in Valparaiso. There were a total of 25 volunteers in Chile, whose training had included Christian Social Doctrine and its relation to politics, economics and international relations. Except for the probable use of CRS-Caritas surplus foods in the community development projects, there was no United States government assistance. American, *USNPO: 1964*, pp. 212, 506. Kevane, pp. 3-4, 6, 8. According to Ivan Illich ("The Seamy Side of Charity," p. 88) the NCWC transferred $1,000,000 from its home missions to the Latin American Bureau in 1960.

The goals of the Precious Blood Sisters (Congregation of the Sisters of the Precious Blood) are: "(t)o train native teachers and catechists; to form adult leaders among the laity; to aid in educational and social work; to help create a middle class; to educate youth in Christian faith and morals as well as in the secular branches; to aid the sick poor in polyclinics or on home visits; to teach mothers the art of homemaking." Their Chilean programs in medicine began in 1964; activities in others probably commenced one or more years earlier.

Medicine and Public Health: In Santa Ines, a polyclinic was staffed and "classes to prepare assistants for the clinic and for general care of the sick" were conducted—all in cooperation with the National Health Service. Health care was provided "for the sick poor in Valdivia." And "foods from Caritas in the mission areas" were distributed.

Community Development: In cooperation with the Municipalidad de San Bernardo, the Sisters assisted "in the development of a cooperative in Santa Ines."

Education: In this area of endeavor, the Sisters have reported that they: "(s)taff and operate San Gaspar school in Santiago with a coed kindergarten for 104 children and preparatory and humanities departments for a total of 925 boys; San Jose school in Santiago with preparatory and humanities departments for 1,485 students; and San Sebastian school in Purranque with preparatory and humanities departments for 520 students. Maintain a kindergarten for 8 children and an education department for 40 adults in Tres Asequias near Santa Ines, the latter with the cooperation of Campana Nacional de Alfabetizacion de la Alianza para el Progresso. One United States Sister, with the assistance of the Fulbright Scholarship program, serves as sub-director of the University English program at Catholic University of Chile in Santiago. United States Sisters, with the assistance of Chilean religious, conduct classes in homemaking, child care and sewing at 'centers for mothers' in Santa Ines, Los Bajos, Calera de Tango and Valdivia for a total of 832 women. Fathers and Sisters of the Congregation of the Precious Blood and the Chilean Government cooperate in this educational work."

Personnel in Chile included: 15 United States Sisters, 18 full and part-time Chilean Sisters, 20 local lay teachers, and "other local religious and lay assistants." Expenditures in Chile "for fiscal year ending 6/30/64 in foreign technical assistance, including gifts in kind and surplus commodities" totaled $59,906.42. American, *USNPO: 1965*, pp. 101, 273.

The goals of the Sisters, Servants of the Immaculate Heart of Mary (General Motherhouse, Pennsylvania) are: "(t)o promote missionary and social work with a view to raising living standards through the medium of education." The Sisters have been in Chile since 1940, but in the 1961-1963 period their program was expanded. Wherever the Sisters are working, clothing, school supplies "and other materials are distributed." At the end of 1964, they were administering the following schools: "Villa Maria Academy (established in 1940), a private day school (kindergarten through high school) for 1,602 girls in Santiago; San Francisco elementary school for the poor (since 1961) in Las Condes with an enrollment of 359 boys and girls; Noviciado Immaculado Corazon de Maria (since

1963), a school in Las Condes which trains native South American Sisters of the order to become qualified school teachers." Personnel at the end of 1964 included "18 U.S. Sisters and 54 local staff members (4 Sisters and 50 lay teachers)." "Cooperating Agencies" were identified as: "Holy Cross Fathers (Mid-West Province, Indiana) cooperate in the operation of the San Francisco School. The Committee for Foreign Relief of Philadelphia processes equipment and materials which are shipped by Catholic Relief Services." American, *USNPO: 1965*, pp. 64, 272.

D. Major Protestant Relief and Service Organizations. The Church World Service began its Chilean program in 1958 in close cooperation with Ayuda Cristiana Evangelica, a division of the Evangelical Council of Chile. In 1963, the program encompassed the following:

Public Health: CWS was providing "U.S.-donated foods for a feeding project for underprivileged families combined with training in diet, health, hygiene, and child care for 120,000 persons, and for a school and institutional feeding project."

Food Production and Agriculture: A demonstration project "in agricultural extension and youth clubs at Calama" was being supported. Preparatory work for a reforestation project in Chol Chol was underway.

Community Development: Support was being given to a "cooperative training project conducted by mobile training unit based in Nueva Imperial."

Education: A demonstration project in vocational training and small crafts industries at Calama was also being supported.

Personnel included: "1 U.S. and 28 Chilean staff members in Santiago office plus about 20 paid staff members in regional offices." During the 1957-1965 period, CWS supplied surplus foods and other supplies for various denominational boards of missions. Shipping charges were paid by the United States government. Data for shipments to Chile are as shown in Table A-11. These figures also include CWS shipments for its own program, which was terminated during 1966. American, *USNPO: 1964*, p. 502. Letter dated June 16, 1967, from John W. Clay, for Richard F. Smith, Secretary for Service.

United States surplus foods and shipping services were first utilized by the Seventh-Day Adventist Welfare Service, Inc., for its programs in Chile during fiscal 1959. Its activities are in the following fields: education; equipment, material aid and relief; food production and agriculture; medicine and public health; and social welfare. No additional information was published in the directory, and the organization declined to answer a letter of inquiry. American, *USNPO: 1964*, p. 226. United States, *Foreign Aid in Action*, p. 12.

Table A-11
U.S. Government Subsidized Church World Service Shipments to Chile,
1957-1965

Year	Net Weight (Lbs.)	Cash Value
1957	91,793	$ 29,791.00
1958	3,039,696	230,454.00
1959	3,039,696	230,453.88
1960	4,620,696	638,198.00
1961	8,155,431	1,093,904.00
1962	10,064,925	985,056.00
1963	10,244,757	1,347,075.00
1964	6,165,891	761,430.00
1965	6,824,957	1,080,847.00

Source: Letter dated June 16, 1967, from John W. Clay, for Richard F. Smith, Secretary for Service.

The objectives of Lutheran World Relief, Inc., are: "(t)o assist needy people outside the U.S. through distribution of material aid, and through rehabilitation, health, self-help and development projects; to help strengthen indigenous groups in developing voluntary social services." Since 1958, it has subsidized and otherwise supported the Social Service Department of the Chilean National Christian Council (Ayuda Cristiana Evangelica). During 1963, the following programs were being assisted:

Medicine and Public Health: Health and education kits were given to 7,000 children, and food to 40,000 persons. Courses in health and sanitation were organized, and supplies were distributed to three hospitals.

Relief: Clothing was given to 40,000 persons.

Social Welfare: Support was given to "community centers in housing projects of Arica, Calama, Santiago (San Gregorio), Concepcion (Jualpencillo), Chillan, Temuco, Valdivia, Puerto Montt, Lota, and Coronel."

Community Development: Assistance was given toward "the establishment of cooperatives in the provinces of Antofagasta, Malleco, Cautin, Valdivia, and Osorno."

Twenty-eight persons employed by Ajuda Cristiana Evangelica were paid with grants from Lutheran World Relief. "In 1963 Lutheran World Relief sent food to Chile valued at $3,945,678 and 1964 food valued at $3,999,626." This was all donated by the United States government, and under the provisions of P.L. 480 had to be used in conjunction with self-help projects. The shipping charges for all of the foodstuffs and most clothing were paid for by the United States government. Exclusive of surplus United States foods which totaled 17,570,955 pounds between 1958 and 1966, "(s)upplies contributed by Lutherans and shipped to Chile totaled 2,117,240 lbs. and were valued at $1,845,471. The U.S. government reimbursed Lutheran World Relief for ocean freight in the amount of $476,660.12." American, *USNPO: 1964*, p. 503. Letters dated April 14, 1967, and May 25, 1967, from Ove R. Nielsen, Assistant Executive Secretary. Lutheran World Relief, *Annual Report for 1966* (New York: Lutheran World Relief, 1966), pp. 2-3, 14.

E. Other Protestant Organizations. The stated purpose of American Women's Hospitals Service, Inc. is "(t)o support medical and hospital services for the care of the indigent sick and prevention of distress due to wars, disasters, etc." During 1963, it provided "financial support to (a) pediatric clinic and hospital ward at Nueva Imperial in cooperation with (the Methodist Church)." The staff included "1 U.S. missionary doctor and 1 Chilean nurse." The organization's "(e)xpenditures for 1962 in foreign assistance including surplus commodities and gifts in kind" were $78,700. There is no indication as to whether such commodities were shipped to the Nueva Imperial hospital. American, *USNPO: 1964*, pp. 44, 500.

"The objectives of the (Board of Missions of the Methodist Church) are religious, philanthropic and educational, designed to diffuse more generally the blessings of Christianity in every part of the world by the promotion and support of all phases of religious, missionary, church and church extension activity in the United States and other countries . . . and to aid in Christianizing personal life and the social order in all lands and among all peoples. . . ." The program in Chile during 1963 encompassed the following:

Medicine and Public Health: Operation of clinics and provision of general medical services at Angol and Nueva Imperial farm centers. The provision of meals for the children of working mothers at a social settlement in Santiago, "which includes central and outlying medical and dental clinics."

Food Production and Agriculture: Support for "El Vergel farm center at Angol with experimental and extension work in land reclamation and reforestation, orchards, and an agricultural school for boys." Maintained the "Duncan Mangum Rural Life Center at Nueva Imperial with an agricultural school, demonstrations and extension work in farming techniques."

Social Welfare: A "social settlement at Santiago including a nursery and kindergarten for 100 children and club and recreation projects" was maintained. It operated a "student center and hostel for 20 students at Concepcion and a recreation project on campgrounds at (the) Angol farm center."

Education: Operation of "Iquique English College which has a total of 460 students in its elementary, secondary and commercial departments." It co-operated "in the support of Santiago College with 890 students in its kindergarten and high school departments." The Board of Missions was also maintaining "primary schools and neighboring rural schools at Angol and Nueva Imperial; and vocational schools at Angol and Nueva Imperial farm centers."

There were "42 U.S. staff members" in Chile, and surplus commodities and other materials were shipped through Church World Service. American, *USNPO: 1964*, pp. 184, 505. Letter dated June 16, 1967, from John W. Clay at CWS.

The goals of the Christian Children's Fund, Inc., are: "(t)o provide housing, clothing, nourishment, medical treatment, education and guidance to orphans, children born out of wedlock, children unwanted or made destitute by family tragedies, wars and natural disasters, and in so doing, to form a person-to-person bond of friendship between the children and their American sponsors." Its Chilean program was initiated in 1956. During 1963, the Fund was: operating one agricultural project for forty-five boys; operating "3 kindergartens for 114 children"; and assisting "300 children living in 7 affiliated homes operated by the Salvation Army." Personnel included "2 U.S. volunteers and 21 local staff members consisting of teachers and institutional personnel." The organization received surplus commodities in 1962, the last year for which financial information was available. American, *USNPO: 1964*, pp. 72, 501.

"To establish national churches and promote the social well being of the people in Chile" are the objectives of the Gospel Mission of South America. In 1964, the mission was operating "1 dispensary in Liquine and 1 in Mechuque, each staffed with a missionary nurse." It was also supervising "30 primary schools in the rural areas of south central Chile." Forty United States missionaries were assigned to Chile, and the expenditures for the Chilean program in the fiscal year ending 3/31/64 were $110,966.21. The Mission distributed surplus commodities during 1960. It was founded in 1940. American, *USNPO: 1965*, pp. 57, 271. Letter during early April 1967, from F.E. Durant, Home Director.

The function of Interchurch Medical Assistance, Inc., is "(t)o serve as a single agent for the collection and distribution of drugs and hospital supplies used in the overseas medical programs of American Protestant churches and agencies." Established in 1961, IMA ships through Church World Service and the Seventh-Day Adventist Welfare Service, Inc., to "medical mission hospitals and clinics" in Chile and other countries. American, *USNPO: 1965*, pp. 66-67. Interchurch Medical Assistance, Inc., *Reach "Round the World with IMA"* (New York: Interchurch Medical Assistance, Inc., n.d.).

The Methodist Committee for Overseas Relief is "(a)n agency of the Methodist Church entrusted with the responsibility for alleviating human distress overseas. . . ." Its Chilean program was initiated in 1962, and by the end of 1963, it encompassed: the operation of five recreation centers and day care nurseries in Camilo Olavarria (Concepcion), Gil de Castro (Valdivia), Lo Vellodor (Santiago),

San Gregorio (Santiago), and Las Cenchas (Talcahuano); and the operation in several depressed areas of one rural and one urban mobile team for community development purposes. Personnel included "1 U.S. administrator, 9 full time and 10 part time local workers." The Committee received surplus commodities. American, *USNPO: 1964*, pp. 186, 505.

The Foreign Mission Board of the Southern Baptist Convention is charged with "(t)he conduct of Christian missions in foreign countries." During 1963, it was operating "1 secondary school in Temuco for 620 students staffed with U.S. missionary teachers and national teachers." "Expenditures for 1962 in foreign assistance including surplus commodities and gifts in kind" totaled $19,966,761.52. But there is no indication as to how much was allocated to Chile. American, *USNPO: 1964*, pp. 228, 506.

The objectives of United Church Women (A Department of the Division of Christian Unity of the National Council of Churches of Christ in the U.S.A.) are: "(t)o unite church women in their allegiance to their Lord and Savior Jesus Christ, through a program looking to their integration in the total life and work of the church and to the building of a world Christian community." UCW intended to "provide support during 1965 for a staff person (probably a local Chilean) to work with Church World Service in a program of community development geared toward the role of woman in the community and the encouragement of responsible parenthood." American, *USNPO: 1965*, pp. 121, 274.

"The functions of the Commission (on Ecumenical Mission and Relations of the United Presbyterian Church in the U.S.A.) include the maintenance, general direction and interpretation of the United Presbyterian Church's mission overseas in the work of evangelism (including industrial evangelism), Christian education and Christian social and welfare services . . . ." Its program in Chile during 1964 encompassed the following:

Medicine: Supported a "maternity clinic operated by the Presbyterian Church in Chile, with a staff of 4 doctors, 3 nurses and 15 others, all nationals."

Social Welfare: Social centers in Santiago and Vina del Mar were maintained in cooperation with Church World Service for social programs.

Community Development: The organization of cooperatives was assisted.

Education: It was sharing "in the support of "6 elementary schools and a secondary school, with a total enrollment of 740 students and a staff of 35 teachers."

Personnel in Chile include "6 U.S. missionaries, 35 nationals in education and 22 in medical work." American, *USNPO: 1965*, pp. 124, 274.

The goals of World Presbyterian Missions include "evangelizing and establishing indigenous churches through various means in accord with historic Presbyterian standards. . . ." Established in 1957, WPM's Chilean activities in 1963 encompassed the following: Relief Work; Disease Control and Medical Services; and Education (Fundamental, Technical and Vocational) for which radio broadcasts were utilized. Surplus commodities were received. American, *USNPO: 1964*, p. 250.

"World Medical Relief is dedicated to the relief of human suffering throughout the world by equipping hospitals, clinics and dispensaries with instruments, supplies and drugs for indigent persons who are unable to pay for medical or dental care." During 1960 and 1963, 233,169 lbs. of equipment and supplies were dispatched to Chilean hospitals, clinics and dispensaries. Similarly, in April-May, 1964, 41,515 lbs. of drugs were shipped to Chile. WMR's programs also extended to the shipment of drugs, equipment and supplies to Medical Civic Action Teams of the United States Armed Forces in Thailand and the Canal Zone since 1962, and to similar teams in Vietnam since January 1965. American, *USNPO: 1964*, p. 248. *World Medical Relief Newsletter*, Vol. I, No. 3.

F. YMCA and Jewish Organizations. "The objective of the International Committee (of the Young Men's Christian Associations of the United States and Canada) is to help strengthen those YMCA Movements abroad with which it has agreed to cooperate, to the end that they may be of maximum effectiveness and fully self-contained." In 1963, it was giving "capital assistance towards building projects in Santiago, Concepcion, Valparaiso, and Antofagasta." YMCA also provided one Fraternal Secretary to give "guidance and counsel in a number of programs which the Associaciones Cristianas de Jovenas (YMCA) carries on itself, including several camps, boys' clubs and work with students, educational courses, sports and recreational projects." The international activities of the YMCA were reported to have been subsidized by the CIA through the Foundation for Youth and Student Affairs. American, *USNPO: 1964*, pp. 257, 507. *New York Times*, Feb. 19, 1967, p. 26.

The goal of the American Jewish Joint Distribution Committee, Inc. is to provide "(a)ll types of assistance to needy Jews in other countries. . . ." In Chile, it has supported "1 loan institution, operated by local Jewish organization, which made 246 loans between 1958 and June 30, 1963." The Committee is registered with the Advisory Committee on Voluntary Foreign Aid, has received surplus commodities as well as funds from "governmental and intergovernmental sources" in the last year for which financial data was available. American, *USNPO: 1964*, pp. 32, 500.

The objective of the United HIAS Service, Inc., is "(t)o assist Jewish refugees and migrants to resettle and integrate in various countries throughout the free world. . . ." In Chile during the early 1960s (and perhaps since 1954), HIAS was providing "(s)ervices for refugees and migrants including reception of migrants, supervision of integration aid by the local Jewish community such as initial relief, inland transportation, provision of housing, interest-free loans, language and citizenship training, vocational guidance and placement, and medical care where necessary." One representative was stationed in Santiago. The "USEP, UNHCR, U.S. Department of State, Government of Chile, local Jewish community, American Jewish Joint Distribution Committee and other international, national, and local voluntary agencies" were cooperating with regard to the program in Chile. HIAS is registered with the Advisory Committee on Voluntary Foreign Aid, and is a member of the American Council of Voluntary Agencies for Foreign Service, Inc. Its financial information for 1963 recorded the receipt of United States "government grants." American, *USNPO: 1965*, pp. 122-23, 274.

G. CARE. The CARE program in Chile was instituted in 1953, "closed in 1955, and reactivated in 1960 following (the) earthquake." "CARE is a non-profit service through which the patrons may supply or make available goods and services in foreign countries for purposes of relief, rehabilitation and construction." The Chilean program in 1963 extended to the following:

Public Health: CARE was operating a "nationwide school-feeding project, involving the distribution of 22.7 million lbs. of milk powder, corn meal, bulgar wheat, rolled wheat, salad oil, and cheese, supplemented by 1,000 cases of donated baby food, to 618,000 school and pre-school children throughout the country."

Social Welfare: It was providing a multiple power tool unit for use in the training of retarded children.

Rural Community Development and Food Production: CARE was supplying "tools and kits to rural villages for development projects under supervision of Peace Corps volunteers; livestock, tools, and donated seed to agricultural cooperatives and isolated Indian villages; poultry brooders, poultry incubators, audiovisual units, and recreational equipment for agricultural extension centers at Ancud, Osorno, Los Alamos, and Longotoma."

Education: Funds were contributed "for the purchase of extensive laboratory equipment for Universidad del Norte in Antofagasta." CARE also provided "sewing machines and equipment to rural sewing cooperatives, kits to trade schools in urban and rural areas, and electrical equipment to assist in training of electrical technicians."
Personnel included "3 U.S. and 5 local employees." "Cooperating agencies" were the "Ministry of Public Education, Peace Corps and (the) Institute of Rural Education." CARE has listed the sources of its 1963 income as: "$12,165,213 — Voluntary contributions (including MEDICO); $43,312,716 — USDA surplus commodities; $13,385,552 — Ocean freight subsidies; $692,630 —

U.S. government contracts (Peace Corps, books, and scientific equipment). Total: $69,556,218." This was, of course, allocated to programs in forty-four countries. American, *USNPO: 1964*, pp. 61-62, 500.

H. Other Secular Relief and Service Organizations. The goals of the American Dietetic Association are: "(t)o improve the nutrition of human beings; to advance the science of dietetics and nutrition; and to promote education in these and allied areas." During 1963, its activities in Chile were in the fields of nutrition and relief. The ADA received surplus commodities in 1962, the last year for which financial information was available. American, *USNPO: 1964*, p. 19.

The purposes of the American Foundation for Overseas Blind, Inc., are "(t)o provide tangible aid and essential services in order to advance the educational and rehabilitation facilities for sightless persons in overseas areas." In 1963, the Foundation was providing the services of a South American representative who was planning a rehabilitation center for blind adults to be opened in 1964 at Valparaiso. It also supplied a large quantity of technical appliances for the center. The Foundation was registered with the Advisory Committee on Voluntary Foreign Aid, and received surplus commodities in 1962, the last year for which financial information was available. Shipment of the "technical appliances" was probably at United States government expense. American, *USNPO: 1964*, pp. 23, 499.

The goals of the American Fund for Czechoslovak Refugees, Inc., are: "(t)o render resettlement aid, material relief and other services to Czechoslovak democratic refugees who escaped from Czechoslovakia following the Communist seizure in February 1948." Its Chilean program encompassed: shipment of clothing, books and other material aids; medical care; support for centers and hostels, homes for the aged and orphanages; and assistance to students. During 1963, the Fund obtained surplus commodities and received funds under a USEP contract. American, *USNPO: 1964*, pp. 30, 712-13.

The objectives of the Rockefeller Brothers Fund endowed American International Association for Economic and Social Development are: "(t)o promote self-development and better standards of living, together with understanding and cooperation, among peoples throughout the world." In the 1962-1964 period, the association—in cooperation with the ministry of education and CORFO—constructed six to eight rural vocational schools near Chillan. The effort involved the organization of local inhabitants into self-help construction committees. The AIA views its program as particularly valuable since "it complements and supplements bilateral and multilateral governmental technical assistance programs, which are often limited by stringent legal requirements in their experimental and exploratory aspects. The fields in which AIA programs operate—rural development and education—are fundamental and involve massive, but usually, inadequate, national programs in each country. The overriding requirement of an AIA program, therefore, is that it must have a significant multiplier effect in relation to the national program in any given field." Plaques "noting the Rockefeller Brothers Fund contribution" were placed on the new schools. The teachers for these schools were trained in vocational subjects and given a course "on youth club organization." During this period, AIA received surplus commodities. The success of this pilot program "in its construction phase is the reason that the U.S. government's Agency for International Development (AID) in Chile decided to use $400,000 of its so-called 'impact program' funds to finance the extension of a Plan Victoria type of program to another area of Chile." Thus, "(e)arly in 1964 the U.S. Agency for International Development (AID) contributed $370,000 for a similar program in the province of Nuble, north of Victoria. The plan there is to construct six new schools at a cost of $275,000. The remaining $95,000 will go to technical work in developing the curriculum and teaching materials needed." "Construction of the Nuble schools started in June, 1964. . . ." AIA is supervising this program under its AID contract. American, *USNPO: 1964*, pp. 31, 499-500. Letter dated April 21, 1967, from Mrs. Sonia Shultz, Administrative Assistant of AIA. *Plan Victoria: An Experiment in Rural Education in Chile* (New York: AIA, 1967), pp. 13-16, 20, 30, 32. American International Association for Economic and Social Development, *Rural Education Program in Chile*, by Ernest D. Maes (New York: AIA, February 1965), p. 18.

The objective of the Association for International Development is "(t)o provide highly motivated and professionally competent personnel to work in collaboration with local leaders for the social economic, cultural and educational development of countries requiring assistance." In 1963, it maintained programs in Chile in the following areas: social welfare; food production and agriculture; community development; communications; cooperatives, credit unions and loans; construction, housing and planning; industrial development; and education. Surplus commodities were received by the Association. American, *USNPO: 1964*, p. 48.

The Direct Relief Foundation was established in 1948 "(t)o help men, women and children in the free world who are in desperate need; the hungry, the cold, the sick or crippled; and those without work, although able and willing." In Chile during 1963, the DRF supplied "food for 10 schools in Puerto Montt and San Jose, 5 summer camps and children's colonies near the Cordillera, Rosario, and Los Vilos, and charitable institutions near Valparaiso." Ocean transportation was provided by Church World Service and Catholic Relief Services. American, *USNPO: 1964*, pp. 101, 502.

The Foundation for International Child Health, Inc., was organized in 1961 "to foster and promote the health and well-being of children worldwide, particularly in the underprivileged and developing countries." A program was initiated in Chile during 1964 which encompassed the provision of medical services, training of pediatricians in the United States and possibly a visiting United States professor. The Foundation received surplus commodities in 1963, the last year for which financial information is available. American, *USNPO: 1964*, p. 117. American, *USNPO: 1965*, p. xxiv.

The Girl Scouts of the USA were carrying out an educational exchange program to promote "international friendship contacts" with Chile in 1963. Other activities in Chile involved the provision of equipment, material aid and/or relief. The Girl Scouts received surplus commodities in 1962, the last year for which financial information is available. American, *USNPO: 1964*, p. 131.

The Institute for Human Progress, Inc. was organized in 1962 to "undertake projects for improving the condition of peoples in other countries, initially concentrating on Latin America." Its Chilean program in 1963 involved activities in the following areas: medicine and public health; social welfare; and education. The Institute provides "consultants' services to overseas private organizations in the preparation of project applications for Alliance for Progress and private foundation assistance" in the fields previously cited. It received surplus commodities in 1962, the last year for which financial information is available. The Institute's publication is *Citizen Groups and the Alliance for Progress*. American, *USNPO: 1964*, pp. 140, 712-13.

Self Help Inc. was established in 1959 "(t)o provide low cost agricultural and industrial machinery to underdeveloped areas of the world through mission stations, cooperatives, credit unions, educational and religious institutions." It has described its program in Chile during 1963 in the following terms: "(t)hrough the Seventh-Day Adventist Welfare Conference, provides Colegio Adventista de Chile in Chillan with equipment for agricultural and industrial development, construction and road building, poultry raising, and dairy processing, plus office machinery, furniture and clothing. Supplies Vincent James in El Vergel, through Methodist Board of Missions, with tractor and miscellaneous implements for crop investment." During 1963, Self Help received surplus commodities, but it is unclear whether they were used in conjunction with the Chilean program. Ocean transport was almost certainly reimbursed by the United States government through the Seventh-Day Adventists and Church World Service. American, *USNPO: 1964*, pp. 225, 506.

The objectives of the Tolstoy Foundation are: "(t)o aid and assist people from Russia and refugees from other nations, without regard to race, nationality or religion, to become loyal and useful members of the society in which they live, by advancing funds or supplies required for their support, education, medication or other needs; to aid and assist writers, artists, scientists, teachers, and other professional men in their efforts to establish themselves in their professions." Organized in 1939, the foundation initiated its Chilean program in 1962. By 1963, its activities were comprised of: distribution of surplus food, medicines and clothing; construction of an Old People's Home in Santiago for 60-80 persons; and assistance to refugees "to establish small industries." The two staff members assigned to Chile were cooperating with Chilean welfare agencies, Chilean government, Red Cross, Hogar de Cristo, Chilean Association for

Refugees and UNHCR. During 1962—the last year for which financial information is available—the foundation received surplus commodities, "governmental and inter-governmental subsidies." American, *USNPO: 1964*, pp. 230, 506-07.

I. Organizations Engaged in Technical Assistance or AID Programs. Section 621 of the Foreign Assistance Act of 1961, as amended in 1962, directs that "(i)n providing technical assistance under this act, the head of any such agency or such officer shall utilize, to the fullest extent practicable, goods and professional and other services from private enterprise on a contract basis. In such fields as education, health, housing, or agriculture, the facilities and resources of other Federal agencies shall be utilized when such facilities are particularly or uniquely suitable for technical assistance, are not competitive with private enterprise, and can be made available without interfering unduly with domestic programs." United States, *Foreign Aid in Action*, p. 79.

The program of the Council for International Progress in Management (USA), Inc. encompasses the "(o)rganization, under contract with USAID, of management study programs in the United States for groups from other countries, and for U.S. citizens, to participate in management seminars abroad. Implementation of similar privately sponsored study programs in the United States for foreign participants. Provision of grants to foreign organizations for aiding management development and to foreign nationals for advanced training in the U.S." Managerial training assistance is given to administrators in governmental, business, labor and non-profit organizations. Activities were being carried out in Chile during 1963. The Chilean organization that was most probably associated with the Council's efforts was ICARE—a managerial training institute which was previously supported by the ICA. American, *USNPO: 1964*, p. 94.

The objectives of the Dairy Society International, Inc. are: "(t)o enhance human health and economic progress by encouraging the development and extension of all phases of the dairy industry throughout the world. DSI acts as a coordinating office in the following areas in industrial responsibility: service to U.S. Government in its wide scale technical assistance program; technical assistance to the dairy industry in the developing countries; guidance to international agencies and/or welfare programs utilizing dairy projects." In Chile, DSI "(m)aintains relationships with milk and ice cream industries and encourages quality improvement of milk and other dairy products for advancing nutritional standards. U.S. Foreign Agricultural Service, U.S. and Chilean government officials, American Dairy Association and local commercial groups cooperate in this project, which began in March 1963 and is maintained by 1 Projects Coordinator for Latin America (located in Santiago), 1 nutritionist, a bilingual secretary and 1 office assistant." The organization receives surplus commodities. American, *USNPO: 1965*, pp. 32, 270.

The International Development Services program in Chile was being carried out pursuant to a "(c)ontract with Ministry of Agriculture (1962-64) to expand program of agricultural improvement and supervised credit on national basis." Personnel included "3 U.S. technicians and about 100 Chilean officers and technicians engaged by counterpart agency." IDS income for 1962 was $2,000.00 – Voluntary contributions, $60,086.58 – Grants; $493,952.38 – U.S. government contracts, international agencies and foreign government contracts. Total: $576,038.96." Given the near financial bankruptcy of the Chilean government during this period, it is probable that an AID loan was necessary to finance this contract. IDS was also providing technical assistance in Costa Rica, Dominican Republic and Guatemala. American, *USNPO: 1964*, p. 144.

During 1963, the National Rural Electric Cooperative Association was providing "the services of a specialist to assist 18 rural electric cooperatives to develop a loan application for funds to extend service to several hundred small farmers." This program was being "carried out under contract with USAID." American, *USNPO: 1964*, p. 506.

"Public Administration Service under a contract with the U.S. Agency for International Development provided technical assistance in financial administration to the Government of Chile between June, 1963, and September, 1965. Total dollar costs reimbursed by AID were $258,037.41." Letter dated April 11, 1967, from G.M. Morris, Field Services Director, PAS. Cf., American, *USNPO: 1965*, p. 106.

J. Population Council and Meals for Millions. An official of the Population Council has reported that "as to the dimensions of our assistance to Chile, also prior to March 1965, I point out that the sum of seven different grants we made to Chile up to that date total $185,200 of which $116,400 was granted to CELADE and the remaining $68,800 was granted to various university clinics for research work in contraception. CELADE . . . is a U.N.-sponsored organization for demographic studies.

In summary, our assistance in Chile is to promote two separate types of activity, the first being demographic and socio-economic surveys, including studies on abortion, and the second being clinical research conducted for the evaluation of various means of contraception." Although the council was given surplus commodities, there is no indication as to whether they were used to facilitate the acceptance of contraceptives by the poor. American, *USNPO: 1964*, p. 215. Letter dated April 10, 1967, from E. Ross Jenney, M.D., of the Council.

"The primary objective (of the Meals for Millions Foundation) is to stimulate, in areas of chronic malnutrition, such production of Multi-Purpose Food and comparable foods, usually from indigenous resources, and to encouarge governments and private agencies to give priority of emphasis to nutritional 'short-cuts' exemplified by MPF." The program in Chile between 1961—when it was initiated—and 1963, provided "(g)rants of Multi-Purpose Food for acceptability demonstration and evaluation (as follows): 10,582 lbs. to National Public Health Service in Santiago; 2,568 lbs. to Caritas in Santiago; 5,022 lbs. to Maryknoll

Fathers in Talca; 621 lbs. to College San Xavier in Puerto Montt; and 1,539 lbs. to Council of Women in Chile." Although this assistance was not subsidized by AID, the Foundation is registered as an "approved" agency with AID's Advisory Committee on Voluntary Foreign Aid, and previously it had received grants from AID for acceptability trials in other countries, and possibly for Chile. Between 1946 and 1960, 12,177 lbs. of MPF had been shipped "to relief and governmental agencies" in Chile. American, *USNPO: 1964*, pp. 178, 505. Letter dated April 19, 1967, from Mrs. Beatriz Azedo, Program Officer of Meals for Millions. Meals for Millions, *Distribution of Relief Shipments: September 1946 - May 15, 1963* (Los Angeles: Meals for Millions, 1963).

K. International Schools Services. ISS "(p)rovides educational services (teacher and school administrator recruitment, curriculum counsel and distribution of educational materials, field consultation, and overseas school conferences) for approximately 225 elementary and secondary multi and bi-national schools." American, *USNPO: 1964*, p. 149.

L. Organizations Cooperating with the Peace Corps. (With regard to TECHO and CARE see Sections C and G, *supra*.) The objectives of the Pan American Development ment Foundation, Inc.—organized "on the initiative of the Organization of American States" in 1963—are: "(t)o provide a direct focus on the Alliance for Progress for citizens, community organizations, businesses and small foundations who wish to participate directly in programs aiding the economic and social development of Latin America, by identifying suitable projects for private sector support." Its program in Chile during 1964 involved: provision of "tools and materials for construction and operation of work centers for serving cooperatives in Ancud and Antofagasta; provision of books to the University of Chile; and provision of supplies "to several schools as part of 'Operation Ninos' campaign." Cooperating agencies include the Peace Corps, CARE and the Pan American Union. American, *USNPO: 1965*, pp. 95, 273. *New York Times*, Feb. 20, 1967.

During the early 1960s, the Experiment in International Living, Inc. contracted with the Peace Corps to train "12 Peace Corps groups in rural development, construction of school buildings and faculty housing, credit unions and cooperatives, English language teaching and physical education." One or more of these groups were assigned to Chile. The Experiment also received State Department subsidies during the period which partly financed visits to North American homes by Chilean youths. American, *USNPO: 1964*, p. 108. U.S., *Departments for 1964*, p. 1500.

VITA provides: "(f)ree technical consultation through correspondence with individual clients in developing countries; development projects; special programs with agencies such as the Peace Corps and CARE." Technical advice has also been given to AID. Although such assistance has been provided in Chile, it is not clear to whom. Nevertheless, given both the important Peace Corps presence since 1961, and the fact that VITA has received "more requests for assistance from Peace Corps volunteers than any other single source," it is probable that some volunteers in Chile have been among the beneficiaries. American, *USNPO: 1964*, p. 241. Letter dated April 10, 1967, from Mrs. Aileene B. Sweetser, VITA Office Coordinator. Volunteers for International Technical Assistance, *VITA: A New Channel for Technical Assistance to Developing Nations* (Schenetady, N.Y.: Volunteers for International Technical Assistance, Inc., n.d.).

The Young Women's Christian Association of the USA's program in Chile during 1963 encompassed the "(p)rovision of 1 U.S. advisory staff member and grant towards the national budget of Asociacion Cristiana Femenina (ACF), an autonomous YWCA whose program emphasized leadership training for civic and social responsibility, community centers in low-cost housing areas, and camping." The YWCA was also implementing a joint program under a contract with the Peace Corps. American, *USNPO: 1964*, pp. 259, 507. U.S., *To Amend the Peace Corps Act*, p. 30.

M. The "People-to-People" Program. Books, pamphlets about Minneapolis, letters from school children and gifts were sent directly to Chilean institutions through the United States Embassy, allegedly because the counterpart Santiago committee was indifferent to the arrangement. Erica Vexler, "La Dificultad de Ser Buen Vecino," *Ercilla* XXX (6 enero 1965), 24-25. "Problemas de la Buena Vecindad," ibid., (13 enero 1965), p. 7.

Under the "People-to-People" program, a group of prominent "non-governmental" United States citizens dispatched a widely publicized letter to the people of Cuba in July 1960. It expressed concern over the deterioration of relations and warned that "Communism presents a grave danger for hemispheric defense and the spiritual unity of the Americas." Apparently the "letter" was publicized in Chile, where the Socialists replied by stressing Cuba's recovery control over her economy from United States corporate interests as well as United States government arrogance, interventions and continuing hostility to the Revolution. It was also noted that during the 1950s there had been no such letters to peoples living under other dictatorships when North American economic interests were not threatened. "Mensaje a Cuba de ciudadanos norteamericanos," *Arauco*, I (julio 1960), 51-52. People-to-People, Inc., which was probably a promotional organization, was reportedly subsidized by the CIA. *New York Times*, Feb. 26, 1967, p. 2.

The background of the People-to-People program and its relation to USIA activities is summarized in the following statement by the Agency:

"The Office of Private Cooperation carries out the mandate of section 1005 of Public Law 402 'to utilize, to the maximum extent practicable, the services and facilities of private agencies.' It stimulates, helps plan and guides work by groups and individuals aimed at improving understanding and developing friendship between Americans and the peoples of other countries."

To further this private supplementation of official diplomacy and communication, a formal people-to-people program was launched in 1956. The Office of Private Cooperation has become the chief channel for the executive branch of the Government in furnishing information, encouragement, and, where necessary, material assistance to the numerous committees through which the program functions. In addition, the Office works with many other private groups and individuals not part of the formal people-to-people organizations. All of these activities help achieve the general—and frequently the specific—objectives of the U.S. Information Agency." The budget of the Office of Private Cooperation for fiscal 1960 was $573,272 (worldwide). Increases were programmed for 1961 and 1962. U.S., *Departments for 1962*, pp. 705-06.

N. Engineers and Scientists Committee. The objectives and general procedures utilized by the Engineers and Scientists Committee are: "(t)o provide libraries, professors and students of colleges in developing countries with journals and technical literature which they normally cannot afford. The material is collected from American engineers and scientists and the work of sorting, allocating and packing is all done by volunteers. . . . Through correspondence with college deans or leaders of groups concerned, the Committee determines what material from its available list is desired, and then arranges to periodically ship quantities of same." Insofar as governmental relations and its Chilean program are concerned, the Committee's President has stated that "(i)n the very beginning of our program, we were assisted by the Office of Private Cooperation in making our first shipments to the Middle East. However, since in my opinion, Congress has stupidly cut the USIA budget to the barest minimum, they are no longer able to give us much help. It is a shame, I think, that this office cannot give valuable assistance to programs like ours which are fostering good will abroad. At any rate, the USIA did not aid us in any way with the one or two shipments of technical literature we sent to Chile prior to 1965. These were sponsored by the Council for Latin America." American, *USNPO: 1965*, p. 38. Letter dated April 28, 1967, from Robert B. Lea, President.

O. Cultural Exchange Organizations. The American Institute for Free Labor Development (AIFLD) was founded in 1962 "(t)o assist in the development of free, democratic trade union structures in Latin America through labor leader training centers and social development programs in such fields as housing, workers' banks, credit unions, consumer and producer cooperatives and related socioeconomic activities." In September 1963, the AIFLD reportedly established a Chilean office under the supervision of Emanual Boggs, a former United States Labor Attache in Bolivia. Between then and the end of 1966, as many as 2,300 Chilean trade union leaders had received urban and trade union leadership training during which room, board and a $2.50 per day living allowance were provided. Thirty-two Chilean union leaders were sent for advanced training to Front

Royal, Va. By August 1967, a total of 3,378 Chilean unionists had participated in one to six week seminars in Chile.

The training includes courses of an anti-Marxist orientation. In conjunction with the training courses, AIFLD in Chile has instituted programs in the following areas: consumer and producer cooperatives, credit unions, workers' housing banks and housing projects. In addition to utilizing USIA pamphlets in its activities, AIFLD in Chile has published its own anti-Communist propaganda such as Dario Rivera's *El Comunismo Internacional y El Sindicalismo Mundial* (Santiago: Instituto Americano para el Desarrollo del Sindicalismo Libre, Imp. 'Soberania', 1964). Published on expensive paper several months before the 1964 election, the tract describes low living standards, the absence of workers' control over unions or the right to strike in East European countries and Cuba: "(l)a propaganda cubana describiendo las condiciones 'ideales' de los trabajadores de esa isla controlada por los communistas esta dirigida principalmente a las organizaciones laborales latino-americanas. Sin embargo, el siniestro historial de Cuba es demasiado bien conocido en todo el resto de la America Latina para que tenga resultados efectivos la propaganda comunista, excepto quizas donde estan mas activos los grupos terroristas partidarios de Castro." P. 29.

The potential trainees in Chile are numerous since there were in the early 1960s more than three thousand small unions, of which about 80 percent were unaffiliated with national or international federations. Some of the more prominent Chilean union leaders who became involved in AIFLD's activities during this period included Juan Lubbiano, Wenceslao Moreno and Arturo Venegas. Venegas, a Radical, became Undersecretary of Labor in the Frei administration. William Thayer, a labor lawyer who was also connected with AIFLD, was appointed by Frei as minister of labor. In 1966, Moreno—then the leader of the Confederacion Maritima de Chile which was affiliated with ORIT—resigned from the Christian Democratic Party in order to maintain his ORIT relationship. Lubbiano was also a maritime leader.

AIFLD was organized in accord with a contract signed in June 1962, by AID and the AFL-CIO. It was founded "primarily in response to the threat of Castroite infiltration . . . of major labor movements within Latin America." During July or August 1966, Joseph Bierne—secretary of AIFLD and then president of the Communications Workers of America—"reported that the AFL-CIO had contributed $200,500 to the institute, business and industry (including some firms not celebrated for their pro-union attitude) about $150,000, and the government Agency for International Development about $3 million in 1965 alone. All in all, about $8 million has been spent since 1961 when the program began. So far, 43,000 unionists in Latin America have been in training under AIFLD, of whom only 455 went either to classes in Washington, D.C. or at Front Royal, Va., where, presumably, the CIA would have a voice in their training." In early 1967, the Institute was reported to have received "funds from the Michigan Fund, a CIA conduit." The Institute's work is directly aided by the Social

Progress Trust Fund of the IADB. "Whenever feasible, the Bank uses the Trust Fund to strengthen the cooperative movement and free trade unions. Assistance to such organizations has been incorporated in loans for housing and rural credit in Peru, Chile, Argentina, and El Salvador, among others." All SPTF aid is subject to a United States veto.

Funds for Chilean operations were increased drastically during the late 1960s. This is evident from the following data on annual expenditures for the program in Chile: FY 1963 ($18,785); FY 1964 ($79,062); FY 1965 ($144,827); FY 1966 ($143,041); FY 1967 ($197,079); FY 1968 ($350,000). American, *USNPO: 1965*, pp. 7, 354. Eduardo Labarca, "Mil Millones de pesos para corromper sindicatos chilenos," *El Siglo*, 24 febrero 1967, p. 3. Eduardo Labarca, "Alemania Occidental Tambien se Trabaja a gremios chilenos," *El Siglo*, 18 marzo 1967, p. 5. Accion Sindical Democrata, *Nace la Union Sindical Democratica*, Pleno de Dirigentes Sindicales (Santiago: Talls. Grafs. 'Rapid', 1964), p. 9. Julio Varela, "USA Quiere Colonizar Movimiento Sindical Chileno," *El Siglo*, 10 febrero 1967, p. 15, 27 febrero, p. 3, 13 marzo, p. 3. *El Mercurio*, 2 junio 1962, p. 31. B.J. Widick, "Vietnam, Race and the Unions," *The Nation*, November 21, 1966, p. 545. "Editorial," *The New Republic*, March 4, 1967, p. 8. U.S., *Foreign Assistance Act of 1963*, V, 947. Cf., *New York Times*, February 19, 1967, p. 26, and U.S., *Castro-Communist Subversion*, pp. 46-47. U.S., Congress, Senate, Committee on Foreign Relations, *Survey of the Alliance for Progress: Labor Policies and Programs—A Study*, prepared at the request of the Sub-committee on American Republics Affairs of the Committee on Foreign Relations, United States Senate, 90th Cong., 2d sess., July 15, 1968, pp. 9, 47, 71, 86.

The objectives of the Cleveland International Program for Youth Leaders and Social Workers, Inc., since 1956 when it was organized, have been "(t)o make a tangible contribution toward international understanding by giving professional people who are engaged in youth work, child welfare services, and community development projects the opportunity to meet and exchange their professional experiences and skills" through an "(a)nnual 4½ month training and exchange program in cooperation with U.S. Department of State for professional and volunteer youth leaders and social workers from foreign countries." "Expenditures for 1964 in training and exchange program amount to approximately $568,000 (including the value of home hospitality). Of this total, approximately 60% came from private contributions and approximately 40% from the Department of State." It is possible that the origin of some of the "private" contributions was the Council for International Programs for Youth Leaders and Social Workers, which was subsidized by the CIA through the Founation for Youth and Student Affairs. The exchange program brought youth leaders and social workers to the United States from many countries, in addition to Chile. The total in 1964 was fifty-seven nations. American, *USNPO: 1965*, pp. 29-30. *New York Times*, Feb. 19, 1967, p. 26.

The purpose of World University Service—founded in 1920—is "(t)o serve voluntarily as an agency through which American students and professors, at the preparatory school, college and university levels, may share materially and intellectually with their needy contemporaries throughout the world." Its Chilean program during 1963 encompassed the following types of activities: disease control and medical services; equipment, material aid and relief; and education. Education may include the "(e)stablishment of libraries, bookstores, and text-book printing projects at universities where books are presently unobtainable or beyond the means of the students; building of dormitories where student housing is desperately needed; scholarships and emergency aid when disaster strikes a university community and services to student refugees. . . ." WUS received financial support from private donors, the Department of State, and the CIA through the Foundation for Youth and Student Affairs. American, *USNPO: 1964*, pp. 252-53, 714-15. *New York Times*, Feb. 19, 1967, p. 26.

"The Commission (for International Development) was formed (during 1960) in response to the need expressed by leaders at home and abroad for a private organization in the U.S. to which they could relate in their commitment to prepare leadership at all levels, for national and international development." CID's Chilean program involved: "(f)ellowships for 3-6 months training in the U.S. in skilled trades for foreign grantees who have some basic technical education," and "(c)ommission-supported 1-3 month study tours in the U.S. for young workers, union, and community leaders from foreign countries aimed at broadening leadership capacities and furthering mutual understanding." Although the Chilean exchange was functioning in 1964, it is not clear when the visits were initiated. CID has stated that "(s)ome programs are maintained with the functional cooperation of the U.S. Departments of Labor and State but are not funded by the Government." American, *USNPO: 1965*, pp. 30-31.

The program of the Overseas Education Fund (established in 1947) of the League of Women Voters is designed "(t)o impart to men and women everywhere a knowledge of the principles and workings of self-government . . . in the belief that an understanding of the process and techniques of popular government and of the essential requirements placed upon citizens can be communicated—and that adaptations to promote organizations with democratic processes help to change attitudes and affect action. We have concentrated on developing leadership to this end." During the 1959-1965 period, the OEF "had 4 Chilean women as participants in 2-3 week leadership seminars who were brought to Washington on leader grants from the State Department, with which OEF has a contract to conduct the seminar program . . . the Chileans were members of multi-national groups. . . . The women went from Washington on a tour of volunteer organizations in various parts of the United States for which (OEF) had no responsibility. (OEF) also had one Chilean woman as a participant in a leadership institute, a year's study under OEF direction in association with a specific university. The costs for this institute are in large part but not entirely financed by A.I.D." The OEF program was also financially supported by "(v)oluntary contributions, funds, foundations, corporations, members and individuals." American, *USNPO: 1964*, p. 163. Letter dated April 26, 1967, from Mrs. Haskell Rosenblum, member of the board of directors.

The National Council of Catholic Women provided clothing and medicines which were shipped to Chile and distributed by Caritas during 1963. CRS assumed responsibility for the shipments. Although the NCCW states that it cooperates "with the Women's Bureau of the U.S. Department of Labor, Department of State and other voluntary agencies in programming for international students and visitors from Latin America, Africa and Asia," there is no indication as to whether the Council provided such services for Chileans. American, *USNPO: 1964*, p. 192.

The goals of the National Farmers Union are: "(t)o provide on-the-job training in rural farm community development for farm leaders from participating Latin American countries and to assist development of democratic farm organizations through program planning, training courses and consultation. To foster assistance through cooperative development programs." Insofar as the Chilean program is concerned, "(t)he project is carried out in two phases: Phase I provides a Spanish-speaking training team of rural organization specialists to participating countries to engage in regional training institutes and consult with leadership people in parallel capacities." "The organizations participating from Chile, primarily involve ANOC, but other individuals are chosen by the (AID) Mission for particular training in campesino affairs." Phase II involves the "(s)election of outstanding farm leaders for 5 months of training in the U.S. in the role and function of farm leaders." "USAID sent 14 (Chilean) participants to the United States (for leadership training programs) in 1963 and 16 participants in 1964. They were in the U.S. for a period of about four months during which time they attended special training courses at colleges, lived and assisted on farms, and participated in a seminar conducted by Farmers Union in Chippewa Falls, Wisconsin." The training programs involved instruction in the formation of cooperatives which must be "non-political," the history of the United States cooperative movement, and United States government—albeit on a rudimentary level, as well as other subjects. NFU received $61,400 from AID and contributed almost $100,000 in funds and services during the two years to the Chilean program. "The ex-participants have organized themselves into a Farmers Union of Chile and are maintaining continued contact among themselves. They come from all organizations in the rural scene in Chile." During 1966, ANOC and the Union de Campesinos Cristianos created the Confederacion Nacional de Campesinos. AID and the NFU have organized cooperative follow-up programs in which ANOC and UCC leaders have been urged to work constructively with Chilean governmental authorities, and INPROA—the Agricultural Promotion (Reform) Institute of the Catholic Church. American, *USNPO: 1965*, pp. 87-88. Letter dated April 12, 1967, from John M. Bailey, NFU African Coordinator. Letter dated May 29, 1967, from John M. Eklund, NFU executive vice-president. Training program schedules and 1966 Chilean seminar reports.

**Appendix III:
Breakdown of U.S. Economic
and Military Assistance**

Table A-12
Post-World War II U.S. Loans and Grants to Chile

[U.S. Fiscal Years—Millions of Dollars]
U.S. Overseas Loans and Grants—Net Obligations and Loan Authorizations

Program	Postwar relief period 1946-48	Marshall plan period 1949-52	Mutual Security Act period					Foreign Assistance Act period				Total, 1946-65	Repayments and interest, 1946-65	Total less repayments and interest
			1953-57	1958	1959	1960	1961	1962	1963	1964	1965			
AID and predecessor agencies—Total		$1.1	$9.8	$12.8	$3.1	$18.3	$31.1	$142.4	$40.4	$78.5	$99.0	$436.5	$5.1	$431.4
Loans			.8	10.0	.3	10.5	8.3	1 140.0	35.0	75.6	96.6	377.0	5.1	371.9
Grants		1.1	9.0	2.8	2.8	7.8	22.9	2.4	5.4	2.9	2.5	59.5		59.5
Social Progress Trust Fund								18.7	4.9	4.5	5.8	33.9	.8	33.1
Food for Peace—Total			32.6	15.0	12.3	8.6	27.7	6.6	26.5	30.5	12.9	172.7	11.5	161.2
Title I (total sales agreements			(38.8)	(—)	(—)	(3.1)	(25.7)	(—)	(—)	(—)	(—)	(67.7)	(—)	(67.7)
Less (planned for U.S. uses)	(—)	(—)	(7.8)	(—)	(—)	(1.0)	(5.1)	(—)	(—)	(—)	(—)	(13.9)	(—)	(13.9)
Title I—Planned for loans and grants	(—)	(—)	31.1			2.1	20.6					53.8	10.0	43.8
104c—Grants for common defense														
104e—Grants for economic development														
104e—Loans to private industry						.8						.8	.2	.6
104g—Loans to government			31.1			1.3	20.6					53.0	9.8	43.2
Title I—Assistance from other country agreements														

Table A-12 (cont.)
Post-World War II U.S. Loans and Grants to Chile

[U.S. Fiscal Years—Millions of Dollars]
U.S. Overseas Loans and Grants—Net Obligations and Loan Authorizations

Program	Postwar relief period 1946-48	Marshall plan period 1949-52	Mutual Security Act period					Foreign Assistance Act period				Total, 1946-65	Repayments and interest, 1946-65	Total less repayments and interest
			1953-57	1958	1959	1960	1961	1962	1963	1964	1965			
Title II—Emergency relief and economic development											4.9	4.9		4.9
Title III—Voluntary relief agencies			1.5	15.0	12.3	6.5	7.1	6.6	5.5	9.6	8.0	72.1		72.1
Title IV—Dollar credit sales									21.0	20.9		41.9	1.5	40.4
Export-Import Bank long-term loans	$41.9	62.1	35.7	15.0	27.5	16.9	74.0	46.4	15.5	16.5	²28.2	²359.7	200.4	159.3
Other U.S. economic programs	4.0	1.1					.1	1.0	.9	1.5	2.7	11.2		11.2 ˢ
Total economic	45.9	64.3	78.1	42.8	42.9	43.8	132.9	215.1	88.2	131.5	128.6	1,014.0	217.8	796.2
Loans	41.9	62.1	67.6	25.0	27.8	29.5	102.8	205.1	76.4	117.5	110.6	866.3	217.8	648.5
Grants	4.0	2.2	10.5	17.8	15.1	14.3	30.1	10.0	11.8	14.0	18.1	147.7		147.7
Military assistance program—(Charge to appropriation)³			$17.3	$6.7	$5.4	$2.7	$4.0	$7.9	$8.0	$7.9	$7.1	$81.1	$0.5	$80.6
Credit assistance										.1	.8	1.1	.5	.6
Grants			17.3	6.7	5.4	2.7	4.0	7.9	8.0	7.8	6.3	80.0		80.0
(Additional grants from excess stocks)	(—)	(—)	(8.3)	(5.2)	(.9)	(1.6)	(.8)	(1.4)	(1.3)	(2.7)	(.6)	(22.8)	(—)	(22.8)

Other military assistance (grants)							5.7	4.4	17.1	1.8	.9	29.9		29.9
Total military			17.3	6.7	5.4	2.7	9.7	12.3	25.1	9.7	8.0	111.0	.5	110.5
Total economic and military	$45.9	$64.3	95.4	49.5	48.3	46.5	142.6	227.4	113.3	141.2	136.6	1,125.0	218.3	906.7
Loans	41.9	62.1	67.6	25.0	27.8	29.5	102.8	205.1	76.4	117.6	111.4	867.4	218.3	649.1
Grants	4.0	2.2	27.8	24.5	20.5	17.0	39.8	22.3	36.9	23.6	25.3	257.6		257.6

[1] Includes $100,000,000 loan for Reconstruction and Rehabilitation.
[2] Excludes refunding of $40,400,000 in fiscal year 1965.
[3] Annual data represent deliveries; total through 1965 is the cumulative program.

Assistance from International Agencies to Which the United States Is a Substantial Contributor

	Fiscal year 1964	Fiscal year 1965	Fiscal years 1946-65
IBRD (World Bank)	$24.0	$4.4	$140.6
U.N. Exp. Prog. (CY)	.6	.8	7.4
U.N. Reg. Prog. (CY)	.2	.2	1.0
U.N. Special Fund	.8	1.7	11.2
Intl. Dev. Assoc.			19.0
Inter-Am. Dev. Bank	18.7	4.9	69.2
Intl. Finance Corp.		.3	9.1

Source: Agency for International Development, Statistics and Reports Division, as reported in U.S., *Foreign Aid in Action*, pp. 13-14.

Notes

Notes

Chapter 1

1. Fidel Castro, *El Partido de la Revolución Socialista: Espina dorsal de la Revolución* (Santiago: Espártaco Editores, 1963), pp. 12-15. Unless Havana is indicated, subsequent references to cities of publication for Spanish language books will be in Chile. Similarly, all Spanish language newspapers and journals are Chilean except where a different country is specified.

2. See chapters 5, 6 and 8. Cf., Russel H. Fitzgibbon, "The Revolution Next Door: Cuba," *Annals*, CCCXXXIV (March 1961), 120-21; J. Halcro-Ferguson, "The Cuban Revolution and Latin America," *International Affairs* (London), XXXVII (July 1961), 90; Herbert Matthews, *The Cuban Story* (New York: Braziller, 1961), pp. 221-22. For similar Leftist views see chapters 6, 7 and: Ramon Ramirez Gomez, "Cuba Socialista," *Ciencias Políticas y Sociales* (Mexico), VIII (abril-junio 1962), 207; "Mensaje del Partido Socialista al Pueblo de Chile," *Arauco*, V (mayo 1964), 4; and Orlando Millas, "Christian Democratic Reformism: The Chilean Experiment," *World Marxist Review*, VIII (November 1965), 48.

3. A brief analysis of this system-maintaining "mobilization of bias" appears in the author's "Chile's Left: Structural Factors Inhibiting an Electoral Victory in 1970," *The Journal of Developing Areas*, III:2 (January 1969), 207-30. A Spanish language translation appears in *Foro Internacional* (El Colegio de Mexico), IX:1 (julio-septiembre de 1968), 43-68.

4. Secular trends in the distribution of wealth and income are discussed in chapter 2 and in the following notes to that chapter: 38, 41, and especially 42, 47-50, and 56. In late 1969, Communist Party Secretary General Luis Corvalan informed the 14th National Congress of the CP that "a privileged sector representing but 10 percent of the population, appropriated for itself more than 50 percent of the national income." *El Siglo*, 24 noviembre 1969, p. 10.

5. Even "developed" political systems seem to be characterized by fairly pervasive cynicism, apathy and modest levels of consensual commitment to civil liberties and Constitutional due process. In the United States, for example, only about a quarter of the adult population were found to be highly committed to "procedural rights." Herbert McClosky, "Consensus and Ideology in American Politics," *American Political Science Review*, LVIII (June 1964), 368.

6. See, for example, S.E. Finer, *The Man on Horseback: The Role of the Military in Politics* (New York: Praeger, 1962).

7. On U.S. support for these interventions, see: David Horowitz, *From Yalta to Vietnam* (London: Penguin Books, 1967); Cheddi Jagan, *The West on Trial* (New York: International Publishers, 1966); Theodore Draper, *The Dominican Revolt* (New York: Commentary Reports, 1968); Irving Louis Horowitz, Josue de Castro and John Gerassi, eds., *Latin American Radicalism* (New York: Random House, 1969); Leon Boramy and Malcolm Caldwell, "Behind the Cambodian Coup," *The Spokesman*, Summer 1970, pp. 3-7.

The priority accorded to economic interests is analyzed in the following: Walter LaFeber, *The New Empire* (Ithaca: Cornell University Press, 1963); William A. Williams, *The Tragedy of American Diplomacy* (New York: Dell, 1962); Gabriel Kolko, *The Roots of American Foreign Policy* (Boston: Beacon, 1969); Harry Magdoff, *The Age of Imperialism* (New York: Monthly Review Press, 1969). Cf., U.S., Congress, Senate, Committee on Foreign Relations, *United States Military Policies and Programs in Latin America, Hearings*, before the Subcommittee on Western Hemisphere Affairs of the Committee on Foreign Relations, Senate, 91st Cong., 1st Sess., 1969, pp. 3, 5, 7, 14, 17, 26-27, 32-33, 46-51, 65, 71-72, 87.

Useful empirical studies of these relationships are: Robert F. Smith, *The United States and Cuba* (New Haven: College and University Press, 1969); Maurice Zeitlin and Robert Scheer, *Cuba: Tragedy in Our Hemisphere* (New York: Grove, 1963); James Petras and Maurice Zeitlin, eds., *Latin America: Reform or Revolution?* (New York: Fawcett,

1968); Gabriel Kolko, *The Politics of War* (New York: Random, 1969); and Bahman Niru-mand, *Iran: The New Imperialism in Action* (New York: Monthly Review Press, 1969).

    8. "Address by Gen. Robert W. Porter, Jr., commander-in-chief, U.S. Southern Command, Presented to the Pan American Society of the United States, New York, N.Y., Tuesday, March 26, 1968," reprinted in U.S., Congress, House, Committee on Foreign Affairs, *Foreign Assistance Act of 1968, Hearings*, before the Committee on Foreign Affairs, House of Representatives, 90th Cong., 2d sess., 1968, pp. 1204-05.

    9. See chapters 5, 6 and 8.

    10. Kenneth F. Johnson, "Causal Factors in Latin American Political Stability," *Western Political Quarterly*, XVII (Summer 1964), 432-46; Harry Eckstein, "On the Etiology of Internal War," *History and Theory*, IV (1965), 133-63; Merle Kling, "Violence and Politics in Latin America," *Latin American Sociological Studies*, ed. Paul Halmos (U.K.: University of Keele, 1967), pp. 119-32; and D.P. Bwy, "Political Instability in Latin America: The Cross-Cultural Test of A Causal Model," *Latin American Research Review*, III (Spring 1968), 17-66.

Chapter 2. Socio-economic Environmental Factors

    1. It has been suggested that relatively few are or have been able to cross the blue collar (*obrero*)–white collar (*empleado*) line of division between the lower classes and the lower middle class. Such factors as slow economic growth, a regressive tax structure, inflation and an influx of immigrants into white collar sectors since the early thirties are frequently referred to in efforts to explain this phenomenon. Similarly, the middle classes are said to shun their social inferiors and to maximize all possible distinctions in an attempt to secure acceptance by those above them. Aspects of this situation during the late fifties and early sixties are discussed in: Kalman H. Silvert, *Chile: Yesterday and Today* (New York: Holt, Rinehart and Winston, 1965), pp. 194-195; Frederick B. Pike, *Chile and the United States: 1880-1962* (Notre Dame: University of Notre Dame Press, 1963), pp. 279, 284-289, 438 (note 40), 442-443; Peter Dorner and Juan Carlos Collarte, "Land Reform in Chile: Proposal for an Institutional Innovation," *Inter-American Economic Affairs*, XIX (Summer 1965), 22; James Petras, "The Latin American Middle Class," *New Politics*, IV (Winter 1965), 74-85; and Federico G. Gil and Charles J. Parrish, *The Chilean Presidential Election of September 4, 1964* (Parts I and II; Washington: Institute for the Comparative Study of Political Systems, 1965), I, 10-13, 15, 17, 22-23. The last two items stress the political roles of the middle classes in recent years.

    2. *Chile: Yesterday and Today*, pp. 26-27.

    3. *Chile and the U.S.*, pp. 292-93.

    4. Jorge Ahumada C., *En Vez de Miseria* (Santiago: Edit. del Pacífico, 1958), p 25. Radomiro Tomic, a PDC leader, once offered the witty comment that "aqui, la ley es típicamente lo que alguna vez se dijo: 'tele de araña que atrapa a los insectos chicos, pero de la cual se burlan los mayores.' " *Unidad y Diversidad de la Democracia Cristiana en el Mundo*. (Santiago: Edit. del Pacífico, 1962).

    5. Lautaro Ojeda Herrera, *Esquema del hambre en Chile* (Santiago, 1959), quoted by Pike, p. 278.

    6. United Nations, Economic and Social Council, *Preliminary Report on the World Social Situation* (New York: United Nations, 1952), pp. 42-43.

    7. W. Stanley Rycroft and Myrtle M. Clemmer, *A Factual Study of Latin America* (New York: United Presbyterian Church in the U.S.A., Commission on Ecumenical Mission and Relations, Office of Research, 1963), pp. 181, 187-188. This study was based on data from U.N. agencies, the Pan American Union and UCLA's Statistical Abstracts of Latin America.

    8. Chile, Servicio Nacional de Salud, *Memoria Anual: 1962* (Santiago: Servicio Nacional de Salud, 1963), p. 11.

9. Meals for Millions Foundation, *Pilot Protein Production and Feeding Program for a Selected Region in Chile (Talca)* (New York: Meals for Millions Foundation, February 1966), p.i.

10. Carlos Jorquera, "Chilenos pierden su Dimensión," *Ercilla*, XXVI (6 abril 1960), 16-17.

11. *Informe de una jornada–Tarud–en la primera línea de combate por los derechos populares* (Santiago: Imp. Horizonte, 1965), p. 59. Cf., Orlando Millas, "El Proyecto de Reajestes Necesita ser Reajustado," *El Siglo*, 20 noviembre 1966, p. 13, and *Las Noticias de Ultima Hora*, 14 junio 1967, p. 7.

12. "Life expectancy at birth for the period 1960-61 was estimated at 55 years for men and 60 for women, which is rather low, taking into account the stage of the country's development. . . . Moreover, the death rate of 11.7 per 1,000 inhabitants (estimates for 1964) is also high. . . . The high proportion of death-causing diseases such as pneumonia and tuberculosis, is unusual in a country as advanced as Chile." Inter-American Development Bank, *Social Progress Trust Fund: Fifth Annual Report, 1965* (Washington: Inter-American Development Bank, 1966), p. 202.
Infant mortality was reported to have risen during the fifties from 112 in 1953 to 127 per 1,000 in 1960. Claudio Veliz, "Chile on the Threshold of Change," *World Today*, XX (May 1964), 226-27. Cf., Pike, p. 279; Oscar Domínguez, *El Condicionamiento de la Reforma Agraria* (Louvain: E. Warney, 1963), p. 65; Donald W. Beatty, "The Chilean Dilemma." *Current History*, IL (December 1965), 345; and *Las Noticias de Ultima Hora*, 21 octubre 1967, p. 2.

13. Studies undertaken by the Latin American Center of Demography and the University of Chile's School of Health during the early sixties reported that there were an estimated 150,000 abortions (80 percent with the husband's consent), and 250,000 live births annually in Chile. Abortions have also been estimated to account for 40 percent of maternal mortality, and there are about 50,000 hospital admissions per year due to complications. Illegitimacy rates among the same period were about 50 percent. Erica Vexler, "Chile: Fábrica de Niños sin Planificación," *Ercilla*, XXX (12 agosto 1964), p. 16. U.S. Congress, Senate, Committee on Government Operations, *United States Aid in Action: A Case Study*, by Hon. Ernest Gruening, Submitted to the Subcommittee on Foreign Aid Expenditures, 89th Cong., 2d. sess. (Washington: Government Printing Office, 1966), p. 116.

14. Due to an inadequate number of beds, two women were reported sharing each one in maternity wards during 1959. In 1966, it was claimed that 75 percent of births were not in hospitals, and that 28 percent did not benefit from any medical assistance. In the early sixties complaints of long waits and complicated bureaucratic procedures were common. During 1967, Dr. Aaron Vantman, a Professor at the University of Chile's School of Medicine and a practicing gynecologist informed the writer that there was an infection rate of up to 42 percent in hospitals operated by the National Health Service, and that this was greatly in excess of that prevailing in private clinics (hospitals). "Dos Madres por cama," *Ercilla*, XXV (28 octubre 1959), 7. M. Angélica Beas, "Un país enfermo," *Punto Final*, I (octubre 1966), 17-18. Robert J. Alexander, *Labor Relations in Argentina, Brazil and Chile* (New York: McGraw-Hill, 1962), pp. 275-276. Cf., Chile, Senado, *Diario*, CCLXXXIV, ses. 25 (26 agosto 1959), pp. 1503-16.

15. Chile, Dirección de Estadística y Censos, *Algunos Resultados del XIII Censo de Población y II de Vivienda* (Santiago: Dirección de Estadística y Censos, 1962), p. 20. Cf., Chile, SNS *Memoria Anual*, p. 12; *Informes de las Comisiones al Congreso Nacional de Trabajadores*, Candidatura Presidencial Eduardo Frei Montalva: 13-14-15-16 agosto-1964 (Santiago: Talls. Grafs. Periodistica, 1964), p. 14; and "Marginalidad," *Reportaje Desal*, I (julio 1966), 4-5.

16. Pike, pp. 276-77. *Las Noticias de Ultima Hora*, 26 abril 1967, p. 6. Cf., Chile, Dirección de Estadística y Censos, *Población del Pais: Características Básicas de la Población, Censo 1960* (Santiago: Dirección de Estadística y Censos, 1964), p. 5; and Federico G. Gil, *The Political System of Chile* (Boston: Houghton Mifflin, 1966), pp. 184-185.

17. Chile, *Algunos Resultados*, p. 27. Chile, *Población del País*, pp. 30, 32. Cf., Partido Comunista de Chile, Volodia Teitelboim, *El Camino de la Juventud*, Texto del informe rendido a nombre de la Comisión Política, por el camarada Volodia Teitelboim, al Pleno del Comité Central del Partido Comunista de Chile, el 28 septiembre de 1962 (Santiago: Imp. Horizonte, 1962), p. 5.

18. Kalman Silvert has reported that in the early 1960s the first year drop-out rate for children beginning school was 23 percent. By the sixth year, 68 percent had left. Elsewhere it has been reported that 53 percent of primary school entrants had left school by the end of two years. In this case, the first year figure was 40 percent. *Chile: Yesterday and Today*, pp. 160-162. *El Mercurio*, 10 noviembre 1960, p. 3.

With regard to such problems as lack of schools, inferior quality of school plants, inferior selection and preparation of teachers, inadequate supervision, shortage of books and materials, lack of coordination among agencies aiding schools, insufficiency of rural education, over-lapping of upper elementary and lower secondary grades, lack of adaptation to pupils' developmental levels, excessive uniformity, lack of definition as to what constitutes essential common learnings, excessively intellectual, abstract and verbalistic content, and lack of time to accomplish goals, see U.S., Department of Health, Education, and Welfare, Office of Education, *Education and Social Change in Chile*, by Clark C. Gill (Washington: Government Printing Office, 1966), pp. 45-48; and *Frente Nacional de Profesores Freístas: Primeras Jornadas de Estudios*, 24-25-26 enero 1964 (Santiago: Edit. del Pacífico, 1964).

19. A prominent Chilean sociologist has warned that many who are officially classified as literate cannot "understand ideas," since they only have to "recognize letters" and "spell words" in addition to signing their name in order to be able to declare they know how to read and write. Domínguez, *Condicionamiento*, p. 69. It is also possible that census takers may have been urged to resolve doubts in favor of literacy, and many persons who had two or three years of schooling may have declined to admit a shameful reality. A *minimum* of three to four years is held necessary to acquire a reading ability. *El Mercurio*, 10 noviembre 1960, p. 3. Furthermore, if one habitually fails to exercise his newly acquired skill, it is likely to be quickly forgotten. According to the 1960 census, 455,900 children between the ages of six and fourteen were illiterates. About 70 percent of them (300,000) were not attending school. Among those fifteen years and older, 717,400 admitted to being illiterate—although 750,833 in that category had never attended school. In addition, 1,535,111 persons had from one to three years of schooling. On the basis of these figures, it could be argued that more than 2,550,000 persons were functionally illiterate. This represents more than 35 percent of the 1960 population of 7,374,115. Furthermore, newspaper circulation data and investigations of mass media usage (to be discussed in subsequent chapters) indicate limited newspaper and magazine reading among the lower classes. Statistics were obtained from: Chile, *Algunos Resultados*, p. 11; and Chile, *Población del País*, pp. 5, 30, 51.

For assertions that functional illiteracy ranges from twenty to forty-two percent for the period in question, see: Silvert, *Chile: Yesterday and Today*, pp. 159-160; Renato Poblete, "Causas de la escasez sacerdotal en Chile," *Mensaje*, no. 130 (julio 1964), p. 310. Frederick B. Pike and Donald W. Bray, "A Vista of Catastrophe: The Future of United States-Chilean Relations," *Review of Politics*, XXII (July 1960), 401; Radomiro Tomic Romero, *Sobre el Sistema Interamericano* (Santiago: Edit. del Pacifico, 1963), pp. 28-29; and Ricardo Donoso, "Chile, en la Encrucijada,: *Cuadernos Americanos* (Mexico), CXIX (noviembre-diciembre 1961), 188. Donoso refers to a study by the Ministry of Education's Center of Economic Planning: "According to that report, 71 percent of the population of the country is beneath the minimum cultural levels that are required by the process of economic growth, the illiteracy rate is 42 percent while only 28 percent of the population has adequate sanitary facilities.

20. Partido Comunista, Teitelboim, *Camino*, pp. 48-49. Cf., Tomic, *Sobre*.

21. These questions were added to the questionnaire at the request of a North American political scientist, James Petras. They did not, therefore, reflect concern by the Frei administration over this situation. The director of CESO, Eduardo Hamuy, worked closely with the Christian Democratic Government. James Petras, *Politics and Social Forces in Chilean Development* (Berkeley: University of California Press, 1969), pp. 307-308, 358.

22. Beatty, "The Chilean Dilemma," p. 346. "En 1954, Chile tenía la tasa más alta de la tierra de muertes por accidente (86.7 por 100,000 habitantes); el 4.0 lugar en las estadísticas mundiales por accidentes automovilísticos, y el primero en relación a muerte de peatones." Julio César Jobet, "Problemas y Contradicciones Fundamentáles en la Crisis Chilena," *Arauco*, IV (Enero 1963), 30. A similar situation prevailed during the succeeding decade.

23. Beatty, "The Chilean Dilemma," p. 345.

24. These assertions are based upon the writer's experience as a Santiago resident from

October 1966 until December 1967. A monthly electric bill was likely to cost five or six dollars, even where no appliances save a refrigerator were operated. Piped gas for a range and an occasionally used small hot water heater was even more dear. It was virtually impossible to obtain a telephone, and the service was abysmally poor. The basic monthly rate was the equivalent of six dollars. With regard to poor telephone service in the late 1950s, see Arturo Olavarría Bravo, *Chile entre dos Alessandri*, (Tomos I-IV; Santiago: Edit. Nascimento, 1962-65), II, 390.

25. On these problems, excessive expense of administration, and high level administrative ineptness, see the following: Gil, pp. 178, 183-84; U.S., *Foreign Aid in Action*, p. 30; U.S., Congress, House, Committee on Foreign Affairs, *Foreign Assistance Act of 1963, Hearings*, before the Committee on Foreign Affairs, House of Representatives, on H.R. 5490, Part. V, 86th Cong., 1st sess., 1963, pp. 943-44; Ahumada, *Miseria*, p. 50; Olavarría, *Alessandri*, II, 457-59. Chile, Senado, *Diario*, CCXCIII, ses. 42, pp. 3429ff. "Proceso a la Burocracia," *Ercilla*, XXX (5 agosto 1964), 3; James Morris, "Chile: Restless Republic," *Saturday Evening Post*, November 25, 1961, p. 70; *Hispanic American Report*, XII (March 1959), 48, XIV (September 1961), 638.

26. *Hispanic American Report*, XII (August 1959), 340-41. *El Mercurio*, 17 noviembre 1960, p. 1. "La Economía Chilena en 1961," *Ercilla*, XXVII (27 diciembre 1961), 6. Partido Democrato Cristiano, *Discursos de una Campaña, por Tomás Pablo Elorza en Concepción, Nuble y Arauco, noviembre de 1960-marzo de 1961* (Concepción: Imp. Original, 1961); Jobet, "Problemas," p. 28.

Between 1962 and 1965, there was a slight decline in unemployment. IADB, *SPTF, 1965 Report*, p. 205.

Actual and hidden middle class unemployment has increased resistance to rationalization of the public bureaucracy. Silvert, *Chile: Yesterday and Today*, p. 203. During August 1959, the Council of the University of Chile submitted a report to the Ministry of Education which deplored the large and increasingly serious flight of newly trained professionals and technicians (especially engineers, agronomists, economists and doctors) from the country where their absence was alleged to be contributing to a deterioration in the provision of vital goods and services. *El Mercurio*, 22 agosto 1959, p. 17.

27. Chile, *Poblacion del Pais*, p. 62. As reported by the census, the exact number of economically active, was 2,388,667. According to this official report, 112,920 were unemployed and 46,685 were looking for work for the first time. It is worth noting, that a survey during 1962 in Greater Santiago undertaken by the University of Chile's Institute of Sociology and the Latin American Center of Demography reported an unemployment rate for those over 14 years of age that reached 47 percent. Chile, SNS, *Memoria Anual*, pp. 12-13.

28. "Es difícil encontrar en América Latina otra ciudad como Santiago con residencias tan lujosas y poblaciones callampas tan miserables. La Hueste de mendigos descalzos, principalmente de niños y mujeres con sus criaturas, la cantidad de gente subempleada en actividades como lustrabotas, vendedores ambulantes, cuidadores de automóviles, improvisados porteros, atestiguan esta extendida pobreza, aun cuando no haya muchos estudios científicos que subrayen el hecho." Joseph H. Fichter, *Cambio Social en Chile* (Santiago: Edit. Universidad Católica, 1962). Cf., Alieto Aldo Guadagni, "La Estructura Ocupacional y el Desarrollo Económico de Chile," *Journal of Inter-American Studies*, VI (April 1964), 197-99. Guadagni notes that while personal services account for 26.2 percent of U.S. employment, in Greater Santiago the corresponding figure is 41 percent. In 1960, too, there were 1,622,009 persons who were excluded from the economically active population because they worked in their homes. If attractive employment opportunities existed, several hundred thousand of these persons would probably have joined the labor force. Data from Chile, *Población del País*, p. 64. Cf., Silvert, *Chile: Yesterday and Today*, pp. 152-156.

29. With regard to the estimate of the blue collar sector, see the census data reported in Gil, p. 19; and Chile, *Población del País*, p. 62.

30. *Hispanic American Report*, XII (March 1959), 48.

31. Gerald Clark, *The Coming Explosion in Latin America* (New York: David McKay, 1963), p. 102. Alexander, p. 278. Comando Nacional Gremial de la Campaña Presidencial del Pueblo, Los Trabajadores en el Gobierno Popular: *Resoluciones de la Asamblea Nacional de Trabajadores Allendistas* (Santiago: Imp. Horizonte, 1964), p. 8.

32. The study referred to in note 36 *infra* reported that 700,000 workers were not

covered. The last reference cited in note 31 *supra* claimed that 800,000 were not covered. According to the 1960 census, cited *supra* at note 29, there were about 1,765,000 blue collar workers.

33. Clark, p. 102. No source is cited.

34. Comando Nacional Allendista de Trabajadores Semi-Fiscales y de Instituciones de Previsión, *Por una Previsión Social-Racional-Igualitaria-Justa: Manifiesto y Compromiso* (Santiago: Imp. Horizonte, 1964), pp. 3-4. Cf., Pike, p. 432, and Gil, p. 181.

35. Alexander, p. 279. Cf., *Hispanic American Report*, XIII (December 1960), 630.

It has also been claimed that employers have unilaterally failed to comply with welfare and social security legislative provisions. Comando Allendista de los Trabajadores de la Industria Textil, *En Santiago, a 31 de mayo de 1964* (Santiago: Imp. Horizonte, 1964). Chile, Senado, *Diario*, CCLXXXVII, ses. 18 (23 noviembre 1960), pp. 889-91, and ses. 30 (1 febrero 1961), pp. 1805-1806.

36. "La Previsión y el Retrato de Dorian Grey," *Ercilla*, XXVIII (21 noviembre 1962), 16-17.

37. During that year, the average annual earnings of 1,388,000 wage earning blue collar workers was E1,100 (less than $275). Chile, Corporación de Fomento de la Producción, *Geografía económica de Chile* (Santiago: CORFO, 1965), p. 405, cited in Gregório Goldenberg, *Después de Frei, ¿Quién?* (Santiago: Edit. Orbe, 1966), p. 85. In October 1964, the government controlled broker's rate for the dollar was E3.25. This has been traditionally below the free rate on international exchanges. An even greater disparity existed on the domestic black market where most non-official conversion was effectuated.

Wages are, in addition, subject to income and social security tax deductions. It was estimated that in 1966, about 10 percent of a typical National Health Service employee's wages would be deducted for such purposes. *El Siglo*, 13 enero 1967, p. 5.

Kalman Silvert has observed that about "nine out of ten persons receiving incomes in Chile cannot maintain an average family of six persons at a minimum adequate standard of living. Indeed, about eight out of ten blue collar workers do not earn enough to support one person decently let alone an entire family. Fewer than one-half of one percent of the laboring groups are able to afford a minimum adequate standard of living for a family of average size." *Chile: Yesterday and Today*, p. 166.

In mid-1965, the daily income of "the average Chilean worker" was about seven escudos (7,000 pesos), while on the black market the dollar could buy 5,500 pesos, "or more." Beatty, "The Chilean Dilemma." pp. 345-46.

The writer's impressions during 1966-1967, were that while food prices ranged from 30-100 percent of those in the United States, cosmetics, textiles, durable goods, and rent were 100 percent or more.

38. Petras, *Politics and Social Forces*, pp. 18, 310. On wage differentials, see Peter Gregory, *Industrial Wages in Chile* (Ithaca, N.Y.: New York State School of Industrial and Labor Relations, Cornell University 1967), pp. 46, 53-76, 79, 93-94.

39. With 1953 as a base (=100), by 1955 the cost of living index was 302 and in 1960 it had reached 1,160. Similarly, using 1958 as a base, the index reported: 155 in 1960, 167 in 1961, 190 in 1962, 274 in 1963, and 400 in 1964. For 1965, it had reached 512. Rycroft and Clemmer, p. 69. *International Financial Statistics*, XIX (March 1966), 76-77.

40. Pike, p. 275. James Petras, "After the Chilean Presidential Election: Reform or Stagnation?" *Journal of Inter-American Studies*, VII (July 1965), 376-77. Jobet, "Problemas," p. 24-25. Alexander, pp. 344-345, 386-87. Silvert, *Reaction and Revolution in Latin America*, (New York, 1959), pp. 236-37. *Hispanic American Report*, XIV (March 1961), 68. "La rodilla en el estómago," *Réplica*, I (enero 1967), 13. Joseph Grunwald, "The 'Structuralist': School on Price Stabilization and Economic Development: The Chilean Case," in *Latin American Issues*, ed. by Albert O. Hirschman (New York: Twentieth Century Fund, 1961), pp. 97-98.

During a 1961 radio debate with Communist Deputy Jose Cademartori, even a Chilean Rightist (Liberal Party Deputy Enrique Edwards) was willing to venture such an opinion: "Yo creo que las masas asalariados están en peor situación que hace 20 años, por culpa de los gobiernos anteriores." See "Frases y Personajes," *Ercilla*, XXVI (4 enero 1961), 23.

41. In 1940, employed and self-employed wage earners received 26.7 percent of the real national income. By 1954, their share had fallen to 21.5 percent, although the number of

blue collar workers in the labor force had risen from 1,344,916 to 1,779,985. During the same period, the share of salaried white collar employees increased from 15.1 percent to 21.1 percent, while their number rose from 244,742 to 372,427. Per capita income during the same period increased at an average of 2.2 percent per annum, while the comparable rate for personal income was 2.6 percent. Chile, Corporación de Fomento de la Producción, Departamento de Planificación y Estudios, *Cuentas Nacionales de Chile: 1940-1954.* (Santiago: Edit. del Pacífico, 1957), pp. 63-64,66, anexo (cuadro #39). During 1954, the last year for which government agencies compiled such figures, less than 10 percent of the economically active population received over 46 percent of the real national income. Poblete, "Causas," p. 310. And it has been claimed that in the early 1960s 40 percent of the national income was being received by 5 percent of the income earners, while 77 percent of the economically active persons obtained only 23 percent. OCEPLAN, Oficina Central de Planificación, *Las Primeras 100 Medidas del Gobierno Popular* (Santiago: Imp. Horizonte, 1964), pp. 19-20.

Between 1954 and 1960, the distribution of national income according to CORFO data was:

	1955	1958	1960
Wages	20.9 percent	18.0 percent	17.1 percent
Salaries	18.2	15.5	15.0
Business Profits	22.4	22.4	22.2
Property Rents	33.9	39.0	40.5

Chile, Senado, *Diario*, CCXCII, ses. 40 (20 agosto 1963), p. 2819.

Because per capita income declined by at least 6 percent between 1953 and 1959, it seems clear that the more than 1,726,700 blue collar workers were affected by a regressive restructuring of existing income shares. Reflective of this process was a 1½ percent decline in the per capita output of traditional consumer goods between 1953 and 1959, while durable consumer goods production increased by 23.8 percent, during the same period on a per capita basis. Grunwald, pp. 97-98. Silvert, *Chile: Yesterday and Today*, pp. 135-36. Cf., Partido Comunista, Teitelboim, *Camino*, p. 10, and Chile, Senado, *Diario*, CCLXXXVIII, ses. 39 (24 agosto 1961), p. 2156. Cf., Petras, *Politics and Social Forces*, pp. 30-31.

Had per capita income risen on an average of 1 percent from 1955 to 1960, a similar if less pronounced redistribution of existing national income would still have occurred. For the 1 percent figure, see: Committee for Economic Development, *How Low Income Countries Can Advance Their Own Growth* (New York: Committee for Economic Development, 1966), p. 29.

A similar phenomenon affected a large sector of the lower middle class, as evidenced by the data on salaries and the fact that at least 40,000 white collar workers were added to the labor force between 1952 and 1960. On labor force composition, see Gil, p. 19, and Chile, *Población del País*, p. 62.

These figures support the conclusion that "between the end of World War II and the present," a "gradual shift away from the working class and toward the middle and upper classes has occurred in the distribution of the national income." Gil and Parrish, I, 22-23. Given the repressive wage policies of the Alessandri and Frei Governments, this trend probably continued into the mid- and late-1960s. With regard to Alessandri's wage policies, see Pike, pp. 273-75, and Gil, pp. 192, 197, 200. For the Frei period see: U.S., *Foreign Aid in Action*, p. 107; Millas, "Proyecto de Reajustes," p. 13; *Las Noticias de Ultima Hora*, 9 noviembre 1967, pp. 2, 15; 13 noviembre, p. 3; and *El Mercurio*, 25 noviembre 1967, p. 5.

42. Domínguez, *Condicionamiento*, p. 106. The redistribution of national income was most immediately caused by the inability of most unions to secure wage increases that fully compensated for previous and current price rises; and by the failure of the labor movement to organize the remainder of the blue collar work force. But even the automatic wage and salary readjustments which were legislated until 1956 did not fully restore the status quo ante.

43. Between 1956 and 1966, tax revenues paid by Chileans were about 2/3 indirect, thus ultimately falling in most cases upon the mass of consumers. Grunwald, p. 114. Rubén Corvalán V., "Jaque Mate al Déficit Fiscal," *Ercilla*, XXIX (16 octubre 1963), 6. *El Siglo*, 18 noviembre 1966, p. 3, and 5 diciembre 1966, p. 6. For an estimate that by 1962, more than 80 percent of taxes paid by Chileans were passed on to the consuming public, see "Talle y Figura de las Grandes Reformas," *Ercilla*, XXVIII (28 marzo 1962), 10.

It has also been argued that the tax structure had become more regressive in the late 1950s, and that such taxes more than compensated for the meager welfare benefits received by the working classes. Pike and Bray, "Vista of Catastrophe," pp. 404-405. Pike, p. 432. Official figures which include taxes paid by foreign mining companies, support this view:

	% of Internal Tax Revenues		
	1951	1958	1960
Sales Taxes	46.9	51.6	51.7
Property Taxes	12.1	10.7	9.8
Income Taxes	41.0	37.0	36.9

Source: Chile, Senado, *Diario*, CCXCII, ses. 29 (12 agosto 1963), p. 2358.

In 1962, some experts estimated that 40 percent of potential tax collections were lost through evasion. Three years later, the Ministry of Finance claimed that 40 percent of sales taxes were not being remitted by merchants, and that a larger amount was lost through defalcations on income taxes. "Talle y Figura de las Grandes Reformas," *Ercilla*, XXVIII (28 marzo 1962), 10, "Cartas a la Dirección: Evasión Tributaria," XXXI (10 febrero 1965), 3. In terms of dollars, it was estimated in 1962 that more than $100,000,000 was being lost due to evasion. *Hispanic American Report*, XV (February 1963), 1146. For an estimate based upon 1965 returns which is considerably higher than this, see Ronald Gold, "Income Tax Evasion in Chile: An Estimate," *Inter-American Economic Affairs*, XXII (Spring 1969), 59-67.

Differential tax rates are discussed by Pike, p. 274, and Rubén Corvalán V., "El Filón Fiscal de las Herencias." *Ercilla* XXIX (6 marzo 1963), 8.

Chilean Governments have met revenue needs by borrowing and by expanding the money supply, which in turn have contributed to the inflationary process. Tom E. Davis, "Eight Decades of Inflation in Chile, 1879-1959," *Journal of Political Economy*, LXXI (August 1963), 392.

44. During the early 1960s, there were reports that many manufacturing industries were working well below installed capacity. OCEPLAN, Comando Nacional de Profesionales y Técnicos, *Planifica con nosotros el renacer de Chile: Jornadas Nacionales de Planificación Popular, Resoluciones*, Santiago, 26-27-28-29 junio 1964 (Santiago: Prensa Latino-americana, 1964), p. 80. "Empresarios: Diques para las Alzas," *Ercilla*, XXXI (17 febrero 1965), 11. More specifically, in 1961 CORFO reported that "industry is working at 2/3 of installed capacity." Chile, Corporación de Fomento de la Producción, *Synopsis of the National Program of Economic Development: 1961-1970* (Santiago: Talls. Grafs. 'La Nación,' 1961), p. 5. Similarly, in 1964 an ECLA team interviewed a random selection of 45 of the 155 Chilean industrialists who employ at least 100 workers. About 58 percent of them reported to be operating at less than full capacity due to a lack of purchasing power by consumers. "La CEPAL Hizo de Confessor," *Ercilla*, XXX (30 diciembre 1964), 18. Given this excess capacity and the continuing capital investment during the period (gross domestic investment was 9 percent of GDP in 1959, and averaged 12.4 percent during 1960-1964; 56 percent was spent on machinery and equipment), it is difficult to discern how much of the 400 percent increase in prices during these years could be attributed to wage-induced *excess* demand. The source for the statistics on inflation appears in note 39. The figures on investment will be found in IADB, *SPTF, 1965*, p. 210. Similarly, studies by CORFO and the Society for the Promotion of Manufacturing have indicated that wages account for only about 15 percent of manufacturing costs. "Un Personaje al Trasluz," *Ercilla*, XXVI (17 febrero 1965), 11. The implication then is that the policies adopted by Chilean Governments since 1955 to control inflation have not only failed to achieve this goal, but rested on faulty premises. In fact, they contributed to the increasingly regressive distribution of national income. On this argument, generally, see Ahumada, *Miseria*, pp. 151-54.

45. CORFO has stressed the problem of low net capital investment. Others have claimed that only about 12 percent of profits are reinvested, the remainder being largely allocated to entrepreneurial sector consumption, i.e., the upper and part of the upper middle classes. This has been contrasted with much higher rates of reinvestment in more developed societies. Chile, *Synopsis*, p. 5. Julio César Jobet, "Democracia Liberal y Subdesarrollo Económico," *Política* (Caracas), No. 5 (enero 1960), p. 99. Pike, p. 433. OCEPLAN, *Planifica con nosotros*, p. 80. OCEPLAN has also claimed that while 40 percent of national income was received by 5 percent of the population, this sector's consumption expenditures were

2½ times average gross investment per annum, and that this group evaded the equivalent of $100,000,000.00 (E400,000,000) in taxes annually. OCEPLAN, *Primeras 100 Medidas*, pp. 19-20. The pattern of upper and middle class disinclination to invest was apparent even before the 1956 initiation of monetary stabilization and wage restraint policies contributed to the stagnation of the economy due to a reduction in consumer purchasing power. Thus, "el ingreso annual per cápita durante el período 1925-1929 era algo más de 400 dólares; en 1955, este ingreso se había reducido a 363 dólares per c apita. Segundo, en el mismo período, 1925-29, el consumo per cápita era de 267.5 dólares; en 1955 este consumo había ascendido a 299 dólares." Poblete, "Causas," p. 309. Cf., Petras, *Politics and Social Forces*, pp. 19-26.

Between 1961 and 1963, capital valued at $167,000,000 left Chile. Tourists legally took $190,000,000 out of Chile from 1958 through 1963. Olavarria, IV, 61-62. The remainder was smuggled out of the country in the form of dollars which could be easily purchased on the black market (even in 1967), or carried out in the form of Escudos. "Todo esto es *perfectamente legal*. El chileno que llena su maleta con billetes de 50 escudos, y los lleva por LAN a Nueva York donde los vende y luego deposita su producto (dólares) en los bancos suizos, *no comete delito*." Luís Alberto Ganderáts, "Fuga de Capitales," *Desfile*, I (9 diciembre 1965), 5.

While it is difficult to ascertain exactly how much has left Chile, in 1962 a businessman while testifying before a U.S. Congressional Committee stated that "$10 billion represents the Latin American amount of flight capital in numbered bank accounts in Switzerland alone. My New York banker friends tell me that the amount of flight capital on deposit in New York, or invested in American securities or bonds, is probably equal to another 10 or 12 billion dollars." *Congressional Record* 87th Congress, May 10 and 11, 1962. Quoted in David Horowitz, *The Free World Colossus* (New York: Hill and Wang, 1965), p. 225. Theodore Moscoso has testified that "from the best possible sources I could find it is estimated that over the past 10 years there has been a flight of capital of less than $300 million a year. But the estimates, themselves, say this is a very difficult thing to measure." U.S., *Foreign Assistance Act of 1963*, V, 876.

46. With 1958 as the base (=100), manufacturing output expanded to 112 in 1960, 131 in 1962 and 144 in 1964. Interest and dividends paid on capital increased as follows: 1956-1960—$66.6 millions of dollars (per annum average), 1960—68.5, 1961—79.2, 1962—88.2, 1963—90.0, and 1964—108.0. Whereas manufacturing production increased by about 44 percent between 1958 and 1964, interest and dividends advanced by about 60 percent during the same period. Committee for Economic Development, p. 69. United Nations, Comisión Económica para América Latina, *Estudio Económico de Américan Latina* (New York: Naciones Unidas, 1965), p. 101.

47. UNESCO, Economical Social Council, Economic Commission for Latin America, Latin American Symposium on Industrial Development, *El desarrollo industrial de Chile*, presented by the Chilean government (ST/ECLA/ Conf. 23/L. 46, February 1966) (Santiago, Chile: March 1966), p. 77, cited in Petras, *Politics and Social Forces*, p. 25.

48. Domínguez, *Condicionamiento*, p. 59. *Idem, Una Oportunidad en la Libertad* (Santiago: Edit. del Pacífico, 1961), pp. 45-50. U.S., Department of Health, *Education*, p. 46. Pike, pp. 439-40. Silvert, *Chile: Yesterday and Today*, pp. 20-21. Juventud Demócrata Cristiana, *Informe del Segundo Congresso Nacional de la Juventud Demócrata Cristiana*, 31 de octubre, 1, 2, y 3 de noviembre de 1963 (Santiago: Imp. 'El Diario Ilustrado,' 1963), pp. 64-65. OCEPLAN, Oficine Central de Planificación, *La Política Agropecuaria del Gobierno Popular* (Santiago: Imp. Horizonte, 1964), p. 34. Humberto Malinarich M., "Los Médicos en el Filo del Bisturí," *Ercilla*, XXVIII (11 abril 1962), 16-17. Dorner and Collarte, "Land Reform in Chile," p. 5. G.M. Korb, "Chile's Exploited Farmers," *America*, CV (September 23, 1961), 798-800. James Becket, "Land Reform in Chile," *Journal of Inter-American Studies*, V (April 1963), 191-92, 207. Chile, Senado, *Diario*, CCLXXXVII, ses. 8 (23 junio 1959), pp. 417-419, CCLXXXVII, ses. 17 (22 noviembre 1960), p. 809, CCXC, ses. 36 (21 agosto 1962), pp. 2519, 2522-23.

49. It has been conservatively estimated that "the upper one percent of the agricultural families receives one-fourth of the total family income, while the bottom 87 percent of the farm labor force received only one-third of the total income." IADB, *SPTF, 1965*, p. 86. Cf., Ahumada, *Miseria*, pp. 84, 108. Gil, pp. 153, 155.

50. Silvert, *Chile: Yesterday and Today*, p. 126. Inter-American Development Bank, *Social Progress Trust Fund: Fourth Annual Report, 1964* (Washington: Inter-American Development Bank, 1965), p. 208. OCEPLAN, *La Política Agropecuaria*, p. 7.

51. Silvert, *Chile: Yesterday and Today*, p. 125. Domínguez, *Oportunidad*, pp. 34-35.

52. Between 1950 and 1960, 548,000 persons moved from rural to urban areas. In the latter year, 34 percent of the population was rural while in 1952, 40 percent had been. "Marginalidad," pp. 4-5. "The Chilean Land Reform: A Laboratory for Alliance-for-Progress Techniques," *Yale Law Journal*, LXXIII (December 1963), 312. Similarly, while 17 percent of the nation's population was in Santiago in 1957, by 1964 the figure was 33 percent. Edwin Lieuwen, *Arms and Politics in Latin America* (New York: Praeger, 1961), p. 44. Orville G. Cope, "The 1964 Presidential Election in Chile: The Politics of Change and Access," *Inter-American Economic Affairs*, XIX (Spring 1966), 25.

Due to the unwillingness of monopolistic businessmen to expand capital investments, the migration resulted in a 14 percent decline of per capita income for "personal services" occupations while public administrators and businessmen increased their per capita income by 52 percent during the same 1940-1960 period. Alieto Aldo Guadagne, "La fuerza de trabajo en Chile, 1930-60." (Santiago, Chile: 1961), p. 93 (mimeographed), cited in Petras, *Politics and Social Forces*, p. 17.

53. Petras, *Politics and Social Forces*, p. 40.

54. Class consciousness has been fairly pronounced at all levels in Chile. Although it might be possible to suggest that the upper classes are more rural oriented than the upper middle class (professionals, high level administrative personnel, etc.), the former have during the last several decades invested heavily in industry, commerce and banking, while the latter have been purchasing small or large rural estates (fundos) and marrying into the lower upper class. Except for a substantial number of family farmers of German origin who are south of the Central Valley, virtually all of the lower middle class elements were in urban areas; they consciously avoided—in most instances—identification with blue collar sectors. Pike, pp. 281, 284, 439. Eduardo Hamuy, "Temas de Nuestro Tiempo," *Cuadernos del Centro de Estudios Socioeconómicos*, N. o 1 (1966), pp. 15-23. Ahumada, *Miseria*, p. 53. Juan Ramón Silva, "La Clase Media," *Desfile*, I (27 enero 1966), p. 10. Petras, "The Latin American Middle Class," pp. 74-85. Francisco A. Encina, *La Educación Económica y el Liceo. La Reforma Agraria, El Momento Sociológico Mundial y los Destinos de los Pueblos Hispanoamericanos* (Santiago: Edit. Nascimento, 1962), p. 225. Rycroft and Clemmer, p. 116. Clark, p. 71. Data on entrepreneurial—rural upper class integration appear in Petras, *Politics and Social Forces*, pp. 53-54.

Worth noting is a 1966 Greater Santiago survey by the Centro de Estudios de Opinion Publica, in which interviewees were asked to identify their social position. Given reformist and radical criticisms of the upper classes during recent years, it was not surprising that few admitted such consciousness. More interesting was the fact that about one third of the blue collar sector wanted to think of themselves as middle class. Since the Left has used the terms in #8 and #9 during recent years, it is unsurprising that less than 3 percent viewed themselves as proletarians. They were probably affiliated with the Marxist parties.

		Socio-Economic Levels			
Categories	Upper	Upper Middle	Lower Middle	Lower	Total
1. Aristocracy	0.0%	0.0%	0.0%	0.0%	0.0%
2. Clase Alta	2.4	0.0	0.0	0.0	0.2
3. Gente Rica	0.0	0.0	0.0	0.0	0.0
4. Burguesía	2.4	1.3	0.8	0.0	1.0
5. Clase Media	64.3	53.9	34.9	24.3	42.3
6. Gente Acomodada	7.1	5.2	2.3	1.2	3.6
7. Proletariado	0.0	1.7	2.3	4.7	2.3
8. Clase Popular	9.5	18.1	27.4	24.7	22.3
9. Gente Humilde	14.3	19.4	31.8	44.9	27.8
No response	0.0	0.0	0.5	0.2	0.5

Source: "Encuestas: Las Clases Sociales," *El Mercurio: Revista del Domingo*, 8 enero 1967, p. 6.

55. IADB, *SPTF, 1964*, p. 214. But holdings of less than one hectare were excluded from the 1955 Agricultural Census. For a critique of its methodology, see the Chile, Senado, *Diario*, CCXC, ses. 19 (24 julio 1962), pp. 1456-58, ses. 25 (26 julio 1962), pp. 1930-31. Similarly, a landowner may hold title to more than one "predio" or holding. Thus, in 1955, 3,250 persons held title to 5,372 predios which accounted for 202,959,444 hectares, while 129,393 persons held title to 171,914 predios which represented 20,513,243 hectares. Chile, Ministerio de Agricultura, *Documentación básica sobre Tenencia de la Tierra en Chile y Materias a fines* (2.a ed., Santiago: Imp. 'Los Andes,' 1962), p. 18. According to the same 1955 Agricultural Census, "9.7 percent of the landowners owned 86 percent of the arable land, while at the other end of the scale 74.6 percent of the landowners owned 5.3 percent of the land. In the provinces of Santiago, Valparaiso and Aconcagua 7 percent of the land-owners possessed 92 percent of the land." Petras, "The Latin American Middle Class," p. 75.

Luís Corvalán has cited the 1960 Agricultural Census as reporting that 6,326 land-owners (4.2 percent of the total) held title to almost 75 percent of the arable land. More than 5.6 million hectares or about 20 percent of the agricultural land were alleged to belong to "600 family groups," Chile, Senado, *Diario*, CCXCIV, ses. 2 (10 junio 1964), p. 34. Cf., Petras, *Politics and Social Forces*, p. 18.

On the other hand, it has been estimated that there are "200,000 landless families" in rural Chile. Becket, "Land Reform," p. 196. They represent 59 percent of the rural labor force. Petras, "After the Election," p. 377. Since the total rural population according to the 1960 census was only 2,346,055, the landless would—assuming an average of four children per family—represent more than half of the persons living in the countryside. Chile, *Población del País*, p. 7.

56. Because of the inflation, such loans were often actually interest free. Small and medium landowners reportedly encountered much greater difficulties in obtaining use of public funds. Pike, pp. 281-82. This tradition dates from the 1879-1925 era. Davis, "Eight Decades of Inflation," p. 389.

57. Becket, "Land Reform," pp. 201-202. Dorner and Collarte, "Land Reform in Chile," p. 14.

58. Law No. 8811 was enacted three months after the expulsion of the Communists from Gonzalez Videla's government in 1947. It required that rural workers who organized unions be literate, undertake never to strike, and constitute at least 25 men on a particular holding. Hence, seventeen years later there were only 22 rural unions with a total of 1,500 members out of a labor force of almost 700,000 in rural areas. Virtually all of the unionized workers were on government-owned *fundos*. Moisés Poblete Troncoso, "El Movimiento Sindical Chileno," *Combate* (San José), IV (Julio y Agosto 1962), 30. Comando Nacional Gremial, *Trabajadores en el Gobierno Popular*, p. 6.

Non-enforcement of rural social welfare and labor codes is discussed in: Pike, pp. 282-83; John Gerassi, *The Great Fear* (New York: MacMillan, 1963), p. 331; and Chile, Senado, *Diario*, CCLXXXVII, ses. 18 (23 noviembre 1960), p. 889.

59. Chile's per capita income in 1961 was $452.90, at the official exchange rate. Rycroft and Clemmer, p. 68.

60. Op. cit., p. 387.

Chapter 3. Aspects of Chilean Political Organization and Behavior

1. Alberto Edwards Vives, *La Fronda Aristocratica* (Santiago: Edit. del Pacifico, 1959, 5th reprinting of 1928 ed.), pp. 20-21.

2. The rule of the oligarchy may have been very harsh, for a substantial number of mestizos, free Negroes and fugitive Indians fled to join these mountain gangs which were "aided clandestinely" by the "peasant population of the Central Valley." Mario Gongora, "Vagabundaje y Sociedad Fronteriza en Chile (Siglos XVII-XIX)," *Cuadernos del Centro de Estudios Socioeconomicos*, No. 2 (1966), pp. 1-41.

3. Fernando Campos Harriet, *Historia Constitucional de Chile* (3 a ed; Santiago: Edit. Juridica de Chile, 1963), p. 135. See pp. 134-36 for a discussion of these developments, and

Alberto Edwards Vives, *La Fronda Aristocratica* (Santiago: Imp. Nacional, 1928), pp. 44-45.

4. The president did not intervene in every case, and on at least some occasions, his efforts were inefficacious. Alberto Edwards Vives y Eduardo Frei Montalva, *Historia de los Partidos Politicos Chilenos*, (Santiago: Edit. del Pacifico, 1949), pp. 30-32, 45-46, 61, 86, 93-94.

5. Until 1888, clergymen could be elected to the Senate or Chamber of Deputies. In the same year, property qualifications for male voters were abolished, and the minimum voting age was lowered from 25 to 21. Since 1874, however, literacy was presumed to establish the property qualification. In 1925, male domestic servants were given the right of suffrage. The Radical Party led the struggle for all of these reforms. Campos, pp. 315, 321.

6. Campos, p. 180. The military revolts and civil war of the 1850s—some inspired by liberal principles—are described in Edwards y Frei, pp. 46, 60-61, 63.

7. Edwards y Frei, pp. 98-99. Silvert, *Reaction*, pp. 57-58. While the issue of constitutionality was uniformly regarded as crucial, who held the better right was problematic. It has been argued that the anti-administration congressional majority was secured only through bribery by Lord North's agents. Some congressmen did support the president and issues involving tax burdens and the utilization of newly discovered nitrate deposits strongly colored the entire controversy. See Luis Vitole, *¿Y Despues del 4, Que Perspectivos de Chile después de las elecciones presidenciales* (Santiago: Prensa Latinoamericana, 1970), p. 51, and Petras, *Politics and Social Forces*, pp. 94-97.

8. During the 1894-1924 period of congressional hegemony, widespread vote-buying replaced electoral intervention by the Executive. There were numerous cabinet changes, and parties differed only at the doctrinal level. Corruption, factionalism and opportunism are said to have characterized the political process. Edwards y Frei, pp. 110-11, 133-44. Silvert, *Reaction*, pp. 58-60. Nevertheless, the attitude favoring compromise was evidenced by the admission of Balmaceda's supporters to the Congress elected in 1894, and many of his measures were retained.

9. On these and related factors, see: Petras, *Politics and Social Forces*, pp. 84-93; Maurice Zeitlin, "The Social Determinants of Political Democracy in Chile," in *Latin America: Reform or Revolution?* ed. by James Petras and Maurice Zeitlin (New York: Fawcett, 1968), pp. 220-34. Cf., Donald W. Beatty, "Middle Class Government in Chile," *Current History*, XLII (February 1962), 106-107; Ernst Halperin, *Nationalism and Communism in Chile* (Cambridge: MIT Press, 1965), pp. 27-30.

10. Alan Angell, "Chile: The Difficulties of Democratic Reform," *International Journal*, XXIV (Summer 1969), 525.

11. Vitale, *Y Despues* pp. 62-63.

12. F.M. Nunn, "Emil Korner and the Prussianization of the Chilean Army," *Hispanic American Historical Review*, L (May 1970), 300-310. LIISA North, *Civil Military Relations in Argentina, Chile and Peru* (Berkeley: Institute of International Studies, University of California, n.d.), pp. 11-13.

13. Edwards, 1928, pp. 249-63.

14. The major provisions of this instrument are summarized by Gil, p. 59.

15. President Figueroa, whom Ibanez had forced out in 1926, had declined to outlaw the Marxists. The major events during the 1925-1927 period are related by Edwards, pp. 278, 286-90, 302.

16. There were, of course, a variety of motives involved. See Pike, pp. 196, 199-200; and John J. Johnson, *Political Change in Latin America* (Stanford: Stanford University Press, 1958), pp. 69-71.

17. This dramatic episode in Chilean militarism is discussed in: Jack Ray Thomas, "The Socialist Republic of Chile," *Journal of Inter-American Studies*, VI (April 1964), 203-20; Edwards y Frei, pp. 210-18; Pike, pp. 209-211; and "La Republica Socialista," *Desfile*, I (23 septiembre 1965), 20-21.

18. Campos, pp. 268-69.

19. "El 'Ariostazo,' " *Desfile*, I (21 octubre 1965), 20-21. "Allende en Televisión: Sexta entrevista realizada 31 de Julio," *Arauco*, V (Agosto 1964), 98-99. Luis Corvalan, "The Peaceful Way—A Form of Revolution," *World Marxist Review*, VI (December 1963), 7.

20. Gil, p. 183.

21. *El Mercurio*, 6 agosto 1960, p. 3. This represents a substantial increment over 1954, when the military received less than 16 percent. In 1954, too, more than 8 percent was budgeted to the *Carabineros* and the court system. Assuming that this figure increased over the succeeding five years, by 1959 probably close to a third of the national budget was being used to equip, entertain and maintain about 38,000 men in the armed forces and the quasi-military national police. Gil, p. 178. *El Mercurio*, 21 noviembre 1959, p. 3.

22. *El Mercurio*, 30 noviembre 1959, p. 21. Mario Díaz B., "Meditacion Electoral," *Punto Final*, I (2.a quincena de marzo de 1967), 2-3.

23. Lieuwen, p. 169. Cf., Gil, p. 296, and Clark, p. 168. In 1961, there was one army colonel for every 200 men and one general per thousand soldiers. *Hispanic American Report*, XIV (September 1961), 637-38.

It has been claimed that during the 1950s, "Ibanez encouraged a military group to plan a coup that would have rid him of parliamentary supervision. The conspirators, the so-called 'Linea Recta' group, were officers with Socialist sympathies and a number of Socialist Party leaders were in the know. The coup failed to materialize because top army leaders took a firm stand against it, and possibly also because Ibanez was not too keen to let it succeed but only wanted to use it to frighten the parliamentary opposition into subservience." Halperin, pp. 132-33.

Again, it was reported in June 1958 that "(a)loof from and disdainful of the four-way race for the presidency, the outlawed military lodge 'Linea Recta' returned to public life, demanding a national movement 'above politics' which would squelch congressional obstreperousness in favor of a strong executive. The group chose to make its reappearance at a time when Charles de Gaulle's return to power in France was a leading concern in the Chilean press. The most notable result was the appointment of a prosecutor by the Chilean courts to investigate the activities of the organization." *Hispanic American Report*, XI (June 1958), 334.

Three years later, Conservative Party leaders publicly criticized the Minister of Defense for alleged favoritism in the promotion of officers known for their "Liberal Party" sympathies. Ibid., XV (November, 1962), 840. By this time a purge that had followed the Cuban Revolution had eliminated virtually all officers with Socialist sympathies. Continued non-Marxist political party interest by the officer corps was reflected by the reported shift of all command positions to those harboring pro-Christian democratic sentiments during the 1964-1965 period.

24. "La Nueva Guerra Subvertiva," *Ercilla*, XXVI (18 mayo 1960), 16-18.

25. The declaration of the general who had served as a Minister of State during the 1950s, also warned that "es tiempo de concitar la opinión pública contra estos desbordes al mismo tiempo que buscar los resortes legales para terminar de una vez por todo con la secta que propende al trastorno institucional." "La Semana Política," *Ercilla* XXVIII (18 abril 1962), 9.

26. "The army officer corps is for the most part composed of persons of middle-class background, with only a few officers possessing an upper-class background. Although some may be described as 'progressive' and interested in social and political reforms, the sense of discipline among Chilean officers is stronger than political sympathies. They are repelled by radicalism and by the expression of it in strikes, riots, and other destructive disorders. These officers do not appear to be as strongly nationalistic as their counterparts in other Latin American countries, and there are no vestiges among them of uncritical anti-imperialist sentiments. The navy, as also is often the case in Latin America, is politically 'liberal' in the best English tradition." Augusto Olivares, "Hablo el General X," *Desfile*, I (6 enero 1966), 6-7 ff. Gil, p. 296.

27. Marxist-resistant attitudinal structures of lower middle and lower class conscripts were reinforced or introduced by the officer corps through systematic inculcation of such sentiments as patriotism and honor. The military definition of such concepts is likely to be substantially at odds with the Marxist class-based interpretation of history and contemporary society. Simultaneously, the good will of conscripts is probably engendered by instruction in literacy, good eating habits, hygiene and vocational fields (tractor driving, carpentry, shoe-making, auto mechanics, radio mechanics, etc.). State sponsored sporting events—very popular in Chile—are also presided over by the military. *El Mercurio*, 21 noviembre 1959, p. 3; 12 septiembre 1960, p. 35.

28. Time (Canadian Ed.), October 9, 1970, p. 30.

29. The gravity of these mutinous conspiracies was reflected upon during a recent hearing on the Rockefeller Report in the U.S. Senate. Both Nelson Rockefeller and Senator Church regarded Chile as "teetering on the brink of a military coup d'etat." U.S., Congress, Senate, Committee on Foreign Relations, *Rockefeller Report on Latin America, Hearing*, before the Subcommittee on Western Hemisphere Affairs of the Committee on Foreign Relations, United States Senate, 91st Cong., 1st sess., November 20, 1969.

30. On the relationship of professionalization and exposure to modernization abroad to military discontent which resulted in intervention during this period, see: Nunn, "Emil Korner and the Prussianization," pp. 312-22.

31. Vitale, *Y Despues?* p. 61.

32. Nunn, "Emil Korner and the Prussianization," p. 307.

33. *New York Times*, December 6, 1970, Section I, p. 2. See article 109 of the Constitution of the Republic of Chile.

34. "The Chilean Socialist leaders are not starry-eyed political novices. They certainly harbor no illusions as to the Communists' aims and intentions in maintaining the alliance. Every single one of them has a long record of political struggle against the Communists. It is true that organizationally the Chilean Communists are greatly superior to the Socialists; but in intensely individualistic Latin America, organizational superiority somehow does not weigh quite so heavily as in other parts of the world. Latin America organizations may look impressive on paper, but they are not very effective in practice since there is not enough discipline, devotion, and self-sacrifice behind them; hence, even such a large communist party as that of Chile is afflicted." Halperin, pp. 120-21.

The Socialist-Communist rivalry and consequential traditional personal animosities weakened the FRAP coalition, especially within a context of proscriptions upon electoral pacts. Halperin's emphasis upon the factor of indiscipline in the above paragraph is worth some comment. Arturo Olavarria Bravo, who was one of Allende's top campaign managers in 1964 and who had supported Alessandri in 1958, has argued (Alessandri, IV, 167) that FRAP lost in the earlier contest only because of inefficient campaign organization while Alessandri's backers—as Frei's did in 1964—possessed sufficient funds to employ professional P.R. firms. And with regard to the latter year, a prominent Communist estimated to the writer that 80 percent of the campaigning was done by Communists. It is not the Chilean lack of organizational commitment and ability in general that is significant here, but that some—the Communists—are relatively less egoistic and more effective organizationally than any other Chilean group save the military. This is one of the major reasons why the Communists were so feared in Chile, Halperin notwithstanding. On the functioning of this system, see: Charles J. Parrish, Arpad J. von Lazar and Jorge Tapia Videla, *The Chilean Congressional Election on March 7, 1965: An Analysis*, (Washington, D.C.: Institute for the Comparative Study of Political Systems, 1967), pp. 19-21.

35. With regard to the pre-1959 practices, see: Gil, p. 224; and *Hispanic American Report*, XI (March 1958), 162-63 (July 1958), 396.

Since 1958, vote-buying techniques have varied. A maid employed by the writer reported that during 1964, Frei supporters distributed parts of a bed, one shoe or half of a ten Escudo note. The remainder would be delivered if Frei won in the district. Similarly, CARITAS foods were distributed by known Frei supporters, some of whom referred to them as "a gift from. . . ." In other instances, it was alleged that homes of known Allendistas were ignored by the food distributors. Charges of such practices appear in Olavarria, *Alessandri*, IV, 114-16, 293, 296, 303; Chile, Senado, *Diario*, CCXC, ses. 43 (4 septiembre 1962), pp. 3283-92; CCXCIII, ses. 50 (29 abril 1964), p. 3926; and Petras, "After the Election," p. 375.

During a lecture by Salomon Corbalan at the Latin American Faculty of Social Sciences in early December 1966, the late secretary general of the Socialist Party charged that government subsidies to Mothers' Centers, Neighbors' Committees, Cultural and Sports Clubs were determined in many instances by which political party was in control of a particular group. Cf., *El Siglo*, 25 diciembre 1966, p. 6.

On the eve of the 1965 congressional election, the government, CARE and other supporting organizations distributed telephones and sewing machines to such centers.

36. Charges of electoral fraud during the 1961-1964 period will be found in *Hispanic*

American Report, XIV (June 1961), 350; XVII (October 1964), 742; and Olavarria, *Alessandri*, IV, 328-29.

37. A cogent analysis of the failure of centrist and rightist parties to cope with the challenge of development will be found in Petras, *Politics and Social Forces*, chapters one to four.

38. ". . . the entire history of the relations between the two parties is one of bitter rivalry, which has been only muted, but by no means eliminated, during periods of political collaboration. There is no love lost between the top-ranking party leaders, and fierce competition and animosity prevail in the union locals and municipalities," Halperin, p. 120. Cf., Alexander, p. 325.

39. The 1958 election marked the emergence of the PDC as the major center-left party, thus supplanting the Radicals in some measure. Despite Alessandri's narrow plurality, the election results indicated a decline in the importance of personalist appeal and the growth of a more leftward and programmatic trend in national politics. Allende received 28.9 percent, Frei 20.7 percent and 3.3 percent were given to Antonio Zamorano, a defrocked priest and former Socialist whose program was reformist.

40. While "considerably less than 10 percent of the Chilean population enjoyed suffrage rights" in 1933, by 1964, approximately 44 percent were eligible to vote. Women first voted in municipal elections in 1934, congressional elections in 1949 and presidential contests in 1952. Pike, p. 252. Gil, p. 212. Between 1958 and 1964, the electoral registration of women increased by 160 percent. Pike, p. 252. Gil, p. 212. Angell, "Chile: The Difficulties," p. 525.

41. According to Petras, in 1964 "the financial resources of the PDC were said to have been nearly fifteen times those of the Left." *Politics and Social Forces*, p. 207.

42. G.S. Grayson, "The Frei Administration and the 1969 Parliamentary Elections," *Inter-American Economic Affairs*, XXIII (Autumn 1969), 60-61, 67.

43. Angell, "Chile: The Difficulties," p. 525.

44. Explicit or implied suggestions of this danger will be found in: Kalman Silvert, *Coda* (American Universities Field Staff, October 10, 1957), p. 10; Pike and Bray "Vista of Catastrophe," p. 396; Editorial, *New York Times*, March 1, 1960, p. 32; Morris, "Chile: Restless Republic," p. 72; and Gil, p. viii.

45. Summaries of supporting data are presented in Appendix I, Part A.

46. Appendix I, Part B.

47. Appendix I, Part C.

48. Petras, *Politics and Social Forces*, pp. 51-71, 139-54, 309-32.

49. With regard to middle class policy orientations: Ibid., pp. 139-54, 309-32; Dale L. Johnson, "The National and Progressive Bourgeoisie of Chile," *Studies in Comparative International Development*, vol. IV, no. 4 (1968-1969), pp. 63-84; Myron Glazer, "Student Politics in a Chilean Society, *Daedalus* XCVII (Winter 1968), 107-108; Alejandro Portes, "Leftist Radicalism in Chile: A Test of Three Hypotheses," *Comparative Politics*, II (January 1970), 255, 269; Vitale, *Y Despues?* pp. 16, 22.

50. Data are from a 1961 University of Chile Survey. Portes, "Leftist Radicalism," pp. 269-70.

51. Angell, "Chile: The Difficulties," p. 20.

52. Portes, "Leftist Radicalism," pp. 255, 269. This finding evidences both stability and consistency with those tabulated in note 55, chapter 2.

53. Portes, "Leftist Radicalism," p. 257. Evidently it takes 8-10 years for effective political socialization to occur within the educational system. Beyond that students may be exposed to crosspressures from youth divisions of political parties. See Glazer, "Student Politics," p. 104. Demographic studies, however, suggest that some caution may be necessary in appraising the political significance of education per se. See: Glancio Soares and Robert L. Hamblin, "Socio-Economic Variables and Voting for the Radical Left," *American Political Science Review*, LXI (December 1967), 1061; Sandra Powell, "Political Change in the Chilean Electorate, 1952-1964," *Western Political Quarterly*, XXIII (June 1970), 373, 375-76; Bernard E. Segal, "Dissatisfaction and Desire for Change Among Chilean Hospital Workers," *American Journal of Sociology*, LXXV (November 1969), 381-82.

54. On female anti-radicalism, see Powell, "Political Change," p. 382.

55. Occupational sub-group and income stratification variables are examined in Portes, "Leftist Radicalism," pp. 255-56.

56. James Petras and Maurice Zeitlin, "Miners and Agrarian Radicalism," *American Sociological Review*, XXXII (August 1967), 578-86. Maurice Zeitlin and James Petras, "The Working Class in Chile: Christian Democracy vs Marxism," *British Journal of Sociology*, XXI (March 1970), 20-25; Segal, "Dissatisfaction," pp. 381-88. Vitale, *Y Despues?* p. 22; Maurice Zeitlin *Revolutionary Politics and the Cuban Working Class*, (Princeton, N.J.: Princeton University Press, 1967).

57. Appendix I, Part D.

58. Appendix I, Part E.

59. Appendix I, Part F.

60. Appendix I, Part G.

61. Campos, pp. 307, 312-13.

62. Ibid., pp. 248-49. Edwards y Frei, pp. 152-56. Johnson, p. 41. G. Kaempfer Villagran, *Bloody Episodes of the Workers' Struggle in Chile (1850-1925)*, Santiago, 1962. Chile, Senado, *Diario*, CCLXXXVIII, ses. 27 (2 agosto 1961), 1539. Petras, *Politics and Social Forces*, pp. 75-78, 81.

63. Charges and/or evidence of such excess of force will be found in "La Protesta contra Batista," *Ercilla*, XXIV (16 abril 1958), 32; "El Unico Incidente," ibid., XXVI (2 marzo 1960), 18; Bibi de Vicenzi, "Yo Fue Golpeado por la Policia," ibid., (18 mayo 1960), p. 17; Emilio Filippi, "Violencia Tras la Marcha del Acero," ibid., XXXVII (22 marzo 1961), 7; Chile, Senado, *Diario*, CCLXXXVI, sec. 15 (12 julio 1960), pp. 742-45, ses. 23 (3 agosto 1960), pp. 1362-63, CCLXXXVIII, ses. 2 (6 junio 1961), pp. 78-80, ses. 3 (7 junio 1961), pp. 149-51; *Hispanic American Report*, XIV (July 1961), 439 (August 1961), p. 543 (May 1962), 257 (January 1963), p. 1043; *El Caso Queirolo: Sensacional Denuncia del Diputado Luis Valente R.* (Santiago: Imp. Horizonte, 1965); Arturo Olavarria Bravo, *Chile bajo la Democracia Cristiana* (Santiago: Edit. Nascimento, 1966), p. 95; Goldenberg, pp. 145-46; and *Las Noticias de Ultima Hora*, 15 abril 1967, p. 3.

64. Petras and Zeitlin, "Miners," pp. 583-84; Vitale, *Y Despues?* p. 43.

65. Grayson, "The Frei Administration," p. 69.

66. Ibid., p. 56.

67. Edwards y Frei, p. 231.

68. Ibid., p. 210.

69. Halperin, p. 45.

70. Ibid., p. 46. Pike, p. 246.

71. Gonzalez Videla's plurality was less than 50,000 votes. Although the Communists only had slightly in excess of 26,000 registered voters, they certainly delivered an equal number of non-party voters.

72. Beipi, "El Partido Comunista de Chile," *Estudios sobre el comunismo*, VIII (octubre-diciembre de 1960), 49-55.

73. Johnson, pp. 86-88. Halperin, pp. 54-55. Partido Comunista de Chile, *Documentos del XI Congreso Nacional*, (Santiago: Talls. Grafs. Lautaro, 1959), p. 10. Cf., U.S., *Foreign Aid in Action*, p. 13.

74. Jules Dubois, *Operation America: The Communist Conspiracy in Latin America* (New York: Walker, 1963), p. 257. Cf., "Allende on Televisión: Quinta entrevista realizada el Viernes 10 de Julio de 1964," *Arauco*, V (Agosto 1964), 80.

75. Halperin, p. 33. The late Jules Dubois has reported (p. 257) that during a serious coal strike in October, 1947, Gonzalez "appealed to the U.S. for assistance, and an emergency supply of coal was shipped from U.S. east coast ports through the Panama Canal to Chile to tide the government over."

The Communist Party's responsiveness to Soviet foreign policy objectives is documented by S. Cole Blasier, "The Cuban and Chilean Communist Parties: Instrumentalities of Soviet Policy, 1935-1948" (unpublished Ph.D. dissertation, Columbia University, 1954).

76. ". . . los asesinatos y las torturas, los campos de concentración y las carceles, las expulsiones de miles de trabajadores y sus familias de las provincias en que vivían, la intervención policial en las organizaciones sindicales y una implacable represion legalizada. . . ." ". . . Solo la primera represión de Gonzalez Videla significó la expulsión de la industria de 17 mil de los mas combativos trabajadores. El decreto Yanez-Koch significó la inhabilidad de 4 mil 500 obreros y empleados para ser dirigentes de los sindicatos. La ilegalidad restringio también nuestra labor de educación política de las masas." Partido Communista, *XI*

Congreso Nacional, pp. 10, 67. Cf., Beipi, "El Partido Comunista de Chile," pp. 52-53. Veliz, "Chile," p. 225. Halperin, p. 55.

77. Olavarria, *Alessandri*, II.

78. Halperin, pp. 127-28. Partido Comunista, *XI Congreso Nacional*, p. 10.

79. Petras, "The Latin American Middle Class," p. 76.

80. The Communists supported Salvador Allende who had resigned from the Popular Socialist Party when it endorsed Ibanez who pledged nationalization, agrarian reform, etc. Allende was then nominated by the Socialist Party of Chile, the rump organization which had formerly supported Gonzalez Videla's persecution of the Communists. Halperin, pp. 132-33.

81. *Reaction*, pp. 188-89. In 1955, the so-called Koch-Yanez circular was decreed by Ibanez's ministers of interior and labor. Under it, all candidates for positions as officers or members of the executive committees of unions had to be investigated by the Political Police. If the latter organization alleged that an individual were a member of the outlawed Communist Party, he could not be elected by the workers. Alexander, pp. 290-91.

82. Silvert, *Reaction*, p. 192.

83. Luis Hernandez Parker, "Elecciones en Tierra Derecha," *Ercilla*, XXVIII (1 febrero 1961). Five had been "Socialists." *Hispanic American Report*, XI (August 1958), 456.

84. Silvert, *Chile: Yesterday and Today*, pp. 81-82. Cf., Olavarria, *Alessandri*, II, 393-95.

85. *Hispanic American Report*, XI (May 1958), 274.

86. Chile, Contraloría General de la República, Secretaría General, *Recopilación de Leyes* (Ed. Oficial, Tomo XLVI, Santiago: Contraloría General de la Republica, 1959), pp. 251-52.

87. *Hispanic American Report*, XII (September 1959), 397. Similarly, within two months of the repeal "of the Law for the Defense of Democracy, which had proscribed Communists from holding positions of union leadership, the Communists had won control of the unions of two large southern coal companies, the Huachipato steel mill, and a large metallurgical plant in Santiago." Ibid., XI (October 1958), 571.

88. *El Mercurio*, 6 diciembre 1959, p. 35. *Hispanic American Report*, XII (November 1959), 506-507, (February 1960), pp. 687-88, XVI (February 1964), 1185. Chile, Senado, *Diario*, CCLXXXVII, ses. 17 (22 noviembre 1960), pp. 815-22.

89. *Hispanic American Report*, XIV (January 1962), 1027-28.

90. Grayson, "The Frei Administration," p. 52.

91. *El Mercurio*, 15 octubre 1960, p. 21. *Hispanic American Report*, XII (January 1960), 622, XIV (December 1961), 926 (January 1962), p. 1028. (December 1963), 999, XVI (January 1064), 1089-90. Even radio broadcasters were not immune from repression. The atmosphere of toleration—or better, its limits—may best be portrayed through the relation of the following case. " 'Bolivia had a port and now doesn't have one due to an unjust peace settlement,' declared Phidias Acevedo on February 20 over Santiago's Radio Portales. Acevedo's broadcast in which he stated his own opinions rather than quoting from other sources, had deep repercussions within the government, whose relations with Bolivia were tense because of Bolivia's demand for an outlet to the sea and a solution to the River Lauca dispute.... 'Chile will have to negotiate, because all of America is against the Chilean stand,' Acevedo stated over the air, concluding that Chile was 'ruthlessly holding back the development of another member of the American family.'

On Feb. 21, Foreign Minister Carlos Martinez Sotomayor, without consulting the vacationing President Jorge Alessandri Rodriguez, declared on Radio Cooperativa Vitalicia that the Acevedo program had 'tried to create, with totally false statements, a difficult position with our neighbors,' and constituted 'treason.' Chile's national broadcasting association suspended Radio Portales' membership; the station's board of directors, which included Liberal Senator Eduardo Alessandri Rodriguez (the President's brother), Radical Senator Julio Duran Neumann, and Conservative Deputy Sergio Diaz Urzua, threatened to resign, but there was no indication that they had done so. Station owner Raul Tarud Siwady (brother of independent leftist Senator Rafael Tarud), refused to be held responsible. Meanwhile, Acevedo and program director Raul Gonzalez Alfaro were arrested for violation of the Internal Security Law." *Hispanic American Report*, XVI (April 1963), 163-64.

92. Grayson, The Frei Administration," pp. 53-4.

93. "The New Press Law in Chile," *Bulletin of the International Commission of Jurists*, No. 20 (September 1964), pp. 16-21. Cf., *Hispanic American Report*, XVII (March 1964), 69-70.

94. Although the percentage of the entire population which votes has increased from about 10 percent during the 1940s to more than 25 percent in the 1963-1965 period, well over seventy percent of the population were not involved in the electoral process and nearly 90 percent were not long-term electoral participants. The entry of new voters is evidenced by the fact that in 1949, less than 11 percent of the population was registered. By 1958, this figure had doubled and tripled by 1963. Gil, pp. 212-13. According to Luis Vitale, only 22 percent of the blue collar workers were registered and but 20 percent actually voted. *Ensayo de Historia del Movimiento Obrero Chileno.* (Santiago: Edit. POR.)

95. Denunciations of such legislation by Socialist Senators were quite vehement. Chile, Senado, *Diario*, CCLXXXVI, ses. 20 (27 julio 1960), pp. 1103-1104, ses. 24 (10 agosto 1960), pp. 1499-1501, ses. 37 (6 septiembre 1960), p. 2599, ses. 39 (7 septiembre 1960), pp. 2723-26. Without a pact, Socialists and Communists have to run on separate lists. In addition to losing votes due to the proportional system, because of traditional hostilities there are followers of each party who won't vote for the other. Electoral pacts were banned for municipal elections in 1960, for deputy contests the following year, and for senators in 1962.

Other structural disadvantages for FRAP originated in the separate voting of men and women. The latter tend to be more conservative.

96. Donoso, "Chile," p. 186, citing from Pike and Bray's "Vista of Catastrophe."

97. *South Pacific Mail*, CIX (August 2, 1963), 13. Frederick Pike related (p. 429) that the Klein-Saks mission "did, indeed, become a hated symbol among the lower-income groups." Some eye-witnesses have stated to the writer that the protest reflected more general underlying discontents and frustrated aspirations which are not articulated for public opinion polls. Interview with Danton Chelen, MIR leader, Santiago, June 29, 1967.

98. Silvert, *Reaction*, pp. 191-92.

99. "Los guatones de la P.P.," *Desfile*, I (13 enero 1966), 14.

100. For a relation of such incidents during the 1924-1925 period see Edwards, 1928, pp. 244-45, 247, 275.

101. Ibid.

102. Kalman H. Silvert, *Elections, Parties and the Law* (American Universities Field Staff, March 10, 1957), p. 1.

103. *Ercilla*, XXIV (13 agosto 1958), 7, 32 (27 agosto 1958), pp. 7-9. During the month of June (the election was in September), an "indoor rally for right-wing candidate Jorge Alessandri underwent repeated tear-gas bombings. Alessandristas, for their part, were charged with attacking a Frente de Accion Popular (FRAP—Popular Action Front) sound truck and stoning the offices of the pro-FRAP newspaper *La Gaceta*." *Hispanic American Report*, XI (June 1958), 333.

104. Olavarria, *Alessandri*, II, 398. During the campaign, Carlos Jorquera, editor of the pro-FRAP Gaceta, published a report indicating "that Alessandri was board chairman or a principal stockholder in 126 corporations which controlled approximatley 200,000 million pesos of capital." He was beaten by unknown assailants one night. *Hispanic American Report*, XI (May 1958), 25.

105. *Ercilla*, XXVII (22 febrero 1961), 10 (8 marzo 1961), p. 32.

106. *El Mercurio*, 16 febrero 1969, p. 25, cited by Grayson, "The Frei Administration," p. 55.

107. *Ercilla*, XXX (18 marzo 1964), 32 (25 marzo 1964), p. 15. Olavarria, *Alessandri*, IV, 114-15.

108. The FRAP National Campaign headquarters was burned down; it had new wiring. In addition, two Socialist Party headquarters were known to have been set afire, and there was a blaze one night at the OCEPLAN (a FRAP planning and research center). Olavarria, *Alessandri*, IV, 319-27.

109. The following two passages—the second by Senator Radomiro Tomic—may fairly portray the climate of violence: "Los compatriotas, a pesar de estar unidos pro un comun destino, siguieron golpeándose; destruyendo la propaganda del contrario; mofándose de sus iniciativas creadoras; ensañádose con los murales y hasta asesinándose entre sí." *Ercilla*,

XXX (19 agosto 1960), 17. "No voy a culpar al Senador Allende de haber dado instrucciones para este asalto, pero es un hecho cierto que este es obra de cierto clima, que está produciendo monstruosas distorciones del proceso democrático." Chile Senado, *Diario*, CCXCIII, ses. 42 (15 abril 1964), pp. 3449-50, CCXCIV, ses. 11 (15 julio 1964), pp. 1095, 1098, ses. 16 (4 agosto 1964), pp. 1742-44, ses. 22 (12 agosto 1964), pp. 2129-31. These instances probably represent a small number of such actions.

110. Chile, Senado, *Diario* CCLXXXIX, ses. 11 (7 noviembre 1961), pp. 527-28.

111. *El Mercurio*, 7 enero 1960, p. 17.

112. Chile, Senado, *Diario*, CCXCII, ses. 27 (agosto 1963), pp. 1744-46.

113. *Hispanic American Report*, XVI (October 1963), 804.

114. Edmundo Espinosa A., 'Los Nazis Porteños," *Ercilla*, XXX (1 abril 1964), p. 6.

115. Grayson, "The Frei Administration," pp. 55-56.

116. On the three disturbances, see: "La Semana Política," *Ercilla*, XXVII (21 junio 1961), 9; *New York Times*, December 4, 1961, p. 2; and "Incidentes universitarios," Mensaje, XIII (diciembre 1964), pp. 613-16.

117. "Invasion pacífica de los 'sin techno'," *Ercilla*, XXVII (26 julio 1961), 163. Ibid. (16 agosto 1961), última pagina. Mario Planet, "Vía Pacífica se Torna Violenta," ibid., (6 diciembre 1961), 16-17. Igor Entrala, "Faltan 225 casas más cada hora." ibid., XXIX (18 diciembre 1963), 4-5. Cesar Cerda, "Chile's Trade Unions," *New Times*, No. 17 (April, 1962), pp. 15-16. *Hispanic American Report*, XVII (March 1964), 69. *El Mercurio*, 8 enero 1964, p. 23. Olavarría, *Alessandri*, IV 19-20, 132-33, 135, 138-39.

118. Samuel Mendoz, *Actividad del Comunismo en Chile en 1961* (Santiago: Congreso por la Libertad de la Cultura, Imp. San Jorge, diciembre 1961), pp. 12-13. "Pasos Públicos y Privados del Complot," *Ercilla*, XXVII (30 agosto 1961), pp. 15-16. Chile, Senado, *Diario*, CCLXXXVIII, ses. 43 (29 agosto 1961), pp. 2405-17, ses. 44 (30 agosto 1961), pp. 2577-89.

119. The Carabineros and each of the three armed services have intelligence units. The ministry of interior's Political Police, which cooperates with at least one anti-Communist intelligence organization in West Germany, concentrates largely upon the Marxist left. It uses wire taps, informers and direct surveillance. The PP recruits poorly paid teachers as spies, and subsidizes university students who are short of funds. Similarly, porters in Leftist periodicals are put on its payroll, as are blue collar workers who have been recommended by their employers. "Los miembros de la P.P. se jactan de que ellos saben perfectamente cuáles serán los próximos pasos de los Partidos Socialista y Comunista. Sobre el medio de información no hacen ningún misterio: 'Tenemos gente adentro', dicen. Fué un problema para la Policia Política cuando surgió una serie de organizaciones neo-marxistas y pekinesas, a partir de 1961. Varios golpes terroristas se desbarataron solo por inexperiencia de sus ejecutores, sin que la P.P. tuviera la menor noticia de ellos, hasta el día de su realización. Sus autores eran elementos jóvenes, sin experiencia política anterior, que no estaban fichados por la P.P. Su desconcierto ante ellos, duró poco: ya están—en su mayoría—infiltrados por la policia secreta." "Los guatones de la P.P.," pp. 13-14.

120. Vitale, *Y Despues?* pp. 16-19. Grayson, "The Frei Administration," pp. 54-56. Normal Gall, "The Chileans Have Elected a Revolution," *New York Times Magazine*, November 1, 1970, p. 27.

121. *El Mercurio*, 18 septiembre 1959, p. 21. "Frases y Personajes," *Ercilla*, XXVI (20 enero 1960), 8.

122. "En el Congreso Pleno: 22 Minutos Fuera de Programa," *Ercilla*, XXVII (24 mayo 1961), 16-18.

On Aug. 27, 1963, the minister of justice and a senator engaged in a fist fight, as did two other senators. In September 1964, two Radicals were exchanging blows in the senate, while a month later a Christian Democratic Deputy and two Radicals altercated in the chamber of deputies. In March 1966, a Socialist and a Christian Democratic Deputy fought, and in December of the same year there was a mass fist fight between FRAP and Christian Democratic members of the same house. Olavarria, *Alessandri*, III, 346-47, IV, 308, 342-44. *Ercilla*, XXX (28 octubre 1964), 1, 15-16. *Desfile*, I (24 marzo 1966), 4. *El Siglo*, 30 diciembre 1966, p. 3.

123. Goldenberg, p. 63. Petras, "After the Election," p. 382. Similarly, after the FRAP Curico victory in March 1964, there was a capital flight and a stock market break. Veliz, "Chile," p. 229.

124. Gall, "The Chileans,: p. 27.

125. Gil, p. viii.

Chapter 4: Revolutionary Cuba Seeks to
Inspire Chileans to Defend the Cuban Revolution and to Struggle for "National Liberation"

1. *El Mercurio*, 28 julio 1960, p. 29, 6 agosto, p. 29.
2. Mendoza, *Comunismo en 1961*, p. 22.
3. U.S., Congress, House, Committee on Foreign Affairs, *Castro-Communist Subversion in the Western Hemisphere, Hearings*, before the Sub-committee on Inter-American Affairs of the Committee on Foreign Affairs, House of Representatives, 88th Cong., 1st sess., 1963, p. 86.
4. This estimate is based upon the Cuban Revolutionary Council figure which is probably the maximum for any five month period. It is likely that after the missile crisis and the refusal of Mexico in 1963 to issue re-entry permits, that the flow was reduced substantially as compared with the 1959-1962 period. During 1963, too, flights from Cuba were terminated from two key entry points; Curacao and Kingston.
5. Quoted from *The Sunday Times* (U.K.), April 19, 1964, in "Asi Nos Ven," *Ercilla*, XXX (17 junio 1964), p. 4.
6. For chapters four and six through eight, the following materials were systematically reviewed: *El Mercurio* (1959-1960); *Ercilla* (1958-1965); *Principios* (1959-1965); *Arauco* (1959-1965); *Politica y Espíritu* (1958-1965); *Mensaje* (1958-1965); *Cuba Socialista* (1961-1965); *New Times* (1959-1965); *Hispanic American Report* (1958-1964); Chile, Senado, *Diario* (1959-1960); Chile, Camara de Diputalos, *Boletín* (May 1963-January 1964); all party and convention or congress reports, declarations and propaganda on file in the Chilean Library of Congress and the National Library; various other books, articles, public opinion surveys and several interviews.
7. Instituto Popular de Chile, *Fidel Castro, Osvaldo Dórticos, Ché Guevara, Carlos R. Rodriguez Hablan para el Instituto Popular de Chile* (Santiago: Instituto Popular de Chile, 1962).
8. Partido Communista de Chile, *Hacia la Conquista de un Gobierno Popular: Documentos del XII Congreso Nacional* (Santiago: Imp. Horizonte, 1962), p. 235.
9. The Chileans included Hernan San Martin and the eminent university researcher and professor, Alejandro Lipschutz. José Solis, "Décimo Congreso Médico y Estomatológico Nacional," *Cuba* (Habana), Año II, No. 11 (1963), pp. 75, 79-80.
10. *Hispanic American Report*, XVI (May 1963), 287. Anibal Bascunan, Dean of the University of Chile's School of Law had also been a visitor. Chile, Senado, *Diario*, CCXCII, ses. 8 (20 junio 1963), p. 357.
11. Lucy Lortsch, *Dos Chilenas en La Habana* (Santiago: ABC Plastigraf Imp., 1963), pp. 11-32.
12. *El Mercurio*, 8 marzo 1959, p. 29. "Voz que Resiste," *Ercilla*, XXVII (12 abril 1961), p. 1. "Matta en La Habana," *Cuba* (Habana), III (mayo 1964), 52-53.
13. These poems, although "bitterly criticizing the United States, also stressed the need for understanding and harmony among the peoples of the hemisphere." *El Mercurio*, 11 diciembre 1960, p. 55.
14. Partido Comunista de Chile, *Pablo Neruda Contesta a Los Obispos*, Conferencia pronunciada por el poeta Pablo Neruda, miembro del CC del Partido Comunista, el 12 de octubre, en el Teatro Caupolican de Santiago (Santiago: Imp. Horizonte, 1962), pp. 13-14.
15. Buenos Aires, Edit. Goyanarte, 1962.
16. Chile, Senado, *Diario*, CCXIV, ses. 11 (15 julio 1964), p. 1095.
17. Both Frei and Allende had endorsed the invitation. *El Mercurio*, 13 febrero 1959, p. 7, 14 febrero, p. 17. *Ercilla*, 18 febrero, p. 8.
18. *La Libertad*, 4 agosto 1959, pp. 8-9. "Cómo vió el PDC la Revolución Cubana," *Vistazo*, VIII (11 agosto 1959), 9. *Ercilla*, XXV (5 agosto 1959), 18.
19. Mendoza, *Comunismo en 1961*, p. 14.
20. Hurtado had allegedly written "La Cortina de Caña" after his return, but the PDC refused to allow him to publish it. *Desfile*, 2 junio 1966, p. 9. "Goodwin: intérprete entre JAR y Kennedy," *Ercilla*, XXVIII (21 febrero 1962), 8. Julio Silva Solar, "Reflexiones sobre La Revolución," *Política y Espíritu*, XVIII (enero-mayo 1964), 18. As late as January

1966, delegations of Christian Democratic deputies were still being invited and going to Havana. Guido Castilla, Santiago Gajardo, Pedro Videla and Alberto Jaramillo were there during that month with a Socialist, Joel Marambio. "Retiro de los Parlamentarios de Cuba y sus Ecos," *Desfile*, I (24 febrero 1966), 4-5.

21. The funds were allegedly given to individuals, and not parties. In addition to Christian Democrats, money was given to members of other centrist and leftist parties. As an indication of amounts, Patricio Hurtado—after his last trip in 1966 or 1967—was known to have sold $30,000 on the Santiago black market upon his return. Hurtado had been expelled from the PDC in early 1966. Information is based on an interview with Rafael Espinosa, a Cuban refugee, on May 5, 1967. Espinosa and four others were sent to Chile in the autumn of 1961 by the CIA. They were subsidized by that organization until the March 1965 congressional elections.

Another congressman who has been identified as a recipient of such funds, was the late Salomon Corbalan. As a senator and secretary general of the Socialist Party, he has been alleged to have used the money for electoral rather than insurrectional purposes. "Pasos Publicos y Privados del Complot," pp. 15-16.

22. Among the deputies were Rolando Schmauk, Mario Saez, Joaquin Morales, Samuel Fuentes and Mario Videla. One or two may have been Liberals. *El Mercurio*, 15 marzo 1959, p. 27, 17 mayo, p. 29.

23. *La Libertad*, 1 agosto 1959, p. 7.

24. Many of these were members of the party's *Juventud*. Their role will be discussed subsequently in connection with the First Latin American Congress of Youth which was held in Havana during July 1960.

25. Other prominent Communists included Mario Zamorano, the leader of their Juventud, and Olga Poblete, who heads the Chilean Peace Movement. Mendoza, *Comunismo en 1961*, p. 23. Zamorano is not identified in this source.

26. *Adios al Cañaveral*, p. 74.

27. Samuel Mendoza, *Comunismo en 1961*, p. 23. *El Mercurio*, 6 septiembre 1959, p. 11. "Anécdotas del 26 de Julio," *Vistazo*, VII (4 agosto 1959), 8. Oscar Waiss, *Socialismo sin Gerentes* (Santiago: Imp. 'Victoria,' 1961). Chile, Senado, *Diario*, CCXCII, ses. 49 (4 septiembre 1963), pp. 3522-25. Interviews with Jaime Ahumada on January 1, 1967, and with Oscar Naranjo on March 26, 1967. Ahumada denied that the Socialist Party ever received any Cuban funds for the purchase of arms. Ampuero is not identified in these sources.

28. *El Mercurio*, 15 agosto 1960, p. 25. Halperin, p. 67. Samuel Mendoza, *Comunismo en 1961*, p. 23. There were several peasant union leaders among the fifteen reported in the *Mercurio* item. The group was taken on a Cuban plane which had returned eighteen Chileans from the *26 de Julio* celebrations and possibly the First Latin American Youth Congress.

29. *El Mercurio*, 7 septiembre 1960, p. 3.

30. *El Mercurio*, 13 junio 1960, p. 25, and 3 agosto, p. 15. It has been alleged that some members of the PDC Youth did attend, as individuals. Samuel Mendoza, "La Actividad del Comunismo en Chile durante 1960," *Estudio sobre el Comunismo*, IX (enero-marzo de 1961), 83-84.

31. But it has been claimed that there were 200 Chilean delegates, and that the expenses of a majority of them were paid for by Cuba or the World Federation of Democratic Youth (WFDY). Chilean organizations represented there included: Partido Radical Juventud; Partido Socialista Juventud; Partido Comunista Juventud; Partido Democrático y Popular Juventud; Vanguardia Nacional del Pueblo Juventud; CUT Depto. Juvenil; and various unions. Mendoza, "Comunismo durante 1960," pp. 83-84.

32. *El Mercurio*, 6 septiembre 1960, p. 3.

33. U.S., *Castro-Communist Subversion*, pp. 289-90. "The CUT-CTC Pact provided for material and moral assistance in the event of external or internal aggression against the democratic institutions or popular interests of either country." *El Mercurio*, 5 agosto 1960, p. 25.

34. U.S., *Castro-Communist Subversion*, pp. 255-56.

35. Ibid., p. 273.

36. "It is an obvious fact that . . . a series of schools and centers of training . . . were organized, in which instruction is being given not only to Cubans but to many other Latin Americans for carrying on subversive activities in various countries of the hemisphere.

Among the many training centers that now function in Cuba, mention may be made of the following:

Blas Roca School, in Los Pinos, Havana Province.

Marcelo Salado School, in the Luyano section of Havana.

El Cortijo School, in Pinar del Rio Province, especially for military personnel.

La Cabana Fort, in Havana, especially for young people.

Minas Rio Frio School, for training guerrillas.

San Lorenzo School, in the Sierra Maestra, Oriente Province, for training guerrillas.

Ciudad Libertad School, in Marianao, Havana Province, under Russian instructors.

Boca Chica School, in Tarara, Havana Province, Director General Alberto Bayo.

Julio Antonia Mella School, in Mar Bella, Havana Province for training and instructing leaders of the Confederacion de Trabajadores de Cuba Revolucionaria (CTCR) (Federation of Workers of Revolutionary Cuba).

A large number of Latin Americans attend these training centers, where they receive instruction not only in Marxist-Leninist theory, but also in propaganda techniques, the use of arms and explosives, sabotage, guerrilla warfare, and so on." Ibid., p. 272.

37. Ibid., p. 151.

38. Claudio Veliz, "The New Cuban Industrial Policy," *World Today*, XIX (September 1963), 373.

39. *Memorias de un Capitán Rebelde* (Santiago: Edit. del Pacífico, 1964).

40. Santiago, Edit. del Pacífico, pp. 29, 33. There were few other direct references to the Cuban Revolution in the 112-page work. Before leaving Chile, Chonchol had been president of the Society of Agrarian Economists and an official in CORFO. *El Mercurio*, 8 septiembre 1959, p. 21.

41. Santiago, Talls. Grafs. de E.H.S. Ltda., 1965.

42. "What is Castroism's Appeal," *New Republic*, CXLVIII (January 12, 1963), 15. It would, however, probably not be justified to conclude that a majority of the Chilean technicians became "embittered" by their experience.

43. After returning from a visit with other journalists, Fernando Murillo, news editor of the Christian Democratic daily *La Libertad*, reflected upon his experiences at the PDC headquarters. He also distributed or exhibited photographs, documents and pamphlets which had been obtained while in Cuba. *El Mercurio*, 5 febrero 1959, p. 15. Several weeks later, a delegation of seven deputies and seven journalists returned after having attended Cuba's national fiesta. *El Mercurio*, 27 febrero 1959, p. 20. Jorge Cash, the director of *La Libertad*, and Mario Carneyro, the Director of the pro-Radical daily *La Tercera*, were invited to the 26 de Julio celebrations during 1959, as was an editor of *La Tercera*, María Eugenia Oyarzún. "Anécdotas del 26 de Julio," p. 8. *La Tercera*, 28 julio 1959, p. 16, 31 julio, p. 16, 1 agosto, pp. 10-11, 10 agosto, p. 1. In January 1960, the Chilean Journalists' Circle received a communication from Cuba's National College of Journalists requesting that good coverage be given to the celebration of the 107th anniversary of Marti's birth. *El Mercurio* 27 enero 1960, p. 11.

One of the reporters who visited Cuba during the first months of the Revolution wrote a book describing the turbulent atmosphere at that time. He emphasized the heroism of the rebels and the aspiration of many for political liberties and social reforms. The author questioned "whether the politician or the guerrilla" in Fidel would ultimately triumph. The book was published by the Christian Democrats. Rafael Otero Echevarría, *Reportaje a una revolución* (Santiago: Edit. del Pacífico, 1959). While in Cuba, Otero represented *Ercilla, El Debate*, and Radio (station) Presidente Balmaceda.

During 1963, a Communist lawyer and journalist for *El Siglo* spent several months in Cuba and returned to publish a very favorable account of the Revolution. Marcos Portnoy, *Testimonio sobre Cuba*, (Santiago: Ediciones del Litoral, 1964). Within a year or so of his return, Portnoy had resigned from the party and affiliated with groups "further to the Left."

44. *El Mercurio*, 23 julio 1960, p. 19, 1 agosto, p. 25. *El Siglo*, 27 octubre 1962, p. 4. *Las Noticias de Ultima Hora*, 15 agosto 1964, p. 5. "En Chile," *Arauco*, IV (julio 1963), 47. *Hispanic American Report*, XVI (September 1963), 713. Mendoza, "Comunismo durante 1960," p. 81. Mendoza, *Comunismo en 1961*, p. 19. Movimiento de Solidaridad y Defensa de la Revolución Cubana, *!Toda América contra el Imperialismo Yanqui!* (Santiago: Imp. Horizonte, 1964).

45. Upon its establishment in December 1959, Matilde Ladrón de Guevara was appointed as its president. The four vice-presidents were Clotário Blest, Jorge MacGinty Dinator, Clodomiro Almeyda Arroyo and Rudecindo Ortega Masson. *El Mercurio*, 2 diciembre 1959, p. 15, and 15 diciembre, p. 19. Of these, only Almeyda—the Socialist editor of *Las Noticias de Ultima Hora*—was a Marxist. After several months, Ladrón was replaced by Alberto Graf Marín. In August 1960, new officers were appointed. Alberto Balta Cortes became president, and the vice-presidencies went to Pablo Neruda and Baltazar Castro Palma. *El Mercurio*, 18 agosto 1960, p. 17. Baltra was a left-wing but non-Marxist Radical, and Castro, though not a Marxist, collaborated with FRAP and would be supported in the 1961 congressional elections by the Communists. Both Baltra and Castro had been Ministers of State—the former under González Videla during the purge of the Communists, and the latter under Ibáñez Campos. Castro had been expelled from the Socialist Party because of his refusal to resign from the Ibáñez cabinet when the Socialists withdrew their support in 1954. Ten years later, Castro withdrew his personalistic Vanguardia Nacional del Pueblo from the Popular Action Front when the Socialists successfully opposed his election as president of FRAP during the final months of the Frei-Allende campaign.

46. *El Mercurio*, 2 diciembre 1959, p. 15. Cf., U.S., *Castro-Communist Subversion*, pp. 111-12. With regard to films, the House Subcommittee *Hearings* report that in Latin America:

"Cuban films have been very limited in number and shown principally by and through the binational centers and Communist-influenced labor and student groups. Films have been produced on Cuban accomplishments in the fields of housing and child care.

A viciously anti-U.S. film on the Bay of Pigs invasion, profuse with corpses of women and children, was probably the most successful anti-U.S. film produced in Cuba. However, its showings have been restricted almost entirely to private or clandestine meetings." Ibid., p. 112.

47. See, for example, *El Mercurio*, 19 mayo 1960, p. 19, and 20 mayo, p. 21.

48. *Las Noticias de Ultima Hora*, 19 abril 1961, p. 16.

49. Personal impressions of the writer who attended several institute functions during early 1967.

50. Samuel Mendoza, *Comunismo en 1961*, p. 19. Mendoza reports that the entire leadership of the Instituto Popular were either members of or sympathizers with the Socialist or Communist parties.

51. Marcos Pinares, "Una chilena ve Cuba," *Cuba*, (Habana), III (enero 1964), 67.

52. Virtually all of the items published by the Communists were printed after Fidel Castro's "I am a Marxist-Leninist and will be one until my dying day" speech. *Fidel Denuncia Otra Invasión* (Santiago: Imp. Horizonte, 1962). *Segunda Declaración de La Habana: La Voz de Cuba*, (Santiago: Imp. Horizonte, 1962). *Cuba-URSS: Una Firme Amistad en Defensa de la Paz*, Declaración conjunta Cubano-Soviética firmada el 23 de Mayo de 1963 en Moscú (Santiago: Imp. Horizonte, 1963). Carlos Rafael Rodríguez, *Cuatro Años de Reforma Agraria en Cuba* (Santiago: Imp. Horizonte, 1963). Fidel Castro, *La Historia me absolverá* (Santiago: Imp. Horizonte, 1964). Alejandro Lipschutz, *Guerra y Paz y Otros Temas Candentes* (Santiago: Edit. Austral, 1964), pp. 93-143.

Even before the 1959 victory, the Socialists were publishing pro-Castro material. *Fidel Castro: Líder y Guerrillero* (Santiago: Prensa Latinoamericana, 1958). José A. Tabares del Real, *La Revolución Cubana: Ensayo de Interpretación*, Prólogo por Salvador Allende (Santiago: Prensa Latinoamericana, 1960). Salvador Allende G., *Cuba, Un Camino* (Santiago: Prensa Latinoamericana, 1960). Alejandro Chelén Rojas, *La Revolución Cubana y sus Proyecciones en América Latina* (Santiago: Prensa Latinoamericana, 1960).

The Christian Democrats published one such item. Osvaldo Dórticos, *Carta del Presidente de Cuba a los Estudiantes Chilenos* (Santiago: Edit. del Pacífico, 1960).

A number of favorable accounts of the Revolution which were published in other countries also probably were distributed by Prensa Latinoamericana and other bookstores. Armando Gimenez, *Sierra Maestra* (Buenos Aires, 1959). Fidel Castro, *La Revolución Cubana* (Buenos Aires: Edit. Palestra, 1960). Alfredo Varela, *Cuba con toda la Barba* (Buenos Aires: Edit. Esfera, 1960). C. Wright Mills, *Escucha, Yanqui* (México: Fondo de Cultura Económica, 1961). Sol Arguedas, *Cuba no es una isla* (México: Ediciones Era, 1961). Waldo Frank, *Cuba, Isla Profética* (Buenos Aires: Edit. Losada, 1961). Alfredo L.

Palacios, *Una Revolución Auténtica: La Reforma Agraria en Cuba* (Buenos Aires: Edit. Palestra, 1961). Enrique González Pedraro, *El Gran Viraje* (México: Ediciones Era, 1961), pp. 161-213. Jean Paul Sartre, *Huracán sobre el Azúcar* (Buenos Aires: Compañía Argentina de Editores, 1962). Rodney Arismendi, *Problemas de una Revolución Continental* (Montevideo: Ediciones Pueblos Unidos, 1962).

53. "Cuba: Una Experiencia Heroica," *Cuadernos de Información Política* (Santiago: Ediciones Socialismo, No. 3 Imp. Lira, 1960). This was published by a neo-Trotskyist group within the Socialist Party.

Fidel Castro, *La Revolución Cubana contra el Sectarismo*, Comentarios de Luis Vitale (Santiago: Edit. POR, 1962). Castro, *El Partido Unido*. Ernesto 'Ché' Guevara, *Contra el Burocratismo* (Santiago: Espártaco Editores, 1963).

54. *El Mercurio*, 16 febrero 1959, p. 17, 16 diciembre, p. 3. Halperin, p. 64. Clark, pp. 225-26.

55. At the official rate of exchange, short wave transistors were selling at $278.00 (U.S.) cash. Monthly payments were $17.50. *El Mercurio*, 4 noviembre 1959, p. 20. Judging from 1966-1967 prices, it is probable that non-transistor models were almost as expensive. Testifying before a congressional appropriations subcommittee in April 1963, the USIA assistant director for Latin America reported that "(w)e do not feel there is a tremendous listening audience" for Cuban shortwave transmissions. U.S., Congress, House, Committee on Appropriations, *Departments of State, Justice, and Commerce, the Judiciary, and Related Agencies Appropriations for 1964, Hearings*, before a subcommittee of the Committee on Appropriations, House of Representatives, 88th Cong., 1st sess., 1963, p. 185.

56. U.S., *Castro-Communist Subversion*, pp. 7, 108-09.

57. In early 1965, Radio Havana was broadcasting in Spanish to Spain and Latin America a total of 144¼ hours per week. U.S., Congress, House, Committee on Appropriations, *Departments of State, Justice and Commerce, the Judiciary and Related Agencies Appropriations for 1966, Hearings*, before a subcommittee of the Committee on Appropriations, House of Representatives, 89th Cong., 1st sess., 1965, p. 462.

58. *New York Times*, March 30, 1966, p. 10.

59. In 1958, short wave broadcasts in Spanish, Portuguese and French to Latin America from all of the Communist nations totaled 104 hours per week. During 1960, Chinese broadcasts rose from 21 to 31 hours weekly, while Soviet transmissions increased from 49 to 56 hours. In the same year, the Communist nations as a whole broadcast 167 hours per week, as compared to 138 hours in 1959. While Soviet transmissions "almost doubled" from 63 hours in 1961 to 120 in 1962, the Chinese increased theirs during the same period to 38½ hours per week. By 1963, all Communist nations taken together were transmitting 415 hours per week. "Actividades de Propaganda Comunista en América Latina en 1958," *Estudios sobre el Comunismo* VII: 26 (Octubre-Diciembre de 1959), p. 125. U.S., Congress, House, Committee on Appropriations, *Departments of State and Justice, the Judiciary and Related Agencies Appropriations for 1962, Hearings*, before a subcommittee of the Committee on Appropriations, House of Representatives, 87th Cong., 1st sess., 1961, p. 26. U.S., *Castro-Communist Subversion*, pp. 108-09.

"It is interesting to note that the Communists have been singularly unsuccessful in placing radio material on local medium wave stations in Latin America and they do little or no television placement. Their prime medium is shortwave broadcasting." U.S., *Castro-Communist Subversion*, p. 109.

"A large portion of the increased communist propaganda aimed at Latin America apparently is not getting through. The broadcasts are being drowned by a stronger Western propaganda transmittor aimed at Russia." *New York Times*, April 20, 1962, p. 3.

60. *El Mercurio*, 7 noviembre 1959, p. 11. Chile, Cámara de Diputados, *Boletín*, ses. 52 (11 septiembre 1963), pp. 4533-35.

61. For both charges and counter-charges regarding the congress, see *El Mercurio*, 9 octubre 1959, p. 3., 16 octubre, p. 3, 20 octubre, p. 15, 21 octubre, p. 3, 22 noviembre, p. 9; and Samuel Mendoza, "El Comunismo en tres congresos realizados en Chile," *Estudios sobre el Comunismo*, VIII (abril-junio de 1960), 79.

62. Mendoza, "Comunismo en tres congresos," p. 79. *El Mercurio*, 16 octubre 1959, p. 15, 18 octubre, p. 11, 21 octubre, p. 3, 27 octubre, p. 21, 19 noviembre, p. 17, 20 noviembre, p. 19, 23 noviembre, p. 23.

63. Enrique Cid, "Ruidos, Rivalidades y Amonestaciones cuando las Faldas Hablan," *Ercilla*, XXV (25 noviembre 1959), 16.

64. *El Mercurio*, 22 noviembre 1959, pp. 22, 35. *Hispanic American Report*, XII (January 1960), 623.

65. Among both non-Marxist and Marxist-led organizations which accepted invitations to attend were the: Juventud Radical; Juventud del Partido Democrático y Nacional (PADENA); Unión de Federaciones Universitarias; Federación de Educadores de Chile; Federación de Estudiantes Comerciales; Juventud Comunista; Depto. Juvenil de CUT; Federación de Estudiantes Secundarios; Federación de Estudiantes Normalistas; Federación Técnica Industrial; Federación de Estudiantes Vespertinos y Nocturnos; Unión de Profesores; Federación Bancaria; Comité de la Joven Chilena; Unión de Mujeres; et al. Samuel Mendoza, "La Reunión del Comité Ejecutivo de la Federación Mundial de la Juventud Democrática," *Estudios sobre el Comunismo*, IX (julio-septiembre de 1961), 71-92.

66. Federación Mundial de Juventud Democrática, *Documentos y Resoluciones del Comité Ejecutivo de la F.M.J.D. (Federación Mundial de Juventud Democrática)*, 16-20 abril 1961, Santiago de Chile (Santiago: Imp. Horizonte, 1961), pp. 72-74.

67. On this event, see: U.S., *Castro-Communist Subversion*, pp. 193-94; and Harold Lavine, "Mexico: The Unfilled Hall," *Newsweek*, March 20, 1961, pp. 57-58.

68. Other prominent Communists included Alfredo de Amesti and Olga Urtúvia. The delegation from Chile included such non-Communists as: Délia Barahona, José Venurelli, Hernán San Martín, Salvador Campos, Hernán Peralta and his wife. Samuel Mendoza, *Comunismo en 1961*, p. 19. Cf., Luis Figueroa, "La Conferencia Lationamericana por la Soberanía Nacional, la Emancipación y la Paz," *Principios*, No. 80 (Abril de 1961), pp. 24-29.

69. Chile, Senado, *Diario*, CCLXXXVII ses. 43 (2 mayo 1961), pp. 2380-83.

70. They were Luís Herrera Fuenzalida and Luís Díaz Jiménez from MADECO, Nelson Sigisfredo Vilchez from the Unión de Obreros Ferroviarios (Santiago), Jorge Astudillo Briones, Cristal Yungay and Jorge Rojas Pino from the Empleados de la ETCE, and Octávio González from the CUT Provincial Committee of Santiago. Laurencio Angél Aparicio, *El Congreso de las Focas Amaestradas y los Lacayos Parlantes de Moscú en Rio de Janéiro* (Santiago: Edit. del Pacífico, 1963), pp. 16-17.

71. Jaime Ahumada, "Hacia el Segundo Congreso Latinoamericano de Juventudes," *Arauco*, IV (enero 1963), 43.

72. Among the Chilean members of the commission were three Communists: Rosendo Rojas, Augusto González and Isabel Rodríguez. Socialists and other non-Communists included: Alejandro Chelén, Ricardo Iturríaga, Mireya Balladares and N. Mellado. Aparicio, *Congreso*, p. 19.

73. Chilean delegates with plenary powers were designees of the following organizations: Federación Nacional de Trabajadores Textiles y del Vestuario, Federación Industrial Ferroviaria de Chile, Federación Nacional del Metal, Federación Nacional Minera, Confederación Nacional de Trabajadores del Cobre, Federación Nacional de Suplementeros de Chile, Depto. Juvenil de CUT, Unión de Obreros Municipales de Chile, Depto. Juvenil de Deporte y Cultura de la FIEMC, Federación Obrera Nacional del Cuero y Calzado, Federación Nacional de Panificadores de Chile, Federación Nacional de Trabajadores de la Salud, Federación Nacional Campesina e Indígena de Chile, Comité Central de Juventudes Comunistas, Juventud Socialista de Chile, Comité Regional de la Juventud Socialista de Valparaíso, Partido Democrático Nacional (PADENA), Alianza Nacional de Trabajadores, Federación de Estudiantes Normalistas de Chile, Federación de Estudiantes Pre-Universitarios de la Universidad Técnica del Estado, Federación de Estudiantes de la Univ. Técnica del Estado, Fed. de Estuds. Industriales de Chile, and the Federación de Estuds. de Concepción.

Chile's twenty-two plenary delegates constituted the largest such group. Brazil and Perú each sent about fifteen, Cuba thirteen, and other countries less.

The presidium of the congress was composed of the following: Sergio Barría Pérez (Juv. Socialista de Chile), Mario Zamorano (Juvs. Comunistas de Chile), Hernán del Canto Riquelme (CUT), Omar Córdova Muñoz (CUT), Miguel Martín (Unión de Jovenes Comunistas de Cuba), Joaquín Mas Martínez (Federación de Estudiantes Universitarios de Cuba), and fourteen others from Venezuela, Uruguay, Bolivia, Brazil, Colombia, Panama, Argentina, México and Puerto Rico.

There were also ninety fraternal delegates. Three were Cuban and fifty-nine were

Chilean. Among the Chileans were members of the following organizations: Juventud Democrática Nacional de Valparaíso, Partido Democrático Nacional, PADENA de Cauquenes, Alianza Nacional de Trabajadores. Among the delegate-observers were representatives of Juventud Radical and organizations in the Soviet Union, German Democratic Republic, Poland, Democratic Republic of Vietnam, Czechoslovakia, the U.S., Zanzibar and Canada. Congreso Latinoamericano de Juventud, *Acuerdos y Resoluciones del II CLAJ (Congreso Latinoamericano de Juventud)*, celebrado en Santiago de Chile del 9 al 13 de marzo de 1964 (Santiago: Imp. Horizonte, 1964), pp. 2-8.

74. Ibid., pp. 15, 43.

75. Ibid., pp. 11-12, 15-16, 19, 25, 27, 31-32, 35, 40, 43-44, 57.

76. *El Mercurio*, 23 mayo 1960, p. 1, 26 mayo, p. 33. This offer was conveyed personally to the Chilean Foreign Minister by Cuba's Minister of Agriculture who made a special trip from Buenos Aires to Santiago for the purpose. *El Mercurio*, 27 mayo 1960, p. 13.

77. *El Mercurio*, 3 julio 1960, p. 37.

78. *El Mercurio*, 1 junio 1960, p. 1, 5 septiembre, p. 23.

79. The vessel reportedly contained enough supplies to fill 110 railroad cars. *El Mercurio*, 27 mayo 1960, p. 13, 30 mayo, p. 17, and 27 junio, p. 28. *Ercilla*, XXVI (29 junio 1960), 32. Chile, Senado, *Diario*, CCLXXXVI, ses. 11 (28 junio 1960), p. 588.

Five years later, when in "August 1965, a hurricane and torrential rains . . . swept across Chile, Castro sent a shipload of sugar to the devastated area." George W. Grayson, Jr., "Significance of the Frei Administration for Latin America," *Orbis*, IX (Fall 1965), 775.

80. *El Mercurio*, 8 agosto 1960, p. 30.

81. *El Mercurio*, 6 agosto, p. 41.

82. "Chilean officials, looking through a ton and a half of earthquake-relief shipments flown in by a Cuban plane, discovered that it was all propaganda and impounded the lot." "Eight distinct types of propaganda leaflets printed in Russia, Communist China, Cuba, and Mexico were found among packages sent to aid quake victims. . . . Upon returning from a tour of the provinces of Valdivia and Osorno, Luis Valdes Larrain, vice-chairman of the Conservative Party, accused the Communists of exploiting Chilean hunger and misery for propaganda purposes." "Revolution for Export," *Time*, August 22, 1960, p. 31. *Hispanic American Report*, XIII (October 1960), 554.

83. Allende and Communist leader César Godoy rejoined that not only were the claims about propaganda highly distorted or false, but that little attention had been given to the Cuban aid in the government newspaper *La Nación* and other mass media. They also charged that the government had failed to thank Cuba. To this, the foreign ministry retorted that it had expressed its appreciation for "the generous offer of the brother country" of 10,000 additional tons, but claimed that no reply had been received regarding further shipments from Cuba. *El Mercurio*, 11 junio 1960, p. 21, 30 septiembre, p. 19, 21 octubre, p. 23. Chile, Senado, *Diario*, CCLXXXVI, ses. 24 (10 agosto 1960), p. 1516, ses. 41 (13 septiembre 1960), p. 2944, and CCLXXXVII, ses. 37 (18 abril 1961), pp. 2104ff. Cesar Godoy, *Terremoto y Miseria* (Santiago: Imp. Lira 363, 1960), p. 15.

84. *El Mercurio*, 17 abril 1960, p. 25. Hernández Parker, "La Semana Política," *Ercilla*, XXV (7 octubre 1959), 8, (9 diciembre), p. 9. Mendoza, *Comunismo en 1961*, pp. 17, 23. Sergio Fernández L., *Y el Comunismo sique su marcha . . .* (Santiago: Edit. del Pregón, 1962), pp. 26, 55-57. Partido Comunista, *XII Congreso*, pp. 321-24.

85. A lunch was arranged at the home of PDC leader Tomás Reyes for the *barbudos*. José Musalem and Alfredo Lorca, two Christian Democratic leaders who had recently been in Cuba where they had invited Castro to visit Chile, were also present. *Ercilla*, XXV (11 marzo 1959), 16-19. *El Mercurio*, 9 marzo 1959, p. 19, 13 marzo, pp. 19, 21.

86. On the question of sanctioning Santo Domingo, Raúl Roa stated that "el Gobierno de Cuba es enteramente contrario a toda intervención de un Estado en otro. ¿Cómo no lo vamos a ser, si hemos vivido intervenidos?

Lo que entraña violación flagrante e intervención son las transmisiones de una emisora oficial. 'La Voz Dominicana', con un programa que se identifica con la mención 'Para Cuba que Sufre'. Es el adiestramiento y la organización de bandas armadas organizadas por un gobierno que públicamente lo admite y hasta las bautiza con el nombre de 'Legion Extranjera' reclutando mercenarios europeos y asiáticos. La contrarrevolución recientemente descubierta en Cuba fue urdida, organizada y financiada en Cuidad Trujillo." "La

Conferencia al Revés y al Derecho," *Ercilla*, XXV (19 agosto 1959), 18. Cf., *El Mercurio*, 5 agosto 1959, pp. 1, 16.

87. Upon his return to Havana, Hart denied charges by Chilean Rightists that he had intervened in Chilean politics. Hart stated that he had been speaking of Cuba's problems, many of which were common to other American countries. *El Mercurio*, 27 agosto, p. 29, 1 septiembre, p. 19.

88. The following Chileans were reported to have attended this meeting: Salvador Allende, Salomón Corbalán (Secretary General of the Socialist Party), Luis Corvalán (Secretary General of the Communist Party), Jorge Costa Canales (President of the Partido Democrático y Popular), Pedro Foncea A. (President of the Partido del Pueblo), Juan Fuentealba (President of the Partido Radical Doctrinario), Mamerto Figueroa (President of the Alianza Nacional de Trabajadores), Osvaldo Pucci (a national leader of the Partido del Trabajo), and Iván Araneda (President of the Partido Intransigencia Radical Antimperialista de Chile). Most of these organizations were affiliated with the FRAP, and with the exception of the first two they had very small followings. Representatives of foreign parties ranged from COPEI of Venezuela to Communists. *El Mercurio*, 23 agosto 1959, p. 33.

89. *El Mercurio*, 17 agosto 1959, p. 23.

90. *El Mercurio*, 20 agosto 1959, pp. 1, 12, 13.

91. *El Mercurio*, 20 agosto 1959, p. 23, 23 agosto, p. 11. *Hispanic American Report*, XII (October 1959), 452.

92. The Conservative youth refused to send a delegation, while the Congress for Cultural Freedom youth were expelled after they demanded to know who was financing and inspiring the projected congress. Then the Liberal youth withdrew. Before the congress was held, the FECH and COPEI *Juventud* withdrew. *El Mercurio*, 21 noviembre 1959, p. 17, 26 noviembre, p. 21, 4 diciembre, p. 3, 6 diciembre, p. 35. Ahumada, "Hacia," pp. 41-42.

93. *New York Times*, August 23, 1959, p. 32.

94. *El Mercurio*, 1 noviembre 1959, p. 37, 14 diciembre, p. 26.

95. *El Mercurio*, 5 marzo 1959, p. 27.

96. Rafael Espinosa, Interview, Santiago, May 5, 1967.

97. Ladrón de Guevara, pp. 37, 179-83.

98. Gomucio was a Christian Democratic leader, and Rojas was a prominent writer who had headed Independents for Allende in 1958. By 1967, Rojas would be President of the Instituto Chileno Cubano de Cultura, and Gomucio, a senator, was elected to the presidency of the PDC in July 1967. Details concerning the "Traveling Letter" and the names of signatories from other Latin American nations will be found in "Viajes Chilenos en Secreto Apoyan a Fidel," *Ercilla*, XXVI (13 abril 1960), 9.

99. *Hispanic American Report*, XIII (September 1960), 477.

100. "La Semana Política," *Ercilla*, XXVII (7 julio 1961), 9.

101. Dubois, p. 11.

102. *Hispanic American Report*, XIV (October 1961), 731.

103. *La Nación*, 22 octubre 1962, p. 2, 24 octubre, p. 2. *New York Times*, October 20, 1962, p. 3. U.S., *Castro-Communist Subversion*, p. 7. *Hispanic American Report*, (December 1962), 949-50.

104. *Hispanic American Report*, XVI (May 1963), 288.

105. Chile, Senado, *Diario*, CCXIV, ses. 16 (4 agosto 1964), pp. 1735-37.

106. "Vacaciones Apolíticas," *Ercilla*, XXVI (10 agosto 1960), 3.

107. This fourteen-page pamphlet contained charges "against the United States for permitting 'fugitives from revolutionary justice' to attack Cuba, conspire against the government, and attempt to re-establish the former 'bloody reign of terror.' " *Hispanic American Report*, XII (January 1960), 600.

108. Habana, Imprenta del Ministerio de Relaciones Exteriores de la República de Cuba, 1960. Also published by Edit. del Pacífico.

109. Boletín Especial de la Embajada de Cuba, Santiago, Chile, junio 1961 (Santiago: Prensa Latinoamericana, 1961).

Chapter 5. Aspects of Chilean-U.S. Relations Which May Have Diminished the Potential Appeal of the Cuban Revolution in Chile

1. On these matters see Campos, pp. 107, 153, 192.
2. Pike, *Chile and United States*, pp. 66-85, 123-69. Halperin, *Nationalism*, p. 46. Lieuwen, *Arms and Politics*, pp. 194-95.
3. "Impuesto Norteamericano Pone el Cobre al Rojo," *Ercilla*, XXIV (16 abril 1958), 8, and (23 abril), p. 10.
4. USIA, *Chilean Attitudes Toward the United States*, pp. 1-2. USIA, *Chilean Attitudes Toward Communism*, Foreword. Eduardo Hamuy, Danilo Salcedo y Orlando Sepulveda, *El Primer Satelite Artificial: sus efectos en la opinión pública* (Santiago: Edit. Universitaria de Chile, 1958), pp. 86, 90-91. CESO, "Stratification Survey" (September 1961). CESO, "Pre-Electoral Survey" (August 1964). Johnson, "National and Progressive Bourgeoisie," p. 74.
5. U.S., Information Agency, Research and Reference Service, *Latin American Views on Political Relations with the United States* (Washington: Report no. 14, September 23, 1957), pp. 7-8. Cf., USIA, *Chilean Attitudes Toward the United States*, pp. 9-10.
6. Hamuy, et al., pp. 56-57.
7. USIA, *Economic and Political Climate*, pp. 14, 41.
8. USIA, *Chilean Attitudes Toward Communism*, pp. 5-7. By December 1962, Chilean sentiment for non-alignment had lessened substantially (39 percent), while those favoring a pro-U.S. position emerged as a majority (51 percent). Three percent opted for a pro-Soviet posture. *Economic and Political Climate*, pp. 44.
9. Hamuy, et al., pp. 102-106. CESO, "Stratification Survey" (September 1961). CESO' "Post-Electoral Survey" (November 1964).
10. USIA, *Chilean Attitudes Toward the United States*, p. 7.
11. USIA, *Latin American Views*, pp. 1, 4.
12. Only 25 percent felt that the United States should have less or no influence. This represented a moderate improvement over the situation in November 1956, when 70 percent viewed the United States as having too much influence. However, in that instance, the alternative of "about the right amount" which obtained 30 percent in 1962 was omitted; hence, the result was more extreme. Ibid., p. 4. USIA, *Economic and Political Climate*, p. 38.
13. USIA, *Chilean Attitudes Toward the United States*, pp. 3-4, 6.
14. Ibid., p. 5.
15. USIA, *Economic and Political Climate*, pp. 27-28, 30-31. By February 1964, 41 percent favored expropriations of the *Gran Minería* while 45 percent were opposed. Males and lower class persons tended to be more radical. Instituto Chileno de Opinion Publica, "Encuesta de Opinión Pública relativa a algunos aspectos de la Realidad Política Chilena" (Santiago: ICOP, Febrero de 1964, unpublished).
16. "Business Abroad: Chile-Why the Copper Men are Getting Edgy," *Business Week*, April 4, 1970, p. 38. Cf., U.S., Congress, House, Committee on Banking and Currency, *Latin American Economic Study*, conducted by the Honorable Thomas M. Rees, 91st Cong., 1st Sess., October 1969, pp. 18-19.
17. Pike, pp. 162-164, 267-269. Campos, p. 224. Veliz, "Chile," p. 224.
18. Petras, *Politics and Social Forces*, p. 116. And in 1964, total "foreign investment in Chile was estimated at about $1,000 million, of which 80 percent was U.S. capital." During the 1950s a similar ratio existed. *Hispanic American Report*, XVII (October 1964), 743-44. U.S., Department of Commerce, Bureau of Foreign Commerce, *Investment in Chile: Basic Information for United States Businessmen*, by Merwin L. Bohan and Morton Pomeranz (Washington: Government Printing Office, 1960), pp. 11-12.
19. "Business Abroad: Chile's Copper Beckons Once Again," *Business Week*, October 1966, p. 76. W. Raymond Duncan, "Chilean Christian Democracy," *Current History*, LIII (November 1967), 267. *El Siglo*, 10 febrero 1967, p. 14. Vitale, *Y Despues?* p. 28.
20. "Chile Starts Chasing the Capitalists," *Time* (Canadian Ed.), January 4, 1971, p. 48.

21. U.S., Department of Commerce, *Economic Trends and Their Implications for the United States in Chile*, (Washington: Bureau of International Commerce, Department of Commerce, July 1970), pp. 12-13.

22. For data on these and other U.S. investments, see U.S., *Investment in Chile*, pp. 12-14, and "Choice for Chile: Which Way to go Left?" *Business Week*, August 8, 1964, p. 48.

23. U.S., *Economic Trends*, p. 12.

24. Pike, pp. 428-29. Gil and Parrish, I, 7-8. Jobet, "Democracia Liberal," pp. 104-107. OCEPLAN, *Planifica con nosotros*, pp. 84-89. Chile, Senado, *Diario de Sesiones del Senado*, CCLXXXVIII, ses. 32 (8 agosto 1961), pp. 1779-81. Pedro Zottele, "News from Chile," *Christian Century*, October 7, 1964, p. 1248.

25. Silvert, *Reaction*, p. 63. Johnson, pp. 86-88, 90-91. Gerassi, pp. 342-43. James Becket and Keith D. Griffin, "Revolution in Chile," *New Republic*, December 29, 1962, p. 9. *Hispanic American Report*, XI (September 1958), 514 (November 1958), p. 628 (December 1958), p. 690, XIV (June 1961), 354 (July 1961), p. 442 (September 1961), pp. 638-39, XV (September 1962), 645 (December 1962), pp. 947-49. Cf., Partido Comunista de Chile, Orlando Millas, *El Fracaso del Gobierno de los Gerentes*, Texto del informe que presentó a nombre de la Comisión Política a la Sesión Plenaria del Comité Central del Partido Comunista de Chile realizada en marzo de 1960 en Santiago (Santiago: Imp. Lautaro, 1960), pp. 28-29.

26. U.S., *Rockefeller Report Hearing*, p. 25. "Business Abroad: Chile's Copper," p. 76.

27. A. Angell, "Christian Democracy in Chile," *Current History*, LVIII (February 1970), 82. Petras, *Politics and Social Forces*, p. 238.

28. U.S., *Latin America Economic Study*, pp. 18-19.

29. Partido Comunista, Millas, *Fracaso*, p. 18.

30. *Information Guide for Doing Business in Chile* (New York: Price Waterhouse and Co., U.S.A., September 1969), pp. 31-32. U.S., Congress, House, Committee on Foreign Affairs, *Foreign Assistance Act of 1969, Hearings*, before the Committee on Foreign Affairs, House of Representatives, 91st Cong., 1st sess., June 1969, p. 208.

31. On these matters, see: *El Mercurio*, 30 julio 1960, p. 15; *Hispanic American Report*, XVI (February 1964), 1185; and U.S., *Foreign Aid in Action*, pp. 158-60.

32. U.S., *Foreign Aid in Action*, pp. 126-27, 129, 133, 136, 148-150, 183, 188, 193, 195, 203. U.S., *Castro Communist Subversion*, pp. 261-62. U.S., *Foreign Assistance Act of 1963*, V, 852, 876-77. U.S., *Departments for 1964*, pp. 338, 399. Eugene P. Dvorin, "Foreign Aid by States," *National Civic Review*, LIII (December 1964), 590.

33. U.S., *Foreign Assistance Act of 1963*, III, 490.

34. *El Mercurio*, 2 octubre 1959, p. 17, 3 octubre, p. 1, 25 noviembre, p. 19, 26 noviembre, p. 1. Chile, Congreso Nacional Senado, *El Presidente Eisenhower en el Congresso de Chile* (Santiago: Zig-Zag, 1960).

35. Based upon an interview with a lawyer and University of Chile professor who served as an ambassador under Alessandri and has represented such companies. These contributions were reportedly given to all major parties, save the Marxists.

36. "Business Abroad: Chile-Why the Copper Men," p. 38.

37. Thus, the Anglo-Lautaro Co. owns *El Mercurio* of Antofagasta, and U.S. firms have a major interest in Radio Gran Mineria. Standard Oil of New Jersey has sponsored the "Esso Reporter" on Chilean radio since 1941.

38. *El Mercurio*, 8 agosto 1959, p. 17. Benjamin Maluenda M., "El Instituto de Educación Rural: Factor en la Reforma Agraria," *Mensaje*, XI (mayo 1962), 170-71.

39. U.S., Information Agency, *12th Review of Operations*, January1-June 30, 1959 (Washington: Government Printing Office, 1959), pp. 11, 27. *16th Report to Congress*, Jan. 1-June 20, 1961 (Washington: Government Printing Office, 1961), p. 31. *17th Review of Operations*, July 1-Dec. 31, 1961 (Washington: Government Printing Office, 1962), p. 14. U.S., *Departments for 1964*, pp. 578-81, 737.

40. U.S., *Foreign Aid in Action*, pp. 13-14. During the 1950-1960 period, Chile received U.S. foreign aid of all types totaling $252,000,000. On a per capita basis, this was exceeded only by Bolivia in Latin America. Charles Wolf, Jr., *The Political Effects of Economic Programs: Some Indications from Latin America* (Santa Monica: Rand Corp., Memo RM-3901-ISA, 1964), p. 18.

41. Joseph S. Tulchin, "Latin America: Focus for U.S. Aid," *Current History*, LI (July 1966), 29.

42. This is inferred from the temporal proximity of congressional authorizations and appropriations to the Conference of San José where Cuban acceptance of Soviet aid was condemned by the OAS Foreign Ministers Meeting. Executive department officials justified the new program not only on humanitarian grounds, but as likely to promote political liberty and "avoid the chaos" of revolution. See, e.g., *El Mercurio*, 5 septiembre 1960, p. 3, 10 noviembre, p. 3, and IADB, *SPTF 1964 Report*, p. 2.

43. U.S., *Foreign Assistance Act of 1963*, V, 852, 854-57, 861, 878, 907, 943, 946, 948-49, 960, 970-971. U.S., Information Agency, *19th Review of Operations*, July 1-Dec. 31, 1962 (Washington: Government Printing Office, 1963), p. 5. U.S., *Castro-Communist Subversion*, pp. 16, 23, 25-26.

44. With regard to the latter point, see Delesseps S. Morrison, *Latin American Mission* (New York: Simon & Schuster, 1965), pp. 179, 181, 189, 218-20, and U.S., *Castro-Communist Subversion*, pp. 27, 37-38.

45. Juan de Onis, "Latin Alliance Revisited," *New York Times*, August 18, 1966, p. 14. "La OEA ante los Golpes Militares," *Ercilla*, XXIX (23 octubre 1963), 7. Alberto Lleras Camargo, "La Alianza después de Kennedy," *Mensaje*, N. o 130 (Julio 1964), pp. 279-80.

The view that during the early 1960s, *the* or *a* major goal of the AFP was to lessen the appeal of the Cuban Revolution has also been articulated by a number of scholars and serious commentators. Ronald M. Schneider, "Five Years of the Cuban Revolution," *Current History*, XLVI (January 1964), 26-33. Pedro C.M. Teichert, "Latin America and the Socio-Economic Impact of the Cuban Revolution." *Journal of Inter-American Studies*, IV (January 1962), 116. "The Chilean Land Reform: A Laboratory," pp. 313-14, 317, 322-25. David Huelin, "Latin America's Development Crisis," *World Today*, XIX (September 1963), 408. John Meslay, "Algo más sobre Cuba," *Mensaje*, XI (Enero-Febrero 1962), 47-49. Luís Hernández Parker, "Punta del Este: 3 Metas Cardinales," *Ercilla*, XXVII (16 agosto 1961), p. 16. Vjekoslav Kosta, "The Cuban Revolution and its International Repercussions," *Review of International Affairs* (Belgrade), XIII (Oct. 20, 1962), 7. *Hispanic American Report*, XIV (July 1961), 455-56. Ann Van Wynen Thomas and A.J. Thomas Jr., *The Organization of American States* (Dallas: Southern Methodist University Press, 1963), p. 327. Silvert, *Chile: Yesterday and Today*, pp. 198-200. Matthews, pp. 198, 217, 277. Horowitz, pp. 217-18.

For Christian Democratic views to this effect, see: "El prestigio de EE.UU. en América Latina," *Política y Espíritu*, XIV (15 noviembre 1960) 11; Jacques Chonchol, "Los factores de aceleración revolucionaria," *Mensaje*, XI (diciembre 1962), 86; Alejandro Magnet, "Commentarios Internacionales: ¿Plan Marshall para America Latina?" *Mensaje*, IX (agosto 1960), pp. 283-84; and Juventud Demócrata Cristiana, *Segundo Congreso*, pp. 39-53.

Similar views by Radical Party President Humberto Aguirre Doolan appear in the Chile, Senado, *Diario*, CCXC, ses. 25 (26 julio 1962), pp. 1903-1904.

Analogous Socialist and Communist evaluations will be found in: Clodomiro Almeyda M., *Reforma Agraria* (Santiago: Prensa Latinoamericana, 1962), pp. 6-10; and Chile, Senado, *Diario*, CCXC, ses. 19 (24 julio 1962), pp. 1472-73.

The Alessandri administration appealed to this objective of the AFP when arguing the necessity of massive aid. "Semana Política," *Ercilla*, XXVII (18 octubre 1961), 9. And in November 1962, it was reported that "high circles in Washington" had decided to give Chile massive aid during 1963 and 1964 because of the danger of her becoming another Cuba. Rubén Corvalán, "Chile, País Clave para USA," *Ibid.*, XXVIII (7 noviembre 1962), 16-17. Cf., Igor Entrala, "Balance de la Gira de Alessandri," *Ibid.* (26 diciembre 1962), p. 16.

46. "The Chilean Land Reform: A Laboratory," p. 313.

47. U.S., *Foreign Aid in Action*, pp. 102-103. For other views that the bill did not encompass basic or structural changes, see: "Editorial: Fidelismo in Cuba (Chile)," *New Republic*, November 24, 1962, p. 8; Becket, "Land Reform in Chile," pp. 209-11; Becket and Griffin, "Revolution in Chile," pp. 10-11; "The Chilean Land Reform: A Laboratory," pp. 315-16, 318-21; and Gil, pp. 150-52. Cf., Luís Hernández Parker, "Informe a los 'Sabios' sobre la Reforma," *Ercilla*, XXVIII (22 agosto 1962), 8-9.

48. Hernández Parker, " 'Cuartelazo' del Congreso a la Reforma," *Ercilla*, XXVIII (25 julio 1962), 7-8.

49. Rubén Corvalán Vera, "Finalizó el Drama: Dólar Libre y Fluctuante en Doble Area," Ibid. (10 octubre 1962), pp. 16-17.

50. U.S., *Foreign Aid in Action*, pp. 25, 50.

51. Olavarría, *Alessandri*, III, pp. 25, 30, 50-54, and IV, pp. 100-102. Cf., U.S., *Foreign Aid in Action*, p. 30.

52. Rubén Corvalán V., "Fin de la Evasión Tributaria," *Ercilla*, XXX (26 febrero 1964), 6-7. Cf., U.S., *Foreign Aid in Action*, pp. 35-36, 39-40, 103.

53. U.S., *Foreign Aid in Action*, pp. 103-106.

54. Ibid., p. viii.

55. Ibid., p. 115. "During the period 1960-64, foreign financing amounted to 40 percent of the total deficit and in 1965 to 65 percent." IADB, *SPTF, 1965 Report*, p. 210. And Gruening notes that "(a)lthough Chile formally met the performance tests, during 1963 and 1964 the annual rate of inflation ran to approximately 40 percent (greater than in the two previous years), the trade deficit widened, and the economic growth rate slackened. In short, the monetary and fiscal commitments assumed by Chile promoted neither stabilization nor development." U.S., *Foreign Aid in Action*, p. 105. According to William D. Rogers, "we cranked in a lot of dough in 1964 before the elections to prevent severe inflation which might have enabled FRAP to win the election." Until 1965, Rogers had been the Deputy Assistant Administrator for Latin America of AID. These remarks were made in the course of an address at Cornell University on July 26, 1966.

56. Morrison, pp. 221-22. Cf., U.S., *Foreign Assistance Act of 1963*, V, 855.

57. Luis Hernandez Parker, "Congreso del PC: Esperando al Zurdo . . . El 64," *Ercilla*, XXVIII (21 marzo 1962), 8. Cf., Ibid., no. 1398 (7 marzo), p. 8.

58. José Musalem, "Misión Goodwin-Moscoso," *Política y Espíritu*, XVI (marzo 1962), 17-18. And Hernández Parker has noted that "(L)a Misión Moscoso-Goodwin no sólo prometió más dólares para Chile: hizo también una crítica a fondo al contenido económico y social de las reformas Agraria y Tributaria, y manifestó sus fundados temores de que 'el país de mayor tradición democrática de América Latina' dejara de serlo, si sus partidos de raíz republicana no hallaban el método con el verdicto de las urnas; es decir, de la democracia representativa. Richard Goodwin expresó muy claramente que una victoria así del FRAP equivaldría 'a la peor catástrofe para el Occidente, y la más dura derrota para el estilo de vida que todos nosotros amamos.' "
. . . Insistió, sí, en una lucha frontal contra el marxismo-leninismo, porque Chile era 'uno de los focos mas calientes del hemisferio, después de Cuba, con el agravante de que aquí la Sierra Maestra podría protagonizarse en las urnas.' " "Misión Moscosco-Goodwin Un Balance para Meditar," *Ercilla*, XXVIII (14 marzo 1962), 8-9.

59. Frei and Tomic held long conversations with Edwin Martin and Latin American division personnel at the Department of State. They were also luncheon guests of the Senate Committee on Foreign Relations. Upon returning to Santiago, they expressed "radiant optimism" at discovering a new type of progressive attitude among high U.S. officials. One of them reported: "(n)o hicimos ninguna concesión y repetimos hasta cansarnos que la alternativa de América Latina era o 'democracia profunda y verdadera—goce de bienestar y libertad para la mayoría—, o la solución marxista-leninista que había insurgido en Cuba'." "Frei y Tomic: 'USA Rechaza a los Moderados,' " *Ercilla*, XXVIII (11 abril 1962), 9. Cf., *Hispanic American Report*, XV (June 1962), 351-52.

60. U.S., *Castro-Communist Subversion*, pp. 12-13.

61. Chile, Senado, *Diario*, CCXCIII, ses. 52 (6 mayo 1964), p. 4144.

62. "Así Nos Ven," *Ercilla*, XXX (9 septiembre 1964), 20-21.

63. U.S., *Economic Trends*, p. 11. *El Siglo*, 28 noviembre 1970, p. 9.

64. U.S., *Latin American Economic Study*, p. 19.

65. Susanne Bodenheimer, " 'Stagnation in Liberty'-The Frei Experiment in Chile," *NACLA Newsletter*, III (March 1969), 4.

66. Steve Weissman, "The Many 'Successes' of the Alliance for Progress," *Pacific Research and World Empire Telegram*, II (November 1970), 2-9. Cf., U.S., *Rockefeller Report*

Hearing, pp. 30, 47-8, 124, 127-28. William Barclay, Joseph Enright and Reid T. Reynolds, "Population Control in the Third World," *NACLA Newsletter*, IV (December 1970), 16.

67. Bodenheimer, " 'Stagnation in Liberty,' " p. 5.

68. Ibid., pp. 2-3. Petras, *Politics and Social Forces*, pp. 225-29. U.S., *Latin American Economic Study*, pp. 17-18.

69. U.S., Congress, House, Committee on Foreign Affairs, *Organization of American States, Hearings*, before the subcommittee on Inter-American Affairs of the Committee on Foreign Affairs, House of Representatives, 91st Cong., 2d. sess., March 17 and 18, 1970, pp. 23, 26, 29.

70. *El Siglo*, 28 noviembre 1970, p. 1. Although data has not yet been released which conclusively demonstrates such an infusion in FY 1970—and indeed foreign exchange holdings may have made it unnecessary—there can be no doubt that such political considerations dominate AID decision making. See: "U.S. A.I.D. in the Dominican Republic-An Inside View," *NACLA Newsletter*, IV (November 1970), 1-10.

71. Gall, "The Chileans," p. 106. *Time* (Canadian Edition), October 9, 1970, p. 32. *El Siglo*, 28 noviembre 1970, p. 5.

72. On the capital flight question, see U.S., *Castro-Communist Subversion*, pp. 261-62.

73. USIA, *17th Review*, p. 14. *19th Review*, p. 5. After 1962, although major priority was assigned to Cuba, even more publicity stressed the goals and "successes" of the AFP. U.S., *Departments for 1964*, p. 161. U.S., Information Agency, *22nd Report to Congress*, Jan. 1-June 30, 1964 (Washington: Government Printing Office, 1964), p. 16.

74. U.S., Congress, House, Committee on Appropriations, *Departments of State and Justice, the Judiciary, and Related Agencies for 1960, Hearings*, before a subcommittee of the Committee on Appropriations, House of Representatives, 86th Cong., 1st sess., 1960, pp. 140, 142. U.S., *Departments for 1962*, p. 240. U.S., *Departments for 1964*, p. 175. U.S., *Departments for 1966*, p. 116.

75. U.S., *Departments for 1962*, pp. 51, 54-55. U.S., *Departments for 1964*, pp. 168-69. U.S., *Departments for 1966*, p. 112.

76. U.S., *Departments for 1962*, pp. 248-49. Cf., pp. 26 and 227.

77. U.S., *Departments for 1960*, p. 818.

78. U.S., Information Agency, *14th Review of Operations*, Jan. 1-June 30, 1960 (Washington: Government Printing Office, 1960), p. 5.

79. U.S., *Departments for 1962*, p. 651.

80. U.S., Information Agency, *Twentieth Review of Operations*, January 1-June 30, 1963 (Washington: Government Printing Office, 1963), p. 49. *23d Report to Congress*, July 1-Dec. 31, 1964 (Washington: Government Printing Office, 1965), p. 40. *24th Report to Congress*, Jan. 1-June 30, 1965 (Washington: Government Printing Office, 1965), p. 27.

81. U.S., *Departments for 1962*, pp. 30, 678-86, 691, 699.

82. According to William D. Rogers—former deputy U.S. coordinator of the AFP and deputy assistant AID administrator for Latin America—USIA packaged programs were "almost certainly" placed on Chilean stations during 1964-1965, "some identified (to the listeners) as such and others not so designated." Cornell University address, July 30, 1966.

83. These figures do not include rebroadcasts of short wave programs. USIA, *14th Review*, p. 26. U.S., *Departments for 1962*, pp. 74, 263.

84. U.S., *Castro-Communist Subversion*, pp. 113-15.

85. U.S., *Departments for 1964*, p. 515.

86. Ibid., pp. 509, 515, 519. *Departments for 1962*, p. 481. *Departments for 1966*, pp. 490-92. USIA, *16th Report*, p. 15.

87. USIA, *17th Review*, p. 11. USIA, *Twentieth Review*, p. 51.

88. Indicative of references will be found in: U.S., Information Agency, *11th Report to Congress*, July 1-Dec. 31, 1958 (Washington: Government Printing Office, 1959), p. 17; USIA, *19th Review*, p. 10; and *22nd Report to Congress*, p. 31. Both *El Mercurio* and *Las Ultimas Noticias* are under common ownership and are produced in the same building.

89. Repeated statements to a Fulbright Program Research Fellow during July 1966.

90. Thus, for example, USIA reported in 1961 that "approximately 25 percent of the 10,000 words daily of Wireless File copy transmitted to field posts has been devoted to the Cuban situation." USIA, *17th Review*, p. 11.

91. Ibid., p. 13.

92. At least five mobile units were in circulation. U.S., *Departments for 1962*, p. 236. U.S., *Departments for 1964*, p. 394.

93. And in 1963, the agency reported that "Cuban communism has been treated in a number of USIA documentaries, including two films, 'The Unfinished Struggle' and 'Cuba Waits,' which were produced after the missile crisis and carry the message of what happens to a country which falls under Communist domination. An animated film on the Cuban agrarian reform has been an effective weapon in demonstrating Castro's betrayal of the revolution." USIA, *16th Report*, p. 15. U.S., *Castro-Communist Subversion*, p. 117.

94. USIA, *22nd Report*, p. 17.

95. Testifying concerning how AFP programs 'directly affect the people,' Teodoro Moscoso observed that "(w)e have 4 million schoolbooks which have been distributed. Obviously this not only affects the child that gets it; it affects the family who looks at the book, perhaps for the first time in their lives." U.S., *Foreign Assistance Act of 1963*, V, 885.

96. U.S., *Departments for 1962*, p. 236. U.S., Information Agency, *21st Report*, July 1-Dec. 31, 1963 (Washington: U.S. Govt. Printing Office, 1964), p. 32.

97. U.S., *Departments for 1962*, pp. 619-28.

98. USIA, *12th Review*, pp. 10-11. The Christian Democratic publishing firm Editorial del Pacífico has been identified as a major Chilean distributor of USIA works published by Edit. del Golfo in Mexico and Edit. del Atlántico in Buenos Aires—both of which are said to be prime contractors. Hector Suarez Bastidas, "Un 'ideologo' anticomunista," *Punto Final*, I (1.a quincena de mayo de 1967), 11.

99. U.S., Information Agency, *13th Review of Operations*, July 1-Dec. 31, 1959 (Washington: Government Printing Office, 1960), p. 12.

100. U.S., *Castro-Communist Subversion*, pp. 120-21.

101. USIA, *19th Review*, p. 31.

102. U.S., *Departments for 1962*, pp. 880, 885-87. U.S., *Departments for 1960*, pp. 920-23. U.S., *Departments for 1964*, p. 694. For additional details about how the program functions, see U.S., *Departments for 1960*, pp. 681, 707, 904, 910.

103. "A 1960 study of the educational attainments of the labor force shows that 40 percent had completed primary school, only 6 percent had completed secondary school, 0.4 percent had completed vocational school, and 1 percent had completed university studies." U.S., *Foreign Aid in Action*, p. 6.

104. USIA, *17th Review*, p. 12.

105. USIA, *Twentieth Review*, pp. 22-23.

106. U.S., Congress, House, Committee on Foreign Affairs, *Foreign Assistance Act of 1964, Hearings*, before the Committee on Foreign Affairs, House of Representatives, 88th Cong., 2d sess., 1964, p. 572. The literacy centers referred to are probably those operated by the Institute for Rural Education, since the writer is aware of no other such program during the period in question. The IER did receive a large AID loan.

107. U.S., *Castro Communist Subversion*, p. 117.

108. U.S., *Departments for 1962*, p. 235. With the exception of the Fernández and Meneses items, the following propaganda does not appear to have been authored by Chileans. All except one violently denounced the Cuban Revolution, and many alleged that an Allende victory would transform Chile into such a tyranny. Only the last three were published by a known political group, the Christian Democratic Party.

R.E. Adams W., *El Mundo Unido: ¿Bajo la Hoz o la Cruz?* (Santiago: Imp. Wilson, Junio 1964).

Victor Franco, *La Revolución Sensual* (Santiago: Edit. Pomaire, 1962).

El cuento del tío Salvador (Santiago: Edit. Nueva Aurora, 1963).

Sergio Fernández L., *Y el comunismo signe su marcha...* (Santiago: Edit. del Pregón, 1962). (This appeared originally in *Estudios sobre el Comunismo*, the USIA-financed Santiago edition of *Problems of Communism*).

Fernando Salvaterra, *Un Mundo Nuevo: Democracia o Comunismo para América Latina* (Santiago: Edit. del Pregón, 1963).

Nuevos Horizontes (Santiago: Imp. Sopech, 1964).

Un Plan que solamente Usted puede derrotar (Santiago: Edit. 'La Portada,' n.d. (Also published in Antófagasta by the same press).

Cristina Meneses Dávila, ¡*Servir al Pueblo!* Santiago, 1960.

Luís Boza Domínguez, *La Situacion Universitaria en Cuba* (Santiago: Edit. del Pacífico, 1962). (Written by a Cuban exile).

Laurencio Angel Aparicio, *Los Malvados no Conocen la Justicia* (Santiago: Edit. del Pacífico, 1962). (Written by a Cuban exile).

, *El Congreso de las Focas Amaestradas y los Lacayos Parlantes de Moscú en Río de Janeiro* (Santiago: Edit. del Pacífico, 1963).

In 1956, the Congress for Cultural Freedom published eulogies by various Chilean intellectuals, political and labor leaders of Stalin upon his decease. See *Así Veían a Stalin*, Santiago, Imp. San Jorge. Among its publications in the early 1960s was a severe condemnation of the Castro regime prepared by exile organizations in the United States. See *La Causa de Cuba: Causa de America* (Santiago: Congreso por la Libertad de la Cultura, 1961). In the early 1960s, the CIA-subsidized Congress moved from very modest to expensive surroundings until after the Frei victory, when it again returned to an inexpensive headquarters. Christian Democratic leaders Jaime Castillo and Jorge Cash—both editors of the party publications—were prominent members of the Congress, as was Conservative Sergio Fernández Larraín. Suarez Bastidas, "Un 'ideólogo' anticomunista," p. 10. *Diccionario Biográfico de Chile*, Duodécima Edición: 1962-1964 (Santiago: Emp. Periodística Chile, 1965), p. 266. *Washington Post*, Feb. 26, 1967, p. E-1.

The intensity of such propaganda is probably reflected by the fact that in June 1963, a group of FRAP leaders solicited and obtained an interview with President Alessandri where they complained of "the anti-Allendist propaganda which the U.S. Embassy was financing and disseminating in the form of pamphlets," Olavarría, *Alessandri*, III, 320. For hard evidence of at least one USIA pamphlet which directly discussed the campaign for the presidency, see the Chile, Senado, *Diario*, CCXCIV, ses. 22 (12 agosto 1964), p. 2134.

109. USIA, *12th Review*, p. 11.
110. U.S., *Departments for 1962*, pp. 993-95.
111. Ibid., p. 51.
112. USIA, *Twentieth Review*, p. 18.
113. U.S., *Castro-Communist Subversion*, p.119.
114. Ibid.
115. On these activities see: U.S., *Departments for 1960*, pp. 151, 159-60, 584-85, 613-14; U.S., *Departments for 1962*, pp. 237-38; U.S., *Departments for 1966*, pp. 115, 389; U.S., *Castro-Communist Subversion*, pp. 115-16, 119-20; U.S., Information Agency, *15th Review of Operations*, July 1-Dec. 31, 1960 (Washington: Government Printing Office, 1961), p. 18; *16th Report*, p. 13; *17th Review*, p. 13; *19th Review*, p. 27; *Twentieth Review*, p. 53; and *22nd Report*, p. 38.
116. U.S., *Chilean Attitudes Toward Communism*, Foreword.
117. U.S., *Departments for 1962*, p. 1272.
118. *El Mercurio*, 31 marzo 1959, p. 3.
119. *El Mercurio*, 11 diciembre 1959. Rycroft and Clemmer, p. 159.
120. U.S., Advisory Commission on International Educational and Cultural Affairs, A Report from the Commission, *A Sequel to A Beacon of Hope: The Exchange of Persons Program* (Washington: Government Printing Office, August 1964), p. 1.
121. U.S., *Departments for 1964*, pp. 1436, 1452, 1454. U.S., *Departments for 1966*, p. 883. For a report of a study indicating that the program has been most effective among Latin Americans in terms of favorable attitudinal modifications, see U.S., Advisory Commission on International Educational and Cultural Affairs, A Report from the Commission, *A Beacon of Hope: The Exchange of Persons Program* (Washington: Government Printing Office, April 1963), p. 160.
122. During 1959, the director of *El Sur* and a cartoonist for *El Mercurio* and *Topazi*

(Chile's leading satirical review) were grantees. *El Mercurio*, 27 junio 1959, p. 16, 13 noviembre, p. 33.

123. "Crónica Nacional," *Ercilla*, XXVII (10 enero 1962), 5.

124. The following list for 1959-1960 is not necessarily inclusive: Ana Eugenia Ugalde (Radical); Inés Enríquez (Radical); María Enriquez (Liberal); Rolando Schmauk; Mario Saez; Joaquín Morales; Samuel Fuentes; Mario Videla; Isauro Torres (Radical); Eduardo Frei (Christian Democrat); Antonio Coloma (Conservative); Guillermo Perez de Arce (National and Popular); Hugo Zepeda (Liberal); Fernando Echavarri (National and Popular); Edmundo Eluchans; Horacio Hevia; Raúl Juliet (Radical); Hugo Rosende; Eugenio Ballesteros (Christian Democrat); Julio Sepulveda (Radical); Manuel José Yrarrazaval (Conservative); *El Mercurio*, 30 enero 1959, p. 21, 6 febrero, p. 13, 12 febrero, p. 1, 15 marzo, p. 27, 21 marzo, p. 1, 1 mayo, p. 17, 1 julio, p. 27, 7 agosto, p. 19, 18 agosto, p. 1, 20 agosto, p. 25, 2 noviembre, p. 21, 17 abril 1960, p. 27, 19 abril, p. 17, 8 mayo, p. 9, 4 septiembre, p. 9, 17 noviembre, p. 21. For testimony concerning the effectiveness of this program, see U.S., *Departments for 1962*, pp. 1301-1302.

125. They included Saez, Torres, Frei, Coloma and Perez de Arce. *El Mercurio*, 17 mayo 1959, p. 29, 1 julio, p. 27. *Ercilla*, XXV (21 octubre 1959), 8. Chile, Senado, *Diario*, CCLXXXVI, ses. 15 (12 julio 1960), pp. 743-48.

126. During 1959, no less than fifty-one union leaders were brought to the United States for brief or extended visits. *El Mercurio*, 23 febrero 1959, p. 17, 27 febrero, p. 17, 27 junio, p. 16, 23 julio, p. 26, 26 septiembre, p. 1, 20 diciembre, p. 47.

127. U.S., *Departments for 1964*, p. 1456. Other U.S. institutions which were involved in such programs included MIT, Cornell, Fordham, California, Indiana and Pittsburgh. Cf., *Foreign Assistance Act of 1963*, V, 869-70, 872.

128. U.S., *A Sequel to a Beacon of Hope*, p. 13.

129. Ibid.

130. U.S., *Departments for 1962*, p. 1302. Cf., U.S., *Departments for 1964*, p. 363.

131. *El Mercurio*, 12 enero 1964, p. 33, 13 enero, p. 31. Cf., USIA, *14th Review*, p. 17.

132. During 1959-1960, visiting U.S. legislators included Barry Goldwater, George Smathers, Burke Hickenlooper, Armistad Selden, Dante Fascell and William Barrett. Additionally, in August 1959, 26 members of the probably CIA-subsidized National Education Association visited Santiago while on a Latin American "fact finding" tour. Three months later, more than 20 U.S. delegates from the National Newspaper Association stopped in Chile during a Latin American tour "to improve understanding." This was probably also Government or CIA-subsidized. A few days later, a probably AID subsidized visit by a Georgia Livestock Association delegation occurred. *El Mercurio*, 4 agosto 1959, p. 16, 19 agosto, p. 16, 21 agosto, p. 1, 3 octubre, p. 19, 4 noviembre, p. 1, 5 noviembre, p. 1, 6 noviembre, p. 16, 26 enero 1960, p. 1, 6 marzo, p. 33, 3 diciembre, pp. 25, 28, 6 diciembre, p. 21, 8 diciembre, p. 27. *New York Times*, Feb. 19, 1967, p. 28. *Washington Post*, Feb. 26, 1967, p. E-1. *Akron Beacon Journal*, Feb. 22, 1967, p. 2.

133. "Obligations for the program since its inception total $6.2 million, with obligations for fiscal year 1965 at $2.7 million." By the end of 1966, there were 475 volunteers in Chile "spending $1,153,000 per annum, exclusive of administrative expenses." U.S., *Foreign Aid in Action*, p. 41. Claudio Aguirre Bianchi, "Los Cuerpos de Paz," *El Siglo*, 31 diciembre 1966, p. 7.

134. U.S., Congress, House, Committee on Appropriations, *Foreign Assistance and Related Agencies Appropriations for 1970, Hearings*, before a subcommittee of the Committee on Appropriations, House of Representatives, 91st Cong., 1st sess., May 1969, p. 484.

135. Augusto Carmona A., "382 Espías 'Voluntarios': Historia de los Cuerpos de Paz en Chile," *Punto Final*, I (1.a quincena de julio de 1967), suplemento, p. 2. Cf., pp. 6-8.

136. "La resistencia interna que despierta el Cuerpo de Paz, parece estar limitada principalmente por la oleada dulzona que levantan los voluntarios con sus actividades. Dirigentes universitarios han declarado que el mayor escollo en su lucha contra la influencia norteamericana, es la 'simpatía que despierta la labor del Cuerpo de Paz entre estudiantes desinformados políticamente'." Ibid., pp. 8-9.

137. "Las siguientes son las instituciones chilenas que trabajan con 'voluntarios' del Cuerpo de Paz: Dirección de Asuntos Indígenas, Ministerio de Agricultura, Junta de Adelanto de Arica, varias intendencias de provincia, Promoción Popular, Corporación de Re-

forma Agraria, Corporación de Servicios Habitacionales, Ministerio del Interior, Universidad de Concepción, Universidad Técnica del Estado, Universidad del Norte, Universidad Austral, Universidad Técnica Federico Santa María, Universidad Católica de Santiago, Centros Regionales de la Universidad de Chile, Instituto Nacional de Capacitación Profesional, Servicio de Cooperación Técnica, Instituto de Educación Cooperativa, Federación de Cooperativas de Ahorro y Créditos Ltda., Instituto de Desarrollo Agropecurario (INDAP), varias cooperativas campesinas a lo largo del país, Instituto Forestal, Ministerio de la Vivienda y Urbanismo, Servicio Nacional de Salud y varios hospitales de la capital y provincias." Although the Peace Corps was not working with a number of these organizations during the 1961-1964 period, the list may be regarded as illustrative. Ibid., p. 6.

138. Ibid., p. 4.

139. Ibid., p. 2. Interviews with several Peace Corps volunteers in Chile during 1966.

140. U.S., Congress, House, Committee on Foreign Affairs, *Peace Corps Act Amendments, Hearings*, before the Committee on Foreign Affairs, House of Representatives, on H.R. 10404, A Bill to Amend the Peace Corps Act, 87th Cong., 2d sess., 1962, pp. 151-52.

The direct relationship between CARITAS and the IER is discussed in Instituto de Educacion Rural, "Un Impulso solidario a la superacion Campesina," Santiago, 1960. (Mimeographed.)

141. Communications with the 402 centrales were strengthened by the "Radio-Escuela, con programas diarios de clases de educación agropecuaria, moral, educación familiar y educación manual, que se transmiten a través de 44 emisoras y son oidas por más de 1,000 escuelas rurales, fiscales y particulares," and through "(p)ublicationes campesinas, que comprenden la revista 'Surco y Semilla' con una tirada mensual de 10,000 ejemplares y toda clase de folletos de crianzas, industrias caseras, atención del hogar, etc." Maluenda, "Instituto," p. 170.

The intensification of IER activities is reflected by the fact that in 1960, it operated only seven training schools, 338 centrales, and broadcast to 812 rural schools. Of the last mentioned, 461 schools had been equipped with new radio receivers for the first time that year so that they could be integrated into the IER program. At that time, too, there were reported to be somewhat more than 2,000 training school alumni. "Cooperating organizations" that year were: Ministry of Agriculture; Ministry of Education; U.S. Technical Assistance Mission' CARITAS and UNESCO. "Economic donations" had been received from the Braden Copper Co., Fundación Helen Lee de Lassen, COVENSA, CARITAS, Ministeries of Agriculture and Education, "and others." Instituto de Educación Rural, "Un Impulso solidario."

142. In that month, the director of the Peace Corps testified that "(i)n Chile, 200 institutes called 'centrales' instructing Chileans in all aspects of rural education have at least 1 volunteer each as a staff member." U.S., Congress, House, Committee on Foreign Affairs, *To Amend the Peace Corps Act, Hearings*, before the Committee on Foreign Affairs, House of Representatives, on H.R. 8754, 88th Cong., 1st sess., 1963, p. 4, cf., p. 14.

143. Maluenda, "Instituto," p. 170.

144. ANOC's role as a competitor with the FRAP-led National Federation of Peasants and Indians is reflected by the following declarations adopted at a Congress in Lautaro during 1962:

"Ninguna organización asociada a la ANOC puede aceptar charlas o choclones políticos en su sede; si se aceptará el uso de los locales con fines políticos muchas personas quedarían excluidas reduciendo la posibilidad de influir y actuar de la ANOC. . . .

La situación actual es aprovechada por agitadores políticos que no buscan la solución de los problemas, sino que buscan conquistarse votos para sus partidos, explotando la desperación y el descontento de quienes no ven otros horizontes. . . .

No estamos contra nadie ni contra ninguna institución, excepto contra la injusticia y la ilegalidad. Se exigirá buen servicio y buena atención médica y educacional y cumplimiento de las leyes de previsión en favor de los campesinos. . . .

Hay urgencia en que el Instituto de Educación Rural y otra institución, efectue cursos sobre cooperativas para especializar delegados de los organizaciones rural.

Se aceptará toda la ayuda que sea constructiva y no limite la independencia de la ANOC." Asociación Nacional de Organizaciones Campesinas (A.N.O.C.), *Discursos y Conclusiones (Extractos) de la 1.a Convención* (Santiago, Abumohor Imp.), 1962), pp. 9, 12, 14,

19. Cf., Oscar Domínguez Correa, "Congreso campesina en Lautaro," *Mensaje*, XI (Junio 1962), 245.

By September 1962, ANOC was closely collaborating with the Christian Democratic Union Department, as were CLASC and ASICH in opposing the FRAP-led Central Unica de Trabajadores (CUT). "La Conferencia Sindical de los Trabajadores de América Latina," Ibid., (octubre 1962), p. 495.

145. U.S., *To Amend the Peace Corps Act*, p. 27. Cf., USIA, *21st Report*, p. 34.

146. Carmona, "382 Espías 'Voluntarios,' " pp. 6, 8-9.

147. U.S., *Peace Corps Act Amendments*, pp. 128-129. U.S., *Departments for 1964*, p. 609. Aguirre, "Los Cuerpos de Paz," p. 7.

148. Aguirre, "Los Cuperos de Paz," p. 7. U.S., *Peace Corps Act Amendments*, pp. 91, 99-101. U.S., *To Amend the Peace Corps Act.*, pp. 45-51, 58-59, 68-69. U.S., *Foreign Assistance Appropriations for 1970*, p. 498.

149. U.S., *Foreign Aid in Action*, p. 178. Cf., U.S., *To Amend the Peace Corps Act*, pp. 3, 44.

150. Section 635 (c) of the amended Foreign Assistance Act of 1961 provides that "(i)t is the sense of Congress that the President, in furthering the purposes of this Act, shall use to the maximum extent practicable the services and facilities of voluntary, non-profit organizations registered with, and approved by, the Advisory Committee on Voluntary Foreign Aid." And Section 216 (a) provides that "(i)n order to further the efficient use of United States voluntary contributions for relief and rehabilitation of friendly peoples, the President is authorized to use funds made available for the purposes of section 211 to pay transportation charges from United States ports or, in the case of excess or surplus property supplied by the United States, from foreign ports to ports of entry abroad . . . on shipments by the American Red Cross and United States voluntary non-profit relief agencies registered with and approved by the Advisory Committee on Voluntary Foreign Aid." U.S., *Foreign Aid in Action*, pp. 132, 173.

151. Net obligations extended under Title III to voluntary relief agencies for their Chilean programs were (in millions of dollars): 1955-1957 (1.5); 1958 (15.0); 1959 (12.3); 1960 (6.5); 1961 (7.1); 1962 (6.6); 1963 (5.5); 1964 (9.6); 1965 (8.0); Total for 1955-1965 (72.1). Ibid., pp. 12-13, 41.

152. "When men and money are sent into a society within the framework of a program, they bring ideas that live after them. It has been pointed out, in the case of the Peace Corps, that the cultural mutation catalyzed by a small foreign group might be more effective than all the immediate services it renders. The same can be true of the North American missioner—close to home, having great means at his disposal, frequently on a short-term assignment—who moves into an area of intense U.S. cultural and economic colonization. He is part of the sphere of influence and, at times, intrigue. . . . The influx of U.S. missioners coincides with the Alliance for Progress, Camelot and CIA projects and looks like a baptism of these. . . . Groups of U.S. missioners cannot avoid projecting the image of 'U.S. outposts.'. . . . The U.S. missioner of necessity is an 'undercover' agent—albeit unconscious—for U.S. social and political consensus."

"Men and money sent with missionary motivation carry a foreign Christian image, a foreign pastoral approach and a foreign political message. They also bear the mark of North American capitalism of the 1950's."

Ivan Illich, "The Seamy Side of Charity," *America*, CXVI (Jan. 21, 1967), 88, 90, 91.

At the time this rather forceful article was written, Illich was "Director of the Center of Inter-Cultural Documentation in Cuernavaca, Mexico, which for many years (had) been preparing missionaries for work in Latin America." Ibid., p. 91. Interestingly, perhaps, the Center was being subsidized by the CIA. *Washington Post* Feb. 26, 1967, p. E-1.

153. In 1955, at an Eucharistic Congress in Río de Janeiro, Latin America's Bishops called upon the Holy See for aid to "revitalize" "the Church" "as a potent force in Latin America." Pope Pius XII then established a Pontifical Commission to study the problem. In August 1960, Pope John XXIII released his Encyclical "Materia y Magestria" with its "historic appeal to laymen." Rev. Raymond A. Kevane, *The Layman Serves Latin America* (Chicago: Papal Volunteers for Latin America, 1965), p. 6.

Insofar as subsequent developments were concerned in 1966, Illich observed:

"Five years ago, U.S. Catholics undertook a peculiar alliance for the progress of the Latin American Church. By 1970, ten percent of the more than 225,000 priests, brothers and sisters would volunteer to be shipped south of the border. In the meantime, the combined U.S. male and female 'clergy' in South America has increased by only 1,622. . . .

The project relied on an impulse supported by uncritical imagination and sentimental judgment. A pointed finger and a 'Call for 20,000' convinced many that 'Latin America needs you.' Nobody dared state why, though the first published propaganda included several references to the 'Red danger' in four pages of text. The Latin American Bureau of the NCWC (National Catholic Welfare Conference) attached the word 'papal' to the program, the volunteers and the call itself.

. . . Let us coldly examine the American Church's outburst of charitable frenzy which resulted in the creation of 'papal' volunteers, student 'mission crusades,' the annual CICOP mass assemblies, numerous diocesan missions and new religious communities . . . the so-called papal plan—(is) part of the many-faceted effort to keep Latin America within the ideologies of the West.

Opinion is divided, of course, on whether the Church went heavily into social projects because it could thus obtain funds 'for the poor,' or whether it went after funds because it could thus contain Castroism and assure its institutional respectability." "The Seamy Side of Charity," pp. 88-89.

154. Appendix II, Sec. A.
155. Ibid., Sec. B.
156. Ibid., Sec. C.
157. Ibid., Sec. D.
158. Ibid., Sec. E.
159. Ibid., Sec. F.
160. Ibid., Sec. G.
161. Ibid., Sec. H.
162. Ibid., Sec. I.
163. Ibid., Sec. J.
164. Ibid., Sec. K.
165. Ibid., Sec. L.
166. Ibid., Sec. M.
167. Ibid., Sec. N.
168. Ibid., Sec. O.
169. "In the pursuit of its overall objectives to encourage the growth of sound and vigorous leadership in the developing countries of Latin America as a prerequisite for social and economic development, the International Development Foundation undertakes programs in three general areas: student leadership, rural leadership, and civic leadership." Its quarterly publication is *Desarrollo y Democracia (Development and Democracy).* IDF described its Chilean program, which was initiated in January 1964, in the following terms: "In cooperation with various indigenous organizations, (it) seeks to engage peasants and slum dwellers in constructive efforts for social reform and to develop strong leaders among them through such activities as courses in leadership training, cooperativism, labor legislation and social security; organization of groups; publications, etc. Headquarters of the projects is Santiago, with affiliated centers located in cities and rural areas throughout the country." "Cooperating Agencies: Instituto de Desarrollo Economico, Corporacion de Centros para el Desarrollo de la Comunidad (CENDES), Asociacion Provincial de Pequenos Agricultores de Osorno (APPAO), Centro para el Desarrollo Economico y Social de America Latina (DESAL), Technical University, USAID." Chilean based personnel included: "2 U.S. staff members (1 country representative, 1 social worker) and 36 local personnel (1 secretary, 35 supervisors)." Financial resources were: "Income for fiscal year ending 6/30/64: Grants-$986,365; other-$1,618; total: $987,983. Expenditures for fiscal year ending 6/30/64 in foreign technical assistance (Brazil, Chile, Colombia, Peru): $768,500." American, *USNPO: 1965*, pp. 67, 272.

With regard to the CIA relationship, it was reported that: "Both of these foundations (International Development Foundation and the Pan American Foundation), which administer many projects in Latin America, were identified last week as the recipients of large annual intelligence agency subsidies that were channeled first through dummy, and then through legitimate, foundations in what is known as a 'pass-through' operation." *New York Times*, Feb. 20, 1967. Cf., "Editorial," *The New Republic*, March 4, 1967, p. 7.

170. "The international Development Foundation has been engaged in organizing anti-Communist peasants unions in Latin America, particularly in Chile, where it sponsors a confederation of rural worker unions against the Communist-led Peasant and Indian Federation." *New York Times*, Feb. 16, 1967. The IDF has subsidized ANOC; the Union of Christian Peasants (UCC) and the Movement of Independent Peasants (MCI). These groups supported Frei in 1964 and managed to elect two of their own deputies in 1965. Under the tutelage of IDF they were organized into the National Peasants' Confederation (CNC). The strategy is to develop an independent political movement which would be allied with but not subordinated to Christian Democracy; i.e., there will be no mutual competition for legislative seats. Interview with Napoleon (Napo) Ruíz in Guatemala City on Dec. 22, 1967. Ruíz is an officer at the IDF training center in Jalapa, Guatemala. The subsidies to ANOC and the UCC were also attested to by IDF Vice-President George W. Wheelwright during conversations with a Columbia University National Defense Fellow in Santiago, Chile. An assistant to former Ambassador Dungan in Chile stated in the presence of the writer that "George" was supporting the UCC. Dates are early 1967 for the latter two conversations.

With reference to UCC strikebraking and other anti-Leftist tactics during the Frei administration, see Petras, *Politics and Social Forces*, p. 225.

171. ORMEU was a confederation of Christian Democratic students in Latin America. It was reportedly organized with the aid and financial support of the CIA-subsidized Foundation for Youth and Student Affairs (FYSA). In 1963, ORMEU sponsored the publication of *Sobre El Sistema Interamericano (On the Inter-American System)*. This was the text of a speech which Christian Democratic leader Radomiro Tomic gave to an ORMEU gathering in San Sebastian, Chile, during February 1962. *El Siglo*, 10 marzo 1967, pp. 1, 3. *New York Times*, Feb. 19, 1967, pp. 1, 26, 28.

The same issue of the *Times* reports CIA subsidies to Pax Romana through the FYSA, as well as subsidies to the International Union of Socialist Youth. Pax Romana activities in Chile are reported by *La Voz*. The Youth of the Radical Party were affiliated with the IUSY. *El Siglo*, 11 marzo 1967, p. 3.

172. "En Chile, concretamente, el 'dirigente estudiantil', Leopoldo Aragon, miembro de la Comisión de Relaciones Internacionales de la NSA mantuvo largo tiempo contacto con los dirigentes democristianos de la UFUCH en los primeros años de esta década. Con esos contactos pudo organizar la división de un Congreso para el movimiento estudiantil latinoamericano. El Congreso se realizó en Natal, Brasil y fué precedido por una reunión de diversos dirigentes de uniones que habían logrado poner bajo la férula de la NSA para planificar la estrategia divisionista. La reunión se realizó en la Ciudad Antigua de Guatemala, con la asistencia de elementos de más de 12 paises latinoamericanos y con la presencia de Aragon, que puso a disposición los fondos necesarios para su realización. Pasajes y estada, en uno de los hoteles mas lujosos de Guatemala, corrieron por cuenta de los yanquis. Fondos de origen semejante siguen sirviendo para la mantención de algunos centros de preparación de cuadros dirigentes en el terreno estudiantil para toda América Latina que funcionan en Chile." *El Siglo*, 18 febrero 1967, p. 1.

At the Third Congress of Latin American Students (Caracas, 1959), fourteen of the eighteen delegations were reportedly controlled by Marxists. Three years later, when the Fourth CLAJ opened in Natal, only eight of the nineteen delegations were controlled by Leftists. The "eight" refused to participate in the sessions until leaders of ten delegations which had previously attended a "caucus" in Guatemala gave "explanations." The "ten" refused, and with one other delegation held the Congress, since eleven were sufficient for a quorum. Otto Boye S., "IV Congreso Latinoamericano de Estudiantes," *Política y Espíritu*, XVI (diciembre-enero 1962), 41-42.

173. Christian Democratic Youth leaders Alberto Sepulveda and Sergio Pizarro were in the Chilean delegation to the Fifth World Assembly of the World Assembly of Youth, which was held at Amherst, Massachusetts during 1964. Sepulveda subsequently characterized the Assembly as "essentially anti-communist" and as serving "one of the world power blocs." Juventud Demócrata Cristiana, *Documentos del Primer Congreso Extraordinario de la Juventud Demócrata Cristiana de América (JUDCA)*, 29 octubre-2 noviembre 1964 (Santiago: Ediciones Rebeldía, Talls. Grafs. 'La Nación,' 1964), pp. 71-73.

CIA subsidies to the National Students Association and the World Assembly of Youth since 1952 are reported in the *New York Times*, Feb. 16, 1967, p. 1 and Feb. 19, 1967, p. 26. Elsewhere it was reported that "(o)ver the years, FYSA has supplied up to 80 percent of NSA's international budget." NSA leadership—in addition to passing along information on the political attitudes of foreign student leaders—also was subject to some cooptation and manipulation by the intelligence agency representatives. "Editorial," *New Republic*, March 4, 1967, p. 6. *Ramparts*, March 1967.

174. During April 1966, *New York Times* staff writers Tom Wicker, John W. Finney, Max Frankel, E.W. Kenworthy, et al., were responsible for a series of articles which identified various types of activities engaged in with some regularity by the intelligence agency. With regard to Latin American politics, they observed: "C.I.A. analysts reading the punchcards of their computers in Virginia can determine that a new youth group in Bogota appears to have fallen under the control of suspected Communists, but it takes an agent on the spot to trade information with the local police, collect photographs and telephone taps of those involved, organize and finance a counter-movement of, say, young Christians or democratic labor youth, and help them erect billboards and turn mimeograph machines at the next election . . . the agency runs dozens of . . . operations throughout the hemisphere.

It provides 'technical assistance' to most Latin nations by helping them establish anti-Communist police forces. It promotes anti-Communist front organizations for students, workers, professional and business men, farmers and political parties. It arranges for contact between these groups and American labor organizations, institutes and foundations.

It has poured money into Latin-American election campaigns in support of moderate candidates and·against leftist leaders such as Cheddi Jagan of British Guiana." *New York Times*, April 27, 1966, p. 28.

For declarations of the Chilean Committee for the Self-Determination of Peoples and the Chilean Committee for the Juridical Defense of Western Democracy which condemned the Cuban Revolution and/or the Second Continental Solidarity (with Cuba) Congress, see: *El Mercurio*, 24 enero 1959, p. 3, 24 marzo 1960, p. 17; and Aparicio, *Congreso*, p. 32.

175. With regard to the direction of the Frei campaign, Christian Democratic Youth leader Alberto Sepulveda charged after Frei's victory that: "Tanto en la campaña como en el poder, el Consejo del PDC fué secundario. No fué el que, antes y ahora, fijo las grandes líneas y ni siquiera administró los fondos que recibimos de todas partes. Fueron personas y organismos ajenos a nosotros. Cuando formulamos estas críticas, se nos tacha de 'inmaduros'; pero resulta que cuando se necesitan brigades de combate, cuando se necesita ganar una universidad o un sindicato, so nos llama a los jóvenes, y entonces, ya no somos inmaduros." Luís Hernández Parker, "Franco Apoyo a Frei . . ., pero Crítico," *Ercilla*, XXX (2 diciembre 1964), 25.

176. Barnard Collier, "Eduardo Frei Is Trying 'A Revolution Without The Execution Wall.' " *New York Times*, Feb. 19, 1967, Section 6. Collier's information was based upon conversations with persons suggested to him by U.S. Embassy personnel in Chile. A Christian Democratic Youth leader and a PDC-appointed Copper Department official both stated to the writer during 1967 that the party had in fact received CIA funds for the 1964 campaign. And in the course of his address at Cornell University on July 30, 1966, former AID Deputy Assistant Administrator for Latin America William P. Rogers admitted that it was "quite conceivable" that CIA funds had subsidized Frei's presidential drive. Cf., note 187, infra.

177. In the course of delivering a Policy Commission Report to the Communist Party's Central Committee on the 28th of that month, Volodia Teitelboim observed: "En últimos tiempos hemos visto al anticomunismo organizarse 'cientificamente,' como una gran industria. Hace el negocio del miedo, explota el pánico, enardece de pavor a los poderosos del dinero al grito apocalíptico de 'viene Fidel Castro,' al cuál torpemente se pinta como un demonio. Instada fábricas de documentos falsos, inunda la prensa, la radio, el cine, los libros y a menudo se aposenta en las catedras y en los púlpitos. Compra periodistas. Afea los muros de las ciudades con propaganda terrorífica y canallesca. Gasta cientos de millones de dólares en su desesperada empresa." Partido Comunista, Teitelboim, *Camino*, pp. 19-20. Partido Comunista, *Neruda Contesta*, pp. 10-11. For references to the propaganda disparity that characterized the Allende-Frei contest, see Gil and Parrish, I, 43-44, and Halperin, pp. 216-217.

178. "Según calculaciones frapistas, Storandt gastaría, solamente en propaganda mural, cada noche, un millón y medio de pesos en el sector céntrico, movilizando alrededor de 50 camiones y 100 automóviles." In addition to Hans Storandt, other PR men included Jorge Fontaine and Fernando Silva. They were joined by Roberto Vergara and the Ducci Claro brothers. FRAP charged that the U.S. Embassy was supplying the financial support for this campaign. In September, Teitelboim had claimed that since PL 480 agreements were first entered into between the U.S. and Chile, more than $10,000,000 had been assigned to the U.S. Embassy for local expenses. He alleged that these funds and contributions from U.S. firms were financing the propaganda campaign. "Reportaje al Comando Secreto," *Ercilla*, XXVIII (7 noviembre 1962), 10-11. Partido Comunista, Teitelboim, *Camino*, pp. 20-21.

179. The effort utilized earlier endorsements of Castro and the Cuban Revolution by Allende and his two major supporting parties to "force an identification for the election. This propaganda became really massive from March on, and was such that the disparity of resources prevented FRAP and Allende from either disassociating themselves from Cuba on one hand, or defending the Cuban Revolution on the other." Interview on May 5, 1967, with Rafael Espinosa. Espinosa and three other FRD activists arrived in Chile during October 1961 as refugees from Cuba. From then until March 1965, their activities—which included compiling a list of every Chilean who had visited Cuba—were subsidized by the CIA. They "placed" anti-Castro propaganda in *El Mercurio, La Tarde, La Segunda*, etc., during and after 1962.

180. In June 1964, the leaders of the Socialist and Communist parties complained that they were unable to buy time on the following stations: Radio Sociedad Nacional de Agricultura (branches in Santiago, Valparaíso, Los Angeles); La Voz de Chile (branches in Antófagasta, Valparaíso, Santiago, Concepción, Temuco and Puerto Montt); Radio Cooperativa Vitalicia; and Corporación Chilena de Broadcasting y Television. Major restrictions (such as broadcasting at one A.M., limitation to twenty sentences or censorship) were charged to Radio Sociedad Nacional Minería and Radio Portales. Chile, Senado, *Diario* CCXCIV, ses. 2 (10 junio 1964), pp. 23-26, 56-57.

181. "Interestingly enough, Allende ended the campaign personally in debt to the Banco de Chile for a considerable amount of money borrowed for the campaign." Gil and Parrish, 1, 43.

For FRAP charges that the disparity of resources was not of minor significance as well as an indication of the magnitude in terms of sound trucks, broadcasts, etc.,—see: Olavarria, *Alessandri*, IV, pp. 205, 293, 307, 313, 323-26, 332-33; Chile, Senado, *Diario*, CCXCIII, ses. 56 (13 mayo 1964), pp. 4390, 4397; CCXCIV, ses. 2 (10 junio 1964), pp. 23-32, 55-57; ses. 12 (21 julio 1964), pp. 1253-57; CCXCVI, ses. 6 (15 diciembre 1964), pp. 378-81.

It is very unlikely that FRAP received significant financial aid from either the Soviet Union or Cuba. The latter country was financially bankrupt and probably lending what material aid it could to Latin Americans who had accepted the preferred "armed road" in Venezuela and Guatemala. And the Soviets had enhanced Frei's image of "independence" by inviting him to Moscow in the last months of 1963. Luis Corvalan—at a private lunch during the weeks preceding the election—expressed the view that it might be desirable for the Christian Democrats to have to confront the problems of developing Chile during the next twenty years. It is unlikely that the Soviet Union and the East European States wanted to support "another Cuba" in 1964.

Consequently, it is unsurprising that the Popular Action Front accepted and urged a congressional investigation into the sources of campaign finances. Although a PDC senator initially proposed this when confronted by reiterated FRAP charges that United States and other foreign money was financing the "campaign of terror," the proposed investigation was vetoed by those directing the Frei campaign and the Christian Democratic leadership. Chile, Senado, *Diario*, CCXCIV, ses. 12 (21 julio 1964), pp. 1253-54, ses. 13 (22 julio 1964), p. 1381.

182. Espinosa stated that he had released the "Uruttía Letter" to the Chilean anti-Allende press. He had also directed a committee which included CIA agents, exiles, Rightists and possibly Christian Democrats, which arranged for the illegal broadcast of the Juanita Castro tape hours before the election when all propaganda is supposed to be prohibited. The tape had been prepared in Brazil where the text had been written for Castro's sister. At least two Christian Democratic activists and another Cuban exile who had formerly worked with

the CIA and was a close friend of Espinosa attested to the PDC involvement in the placing of the tape. Espinosa, however, claimed that only the Conservatives had assisted his group.

Exile anti-Castro propaganda activities in Chile began as early as 1960. By December 1961, there was a Chilean Committee for Cuban Freedom which was able to organize a meeting for 2,000 persons. In October 1963, the Inter-American Commission on Human Rights was authorized by the Chilean government to schedule an eighteen day session in Santiago. This represented a new precedent for the commission which generally held its sessions in Washington. During its hearings in Santiago, the Cuban Committee for Human Rights "supplied documentation on violations of these rights in Cuba." Presumably, this was broadly diffused in the Chilean mass media. The exiles in Chile were also publishing the weekly *Liborio*. In its April-May 1964 issue, a major critique of the Cuban regime was published under the authorship of René Dumont. Another interesting aspect of the "campaign of terror" involved the publication in Chile of a number of pamphlets which were edited abroad: *Libertad o esclavitud; La Hora de escoger ha llegado; En sus manos esta la decisión; Los próximas elecciones serán la prueba de fuego para el castrismo en hispanoamérica;* and *¿Entre Rusia y Chile, decidase por Chile, doctor Allende?* Similarly, on file in the National Library are such interesting compilations as: *Acción Chilena: Los avisos reproducidos en el presente folleto y otros de la misma índole fueron publicados en diarios y revistas de Chile durante los meses que precedieron al 4 de Septiembre de 1964, día en que la República eligió un nuevo Presidente* (Santiago: Imp. Sopech, 1964), 18 pp., and *Chile en la Encrucijada,* Foro de la Libertad del Trabajo, Relación de los avisos de prensa de la campaña 'Chile en la Encrucijada' reproducidos en el presente folleto (Santiago: Imp. Sopech, 1964), 21 pp. The Cuban Revolution was prominent in both collections of political insertions. References to the matters referred to at the beginning of this paragraph will be found in the following: *El Mercurio*, 16 agosto 1960, p. 25; 20 agosto, p. 17; 22 noviembre, p. 17; 10 diciembre, p. 23; 12 diciembre, p. 27; 13 diciembre, p. 21; 16 diciembre, p. 35; 17 diciembre, p. 25. *New York Times*, Dec. 4, 1961, p. 2. Organization of American States (OAS), *Report of the Secretary General to the Council of the Organization, January 1, 1963-June 30, 1964* (Washington: Pan American Union, 1964), pp. 15-16. Theodore Draper, *Castroism: Theory and Practice* (New York: Praeger, 1965), p. 177. Chile, Senado, *Diario*, CCXCVI, ses. 6 (15 diciembre 1964), p. 386.

183. This is the view of everyone with whom the writer discussed the event during 1966 and 1967. They included maids, university professors, Christian Democrats and FRAPists.

184. Statements to the writer by U.S. Press Attaché Charles Wolfolk on April 4, 1967. According to William P. Rogers, in order "to help Frei, Ambassador Cole was instructed not to make any public statements during the last months of the campaign." Cornell University address on July 30, 1966.

185. Ibid., Wolfolk.

186. Socialist leader Aniceto Rodríguez claimed in the Senate that the meeting was arranged with Allende at Durán's request. Since the latter was a leader of the right wing of the Radical Party and had framed his campaign around the Cuban-Communist issue, this contention appears reasonable. Others have alleged that Allende solicited the interview, and that Anaconda President Rodolfo Michels was with Jova during the subsequent conversation with Durán. Thus, the copper firms may well have aided in financing the anti-FRAP campaign(s). On these matters, see: Chile, Senado, *Diario*, CCXCIII, ses. 56 (13 mayo 1964), p. 4389. "Así Nos Ven," *Ercilla*, XXX (26 agosto 1964), 4 (9 septiembre 1964), p. 11; Gil and Parrish, I, 37-39. M. Gornov, "Who Will be President of Chile?" *New Times*, No. 24 (June 17, 1964), p. 16.

187. The fiscal 1963 Food for Peace agreement which was signed on August 7, 1962, provided that 80 percent of the return on sales be used for economic development purposes. But 20 percent of the $21,011,000 was reserved for embassy purposes. A fiscal 1964 agreement was signed for $20,900,000 with a similar arrangement. It is impossible to ascertain what portion of these embassy funds were used for its maintenance, the USIA program, the Cultural Exchange Program or for assisting anti-Communist groups. The possibility that such aid may have been provided has been implied by a former Washington correspondent of the *Wall Street Journal*: "Disimulo fué la palabra indicada para la actitud de Johnson con respecto a Chile, aunque durante toda la primavera y el verano del año 1964 hubo al menos una fuerte posibilidad de que Chile se hubiera convertido en la primera Nacion que en la

historia hubiera elegido el comunismo por la vía electoral. . . . La Administración Johnson
. . . deseaba fervientemente hacer triunfar al principal oponente de Allende: Eduardo Frei,
y, desde esta evidencia, no estaba dispuesta a dejarlo todo a la suerte. Pero el apoyo abierto
o cualquier actividad pública en favor de Frei, nuevamente habría sido casi un tiro por la
culata. De esa manera Johnson sólo podía perder; nadie iba a creerle en las posibilidades de
victoria de Frei. Pero el triunfo de Allende en septiembre de 1964, exactamente antes de las
elecciones en Estados Unidos hubiera sido un punto negro en contra de la Administración de
Johnson y de los demócratas, a pesar de lo que pudieran hacer para evitarlo.

Lo que debía hacerse no podía ser conocido; había muchas maneras de que la influencia norteamericana se manifestara: con fondos para la campaña, con oportunas declaraciones de simpatía para objetivos específicos de Frei y muchas otras formas que los repre-
sentantes oficiales del gobierno de Estados Unidos estaban comprensiblemente impedidos de
explicar. Lo único que estaba absolutamente claro era—como un ayudante del Presidente
Johnson dijo—que 'ayudamos a Frei silenciosamente, detrás de bastidores." Philip L.
Geyelin, *Lyndon B. Johnson and The World* (New York: Praeger, 1966), p. 122, quoted
from "Johnson ?es chileno?" *Punto Final*, I (2.a quincena de julio de 1967), 13. With regard
to the Food for Peace agreements, see Chile, Senado, *Diario*, CCXCIII, ses. 4 (22 octubre
1963), p. 338; Jaime Barros P.C., *Muerte al Imperialismo Yanqui* (Santiago: Imp. Entrecerros, 1965), p. 27; U.S., *Foreign Aid In Action*, p. 13, U.S., *Department of State Bulletin*,
XLII (February 22, 1960), 309.

188. Between sixty and seventy thousand dollars worth of CARITAS U.S.-donated
foods were diverted to Christian Democratic campaigners during the 1964 campaign. This
was "discovered" in a post-election audit by AID. Statement during April 1967 by AID
Program Loan Administrator Andrew Moorhead to Philip O'Brien, Ford Foundation Fellow.
The amount involved was confirmed by AID official Charles Johnson during a conversation
with the writer on August 9, 1967. Both were stationed in Chile.

189. On the post-victory panic, see *Time* (Canadian Edition), October 9, 1970, p. 26.

190. Bodenheimer, "Stagnation in Liberty," p. 4.

191. *Time* (Canadian Edition), October 9, 1970, p. 25.

192. "A traves del Mundo: Chile," *Bohemia* (La Habana), 25 de diciembre de 1970, p.
80.

193. Ibid., p. 32.

194. The yearly amounts were: 17.3 (1953-1957); 6.7 (1958); 5.4 (1959); 2.7 (1960);
9.7 (1961); 12.3 (1962); 25.1 (1963); 9.7 (1964); and 8.0 (1965). U.S., *Foreign Aid in
Action*, p. 14.

195. U.S., *Foreign Assistance Act of 1963*, V, 874-75.

196. Vitale, *Y Despues*? pp. 110-12. Bodenheimer, " 'Stagnation in Liberty,' " p. 4.

197. U.S., Department of Defense, *Military Assistance and Sales Facts: March 1970*
(Washington: Office of the Assistant Secretary of Defense for International Security Affairs,
1970), pp. 13, 15.

198. "Police Assistance-Worldwide 1961-69," *NACLA Newsletter*, IV November 1970,
18-21. Cf., Bodenheimer, " 'Stagnation in Liberty,' " p. 18.

199. *El Siglo*, 10 noviembre 1966, p. 3. U.S., *Castro-Communist Subversion*, pp. 18-19.

In 1961, the Carabineros were reported to be receiving U.S. technical assistance in
criminal investigation and "rural policing." The latter may have encompassed counterinsurgency training. "Carabineros exporta nuevas Técnicas Policiales," *Ercilla*, XXVII (26 abril
1961), p. 8.

200. U.S., Department of Defense, *Military Assistance Facts: May 1969* (Washington:
Office of the Assistant Secretary of Defense for International Security Affairs, 1969), p. 21.

201. U.S., *Foreign Assistance Act of 1963*, V, 919.

202. See, e.g., Escuela De Los Americos, Comite de Seguridad, *Teoria, Practica E Insti-
tuciones De Los Gobiernos Totalitarios* (Fuerte Gulick, Zona del Canal: Ejercita De Los EE.
UU. MI 4606, 1-69), passim. There are many pamphlets similar to: *Folleto No. 8-Como
Controla El Comunismo La Vida Del Pueblo*.

203. Testifying in 1963, Gen. Carroll observed that: "As I have already mentioned, the Latin American military generally is alert to the danger posed by international communism. However, there has been a tendency in some nations to depreciate the threat posed by indigenous Communist elements. In these countries, the Communist Party is looked upon as just another element in the political life of the country, and the relationship between local Communists and Moscow Communists is not generally acknowledged.

Nonetheless, over the past 2 or 3 years, there has been an increasing willingness on the part of the great majority of the Latin American armed forces to relate indigenous Communists to the International Communist movement, with a subsequent increase in their own counter-intelligence efforts.

A number of these countries have been exchanging information on subversive movements across their borders." U.S., *Castro-Communist Subversion*, p. 152.

204. And sixteen months later, the commission reported that "(f)ollowing a joint review with the State Department and USIA, the secretary of defense has asked the services and commanders to modify training programs, manuals, and facilities in such a way as to give foreign military trainees a balanced understanding of our society, institutions, and ideas. Some of the subjects to be added to the curriculum are: U.S. government institutions; the judicial system and the doctrine of judicial review; the role of the opposition in a two-party system; the role of the press, radio and television in American life; the position of minority groups in the United States; the diversity of American society; agriculture; the economy; labor; and education." During the early 1960s, about 16,000 foreign military personnel were visiting the United States each year, "as compared with 5,400 or more grantees brought here under the State Department's educational exchange program." U.S., Advisory, *Beacon*, p. 54. U.S., Advisory, *Sequel*, pp. 18, 54.

205. U.S., Department of the Navy, *Informational Program for Foreign Military Trainees and Visitors in the United States* (OPNAVINST 4950. ID CH-1, 14 Dec., 1966), Ch. VI, pp. 31-71. U.S. Army Command and Staff College, *Lesson Plan for the Communist Powers: China* (Fort Leavenworth: Command and General Staff Officer Course, Subject R2811-2/0, School Year 1969-1970), passim. U.S. Armed Forces Institute, *Informational Program on American Life and Institutions* (Madison, Wisconsin: Volumes I-VI, 1965).

206. Olavarría, *Alessandri*, III, 175. *Hispanic American Report*, XIV (March 1961), 65. Edwin Lieuwen speaks (p. 169) of a "sort of Gentleman's Agreement" which conditions non-intervention by the Chilean military. This allegedly requires that the armed forces be allowed "to function unmolested and to look after their own affairs."

207. Writing in 1962, Socialist leader Raúl Ampuero observed that "(a)t present the Republican Militia is being clandestinely organized, and in the armed forces they are eliminating without inhibitions every officer who manifests a progressive mentality or, because of his disciplined attitude, is considered a danger to the perpetuation of the oligarchic system." Halperin, pp. 151-52.

208. The following exchange between Assistant Secretary of State Edwin Martin and Congressman Smith may be instructive on this question:

"Mr. Smith. With regard to the Air Force Latin American College in Panama, that has been going on for some 10 years or more, is it likely to produce some good results in terms of getting them to realize the military should not take over political affairs?

Mr. Martin. My impression is that the air force institution to which you referred, tends to be primarily at a technical level dealing with engine maintenance and matters like this. Largely non-commissioned officer grades are involved. I think that this kind of training lends itself less well to this indoctrination to which you refer than the staff colleges and the school at Fort Gulick where the Army teaches counterinsurgency and other matters of this character.

We tried to see that all of these colleges introduces this concept and we try to promote this kind of approach.

Mr. Smith. When these top people who, 10 years ago, were in the same school in Panama and simultaneously come to the top in the military establishments in their respective countries, this can either be good or bad, can it not?

Mr. Martin. Yes, it can.

Mr. Smith. It could be very good?

Mr. Martin. Yes, sir.

Mr. Smith. I assume that there is a lot of thought going into what could happen in the way of bad results?

Mr. Martin. There is; that is right.

Mr. Smith. By coordinating their small air forces in the various countries, they could help another classmate who is not yet in power in another country.

Mr. Martin. They could, but I think, on the whole, the OAS system is designed to prevent this and I think by this school training they get a contact with the United States which gives us a chance to intervene and influence them in the opposite direction but it is something to be watched." U.S., *Departments for 1964*, pp. 416-17.

Where a perceived Communist threat existed, such "influence" might well operate in a contrary direction. And in the course of his July 30, 1966 address at Cornell University, former Assistant Coordinator for the AFP William P. Rogers accepted the possibility that "in some cases" U.S. military officers in Latin America have "influenced" their Latin American counterparts in the direction of intervention. An officer who has instructed Latin Americans informed the writer during the same summer that in his judgment, social relationships and entertainment have been of greater importance than technical training in the program.

209. Between February 1959 and January 1960, the following were among the officers and missions visiting Chile: in February eleven USAF officers arrived for six days on a mission to check the use of U.S. equipment and to ascertain "what is needed"; in March several USAF officers arrived in Santiago for an International Civil Air Patrol Conference in which the exchange of cadets was to be discussed; a month later, Gen. Randolph McCall Pate, commandant of the USMC, stopped in Chile for a one day "fact finding" visit; during November, Maj. Gen. Leland S. Stranathan, chief of the USAF Caribbean Command, arrived for a stay during which he was to hold conversations with the commander of the Chilean Air Force and the minister of defense; in December, a U.S. Military Mission plane flew the commander of the Chilean Air Force to the Canal Zone so that he could be present at the graduation of the Albrook Field Latin American School; and during January 1960, high defense department and military officials stopped in Chile while on a Latin American "fact finding" tour to survey nutritional problems. *El Mercurio*, 22 febrero 1959, p. 23, 28 febrero, 1 marzo, p. 23, 2 marzo, p. 17, 3 marzo, p. 13, 4 marzo, p. 1, 7 marzo, p. 1, 4 abril, p. 17, 6 abril, p. 19, 8 noviembre, p. 29, 11 noviembre, p. 1, 6 diciembre, p. 39, 5 enero 1960, p. 17.

210. The year 1959 will again be used for illustrative purposes. The list which follows may not be wholly inclusive: U.S. Ambassador Howe conferred the Legion of Merit on Col. Humberto Zamorano who had served as military attaché in the Chilean Embassy at Washington; the Chilean Armed Forces decorated Gen. Wesley W. Scott, chief of the U.S. Military Mission in Chile on his return to the United States; at the Chilean Airforce Club and in the presence of high ranking Chilean officers, Ambassador Howe conferred the Legion of Merit upon Col. Osvaldo Croquevielle Cardemil, a former Air Force attaché at the embassy in Washington; the commander-in-chief of the Chilean Army invited Gen. Charles I. Dasher, commander-in-chief of U.S. Armed Forces in the Canal Zone, to be an honored guest at the Chilean Independence Day celebrations; Dasher was awarded the Great Star of Military Valor ("El general Izurieta, quien confirió la distinción, entre otros conceptos señaló que con especial complacencia tenía el honor de expresar el sincero afecto y calido reconocimiento del Ejército chileno hacia el general Dasher con motivo de su visita al país para asistir a las festividades patrias. El general Dasher al agradecer, dijo: 'Esas palabras, salidas, desde el fondo de un corazón bien puestopuesto, comprometen mi gratitud. Quisiera tomarías, más que como un homenje a mi persona y a mis modestos servicios profesionales en el Ejército, como una expresión del afecto que usted ha demostrado a través de su vida hacia nuestra patria y hacia nuestras instituciones.' "); the Commander in Chief of the Chilean Air Force presented to Major Thomas Manjak (USAF) "las distinciones 'Piloto de Guerra Honorario' y 'Estrella Militar' en reconocimiento a la labor desarrollada en la FACH, y a su valiosa cooperación prestada a nuestro país." *El Mercurio*, 9 abril 1959, p. 1, 10 abril, p. 15, 29 julio, p. 14, 1 septiembre, p. 18, 17 septiembre, p. 21, 18 septiembre, p. 20, 20 septiembre, p. 21, 22 septiembre, p. 17, 23 septiembre, p. 19, 14 octubre, p. 17.

Other efforts to promote favorable images have involved performances by U.S. Navy and Air Force bands in Santiago, "Good Neighbor" visits by U.S. naval vessels, and at least one U.S. Navy maritime exhibit. *El Mercurio* 6 febrero 1959, p. 1, 26 abril, p. 43, 20 octubre 1960, p. 1. U.S., Information Agency, *18th Report to Congress*, January 1-June 30, 1962 (Washington: Government Printing Office, 1962), p. 26.

211. Quoted from the U.S., Air Force, *Bibliography for Latin America* (Albrook Air Force Base, Canal Zone: Caribbean Air Command, Historical Division, Office of Information, 1959), Foreword. During the last week in January 1967, Secretary of State Rusk was described as telling a group of senators, who were opposed to the resumption of economic and military aid to Indonesia, that within "a few weeks" Sukarno would resign or be deposed. "Defendiendo anto los senadores el nuevo plan de Johnson, Rusk afirmó que la ayuda prestada anteriormente a Indonesia 'contribuyó a crear lazos y amistades con los dirigentes militares,' y que esa ayuda 'había sido una de las mejores inversiones hechas por este país,' " Sukarno was deposed on February 21st. Fernando Murillo V., "15 millones de dólares por Sukarno," *Punto Final*, I (1.a quincena de abril de 1967), 26.

212. U.S., *Departments for 1964*, p. 394.

213. The delegation included or was led by a Brig. Gen. named Walters. In 1962, Walters, who had worked as a liaison official with Gen. Costelo Branco in Italy during World War II, had been appointed as a military attaché in Río. *Newsweek* of November 10, 1966, has been quoted as reporting that "una semana antes del golpe de Estado (1964), Walters cablegrafió todos los detalles de su organización a Washington, y el día después que Castello Branco tomara posesión como Presidente, almorzó con él privadamente en el palacio presidencial." L. Kamynin, "Chile: Pre-election Volcano," *International Affairs* (Moscow), no. 8 (August 1964), p. 60. "Está en Chile el yanqui que derrocó a Goulart," *Punto Final*, I (diciembre 1966), 7.

214. Fear of an impending golpe by the military was reported to be prevalent among Freístas and especially in the FRAP. Several FRAP leaders were so concerned that they obtained an interview with Alessandri and held conversations with the Minister of Interior. Luís Hernández Parker, "Al Final: la Batalla Psicológica," *Ercilla*, XXX (19 agosto 1964), 16-17.

215. "President of the Senate Hugh Zepeda Barros made it clear that Congress would never confirm the FRAP candidate as president even if he got the largest number of votes. . . ." Kamyn, "Chile," p. 60. Given the refusal of some FRAPist Congressmen to vote for Alessandri in 1958, and the intense fear and hatred that infused the 1964 campaign, this appears to be a reasonable prognostication. The feeling that a FRAP victory would mean the end of the system was sensed and articulated generally—except by the FRAP leadership for tactical reasons. The joint maneuvers, which would involve the landing of 4,000 U.S. sailors and marines, were denounced by FRAP Senators. Chile, Senado, *Diario*, CCXCIV, ses. 23 (18 agosto 1964), pp. 2197-2209. Had the Congress refused to vote for Allende—assuming he had received a plurality—it is virtually certain that there would have been a general strike and violent demonstrations on a massive scale. Had Chilean internal security forces been unable to cope with the outraged demonstrators, there is at least a fair probability that the United States would have intervened. The following exchange may be instructive in this regard:

"Mr. Selden. . . .In the event Communist subversion reaches the point that some freely elected government in Latin America is overthrown as a result of Communist infiltration and subversion, and this freely elected government requests the United States to move in and help them, are we prepared to do so or has any policy decision been made along that line?

Mr. Martin. I do think it is difficult to anticipate all the circumstances in which military force may or may not be used, military force being what it is and having chain reactions. Nevertheless, the Declaration of Punta del Este contemplates bilateral assistance on request in dealing with Communist subversion. And our basic position is that any government which asks us for help in this matter will receive help. We are prepared militarily in anticipation of a political decision to give it." U.S., *Castro-Communist Subversion*, p. 48.

216. U.S., *Rockefeller Report Hearing*, pp. 8-11, 26, 35-6, 120-22.

217. U.S., Congress, House, Committee on Foreign Affairs, *Cuba and the Caribbean*, Hearings, before the Subcommittee on Inter-American Affairs of the Committee on Foreign Affairs, House of Representatives, 91st Cong., 2nd sess., July-August 1970, pp. 91-2.

218. Ibid., pp. 97-9. Cf., *Rockefeller Report Hearing*, pp. 85, 93, 117-19.

219. *El Siglo*, 28 noviembre 1970, p. 7.
220. *Time* (Canadian Ed.), November 2, 1970, p. 20. *Granma* (Weekly Review), November 1, 1970, p. 12.
221. *Time* (Canadian Ed.), October 9, 1970, p. 30.
222. Aid to the other non-governmental organizations also tended to alleviate discontent and promote non-receptive attitudinal orientations among lower class persons towards FRAP propaganda. The Peace Corps similarly contributed to such an outcome.
223 It is worth noting that between the mid-1950s and 1962, there was a rise in pro-United States sentiment both generally and in terms of Cold War alignment. By 1964, there was a measurable decline in sentiment favoring nationalization of foreign firms. And between 1961 and 1964, public opinion polls indicated a marked decline in the popularity of Castro as well as the Cuban Revolution—and an even more marked rise in hostile sentiments. See earlier sections of this chapter and chapter 9.

Chapter 6. Discomfort and Antagonism:
The Response of the Chilean Right

1. The classification of these sectors as "right" is in accord with common usage in contemporary Chilean politics. In general, the various Marxist tendencies and groups are characterized as "left," while the "center" parties are the Radicals (PR) and Christian Democrats (PDC).
2. On these matters, see: Gil, pp. 248-50; Pike, p. 243; Peter G. Snow, "The Political Party Spectrum in Chile," *South Atlantic Quarterly*, LXII (Autumn 1963), 475; and Petras, *Politics and Social Forces*, p. 103.
3. "El Partido Conservador busca ajustar su Programa más que a declaraciones Teóricas, a un análisis realista de lo que es nuestro país; y, como confome a sus doctrinas y su acción a las enseñanzas de la Iglesia Católica, en ellas inspira todas las soluciones que propone." "Discurso del señor Prieto (Jorge Prieto Letelier, Presidente Nacional del Partido Conservador)," *Acción Conservadora*, I (octubre-noviembre 1959), 10. Cf., Gil, pp. 246-48.
4. *El Mercurio*, 25 mayo 1959, pp. 2. Cf., Juventud Conservadora, *El Partido Conservador: su Programa, su Labor*, Redactado y Editado por la Juventud Conservadora (Santiago: Imp. Arancibia Hnos., n.d. (deposited at the National Library in August 1964), 18p.
5. Fernando Aldunate, *?Por Qué los Conservadores estamos con Julio Durán?* (Santiago: 'El Diario Ilustrado,' febrero 1964).
6. Edwards y Frei, p. 223.
7. At its National Convention in 1959, the party called for: the outlawing of communism; a "new agricultural policy" not involving land distribution; an end of the University of Chile's authority over curricula in private schools and the introduction of religious instruction in public schools; and the use of the State to curb monopolistic abuses and to promote private business enterprise. "Convención PCU por Dentro: FRIA, Pero Quema," *Ercilla*, XXV (28 octubre 1959), 8-9. *El Mercurio*, 26 octubre 1959, p. 23.
8. Social legislation proposed in Congress by Conservatives from 1906 to 1959 is itemized in the Chile, Senado, *Diario*, CCLXXXVIII, ses. 36 (22 agosto 1961), pp. 1966-69.
9. "La Elección," *Ercilla*, XXIV (3 septiembre 1958), 7-8.
10. When they had decided to support the illegalization of the Communists, a civil libertarian wing of the Conservative Party had withdrawn and organized the Social Christian Party. In 1957, the bulk of this group merged with the National Falange to become the Christian Democratic Party. A small faction rejoined the Conservatives whose name was changed to United Conservative Party (PCU).
11. Jorge Alessandri, *Discurso —Programa del candidato Independiente don Jorge Alessandri Rodríguez* (Santiago: Edit. Lord Cochrane, 1958), pp. 3-24. *Hispanic American Report*, XI (August 1958), 455, (September 1958), p. 514.
12. See, e.g., the editorial page column on July 3, 1958, p. 3. With regard to the intimate relationship between this daily and the PCU leadership, see "Un personaje al Trasluz," *Ercilla*, XXVII (17 mayo 1961), 11.

13. *El Mercurio*, 12 agosto, 1959, p. 19.

14. *El Mercurio*, 27 agosto 1959, p. 29. 1 septiembre, p. 19.

15. Cristian Perez Fernández, "Juventud y Señorio," *Acción Conservadora*, I (Septiembre 1959), 1-3.

16. 6 noviembre, p. 3.

17. Interview with Rafael Espinosa, May 5, 1967.

18. Five days after his initial attempt, Coloma succeeded in having the five page "Cuba Denounces the Communist Conspiracy and the Betrayal by the Castro Regime of the Ideals of the Cuban Revolution" inserted with the backing of Radical and Christian Democratic votes. Chile, Senado, *Diario*, CCLXXXVI, ses. 25 (16 agosto 1960), pp. 1568-73, ses. 29 (23 agosto 1960), pp. 1956-66.

19. *Hispanic American Report*, XIII (October 1960), 554.

20. *El Mercurio*, 29 diciembre 1960, p. 17.

21. *Las Noticias de Ultimate Hora*, 18 abril 1961, p. 9. *La Nacion*, 20 abril 1961, p. 5, 22 abril, p. 1.

22. During the debate, Bulnes charged that the "alleged social reforms" of the Revolutionary Government had been used to justify all attacks upon human dignity, civil liberties and religious freedom. He rejected the view that mass demonstrations by hundreds of thousands in support of the Revolution were sufficient to give it a democratic basis. He also denied that the course of the Castro government could be defended by referring to the corruption or U.S. dominance that characterized Cuba under Batista. Bulnes went on to ask why the FRAPists had not been so critical of Soviet intervention and dominance in Eastern Europe, Hungary or Tibet. Turning to the Chilean scene, the Conservative leader denied that the masses wanted a revolution, and stated that the willingness of dominant groups to provide greater social opportunities would reinforce that orientation. Chile, Senado, *Diario*, CCLXXXVII, ses. 37 (18 abril 1961), pp. 2123-27. Cf., ses. 43 (2 mayo 1961), pp. 2391-95.

23. "Semana Política," *Ercilla*, XXVII (25 octubre 1961), 8-9. "Semana Política," Ibid., (29 noviembre 1961), p. 7. "La 'Batalla' del Senado," Ibid. (13 diciembre 1961), p. 8. L.H.P., "Semana Política," Ibid., XXVIII (31 enero 1961), 8-9.

24. Collective armed intervention was also advocated, as were measures to halt the Cuban sponsored "infiltration of Communism," "Un Personaje al Trasluz," *Ercilla*, XXVII (17 mayo 1961), 11. "Juicio Secreto de los Partidos," ibid., XXVIII (7 febrero 1962), 7-8. L.H.P., "Ofensiva Anti-PC en Dos Dimensiones," ibid., (15 agosto 1962), p. 7. "La SIP: Vigorosa Defensa de la Libertad de Prensa," ibid., (24 octubre 1962), pp. 16-17. "Chile: El Bloqueo no Llegó al Río," ibid., (31 octubre 1962), p. 9. *El Siglo*, 30 Octubre 1962, p. 1.

25. In the 1957 congressional election, the PCU had received more than 16 percent of the vote. This declined to 14.9 percent in the 1960 municipal election, and now fell to 14.7 percent. Despite the small decline a net loss of seats resulted. The Marxist parties increased from about 18 percent in 1960 to 22.5 percent in 1961. Gil, pp. 238, 310.

26. "La Semana Política," *Ercilla*, XXVII (12 julio 1961), 8.

27. "Semana Política," ibid. (19 julio 1961), p. 9.

28. "La Semana Política," ibid. (2 agosto 1961), pp. 8-9. Cf., Juventud Conservadora, *Acuerdos Adoptados por la Asamblea Plenaria en la Reunión Ampliada Efectuada por la Juventud Conservadora*, El Dia 2 de Diciembre de 1962, Y Otros Acuerdos (Santiago: Juventud Conservadora, 1963).

29. Gil, p. 247.

30. Yet other planks endorsed: state promotion of industrial growth through incentives to private capital; the avoidance of "excessive" taxation; relaxation of the state oil monopoly and the sale of other state enterprises once they had become profitable; encouragement of foreign capital to invest in the country; taxation of large farms only in accord with their productive potential; and the promotion of private education. Juventud Conservadora, pp. 4-12.

31. After also suggesting that the United States support higher stabilized prices for Latin American exports and that U.S. firms be required to invest more of their profits, Bulnes concluded: "Si están dispuestos a ello, bienvenida sea la Alianza para el Progreso. Si no es ese su propósito, mejor sería que los gobernantes y la prensa norteamericana dejarán de agitar nuestros problemas económico-sociales. No sea que al ponerlos más de relieve, sin darnos soluciones adecuadas, contribuyen a precipitar la caída en régimenes análogos al de Cuba." "La Semana Política," *Ercilla*, XXVII (5 julio 1961), 9.

32. When the FD agreement was first publicized at a May 1962 meeting of leaders from the Liberal, Conservative and Radical parties, it was reported that "(t)odos fueron estremecidos por los oráculos 'made in USA' de las pitonizas de la Alianza para el Progreso. Que si no hacían profundas reformas y les quitaban los latifundios a los poderosos, era fatal el triunfo del comunismo. En Chile sólo la unión de todas fuerzas democráticas (de conservadoras a democratacristianos y padenistas) podría impedir el triunfo ineluctable de Salvador Allende, portador y portavoz de la revolución cubana." LHP, "Listo Frente Democrático: Nace con Cuentas Alegres," *Ercilla, XXVIII* (30 mayo 1962), 9.

33. The PCU percentage of the total vote declined from 14.7 in 1961 to 11.4 in this contest. Gil, p. 238.

34. Francisco Bulnes Sanfuentes, *Cuenta del Presidente del Partido Conservador Don Francisco Bulnes Sanfuentes ante el Directorio General del Partido celebrado el l. o de 1963* (Santiago: Imp Sopech, 1963), pp. 3ff. Cf., Aldunate, pp. 4f.

35. LHP, "Curico Borró la Duda," *Ercilla*, XXX (18 marzo 1964), 15-17.

36. Gil, p. 248. Cf., " 'Americanos del Sur, Unidos!' " *Ercilla*, XXVI (3 febrero 1960), 9.

37. Edwards y Frei, p. 222. Gil, pp. 254-55. Petras, *Politics and Social Forces*, pp. 101-103.

38. See, e.g., Igor Entrala, "Divorcio separa a los Partidos," ibid., XXX (12 agosto 1964), 10-11. Cf., *El Mercurio*, 17 enero 1960, p. 11.

39. Raul Mellado, "Liberales no se oponen a relaciones con la URSS," *Vistazo*, VII (11 agosto 1959), 8. "Tema Polémico en Cóctel Abigarrado Relaciones con la URSS," *Ercilla*, XXV (26 agosto 1959), 8.

And in April 1961, the Liberal Youth even participated in the open Executive Committee meeting in Santiago of the Prague-based World Federation of Democratic Youth. *Hispanic American Report*, XIV (June 1961), 353.

40. In October 1959, for example, the Liberal Party conferred the title of "Honorary Director" upon Rafael Maluenda for "his services to the party, its doctrines and the fatherland." Maluenda was then Director of the daily. Its owner, Augustin Edwards Eastman is one of the most plutocratic industrialist-financiers in Chile, *El Mercurio*, 12 octubre 1959, p. 27. "Dime con quién andas y te diré quién eres," *Punto Final*, Año I, N. o 20 (enero 1967), pp. 18-19.

Yet, between 1964 (or earlier) and 1967, the daily's Director was Rene Silva Espejo, an individual of distinctly "non-liberal" origins. "Rene Silva fué el creador de los diarios 'El Sol' y 'El Trabajo', ambos voceros del nazismo en vísperas de la Segunda Guerra Mundial. El subdirector de 'El Mercurio', Arturo Fontaine, perteneció al equipo de la revista de corte fascista 'Estanquero' y es redactor de los artículos políticos del matutino del grupo Edwards que llevan la firma Kleck." *Las Noticias de Ultima Hora*, 14 Julio 1967, p. 2. Olavarría, *Alessandri*, IV, 231-32.

41. For examples of firm opposition to trade relations with the Soviet Union, see columns and editorials which appeared on 16 diciembre 1959, p. 3, 19 enero 1960, p. 3, 3 marzo 1960, p. 3. Its position had not changed when Frei—whom it had supported in the presidential campaign established diplomatic relations with the USSR in November 1964. Joaquin Gutierrez, "Chile and the Socialist Countries," *New Times*, No. 13 (March 31, 1965). With respect to the 1970 campaign and its aftermath, see *The Halifax Chronicle Herald* (Canada), December 21, 1970.

42. Gil, p. 253.

43. Ibid., p. 254.

44. Partido Liberal, Juventud Liberal, *Principios, Estatutos y Reglamentos Aprobados en la 7. a Convención Nacional celebrada en Santiago los días 24, 25 y 26 de Abril de 1959* (Santiago: Imp. Chile, 1959), pp. 3-6. Cf., Juventud Liberal, *Principios, Estatutos y Reglamentos Aprobados en la VI Convención Nacional celebrada en Santiago los días 6 y 7 de Mayo de 1950* (Santiago: Duble Almeyda 1386, 1958), p. 4.

45. Gil, p. 310.

46. *El Mercurio*, 5 noviembre 1959, p. 19.

47. *El Mercurio*, 14 diciembre 1959, p. 3, 15 enero, 1960, p. 1, 18 enero, p. 3.

48. Chile, Senado, *Diario*, CCLXXXVI, ses. 11 (28 junio 1960), p. 586.

49. *El Mercurio*, 16 diciembre 1960, p. 35.

352

50. *La Nación*, 22 abril 1961, p. 1. *Hispanic American Report*, XIV (June 1961), 352-53.

51. Chile, Senado, *Diario*, CCLXXXVII, ses. 45 (9 mayo 1961), pp. 2528-32.

52. "The delegates to the congress, representing traditional liberal parties, devoted themselves to repeated and vehement denunciations of Communism and its adopted son, Fidel Castro. Composed of delegations from 15 Latin American nations and representatives of exile organizations from others, the congress called on the OAS to adopt an 'interventionist attitude' until plebiscites under its supervision brought democracy to the 'tyrannical governments' of Nicaragua, Paraguay, Cuba and Haiti. One indication that representatives from Christian Democratic parties were numerous was the congress' declaration that a new America must be built and based on a concept of 'bread, liberty and faith.' There was relatively little criticism of U.S. policies. Significantly, the honorary chairman was a Cuban leader, Luis Conte Aguero." *Hispanic American Report*, XIV (August 1961), p. 565.

53. Humberto Malinarich M., "Chile Hierve con la Guerra Fría," *Ercilla*, XXVII (26 abril 1961), 17-18.

54. *El Mercurio*, 22 marzo 1958, p. 3, 4 abril, p. 3. Although a few exceptional commentaries were at variance with the textual statements, the latter are fairly based upon a systematic reading of all columns and editorials published from Jan. 1, 1959 until Jan. 1, 1961.

55. While enjoying his "leader grant" in the United States, the former PL President publicly called attention to the danger of Communism in the hemisphere, and stated that the United States must lead in the effort to combat this menace. He characterized Castro as "demagogic" and harmful for Latin America. *El Mercurio*, 8 mayo 1960, p. 9.

56. Chile, Senado, *Diario*, CCLXXXVIII, ses. 36 (22 agosto 1961), pp. 1958-65.

57. Ibid., ses. 38 (23 agosto 1961), pp. 2111-12; ses. 49 (12 septiembre 1961), pp. 2945-46, CCXC, ses. 27 (27 julio 1962), pp. 2017-26; ses. 38 (22 agosto 1962), p. 2809, CCXCII, ses. 27 (7 agosto 1963), pp. 1742-45, ses. 49 (4 septiembre 1963), p. 3517, CCXCIII, ses. 56 (13 mayo 1964), pp. 4353-64, CCXCIV, ses. 11 (15 julio 1964), p. 1095, ses. 16 (4 agosto 1964), pp. 1732-39.

58. "Chile: El Bloqueo no Llegó al Río," *Ercilla*, XXVIII (31 octubre 1962), 9.

59. Humberto Malinarich M., "Confesiones a 10 mil metros de altura," ibid., XXVII (18 octubre 1961), 6.

60. ". . . en la colectividad más individualista, tradicional y derechista se impuso, por abrumadora mayoría, el reclamo brutal de las urgencias de 'hacer algo por la vía democrática, antes que soportar mucho por la revolución violenta.' " "Semana Política," ibid., (22 noviembre 1961), 9. Cf., "Lección de Decano: 'Alarmese el Senado,' "ibid., (11 octubre 1961), p. 9, and Malinarich, "Confesiones."

61. Chile, Senado, *Diario*, CCXC, ses. 20 (25 julio 1962), pp. 1646-70, ses. 27 (27 julio 1962), p. 2082, ses. 38 (22 agosto 1962), pp. 2814-15.

62. Some, such as Julio von Muhlenbrock, actually extolled the AFP as well as the United States. Ibid., ses. 20 (24 julio 1962), pp. 1672-73. Cf., Malinarich, "Confesiones."

63. LHP, "Listo Frente Democrático." *Hispanic American Report*, XIV (August 1961), 543, (December 1962), 946-47.

64. In March 1963, it was reported that some Liberal leaders had joined their PCU colleagues in attempting to persuade the Christian Democrats to enter the FD. There were even hints that Frei might be acceptable as a presidential nominee. But after major gains in the 1963 municipal elections, the PDC had decided to field its own candidate. See LHP, "Cerco Derechista al PDC Inquieta al P. Radical," *Ercilla*, XXIX (27 marzo 1963), 19.

65. "La Elección."

66. In the March 1965 congressional election, the PL obtained about 8 percent of the vote. It had fallen from 16.5 in 1961, and 13.2 in the 1963 municipal election. Gil, pp. 238, 310.

67. "Semana Política," *Ercilla*, XXVII (18 octubre 1961), 9.

68. On these matters, see: LHP, "La Silenciosa 'Batalla' de La Misión Molina - Piñera," ibid., XXVIII (28 noviembre 1962), 16-17; Olavarría, *Alessandri*, III, 116-22; U.S., *Foreign Aid in Action*, p. 30; Chile, Ministerio de Relaciones Exteriores de Chile, *Gira Continental del Presidente de la República Excmo. Señor Jorge Alessandri Rodríquez: 9 al 21 diciembre 1962* (Santiago: Zig-Zag, 1963), pp. 36, 38; Igor Entrala, "Balance."

69. *El Mercurio*, 21 enero 1959, p. 19, 22 enero, p. 21, 27 enero; p. 1, 29 enero, p. 1, 6 febrero, p. 18, 18 febrero, p. 1, 22 febrero, p. 31, 18 marzo, p. 28.

70. *New York Times*, November 4, 1961, p. 7.

71. "Semana Política," *Ercilla*, XXVII (8 noviembre 1961), 16.

72. Ibid. (15 noviembre 1961), p. 2.

73. In fact, Foreign Minister Vergara had delivered a note of protest to Cuban Ambassador Lechuga who issued a conciliatory statement in reply. *El Mercurio*, 18 agosto 1959, pp. 1, 12.

74. *Hispanic American Report*, XII (October 1959), 452.

75. "Frases y Personajes," *Ercilla*, XXV (16 agosto 1959), 10.

76. United Nations, Office of Public Information, *Yearbook of the United Nations, 1960* (New York: United Nations, 1961), pp. 158-59. United Nations, General Assembly, 15th Session, November 1, 1960, *Official Records: 910th Plenary Meeting*, p. 817. United Nations, Office of Public Information, *Yearbook of the United Nations, 1961* (New York: United Nations, 1963), pp. 118-19. United Nations, General Assembly, 16th Session, First Committee, February 9, 1962, *Official Records; 1235th Meeting*, pp. 393-94, February 15, 1962, *Official Records: 1243rd Meeting*, pp. 436-37. United Nations, *Yearbook of the United Nations, 1962* (New York: Columbia University Press in Cooperation with the United Nations, 1964), pp. 101-104, 111. United Nations, Security Council, February 27, 1962, *Official Records: 991st Meeting*, pp. 3-4, March 16, 1962, *Official Records: 994th Meeting*, pp. 7-15. Cf., *Hispanic American Report*, XIII (November 1960), 605, XIV (July 1961), 409, and Edward B. Glick, "Cuba and the Fifteenth UN General Assembly: A Case Study in Regional Disassociation," *Journal of Inter-American Studies*, VI (April 1964), 236-42.

77. United Nations, *Yearbook for 1960*, pp. 154-56.

78. Ibid., pp. 157-58. United Nations, Security Council, Jan. 5, 1961, *Official Records: 923rd Meeting*, pp. 8-11. *New York Times*, Jan. 5, 1961, pp. 1, 8.

79. United Nations, *Yearbook for 1960*, pp. 159-64. United Nations, General Assembly, 15th Session, First Committee, April 21, 1961, *Official Records: 1160th Meeting*, p. 106.

80. *Hispanic American Report*, XI (August 1958), 455 (September 1958), p. 514.

81. The credits were extended by U.S. Government lending institutions and private banks. Three-quarters of the total were earmarked for "economic development." At the same time Chile had signed an exchange stabilization agreement. *El Mercurio*, 19 mayo 1959, p. 1, 20 mayo, p. 1. *Hispanic American Report*, XII (July 1959), 284.

82. *El Mercurio*, 11 julio 1959, p. 1.

83. *El Mercurio*, 1 agosto 1959, p. 1, 6 agosto, p. 17. Cf., Hernández Parker, "La Semana Política," *Ercilla*, XXV (5 agosto 1959), 8.

84. *El Mercurio*, 13 agosto 1959, p. 3. *South Pacific Mail*, Aug. 14, 1959, p. 17.

85. With regard to the U.S. position, see the *New York Times*, Aug. 12, 1959, p. 8, Aug. 14, p. 2.

86. During the conference the FRAP had sponsored a rally in Santiago to protest the defeat of the Cuban position on the agenda. Armando Hart's remarks at the demonstration have already been commented upon. With regard to Roa's, see *El Mercurio*, 24 agosto 1959, p. 24.

87. *El Mercurio*, 3 septiembre 1959, p. 23.

88. 28 enero 1960, p. 3.

89. "Mas AYUDA, Menos Armas para la América Latina," *Ercilla*, XXVI (10 febrero 1960), 22.

90. *Hispanic American Report*, XIII (April 1960), 126.

91. *El Mercurio*, 8 marzo 1960, p. 26.

92. *El Mercurio*, 1 diciembre 1959, p. 1. *Hispanic American Report*, XIII (May 1960), 199. U.S., Department of State, "Joint Statement, Santiago, March 1," *Bulletin*, XLII (March 28, 1960), 483.

93. *El Mercurio*, 8 marzo 1960, p. 1.

94. *Hispanic American Report*, XIII (May 1960), 200.

95. Ibid., (July 1960), p. 311.

96. *El Mercurio*, 16 agosto 1960, p. 1, 17 agosto, p. 23, 20 agosto, p. 28.

97. *Hispanic American Report*, XIII (October 1960), 572-74.

354

98. *El Mercurio*, 18 agosto 1960, p. 14, 25 agosto, p. 16, 29 agosto, p. 29.
99. Luís Hernández Parker, "Reportaje al Juicio de los Cancilleres," *Ercilla*, XXVI (24 agosto 1960), 16-17. LHP, "El fracaso de conciliación chilena," ibid. (7 septiembre 1960), pp. 16-17. Chile, Senado, *Diario*, CCLXXXVI, ses. 41 (13 septiembre 1960), pp. 2953-55.
100. *New York Times*, Jan. 9, 1961, p. 8.
101. *Hispanic American Report*, XIV (June 1961), 352.
102. *Las Noticias de Ultima Hora*, 21 abril 1961, p. 3.
103. *Hispanic American Report*, XIV (June 1961), 352-53. The commentary suggests that Vergara's decision was motivated by disappointment at the failure of Chile to publicly criticize the U.S. role.
104. *La Tercera de la Hora*, 23 abril 1961, p. 2. *New York Times*, April 23, 1961, p. 27.
105. "Torbellinos en el PS," *Ercilla*, XXVII (10 mayo 1961), 7. Cf., *Hispanic American Report*, XIV (June 1961), 371. (July 1961), pp. 458-59.
106. Morrison, p. 87.
107. Hernández Parker, "Punta del Este," Cf., "Semana Política," *Ercilla*, XXVII (23 agosto 1961), 8.
108. *Hispanic American Report*, XIV (January 1962), 988 (February 1962), p. 1125.
109. "Semana Política," *Ercilla*, XXVII (25 octubre 1961), 8 (6 diciembre 1961), p. 8.
110. *Hispanic American Report*, XIV (February 1962), 1125. 'Cuba se coloca Escudo Neutral," *Ercilla*, XXVII (3 enero 1962), 23.
111. And it had been implied that unless some strong action were taken, the U.S. Congress might be less than generous in appropriating funds for AFP. Morrison, pp. 181, 189. "USA Elabora Estrategia Frente a Cuba y la URSS," *Ercilla*, XXVII (20 diciembre 1961), 21. Humberto Malinarich, "Punta del Este: La Difícil Cita de los '21,' ibid., XXVIII (31 enero 1962), 15-18. LHP, "Semana Política," ibid., p. 8. Humberto Malinarich, "El Infierno de 'Dantas,' " ibid., (7 febrero 1961), 15-16. Escalona L. Aragon, "Division in the Americas," *New Republic*, February 26, 1962, pp. 9-10. *Hispanic American Report*, XV (March 1962), 79-82. U.S., *Foreign Aid in Action*, p. 15. U.S., *Castro-Communist Subversion*, pp. 225-26. Organization of American States (OAS), *Annual Report of the Secretary General to the Council of the Organization, 1962* (Washington: Pan American Union, 1963), p. 3. Thomas and Thomas, p. 329.
112. OAS, *Report for 1962*, pp. 17-18. Thomas and Thomas, p. 329. Alejandro Magnet, "Bloqueo de Cuba—Elecciones en EE. UU.," *Mensaje*, XI (noviembre 1962), 523. Humberto Malinarich M., "El Mitin de los 20," *Ercilla*, XXVIII (10 octubre 1962), 2.
113. *New York Times*, Oct. 20, 1962, 16.
114. OAS, *Report for 1962*, pp. 3-4. *New York Times*, Oct. 28, 1962, Sec. 4, pp. 4, 6. "Chile: El Bloqueo."
115. *South Pacific Mail*, CVII (Nov. 2, 1962), 16.
116. *La Nación*, 24 octubre 1962, p. 1. Olavarría, *Alessandri*, III, 94-95. Jorge Alessandri, "Mensaje de S.E. El Presidente de la República don Jorge Alessandri Rodríguez al Congreso Nacional al inaugurar el periodo ordinario de sesiones, 21 de mayo de 1963, "Chile, Senado, *Diario*, CCXCII, p. 34.
117. Based upon a statement by a Chilean who was present. Interview with Rafael Espinosa, May 5, 1967.
118. Chile, Senado, *Diario*, CCXCII, ses. 8. (20 junio 1963), pp. 349-53, OAS, *Report for 1962*, pp. 9, 18. OAS, *Report for 1963-64*, p. 10. "Suecedió en junio: en Chile," *Arauco*, IV (Junio 1963), 47. *Hispanic American Report*, XVI (September 1963), 714-15.
119. *Hispanic American Report*, XVI (September 1963), 735.
120. U.S., *Foreign Aid in Action*, pp. 157-58. Alejandro Magnet, "Comentarios Internacionales," *Mensaje*, no.127 (marzo-abril 1964), p. 70.
121. LHP, "Cuba y Chile en Cita de Cancilleres," *Ercilla*, XXX (1 julio 1964), 10. Cf., LHP, "Cancilleres en USA Miran a Cuba," ibid. (22 julio 1964), p. 17.
122. LHP, "Cancilleres en USA." Mario Planet, "La Guerra de los Cancilleres," Ibid., XXX (29 julio 1964), 17. Igor Entrala, "JAR le Quitó el Saludo a Fidel Castro," ibid., (19 agosto 1964), p. 10, OAS, *Report for 1963-64*, pp. 3-4.
123. "Peligrosa Aventura Argentina," *Ercilla*, XXX (29 julio 1964), 25.
124. LHP, "Cancilleres en USA."
125. "Así Nos Ven," *Ercilla*, XXX (26 agosto, 1964), 4. Olavarría, *Alessandri*, IV, pp. 241, 243-44, 248-52.

126. *Hispanic American Report*, XVII (October 1964), 710.

127. Hernández Parker, "Al Final," p. 17.

128. Entrala, "JAR le Quitó," p. 11. For the text of Alessandri's statement, see *Las Noticias de Ultima Hora*, 12 agosto 1964, p. 8. Cf., Olavarría, *Alessandri*, IV, 258-60.

129. *Las Noticias de Ultima Hora*, 14 agosto 1964, p. 3. Cf., Olavarría, *Alessandri*, IV, 267-68.

130. *Hispanic American Report*, XVII (October 1964), 710.

131. LHP, "Cancilleres en USA."

132. Gil and Parrish, I, 44.

133. Alejandro Magnet, "La Novena Reunión de Cancilleres," *Mensaje*, XIII (Septiembre 1964), 407. Igor Entrala, "JAR le Quitó," p. 10.

134. Petras, *Politics and Social Forces*, pp. 217-19.

135. Ibid., p. 224.

136. Weston H. Agor, "Senate vs. CORA: An attempt to Evaluate Chile's Agrarian Reform to Date " *Inter-American Economic Affairs*, XII (Autumn 1968), 47-53.

137. Ronald Gold, "Income Tax Evasion in Chile: An Estimate," *Inter-American Economic Affairs*, XXII (Spring 1969), 59-67.

138. Grayson,"The Frei Administration," p. 52.

139. Selden Rodman, "October Revolution in Chile," *National Review*, October 6, 1970, p. 1054.

140. Grayson, "The Frei Administration," p. 59.

141. Ibid., pp. 62-65.

142. U.S., *Economic Trends*, p. 5.

143. Rodman, "October Revolution," p. 1054. *Granma* (Weekly Review), Nov. 1, 1970, p. 10. U.S., *Cuba and the Caribbean*, p. 200.

144. Vitale, *?Y Despues?*, p. 39.

145. Ibid., p. 41.

146. Rodman, "October Revolution," p. 1054.

147. See the "Programa de Jorge Alessandri," *Política Y Espiritu*, No. 317 (Agosto 1970).

148. Vitale,¿ *Y Despues?*, pp. 42-43. Petras and Zeitlin, "Agrarian Radicalism," p. 264.

149. Vitale,¿ *Y Despues?*, pp. 49-58, 64.

150. Although Frei was personally disliked by Alessandri, it is reasonable to suppose that he was by far the lesser evil in the opinion of the President. The effect of the "Campaign of Terror" was to *exclusively* identify Allende and FRAP with a highly negative image of the Cuban Revolution. Not only FRAP, but the PDC as well had consistently opposed the projected OAS mandate to force an end to diplomatic relations with Havana. Had Alessandri supported instead of opposed the sanctions, the PDC would have been compelled to join FRAP in criticizing the government for failing to defend Chilean self-determination on the crucial matter of diplomatic ties. Similarly, the PDC had long argued that further isolation would drive Cuba even closer to the East. Hence, by being forced to join the FRAP in denouncing Alessandri on the Cuban issue, the PDC would have undermined the propaganda effort to *exclusively* identify Allende with the Castro regime. Thus, Alessandri's firm opposition to sanctions saved the PDC from such a situation, and maximized the effect of the propaganda campaign.

Chapter 7. Radicalization and Equivocation: FRAP Responses to the Cuban Revolution

1. Nationalization also was proposed for: public utilities; coal; foreign commerce; credit, banking and monopolies; and all other basic industries. Additional planks included: tax reform; increasing wages and welfare benefits for the lower classes; facilitation of unionization in rural areas; and the promotion of industrialization. The party's agrarian reform envisaged: elimination of both minifundia and latifundia; the distribution of fallow and

356

state lands to cooperatives and state farms; higher rural wages and improved social legislation. Partido Socialista de Chile, *Programa del Partido Socialista: Fundamentación Teórica y Directivas Programáticas*, I (Santiago: Prensa Latinoamericana, 1961), pp. 1-2, 15.

2. Halperin, pp. 128, 136.

3. Since most of the Socialists had followed Ampuero into the PSP, Allende's percentage may indicate how severely outlawry had weakened the Communist organization. In the 1947 municipal election, their last before González Videla's suppression, the PC alone had won more than 16 percent of the total vote.

4. Soares and Hamblin, "Socio-Economic Variables," p. 1061.

5. Petras and Zeitlin, "Miners," pp. 583-84.

6. Petras, *Politics and Social Forces*, pp. 102-103, 161.

7. Gall, "The Chileans," p. 106.

8. Ibid., p. 107.

9. Reference was made in chapter 3 to governmental suppression to which the CUT was subjected during the mid-1950s. And even in the 1960s, the CUT hardly warranted being described as an "organization."

10. *El Mercurio*, 30 septiembre 1959, p. 3, 2 octubre, p. 19. LHP, "Las 4 Caras del Torneo de la CUT," *Ercilla*, XXVIII (8 agosto 1962), 8.

11. *Informes de las Comisiones al Congreso Nacional de Trabajadores*, p. 2. Rycroft and Clemmer, p. 72.

During 1963, the University of Chile's Institute of Organization and Administration interviewed 231 labor leaders. About half represented unions with at least 500 members. One hundred and fifty were from Santiago, 47 from Valparaíso and 34 lived in Concepción. Among other questions, they were asked: Do you believe that what helps the business firm also helps the union? Only 16 percent replied categorically in the negative, indicating a Marxist class struggle orientation. Seventy-four percent replied that the union benefits in varying degree, and 10 percent replied wholly in the affirmative. Yet 43 percent said that FRAP was the political grouping "most concerned with the problems of the working class," 23 percent identified the PDC, 6 percent the Radicals and 4 percent opted for the PL or the PCU. Nineteen percent stated that "no party" was so committed. Eight years earlier, a USIA survey reported that among the rank and file, only 15 percent believed that if the Communists came to power that their work or income would be "favorably" affected. The percentage "of union members who (thought) communism would hurt unions (was) larger than in the general population. . . ." Rubén Corvalán V., "Habla la Elite Sindical," *Ercilla*, XXIX (20 noviembre 1963), 10-11. USIA, *Chilean Attitudes Toward Communism*, p. 9.

12. Petras, *Politics and Social Forces*, pp. 168-73.

13. Halperin, pp. 132-33.

14. Luís Vitale, "Which Road for Chile," *International Socialist Review*, XXV (Summer 1964), 70. Although Vitale, a Trotskyist, claims the move was wholly a Communist one, in conversations with the writer, Chilean Communists stressed the catalyzing role of Allende.

15. The Eleventh National Congress of the PC proposed that such a broadened coalition be forged upon the basis of the following: defense and expansion of civil liberties; defense of the economic interests of the working class; ending unemployment; raising peasant wage scales, and establishing their right to organize; defense of oil and other natural resources from foreign exploitation; development of diplomatic and economic relations with the USSR and other Socialist states. The program *did not include* agrarian reform, nationalization of U.S. mining firms or major Chilean financial and industrial operations, abrogation of military pacts, withdrawal from the OAS, etc. Partido Comunista, *XI Congreso Nacional*, p. 60.

16. The 1947 PS program was ratified, but the Unity Congress now called for *immediate* agrarian reform as well as "lucha por la supresión de la organización de Estados Americanos." Several small neo-Trotskyist groups also participated in the merger. Jaime Faivovich, "¿Tiene vigencia el Frente de Trabajadores?"*Punto Final*, I (2.a quincena de agosto de 1967), 38. Partido Socialista de Chile, *Tesis Política Sindical y Organizativa Aprobadas por el Congreso de Unidad Socialista, Julio 1957* (Santiago: Prensa Latinoamericana, 1958), pp. 7-8.

17. Although he condemned Soviet intervention in Hungary, Allende had also eulogized Stalin in 1953. In 1959, the PS forced both Allende and Humberto Martones to withdraw

from the World Peace Council. Despite his showing in 1958, which eliminated the alliance with the Communists as an issue within the Socialist Party, differences between the two Marxist groupings remained. In addition to international non-alignment and coalition tactics, they included: Socialist rejection of the pretension that the USSR or the Communist parties are the authoritative interpreters of Marxism or Marxism-Leninism; Socialist denial that the highest priority be accorded to the defense of the "Socialist Camp" and the assumption that its economic successes are the most important factor in strengthening socialism in the world; Socialist denial that the promotion of peaceful coexistence is necessarily in the interest of the revolutionary forces in the underdeveloped world; and Communist identification with the USSR in the Sino-Soviet conflict. On some of these matters, see Halperin, pp. 145-52, 156-57. And with regard to the Socialist definition of Marxism in terms of nationalism, antiparliamentarianism, socialism and proletarianism, see pp. 142-44.

18. The Communists had in fact unsuccessfully attempted to persuade the Socialists to withdraw Allende and to modify the program in furtherance of a broadened coalition. Only in the absence of such a concession on Allende's candidacy would the Socialists accept the Radicals. *Hispanic American Report*, XI (June 1958), 334. Jaime Faivovich, "¿Tiene vigencia el Frente de Trabajadores?" p. 39.

19. They included the following: Partido Democrático del Pueblo; Partido del Trabajo; Partido Radical Doctrinario; Alianza Nacional; and a sector of the Partido Democrático. Some of these represented little more than the personal following of a leader, and one may have contained neo-Trotskyist elements.

20. Gil, p. 231.

21. Fernández, p. 9.

22. Gil, p. 233.

23. Asociación Nacional de Agricultores de Chile, *Proyecto de Ley de 'Reforma Agraria'* (Santiago: Imp. Lautaro, 1958). *Convención Nacional de Profesionales y Técnicos de la Candidatura de Salvador Allende: Medidas Concretas del Gobierno Popular* (Santiago: Imp. Lautaro, 1958), pp. 45-48.

24. *Convención Nacional de Profesionales y Técnicos de la Candidatura de Salvador Allende, passim. Hispanic American Report*, XI (May 1958), 455.

25. Olavarría, *Alessandri*, IV, 277.

26. Allende received 32.4 percent of the male vote, but only 22.3 percent of the female ballots. Zamorano obtained 3.3 percent of the total vote. An ex-FRAP candidate (1957), he campaigned on a platform similar to Allende's.

27. Petras, *Politics and Social Forces*, pp. 194-95. Petras and Zeitlin, "Agrarian Radicalism," pp. 260-62. Zeitlin and Petras, "The Working Class," pp. 20-25. Petras and Zeitlin, "Miners," p. 583.

28. *El Mercurio*, 1 marzo 1959, p. 7, 8 junio, p. 19. Chile, Senado, *Diario*, CCLXXXVI, ses. 20 (27 julio 1960), pp. 1057-82, ses. 41 (13 septiembre 1960), pp. 2961-74. "Pleno Nacional del Partido Socialista: Solidaridad Nacional con la Revolución Cubana," *Arauco*, II (Agosto 1961), 21. *Hispanic American Report*, XV (June 1962), 352, XVI (October 1963), 804-05. "El Congreso de Niteroi: Vigorosa Jornada Internacional de Solidaridad con Cuba," *Cuba Socialista*, 21 (mayo 1963), p. 106. "Crisis en el FRAP y Algo Más," *Ercilla*, XXX (13 enero 1965), 11. Partido Socialista de Chile, *XVIII Congreso Nacional* (Santiago: Prensa Latinoamericana, 1959), pp. 92-93, 101, 103, 112, 114-15. Aniceto Rodríguez, *La Conspiracion contra Chile* (Santiago: Prensa Latinoamericana, 1964), pp. 13-15. Partido Comunista de Chile, Luís Corvalán L., *Chile y El Nuevo Panorama Mundial*, Informe a la Sesión Plenaria del Comité Central del Partido Comunista de Chile, rendido en un Acto de Masas en el Teatro Caupé el 10 de Mayo de 1959 (Santiago: Talls. Grafs. Lautaro, 1959), pp. 23, 25, 26-27, 29, 30-32.

29. *El Mercurio*, 8 junio 1959, p. 19, 24 julio, 1960, p. 9. *El Siglo*, 16 abril 1961, p. 14. *New York Times*, Oct. 28, 1962, p. 35. Luís Hernández Parker, "La Semana Política," *Ercilla*, XXVI (20 julio 1960), 9. "La 'Batalla' del Senado," ibid., XXVII (13 diciembre 1961), 8. "Chile: El Bloqueo." Chile, Senado, *Diario*, CCLXXXIV, ses. 19 (4 agosto 1959), pp. 1108-18, CCLXXXVI, ses. 22 (3 agosto 1960), pp. 1354-61, ses. 41 (13 septiembre 1960), pp. 2961-74, CCXC, ses. 53 (13 septiembre 1962), p. 4087, CCXCII, 8 (20 junio 1963), CCXCIV, ses. 21 (11 agosto 1964), p. 2028, CCXCVI, ses. 5 (9 diciembre 1964). Olavarría, *Alessandri*, IV, 262-65. Mendoza, *Comunismo en 1961*, p. 8.

30. Chile, Senado, *Diario*, CCLXXXVI, ses. 11 (28 junio 1960), pp. 582, 587, ses. 20 (27 julio 1960), pp. 1057-82, ses. 39 (7 septiembre 1960), pp. 2727-37, ses. 41 (13 septiembre 1960), pp. 2924-31, 2977-78, CCLXXXVII, ses. 37 (18 abril 1961), pp. 2103-17, 2130, 2134-36, ses. 39 (25 abril 1961), pp. 2241-46, ses. 43 (2 mayo 1961), pp. 2377-85, CCLXXXVIII, ses. 2 (6 junio 1961), pp. 93-105, ses. 17 (12 julio 1961), pp. 890-91, ses. 24 (26 julio 1961), pp. 1298-1302, ses. 32 (8 agosto 1961), pp. 1757-58, 1775, 1779-85, CCXC, ses. 19 (24 julio 1962), pp. 1462-77, ses. 48 (11 septiembre 1962), pp. 3708-12. Chile, Cámara de Diputados, *Boletín de Sesiones*, ses. 29 (31 julio 1963), pp. 2608-10. *El Mercurio*, 4 agosto 1959, p. 17, 15 julio 1960, p. 19, 26 julio, p. 24. *Las Noticas de Ultima Hora*, 18 abril 1961, p. 16. Aniceto Rodríguez, pp. 13-15. Partido Communista, *XII Congreso*, pp. 3-4, 8-9, 12, 23, 26-27, 29, 30-33, 37-38, 41, 43-47, 52, 55, 60-61, 59-70, 100, 105, 210-12, 220-21. Partido Comunista de Chile, Orlando Millas, *Derrotar a la Derecha*, Texto completo del Informe rendido en numbre de la Comisión Política por el Diputado Orlando Millas a la Sesión Plenaria del Comité Central del Partido Comunista de Chile, el día 6 de Junio de 1963 (Santiago: Imp. Horizonte, 1963), pp. 27-28. Partido Comunista, Teitelboim, *Camino*, pp. 26-27. See also the following numbers of *Principios*, the organ of the PC's Central Committee: 60, 61, 63, 64, and 99.

31. Partido Comunista, *XII Congreso*, pp. 24, 170, 381-86. Partido Comunista de Chile, *Sesión Plenaria del Comité Central del Partido Comunista de Chile, 19 al 21 de Diciembre de 1963*, Informe Central rendido a nombre de la Comisión Política por el camarada Oscar Astudillo, Intervención de Resumen del Subsecretario General del Partido, camarada José González (Santiago: Imp. Horizonte, 1964), pp. 7, 35-36. Lipschutz, pp. 109-23. Partido Comunista, *Neruda Contesta*, pp. 13, 15, 25, 38. Partido Comunista de Chile, Luís Corvalán, *Todo Chile contra la Política Reaccionaria de Alessandri*, Informe a la X Conferencia Nacional del Partido Comunista de Chile, celebrada los días 16, 17 y 18 de octubre de 1960, rendido por el Secretario General, camarada Luís Corvalán, en al acto Publico del día domingo 16 en el Teatro Banquedano (Santiago: Imp. Lira 363, 1960), pp. 21-22, 26, 38-40. "Mensaje del Partido Socialista al Pueblo de Chile," *Hispanic American Report*, XII (July 1959), 283. *El Mercurio*, 17 octubre 1960, p. 23, 21 octubre, p. 21. "Editorial: Solidaridad con Cuba, deber de nuestros pueblos," *Principios*, No. 81 (mayo 1961), pp. 3-9. Mendoza, *Comunismo en 1961*, p. 4.

32. *El Mercurio*, 8 agosto 1959, p. 19.

33. "Puntos de Vista," *Política y Espíritu*, XIV (1 agosto 1959), p. 1.

34. *El Mercurio*, 20 agosto 1959, p. 23, 23 agosto, p. 11. *New York Times*, August 23, 1959, p. 32.

35. *Hispanic American Report*, XIII (April 1960), 124. Chile, *El Presidente Eisenhower*.

36. *Hispanic American Report*, XIII (September 1960), 477. "La Semana Política," *Ercilla*, XXVI (20 julio 1960), 9. *El Mercurio*, 24 julio 1960, p. 9.

37. Mendoza, *Comunismo en 1961*, p. 18. *Las Notícias de Ultima Hora*, 18 abril 1961, p. 16.

38. *Las Notícias de Ultima Hora*, 18 abril 1961, p. 16, 19 abril, pp. 8, 16. *La Nación*, 20 abril 1961, pp. 3-4. "Cuba: Medita la Moneda," *Ercilla*, XXVII (3 mayo 1961), 8. Mendoza, *Comunismo en 1961*, p. 18.

39. Estimated attendance was 2,000 in 1960, 5,000 in 1961 and 8,000 the following year. *El Mercurio*, 2 mayo 1960, p. 21. Mendoza, *Comunismo en 1961*, pp. 18-19. *Hispanic American Report*, XV (July 1962), 449.

40. "Goodwin: Intérprete entre JAR y Kennedy," *Ercilla*, XXVIII (21 febrero 1962), 8. *Hispanic American Report*, XV (May 1962), 247.

41. Yet within the Senate, Allende delivered a forceful denunciation of the blockade for the coalition, and defended the social and economic measures of the Cuban Government. But in the course of this, he reiterated FRAP's commitment to civil liberties and the rule of law. In the Chamber of Deputies, the FRAP introduced a resolution calling upon the U.S. to lift the blockade. Pablo Neruda sent a letter upon behalf of the FRAP to Alessandri asking that he maintain relations with Havana and adopt a neutral position during the crisis. Cables were dispatched to Dórticos expressing support and to U Thant requesting his intervention. *El Siglo*, 29 octubre 1962, p. 7. *New York Times*, Oct. 28, 1962, p. 35. "Chile: El Bloqueo."

42. *Las Noticias de Ultima Hora*, 15 agosto 1964, p. 5. *El Diario Ilustrado*, 15 agosto 1964, pp. 1, 8. Igor Entrala, "JAR le Quitó," pp. 10-11.

At this time, according to statements by FRAPists in 1967, the leftists were extremely fearful of giving the slightest pretext for governmental suppression.

43. LHP, "Un Gobierno con Compromiso," *Ercilla*, XXX (4 noviembre 1964), 25. Cf., Chile, Senado, *Diario*, CCXCVI, ses. 15 (6 enero 1965), pp. 873-76.

44. Duncan, "Chilean Christian Democracy," p. 269. "Chile: Frei and Frap," *Economist*, May 27, 1967, p. 904.

45. Gall, "The Chileans," p. 106.

46. Ibid., p. 26. Rodman, "October Revolution," p. 1054.

47. U.S., *Cuba and the Caribbean, Hearings*, p. 27.

48. *Time* (Canadian Edition), October 9, 1970, pp. 31-2.

49. Gall, "The Chileans," pp. 26, 106.

50. Partido Comunista, Millas, *Fracaso*, pp. 73-74.

51. Conversations with Alejandro Chelén, a former Socialist Senator, August 1967.

52. LHP, "GGV: Polémico Retorno," *Ercilla*, XXIX (19 junio 1963), 6-7. Gil, p. 236. Petras, *Politics and Social Forces*, pp. 188-89.

53. Conversations with Alejandro Chelén, August 1967.

54. By early 1961, the following CUT-associated pro-FRAP organizations—some old and others new—were in existence: Asociación Nacional de Agricultores; Asociación Nacional Indígena; Frente de Trabajadores de la Tierra; Unión de Indios Huiliches; and the Federación Nacional de Trabajadores Agrícolas. In May 1961, FRAP and CUT sponsored the First National Peasants' Congress which launched the Movimiento Nacional Campesino. Three Cuban delegates attended the congress, and Pablo Neruda extolled the Cuban Agrarian Reform before more than a thousand representatives of 326 peasant syndicates, committees, unions, associations and communities. Mendoza, *Comunismo en 1961*, p. 17. Fernández, pp. 9-10, 31-43.

Despite its propitious beginning, the predominantly Socialist-led FNCI (National Federation of Peasants and Indígenes) which had been constituted at the congress, soon mirrored the CUT in its organizational inefficacy. Raúl Ampuero reported to the Twentieth Congress of the PS during February 1964, that "(l)a Federación Campesina vive un peligroso período de estancamiento y ha sido incapaz de establecer direcciones provinciales estables en aquellas zonas donde logró constituirse." Partido Socialista de Chile, Raúl Ampuero Díaz, *1964: Año de Prueba para la Revolución Chilena*, Informe del c. Raúl Ampuero Díaz al XX Congreso General del Partido Socialista, Concepción, Febrero de 1964 (Santiago: Imp. Prensa Latinoamericana, 1964), p. 41.

55. "Semana Política," *Ercilla*, XXVII (9 agosto 1961), 7. "La 'Weltanschaung' del Ministro," ibid., XXVIII (7 febrero 1962), 9. Emilio Filippi, "El explosivo caso de la Isla Ranquilco," ibid., (14 marzo 1962), p. 2. Emilio Filippi, "Eclosión Mapuche en Arauco y Malleco," ibid. (16 mayo 1962), pp. 15, 18. Corvalán, "Chile, País Clave para USA," p. 17. Igor Entrala, "Faltan 225 casas mas cada Hora," ibid., XXIX (18 diciembre 1963), 4-5. *El Mercurio*, 8 enero 1964, p. 23, 10 enero, p. 21. Cerda, "Chile's Trade Unions," p. 16. Vitale, "Which Road for Chile," p. 70.

56. In other respects, the program paralleled that of 1958. Partido Comunista, *XII Congreso*, p. 396. *Hispanic American Report*, XIV (March 1961), 65-66.

57. Halperin, pp. 231-32.

58. Goldenberg, p. 52. *Candidatura de Oposición, un diputado valiente, sin pelos en la lengua, estudioso y que sabe lo que dice: Orlando Millas, Frente de Acción Popular* (Santiago: Imp. Lira, 1961). *Hispanic American Report*, XII (February 1961), 914, XIII (May 1961), 247-49. Since Communist campaigns are centrally controlled, the Millas pamphlet almost certainly reflected party policy.

59. Pike, p. 265. Gil, pp. 234, 236, 310. Petras, *Politics and Social Forces*, pp. 178-80.

60. According to official data, the Consumer Price Index increased by 39 percent in 1959, 12 percent in 1960, 8 percent in 1961, 14 percent in 1962, and 44 percent in 1963. Cited in Gregory, *Industrial Wages*, p. 2.

61. What the Socialists did, in fact, was to impose their 1957 program upon the coalition. This marked the total defeat of the Communist strategy outlined at the Eleventh Congress of that party. According to Alejandro Chelén (conversation, August 1967), it was the PS that was responsible for this programmatic radicalization. But even the Communists had been moved by the Cuban successes. See: Luís Hernández Parker, "La Semana Política,"

Ercilla, XXVI (26 octubre 1960), 8; Luís Hernández Parker, "La Semana Política," ibid. (5 octubre 1960); Partido Comunista, Millas, *Fracaso*, pp. 14-15; Halperin, pp. 64-65.

With regard to Communist efforts to obtain Centrist backing—which Socialists accepted so long as it did not involve sacrificing Allende's position at the head of the ticket, or the program—see: "FRAP: Apertura a al Partido Radical," *Ercilla*, XXVIII (20 junio 1962), 9; and LHP, "Larga Maratón con Sorpresas," ibid., XXIX (12 junio 1963), 10.

62. It is somewhat ironical that despite the firm PS-PC alliance, even in 1967 a number of Communists expressed the view that many Socialists *were in fact anti-Communist*. They also said that 80 percent of the campaigning during the 1964 contest had been done by Communists. It is unremarkable, then, that following Frei's victory it was reported that "Allende had become an advocate of the Cuban dictatorship, making clear that he staunchly supported the economic and social policies of Fidel Castro. As a result of his stand, many Socialists abandoned his ranks and organized what they called the Socialist Democratic Party." Zottele, "News from Chile," p. 1246. This also attests to the effectiveness of the "campaign of terror."

63. At its First National Convention in December 1961, PADENA resolved to remain in the FRAP as a "catalyzing force" for the unification of both the PDC and the FRAP behind a single candidate—hopefully PADENA President Carlos Montero. " 'Yugoslavo' Fué Congreso Socialista," *Ercilla*, XXVII (13 diciembre 1961), 9.

64. LHP, "La Semana Política," ibid., XXVIII (25 julio 1962), 7-8.

65. LHP, "Acuerdos del PDC y Padena, ibid. (31 octubre 1962), p. 8. LHP, "JAR: 'No soy candidato,' Listo Frei," ibid. (21 octubre 1964), p. 6. *Hispanic American Report*, XV (December 1962), 947, XVI (September 1963), 712. Olavarría, *Alessandri*, III, 77-81. *South Pacific Mail*, CVIII (June 28, 1963), 3.

66. By this date (Nov. 1962) the program had been further radicalized to include economic crimes and withdrawal from the OAS. In the opinion of Ernst Halperin, the contemplated FRAP goals were "so sweeping that they could not be implemented within the framework of Chile's existing democratic institutions. . . . It is evident that the authors of this platform had in mind a revolution similar to that carried out by Castro." Op. cit., pp. 140-41. Gil, p. 300. Olavarría, *Alessandri*, IV, 88, 199. "Rebase del Frap en Las Vertientes," *Ercilla*, XXVIII (9 enero 1963), 7. Cf., OCEPLAN, *Primeras 100 Medidas*, pp. 7-21; OCEPLAN, *La Política Agropecuaria*, pp. 15-23; OCEPLAN, *Planifica con nosotros*, pp. 5-94; and Salvador Allende, "Significado de la Conquista de un Gobierno Popular para Chile," *Cuadernos Americanos*, (México) XXIII (Septiembre-Octubre 1964), 7-24.

67. Olavarría, *Alessandri*, III, 73-75. The word "reversal" as used in the text signifies only a major shift in emphasis. As early as 1960—the year when Allende's identification with the Cuban Revolution was most passionate—he was careful to distinguish the methods that would be used in Chile from the violence that characterized Cuba under Castro. The latter was attributable to a reaction against U.S. domination and great corruption as well as soci-economic injustices. Because the Chilean mentality, psychology and civil libertarian tradition were distinctive, the Chilean revolution would imply "neither violence, nor abuses, nor reproachable acts." *El Mercurio*, 27 febrero 1960, p. 15. Chile, Senado, *Diario*, CCLXXXVI, ses. 41 (13 septiembre 1960), pp. 2961-74. Cf., *New York Times*, August 12, 1962, p. 15.

68. Partido Democrático Nacional, PADENA, *Candidato de la Unidad Popular, La Oposición Unida:, dará el triunfo al pueblo, Carlos Montero Sch., Candidato a la Presidencia de la República del Partido Democrático Nacional* (Santiago: Talls. Grafs. Periodística Chile Ltda., 1963), p. 6.

69. And by January 1963, Montero—a one time *invitado* who had still been praising the Castro regime as late as October 1962—declared himself against *el paredón* (symbolic of the Cuban execution wall) in the course of a radio address. *Hispanic American Report*, XV (November 1962), 838-39. Partido Comunista, *XII Congreso Nacional del Partido Comunista de Chile*, p. 391. LHP, " 'New Look' del PC chileno," *Ercilla*, XXVIII (9 enero 1963), 7.

70. "Los redactores (comunistas) incluyeron buena dosis del mismo calmante utilizado desde fines del año pasado, para que nadie crea, que el triunfo de Allende podría significar un 'cubanazo.' Para eso pusieron especial énfasis en sostener que en esencia los objetivos de la revolución cubana son los mismos que éstan planteados en toda América latina, pero que

en cuanto a métodos y formas siempre han sostenido que no se dan en la historia dos revoluciones absolutamente iguales. Es decir, que en este aspecto habrá diferencias entre la revolución chilena y la revolución cubana." Igor Entrala, "El PC Envía Paloma de la Paz al PDC," *Ercilla*, XXIX (13 febrero 1963), 8. *Hispanic American Report*, XVI (April 1963).

71. Gil, pp. 237-39.

72. Olavarría, *Alessandri*, III, 320-23. Nueva Izquierda Democrática, *Por Que Triunfará Frei* (Santiago: Imp. Fantasia, 1963). Partido Democracia Agrario Laborista, *Declaración de Principios Estatutos* (Santiago: Imp. Stanley, 1964). Cf., *Hispanic American Report*, XVII (March 1964), 68.

73. LHP, "Los Cuatro Naipes de la Duda," *Ercilla*, XXIX (22 mayo 1963), 15.

74. Halperin, pp. 216-17.

75. Olavarría, *Alessandri*, IV, 193, 276-77. Cf.: Gil and Parrish, I, 39, 42; and LHP, "Frei, Allende y Durán ante la Meta," *Ercilla*, XXX (12 agosto 1964), 9.

76. They also noted that "the Christian Democrats and their allies were doing their best to make the Cuban revolution an issue in the campaign. . . .

The second aspect of the Communist (issue) was its effectiveness as a campaign weapon against Allende. This matter was drummed persistently into the consciousness of the Chilean electorate, and there is no doubt of its great effect. While the more blatant propaganda was laughed off in typical Chilean fashion, one must believe that even this left its mark. Allende was constantly on the defensive concerning this issue and found it necessary . . . to protest the charge of communism. Defeat left the FRAP in a very bitter mood, and it denounced the 'Campaign of Terror' that had driven voters to Frei through 'fear.' This assertion may contain more than a grain of truth. The fact is that many voters were so frightened before the election that they laid in a week's supply of food in case of riots or other political upsets that might be attendant on a FRAP victory. Another indication of this anxiety was the fact that airline reservations were booked out of Chile for several months after the elections as a hedge against a FRAP victory. When people are prepared to leave their country because they have supported a losing political candidate, it is safe to say that they are indeed alarmed." Gill and Parrish, I, pp. 40, 43, 49.

And during June 1964, a high-strung Communist senator provided bountiful source material for the anti-FRAP coalition. In the course of denouncing Church support for Frei, he used violent language that reflected hostility to religion itself. Although immediately repudiated by the PC, his remarks were freely quoted. One observer depicted them as a "bomba que rompió primero los vidrios y amenazó luego con los cimientos del llamado Movimiento Católico Allendista, y que en buena medida dañó seriamente todo el paciente trabajo hecho por el FRAP para demostrar que, aunque de concepción marxista, respeta lo mismo a la Iglesia que a quienes van a ella." Igor Entrala, "De los Arrepentidos," *Ercilla*, XXX (1 julio 1964), 8-9, 10.

77. See note 62, *supra*, and chapter 9.

78. Olavarría, *Alessandri*, IV, 53, 279-81, 296. Chile, Senado, *Diario*, CCXCIII, ses. 52 (6 mayo 1964), p. 4153, CCXCIV, ses. 4 (17 junio 1964), p. 289, CCXCVI, ses. 6 (15 diciembre 1964), pp. 378-81.

As for non-FRAP sources, Gil and Parrish have reported "their impression that the Christian Democratic candidate was supported by more numerous campaign posters, radio spot announcements, and newspaper advertisements than the FRAP candidate. But how much more money was available to Frei than to Allende simply cannot be determined." Op. cit., I, 44.

79. Bodenheimer, "Stagnation in Liberty," p. 9.

80. In the course of a Senate address during November 1966, Carlos Altamirano (PS) listed the following circulation figures for newspapers that had supported Allende in 1964; *Ultima Hora* (30,000); *El Siglo* (25,000); and *Clarín* (85,000). The remaining Chilean newspapers—virtually all of which had probably opposed the Marxist candidate—accounted for a combined circulation of 531,300. Insofar as the more widely used radio was concerned, Altamirano admitted that two small provincial stations were owned by persons sympathetic to the PS. None were operated by Communist sympathizers, while 128—including the nine principal broadcasters—were charged with slanting their programs against the FRAP. For 1966, similar allegations were applied to all newspapers, save *El Siglo* and *Ultima Hora. El Mercurio*, 17 noviembre 1966, p. 15.

The problem associated with the refusal by major radio networks to sell any or prime listening time was discussed in chapter 5. Cf.: "Allende en Televisión: Cuarta entrevista realizada el 19 de Junio de 1964," and "Allende en Televisión: Quinta entrevista," *Arauco*, V (Agosto 1964), 74-76, 81-82; and Chile, Senado, *Diario*, CCXCIV, ses. 4 (17 junio 1964), pp. 282-83.

81. Thus, in August 1964, PS Secretary General Solomón Corbalán inserted into the Senate proceedings a letter which he had written to the Minister of the Interior. Corbalán charged that a Hungarian had projected seven USIA supplied films before 3,810 persons affiliated with twelve educational institutions and social clubs. The features were: "Tierra Prometida"; "Danza Hacia la Libertad"; "La Revolución Traicionada"; "Preguntad a Quienes Saben"; "Lucha por la Libertad"; "La Isla Desdichada"; and "Hungría Lucha por su Libertad." He also charged that "(u)n documento emanado de un supuesto servicio informativo y que se titula 'Enseñanza de tres elecciones'. Al final dice: 'Santiago de Chile: · Es posible que los millones y millones de refugiados alemanes, húngaros, cubanos, polacos, rusos, chinos, tibetanos, etc., no sean suficientes testigos para una parte de la población de Chile? ¿Es posible que a pesar de los hechos trágicos del mundo comunista, como los diez millones de presos políticos de Rusia, la destrucción de la democracia, el ultraje de las libertades, la colonización soviética de naciones millenarias, la miseria espentosa, las revoluciones desesperadas de los pueblos oprimidos detrás de la cortina de hierro, y tantos otros argumentos más sobre el régimen más injusto, más antipopular de la historia, todavía existen 250 mil personas en Chile que dan su voto por el comunismo internacional? ¿Es decir, viven en Chile 250,000 cuidadanos engañados, quienes, como los ciegos, no creen en la verdad y sólo escuchan el viejo disco de la propaganda grabada en Moscú y transmitida por los agentes bien pagados de Khruschev en Santiago.' " Chile, Senado, *Diario*, CCXCIV, ses. 22 (12 agosto 1964), pp. 2133-34.

82. With regard to this continuing FRAP fear, see: Olavarría, *Alessandri*, III, 213; Chile, Senado, *Diario*, CCXCIII, ses. 52 (6 mayo 1964), p. 4151, CCXCIV, ses. 23 (18 agosto 1964), 2208-09; Gil and Parrish, I, 44; and *Hispanic American Report*, XVII (September 1964), 647. Cf., Mario Díaz B., "Meditación Electoral," *Punto Final*, I (15 Marzo 1967), 2-3.

Even among some leading Frei backers this apprehension was not unknown. Hernández Parker, "Al Final," pp. 16-17.

83. Gil and Parrish, I, 47. Cf., Glaucio Soares and Robert L. Hamblin, "Socio-economic Variables and Voting for the Radical Left: Chile, 1952," *American Political Science Review*, LXI (December 1967), 1062.

84. Petras, *Politics and Social Forces*, pp. 194-95; Zeitlin and Petras, "The Working Class," pp. 20-27. Petras and Zeitlin, "Agrarian Radicalism," pp. 260-62. Gil and Parrish, II, 9-11. Cf., Powell, "Political Change," pp. 375-76, 382.

85. The term was used by Oscar Naranjo during an interview on March 26, 1967. According to this Socialist Deputy, it was a "great mistake." Naranjo had visited Cuba, and Cuban flags were flying above Chilean ones during an election rally for the municipal campaign then in progress.

86. LHP, "PDC y FRAP Piden el Bis para Marzo," *Ercilla*, XXX (23 septiembre 1964), 15. *Hispanic American Report*, XVII (November 1964), 837. Norman Gall, "Chile Goes to The Polls," *New Leader*, XLVIII (March 1, 1965), 13-14. Sergio De Santis, "Chile," *International Socialist Journal*, II (August 1965), 465-66. Olavarría, *Democracia*, pp. 26-27. Carlos Santana, "Ha Faltado Muñequeo Político," *Ercilla*, XXX (13 enero 1965), 10. Santana, "Conflicto con Cara de Marzo," ibid., XXXI (20 enero 1965), 8-9. Quoted passages are from Parrish, Von Lazar and Tapia, *Chilean Congressional Election*, pp. 15-16.

87. Gil, pp. 308-10.

88. LHP, "Tensa Pugna: control del Parlamento," *Ercilla*, XXXI (3 febrero 1965), 9. LHP, "La DC Destrozó los Cronómetros," ibid. (10 marzo 1965), pp. 18-19. Olavarría, *Democracia*, pp. 25-26, 35.

89. Parrish, Von Lazar and Tapia, *Chilean Congressional Election*, pp. 4-6. Cf., Petras, *Politics and Social Forces*, p. 186.

90. Petras, *Politics and Social Forces*, pp. 184-88, 218-19, 239-46. Grayson, "The Frei Administration," pp. 54-55. Angell, "Chile: The Difficulties," pp. 518-19, 522-23, 527-28. Duncan, "Chilean Christian Democracy," p. 365. Petras and Zeitlin, "Miners," pp. 583-84.

91. Petras, *Politics and Social Forces*, p. 196.
92. "Ampuero and Chadwick charge that the central committee is changing the traditional party line to form an alliance with the Radicals." Duncan, "Chilean Christian Democracy," p. 266.
93. Ibid., p. 265.
94. Federico G. Gil, "Chile: 'Revolution in Liberty,'" *Current History*, LI (November 1966), 295.
95. Angell, "Chile: The Difficulties," p. 523, Petras, *Politics and Social Forces*, pp. 225-26.
96. Vitale, ¿*Y Despues?*, pp. 17-22.
97. On the election, see: Grayson, "The Frei Administration," pp. 59-66. Cf., Angell, "Christian Democracy," p. 84.
98. Grayson, "The Frei Administration," pp. 71-74.
99. *Programa Basico de Gobierno de la Unidad Popular: Candidatura Presidencial de Salvador Allende* (Santiago: Horizonte, n.d.), *passim*.
100. Ibid., Gall, "The Chileans," pp. 27, 106.
101. Ibid., Vitale, ¿*Y Despues?*, pp. 41-44. With regard to the Castro-Communist "Campaign of Terror" in 1970, see: *Granma* (Weekly Review), November 1, 1970, p. 10.
102. These developments are discussed with greater length in the chapter that follows.
103. On these and related matters, see: Gall, "The Chileans," p. 106; *Time* (Canadian Edition), Oct. 9, 1970, pp. 29-30; *Granma* (Weekly Review), Nov. 8, 1970, p. 1, Nov. 15, 1970, pp. 1, 5, Nov. 22, 1970, pp. 1, 4, Nov. 29, 1970, p. 1.
104. *Granma* (Weekly Review), November 15, 1970, p. 4.
105. "Chile Starts Chasing," p. 48. *El Siglo*, 28 noviembre 1970, p. 1, 17 diciembre 1970, pp. 1, 5, 8.
106. Vitale, ¿*Y Despues?*, pp. 89-92.
107. U.S., *Rockefeller Report, Hearing*, pp. 85, 93, 117-19.
108. See note 67, *supra*.
109. *Time* (Canadian Edition), Oct. 9, 1970, p. 29.
110. Chile, Senado, *Diario*, CCLXXXVI, ses. 20 (27 julio 1960), pp. 1083-1104, 17 (12 julio 1961), pp. 890-91. The citations refer to speeches by Allende and Alejandro Chelén. Chelén has never visited Cuba. For a similar approach by Luis Corvalán, see Partido Comunista XII Congreso, pp. 3-4, 8-9, 12, 23, 26-27, 29, 30-33, 37-38, 41, 43-47, 52, 55, 60-61, 69-70, 100, 105, 210-12, 220-21.
111. *El Mercurio*, 7 septiembre 1960, p. 3.
112. *Fidel Castro: Líder y Guerrilero*, 78pp.
113. When interviewed in his jail cell, Blest not only again lauded the Cuban Revolution, but he "denuncio que el comunismo dentro de la CUT actua 'con miras a la elección parlamentaria y ne se preocupa de la marcha sindical . Señaló también que socialistas, socialcristianos y anarquistas 'están por la acción rápida para hacer inmediatamente los cambios sustanciales en la política económica actual.'" *El Mercurio*, 6 noviembre 1960, p. 21, 8 noviembre, p. 3, 13 noviembre, p. 21, 23 noviembre, p. 21, 27 noviembre, p. 21. *Hispanic American Report*, XIII (January 1961), 824-25. Luís Vitale, *Los Discursos de Clotario Blest y la Revolución Chilean* (Santiago: Edit. POR, Imp. 'Victoria,' 1961), pp. 10-11, 20.
114. It is clear that the Communist and Socialist leaders were opposed to a general strike. Whether their opposition was based upon an estimate of inadequate support from the rank and file, or conditioned by other considerations is less apparent. "Semana Política," *Ercilla*, XXVII (6 septiembre 1961), 9. Poblete, "El Movimiento Sindical Chileno," p. 32. *Hispanic American Report*, XIV (October 1961), 728-29 (November 1961), p. 826. Halperin, pp. 71-73. Mendoza, *Comunismo en 1961*, pp. 15-16.
115. Thus, while addressing a "huge rally in the Plaza de la Revolucion in Havana" on July 26, 1963, "Prime Minister Castro called the Cuban Revolution the example for Latin America to follow. Pre-revolutionary conditions were better *in several* Latin American countries than those that had existed in Cuba, he said, while the duty of the revolutionaries was to grasp existing opportunities and actively struggle to overthrow the old orders, by force, *if necessary*." (Emphasis added). *Hispanic American Report*, XVI, (September 1963), 670. Vitale, "Which Road for Chile," Cf., Draper, pp. 65-66.
Draper also reports (pp. 46-47) that in the course of a July 1964 interview, Castro endorsed the peaceful road as probably most appropriate for Chile.

116. In the course of addressing graduating medical students on Sept. 10, 1964, Castro noted with satisfaction that the FRAP with a revolutionary program had increased its voting support from about 350,000 in 1958 to almost a million. Accepting FRAP evaluations, Castro attributed Frei's victory to massive propaganda and aid from both the Right and the United States. But rather than suggesting that armed insurrection was the order of the day for Chile, the Cuban leader observed: "Pero es el hecho cierto que a partir del triunfo de la Revolución Cubana toda la política continental demuestra y expresa la influencia que nuestra Revolución ha tenido en el Continente en las posiciones de todos los políticos. Y así, ya la lucha en Chile no se libró entre extrema derecha y extrema izquierda, entre revolucionarios y reaccionarios—en el más cabal sentido de la palabra—sino entre reformistas y revolucionarios. . . . Aparentemente, los imperialistas quieren presentar el ejemplo de Chile como un ejemplo frente a nuestro ejemplo: aparentemente quieren poner la experiencia chilena a emular con la experiencia cubana. Pués bien, ¡estamos encantados de esa emulación! Y aún cuando tengamos en contra a los imperialistas con todos sus medicos, y todos sus recursos y todo su bloqueo, y aún cuando los imperialistas apoyaran esa experiencia con todos sus recursos, y aún cuando ningún bloqueo y ningun obstáculo se interpusiera en la gestión de ese gobierno, aceptamos esa emulación, aceptamos encantados esa emulación, para ver que país avanza más, que experiencia llega más lejos, cual de ellas resuelve los problemas esenciales y verdaderos de los pueblo y en cuanto tiempe los resuelve. Mejor, los revolucionarios cubanos nos sentiremos estimulados a luchar más, a trabajar mas, y a demostrar la justeza de nuestra causa y las virtudes de nuestro camino revolucionario." Fidel Castro, "Las elecciones chilenas," *Principios*, N. o 102 (Septiembre-Octubre 1964), pp. 64-70.

117. *Time* (Canadian Edition), October 9, 1970, pp. 29-30. Cf., *Granma* (Weekly Review), November 1,1970, p. 12.

118. With regard to the relevant polemics and factional activities, see: Halperin, pp. 6, 73-74, 89-90, 103, 113-14, 116, 151-52, 170-76; Mendoza, *Comunismo en 1961*, p. 10; Luís Corvalán, "The Struggle for a People's Government in Chile," *World Marxist Review* (December 1962), 19-25; Corvalán, "The Peaceful Way," 3-7; "Political Crisis Splits the Chilean Socialist Party," *International Socialist Review*, XXV (Summer 1964), 73; LHP, "Puga Interna en el PS," *Ercilla*, XXX (22 enero 1964), 8, 23; Igor Entrala, "Pacífica Reeleccion de Ampuero," ibid. (19 febrero 1964), p. 9; *Hispanic American Report*, VIII (April 1964), 160-61.

119. Following its legalization, PC membership increased by 35 percent in 1958 and by 100 percent the following year. In April 1963, the Department of State estimated that total membership ranged from 20,000 to 25,000. By 1967, U.S. Embassy sources estimated it at 30,000, while the Socialists had a "substantially" smaller membership. In both parties, however, the quality of theoretical indoctrination of the rank and file was reportedly quite low, and entry easy. *Hispanic American Report*, XI (September 1959), 397. *South Pacific Mail* CVIII (April 26, 1963), 3. Conversation with Richard Pogue (an assistant to the Ambassador) and Charles Wolfolk (Press Attache) on April 4, 1967. Partido Socialista, *Ampuero, 1964*, p. 36. Conversations with N.B. and E.M., the former a PC member and the latter an ex-PC member, during early 1967.

120. See Blasier, "The Cuban and Chilean Communist Parties."

121. LHP, "Reformistas Izaron a JAR; el PC y Frei," *Ercilla*, XXIX (23 octubre 1963), 11.

122. Thus, in welcoming seventy new PS members during October 1964, Raúl Ampuero observed that "(h)emos solidarizado con las revoluciones en Cuba, en Argelia y demás naciones subdesarrolladas. Pero esta aceptación cabal de la solidaridad internacional no significa sumisión a las ideologias en muchos movimientos y procesos que han tenido lugar lejos de nuestras fronteras. El PC ni en Cuba ni en Argelia comandaron las revoluciones de sus pueblos, y hoy nada es mas dañino a la causa del internacionalismo proletario que la pugna entre los partidos comunistas de la Unión Soviética y de China Popular." LHP, "El Congreso Pleno: Alerta para Eduardo Frei," ibid., XXX (28 octubre 1964), 17.

123. Gil, pp. 285-90. alperin, pp. 118-44. Julio César Jobet, "Acción e Historia del Socialismo Chileno," *Combate* (San José), II (septiembre-octubre 1960), 32-45, III (enero-Febrero 1961), 39-49.

124. Chile, Senado, *Diario*, CCLXXXIV, ses. 29 (9 septiembre 1959), pp. 1768-69, CCLXXXV, ses. 4 (20 octubre 1959), p. 152. Partido Socialista, *XVIII Congreso Nacional*,

pp. 92-93, 101, 103, 112, 114-15. Partido Comunista, Corvalán, *Chile y el Nuevo Panorama Mundial*, pp. 23, 25, 26-27, 29, 30-32. *Hispanic American Report*, XII (July 1959), 283.

125. The appeal of Titoism and its relation to earlier and subsequent "fashion" attractions is treated by Halperin, pp. 137-42, 154-55, 158. Cf., Julio César Jobet, "Yugoslavia, Democracia Socialista," *Arauco*, III (Noviembre 1961), 26-37.

126. Even the Nixon administration admitted in 1969 that despite substantial Soviet influence in Cuba, that its Revolutionary Government was not a satellite regime. U.S., *Cuba and the Caribbean, Hearings*, p. 30.

127. Op. cit., p. 243.

128. Juventud Socialista Popular, *Contra el Democristianismo Burgués: Contra el Reformismo Antirevolucionario: ¡Por Una Victoria Revolucionaria del FRAP!* (Santiago: Astudillo e Hijos, 1964), 2pp.

129. *El Espejismo del 64* (Santiago: Imp. 'Victoria,' 1962), p. 10.

130. Ibid., pp. 7-9, 13-14.

131. Vanguardia Revolucionaria Marxista, *Tesis Políticas Aprobadas por el Primer Congreso Nacional* (Santiago: Imp. Entrecerros, 1964), pp. 6, 15, 17, 22.

132. Halperin, p. 245. Vanguardia Revolucionaria Marxista, *¡Insurrección Socialista!* (Santiago: Imp. Entrecerros, 1964), 4pp.

133. *Ensayo de Historia*, pp. 116, 121. Interestingly, the view that the Chilean masses were not intensely committed to the norms and institutions associated with parliamentary democracy was shared by a leading member of the Ampuero faction of the PS. The late Secretary General of the party, Solomón Corbalán, presented this proposition and supported it by referring to the mass support given Ibáñez in 1952 when many believed that he would—when victorious—institute a neo-authoritarian regime. Lecture at the Latin American Faculty of Social Sciences on Dec. 5, 1966.

134. Pp. 99-101.

135. LHP, "A 360 Días de las Elecciones Presidenciales," *Ercilla*, XXIX (11 septiembre 1963), 9. LHP, "Retorno a la Libertad," ibid. (2 octubre 1963), p. 30. LHP, "PR: Dura Ataque a la 'Reforma,' " ibid. (16 octubre 1963), p. 9. "Chilean Marxists Form New Party," and Vitale, "Which Road for Chile," pp. 70-72. Cf., Halperin, pp. 94, 107-10.

136. Peter Roman, "Can Chile's Allende Move Far to the Left?" *Guardian*, November 7, 1970, p. 16.

137. Vitale, *¿Y Despues?*, pp. 25, 36-37.

138. Vitale, "Which Road for Chile," pp. 71-72. Vanguardia Revolucionaria Marxista, *¡Movilización permanente de los Comites Allendistas para Imponer por la Razon y la Fuerza, el Triunfo de Allende!* (Santiago: Imp. Delta, 1964), 1h. Vanguardia Revolucionaria Marxista, Comité Central, *Pueblo de Chile: Organizaté para Defender tu Victoria Electoral* (Santiago: Imp. Entrecerros, 1964), 1h.

139. Partido Socialista Popular, Comité Central; *¡Una Nueva Dirección para los Trabajadores Chilenos!* (Santiago: Imp. Astudillo e Hijos Ltda, 1964), 2pp. Halperin, pp. 223-24. LHP, "Un Arqueo Político a los 45 Días," *Ercilla*, XXX (16 diciembre 1964), 8-9.

140. Vanguardia Revolucionaria Marxista, *El Verdadero Camino después del 4 de Septiembre* (Santiago: Imp. Entrecerros, 1964), pp. 7-8, 17.

141. Partido Socialista Popular, *¡Una Nueva Dirección!* In 1965, 70,680 null and blank ballots were cast. This represented approximately 3 percent of the total. Comparative figures for the 1963 municipal elections were 70,576 and 3.4 percent.

142. The ultraleft appears to have been largely urban-oriented. The closest they came to rural insurrection was an attempted land seizure in January 1964, when the "government authorities discovered a 'terrorist' plot to occupy private lands in the Central Valley. Military troops occupied the San Dionisio estate belonging to the Archbishop of Linares in order to prevent a proposed peasant land grab. According to the news service Orbe Latinoamericana, police detained three agitators carrying plans for a series of such take-overs. Undersecretary of the Interior Jaime Silva, noting that a copy of El Rebelde, organ of the extreme left Vanguardia Revolucionaria Marxists, had been found on one of the prisoners, blamed the far left for provoking incidents 'to create an artificial climate of disorder.' " *Hispanic American Report*, XVII (March 1964), 69.

143. Grayson, "The Frei Administration," p. 62.

144. Vitale, *?Y Despues?*, pp. 91, 93.

145. *Granma*, (Weekly Review), November 1, 1970, p. 12.
146. Vitale, *¿ Despues?*
147. Following these arrests, four "Fidelistas" with rifles were also arrested. The police claimed they intended to start a *foco* "or other trouble." "Pasos Públicos y Privados del Complot." " 'Doc' del otro complot al tribunal psiquiátrico," *Ercilla*, XXVII (6 septiembre 1961), 2. Samuel Mendoza, *Comunismo en 1961*, pp. 12-13.
148. Chile, Senado, *Diario*, CCLXXXVIII, ses. 43 (29 agosto 1961), pp. 2405-17.
149. "Los que hayan visto los afiches electorales y escuchado las audiciones radiales de ciertos candidatos del partido, saben de antimano lo que se hizo con la plata." Waiss, *Socialismo sin Gerentes*.
150. "Una Torpe Aventura Terrorista," *Ercilla*, XXVIII (31 octubre 1962), 11. *El Siglo*, 31 octubre 1962, p. 1.
151. *South Pacific Mail*, CVII (November 2, 1962), 6.
152. Carlos Hugembert, "Persecutions in Chile for Pro-Cuban Actions," *The Militant* (New York), Dec. 3, 1962, p. 3.
153. Thus, while addressing several thousand Socialist members and sympathizers in June 1962, Raúl Ampuero observed that "en el corazón de los latinoamericanos, se apresura el latido cuando sentimos vibrar el nombre de Cuba y recordar la gesta de Fidel Castro." Raúl Ampuero Díaz, "Los trabajadores chilenos harán por si mismos, su tarea revolucionaria," *Arauco*, III (Junio 1962), 7.
154. Aniceto Rodríguez Arenas, "Veinticinco mil obreros y campesinos ingresaron al Partido Socialista con el Contingente 'Fidel Castro,' " ibid., p. 16.

Chapter 8. Self-Determination and Rejection: Chile's Center Groups

1. Olavarría, *Alessandri*, III, 483-84. Gil, pp. 260-63. Millas, "Christian Democratic Reformism," p. 46. Moulian, p. 46. Angell, "Chile: The Difficulties," pp. 520, 527.
2. Aldunate, p. 8. Cf., Olavarría, *Alessandri*, IV, 239-40, 276; Donoso, "Chile, en la Encrucijada," *Mensaje*, no. 118 (mayo 1963), p. 182; 'Renace el Ibañismo," *Ercilla*, XXIX (26 junio 1963), 8; LHP, "Batalla de los Rumores," Ibid., XXX (29 julio 1964), 9; and Igor Entrala, "Divorcio separa a los Partidos,: pp. 10-11. Petras, *Politics and Social Forces*, pp. 10-12, 99-101, 123-132, 338-41.
3. Petras, *Politics and Social Forces*, p. 330.
4. Trends in party policies, and its dominance by conservative elements in recent years are discussed in the following: Johnson, pp. 72-75, 83-90; Pike, pp. 245-48. Campos, p. 244. Gil and Parrish, I, 13-15; Olavarría, *Democracia Cristiana*, pp. 7-8; Alexander, pp. 240-41; Silvert, *Chile: Yesterday and Today*, pp. 138-41; Halperin, pp. 124, 126; Petras, "The Latin American Middle Class," pp. 76-77; Veliz, "Chile," p. 244; De Santis, "Chile," pp. 347-48; Beatty, "Middle Class," p. 112; and "Ensimismamiento en Palabras Vacías..," *Ercilla*, XXXIII (15 febrero 1967), 3.
With regard to the problems of factionalism and especially indiscipline, see LHP, "Exequiel González Madariaga, Castigado el Niño Terrible del PR," *Ercilla*, XXX (10 junio 1964), 9. Cf., Gil, p. 265, and Pike, pp. 244-45.
Survey research data is summarized in Petras, *Politics and Social Forces*, pp. 101-103. Cf., pp. 66-71.
5. Jorge Mario Quinzio Figueiredo, *El Partido Radical: Origen-Doctrina-Convenciones* (Santiago: Imp. 'Bio-Bio,' 1964), pp. 77-79.
6. *Hispanic American Report*, XI (August 1958), 455.
7. Ibid. (June 1958), p. 334, (September 1958), p. 514. LHP, "Exequiel González Madariaga," p. 9.
8. *El Mercurio*, 11 agosto 1959, p. 21, 12 agosto, p. 19.
9. *La Libertad*, 1 agosto 1959, p. 7.
10. Yet the August 11th CUT-FRAP rally to protest the OAS agenda was ignored by the daily. *La Tercera de la Hora*, 28 julio 1959, p. 16, 31 julio, p. 16, 1 agosto, pp. 10-11, 2 agosto, p. 5, 4 agosto, p. 5, 10 agosto, p. 1.

11. Chile, Senado, *Diario*, CCLXXXIV, ses. 17 (28 julio 1959), pp. 969-72.

12. Hernández Parker, "La Semana Política," *Ercilla*, XXV (5 agosto 1959), 8. *El Mercurio*, 25 agosto 1959, p. 19.

13. "Viajes chilenos en secreto apoyan a Fidel," p. 9.

14. *El Mercurio*, 27 febrero 1960, p. 15.

15. *El Mercurio*, 1 agosto 1960, p. 25.

16. Chile, Senado, *Diario*, CCLXXXVI, ses. 41 (13 septiembre 1960), pp. 2943-52, 2981-85.

17. *Las Noticias de Ultima Hora*, 19 abril 1961, p. 8, 20 abril, pp. 8-9. *La Tercera de la Hora*, 26 abril 1961, p. 5. Humberto Malinarich M., "Chile Hierve con la Guerra Fria," p. 18. "Cuba: Medita la Moneda," p. 8. And on April 18th, although *La Tercera* editorially concurred with Vergara's opposition to "foreign intervention," it openly sympathized with the invaders—that Castro had brought this on himself by economic mismanagement and the destruction of civil liberties.

18. "Un Personaje al Trasluz," *Ercilla*, XXVII (5 julio 1961), 7-8.

19. *South Pacific Mail*, no. 2423 (Jan. 5, 1962), p. 2.

20. "Chile: El Bloqueo," p. 9. "Suspenso en Torno a Cuba," *Ercilla*, XXVIII (7 noviembre 1962), 6. Olavarría, *Alessandri*, III, 96-98.

21. LHP, "La campaña tomando la Recta," *Ercilla*, XXX (22 julio 1964), 9.

22. Ibid.

23. *El Mercurio*, 15 abril 1960, p. 17, 17 abril, p. 25, 6 septiembre, p. 3. *Las Noticias de Ultima Hora*, 18 abril 1961, p. 9, 19 abril, p. 8, 20 abril, pp. 8-9. Ladrón de Guevara, pp. 179-81. Federacion Mùndial de Juventud Democrática, *Documentos y Resoluciones del Comite Ejecutivo de la F.M.J.D.*, pp. 60-62, 72-74, 88-96.

24. And when former PR President Alberto Baltra addressed a rally organized by the Movement for Solidarity and Defense of the Cuban Revolution to protest the blockade, he referred to "the heroic island of Cuba, Marxist or not." *El Siglo*, 25 octubre 1962, p. 3, 26 octubre, p. 8.

25. *Ercilla*, XXV (27 mayo 1959), 9.

26. Chile, Senado, *Diario*, CCLXXXVI, ses. 41 (13 septiembre 1960), pp. 2981-85.

27. Ibid., CCLXXXVII, ses. 35 (11 abril 1961), pp. 2047-53. Hernandez Parker, "La Semana Política," *Ercilla*, XXV (23 diciembre 1959).

28. With regard to this stipulation and Alessandri's affirmative response expressed via a letter to the convention, see: "La Semana Política," *Ercilla*, XXVII (14 junio 1961), 9; "La Semana Política," Ibid. (21 junio 1961), pp. 8-9; and Humberto Malinarich M., "Los Secretos del Plan Marshall para América Latina," Ibid. (28 junio 1961), p. 7.

29. Quinzio, pp. 81-84. Cf., *Radicalismo*, I, nos. 2-3 (Enero 1962), (Febrero-Marzo 1962), pp. 19-21, 20-21; and Olavarría, *Alessandri*, II, 419.

30. They impugned the leadership for betrayal to the ideals of the party in exchange for the spoils of office. Olavarría, *Alessandri*, II, 437-38. *Hispanic American Report*, XVI (April 1963), 163.

31. LHP, "La Semana Política," *Ercilla*, XXVIII (11 abril 1962), 8.

32. "The Chilean Land Reform: A Laboratory," p. 314. Gil and Parrish, I, 30.

33. "Semana Económica: Partió la Reforma Agraria," *Ercilla*, XXVIII (23 Mayo 1962), 9.

34. Chile, Senado, *Diario*, CCXC, ses. 22 (25 julio 1962), pp. 1819-21, ses. 25 (26 julio 1962), pp. 1903-05.

35. LHP, "Reforma Agraria sin FF. EE.," *Ercilla*, XXVIII (18 julio 1962), 7.

36. Olavarría, *Alessandri*, III, 67-70. *Hispanic American Report*, XV (December 1962), 946-47.

37. "Desde dos Extremos partió la Presidencial," *Ercilla*, XXVIII (19 diciembre 1962), 17.

38. *Hispanic American Report*, XV (February 1963), 1144.

39. LHP, "Larga Maratón con Sorpresas," *Ercilla*, XXIX (12 junio 1963), 10; LHP, "Frei, Allende y Durán ante la Meta," p. 9; "Así Nos Ven," Ibid. (26 agosto 1964), p. 4; Ibid. (9 septiembre 1964), p. 11; Gil and Parrish, I, 35; and Gil, p. 299.

40. Olavarría, *Alessandri*, III, 184-85, 202, 222-23, 313-14.

41. *Hispanic American Report*, XVI (November 1963), 900. Cf., *New York Times*, Sept. 19, 1963, p. 12.

368

42. Petras, *Politics and Social Forces*, pp. 154-55.
43. *Hispanic American Report*, XVI (December 1963), 997-98.
44. Interview with Oscar Naranjo, March 26, 1967.
45. Gil, p. 242.
46. On Joseph Jova's intervention in the 1964 campaign and his association with PR leaders, see chapter 5.
47. Olavarría, *Alessandri*, IV, 124, 127-28, 131, 133, 143-44. LHP, "Derecha: Frei; PR; Allende; Mutis de Prat," *Ercilla*, XXX (25 marzo 1964), 17-18. LHP, "Durán Marcó el Destino de Radicales," Ibid. (8 abril 1964), pp. 8-9.
48. Gil and Parrish, I, 33-34.
49. For reports that a majority of rank and file Radical followers and members were believed by Radical leaders, FRAP leaders and other qualified observers to be more likely to support Allende than Frei, see: LHP, "Derecha: Frei; PR; Allende; Mutis de Prat," pp. 16-18; Olavarría, *Alessandri*, IV, 147-48, 165-68, 170-71, 174, 176-79, 194, 197; and Veliz, "Chile," p. 228. Cf., Gil and Parrish, I, 35, and Bulnes, pp. 9-10.
50. Gil and Parrish, I, 16-17.
51. "Ese es el papel del duranismo: mantenerse hasta el final para impedir un 'vaciado' del PR hacia Allende, en su mayoría, y hacia Frei, en su minoría; pero sobre todo, disponer con la Derecha y la DC el control del Congreso Pleno en el case que ninguno de los aspirantes definitivos (frei-Allende) obtuvieron la mayoría absoluta (50,0001 percent). . . ." LHP, "Mi Capitán Prat Bajose sin Disparar," *Ercilla*, XXX (29 abril 1964), 8.
52. Zeitlin and Petras, "The Working Class," p. 17.
53. Consistent with this view is not only the fact that his campaign had stressed the Cuban-Communist issue against Allende, but that in his letter of resignation as the FD candidate after Curico, Durán had "maintained that he was withdrawing his name in order to facilitate the Frente's search for solutions that would permit the defense of democracy and liberty," Gil and Parrish, I, 33.
54. "Nueva Táctica anti FRAP," *Ercilla*, XXX (15 abril 1964), 9. Olavarría, *Alessandri*, IV, 145-46.
55. Carlos Santana, "PR en 'Oposición Radical'," *Ercilla*, XXX (14 octubre 1964), 9. Santana, "Críticas para Frei y Allende," Ibid. (4 noviembre 1964), pp. 28-29.
56. On the pace and bargaining with regard to Frei's agrarian program, see Robert R. Kaufman, *The Chilean Political Right and Agrarian Reform: Resistance and Moderation* (Washington: Institute for the Comparative Study of Political Systems, 1967), pp. 3-4.
57. Gil, "Chile: 'Revolution,' " p. 294.
58. See chapter 4.
59. See data tables in: Grayson, "The Frei Administration," p. 57; Parrish, von Lazar and Tapia, *Chilean Congressional Election*, pp. 34-40.
60. Grayson, "The Frei Administration," p. 56.
61. PDC background and history is summarized by Halperin, pp. 179-93.
62. Moulian, p. 48. Gil, pp. 271-74. Grayson, "Significance," pp. 762, 764. Millas, "Christian Democratic Reformism," p. 45. Gall, "Chile Goes," p. 14.
63. *Ercilla*, 4 octubre 1961, p. 10. "DC: Pugna por el Mando y la Táctica," Ibid., XXX (18 noviembre 1964), 11. "Pablo Gomucio: constructor, banquero, publicista, industrial, pescador y etcéteras. . . ." *Punto Final*, I (1.a quincena de enero de 1967), 16-17, 28. "Dime con quien andas," pp. 16-19. Alfonso Bravo R., "Entre bueyes no hay cornadas," *Punto Final*, I (1.a quincena de abril de 1967), 10-11. Olavarría, *Democracia Cristiana*, pp. 81-82. Goldenberg, p. 81. Cf.: *El Siglo*, 30 enero 1967, p. 3; Grayson, "Significance," p. 763; Angel, "Chile: The Difficulties," p. 528.
64. Interview with David Baytelbaum, an agricultural engineer with CORFO, on May 6, 1967.
65. Petras, *Politics and Social Forces*, p. 207. This, of course, included funds contributed by businessmen, international Christian Democratic entities and U.S. sources.
66. Goldenberg, pp. 113-14. Edwards y Frei, pp. 242-45. Halperin, pp. 196-200. Pike, pp. 259-61. "Principios del Comunitarismo," *Política y Espíritu*, Ano XVI, N. o 272 (julio 1962), pp. 43-46, N. o 273 (agosto 1962), pp. 40-44. De Santis, "Chile," pp. 454-56. James K. Weekly, "Christian Democracy in Chile-Ideology and Economic Development," *South Atlantic Quarterly*, LXVI (Autumn 1967), 523-24.

In the course of a lecture on Dec. 6, 1966 at the Latin American Faculty of Social Sciences, PDC Senator and President Rafael A. Gomucio stated that "only a small minority" in the party had internalized Communitarian principles. Similarly, an examination of Frei's thinking during the 1950's reveals little concern by him with such goals. Although there were some references to the need for agrarian reform, Frei did not envisage this as involving significant expropriations from existing *fundo* owners. On the otherhand, a definite stress was placed upon urban welfare programs, raising the wages of low income groups and requiring the Gran Mineria to reinvest its earnings in Chile. *La Verdad Tiene Su Hora* (Santiago: Edit. del Pacífico, 1955), pp. 63-64; and *Pensamiento y Acción* (Santiago: Edit. del Pacífico, 1956), pp. 11-12, 18, 44-48, 94-112, 150-75, 196.

67. Frei had written a letter to the Liberals soliciting their backing, but declined Conservative requests that he also write them a letter. Given his earlier Falange role in challenging and defying the Conservatives, a letter would have symbolized a humiliating confession of partial failure for the egotistic Frei. Subsequently, he was to denounce these parties as "oligarchic," and for this many Rightists—and especially Liberals—would prove unable to forgive him in 1964 when an abortive attempt was made to run Jorge Prat. But because the system was clearly threatened, even he withdrew. On these matters, see: "La Elección," pp. 7-8; LHP, "4 Candidatos en el Punto de Partida," *Ercilla*, XXIX (29 mayo 1963), 10; and Chile, Senado, *Diario*, CCXCIII, ses. 56 (13 mayo 1964), p. 4399.

68. Hector Valenzuela Valderrama, "El Dilema Político de Hoy," *Política y Espíritu*, XIII (mayo 1958), 22-26. Francisco A. Pinto, "La Democracia Cristiana y La Economía," Ibid. (15 agosto 1958), pp. 22-30. *Hispanic American Report*, XI (August 1958), 455.

69. Gil and Parrish, II, 29. Halperin, p. 193. Powell, "Political Change," pp. 373-74.

70. Alejandro Magnet and Radomiro Tomic were also members of the Congress for Cultural Freedom. *El Mercurio*, 30 julio 1959, p. 3.

71. "Puntos de Vista," XIV, 1.

72. Ibid. (15 julio 1959), p. 1.

73. Ibid. (1 septiembre 1959), p. 1. Ibid. (1 noviembre 1959), pp. 7-8. "La Crisis Cubano-Norteamericana," Ibid. (1 abril 1960), pp. 10-11. "Castro: Camino de la Dictadura Total," Ibid. (15 mayo 1960), pp. 8-9. "Puntos de Vista" (15 julio 1960), p. 1. "Presiones sobre la Democracia," Ibid. (15 octubre 1960), pp. 5-7. "Atentados Contra la Democracia Venezolana," Ibid. (1 diciembre 1960), p. 1. "Constitución de la Vanguardia Demócrata Cristiana Cubana," Ibid., pp. 30-31. "Documentos: El Problema Sindical en Cuba," Ibid. (15 diciembre 1960), pp. 25-28. "Una situación aclarada," Ibid., XV (noviembre 1961), 1-2. "La Política de Bloques," Ibid., XVI (abril 1962), 33-37.

74. "Cuba, Un Año Después," Ibid., XIV (1 enero 1960), 8-9. "Declaración del Movimiento D.C. de Cuba," Ibid. (1 junio 1960), pp. 30-31.

75. "Cuba: Ante una provocación comunista los católicos plantean su posición social," Ibid. (1 junio 1960), pp. 21-22. "La Iglesia Católica, el Régimen Cubano y el Partido Communista," Ibid. (1 septiembre 1960), pp. 23-24. "Declaración de la CLASC Sobre La Revolución Cubana y El Gobierno de Fidel Castro," Ibid. (15 noviembre 1960), pp. 31-32.

76. This, despite the fact that Jaime Castillo, Radomiro Tomic, Jorge Cash (Director of *La Libertad*), and Alejandro Magnet (an editor of *Política y Espíritu* and a very frequent contributor to the Jesuit monthly *Mensaje*) had been *invitados* for Cuba's 26th of July celebrations. These four members of the party's National Council returned voicing largely sympathetic reports of the Castro regime. With regard to this and the matters referred to in the text, see: *El Mercurio*, 8 agosto 1959, p. 35; *La Libertad*, 4 agosto 1959, pp. 8-9, 8 agosto, p. 4; "La Semana Política," *Ercilla*, XXV (22 julio 1959), 8; and "Como vió el PDC la Revolución Cubana," p. 9.

77. *La Libertad*, 22 agosto 1960, p. 3. "La Doble Conferencia de Cancilleres," *Política y Espíritu*, XIV (1 septiembre 1960), 1.

78. And in a letter published at about the same time by the *New York Times*, Eduardo Frei categorically denied imputations that the PDC held *any* sympathy for the Communistic Castro regime: "El PDC no pertenece al bloque marxista. Es abierta y definitivamente anticommunista, no promueve la nacionalización de todas las industrias mineras sino solamente de algunas actividades muy definidas, como el petróleo, por ejemplo, y no es 'fidelista' habiendo criticado large tiempo e implacablemente, al régimen cubano." "El PDC Busca una Postura Revolucionaria," *Ercilla*, XXVII (12 abril 1961), 7. Frei's criticism of Castro's rule dated from April 1960. *El Mercurio*, 25 abril 1960, p. 3, 27 abril, p. 17, 28 abril, p. 23, 1 mayo, p. 9.

79. "Suspenso en la Política Nacional," *Ercilla*, XXVII (19 abril 1961), 7.
80. *Las Noticias de Ultima Hora*, 20 abril 1961, pp. 8-9. *Hispanic American Report*, XIV (June 1961), 351-52.
81. "Chile: El Bloqueo," p. 9.
82. "El Pensamiento de la Democracia Cristiana Frente a la Situación Internacional," *Política y Espíritu*, XVI (octubre 1962), 36.
83. Matilde Ladrón de Guevara, *Adiós al Cañaveral*,—this had already been published by Edit. Goyanarte in Buenos Aires—(Santiago: Edit. del Pacífico, 1962). Luís Boza Domínguez, *La Situación Universitaria en Cuba* (Santiago: Edit. del Pacífico, 1962). Laurencio Angel Aparicio, *Los Malvados No Conocen La Justicia* (Santiago: Edit. del Pacífico, 1963). Aparicio, *El Congreso de las Focas Amaestradas y los Lacayos Parlantes de Moscú en Río de Janeiro* (Santiago: Edit. del Pacífico, 1963).
84. Grayson, "Significance," p. 774.
85. And Frei was reported to have stated on a campaign tour in the north that if Alessandri did not sever relations, he would be compelled to do so. *Las Noticias de Ultima Hora*, 12 agosto 1964, p. 3, 14 agosto, p. 8.
86. Igor Entrala, "JAR le Quitó," p. 11. Although the PDC Youth had been reportedly "pressured" not to take a position against the break, the Federation of Chilean Students—controlled by the PDC Youth—did release such a declaration which attributed Alessandri's decision to "la existencia de conflictos limítrofes en la región de Palena provocados por la Gendarmería Argentina, han sido utilizados como un elemento de persuasión internacional en contra el del Gobierno de Chile que se vió colocado en la alternativa de romper relaciones con Cuba o qurdar expuesto a la marginación de la garantías del Tratado de Asistencia Recíproca de Río de Janeiro ante un caso de Agresión." *Las Noticias de Ultima Hora*, 12 agosto 1964, p. 9, 14 agosto, p. 8.
87. Erica Vexler, "Frei en la antesala de la Moneda," *Ercilla*, XXX (9 septiembre 1964), 20. Grayson, "Significance," pp. 774-75. *New York Times*, Dec. 28, 1964, p. 14. Gabriel Valdes Subercaseaux, *Address delivered by the Minister of Foreign Affairs before the Senate, on 6 January 1965* (Santiago: South Pacific Mail, 1965), 8 pp. Olavarría, *Alessandri*, IV, 339. Chile, Senado, *Diario*, CCXCVI, ses. 15 (6 enero 1965), pp. 870-71. Cf., "Lo que Tomic hará en USA," *Ercilla*, XXX (13 enero 1965), 15.
88. For statements by Radomiro Tomic, see: "La Democracia y La Revolución," *Política y Espíritu*, XIV (15 marzo 1959), 19-29; "Sobre la Revolución Cubana," Ibid. (1 mayo 1960), pp. 10-12; *El Mercurio*, 20 julio 1959, p. 3, 10 septiembre 1960, p. 3; *La Libertad*, 4 agosto 1959, pp. 8-9, 8 agosto, p. 4; *Las Noticias de Ultima Hora*, 18 abril 1961, p. 9; *El Siglo*, 30 octubre 1962, p. 1; "Como vió el PDC la Revolución Cubana," p. 9; "Tomic: Salvar a Cuba para la Democracia," *Ercilla*, XXVI (20 julio 1960), 8; "La 'Batalla' del Senado," p. 8; Chile, Senado, *Diario*, CCLXXXVIII, ses. 3 (7 junio 1961), p. 135, CCXCII, ses. 8 (20 junio 1963), pp. 358-63, CCXCIII, ses. 37 (22 enero 1964), p. 2835, CCXCIV, ses. 21 (11 agosto 1964), pp. 2036-45; and his *Sobre el Sistema Interamericano*, pp. 38-40, 47.

References to the views and acts of other PDC leaders who in varying degree shared the Tomic approach will be found in: "Como vió el PDC la Revolución Cubana," p. 9; "En la Plaza Banquedano hablará Fidel Castro," *Vistazo*, VIII (11 agosto 1959), 9. "Dos juicios sobre las relaciones interamericanas," *Política y Espíritu*, XIV (15 mayo 1960), 18-22; Jorge Cash, "Cuba y la Política de Bloques," Ibid., XVI (marzo 1962), 32-34; Julio Silva, "Reflexiones sobre la Revolución," Julio Silva S., "Declaración del PDC," *Las Noticias de Ultima Hora*, 17 abril 1961, p. 2, 12 agosto 1964, p. 3, 14 agosto, p. 8; *El Siglo*, 26 octubre 1962, pp. 1, 7, 8; "Goodwin: intérprete entre JAR y Kennedy," p. 8; Jacques Chonchol, "La Reforma Agraria Cubana," *Panorama Económico*, Año XV, N. o 227 (Enero 1962), pp. 16-24, No. 228 (marzo 1962), pp. 38-47, No. 229 (abril 1962), pp. 97-106; Jorge Ahumada, *La Crisis Integral de Chile* (Santiago: Edit. Universitaria, 1966), pp. 23-25; and Partido Democratico Cristiano, *Primer Congreso Nacional de Profesionales y Técnicos de la Democracia Cristiana e Independientes: III Política Internacional Apartado, No. 1 al Informe Preliminar* (Santiago: Imp del Pacífico, n.d. 1963), pp. 6-13.

89. The more radical views and conduct of the party's youth, as expressed directly and through the Federation of Chilean Students are found in: *El Mercurio*, 6 diciembre 1959, p. 35, 6 julio 1960, p. 21, 1 agosto, p. 25, 3 agosto, p. 15; *La Nación*, 18 abril 1961, p. 2, 24 octubre 1962, p. 5; *Las Noticias de Ultima Hora*, 18 abril 1961, p. 16, 11 agosto 1964, pp.

8-9, 15, 15 agosto, p. 5; *El Siglo*, 26 octubre 1962, pp. 1, 7, 8, 30 octubre, p. 7; Malinarich, "Chile Hierve con la Guerra Fría," p. 17, LHP, "Listo Frente Democratico, p. 9; U.S., Department of State, "Text of Chilean 'Federation of the Students of Chile' Letter," *Bulletin*, XLII (April 25, 1960), 656-58; *Informe del Segundo Congreso Nacional de la Juventud Demócrata Cristiana*, pp. 39-53, 69; and Congreso Latinoamericano, *Acuerdos y Resoluciones del II CLAJ*, pp. 5-8.

90. See "The Consensus of Viña del Mar," *LADOC*, I (October 1970), 1-9.

91. U.S., *Organization of American States Hearings*, p. 26.

92. "La Primera Convención del Partido Demócrata Cristiana," *Política y Espíritu*, XIV (15 junio 1959), 12, 17-22; *Convención Nacional del Partido Demócrata Cristiano*, 1.a, Santiago, 1959, Resolución sobre política nacional, Declaración de Principios (Santiago: Edit. del Pacífico, 1959), 15 pp. *Documentos de la Convención Nacional del Partido Demócrata Cristiano*, 1.a, Santiago, 1959, Resolución sobre política, Declaración de Principios (Santiago: Edit. del Pacífico, 1959), p. 2.

93. *El Mercurio*, 30 mayo 1959, p. 15. Halperin, pp. 191-92. Cf., Pike, pp. 265-66.

94. Chile, Senado, *Diario*, CCLXXXIV, ses. 17 (28 julio 1959), pp. 947-53. *El Mercurio*, 2 septiembre 1959, p. 17. *Hispanic American Report*, XII (November 1959), 507.

95. *El Mercurio*, 6 marzo 1960, p. 11.

96. *El Mercurio*, 8 marzo 1960, p. 1.

97. "El PDC Busca Una Postura Revolucionaria," p. 7. Gil, p. 237.

98. *Hispanic American Report*, XIV (July 1961), 440-41.

99. Chile, Senado, *Diario*, CCLXXXVIII, ses. 20 (18 julio 1961).

100. "Torneo D.C.: una estrategia y dos tácticas frente al PC," *Ercilla*, XXVII (2 agosto 1961), 16-17.

101. Chile, Senado, *Diario*, CCLXXXVIII, ses. 37 (22 agosto 1961), pp. 2058-60, CCXC, ses. 38 (22 agosto 1962), pp. 2763-64.

102. *Hispanic American Report*, XVI (March 1963), 68-69.

103. Unlike 1958, it was also argued that such a coalition would require that the party compromise its new vigorous reformism. LHP, "La Semana Política," *Ercilla*, XXVIII (28 marzo 1962), 9. For other instances of stress being placed in 1962 upon the contention that "la única fuerza capaz de combatir eficazmente al comunismo es la Democracia Cristiana," see: "Rebase del FRAP en Las Vertientes," Ibid. (7 marzo 1962), p. 15; and Instituto de Estudios Políticos del PDC de Concepción, *El a-b-c de la Democracia Cristiana* (Santiago: Edit. del Pacífico, 1962).

104. LHP, "Partió el FRAP con Allende, *Ercilla*, XXVIII (4 julio 1962), 7. Hernández Parker, "Semana Política," Ibid. (25 julio 1962), p. 8. Cf., *New York Times*, Oct. 28, 1962, p. 35.

105. "Oposición sigue sendas separadas," *Ercilla*, XXVIII (26 diciembre 1962), 10.

106. Partido Demócrata Cristiano, Consejo Nacional, *Nosotros creemos que la Democracia es la forma política de la Revolución y nos negamos a aceptar que en nombre de esta última, transitoria o definitivamente, se acabe con la libertad: Dice la Democracia Cristiana a los Partidos Comunista y Socialista, 31 de Enero de 1963*, (Santiago: Edit. del Pacífico, 1963), pp. 3, 7.

107. Igor Entrala, "El PC Envía Paloma," p. 8. "Otra vez Deciden la Mujeres," *Ercilla*, XXIX (20 febrero 1963), 7. *Hispanic American Report*, XVI (April 1963), 161-63.

108. LHP, "La Elección Municipal: Primer Pie," *Ercilla*, XXIX (3 abril 1963), 8. LHP, "4 Candidatos," p. 11. Gil and Parrish, 21-22.

109. "Frases y Personajes," *Ercilla*, XXIX (24 abril 1963), 9.

110. LHP, "Las Mujeres se 'Toman' la Política," Ibid. (28 agosto 1963), pp. 8-9. Cf., Partido Demócrata Cristiano, *Congreso Nacional de Mujeres Demócratas Cristianas e Independientes: Congreso de la Mujer Chilena, 23, 24 y 25 de Agosto, Valparaíso, 1963* (Santiago: Imp. Sopech, 1963), 16 pp.

111. LHP, "Reformistas Izaron a JAR," p. 11.

112. "Frases y Personajes," *Ercilla*, XXX (6 mayo 1964), 9.

113. Igor Entrala, "El Error del Plebiscito," Ibid. (18 marzo 1964) p. 17.

114. Gil and Parrish, I, 39-40, 42, 43, 49. For examples of leading PDC figures (Frei Pablo and Fuentealba) and the party stressing that an Allende victory would Cubanize and/ or Communize Chile, see: Chile, Senado, *Diario* CCXCIII, ses. 56 (13 mayo 1964), p. 4365;

Eduardo Frei Montalva, *Dos Discursos* (Santiago: Edit. del Pacífico, 1964), pp. 16, 49; Renán Fuentealba Moena, *A Los Pobladores*, Discurso del Presidente Nacional de la Democracia Cristiana, Diputado R. Fuentealba, 1. o de Mayo 1964 (Santiago: Imp. 'Soberanía', 1964); Partido Democrático Cristiano, Departamento Nacional Campesino, *Principios Fundamentales: Jornadas Campesinas*, Democracia Cristiana (Santiago: 'El Diario Ilustrado,' 1964); *Ahora el Pueblo Busca su Camino Mano a Mano con Frei* (Santiago: Edit. del Pacífico, 1964), p. 7; and *Hispanic American Report*, XVII (May 1964), 257.

115. LHP, "Frei, Allende y Durán," p. 8. Cope, "The 1964 Presidential Election," pp. 12-13. Gil and Parrish, I, 49, 51.

116. The USIA chief in Chile, James Echols, informed the writer late in 1966 that "public opinion surveys"—such as those referred to in chapters 3, 5, and 9—were undertaken for the Agency by Salas Reyes, Eduardo Hamuy and the McCann Erikson local affiliate. During the exposure of CIA subsidies in February 1967, International Research Associates was identified by the *Washington Post* on Feb. 26, 1967, as a recipient of such funds.

117. Partido Democrático Cristiana, *Democracia Cristiana: Tercera Declaración de Millahue y Cuenta Política del Presidente Nacional de la DC, Diputado Renán Fuentealba*, (Santiago: imp. El Imparcial, Abril 1964), 16pp. The textual summary is based upon the restatement of the program that appears in the *Informes de las comisiones al Congreso Nacional de Trabajadores*. Cf.; *Frente Nacional de Profesores Freístas: Primeras Jornadas de Estudios*; LHP, "DC: Allende o Frei es la alternativa," *Ercilla*, XXX (22 abril 1964), 8-9; Gil, pp. 301-303; Weekly, "Christian Democracy," pp. 529-30.

In order to compare this with the greater moderation in a number of fields (e.g., scholarships and housing) as of late 1962, see the Partido Democrático Cristiano, *Informe Preliminar para un Programa de Gobierno de la Democracia Cristiana del Primer Congreso Nacional de Professionales y Técnicos de la Democracia Cristiana e Independientes, 6-7-8 y 9 de Diciembre de 1962* (Santiago: Edit. del Pacífico, 1963), 108pp.

With regard to the issue of nationalizing the Gran Mineria, the PDC claimed that FRAP favored this in order to justify Soviet aid, and called the attention of the miners to the fact that "Cuba nacionalizó todas sus riquezas, pero tuvo que pagar el precio de vincularse al bloque soviético y de aceptar las imposiciones políticas de dicho bloque al igual que los gobiernos obsecuentes de América Latina aceptan las imposiciones de la política norteamericana." It was also alleged that nationalization would require a reduction in the wages and benefits of the miners. The PDC justified "Chileanization" by denying that the nation possessed sufficient resources to compensate the U.S. owners of the mines, and by arguing that available funds should be allocated to other programs. Frei would force an expansion in mining production. It was denied that rejection of nationalization—a possible long range goal—was motivated by fear of U.S. reprisals, although Radomiro Tomic was reported to have warned that such measures "could lead to the kind of situation Cuba is in—asphyxiation, or worse." *Los Trabajadores y la Nacionalización del Cobre* (Santiago: Edit. del Pacífico, Julio 1964), pp. 9-15. Partido Democrático Cristiano, *Informe Preliminar para un Programa de Gobierno*, p. 75. *El Mercurio*, 5 enero 1964, p. 43. De Santis, "Chile" pp. 355-358.

118. LHP, "Durán Marca el Destina de Radicales," *Ercilla*, XXX (1 abril 1964), 8.

119. Goldenberg, p. 53. Conversations with persons present at the time.

120. Conversations with R.M., a close friend of Rafael Espinosa who was in charge of the operation. The PDC role was also attested to by at least two party members in their late twenties, E.M., and N.C., in the course of conversations during March and April 1967.

121. A CESO "Post-Electoral Survey" in November 1964, reported that 20 percent of the Greater Santiago interviewees believed that communism had been the most important factor in the Frei victory. Another twenty percent expressed the view that it was the second most important factor. Cf., Petras, *Politics and Social Forces*, pp. 205-207; Powell, "Political Change," pp. 377-82.

122. LHP, "Se 'Exporta' el Plan Frei," *Ercilla*, XXX (7 octubre 1964), 8-9. LHP, "Frei Pone Cascabeles al Gate," Ibid. (18 noviembre 1964), pp. 10-11.

123. William P. Lineberry, "Chile's Struggle on the Left," *New Leader*, XLIX (May 23, 1966), 6.

124. Parrish, von Lazar and Tapia, *Chilean Congressional Election*, p. 11.

125. Frei also advanced the date for primary school registration and promised that a

place would be found in school for every child. In a not wholly successful effort to realize this goal, university students of all political tendencies devoted part of their summer vacations between January and March 1965 to constructing buildings for primary schools. In addition, shortly before the March election and with great publicity, 5,000 sewing machines, telephones and some TV sets were distributed through "Promoción Popular" in slum districts by the Government or through its efforts and those of cooperating agencies and organizations. LHP, "Tensa Pugna," p. 9. LHP, "La DC Destrozó," pp. 18-19. Olavarría, *Democracia Cristiana*, pp. 25-26, 35.

126. Descriptions of these proposals and the differential responses of the various parties will be found in: LHP, "Un Arqueo Político," pp. 8-9. Carlos Santana, "Ha Faltado," pp. 10-11. LHP, "Tensa Pugna," p. 8; Carlos Santana, "PDC contra todas; todos contra PDC," *Ercilla*, XXX (17 febrero 1965), 8; LHP, "Tres Bloques dan examen el Domingo," Ibid. (3 marzo 1965), p. 17; Beatty, "The Chilean Dilemma," p. 348; Grayson, "Significance," pp. 765-71; Gall, "Chile Goes," pp. 13-14; Petras, "After the Election," pp. 382-83; De Santis, "Chile," pp. 358-59; and Parrish, von Lazar and Tapia Videla, *Chilean Congressional Election*, pp. 11-17.

127. Parrish, von Lazar and Tapia, *Chilean Congressional Election*, pp. 21-22, 24-26.

128. Ibid., p. 27.

129. Bodenheimer, " 'Stagnation in Liberty,' " p. 6.

130. U.S., *Rockefeller Report Hearing*, p. 25. Cf., chapter 5.

131. Petras, *Politics and Social Forces*, p. 238. "Business Abroad: Chile-Why the Copper Men," p. 38.

132. Bodenheimer, " 'Stagnation in Liberty,' " p. 6. Cf., Angell, "Chile: The Difficulties," p. 522.

133. Parrish, von Lazar and Tapia, *Chilean Congressional Election*, p. 10.

134. Kaufman, *The Chilean Political Right*, pp. 1-5.

135. Manuel Barrera, "Participation by Occupational Organizations in Economic and Social Planning in Chile," *International Labor Review*, XCVI (August 1967), 175.

136. Johnson, "The National and Progressive Bourgeoisie," pp. 63-84.

137. Bodenheimer, " 'Stagnation in Liberty,' " p. 3.

138. James Petras, *Chilean Christian Democracy: Politics and Social Forces* (Berkeley: Institute of International Studies, University of California, 1967), pp. 15, 40-50.

139. Bodenheimer, " 'Stagnation in Liberty,' " pp. 2-3.

140. Petras, *Politics and Social Forces*, pp. 239-45.

141. "Ninth National Congress of the Christian Workers' Confederation of Chile," *International Labour Review*, XCVI (July 1967), 110-13.

142. Petras, *Chilean Christian Democracy*, p. 15. Angell, "Chile: The Difficulties," pp. 518-19. Barrera, "Participation," pp. 170-71.

143. Petras, *Politics and Social Forces*, pp. 217-19, 246-53.

144. Vitale, *¿Y Después?* pp. 27-28. Cf., Grayson, "The Frei Administration," pp. 54-55; "Business Abroad: Chile-Why the Copper Men are Getting Edgy," *Business Week*, April 4, 1970, pp. 38-39.

145. Petras, *Politics and Social Forces*, pp. 246-52.

146. Kaufman, *The Chilean Political Right*, pp. 3-5. Petras, *Politics and Social Forces*, pp. 207-209, 225-29. "Chilean Campesino Unionization Law," *Labor Developments Abroad*, XIII (February 1968), 6-9.

147. Grayson, "The Frei Administration," p. 52.

148. Vitale, *¿Y Después?* p. 37.

149. Ibid.

150. *Time* (Canadian Edition), October 9, 1970, p. 30. This may be another case of doctored official figures. According to the new UP Government, only 10,000 had actually "received their own land by 1970." Richard O'Mara, "Chile: A Good Neighbor," *Nation*, February 8, 1971, p. 181.

151. Angell, "Christian Democracy," pp. 81-82.

152. Agor, "Senate vs. CORA," pp. 47-53.

153. For data on this organization see: Petras, *Politics and Social Forces*, pp. 227-28; Angell, "Christian Democracy," p. 82.

154. Vitale, *¿Y Después?* pp. 19, 23.

155. Based upon interviews with UCC leaders. Petras, *Politics and Social Forces*, pp. 220-23.

156. At the earlier date, an additional 15,000 peasants were "influenced" by the UCC. Ibid.

157. Angell, "Christian Democracy," pp. 81-82.

158. U.S., *Economic Trends*, p. 7.

159. U.S., Department of Agriculture, *Agricultural Prospects in Chile*, by Francis S. Urban (Washington: Economic Research Service, Foreign Regional Analysis Division, U.S. Department of Agriculture, January 1970), pp. 7-11.

160. U.S., *Economic Trends*, pp. 6-7.

161. Angell, "Christian Democracy," p. 81.

162. Vitale, *¿Y Después?* p. 25.

163. U.S., *Economic Trends*, p. 3. Joseph Kraft, "Letter from Santiago," *The New Yorker*, Jan. 30, 1971, p. 85.

164. Ibid., pp. 2, 12.

165. Ibid., pp. 2-3.

166. Ibid., pp. 10, 13. U.S., *Latin American Economic Study*, pp. 31-32.

167. U.S., *Economic Trends*, pp. 2, 11-12.

168. Angell, "Chile: The Difficulties," pp. 521-22, 527-28.

169. Cited in Vitale, *¿Y Después?* p. 23.

170. Barrera, "Participation by Occupational Organizations," p. 169.

171. "Ninth National Congress" pp. 110-11.

172. Petras, *Politics and Social Forces*, pp. 231-36. Cf., Weekly, "Christian Democracy," p. 529.

173. Duncan, "Chilean Christian Democracy," pp. 267-68.

174. *Time* (Canadian Edition), Oct. 9, 1970, p. 30.

175. Ibid.

176. Angell, "Chile: The Difficulties," p. 525.

177. U.S., *Latin American Economic Study*, p. 18.

178. Angell, "Christian Democracy," p. 82. Petras, *Politics and Social Forces*, p. 238.

179. Angell, "Christian Democracy," p. 83.

180. *Time* (Canadian Edition), Oct. 9, 1970, p. 31. Gall, "The Chileans," p. 110.

181. U.S., *Economic Trends*, p. 5.

182. Gold, "Income Tax Evasion," pp. 55-66.

183. U.S., *Economic Trends*, p. 9. *Time* (Canadian Edition), October 9, 1970, p. 30.

184. U.S., *Latin American Economic Study*, p. 18.

185. Petras, *Politics and Social Forces*, pp. 347-48.

186. Vitale, *¿Y Después?* p. 9. Angell, "Chile: The Difficulties," pp. 527-28.

187. Address to the Nation by the President of Chile on February 18, 1965. Cited in Parrish, von Lazar, and Tapia, *Chilean Congressional Election*, p. 17.

188. *El Siglo*, 28 Noviembre 1970, p. 9, 17 Diciembre 1970, p. 1.

189. Petras, *Politics and Social Forces*, p. 254.

190. Ibid., p. 255.

191. Petras, *Chilean Christian Democracy*, p. 15.

192. Duncan, "Chilean Christian Democracy," p. 265.

193. Petras, *Politics and Social Forces*, p. 219. Parrish, von Lazar and Tapia, *Chilean Congressional Election*, p. 28.

194. Petras, *Politics and Social Forces*, p. 219.

195. Bodenheimer, " 'Stagnation in Liberty,' " pp. 6-7.

196. Percentages are from Grayson, "The Frei Administration," p. 68.

197. Bodenheimer, " 'Stagnation in Liberty,' " p. 9.

198. Grayson, "The Frei Administration," p. 65.

199. Ibid., p. 71.

200. Ibid.

201. *Las Noticias de Ultima Hora*, 8 enero 1971, pp. 3, 8-9.

202. Vitale, *¿Y Después?* pp. 38-39. "Programa de Radomiro Tomic," *Politica y Espiritu*, no. 317 (Agosto de 1970). Grayson, "The Frei Administration," pp. 63-68. Angell, "Christian Democracy," pp. 82-83. U.S., *Organization of American States, Hearings*, p. 26.

203. Vitale, ¿Y Después? pp. 40, 44. U.S., *Cuba and the Caribbean*, p. 200.

204. Ibid.

205. U.S., *Economic Trends*, p. 10.

206. "A Traves del Mundo," *Bohemia* (La Habana), 25 diciembre 1970, p. 80.

207. Vitale, ¿Y Después? p. 89.

208. Ibid., pp. 60-64. Gall, "The Chileans," pp. 26, 106, 109. Rodman, "October Revolution," pp. 1054-55. *Time* (Canadian Edition), Oct. 9, 1970, pp. 26, 29, November 2, 1970, p. 20. *New York Times*, Nov. 1, 1970, Section I, p. 2. *Chronicle Herald* (Halifax, Nova Scotia), Dec. 21, 1970.

209. Entrala, "Divorcio," pp. 10-11.

210. Upper class annulment frauds are discussed in Enrique Cid, "Revision de 6 Mil Nulidades Matrimoniales," *Ercilla*, XXV (9 septiembre 1959), 10.

211. Fichter, pp. 17-18. IADB, *SPTF, 1964 Report*, pp. 212-13. "A proposito de un discurso extraño," *Mensaje*, N. o 131 (Agosto 1964), p. 345. *Frente Nacional de Profesores Freistas: Primeras Jornadas de Estudios*, Chile, Senado, *Diario*, CCXCIII, ses. 34 (15 enero 1964), p. 2635.

212. Hamuy, et al., p. 25. CESO, "Survey" (January 1965).

213. CESO, "Post-Electoral Survey" (November 1964).

214. Rycroft and Clemmer, p. 207. Silvert, *Chile: Yesterday and Today*, p. 170.

215. The data cited in the text would imply that in an ordinary presidential contest about 45 percent would not vote for an anti-clerical candidate 'or one clearly opposed by their Church. Where the candidate was identified as an agent of communism (the modern equivalent for the devil), the percentage might well be over fifty. Yet, Ernst Halperin estimates that effective Church influence extends only to one third of the population. Op. cit., p. 202. Cf., Soares and Hamblin, "Socio-economic Variables," p. 1061.

216. Pedro Zottele, "Chile: Orienting the Faithful," *Christian Century*, May 22, 1968, p. 697.

217. During 1964, Chile ranked with Colombia as the highest in priests per person for Latin America. There was one priest or member of a holy order for every 2,783 Catholics (or 3,127 inhabitants, including non-Catholics). This represented an improvement over the situation in 1930 when the ratio had been one priest per 3,266 Catholics. By 1968, the situation had deteriorated considerably to one priest per 7,448 Catholics. Poblete, "Causas," p. 307. Zottele, "Chile: Orienting," p. 697.

218. And in 1964, USEC was propagandizing for a Communitarian reform of business firms. The conclusions of the 1960 conference on agrarian reform—held at Catholic University—were published by the PDC. Fernando Illanes Abbott, *Reforma Agraria*, Foro efectuada por USEC en la Universidad Católica el 13 de octubre de 1960 (Santiago: Edit. del Pacífico, 1961), 16pp. "USEC y la reforma de la empresa," *Mensaje*, No. 131 (agosto 1964), pp. 373-374.

219. Within a year, the UCC boasted of an estimated 20,000 members. In May 1962, the National Association of Peasant Organizations (ANOC) was organized to: 1) represent peasants before groups or the Government; 2) train leaders, creating "a communitarian conscience"; and 3) provide credit and marketing services for peasants. During November 1962, the Central Nacional de Pobladores (CENAPO) was organized as an affiliate of CLASC. Its goal was to organize and represent slum dwellers in the promotion of such goals as "full liberty, work, justice, love and human dignity." Years earlier in 1956 the Federación Gremialista de Chile (FEGRECH) had been constituted as "a movement of penetration and proselytization within the rank and file of existing unions." It sought to group all democratic unionists in a struggle "against dictatorship and totalitarianism" and for private or Communitarian property. All of these organizations coordinated their efforts by forming or joining the Movimiento Unitario de Trabajadores de Chile (MUTCH) in 1961 or 1962. Its function was to unite Catholic and non-Catholic labor for a struggle against the Marxist-led unions. Associated with the MUTCH as a leadership training organization was the Instituto de Capacitación Sindical y Social del MUTCH (INCASIS), which was subsidized by the German Bishop's Foundation "MISEREOR" and the *Institute of International Solidarity*. Some INCASIS leadership training courses were organized at the CARITAS summer center in Penalolen. And it was reported that Hernán Troncoso, a Labor advisor to the U.S. Embassy,

edited INCASIS training materials. Although these organizations were not formally linked with the PDC, a close relationship was evidenced by: 1) similarity of doctrine and goals; 2) interchange of personnel or the exercise of dual roles by individuals; and 3) voting coordination within the CUT under leadership of the PDC union department. *Movimiento Unitario de Trabajadores de Chile (MUTCH)* (Santiago: Imp. Sopech, 1963), pp. 3-6, 19-27, 30. Acción Sindical Chilena (ASICH), *Tierra y Libertad por la Reforma Agraria*, A pedido de la Unión de Campesinos Cristianos de Chile (Santiago: Escuela Tipo-Litográfica 'La Gratitud Nacional,' Abril de 1961), pp. 3-4. Gonzalo Arroyo C., "Sindicalismo y Promoción campesina," *Mensaje*, XV (Junio 1966), 245. "La conferencia sindical de los Trabajadores de América Latina," Ibid., XI (octubre 1962), 495-96. *Ercilla*, XXV (3 junio 1959), 8. "Semana Política," Ibid., XXVIII (24 febrero 1962), 7, 18. LHP, "Las 4 Caras," p. 8. Eduardo Labarca, "Luís Quiroga y un Instituto con 160 millones," *El Siglo*, 13 marzo 1967, p. 3. Labarca, "Alemania Occidental también se trabaja a gremios chilenos," p. 5.

220. Acción Sindical Chilena (ASICH), *Tierra y Libertad por la Reforma Agraria.*

221. CLASC, Confederación Latinoamericana de Sindicalistas Cristianos, *1.a Jornada de Solidaridad Latinoamericana con los Trabajadores y el Pueblo de Cuba 26 al 31 de Julio 1964* (Santiago: Imp Sopech, 1964). Both MUTCH and the Movement of Independent Peasants (MCI) disseminated propaganda stressing the same theme during 1963 and 1964. The MCI, a union of Christian inspiration, was constituted in 1964 and directly urged peasants to vote for Frei. *Movimiento Unitario de Trabajadores de Chile (MUTCH)*, p. 5. Arroyo, "Sindicalismo y Promoción campesina," p. 245. *Movimiento Campesino Independiente: Informe a los Campesinos de Chile*, (Santiago: 'La Nación,' 1964), 20 pp.

222. In April 1961, *Ercilla*, had characterized *La Voz* as the "periódico vinculado directamente a la curia metropolitana" and as the "periódico católico y de tendencia demócratacristiana." When the Archbishop and the bishops declared their support for structural reforms in October 1962, this was immediately reflected by both *La Voz* and Radio Chilena. Humberto Malinarich, "Reforma Agraria Divide a Católicos," *Ercilla*, XXVII (5 abril 1961), 10. "El PDC Busca una Postura Revolucionaria," p. 7. "El Anti 'Mensaje' del Ilustrado," Ibid., XXIX (30 enero 1963), 10.

With regard to *La Voz* circulation figures, see the *South Pacific Mail*, CIX (August 23, 1963), 5, and *La Voz*, N. o 194 (23 abril 1961), p. 2.

223. This was admitted in an interview given by Veckemans to *Zig Zag* during October 1964. Olavarría, *Alessandri*, IV, 293, 324-26, 332-33. For other indications of conduct supporting Frei by Veckemans or DESAL, see: LHP, "Elección de Congreso a la Vista," *Ercilla*, XXX (30 septiembre 1964), 6; DESAL, *Una Estrategia contra la Miseria* (Santiago: DESAL, n.d. (pub. between 1964 and 1966)); and *Punto Final*, 15 mayo 1967, p. 5.

224. "Reforma Agraria en Cuba," VIII (Marzo-Abril 1959), 91-92.

225. H.L.S., "Justicia de Vencedores," VIII, N. o 79, pp. 169-71. José Ignacio Lasaga, "La Reforma Agraria y el comunismo," VIII (septiembre 1959), 373-76. Alejandro Magnet, "Rebajada la Cuota de Azúcar," IX (agosto 1960), 282-83. Manuel Aguirre, "Anverso y Reverso de la Revolución Cubana" (septiembre 1960), pp. 376-77. "La ley de reforma agraria en Cuba," X (marzo-abril 1961), 107-12. "Los tractores valen mas" (julio 1961), pp. 265-68, 290-94. "Cuba: Primera navidad socialista," XI (marzo-abril 1962), 103. Alejandro Magnet, "Cuba, o la revolución traicionada," XII (octubre 1963), 663-66. Magnet, "La Novena Reunión de Cancilleres," 406-408, Magnet, "La 'Revolución en Libertad' en América Latina," XIII (octubre 1964), 480-82. *La Voz*, 5 julio 1964, p. 12.

226. "La CLASC y la Revolución Cubana: Declaración . . ," *Mensaje*, IX (diciembre 1960), 541-42.

227. "Alianza contra Castro," *La Voz*, 9 abril 1961, p. 4. "Problema Cuadrangular: URSS, Cuba, USA, América Latina," *La Voz*, 23 abril 1961, p. 5. Malinarich M., "Chile Hierve con la Guerra Fría," p. 17.

228. "¿Era lícito intervonir?" X (junio 1961), 199-201. Alejandro Magnet, "La aventura cubana," Ibid., pp. 196-98. John Meslay, "Algo mas sobre Cuba," 47-49. Alejandro Magnet, "Comentarios Internacionales," XIII (abril 1964), 202-204.

229. Alejandro Magnet, "Comentarios Internacionales: ¿Plan Marshall para América Latina? " IX (agosto 1960), 283-84. Chonchol, "Los factores de aceleración revolucionaria," pp. 82-86. Lleras Camargo, "La Alianza después de Kennedy," pp. 278-83.

230. "La ley agraria cubana: Declaraciones de Mons. Martín Villaverde, Obispo de

Matanzas, Cuba," VII (septiembre 1959), 371-73. "Mons. Perez Serantes Condena al Comunismo," IX (julio 1960), 263-65. "Martires universitarios en Cuba," X (marzo-abril) 1961, 121-22. Mons. Dr., Eduardo Boza Masvidal, "¿Es cristiana la Revolución Social que se esta verificando en Cuba?" Ibid., pp. 128-28b. G.A.J., "Cuba: La Iglesia Católica y Fidel Castro," X (junio 1961), 235-39. "¿Es la Iglesia católica en Cuba una Iglesia perseguida?" XII (mayo1963) 184-87.

231. Santiago, Departmento de Publicaciones del Secretariado de Difusión.

232. With regard to *Mensaje's* perspective on revolutionary tendencies in Colombia, Peru, Brazil, Paraguay, Argentina, and Chile prior to the UP victory, see: "Cardinal Rossi's Puzzling Statements," *Mensaje*, July 1970, reprinted in LADOC, I (August 1970), 1-2; Gonzalo Arroyo, "Catholics of the Left in Latin America," *Mensaje*, August 1970, reprinted in LADOC, I (January 1971), 1-8. On vastly improved Church-State relations in Revolucionary Cuba, the following are quite useful: "Radio Interview with Bishop Oves of Cuba." Cristianismo y Revolución (Argentina), July 1969, reprinted in LADOC, I (August 1970), 1-4; "First Pastoral Letter of the Cuban Bishops (Dated April 10, 1969, and read in all Cuban churches April 20)," *LADOC*, I (September 1970), 1-5.

233. *Granma* (Weekly Review), Nov. 29, 1970, p. 5.

234. Mons. Manuel Larraín E., Obispo de Talca, *Escritos Sociales* (Santiago: Edit. del Pacífico, 1963), p. 39. Cf., pp. 126-127.

235. The principal political questions of interest to the Church in 1957, for example, centered upon continued denial of the liberty of divorce and an increase in state subsidies to religious schools. Silvert, *Elections, Parties, and the Law*, p. 15.

236. "Gestiones ante el Cardenal," *Ercilla*, XXIV (30 abril 1958), 9. *Hispanic American Report*, XI (July 1958), 396 97.

237. Ibid. (August 1958), p. 454, (November 1958), p. 626.

238. "Puntos de Vista," XIV (15 marzo 1959), 1.

239. Ibid. (15 abril 1959), p. 1.

240. "No pueden los Católicos favorecer al Comunismo," LXII (mayo a agosto de 1959), 2332.

241. "La Iglesia y el Problema de la Tierra en Latinoamerica," *Política y Espíritu*, XV (abril 1961), 43-47. Cf., "Declaración del Consejo Episcopal Latinoamericano reunido en Bogotá," *Revista Católica*, LVII (septiembre a diciembre1959), 2466-2467.

242. "El Arzobispo se Confiesa," *Ercilla*, XXVII (5 julio 1961), 16-17.

243. "Semana Política," Ibid. (9 agosto 1961), p. 7.

244. LHP, "La Semana Política," Ibid., XXVIII (21 marzo 1962), 9.

245. "La Iglesia Abrió Primer Surco de la Reforma Agraria," Ibid. (4 julio 1962), pp. 16-17. Olavarría, *Alessandri*, III, 18.

246. "La Alianza para el progreso," XI (mayo 1962), 148-150f.

247. *Mensaje*, XI (mayo 1962), 185-94a.

248. "El Cardenal con S.E.," *Ercilla*, XXVIII (25 julio 1962), 2.

249. "Polémica Pastoral de la Iglesia," Ibid. (26 septiembre 1962), p. 8. "Tres Cartas en la Manga de la Nueva Mesa del PR," Ibid. (3 octubre 1962), p. 8. "Tres Partidos Frente a la Pastoral," Ibid., p. 14. "El Deber Social y Político en la Hora Presente," *Política y Espíritu*, XVI (septiembre 1962), 29. Aldunate, p. 10. Fernando Sanhueza Herbage y Juan Orellana Peralta, *La Juventud la Estrategia del Comunismo Internacional* (Santiago: Edit. Universidad Católica, 1962), p. 34. Sergio Vuskovic y Osvaldo Fernandez, *Teoría de la Ambiquedad: Bases Ideológicas de la Democracia Cristiana* (Santiago: Edit. Austral, 1964), p. 68. Cf., "Declaraciones del Cardenal Arzobispo Monseñor Raul Silva Henriquez," *Política y Espítiru*, XVI (septiembre 1962), 33, 35; and *Hispanic American Report*, XV (November 1962), 32.

250. De Santis, "Chile," p. 457.

251. *Chile: Yesterday and Today*, pp. 168, 171. Cf., Millas, "Christian Democratic Reformism," p. 48.

252. Ruben Corvalán V., "Diálogo con el Cardenal," *Ercilla*, XXIX (25 diciembre 1962), 11.

253. Vol. XI (diciembre 1962), 9-12.

254. "New Trends in Catholicism and the Policy of the Chilean Communists," *World Marxist Review*, VII (March 1964), 25-26.

255. Rycroft and Clemmer, p. 215.

256. "There is currently in progress a resurgence of clerical activity in politics. . . . The occasion for this is the promotion of a strong anti-Communist offensive, prompted by the favorable attitude toward Communism and the Soviet bloc shown by Fidel Castro, and designed to counteract incursions of *fidelismo* in other states of the Americas." *Latin American Politics in Perspective* (New York: Van Nostrand, 1963), p. 43. Cf., Illich, "The Seamy Side of Charity," pp. 88, 90.

257. Simultaneously, both *La Voz* and Radio Chilena were calling for structural reforms. *Ercilla*, XXIX (30 enero 1963), 3, 10.

258. *Hispanic American Report*, XVI (March 1963), 70.

259. Olavarría, *Democracia Cristiana*, pp. 16-17. In 1963, CARITAS was feeding about 1,100,000 persons or about 12 percent of the population. And a U.S. Embassy report stated that 28.6 percent of the Chilean population was receiving P.L. 480 surplus foods through all channels—private and inter-governmental—that year. According to one PDC member in his late twenties, frequently the same persons who distributed the CARITAS foodstuffs in the slums would return in behalf of the PDC candidate. An alternative technique, was to say—when distributing the needed foods—"this is a gift from (the party's candidate)." Chile, Senado, *Diario*, CCXCIII (15 enero 1964), 2579, ses. 37 (22 enero 1964), pp. 2823, 2835. Interview with N.C. on April 5, 1967.

260. Frederick B. Pike and William V. D'Antonio, eds., *Religion, Revolution and Reform: New Forces for Change in Latin America* (New York: Praeger, 1964), p. 112.

261. Interview with David Baytelbaum on May 6, 1967. Baytelbaum is an agricultural engineer with CORFO, and was a top advisor to Allende in 1964 on agricultural problems. This conformed to similar views regarding the pro-PDC political roles of some rural priests which were held by N.C. Interview on April 5, 1967.

262. Olavarría, *Alessandri*, III, 308-309.

263. Partido Comunista de Chile, Teitelboim, *El Significado de la Candidatura de Frei*, Intervención del dia 21 de diciembre de 1963, en la Sesión Plenaria del Comité Central del Partido Comunista de Chile (Santiago: Imp. Horizonte, 1964), pp. 15-16.

264. *Hispanic American Report*, XVII (April 1964), 163.

265. *Instituto de Promoción Agraria La Tierra Nuestra* (Santiago: Imp. Lord Cochrane, 1964).

266. Jean Ives Cálvez, José Miguel Ibáñez, Roger Veckemans, Máximo Pacheco, William Thayer, Jaime Castillo, (Santiago: Edit. del Pacífico), 306pp. Partido Demócrata Cristiano, *Revolución en Libertad*, Por Dr. Antonio Morales Delpiano, Departamento de Capitación, Séptima Comuna, Lira No. 92-A (Santiago: Imp. Entrecerros, 1964), 16pp.

267. Perceval (pseud.), ¡Gano Allende! (Santiago: Nueva Aurora, Imp. Edit. Universidad Católica, 1964), pp. 30-31, 34, 45-46, 68-70, 123-124.

268. "Así Nos Ven," XXX (17 junio 1964), 4.

269. Chile, Senado, *Diario*, CCXCIII, ses. 52 (6 mayo 1964), p. 4154.

270. Ibid., CCXCIV, ses. 5 (23 junio 1964), pp. 267, 370. Cf., Ibid., CCXCIII, ses. 52 (6 mayo 1964), pp. 4153-54; and LHP, "Final: Frei o Allende; pero Clave, Durán," *Ercilla*, XXX (29 abril 1964), 9.

271. Olavarría, *Alessandri*, IV, 210-11, 295, 297. Idem. *Democracia Cristiana*, p. 50.

272. Interview with N.C., April 5, 1967.

273. OCEPLAN, *La Política Agropecuaria*, p. 9.

274. Erica Vexler, "Golpes Bajo el Cinturón," *Ercilla*, XXX (10 junio 1964), 10. During May, Socialist Senator Aniceto Rodríguez had charged: "Violencia moral y desprecio espiritual existen, cuando haciendo escarnio de la coridad cristiana se lleva el paquete Caritas, la dádiva, la fonolita o el fréjoles que se repartió en la población José María Caro, antes de la visita del candidato de la Derecha (Frei), con el compromiso de colocar su efigie en la ventana de la humilde casa." And in early June, he observed "¿No se ha visto, en numerosas poblaciones, como esa caridad se hace sólo con quienes estan 'matriculados'; en forma efectiva o simulada, con la candidatura democratacristiana, y pasan por alto, en la distribución de alimentos, las casas cuyos ocupantes han declarado en público su adhesión al Senador señor Allende, aunque sean tan pobres como las otras?" Although Radomiro Tomic denied these charges, with regard to Church support generally, he stated "(e)so habría que

probarlo." Chile, Senado, *Diario*, CCXCIII, ses. 52 (6 mayo 1964), p. 4168, CCXCIV, ses. 6 (24 junio 1964), pp. 482, 484, 486. Reference has already been made in chapter 5 to the postelectoral AID audit that proved the conversion of $70,000 (perhaps two hundred thousand donations) worth of CARITAS foodstuffs by the PDC.

275. Chile, Senado, *Diario*, CCXCIV, ses. 22 (12 agosto 1964), p. 2135. Cf., chapter 5.

276. Instituto de Capacitación Sindical y Social (INCASIS), *Memoria del Instituto de Capacitación Sindical y Social Correspondiente al Periódo 1.o de Enero al 31 de Diciembre de 1964* (Santiago: INCASIS, 1964).

277. Gastón Cruzat, "Propaganda y estrategia," "Responsabilidad de los políticos," XIII, 269-71, 275-77.

278. "En torno al 4 de septiembre," XIII (Septiembre 1964), 409-13.

279. Grayson, "Significance," p. 762.

280. Frei received 756,117 female votes and 652,895 male votes. Comparable figures for Allende were 384,132 and 593,770. Gil and Parrish, II, 10-11.

281. "The Chilean Dilemma," p. 347.

282. LHP, "Frei: Revolución en las Urnas," *Ercilla*, XXX (9 septiembre 1964), 10-11.

283. "Chile Goes," p. 14.

284. Rodman, "October Revolution," p. 1054.

285. "Ninth National Congress," pp. 111-13.

286. Pedro Zottele, "Chilean Students Ignite Revolt," *Christian Century*, October 16, 1968, p. 138.

287. *Granma* (Weekly Review), November 15, 1970, p. 5.

288. Quoted in Zottele, "Chilean Students," p. 1318.

289. Ibid., p. 1319.

290. Ibid., p. 1320.

291. *Granma* (Weekly Review), Nov. 1, 1970, p. 10.

292. "Cardinal Rossi's," pp. 1-2.

293. Zottele, "Orienting," pp. 696-97.

294. "Preguntas a las candidaturas presidenciales," Nos. 190 and 191, July – August 1970.

295. "Editorial: The Victory of the 'Popular Unity' Coalition in Chile," *Mensaje*, October 1970, reprinted in *LADOC*, I (October 1970), 1-3.

296. *Granma* (Weekly Review), Nov. 15, 1970, p. 5.

297. Ibid., November 29, 1970, p. 5.

298. "Chile: Sept. 4 to Nov. 3," *Monthly Review*, XXII (January 1971), 27.

Chapter 9. Public Opinion and Activism

1. The written questionnaires were distributed to a random sampling of students who did not indicate their identities on them. Nevertheless, they were distributed in only five of the University of Chile's twenty-three schools. In addition, Leftist student leaders refused to disseminate them, and 350 were not returned. "Universitarios Chilenos Enjuician a USA y la URSS," *Ercilla*, XXV (16 diciembre 1959), 16-18.

2. USIA, *Economic and Political Climate*, p. 33.

3. Ibid., p. iv. USIA, *Economic and Political Climate, Appendix*, p. 5.

4. Kaplan, et al.

5. U.S., Information Agency, Research and Reference Service, *Latin American Attitudes Toward Certain Anti-Castro Measures: The Arms Cache Resolution and the Cuban Overflights* (Washington, D.C.: USIA, R-75-64, June 10, 1964), pp. 4-5.

6. CESO, "Post-Electoral Survey" (November 1964).

7. *El Mercurio*, 8 agosto 1959, p. 19. *La Libertad*, 12 agosto 1959, p. 6. "En la Plaza Banquedano hablará Fidel Castro," p. 9.

8. *El Mercurio*, 16 mayo 1960, p. 21.

9. *Hispanic American Report*, XIII (April 1960), 124. But many may have been government employees released from their work for this purpose.

10. Ibid. (September 1960), p. 477.

11. *El Mercurio*, 26 agosto 1960, p. 20. Mendoza, "Comunismo durante 1960," p. 81.
12. 27 septiembre 1960, p. 3.
13. *Las Noticias de Ultima Hora*, 20 abril 1961, p. 4.
14. Ibid., and 19 abril 1961, p. 16.
15. "Cuba: Medita la Moneda," p. 8.
16. *Las Noticias de Ultima Hora*, 18 abril 1961, pp. 2, 8-9. *La Nación*, 19 abril 1961, p. 2, 20 abril, pp. 1, 3, 21 abril, p. 4. Mendoza, *Comunismo en 1961*, pp. 18-19.
17. Mendoza *Comunismo en 1961*, pp. 18-19.
18. *Hispanic American Report*, XIV (August 1961), 543.
19. "Goodwin: intérprete entre JAR y Kennedy," p. 8.
20. *Hispanic American Report*, XV (July 1962), 449.
21. *South Pacific Mail*, CVII (Oct. 26, 1962), 16.
22. 23 octubre 1962, pp. 1, 7, 24 octubre, p. 1, 26 octubre, pp. 1, 7, 8. *La Nación*, 24 octubre 1962, p. 2. "Chile: El Bloqueo," p. 9. *New York Times*, October 28, 1962, Section 4, p. 4. *Hispanic American Report*, XV (December 1962), 950.
23. *New York Times*, Oct. 29, 1962, p. 19.
24. Chile, Senado, *Diario*, CCXCII, ses. 27 (7 agosto 1963), p. 1749.
25. Ibid.
26. *El Diario Ilustrado*, 15 agosto 1964, p. 1.
27. Igor Entrala, "JAR le Quitó," pp. 10-11.
28. Thomas R. Dye and L. Harmon Zeigler, *The Irony of Democracy* (Belmont, Cal.: Wadsworth, 1970), pp. 127-40, and the survey research cited therein.
29. Parrish, von Lazar and Tapia, *Chilean Congressional Election*, p. 16. Appendix I, Parts E, F, G. Cf., chapter 3.

Chapter 10. Conclusions

1. U.S., *Cuba and the Caribbean*, p. 98. Cf.: U.S., *Rockefeller Report Hearing*, pp. 6-12, 35-36; Lloyd C. Gardner, *Economic Aspects of New Deal Diplomacy* (Madison: University of Wisconsin Press, 1964); Harry Magdoff, *The Age of Imperialism* (New York: Monthly Review Press, 1969); Andre Gunder Frank, *Capitalism and Underdevelopment in Latin America* (New York: Monthly Review Press, 1967).
2. Rene Dumont, Cuba: *Socialism and Development* (New York: Grove Press, 1970). Cf., Leo Huberman and Paul M. Sweezy, *Socialism in Cuba* (New York: Monthly Review Press, 1969).
3. "Doctrine and Dilemmas of the Latin American 'New Left,' " *World Politics*, XXII (January 1970), 196.
4. From the text of his address as reprinted in the *Granma* (Weekly Review), Nov. 15, 1970, p. 5.
5. Peter Roman, "The Left is Uniting in Chile," *Guardian*, Jan. 16, 1971, p. 12.
6. *Granma* (Weekly Review), Nov. 1, 1960, p. 10.
7. Angell, "Christian Democracy," p. 84.
8. Bodenheimer, " 'Stagnation,' ", p. 10.
9. See "Chile: Peaceful Transition to Socialism," and Oscar Lange, "On the Policy of Transition," *Monthly Review*, XXII (January 1971), 1-18, 38-44.
10. These elements suffered a temporary setback after the attempted kidnapping and murder of General Schneider was quickly linked to the Right. Several high ranking officers and former commanders were arrested and Allende emerged with greater stature as a symbol of Constitutional legitimacy.
11. U.S., *Rockefeller Report Hearing*, p. 93. Cf., pp. 85, 117-19.
12. "Address by Gen. Robert W. Porter, Jr., Commander in Chief, U.S. Southern Command, Presented to the Pan American Society of the United States, New York, N.Y., Tuesday, March 26, 1968," reprinted in U.S., Congress, House, Committee on Foreign Affairs, *Foreign Assistance Act of 1968, Hearings*, before the Committee on Foreign Affairs, House of Representatives, 90th Cong., 2d sess., pp. 1204-05.
13. Unless domestic or foreign enemies resort to violence, Allende has pledged his coali-

tion to respect for "pluralism," "majoritarianism," political democracy and liberty. This will be Chile's "distinctive road" to socialism—one which if fully endorsed in Habana. *Granma* (Weekly Review), Nov. 15, 1970, p. 4.

14. Vitale, *?Y Despues?*, pp. 87-98.

15. On these day-to-day activities, see Petras, *Politics and Social Forces*, pp. 185-87.

16. "Indirect" intervention may also have been reflected by the well-publicized nation-wide "anti-subversive" exercises by the armed forces during the final days of the 1964 campaign. Similarly, joint U.S.-Chilean-Peruvian naval-air maneuvers involving the landing of 5,000 U.S. marines and sailors were scheduled to coincide with a possible special session of Congress if no candidate had received an absolute majority. In the immediate background were the Argentine border provocations and the recent military deposition of Brazilian President Goulart—a man who unlike Allende didn't even claim to be a Marxist-Leninist.

17. On the latter, see Barclay, Enright and Reynolds, "Population Control," p. 16.

18. With regard to the oblique UP approach to the Armed Forces see the *Programa Basico*, pp. 18-19. On the size of the U.S. MILGRP stationed in Santiago as of July 1, 1970, see: "U.S. Military Aid Missions Abroad," *NACLA Newsletter*, IV (December 1970), 13.

19. This is due to its failure to "take in" voters who identify with the middle class. As for militant *obreros*, Petras has suggested that it exaggerates the cleavage between domestic and foreign capitalists. The former are just as if not more likely to be perceived as exploiters by class conscious workers. *Politics and Social Forces*, pp. 187-88.

20. Martin and Carolyn Needleman, "Marx and the Problem of Causation," *Science & Society*, XXXIII (Summer-Fall 1969), 322-39. Portes, "Leftist Radicalism," pp. 251-74. Powell, "Political Change," pp. 364-83. Soares and Hamblin, "Socio-Economic Variables," pp. 1053-65.

Bibliography

Bibliography

Books, Articles, Pamphlets (Individual Author(s) Identified*)

Adams, W., R.E. *El Mundo Unido: ¿Bajo la Hoz o la Cruz?* Santiago: Imp. Wilson, junio 1964.

Agor, Weston H. "Senate vs. CORA: An Attempt to Evaluate Chile's Agrarian Reform to Date," *Inter-American Economic Affairs*, XII (Autumn 1968), 47-53.

Aguirre, Manuel. "Anverso y Reverso de la Revolución Cubana," *Mensaje*, IX (septiembre 1960), 376-77.

Aguirre Bianchi, Claudio. "Los Cuerpos de Paz," *El Siglo*, 31 diciembre 1966, p. 7.

Ahumada, Jaime. "Hacia el Segundo Congreso Latinoamericano de Juventudes," *Arauco*, IV (Enero 1963), 41-42.

Ahumada C., Jorge. *En Vez de Miseria.* Santiago: Edit. del Pacífico, 1958.

Ahumada, Jorge. *La Crisis Integral de Chile.* Santiago: Edit. Universitaria, 1966.

Aldunate, Fernando. *¿Por Que los Conservadores estamos con Julio Durán?* Santiago: 'El Diario Ilustrado,' febrero 1964.

Alessandri, Jorge. *Discurso–Programa del candidato Independiente don Alessandri Rodríguez.* Santiago: Edit. Lord Cochrane, 1958.

Alessandri, Jorge. "Mensaje de S.E. El Presidente de la República don Jorge Alessandri Rodríguez al Congreso Nacional al inaugurar el periodo ordinario de sesiones, 21 de mayo de 1963." Chile, Senado, *Diario de Sesiones*, CCXCII.

Alexander, Robert J. *Labor Relations in Argentina, Brazil and Chile.* New York: McGraw-Hill, 1962.

Allende G., Salvador. *Cuba, Un Camino.* Santiago: Prensa Latinoamericana, 1960.

"Allende en Televisión: Cuarta entrevista realizada el 19 de Junio de 1964," *Arauco*, V (Agosto 1964), 56-76.

"Allende en Televisión: Quinta entrevista realizada el Viernes 10 de Julio de 1964," *Arauco*, V (Agosto 1964), pp. 77-90.

"Allende en Televisión: Sexta entrevista realizada el 31 de Julio," *Arauco*, V (agosto 1964), 91-109.

Allende, Salvador. "Significado de la Conquista de un Gobierno Popular para Chile," *Cuadernos Americanos* (Mexico), XXIII (septiembre-octubre 1964), 7-24.

Almeyda M., Clodomiro. *Reforma Agraria.* Santiago: Prensa Latinoamericana, 1962.

Ampuero Díaz, Raúl. "Los Trabajadores chilenos harán por si mismos, su tarea revolucionaria," *Arauco*, III (junio 1962), 5-8.

Angell, Alan. "Chile: The Difficulties of Democratic Reform," *International Journal*, XXIV (Summer 1969), 515-28.

Angell, Alan. "Christian Democracy in Chile," *Current History*, LVIII (February 1970), 79-84.

Aparicio, Laurencio Angel. *El Congreso de las Focas Amaestradas y los Lacayos Parlantes de Moscu en Río de Janeiro.* Santiago: Edit. del Pacífico, 1963.

Aparicio, Laurencio Angel. *Los Malvados no Conocen la Justicia.* Santiago: Edit. del Pacífico, 1962.

Aragon, Escalona L. "División in the Americas," *New Republic*, February 26, 1962, pp. 9-10.

Arguedas, Sol. "El Saldo de las elecciones chilenas," *Cuadernos Americanos*, CXXXVIII (enero-febrero 1965), 28-44.

Arroyo C., Gonzalo. "Sindicalismo y Promoción campesina," *Mensaje*, XV (junio 1966).

Barclay, William, Enright, Joseph, and Reynolds, Reid T. "Population Control in the Third World," *NACLA Newsletter*, IV (December 1970), 1-17.

Barrera, Manuel. "Participation by Occupational Organizations in Economic and Social Planning in Chile," *International Labor Review*, XCVI (August 1967), 151-76.

*See next classification (Partido Comunista de Chile) for speeches by Corvalan, Millas, Neruda and Teitelboim.

Barros P.C., Jaime. *Muerte al Imperialismo Yanqui*. Santiago: Imp. Entrecerros, 1965.
Beatty, Donald W. "The Chilean Dilemma," *Current History*, IL (December 1965), 342-48, 367-68.
Beatty, Donald W. "Middle Class Government in Chile," *Current History*, XLII (February 1962), 106-13.
Becket, James. "Land Reform in Chile," *Journal of Inter-American Studies*, V (April 1963), 177-211.
Becket, James, and Griffin, Keith D. "Revolution in Chile," *New Republic*, December 29, 1962, pp. 9-11.
Beipi. "El Partido Comunista de Chile," *Estudios sobre el Comunismo*, VIII (octubre-diciembre de 1960), 49-55.
Blasier, S. Cole. "The Cuban and Chilean Communist Parties: Instrumentalities of Soviet Policy, 1935-1948." Unpublished Ph.D. dissertation, Columbia University, 1954.
Bodenheimer, Susanne. " 'Stagnation in Liberty'–The Frei Experiment in Chile," *NACLA Newsletter*, III (March 1969), 1-11.
Boye, S., Otto. "IV Congreso Latinoamericano de Estudiantes," *Política y Espíritu*, XVI (diciembre-enero 1962), 41-42.
Boza Domínguez, Luís. *La Situación Universitaria en Cuba*. Santiago: Edit. del Pacífico, 1962.
Boza Masvidal, Mons. Dr. Eduardo. "¿Es cristiana la Revolución Social que está verificando en Cuba?" *Mensaje*, X (marzo-abril 1961), 128-286.
Bravo R., Alfonso. "Entre bueyes no hay cornadas," *Punto Final*, I (1.a quincena de abril de 1967), 10-11.
Briones, Guillermo. "La Estructura Social y La Participación Política," *Revista Interamericana de Ciencias Sociales*, Vol. II, No. 3 (1963), pp. 376-404.
Bulnes Sanfuentes, Francisco. *Cuenta del Presidente del Partido Conservador Don Francisco Bulnes Sanfuentes ante el Directorio General del Partido celebrado el 1.o de Junio de 1963*. Santiago: Imp. Sopech, 1963.
Calvez, Jean Ives; Ibáñez, José Miguel; Veckemans, Roger; Pacheco, Máximo; Thayer, William; y Castillo, Jaime. *El Marxismo: Teoría y Acción*. Santiago: Edit. del Pacífico, 1964.
Campos Harriet, Fernando. *Historia Constitucional de Chile*. 3.a ed. Santiago: Edit. Jurídica de Chile, 1963.
Campusano, Julieta. "The Role of Women in Modern Society (Chile)," *World Marxist Review*, V (August 1962).
Carmona A., Augusto. "382 Espías 'Voluntarios' Historia de los Cuerpos de Paz en Chile," *Punto Final*, I (1.a quincena de julio de 1967), suplemento.
Carter, Roy E., Jr., and Sepulveda, Orlando. "Some Patterns of Mass Media Use in Santiago de Chile," *Journalism Quarterly*, XLI (Spring 1964), 215-24.
Cash, Jorge. "Cuba y la Política de Bloques," *Política y Espíritu*, XVI (marzo 1962), 32-34.
Castro, Fidel. "Las elecciones chilenas," *Principios*, N.o 102 (septiembre-octubre 1964), 64-70.
Castro, Fidel. *La Historia me absolverá*. Santiago: Horizonte, 1964.
Castro, Fidel. *El Partido Unido de la Revolución Socialista: Espina dorsal de la Revolución*. Santiago: Espartaco Editores, 1963.
Castro, Fidel. *La Revolución Cubana contra el Sectarismo*. Comentarios de Luís Vitale. Santiago: Edit. POR, 1962.
Cerda, Cesar. "Chile's Trade Unions," *New Times*, No. 17 (April 25, 1962), pp. 15-16.
Chelen Rojas, Alejandro. *La Revolución Cubana y sus Proyecciones en América Latina*. Santiago: Prensa Latinoamericana, 1960.
Chonchol, Jacques. *El Desarrollo de América Latina y la Reforma Agraria*. Santiago: Edit. del Pacífico, 1964.
Chonchol, Jacques. "La Reforma Agraria Cubana," *Panorama Económico*, Ano XV, N.o 227 (enero 1962), pp. 16-24, N.o 228 (marzo 1962), pp. 38-47, N.o 229 (abril 1962), pp. 97-106.
Chonchol, Jacques. "Los factores de aceleración revolucionaria," *Mensaje*, XI (diciembre 1962), 82-86.
Clark, Gerald. *The Coming Explosion in Latin America*. New York: David McKay, 1963.
Collier, Barnard. "Eduardo Frei Is Trying 'A Revolution Without the Execution Wall,' " *New York Times*, Section 6.

Cope, Orville G. "The 1964 Presidential Election in Chile: The Politics of Change and Access," *Inter-American Economic Affairs*, XIX (Spring 1966), 1-29.

Covalán, Luís. "The Peaceful Way—A Form of Revolution," *World Marxist Review*, VI (December 1963), 3-10.

Corvalán, Luís. "The Struggle for a People's Government in Chile," *World Marxist Review*, V (December 1962), 19-25.

Corvalán, Rubén. "Chile, País Clave para USA," *Ercilla*, XXVIII (7 noviembre 1962), 16-17.

Corvalán. V., Rubén. "Diálogo con el Cardenal," *Ercilla*, XXIX (25 diciembre 1962), 11.

Corvalán Vera, Rubén. "finalizó el Drama: Dólar Libre y Fluctuante en Doble Area," *Ercilla*, XXVIII (10 octubre 1962), 16-17.

Corvalán V., Rubén. "Habla la Elite Sindical," *Ercilla*, XXIX (20 noviembre 1963), 10-11.

Cruzat, Gastón. "Propaganda y estrategia," "Responsabilidad de los políticos," *Mensaje*, XIII (julio 1964), 269-71, 275-77.

Davis, Tom E. "Eight Decades of Inflation in Chile, 1879-1959," *Journal of Political Economy*, LXXI (August 1963), 379-97.

De Santis, Sergio. "Chile," *International Socialist Journal*, II (June 1965), 342-63 (August 1965), 446-68.

Díaz B., Mario. "Meditación Electoral," *Punto Final*, I (2.a quincena de marzo de 1967), 2-3.

"Dime con quien andas y te diré quien eres," *Punto Final*, Año I, N.o 20 (enero 1967), pp. 18-19.

Domínguez Correa, Oscar. "Congreso campesino en Lautaro," *Mensaje*, XI (junio 1962).

Domínguez Correa, Oscar. *El Condicionamiento de la Reforma Agraria*. Louvain: E. Warny, 1963.

Dominguez Correa, Oscar. *Una Oportunidad en la Libertad*. Santiago: Edit. del Pacífico, 1961.

Donoso, Ricardo. "Chile, en la Encrucijada," *Cuadernos Americanos* (México), CXIX (noviembre–diciembre 1961), 173-93.

Dorner, Peter, and Collarte, Juan Carlos. "Land Reform in Chile: Proposal for an Institutional Innovation," *Inter-American Economic Affairs*, XIX (Summer 1965), 3-22.

Dórticos, Osvaldo. *Carta del Presidente de Cuba a los Estudiantes Chilenos*. Santiago: Edit. del Pacífico, 1960.

Draper, Theodore. *Castroism: Theory and Practice*. New York: Praeger, 1965.

Dubois, Jules. *Operation America: The Communist Conspiracy in Latin America*. New York: Walker, 1963.

Duncan, W. Raymond. "Chilean Christian Democracy," *Current History*, LIII (November 1967), 263-69.

Dvorin, Eugene P. "Foreign Aid by States," *National Civic Review*, LIII (December 1964), 585-90, 622.

Edwards Vives, Alberto. *La Fronda Aristocrática*. Santiago: Edit. del Pacífico, 1959 (5th reprinting of 1928 ed.). Santiago: Imp. Nacional, 1928.

Edwards Vives, Alberto, y Frei Montalva, Eduardo. *Historia de los Partidos Políticos Chilenos*. Santiago: Edit. del Pacífico, 1949.

Entrala, Igor. "Balance de la Gira de Alessandri," *Ercilla*, XXVIII (26 diciembre 1962), 15-16.

Entrala, Igor. "Divorcio separa a los Partidos," *Ercilla*, XXX (12 agosto 1964), 10-11.

Entrala, Igor. "El Error del Plebiscito," *Ercilla*, XXX (18 marzo 1964), 17.

Entrala, Igor. "El PC Envía Paloma de la Paz al PDC," *Ercilla*,XXIX (13 febrero 1963), 8.

Entrala, Igor. "Faltan 225 casas más cada Hora," *Ercilla*, XXIX (18 diciembre 1963), 4-5.

Entrala, Igor. "JAR le Quitó el Saludo a Fidel Castro," *Ercilla*, XXX (19 agosto 1964), 10-11.

Entrala, Igor. "Pacífica Reelección de Ampuero," *Ercilla*, XXX (19 febrero 1964), 9.

Espinosa A., Edmundo. "Los Nazis Porteños," *Ercilla*, XXX (1 abril 1964), 6.

Faivovich, Jaime. "¿Tiene vigencia el Frente de Trabajadores?" *Punto Final*, I (2.a quincena de agosto de 1967), 38-39.

Fernández L., Sergio. *Y el Comunismo sigue su marcha*. Santiago: Edit. del Pregon, 1962.

Fichter, Joseph. *Cambio Social en Chile*. Santiago: Edit. Universidad Católica, 1962.

Figueroa, Luís. "La Conferencia Latinoamericana por la Soberania Nacional, la Emancipación Económica y la Paz," *Principios*, N.o 80 (abril de 1961), pp. 24-29.

388

Filippi, Emilio. "Eclosión Mapuche en Arauco y Malleco," *Ercilla*, XXVII (16 mayo 1962), 15, 18.
Filippi, Emilio. "El explosivo caso de la Isla Ranquilco," *Ercilla*, XXVII (14 marzo 1962), 2.
Fitzgibbon, Russel H. "The Revolution Next Door: Cuba," *Annals*, CCCXXXIV (March 1961), 113-122.
Fonseca, Jaime. "Reforma Agraria en Cuba," *Mensaje*, VIII (marzo–abril 1959), 91-92.
Franco, Victor. *La Revolución Sensual*. Santiago: Edit. Pomaire, 1962.
Frei Montalva, Eduardo. *Dos Discursos*. Santiago: Edit. del Pacífico, 1964.
Frei Montalva, Eduardo. *La Verdad Tiene Su Hora*. Santiago: Edit. del Pacífico, 1955.
Frei Montalva, Eduardo. *Pensamiento y Acción*. Santiago: Edit. del Pacífico, 1956.
Fuentealba Maena, Renán. *A Los Pobladores*. Discurso del Presidente Nacional de la Democracia Cristiana, Diputado R. Fuentealba, 1.o de mayo 1964. Santiago: Imp. 'Soberanía', 1964.
G.A.J. "Cuba: La Iglesia Católica y Fidel Castro," *Mensaje*, X (junio 1961), 235-39.
Gall, Norman. "Chile Goes To The Polls," *New Leader*, XLVIII (March 1, 1965), 13-14.
Gall, Norman. "The Chileans Have Elected a Revolution," *New York Times Magazine*, November 1, 1970, pp. 26-27, ff.
Ganderats, Luis Alberto. "Fuga de Capitales," *Desfile*, I (9 diciembre 1965), 5.
Gerassi, John. *The Great Fear*. New York: Macmillan, 1963.
Gerassi, John. "What is Castroism's Appeal," *New Republic*, CXLVIII (January 12, 1963), 13-15.
Geyelin, Philip L. *Lyndon B. Johnson and The World*. New York: Praeger, 1966.
Gil, Federico G. "Chile: 'Revolution in Liberty,' " *Current History*, LI (November 1966), 291-95.
Gil, Federico G. *The Political System of Chile*. Boston: Houghton Mifflin, 1966.
Gil, Federico G., and Parrish, Charles J. *The Chilean Presidential Election of September 4, 1964*. Parts I and II. Washington: Institute for the Comparative Study of Political Systems, 1965.
Glazer, Myron. "Student Politics in a Chilean Society," *Daedalus*, XCVII (Winter 1968), 99-115.
Glick, Edward B. "Cuba and the Fifteenth UN General Assembly: A Case Study in Regional Disassociation." *Journal of Inter-American Studies*, VI (April 1964), 236-42.
Godoy, César. *Terremoto y Miseria*. Santiago: Imp. Lira 363, 1960.
Gold, Ronald. "Income Tax Evasion in Chile: An Estimate," *Inter-American Economic Affairs*, XXII (Spring 1969), 59-67.
Goldenberg, Gregorio. *Después de Frei, ¿Quien?* Santiago: Edit. Orbe, 1966.
Gongora, Mario. "Vagabundaje y Sociedad Fronteriza en Chile (Siglos XVII-XIX)," *Cuadernos del Centro de Estudios Socioeconomicos*, N.o 2 (1966), pp. 1-41.
Gornov, M. "Who Will Be President of Chile?" *New Times*, No. 24 (June 17, 1964), p. 16.
Grayson, George W., Jr. "Significance of the Frei Administration for Latin America," *Orbis*, IX (Fall 1965), 760-79.
Grayson, George W. "The Frei Administration and the 1969 Parliamentary Elections," *Inter-American Economic Affairs*, XXIII (Autumn 1969), 49-74.
Gregory, Peter. *Industrial Wages in Chile*. Ithaca, N.Y.: New York State School of Industrial and Labor Relations, Cornell University, 1967.
Grunwald, Joseph. "The 'Structuralist' School on Price Stabilization and Economic Development: The Chilean Case." *Latin American Issues*. Edited by Albert O. Hirschman. New York: Twentieth Century Fund, 1961.
Guadagni, Alieto Aldo. "La Estructura Ocupacional y el Desarrollo Económico de Chile," *Journal of Inter-American Studies*, VI (April 1964), 187-201.
Guevara, Ernesto 'Ché.' *Contra el Burocratismo*. Santiago: Espartaco Editores, 1963.
Gutierrez, Joaquin. "Chile and the Socialist Countries," *New Times*, No. 13 (March 31, 1965).
H.L.S., "Justicia de Vencedores," *Mensaje*, VIII, N.o 79, pp. 169-71.
Halcro-Ferguson, J. "The Cuban Revolution and Latin America," *International Affairs* (London), XXXVII (July 1961).
Halperin, Ernst. *Nationalism and Communism in Chile*. Cambridge: MIT Press, 1965.

Hamuy, Eduardo. "Temas de Nuestro Tiempo," *Cuadernos del Centro de Estudios Socioeconomicos*, N.o 1 (1966), pp. 15-23.
Hamuy, Eduardo, Salcedo, Danilo, y Sepulveda, Orlando. *El Primer Satelite Artificial: sus efectos en la opinion publica*. Santiago: Edit. Universitaria de Chile, 1958.
Hernández Parker, Luís. "Al Final: la Batalla Psicologica," *Ercilla*, XXX (19 agosto 1964), 16-17.
Hernández Parker, Luís. "Congreso del PC: Esperando al Zurdo . . . El 64," *Ercilla*, XXVIII (21 marzo 1962), 8.
Hernández Parker, Luís. "'Cuartelazo' del Congreso a la Reforma," *Ercilla*, XXVIII (25 julio 1962), 7-8.
Hernández Parker, Luís. "Franco Apoyo a Frei . . . , pero Crítico," *Ercilla*, XXX (2 diciembre 1964), 25.
Hernández Parker, Luís. "Informe a los 'Sabios' sobre la Reforma," *Ercilla*, XXVIII (22 agosto 1962), 8-9.
Hernández Parker, Luís. "Punta del Este: 3 Metas Cardinales," *Ercilla*, XXVII (16 agosto 1961), 16-17.
Hernández Parker, Luís. "Reportaje al Juicio de los Cancilleres," *Ercilla*, XXVI (24 agosto 1960), 16-17.
Hernández Parker, Luís. "Semana Política," *Ercilla*, XXVIII (25 julio 1962), 8.
Horowitz, David. *The Free World Colossus*. New York: Hill and Wang, 1963.
Huelin, David. "Latin America's Development Crisis," *World Today*, XIX (September 1963).
Hugembert, Carlos. "Persecutions in Chile for Pro-Cuba Actions," *The Militant* (New York), December 3, 1962, p. 3.
Illich, Ivan. "The Seamy Side of Charity," *America*, CXVI (January 21, 1967), 87-91.
Jobet, Julio César. "Acción e Historia del Socialismo Chileno," *Combate* (San Jose), II (septiembre–octubre 1960), 32-45, III (enero–febrero 1961), 39-49.
Jobet, Julio César. "Democracia Liberal y Subdesarrollo Económico," *Politica* (Caracas), N.o 5 (enero 1960), pp. 96-107.
Jobet, Julio César. "Problemas y Contradicciones en la Crisis Chilena," *Arauco*, IV (enero 1963).
Jobet, Julio César. "Yugoslavia, Democracia Socialista," *Arauco*, III (noviembre 1961), 26-37.
Johnson, Dale L. "The National and Progressive Bourgeosie of Chile," *Studies in Comparative International Development*, vol. IV, no. 4 (1968-1969), pp. 63-84.
Johnson, John J. *Political Change in Latin America*. Stanford: Stanford University Press, 1958.
Kamynin, L. "Chile: Pre-election Volcano," *International Affairs* (Moscow), No. 8 (August 1964), pp. 57-60, 82.
Kaplan B., Frida; Navarrete R., Yolanda; y Rubens F., Daniela. "Algunos Factores que Determinan la Conducta Electoral de la Mujer." Memoria para Optar al Título de Psicológico, Universidad de Chile, Facultad de Filosofía y Educación, Escuela de Psicología, Santiago, 1964. No pages enumerated.
Kaufman, Robert R. *The Chilean Political Right and Agrarian Reform: Resistance and Moderation*. Washington: Institute for the Comparative Study of Political Systems, 1967.
Korb, G.M. "Chile's Exploited Farmers," *America*, CV (September 23, 1961).
Kosta, Vjekoslav. "The Cuban Revolution and its International Repercussions," *Review of International Affairs* (Belgrade), XIII (October 20, 1962).
LHP. "A 360 Días de las Elecciones Presidenciales," *Ercilla*, XXIX (11 septiembre 1963), 9.
LHP. "Acuerdos del PDC y Padena," *Ercilla*, XXVIII (31 octubre 1962), 8.
LHP. "Batalla de los Rumores," *Ercilla*, XXIX (19 julio 1964), 9.
LHP. "Cancilleres en USA Miran a Cuba," *Ercilla*, XXX (22 julio 1964), 17.
LHP. "Cerco Derechista al PDC Inquieta al P. Radical," *Ercilla*, XXIX (27 marzo 1963), 19.
LHP. "4 Candidatos en el Punto de Partida," *Ercilla*, XXIX (29 mayo 1963), 10.
LHP. "Cuba y Chile en Cita de Cancilleres," *Ercilla*, XXX (1 julio 1964), 10.

LHP. "El Congreso Pleno: Alerta para Eduardo Frei," *Ercilla*, XXX (28 octubre 1964), 17.
LHP. "Curico Borró la Duda," *Ercilla*, XXX (18 marzo 1964), 15-17.
LHP. "DC: Allende o Frei es la alternativa," *Ercilla*, XXX (22 abril 1964), 8-9.
LHP. "Derecha: Frei; PR; Allende; Mutis de Prat," *Ercilla*, XXX (25 marzo 1964), 17-18.
LHP. "Durán Marca el Destino de Radicales," *Ercilla*, XXX (1 abril 1964), 8.
LHP. "Durán Marcó el Destino de Radicales," *Ercilla*, XXX (8 abril 1964), 8-9.
LHP. "El fracaso de conciliación chilena," *Ercilla*, XXVI (7 septiembre 1960), 16-17.
LHP. "Elección de Congreso a la Vista," *Ercilla*, XXX (30 septiembre 1964), 6.
LHP. "Exequiel González Madariaga, Castigado el Niño Terrible del PR," *Ercilla*, XXX (10 junio 1964), 9.
LHP. "Final: Frei o Allende; pero Clave, Durán," *Ercilla*, XXX (29 abril 1964), 9.
LHP. "Frei, Allende y Durán ante la Meta," *Ercilla*, XXX (12 agosto 1964), 8-9.
LHP. "Frei: Revolución en las Urnas," *Ercilla*, XXX (9 septiembre 1964), 10-11.
LHP. "La Campana tomando la Recta," *Ercilla*, XXX (22 julio 1964), 9.
LHP. "La DC Destrozó los Cronómetros," *Ercilla*, XXXI (10 marzo 1965), 18-19.
LHP. "La Elección Municipal: Primer Pie," *Ercilla*, XXIX (3 abril 1963), 8.
LHP. "La Semana Política," *Ercilla*, XXVIII (28 marzo 1962), 9.
LHP. "La Silenciosa 'Batalla' de La Misión Molina–Pinera," *Ercilla*, XXVIII (28 noviembre 1962), 16-17.
LHP. "Las 4 Caras del Torneo de la CUT," *Ercilla*, XXVIII (8 agosto 1962), 8.
LHP. "Las Mujeres se 'Toman' la Política," *Ercilla*, XXIX (28 agosto 1963), 8-9.
LHP. "Larga Maratón con Sorpresas," *Ercilla*, XXIX (12 junio 1963), 10.
LHP. "Listo Frente Democrático: Nace con Cuentas Alegres," *Ercilla*, XXVIII (30 mayo 1962), 9.
LHP. "Mi Capitán Prat Bajose sin Disparar," *Ercilla*, XXX (29 abril 1964), 8.
LHP. " 'New Look' del PC chileno," *Ercilla*, XXVIII (9 enero 1963), 7.
LHP. "PDC y FRAP Piden el Bis para Marzo," *Ercilla*, XXX (23 septiembre 1964), 15.
LHP. "PR: Dura Atague a la 'Reforma,' " *Ercilla*, XXIX (16 octubre 1963), 9.
LHP. "Partió el FRAP con Allende," *Ercilla*, XXVIII (4 julio 1962), 7.
LHP. "Pugna Interna en el PS," *Ercilla*, XXX (22 enero 1964), 8, 23.
LHP. "Reforma Agraria sin FF. EE.," *Ercilla*, XXVIII (18 julio 1962), 7.
LHP. "Reformistas Izaron a JAR; el PC y Frei," *Ercilla*, XXIX (23 octubre 1963), 11.
LHP. "Se 'Exporta' el Plan Frei," *Ercilla*, XXX (7 octubre 1964), 8-9.
LHP. "Tensa Pugna: control del Parlamento," *Ercilla*, XXXI (3 febrero 1965), 9.
LHP. "Tres Bloques dan examen el Domingo," *Ercilla*, XXX (3 marzo 1965), 17.
LHP. "Un Arqueo Político a los 45 Dias," *Ercilla*, XXX (16 diciembre 1964), 8-9.
Labarca, Eduardo. "Alemania Occidental Tambien se Trabaja a gremios chilenos," *El Siglo*, 18 marzo 1967, p. 3.
Labarca, Eduardo. "Luís Quiroga y un Instiuto con 160 millones," *El Siglo*, 13 marzo 1967, p. 3.
Labarca, Eduardo. "Mil Millones de pesos para corromper sindicatos chilenos," *El Siglo*, 24 febrero 1967, p. 3.
Ladrón de Guevara, Matilde. *Adios al Canaveral: Diario de una Mujer en Cuba*. Buenos Aires: Edit. Goyanarte, 1962.
Larrain E., Mons. Manuel, Obispo de Talca. *Escritos Sociales*. Santiago: Edit. del Pacífico, 1963.
Lasaga, Jose Ignacio. "La Reforma Agraria y el Comunismo," *Mensaje*, VIII (Septiembre 1959), 373-76.
Lieuwen, Edwin. *Arms and Politics in Latin America*. New York: Praeger, 1961.
Lineberry, William P. "Chile's Struggle on the Left," *New Leader*, XLIX (May 23, 1966), 3-6.
Lipschutz, Alejandro. *Guerra y Paz y Otros Temas Candentes*. Santiago: Edit. Austral, 1964.
Lleras Camargo, Alberto. "La Alianza después de Kennedy," *Mensaje*, N.o 130 (julio 1964), 278-83.
Lortsch, Lucy. *Dos Chilenas en La Habana*. Santiago: ABC Plastigraf Imp., 1963.
Magnet, Alejandro. "Bloqueo de Cuba–Elecciones en EE. UU.," *Mensaje*, XI (noviembre 1962), 523.
Magnet, Alejandro. "Comentarios Internacionales: Plan Marshall para América Latina?" *Mensaje*, IX (agosto 1960), 283-84.

Magnet, Alejandro. "Cuba, o la revolución traicionada," *Mensaje*, XII (octubre 1963), 663-66.
Magnet, Alejandro. "La aventura cubana," *Mensaje*, X (junio 1961), 196-98.
Magnet, Alejandro. "La Novena Reunión de Cancilleres," *Mensaje*, XIII (septiembre 1964).
Magnet, Alejandro. "La 'Revolución en Libertad' en América Latina," *Mensaje*, XII (octubre 1964), 480-82.
Malinarich M., Humberto. "Chile Hierve con la Guerra Fría," *Ercilla*, XXVII (26 abril 1961), 17-18.
Malinarich M., Humberto. "Confesiones a 10 mil metros de altura," *Ercilla*, XXVII (18 octubre 1961), 6.
Malinarich M., Humberto. "El Mitin de los 20," *Ercilla*, XXVIII (10 octubre 1962), 2.
Malinarich, Humberto. "Los Secretos del Plan Marshall para América Latina," *Ercilla*, XXVII (28 junio 1961), 7.
Malinarich, Humberto. "Punta del Este: La Dificil Cita de los '21,' " *Ercilla*, XXVIII (31 enero 1962), 15-18.
Malinarich, Humberto. "Reforma Agraria Divide a Católicos," *Ercilla*, XXVII (5 abril 1961), 10.
Maluenda M., Benjamin. "El Instituto de Educación Rural: Factor en la Reforma Agraria," *Mensaje*, XI (Mayo 1962), 170-171.
Martz, John D. "Doctrine and Dilemmas of the Latin American 'New Left,' " *World Politics*, XXII (January 1970), 170-96.
Matthews, Herbert. *The Cuban Story*. New York: George Braziller, 1961.
Mellado, Raul. "Liberales no se oponen a relaciones con la URSS," *Vistazo*, VII (11 agosto 1959), 8.
Mendoza, Samuel. *Actividad del Comunismo en Chile en 1961*. Santiago: Congreso por la Libertad de la Cultura, Imp. San Jorge, diciembre 1961.
Mendoza, Samuel. "El Comunismo en tres congresos realizados en Chile," *Estudios sobre el Comunismo*, VIII (abril–junio de 1960).
Mendoza, Samuel. "La Actividad del Comunismo en Chile durante 1960," *Estudios sobre el Comunismo*, IX (enero–marzo de 1961), 83-84.
Mendoza, Samuel. "La Reunión del Comité Ejecutive de la Federación Mundial de la Juventud Democrática," *Estudios sobre el Comunismo*, IX (julio–septiembre de 1961), 71-92.
Meneses Davila, Cristina. *¡Servir al Pueblo!* Santiago, 1960.
Meslay, John. "Algo más sobre Cuba," *Mensaje*, XI (enero–febrero 1962), 47-49.
Millas, Orlando. "Christian Democratic Reformism: The Chilean Experiment," *World Marxist Review*, VIII (November 1965), 45-48.
Millas, Orlando. "El Proyecto de Reajustes Necesita ser Reajustado," *El Siglo*, 20 noviembre 1966, p. 13.
Millas, Orlando. "New Trends in Catholicism and the Policy of the Chilean Communists," *World Marxist Review*, VII (March 1964), 25-30.
Morris, James. "Chile: Restless Republic," *Saturday Evening Post*, November 25, 1961.
Morrison, Delesseps S. *Latin American Mission*. New York: Simon and Schuster, 1965.
Murillo V., Fernando. "15 millones de dolares por Sukarno," *Punto Final*, I (1.a quincena de abril de 1967), 26.
Musalem, Jose. "Misión Goodwin–Moscoso," *Política y Espíritu*, XVI (marzo 1962), 17-18.
Needler, Martin. *Latin American Politics in Perspective*. New York: Van Nostrand, 1963.
North, Liisa. *Civil Military Relations in Argentina, Chile and Peru*. Berkeley: Institute of International Studies, University of California, n.d.
Nuñez Jimenez, Antonio. *Dos Años de Reforma Agraria*. Boletín Especial de la Embajada de Cuba, Santiago, Chile, Junio 1961. Santiago: Prensa Latinoamericana, 1961.
Nunn, F.M. "Emil Korner and the Prussianization of the Chilean Army," *Hispanic American Historical Review*, L (May 1970), 300-22.
Olavarría Bravo, Arturo. *Chile bajo la Democracia Cristiana*. Santiago: Edit. Nascimento, 1966.
Olavarría Bravo, Arturo. *Chile entre dos Alessandri*. Tomos I-IV. Santiago: Edit. Nascimento, 1962-65.
Olivares, Augusto. "Habló el General X," *Desfile*, I (6 enero 1966), 6-7 ff.

Olivares, Augusto. "La Joventud en una población callampa," *Desfile*, I (9 diciembre 1965), 18-19.

Onis, Juan de. "Latin Alliance Revisted," *New York Times*, August 18, 1966, p. 14.

Otero Echeverría, Rafael. *Reportaje a una revolución*. Santiago: Edit. del Pacífico, 1959.

Parrish, Carles J., Lazar, Arpad J. von; and Tapia Videla, Jorge. *The Chilean Congressional Election of March 7, 1965: An Analysis*. Washington: Institute for the Comparative Study of Political Systems, 1967.

Perceval(pseud.). *¡Ganó Allende!* Santiago: Nueva Aurora, Imp. Edit. Universidad Católica, 1964.

Perez Fernández, Cristian. "Juventud Senorio," *Acción Conservadora*, I (septiembre 1959), 1-3.

"Mons. Perez Serantes Condena al Comunismo," *Mensaje*, IX (Julio 1960), 263-65.

Petras, James. "After the Chilean Presidential Election: Reform or Stagnation?" *Journal of Inter-American Studies*, VII (July 1965), 375-85.

Petras, James. *Chilean Christian Democracy: Politics and Social Forces*. Berkeley: Institute of International Studies, University of California, 1967.

Petras, James. *Politics and Social Forces in Chilean Development*. Berkeley: University of California Press.

Petras, James. "The Latin American Middle Class," *New Politics*, IV (Winter 1965), 74-85.

Petras, James, and Zeitlin, Maurice. "Agrarian Radicalism in Chile," *British Journal of Sociology*, XIX (September 1969), 254-70.

Petras, James and Zeitlin, Maurice. "Miners and Agrarian Radicalism," *American Sociological Review*, XXXII (August 1967), 578-86.

Pike, Frederick B. *Chile and the United States: 1880-1962*. Notre Dame: University of Notre Dame Press, 1963.

Pike, Frederick B., and Bray, Donald W. "A Vista of Catastrophe: The Future of United States—Chilean Relations," *Review of Politics*, XXII (July 1960), 393-418.

Pike, Frederick B., and D'Antonio, William V., eds. *Religion, Revolution and Reform: New Forces for Change in Latin America*. New York: Praeger, 1964.

Pinares, Marcos. "Una chilena ve Cuba," *Cuba* (Habana), III (enero 1964), 67.

Pinto, Francisco A. "La Democracia Cristiana y La Economía," *Política y Espíritu*, XIII (15 agosto 1958), 22-30.

Planet, Mario. "La Guerra de los Cancilleres," *Ercilla*, XXX (29 julio 1964), 17.

Poblete, Renato. "Causas de la escasez sacerdotal en Chile," *Mensaje*, N.o 130 (julio 1964).

Poblete Troncoso, Moises. "El Movimiento Sindical Chileno," *Combate* (San Jose), IV (julio y agosto 1962), 25-34.

Portes, Alejandro. "Leftist Radicalism in Chile: A Test of Three Hypotheses," *Comparative Politics*, II (January 1970), 251-74.

Portnoy, Marcos. *Testimonio sobre Cuba*. Santiago: Ediciones del Litoral, 1964.

Powell, Sandra. "Political Change in the Chilean Electorate, 1952-1964," *Western Political Quarterly*, XXIII (June 1970), 364-83.

Prieto Letelier, Jorge. "Discurso del Señor Prieto (Presidente Nacional del Partido Conservador)," *Acción Conservadora*, I (octubre—noviembre 1959).

Quinzio Figueiredo, Jorge Mario. *El Partido Radical: Origen—Doctrina—Convenciones*. Santiago: Imp. 'Bío-Bío,' 1964.

Ramírez Gomez, Ramon. "Cuba Socialista," *Ciencias Políticas y Sociales* (Mexico), VIII (abril—junio 1962), 175-209.

Rodman, Selden. "October Revolution in Chile," *National Review*, October 6, 1970, pp. 1053-55.

Rodríguez, Carlos Rafael. *Cuatro Años de Reforma Agraria en Cuba*. Santiago: Imp. Horizonte, 1963.

Rodríguez, Arenas Aniceto. *La Conspiración contra Chile*. Santiago: Prensa Latinoamericana, 1964.

Rodríguez, Arenas, Aniceto. "Veinticinco mil obreros y campesinos ingresaron al Partido Socialista con el Contingente 'Fidel Castro,'" *Arauco*, III (Junio 1962), 16-23.

Roman, Peter. "Can Chile's Allende Move Far to the Left?" *Guardian*, November 7, 1970, p. 16.

Rosman, Alan. *La Nueva Cuba*. Santiago: Talls. Grafs. de E.H.S. Ltda., 1965.

Rycroft, W. Stanley, and Clemmer, Myrtle M. *A Factual Study of Latin America.* New York: United Presbyterian Church in the U.S.A., Commission on Ecumenical Mission and Relations, Office of Research, 1963.

Salvaterra, Fernando. *Un Mundo Nuevo: Democracia o Comunismo para America Latina.* Santiago: Edit. del Pregón, 1963.

Sanhueza Herbage, Fernando, y Orellana Peralta, Juan. *La Juventud y la Estrategia del Comunismo Internacional.* Santiago: Edit. Universidad Católica, 1962.

Santana, Carlos. "Conflicto con Cara de Marzo," *Ercilla,* XXXI (20 enero 1965), 8-9.

Santana, Carlos. "Ha Faltado Muñequeo Político," *Ercilla,* XXX (13 enero 1965), 10.

Santana, Carlos. "PDC contra todos; todos contra PDC," *Ercilla,* XXX (17 febrero 1965), 8.

Schneider, Ronald M. "Five Years of the Cuban Revolution," *Current History,* XLVI (January 1964), 26-33.

Segal, Bernard E. "Dissatisfaction and Desire for Change Among Chilean Hospital Workers," *American Journal of Sociology,* LXXV (November 1969), 375-88.

Sepulveda, Orlando. "Medios de Communición de Masas y Cambio Social." Universidad de Chile, Instituto de Sociología, Santiago, 1966. (Mimeographed.)

Silva, Juan Ramon. "La Clase Media," *Desfile,* I (27 enero 1966), 9-11.

Silva Solar, Julio. "Declaracion del PDC," *Las Noticias de Ultima Hora,* 17 abril 1961, p. 2.

Silva Solar, Julio. "Reflexiones La Revolución," *Política y Espíritu,* XVIII (enero—mayo 1964), 18-25.

Silvert, Kalman H. *Chile: Yesterday and Today.* New York: Holt, Rinehart and Winston, 1965.

Silvert, Kalman H. *Coda.* American Universities Field Staff, October 10, 1957.

Silvert, Kalman H. *Elections, Parties and the Law.* American Universities Field Staff, March 10, 1957.

Silvert, Kalman H. *Reaction and Revolution in Latin America.* New York, 1959.

Snow, Peter G. "The Political Party Spectrum in Chile," *South Atlantic Quarterly,* LXII (Autumn 1963), 474-87.

Soares, Glaucio, and Hamblin, Robert L. "Socio-economic Variables and Voting for the Radical Left: Chile, 1952," *American Political Science Review,* LXI (December 1967), 1053-65.

Solis, José. "Décimo Congreso Médico y Estomatológico Nacional," *Cuba* (Habana), Ano II, No. 11 (1963), pp. 75-80.

Suarez Bastidas, Hector. "Un 'ideólogo' anticomunista," *Punto Final,* I (1.a quincena de mayo de 1967), 10-11.

Tábares del Real, Jose A. *La Revolución Cubana: Ensayo de Interpretación.* Prologo por Salvador Allende. Santiago: Prensa Latinoamericana, 1960.

Teichert, Pedro C.M. "Latin America and the Socio-Economic Impact of the Cuban Revolution," *Journal of Inter-American Studies,* IV (January 1962), 105-20.

Thomas, Ann Van Wynen, and Thomas, A.J., Jr. *The Organization of American States.* Dallas: Southern Methodist University Press, 1963.

Thomas, Jack Ray. "The Socialist Republic of Chile," *Journal of Inter-American Studies,* VI (April 1964), 203-20.

Tomic Romero, Radomiro. *Sobre el Sistema Interamericano.* Santiago: Edit. del Pacífico, 1963.

Tomic Romero, Radomiro. "Sobre la Revolución Cubana," *Política y Espíritu,* XIV (1 mayo 1960), 10-12.

Tomic Romero, Radomiro. *Unidad y Diversidad de la Democracia Cristiana en el Mundo.* Santiago: Edit. del Pacífico, 1962.

Tulchin, Joseph S. "Latin America: Focus for U.S. Aid," *Current History,* LI (July 1966), 28-35.

Valdes Subercaseaux, Gabriel. *Address delivered by the Minister of Foreign Affairs before the Senate, on 6 January 1965.* Santiago: South Pacific Mail, 1965.

Valenzuela Valderrama, Hector. "El Dilema Político de Hoy," *Política y Espíritu,* XIII (mayo 1958), 22-26.

Varela, Julio. "USA Quiere Colonizar Movimiento Sindical Chileno," *El Siglo,* 10 febrero 1967, p. 15.

Veliz, Claudio. "Chile on the Threshold of Change," *World Today,* XX (May 1964), 223-230.

Veliz, Claudio. "The New Cuban Industrial Policy," *World Today*, XIX (September 1963), 371-74.

Vexler, Erica. "Frei en la antesala de la Moneda," *Ercilla*, XXX (9 septiembre 1964), 20.

Vexler, Erica. "Golpes Bajo el Cinturón," *Ercilla*, XXX (10 junio 1964), 10.

Vexler, Erica. "La Dificultad de Ser Buen Vecino," *Ercilla*, XXX (6 enero 1965), 24-25.

Vexler, Erica. "Lenguaje Político Gastado," *Ercilla*, XXIX (17 julio 1963), 11.

Vitale, Luís. *Ensayo de Historia del Movimiento Obrero Chileno.* Santiago: Edit. POR, Imp. 'Victoria,' 1961.

Vitale, Luís. *¿Y Despues del 4, Que? Perspectivas de Chile despues de las elecciones presidenciales* (Santiago: Prensa Latinoamericana, 1970).

Vitale, Luís. *Los Discursos de Clotario Blest y la Revolución Chilena.* Santiago: Edit. POR, Imp. 'Victoria,' 1961.

Vitale, Luís. "Which Road for Chile?" *International Socialist Review*, XXV (Summer 1964), 67-72.

Vúskovic, Sergio, y Fernández, Osvaldo. *Teoría de la Ambigüedad: Bases Ideológicas de la Democracia Cristiana.* Santiago: Edit. Austral, 1964.

Waiss, Oscar. *El Espejismo del 64.* Santiago: Imp. 'Victoria,' 1962.

Waiss, Oscar. *Socialismo sin Gerentes.* Santiago: Imp. 'Victoria,' 1961.

Weekly, James K. "Christian Democracy in Chile–Ideology and Economic Development," *South Atlantic Quarterly*, LXVI (Autumn 1967).

Weissman, Steve. "The Many 'Successes' of the Alliance for Progress," *Pacific Research and World Empire Telegram*, II (November 1970), 2-9.

Widick, B.J. "Vietnam, Race and the Unions," *Nation*, November 21, 1966.

Wilkerson, Loree. *Fidel Castro's Political Programs from Reformism to 'Marxism-Leninism.'* Gainesville: University of Florida Press, 1965.

Wolf, Charles, Jr. *The Political Effects of Economic Programs: Some Indications from Latin America.* Santa Monica: Rand Corp., Memo RM-3901-ISA, 1964.

Wolfe, Marshall. "Rural Settlement Patterns and Social Change in Latin America," *Latin American Research Review*, vol. I, no. 2 (1966).

Zeitlin, Maurice. "The Social Determinants of Political Democracy in Chile." *Latin America: Reform or Revolution.* Edited by James Petras and Maurice Zeitlin. New York: Fawcett, 1968.

Zeitlin, Maurice, and Petras, James. "The Working Class in Chile: Christian Democracy vs. Marxism," *British Journal of Sociology*, XXI (March 1970), 16-29.

Zottele, Pedro. "Chile: Orienting the Faithful," *Christian Century*, May 22, 1968, 696-98.

Zottele, Pedro. "Chilean Students Ignite Revolt," *Christian Century*, October 16, 1968, 1318-20.

Zottele, Pedro. "News from Chile," *Christian Century*, October 7, 1964, pp. 1246-49.

Propaganda, Reports, Articles (Corporate Author or Anonymous)

"A Traves del Mundo," *Bohemia* (La Habana), 25 diciembre 1970, p. 80.

Acción Chilena. Los avisos reproducidos en el presente folleto y otros de la misma índole fueron publicados en diarios y revistas de Chile durante los meses que precedieron al 4 de Septiembre de 1964, día en que la República eligió un nuevo Presidente. Santiago: Imp. Sopech, 1964, 18pp.

Acción Sindical Chilena (ASICH). *Tierra y Libertad por la Reforma Agraria.* A pedido de la Unión de Campesinos Cristianos de Chile. Santiago: Tipo-Litográfica 'La Gratitud Nacional,' abril de 1961.

Acción Sindical Demócrata. *Nace la Unión Sindical Democrática.* Pleno de Dirigentes Sindicales. Santiago: Talls. Grafs. 'Rapid,' 1964.

Ahora el Pueblo Busca su Camino Mano a Mano con Frei. Santiago: Edit. del Pacífico, 1964.

American Council of Voluntary Agencies for Foreign Service, Inc. Technical Assistance Information Clearing House. *U.S. Non-Profit Organizations (Voluntary Agencies, Missions and Foundations Participating in Technical Assistance Abroad): A Directory for 1964.* New York: Technical Assistance Information Clearing House of the American Council of Voluntary Agencies for Foreign Service, Inc., 1964.

American Council of Voluntary Agencies for Foreign Service, Inc. Technical Assistance Information Clearing House. *U.S. Non-Profit Organizations (Voluntary Agencies, Missions and Foundations Participating in Technical Assistance Abroad): Supplement for 1965.* New York: Technical Assistance Information Clearing House of the American Council of Voluntary Agencies for Foreign Service, Inc., 1965.

American International Association for Economic and Social Development. *Rural Education in Chile,* by Ernest E. Maes. New York: AIA, February 1965.

"Anécdotas del 26 de julio," *Vistazo,* VII (4 agosto 1959), 8.

"El Anti 'Mensaje' del Ilustrado," *Ercilla,* XXIX (30 enero 1963), 10.

"El 'Ariostazo,' " *Desfile,* I (21 octubre 1965), 20-21.

"El Arzobispo se Confiesa," *Ercilla,* XXVII (5 julio 1961), 16-17.

Asociación Nacional de Agricultores de Chile. *Proyecto de Ley de 'Reforma Agraria.'* Santiago: Imp. Lautaro, 1958.

Asociación Nacional de Organizaciones Campesinas (A.N.O.C.), *Discursos y Conclusiones (Extractos) de la 1.a Convención.* Santiago: Abumohor Imp., 1962.

"Atentados Contra la Democracia Venezolana," *Política y Espíritu,* XIV (1 diciembre 1960), 1.

"La 'Batalla' del Senado," *Ercilla,* XXVII (13 diciembre 1961), 8.

"Business Abroad: Chile's Copper Beckons Once Again," *Business Week,* October 1966, pp. 76-78.

"Business Abroad: Chile—Why the Copper Men are Getting Edgy," *Business Week,* April 4, 1970, pp. 38-39.

Candidatura de Oposición, un diputado valiente, sin pelos en la lengua, estudioso y que sabe lo que dice: Orlando Millas, Frente de Accion Popular. Santiago: Imp. Lira, 1961.

"Carabineros exporta nuevas Técnicas Policiales," *Ercilla,* XXVII (26 abril 1961), 8.

"Cardinal Rossi's Puzzling Statements," *Mensaje,* July 1970, reprinted in *LADOC,* I (August 1970), 1-2.

"El Cardenal con S.E.," *Ercilla,* XXVIII (25 julio 1962), 2.

"Castro: Camino de la Dictadura Total," *Política y Espíritu,* XIV (15 mayo 1960), 8-9.

CESO. Centro de Estudios Socioeconómicos. Instituto de Economía. Universidad de Chile. Greater Santiago Surveys. "Stratification," September 1961; "Pre-Electoral," August 1964; "Post-Electoral," November 1964; January 1965. Unpublished.

CESO. Centro de Estudios Socioeconómicos. Instituto de Economía. Universidad de Chile. "Patrones Socio-Culturales del Comportamiento Economico." *Informe Preliminar No. 1.* Julio 1966.

"Chile: El Bloqueo no Llegó al Río," *Ercilla,* XXVIII (31 octubre 1962), 9.

Chile en la Encrucijada. Foro de la Libertad del Trabajo. Relacion de los avisos de prensa de la campaña 'Chile en la Encrucijada' reproducidos en el presente folleto. Santiago: Imp. Sopech, 1964, 21pp.

"Chilean Campesino Unionization Law," *Labor Developments Abroad,* XIII (February 1968), 6-9.

"The Chilean Land Reform: A Laboratory for Alliance-for-Progress Techniques," *Yale Law Journal,* LXXIII (December 1963), 310-33.

"Chile: September 4 to November 3," *Monthly Review,* XXII (January 1971), 520-33.

"Chile Starts Chasing the Capitalists," *Time* (Canadian Edition), January 4, 1971, p. 48.

"Choice for Chile: Which Way to go Left?" *Business Week,* August 8, 1964.

CLASC. Confederación Latinoamericana de Sindicalistas Cristianas. *1.a Jornada de Solidaridad Latinoamerica con los Trabajadores y el Pueblo de Cuba 26 al 31 de Julio 1964.* Santiago: Imp. Sopech, 1964.

"La CLASC y la Revolución Cubana: Declaración . . . ," *Mensaje,* IX (diciembre 1960), 541-42.

Comando Allendista de los Trabajadores de la Industria Textil. *En Santiago, a 31 de mayo de 1964.* Santiago: Imp. Horizonte, 1964.

Comando Nacional Allendista de Trabajadores Semi-Fiscales y de Instituciones de Previsión. *Por una Previsión Social—Racional—Igualitaria—Justa: Manifesto y Compromiso.* Santiago: Imp. Horizonte, 1964.

Comando Nacional Gremial de la Campaña Presidencial del Pueblo. *Los Trabajadores en el Gobierno Popular: Resoluciones de la Asamblea Nacional de Trabajadores Allendistas.* Santiago: Imp. Horizonte, 1964.

Committee for Economic Development. *How Low Income Countries Can Advance Their Own Growth.* New York: Committee for Economic Development, 1966.

"Cómo vió el PDC la Revolución Cubana," *Vistazo*, VIII (11 agosto 1959), 9.

"La Conferencia Sindical de los Trabajadores de América Latina," *Mensaje*, XI (octubre 1962).

"El Congreso de Niteroi: Vigorosa Jornada Internacional de Solidaridad con Cuba," *Cuba Socialista*, No. 21 (mayo 1963).

Congreso Latinoamericano de Juventud. *Acuerdos y Resoluciones del II CLAJ (Congreso Latinoamericano de Juventud).* Celebrado en Santiago de Chile del 9 al 13 de Marzo de 1964. Santiago: Imp. Horizonte, 1964.

Congreso por la Libertad de la Cultura. *Así Veían a Stalin.* Santiago: Imp. San Jorge, 1956.

Congreso por la Libertad de la Cultura. *La Causa de Cuba: Causa de America.* Santiago: Congreso por la Libertad de la Cultura, 1961.

"Constitución de la Vanquardia Democrata Cristiana Cubano," *Política y Espíritu*, XIV (1 diciembre 1960), 30-31.

Convención Nacional de Profesionales y Técnicos de la Candidatura de Salvador Allende: Medidas Concretas del Gobierno Popular. Santiago: Imp. Lautaro, 1958.

"Convención PCU por Dentro: FRIA, Pero Quema," *Ercilla*, XXV (28 octubre 1959), 8-9.

"La Crisis Cubano-Norteamericana," *Política y Espíritu*, XIV (1 abril 1960), 10-11.

"Crisis en el FRAP y Algo Mas," *Ercilla*, XXX (13 enero 1965), 11.

"Cuba: Ante una provocación comunista los católicos plantean su posición social," *Política y Espíritu*, XIV (1 junio 1960), 21-22.

"Cuba: Medita la Moneda," *Ercilla*, XXVII (3 mayo 1961), 8.

"Cuba: Primera navidad socialista," *Mensaje*, XI (marzo-abril 1962), 103.

"Cuba, Un Año Después," *Política y Espíritu*, XIV (1 enero 1960), 8-9.

"Cuba: Una Experiencia Heroica." *Cuadernos de Información Política.* Santiago: Ediciones Socialismo, N.o 3, Edit. POR, 1962.

Cuba—URSS: Una Firme Amistad en Defensa de la Paz. Declaración conjunta Cubano-Sovietica firmada el 23 de Mayo de 1963 en Moscú. Santiago: Imp. Horizonte, 1963.

El Cuento del tío Salvador. Santiago: Edit. Nueva Aurora, 1963.

"DC: Pugna por el Mando y la Táctica," *Ercilla*, XXX (18 noviembre 1964), 11.

"El Deber Social y Político en la Hora Presente," *Política y Espíritu*, XVI (septiembre 1962).

"Declaración de la CLASC Sobre La Revolución Cubana y El Gobierno de Fidel Castro," *Política y Espíritu*, XIV (15 noviembre 1960), 31-32.

"Declaración del Consejo Episcopal Latinoamericano reunido en Bogotá," *Revista Catolica*, LVII (septiembre a diciembre 1959), 2466-67.

"Declaración del Movimiento D.C. de Cuba," *Política y Espíritu*, XIV (1 junio 1960), 30-31.

"Declaraciones del Cardenal Arzobispo Monseñor Raúl Silva Henríquez," *Política y Espíritu*, (septiembre 1962), 33-35.

"La Democracia y La Revolución," *Política y Espíritu*, XIV (15 marzo 1959), 19-29.

DESAL. *Una Estrategia contra la Miseria.* Santiago: DESAL, n.d. (published between 1964 and 1966).

"Desde dos Extremos partió la Presidencial," *Ercilla*, XXVIII (19 diciembre 1962), 17.

Diccionario Biográfico de Chile. Duodécima Edición: 1962-1964. Santiago: Emp. Periodística Chile, 1965.

"La Doble Conferencia de Cancilleres," *Política y Espíritu*, XIV (1 septiembre 1960), 1.

" 'Doc' del otro complot al tribunal psiquiátrico," *Ercilla*, XXII (6 septiembre 1961), 2.

"Documentos: El Problema Sindical en Cuba," *Política y Espíritu*, XIV (15 diciembre 1960), 25-28.

"Dos juicos sobre las relaciones interamericanas,"*Política y Espíritu*, XIV (15 mayo 1960), 18-22.

"Editorial: Fidelismo en Cuba (Chile)," *New Republic*, November 24, 1962, p. 8.

"Editorial: Solidaridad con Cuba, deber de nuestros pueblos," *Principios*, N.o 81 (Mayo 1961), 3-9.

"Editorial: The Victory of the 'Popular Unity' Coalition in Chile," *Mensaje*, October 1970, reprinted in *LADOC*, I (October 1970), 1-3.

"La Elección," *Ercilla*, XXIV (3 septiembre 1958), 7-8.

"Encuesta Gallup en Chile," *Ercilla*, XXIX (20 febrero 1963), 15.
"Encuestas: Las Clases Sociales," *El Mercurio: Revista del Domingo*, 8 enero 1967, p. 6.
"Era lícito intervenir?" *Mensaje*, X (junio 1961), 199-201.
"Es la Iglesia católica en Cuba una Iglesia persequida?" *Mensaje*, XII (Mayo 1963), 184-87.
"Está en Chile el yanqui que derrocó a Goulart," *Punto Final*, I (diciembre 1966), 7.
Federación Mundial de Juventud Democrática. *Documentos y Resoluciones del Comite Ejecutivo de la F.M.J.D. (Federación Mundial de Juventud Democrática)*. 16-20 abril 1961, Santiago de Chile. Santiago: Imp. Horizonte, 1961.
Fidel Castro: Líder y Guerrillero. Santiago: Prensa Latinoamericana, 1958.
Fidel Denuncia Otra Invasión. Santiago: Imp. Horizonte, 1962.
"FRAP: Apertura al Partido Radical," *Ercilla*, XXVIII (20 junio 1962), 9.
"Frei y Tomic: 'USA Rechaza a los Moderados,' " *Ercilla*, XXVIII (11 abril 1962), 9.
Frente Nacional de Profesores Freistas: Primeras Jornadas de Estudios. 24-25-26 enero 1964. Santiago: Edit. del Pacífico, 1964.
"Goodwin: Intérprete entre JAR y Kennedy," *Ercilla*, XXVIII (21 febrero 1962), 8.
"Los guatones de la P.P.," *Desfile*, I (13 enero 1966), 14.
"La Iglesia Abrió Primer Surco de la Reforma," *Ercilla*, XXVIII (4 julio 1962), 16-17.
"La Iglesia Católica, el Régimen Cubano y el Partido Comunista," *Política y Espíritu*, XIV (1 septiembre 1960), 23-24.
"La Iglesia y el Problema de la Tierra en Latinoamerica," *Politica y Espiritu*, XV (abril 1961), 43-47.
"La Iglesia y el problema del campesino chileno," *Mensaje*, XL (mayo 1962), 185-94a.
Information Guide for Doing Business in Chile. New York: Price Waterhouse and Co., U.S.A., September 1969.
Informe de una jornada-Tarud-en la primera línea de combate por los derechos populares. Santiago: Imp. Horizonte, 1965.
Informes de las Comisiones al Congreso Nacional de Trabajadores. Candidatura Presidencial Eduardo Frei Montalva: 13-14-15-16 agosto 1964. Santiago: Talls. Grafs. Periodística, 1964.
Instituto Chileno de Opinión Pública. "Encuesta de Opinion relativa a algunos aspectos de la Realidad Política Chilena." Santiago: ICOP, Febrero de 1964, unpublished.
Instituto de Capacitación Sindical y Social (INCASIS). *Memoria del Instituto de Capacitación Sindical y Social Correspondiente al Periodo 1.o de Enero al 31 de Diciembre de 1964*. INCASIS, 1964.
Instituto de Educación Rural. "Un Impulso solidario a la superación Campesina," Santiago, 1960. (Mimeographed.)
Instituto de Estudios Políticos del PDC de Concepción. *El a-b-c de la Democracia Cristiana*. Santiago: Edit. del Pacífico, 1962.
Instituto de Promoción Agraria. *La Tierra Nuestra*. Santiago: Imp. Lord Cochrane, 1964.
Instituto para el Desarrollo del Sindicalismo Libre. *El Comunismo Internacional y El Sindicalismo Mundial*, por Dario Rivera. Santiago: Instituto para el Desarrollo del Sindicalismo Libre, Imp. 'Soberanía,' 1964.
Instituto Popular de Chile. *Fidel Castro, Osvaldo Dórticos, Ché Guevara, Carlos R. Rodríguez Hablan para el Instituto Popular de Chile*. Santiago: Instituto Popular de Chile, 1962.
Interchurch Medical Assistance, Inc. *Reach 'Round the World with IMA.'* New York: Interchurch Medical Assistance, Inc., n.d.
"Johnson ¿es chileno?" *Punto Final*, I (2.a quincena de julio de 1967).
Juventud Conservadora. *El Partido Conservador: su Programa, su Labor*. Redactado y Editado por la, Juventud Conservadora. Santiago: Imp. Arancibía Hnos., n.d. (deposited at the National Library in August, 1964).
Juventud Demócrata Cristiana. *Documentos del Primer Congreso Extraordinario de la Juventud Demócrata Cristiana de America (JUDCA)*. 29 octubre-2 noviembre 1964. Santiago: Ediciones Rebeldia, Talls. Grafs. 'La Nación,' 1964.
Juventud Demócrata Cristiana. *Informe del Segundo Congreso Nacional de la Juventud Demócrata Cristiana*. 31 de octubre, 1, 2 y 3 de noviembre de 1963. Santiago: Imp. 'El Diario Ilustrado,' 1963.
Juventud Liberal. *Principios, Estatutos y Reglamentos Aprobados en la VI Convención*

398

Nacional Celebrada en Santiago los días 6 y 7 de Mayo de 1950. Santiago: Doble Almeyda 1368, 1958.

Juventud Socialista Popular. *Contra el Democristianismo Burques: Contra el Reformismo Antirevolucionario: ¡Por Una Victoria Revolucionaria del FRAP!* Santiago: Astudillo e Hijos, 1964.

"La ley agraria cubana: Declaraciones de Mons. Martín Villaverde, Obispo de Matanzas, Cuba," *Mensaje,* VII (Septiembre 1959), 371-73.

"La ley de reforma agraria en Cuba," *Mensaje,* X (marzo—abril 1961), 107-12.

Lutheran World Relief. *Annual Report for 1966.* New York: Lutheran World Relief, 1966.

"Marginalidad," *Reportaje Desal,* I (julio 1966), 4-5.

"Martires universitarios en Cuba," *Mensaje,* X (marzo—abril 1961), 121-22.

"Matta en La Habana," *Cuba* (Habana), III (mayo 1964), 52-53.

Meals for Millions Foundation. *Distribution of Relief Shipments: September 1946—May 15, 1963.* Los Angeles: Meals for Millions, 1963.

Meals for Millions Foundation. *Pilot Protein Production and Feeding Program for a Selected Region in Chile (Talca).* New York: Meals for Millions Foundation, February 1966.

"Mensaje del Partido Socialista al Pueblo de Chile,"*Arauco,* V (mayo 1964), 4.

"Misión Moscoso-Goodwin: Un Balance para Meditar," *Ercilla,* XXVIII (14 marzo 1962), 8-9.

Movimiento de Solidaridad y Defensa de la Revolución Cubana. *¡Toda América contra el Imperialismo Yanqui!* Santiago: Imp. Horizonte, 1964.

Movimiento Unitario de Trabajadores de Chile (MUTCH). Santiago: Imp. Sopech, 1963.

"The New Press Law in Chile," *Bulletin of the International Commission of Jurists,* No. 20 (September 1964), pp. 16-21.

"Ninth National Congress of the Christian Workers' Confederation of Chile," *International Labour Review,* XCVI (July 1967), 111-13.

"No pueden los Católicos favorecer al Comunismo," *Revista Católica,* LVII (mayo a agosto de 1959), 2332.

"La Nueva Guerra Subvertiva," *Ercilla,* XXVI (18 mayo 1960), 16-18.

Nueva Izquierda Democrática. *Por Qué Triunfará Frei.* Santiago: Imp. Fantasía, 1963.

"Nueva Táctica anti FRAP," *Ercilla,* XXX (15 abril 1964), 9.

Nuevos Horizontes. Santiago: Imp. Sopech, 1964.

OCEPLAN. Comando Nacional de Profesionales y Técnicos. *Planifica con nosotros el renacer de Chile: Jornadas Nacionales de Planificación Popular, Resoluciones,* Santiago, 26-27-28-29 junio 1964. Santiago: Prensa Latinoamericana, 1964.

OCEPLAN. Oficina Central de Planificación. *La Política Agropecuaria del Gobierno Popular.* Santiago: Imp. Horizonte, 1964.

OCEPLAN. Oficina Central de Planificación. *Las Primeras 100 Medidas del Gobierno Popular.* Santiago: Imp. Horizonte, 1964.

"Pablo Gomucio: constructor, banquero, publicista, industrial, pescador y etcéteras... " *Punto Final,* I (1.a quincena de enero de 1967), 16-17, 28.

Partido Comunista de Chile. *Documentos del XI Congreso Nacional.* Santiago: Talls. Grafs. Lautaro, 1959.

Partido Comunista de Chile. *Hacia la Conquista de un Gobierno Popular: Documentos del XII Congreso Nacional.* Santiago: Imp. Horizonte, 1962.

Partido Comunista de Chile. Luís Corvalán L. *Chile y El Nuevo Panorama Mundial.* Informe a la Sesion Plenaria del Comité Central del Partido Comunista de Chile, rendido en un Acto de Masas en el Teatro Caupólican de Santiago, el 10 de Mayo de 1959. Santiago: Talls. Grafs. Lautaro, 1959.

Partido Comunista de Chile. Luís Corvalán. *Todo Chile contra la Política Reaccionaria de Alessandri.* Informe a la X Conferencia Nacional del Partido Comunista de Chile, celebrada los dias 16, 17 y 18 de octubre de 1960, rendido por el Secretario General, Camarada Luís Corvalán, en el acto publico del día domingo 16 en el Teatro Banquedano. Santiago: Imp. Lira 363, 1960.

Partido Comunista de Chile. Orlando Millas. *Derrotar a la Derecha.* Texto completo del Informe rendido en nombre de la Comisión Política por el Diputado Orlando Millas a la Sesion Plenaria del Comité Central del Partido Comunista de Chile, el día 6 de Junio de 1963. Santiago: Imp. Horizonte, 1963.

Partido Comunista de Chile. Orlando Millas. *El Fracaso del Gobierno de los Gerentes.* Texto del informe que presento a nombre de la Comision Política a la Sesión Plenaria del Comité Central del Partido Comunista de Chile realizada en marzo de 1960 en Santiago. Santiago: Imp. Lautaro, 1960.

Partido Comunista de Chile. *Pablo Neruda Contesta a Los Obispos.* Conferencia pronunciada por el poeta Pablo Neruda, miembro del CC del Partido Comunista, el 12 de Octubre, en el Teatro Caupólican de Santiago. Santiago: Imp. Horizonte, 1962.

Partido Comunista de Chile. *Sesión Plenaria del Comité Central del Partido Comunista de Chile, 19 al 21 de Diciembre de 1963.* Informe Central rendido a nombre de la Comisión Política por el camarada Oscar Astudillo, Intervención de Resumen del Subsecretario General del Partido, camarada José González. Santiago: Imp. Horizonte, 1964.

Partido Comunista de Chile, Volodia Teitelboim. *El Camino de la Juventud.* Texto del informe rendido a nombre de la Comision Política, por el camarada Volodia Teitelboim, al Pleno del Comité Central del Partido Comunista de Chile, el 28 de septiembre de 1962. Santiago: Imp. Horizonte, 1962.

Partido Comunista de Chile. Volodia Teitelboim. *El Significado de la Candidatura de Frei.* Intervención del dia 21 de diciembre de 1963, en la Sesión Plenaria del Comité Central del Partido Comunista de Chile. Santiago: Imp. Horizonte, 1964.

Partido Democracia Agraria Laborista. *Declaración de Principios, Estatutos.* Santiago: Imp. Stanley, 1964.

Partido Demócrata Cristiano. *Congreso Nacional de Mujeres Demócratas Cristianas e Independientes: Congreso `de la Mujer Chilena.* 23, 24 y 25 de Agosto, Valparaiso, 1963. Santiago: Imp. Sopech, 1963.

Partido Demócrata Cristiano. Consejo Nacional. *Nosotros creemos que la Democracia es la forma política de la Revolución y nos negamos a aceptar que en nombre de esta última, transitoria o definitivamente, se acabe con la libertad: Dice la Democracia Cristiana a los Partido Comunista y Socialista, 31 de Enero de 1963.* Santiago: Edit. del Pacífico, 1963.

Partido Demócrata Cristiano. *Convención Nacional del Partido Demócrata Cristiano.* 1.a, Santiago, 1959, Resolución sobre política nacional, Declaración de Principios, Santiago: Edit. del Pacífico, 1959.

Partido Democrático Cristiano. *Democracia Cristiana: Tercera Declaración de Millahue y Cuenta Política del Presidente Nacional de la DC, Diputado Renan Fuentealba.* Santiago: Imp. El Imparacial, abril 1964.

Partido Democrático Cristiano. Departamento Nacional Campesino. *Principios Fundamentales: Jornadas Campesinas.* Democracia Cristiana. Santiago: 'El Diario Ilustrado,' 1964.

Partido Demócrata Cristiano. *Documentos de la Convención Nacional del Partido Demócrata Cristiano.* 1.a, Santiago, 1959, Resolucíon sobre política, Declaración de Principios. Santiago: Edit. del Pacifico, 1959.

Partido Demócrata Cristiano. *Discursos de una Campana, por Tomás Pablo Elorza en Concepción, Nuble y Arauco, Noviembre de 1960–Marzo de 1961.* Concepción: Imp. Original, 1961.

Partido Democrático Cristiano. *Informe Preliminar para un Programa de Gobierno de la Democracia Cristiana del Primer Congreso Nacional de Profesionales y Técnicos de la Democracia Cristiana e Independientes, 6-7-8 y 9, de Diciembre de 1962.* Santiago: Edit. del Pacífico, 1963.

Partido Democrático Cristiano. *Primer Congreso Nacional de Profesionales y Técnicos de la Democracia Cristiana e Independientes: III Política Internacional, Apartado N.o al Informe Preliminar.* Santiago: Imp. del Pacífico, n.d. (1963).

Partido Demócrata Cristiano. *Revolución en Libertad.* Por Dr. Antonio Morales Delpiano, Departamento de Capitación, Séptima Comuna, Lira N.o 92-A. Santiago: Imp. Entrecerros, 1964.

"El PDC Busca una Postura Revolucionaria," *Ercilla,* XXVII (12 abril 1961), 7.

Partido Democrático Nacional, PADENA. *Candidato de la Unidad Popular, La Oposición Unida: dará el triunfo al pueblo, Carlos Montero Sch., Candidato a la Presidencia de la República del Partido Democratico Nacional.* Santiago: Talls. Grafs. Periodística Chile Ltda., 1963.

Partido Liberal. Juventud Liberal. *Principios, Estatutos y Reglamentos Aprobados en la 7.a*

Convención Nacional celebrada en Santiago los dias 24, 25 y 26 de Abril de 1959. Santiago: Imp. Chile, 1959.

Partido Socialista de Chile. *XVIII Congreso Nacional.* Santiago: Prensa Latinoamericana, 1959.

Partido Socialista de Chile. *Programa del Partido Socialista: Fundamentación Teórica y Directivas Programáticas.* I. Santiago: Prensa Latinoamericana, 1961.

Partido Socialista de Chile. Raul Ampuero Diaz. *1964: Año de Prueba para la Revolución Chilena.* Informe del c. Raul Ampuero Diaz al XX Congreso General del Partido Socialista, Concepción, Febrero de 1964. Santiago: Imp. Prensa Latinoamericana, 1964.

Partido Socialista de Chile. *Tesis Política Sindical y Organizativa Aprobadas por el Congreso de Unidad Socialista, Julio 1957.* Santiago: Prensa Latinoamericana, 1958.

Partido Socialista Popular. Comité Central. *Una Nueva Dirección para los Trabajadores Chilenos!* Santiago: Imp. Astudillo e Hijos Ltda., 1964.

Pasión de Cristo en Cuba: Testimonio de un Sacerdote. Santiago: Departamento de Publicaciones del Secretariado de Difusion, 1962.

"Pasos Públicos y Privados del Complot," *Ercilla,* XXVII (30 agosto 1961), 15-16.

"Peligrosa Aventura Argentina," *Ercilla,* XXX (29 julio 1964), 25.

"El Pensamiento de la Democracia Cristiana Frente a la Situación Internacional," *Política y Espíritu,* XVI (octubre 1962), 36.

Un Plan que solamente Usted puede derrotar. Santiago y Antófagasta: Edit. 'La Portada,' n.d. 1961 or 1962.

"En la Plaza Banquedano hablará Fidel Castro," *Vistazo,* VIII (11 agosto 1959), 9.

"Pleno Nacional del Partido Socialista: Solidaridad Nacional con la Revolución Cubana," *Arauco,* II (agosto 1961), 21.

"Polémica Pastoral de la Iglesia," *Ercilla,* XXVIII (26 septiembre 1962).

"La Política de Bloques," *Política y Espíritu,* XVI (abril 1962), 33-37.

"Politicai Crisis Splits the Chilean Socialist Party," *International Socialist Review,* XXV (Summer 1964), 73.

"Presiones sobre la Democracia," *Política y Espíritu,* XIV (15 octubre 1960), 5-7.

"El Prestígio de EE. UU. en América Latina," *Política y Espíritu,* XIV (15 noviembre 1960), 11.

"La Primera Convención del Partido Demócrata Cristiano," *Política y Espíritu,* XIV (15 junio 1959), 12, 17-22.

"Principios del Comunitarismo," *Política y Espíritu,* Año XVI, N.o 272 (julio 1962), pp. 43-46, N.o 273 (agosto 1962), pp. 40-44.

"Programa de Jorge Alessandri," *Política y Espíritu,* No. 317 (agosto 1970).

"Programa de Radomiro Tomic," *Política y Espíritu,* No. 317 (agosto de 1970).

"Puntos de Vista," *Política y Espíritu,* XIV, N.os 216, 226, 229, 233, 247 (enero 1959—julio 1960).

"Rebase del FRAP en Las Vertientes," *Ercilla,* XXVIII (7 marzo 1962), 15.

"Rebase del FRAP en Las Vertientes," *Ercilla,* XXVIII (9 enero 1963), 7.

"Reportaje al Comando Secreto," *Ercilla,* XXVIII (7 noviembre 1962), 10-11.

"La República Socialista," *Desfile,* I (23 septiembre 1965), 20-21.

"Revolution for Export," *Time,* August 22, 1960.

Segunda Declaración de La Habana: La Voz de Cuba. Santiago: Imp. Horizonte, 1962.

"Semana Económica: Partió la Reforma Agraria," *Ercilla,* XXVIII (23 mayo 1962), 9.

Statistical Abstract of Latin America: 1966. Los Angeles: Latin American Center of the University of California, 1967.

"Suspenso en la Política Nacional," *Ercilla,* XXVII (19 abril 1961), 7.

"Tomic: Salvar a Cuba para la Democracia," *Ercilla,* XXVI (20 julio 1960), 8.

"Lo que Tomic hará en USA," *Ercilla,* XXX (13 enero 1965), 15.

"Torneo D.C.: una estrategia y dos tácticas frente al PC," *Ercilla,* XXVII (2 agosto 1961), 16-17.

"En torno al 4 de septiembre," *Mensaje,* XIII (septiembre 1964), 409-13.

"Una Torpe Aventura Terrorista," *Ercilla,* XXVIII (31 octubre 1962), 11.

Los Trabajadores y la Nacionalización del Cobre. Santiago: Edit. del Pacífico, Julio 1964.

"Los tractores valen mas," *Mensaje,* X (julio 1961), 265-68, 290-94.

"Tres Partidos Frente a la Pastoral," *Ercilla,* XXVIII (3 octubre 1962), 14.

"USA Elabora Estrategia Frente a Cuba y la URSS," *Ercilla*, XXVII (20 diciembre 1961), 21.

"Universitarios Chilenos Enjuician a USA y la URSS," *Ercilla*, XXV (16 diciembre 1959), 16-18.

Vanguardia Revolucionaria Marxista. Comité Central. *Pueblo de Chile: Organizaté para Defender tu Victoria Electoral.* Santiago: Imp. Entrecerros, 1964.

Vanguardia Revolucionaria Marxista. *El Verdadero Gamino después del 4 de Septiembre.* Santiago: Imp. Entrecerros, 1964.

Vanguardia Revolucionaria Marxista. *¡Insurrección Socialista!* Santiago: Imp. Entrecerros, 1964.

Vanguardia Revolucionaria Marxista. *¡Movilización permanente de los Comités Allendistas para Imponer por la Razón y la Fuerza, el Triunfo de Allende!* Santiago: Imp. Delta, 1964.

Vanguardia Revolucionaria Marxista. *Tesis Políticas Aprobadas por el Primer Congreso Nacional.* Santiago: Imp. Entrecerros, 1964.

"Viajes Chilenos en Secreto Apoyan a Fidel," *Ercilla*, XXVI (13 abril 1960), 9.

"Vision Cristiana de la Revolución en América Latina," *Mensaje*, XI (Diciembre 1962), 9-12.

Volunteers for International Technical Assistance. *VITA: A New Channel for Technical Assistance to Developing Nations.* Schenectady (N.Y.): Volunteers for International Technical Assistance, Inc., n.d.

" 'Yugoslavo' Fué Congreso Socialista," *Ercilla*, XXVII (13 diciembre 1961), 9.

Public Documents (Chile, U.S., U.N., OAA, IADB)

Chile. Congreso Nacional. Senado, *El Presidente Eisenhower en el Congreso de Chile.* Santiago: Zig-Zag, 1960.

Chile. Controloría General de la República. Secretaria General. *Recopliación de Leyes.* Edición Oficial. Tomo XLVI. Santiago: Controloría General de la República, 1959.

Chile. Corporación de Fomento de la Producción. Departamento de Planificación y Estudios. *Quentas Nacionales de Chile: 1940-1954.* Santiago: Edit. del Pacífico, 1957.

Chile. Corporación de Fomento de la Producción. *Synopsis of the National Program of Economic Development: 1961-1970.* Santiago: Talls. Grafs. 'La Nación,' 1961.

Chile. Dirección de Estadística y Censos. *Algunos Resultados del XIII Censo de Poblacion y II de Vivienda.* Santiago: Direccion de Estadistica y Censos, 1962.

Chile. Dirección de Estadística y Censos. *Población del País: Características Básicas de la Población, Censo 1960.* Santiago: Dirección de Estadística y Censos, 1964.

Chile. Ministerio de Agricultura. *Documentación básica sobre Tenencia de la Tierra en Chile y Materias afines.* 2.a ed. Santiago: Imp. 'Les Andes,' 1962.

Chile. Ministerio de Relaciones Exteriores de Chile. *Gira Continental del Presidente de la República Excmo. Senor Jorge Alessandri Rodríguez: 9 al 21 de diciembre de 1962.* Santiago: Zig-Zag, 1963.

Chile. Servicio Nacional de Salud. *Memória Anual: 1962.* Santiago: Servicio Nacional de Salud, V Zona, 1963.

Inter-American Development Bank. *Social Progress Trust Fund: Fourth Annual Report, 1964.* Washington, D.C.: Inter-American Development Bank, 1965.

Inter-American Development Bank. *Social Progress Trust Fund: Fifth Annual Report, 1965.* Washington: Inter-American Development Bank, 1966.

Organization of American States (OAS). *Annual Report of the Secretary General to the Council of the Organization, 1962.* Washington, D.C.: Pan American Union, 1963.

Organization of American States (OAS). *Report of the Secretary General to the Council of the Organization, January 1, 1963-June 30, 1964.* Washington, D.C.: Pan American Union, 1964.

United Nations. Comision Económica para America Latina. *Estudio Económico de America Latina.* New York: Naciones Unidas, 1965.

United Nations. Economic and Social Council. *Preliminary Report on the World Social Situation.* New York: United Nations, 1952.

United Nations. General Assembly, 15th Session, November 1, 1960. *Official Records: 910th Plenary Meeting.*

United Nations. General Assembly, 15th Session, First Committee, April 21, 1961. *Official Records: 1160th Meeting.* February 9, 1962. *Official Records: 1235th Meeting.* February 15, 1962. *Official Records: 1243rd Meeting.*

United Nations. Security Council, January 5, 1961. *Official Records: 923rd Meeting.* February 27, 1962. *Official Records: 991st Meeting.* March 16, 1962. *Official Records: 994th Meeting.*

United Nations. Office of Public Information. *Yearbook of the United Nations, 1960.* New York: United Nations, 1961.

United Nations. Office of Public Information. *Yearbook of the United Nations, 1961.* New York: United Nations, 1963.

United Nations. *Yearbook of the United Nations, 1962.* New York: Columbia University in Cooperation with the United Nations, 1964.

U.S. Advisory Commission on International Educational and Cultural Affairs. A Report from the Commission. *A Beacon of Hope: The Exchange of Persons Program.* Washington, D.C.: Government Printing Office, 1963.

U.S. Advisory Commission on International Educational and Cultural Affairs. A Report from the Comission. *A Sequel to a Beacon of Hope: The Exchange of Persons Program.* Washington, D.C.: Government Printing Office, 1964.

U.S. Air Force. *Bibliography for Latin America.* Albrook Air Force Base (Canal Zone): Caribbean Air Command, Historical Division, Office of Information, 1959.

U.S. Congress. House. Committee on Appropriations. *Departments of State and Justice, the Judiciary, and Related Agencies for 1960. Hearings* before a subcommittee of the Committee on Appropriations, House of Representatives, 86th Cong., 1st sess., 1960.

U.S. Congress. House. Committee on Appropriations. *Departments of State and Justice, the Judiciary and Related Agencies Appropriations for 1962. Hearings* before a subcommittee of the Committee on Appropriations, House of Representatives, 87th Cong., 1st sess., 1961.

U.S. Congress. House. Committee on Appropriations. *Departments of State, Justice, and Commerce, the Judiciary, and Related Agencies Appropriations for 1964. Hearings* before a subcommittee of the Committee on Appropriations, House of Representatives, 88th Cong., 1st sess., 1963.

U.S. Congress. House. Committee on Appropriations. *Departments of State, Justice and Commerce, the Judiciary and Related Agencies Appropriations for 1966. Hearings* before a subcommittee of the Committee on Appropriations, House of Representatives, 89th Cong., 1st sess., 1965.

U.S. Congress. House. Committee on Banking and Currency. *Latin American Economic Study.* Conducted by the Honorable Thomas M. Rees. House of Representatives, 91st Cong., 1st sess., October 1969.

U.S. Congress. House. Committee on Foreign Affairs. *Castro-Communist Subversion in the Western Hemisphere. Hearings* before the Subcommittee on Inter-American Affairs of the Committee on Foreign Affairs, House of Representatives, 88th Cong., 1st sess., 1963.

U.S. Congress. House. Committee on Foreign Affairs. *Cuba and the Caribbean. Hearings* before the subcommittee on Inter-American Affairs of the Committee on Foreign Affairs, House of Representatives, 91st Cong., 2nd sess., July-August 1970.

U.S. Congress. House. Committee on Foreign Affairs. *Foreign Assistance Act of 1963. Hearings* before the Committee on Foreign Affairs, House of Representatives, on H.R. 5490, Parts III and V, 86th Cong., 1st sess., 1963.

U.S. Congress. House. Committee on Foreign Affairs. *Foreign Assistance Act of 1964. Hearings* before the Committee on Foreign Affairs, 88th Cong., 1st sess., 1964.

U.S. Congress. House. Committee on Foreign Affairs. *Foreign Assistance Act of 1969. Hearings* before the Committee on Foreign Affairs, House of Representatives, 91st Cong., 2nd sess., June 1969.

U.S. Congress. House. Committee on Foreign Affairs. *Organization of American States. Hearings* before the Subcommittee on Inter-American Affairs of the Committee on Foreign Affairs, House of Representatives, 91st Cong., 2nd sess., March 1970.

U. S. Congress. House. Committee on Foreign Affairs. *Peace Corps Act Amendments. Hearings* before the Committee on Foreign Affairs, House of Representatives, on H.R. 10404, A Bill to Amend the Peace Corps Act, 87 Cong., 2nd sess., 1962.

U.S. Congress. House. Committee on Foreign Affairs. *To Amend the Peace Corps Act. Hearings* before the Committee on Foreign Affairs, House of Representatives, on H.R. 8754, 88th Cong., 1st sess., 1963.

U.S. Congress. Senate. Committee on Foreign Relations. *Rockefeller Report on Latin America*. Hearing before the Subcommittee on Western Hemisphere Affairs of the Committee on Foreign Relations, United States Senate, 91st Cong., 1st sess., November 20, 1969.

U.S. Congress. Senate. Committee on Government Operations. *United States Foreign Aid in Action: A Case Study*, by Hon. Ernest Gruening. Submitted to the Subcommittee on Foreign Aid Expenditures, 89th Cong., 2nd sess. Washington, D.C.: Government Printing Office, 1966.

U.S. Department of Agriculture. *Agricultural Prospects in Chile*. By Francis S. Urban. Washington: Economic Research, Foreign Regional Analysis Division, U.S. Department of Agriculture, January 1970.

U.S. Department of Commerce. Bureau of Foreign Commerce. *Investment in Chile: Basic Information for United States Businessmen*, by Merwin L. Bohan and Morton Pomeranz. Washington: Government Printing Office, 1960.

U.S. Department of Commerce. *Economic Trends and Their Implications for the United States in Chile*. Washington, D.C.: Bureau of International Commerce, Department of Commerce, July 1970.

U.S. Department of Health, Education and Welfare. Office of Education. *Education and Social Change in Chile* by Clark C. Gill. Washington, D.C.: Government Printing Office, 1966.

U.S. Department of State. "Joint Statement, Santiago, March 1," *Bulletin*, XLII (March 28, 1960).

U.S. Department of State. "Text of Chilean 'Federation of the Students of Chile' Letter," *Bulletin*, XLII (April 25, 1960), 656-58.

U.S. Information Agency. *11th Report to Congress*. July 1-December 31, 1958. Washington, D.C.: Government Printing Office, 1959.

U.S. Information Agency. *12th Review of Operations*. January 1-June 30, 1959. Washington, D.C.: Government Printing Office, 1959.

U.S. Information Agency. *13th Review of Operations*. July 1-December 31, 1959. Washington, D.C.: Government Printing Office, 1960.

U.S. Information Agency. *14th Review of Operations*. January 1-June 30, 1960. Washington, D.C.: Government Printing Office, 1960.

U.S. Information Agency. *15th Review of Operations*. July 1-December 31, 1960. Washington, D.C.: Government Printing Office, 1961.

U.S. Information Agency. *16th Report to Congress*. January 1-June 30, 1961. Washington, D.C.: Government Printing Office, 1961.

U.S. Information Agency. *17th Review of Operations*. July 1-December 31, 1961. Washington, D.C.: Government Printing Office, 1962.

U.S. Information Agency. *18th Report to Congress*. January 1-June 30, 1962. Washington, D.C.: Government Printing Office, 1962.

U.S. Information Agency. *19th Review of Operations*. July 1-December 31, 1962. Washington, D.C.: Government Printing Office, 1963.

U.S. Information Agency. *Twentieth Review of Operations*. January 1-June 30, 1963. Washington, D.C.: Government Printing Office, 1963.

U.S. Information Agency. *21st Report to Congress*. July 1-December 31, 1963. Washington, D.C.: Government Printing Office, 1964.

U.S. Information Agency. *22nd Report to Congress*. January 1-June 30, 1964. Washington, D.C.: Government Printing Office, 1964.

U.S. Information Agency. *23rd Report to Congress*. July 1-December 31, 1964. Washington, D.C.: Government Printing Office, 1965.

U.S. Information Agency. *24th Report to Congress*. January 1-June 30, 1965. Washington, D.C.: Government Printing Office, 1965.

U.S. Information Agency. Research and Reference Service. *Chilean Attitudes Toward Communism and the East-West Conflict*. Washington, D.C.: USIA, Report No. 4, December 16, 1955.

U.S. Information Agency. Research and Reference Service. *Chilean Attitudes Toward the United States and U.S. Economic Policies.* Washington, D.C.: USIA, Report No. 3, October 31, 1955.

U.S. Information Agency. Research and Reference Service. *Latin American Attitudes Toward Certain Anti-Castro Measures: The Arms Cache Resolution and the Cuban Overflights.* Washington, D.C.: USIA, R-75-64, June 10, 1964.

U.S. Information Agency. Research and Reference Service. *Latin American Views on Political Relations with the United States.* Washington, D.C.: USIA, Report No. 14, September 23, 1957.

U.S. Information Agency. Research and Reference Service. *The Economic and Political Climate of Opinion in Latin America and Attitudes Toward the Alliance for Progress.* Washington, D.C.: USIA, R-110-63(R), June 1963.

U.S. Information Agency. Research and Reference Service. *The Economic And Political Climate of Opinion in Latin America and Attitudes Toward the Alliance for Progress: Appendix I, Breakdowns by Economic Sub-Groups within the Urban Sample.* Washington, D.C.: USIA, R-50-64, April 30, 1964.

"U.S. Military Aid Missions Abroad," *NACLA Newsletter* IV (December 1970), 13.

Newspaper and Periodical References

Akron Beacon Journal. February 22, 1967.

El Diario Ilustrado. 15 agosto 1964.

La Libertad.
1 agosto 1959.
4 agosto 1959.
8 agosto 1959.
12 agosto 1959.
22 agosto 1959.

La Nacion.
18 abril 1961.
19 abril 1961.
20 abril 1961.
21 abril 1961.
22 abril 1961.
24 octubre 1962.
11 agosto 1964.

New Republic. Editorial, March 4, 1967.

New York Times.
August 23, 1959.
January 9, 1961.
April 23, 1961.
December 4, 1961.
August 12, 1962.
October 20, 1962.
October 28, 1962.
October 29, 1962.
September 19, 1963.
February 27, 1966.
February 16, 1967.
February 19, 1967.
February 20, 1967.
February 26, 1967.

New York Times. Editorial, March 1, 1960.

Las Noticias de Ultima Hora.
17 abril 1961.
18 abril 1961.
19 abril 1961.
20 abril 1961.
11 agosto 1964.
12 agosto 1964.
14 agosto 1964.
15 agosto 1964.

Ramparts. March 1967.

El Siglo.
23 octubre 1962.
24 octubre 1962.
25 octubre 1962.
26 octubre 1962.
10 noviembre 1966.
30 enero 1967.
27 febrero 1967.
13 marzo 1967.

El Siglo (cont). 29 octubre 1962.
30 octubre 1962.
31 octubre 1962.

South Pacific Mail. January 5, 1962.
October 26, 1962.
November 2, 1962.
April 26, 1963.
August 23, 1963.

La Tercera de la Hora.

18 abril 1961.	1 agosto 1959.
26 abril 1961.	2 agosto 1959.
28 julio 1959.	4 agosto 1959.
31 julio 1959.	10 agosto 1959.

La Voz. 9 abril 1961.
23 abril 1961.
5 julio 1964.

Washington Post. February 26, 1967. E-1.

World Medical Relief Newsletter. Vol. I, No. 3.

Interviews, Conversations, Letters, Addresses

Altamirano, Carlos. *Address at the Sala Arauco.* Santiago, May 12, 1967.

Azedo, Beatriz. Program Officer. Meals for Millions. Santa Monica, California. Letter. April 19, 1967.

B., N. Chilean Communist Party activist. Conversations. Santiago, 1967.

Bailey, John M. African Coordinator. National Farmers Union. Washington, D.C. Letter. April 12, 1967.

Baytelbaum, David. CORFO, Agricultural Engineer. Interview. Santiago, May 6, 1967.

C., N. PDC youth activist and student at the University of Chile's School of Political and Administrative Sciences. Interview. Santiago, April 5, 1967.

Chelen, Alejandro. Socialist Leader and former Senator. Conversations. Santiago, August 1967.

Chelen, Danton. MIR leader. Interview. Santiago, June 29, 1967.

Clay, John W. Assistant to Richard F. Smith, Secretary for Service, Church World Service. New York. Letter. June 16, 1967.

Corbalan, Salomon. *Address at the Facultad Latinoamericana de Ciencias Sociales.* Santiago, December 5, 1966.

Durant, F.E. Home Director, Gospel Mission of South America. Pompton Plains, New Jersey. Letter. April 1967.

Echols, James. Mission Chief, USIS. Conversation. Santiago, November 1966.

Eklund, John M. Executive Vice-President. National Farmers Union. Washington, D.C.: Letter. May 29, 1967.

Espinosa, Rafael. FRD-CIA Propagandist in Chile. Cuban Refugee. Interview. Santiago, May 5, 1967.

Gomucio, Rafael A. *Address at the Facultad Latinoamericana de Ciencias Sociales.* Santiago, December 6, 1966.

Jenney, E. Ross, M.D. Population Council. New York. Letter April 10, 1967.

Johnson, Charles. Officer, AID. Conversation. Santiago. August 9, 1967.

Kinch, Joan. TECHO Foundation. Briarcliff Manor, New York. Letter. April 22, 1967.

Lea, Robert B. President. Engineers and Scientists Committee. New Hyde Park, Long Island. Letter. April 28, 1967.

M., E. Christian Democrat and former Communist activist. Conversations. Santiago. 1966-67.

M., R. Former anti-Castro operative in Cuba, close friend of Rafael Espinosa. Conversations. Santiago, 1967.

Morris, G.M. Field Services Director, Public Administration Service. Chicago. Letter. April 11, 1967.

Naranjo, Oscar. Socialist Leader. Interview. Curico, March 26, 1967.

Nielsen, Ove R. Assistant Executive Secretary, Lutheran World Relief. New York. Letters. April 14, and May 25, 1967.

O'Brien, Evelyn. Secretary to Rev. C.J. Ryan, S.J., President of International Educational Development, Inc. New York. Letter. April 11, 1967.

Pogue, Richard. An assistant to Ambassador Dungan. Conversation. Santiago, April 14, 1967.

Rogers, William D. Former Deputy Assistant Administrator of the Agency for International Development, and former Deputy U.S. Coordinator of the Alliance for Progress. Address. Cornell University, July 29, 1966.

Rosenblum, Haskell. Member of the Board of Directors. Overseas Education Fund of the League of Women Voters. Washington, D.C.: Letter. April 26, 1967.

Ruiz, Napoleon ("Napo"). Official of the CIA-related International Development Foundation. Interview. Guatemala City, December 22, 1967.

Sacci, Rocco A. Public Relations, Catholic Relief Services, New York. Letter. June 19, 1967.

Schultz, Sonia. Administrative Assistant, American International Association for Economic and Social Development. New York. Letter. April 21, 1967.

Sweetser, Aileene B. Officer Coordinator. Volunteers for International Technical Assistance, Inc. Schenectady, N.Y. Letter. April 10, 1967.

Vahey, Very Rev. Richard E., O.P., P.G. Director of Mission. Sacred Order of Friars Preachers, Province of St. Joseph. New York. Letter. April 18, 1967.

Wolfolk, Charles. Press Attache, U.S. Embassy. Conversation. Santiago. April 4, 1967.

Periodicals and Newspapers Systematically Examined

Arauco.	(1959-1965)
Chile, Cámara de Diputados.	
Boletín de Sesiones.	(1963-1964)
Chile. Senado. *Diario de*	
Sesiones.	(1959-1965)
Cuba Socialista.	(1961-1965)
Desfile.	(1965)
Ercilla.	(1958-1965)
Hispanic American Report.	(1959-1964)
Mensaje.	(1958-1965)
El Mercurio.	(1959-1960)
New Times.	(1959-1965)
New York Times.	(1959-1965)
Política y Espíritu.	(1958-1965)
Principios.	(1958-1965)
Revista Católica.	(1958-1964)
South Pacific Mail.	(1959-1965)
Vistazo.	(1959)

Index

407

Miles D. Wolpin was born in Mount Vernon, New York in 1937. After attending the London School of Economics, he received his B.S. from the University of Pennsylvania. Following graduate study, Wolpin was awarded a J.D., and a Ph.D. in international politics by Columbia University. He conducted research in Chile on a Ford Foundation grant administered by the Latin American Teaching Fellowship Program at the Fletcher School of Law and Diplomacy. Dr. Wolpin has published articles in a number of scholarly journals and is currently at work on a study of Military Assistance and Counterrevolution in the Third World. He is Assistant Professor of Political Science at St. Francis Xavier University, Antigonish, Nova Scotia.